MODERN PRODUCTION/ OPERATIONS MANAGEMENT

ELWOOD S. BUFFA

University of California, Los Angeles

MODERN PRODUCTION/ OPERATIONS MANAGEMENT

7/e

JOHN WILEY & SONS

New York   Chichester   Brisbane   Toronto   Singapore

Library of Congress Cataloging in Publication Data:

Buffa, Elwood Spencer, 1923-
    Modern production/operations management.

    Includes bibliographies and indexes.
    1. Production management.   I. Title.
TS155.B723   1982   658.5   82-10860
ISBN 0-471-86384-X

Printed in the United States of America

10 9 8 7 6 5

To Betty

ABOUT THE AUTHOR

Elwood S. Buffa is professor of production and operations management and management science, and Director of the Executive MBA Program at the Graduate School of Management of the University of California, Los Angeles. He received his B.S. and M.B.A. degrees from the University of Wisconsin, and his Ph.D. from the University of California, Los Angeles. He worked as an operations analyst at the Eastman Kodak Company before entering the teaching profession, and has engaged in consulting activities in a wide variety of settings during the past twenty-five years. He has served as assistant dean and associate dean at the Graduate School of Management, Chairman of UCLA's Academic Senate, and has held visiting appointments at IPSOA in Turin, Italy, and at the Harvard Business School. Professor Buffa has published many research papers in management science and operations management. He is the author of other books published by Wiley, including *OPERATIONS MANAGEMENT: The Management of Productive Systems; OPERATIONS MANAGEMENT: Problems and Models; BASIC PRODUCTION MANAGEMENT;* and, coauthored with James S. Dyer, *MANAGEMENT SCIENCE/OPERATIONS RESEARCH: Model Formulation and Solution Methods*. In addition, Professor Buffa serves on the board of directors of The Planning Decisions Group, Inc.

PREFACE

As the production/operations management field has matured, its technical content has stabilized and the emphasis has returned to P/OM as a functional field of management. As such, there is a reemphasis on "management." Many of the changes that were introduced in the sixth edition to strengthen the managerial orientation of P/OM have been carried further in the seventh edition.

There is a new awareness of the importance of the operations function in America. The productivity crisis in the United States, and the lack of international competitiveness of many sectors of the economy have spurred many managers into action to "reindustrialize." To these managers, this means an emphasis on productivity and on the operations function in general. Many articles on this trend have been published in *Fortune, Business Week, The Wall Street Journal,* and the *Harvard Business Review.* Some of the titles are themselves foretelling of a rebirth of managerial emphasis on production and the operations function: "Rediscovering the Factory," "Business Refocuses on the Factory Floor," and "Schools Again Offer Courses on Production."

Today there has also developed a keen interest in Japan, and in understanding why the Japanese are able to produce higher quality products, of outstanding design, and for competitive costs. Again, the literature is filled with explanations of quality circles, descriptions of the Kanban system, and analyses of the strategic approach of Japanese managers to production and operations.

The interest of managers in productivity and international competitiveness represents an interest in the operations function. What other group in academic and professional life takes as one of its prime objectives the improvement of productivity? In studying production and operations management, students have the opportunity to reap the benefits of being in the right place at the right time. Managers of productive systems will be heard as never before, and will have opportunities to move into general management as never before.

MAJOR CHANGES IN THE SEVENTH EDITION

The major additions in this new edition include:

New chapter on Strategic Planning Decisions for Operations—Chapter 2
New Supplement on Assembly Line Balancing—added to Chapter 7
New chapter on Operations Planning and Control—Chapter 8

New supplement on Linear Programming Methods of Aggregate Planning—added to Chapter 9

New supplement on Statistical Quality Control to support the materials in Chapter 15

The new chapters both introduce these major sections of the book and cover important topics. Both chapters contain materials that are entirely new to the seventh edition, as well as materials drawn from other chapters. Chapter 2, "Strategic Planning Decisions for Operations," considers the experience curve phenomenon and its strategic implications, joint product/process strategies, focus, and the organization of the operations function. Chapter 8, "Operations Planning and Control," examines the nature of production-distribution systems, the role of system inventories, system dynamics and its managerial implications, the role of comprehensive planning, control systems, the concept of the materials manager, and the unique features of service systems for planning and control.

Other additions are discussions of the productivity crisis (Chapter 1), descriptions of the Toyota production system including Kanban and Japanese quality control circles, discussions of automation, robotics, and CAD/CAM (computer aided design and manufacturing), lists of important terms at the ends of chapters with page references, and new short cases. These short cases were well accepted in the sixth edition, and their number has been expanded considerably in the seventh edition. Another important addition is to the *Instructor's Manual*, where transparency masters of key illustrations in the text have been reproduced, together with masters of illustrations and tables from the manual that are related to problems and situations.

Numerous other changes throughout the book include new and updated references and the addition and deletion of material to place more emphasis on the managerial function. Many of these changes are in response to excellent suggestions by reviewers of the sixth edition. For example, long-range forecasting materials have been combined with the major chapter on forecasting and are now relocated as the new Chapter 3. Chapter 7, "Processes, Jobs, and Facility Layout," is a combination of two previous chapters. In combining them, I have regarded these topics as elements of one topic; the design of the physical system for a managerial point of view. Somewhat less emphasis on the technical aspects of layout results. The former chapter on aggregate planning is introduced with a discussion of managerial actions to smooth demand. Simulation of project networks is introduced in Chapter 13 because it provides important information for decision making. New materials on scheduling personnel are introduced in Chapter 14.

The balance between manufacturing and service systems of the sixth edition is retained in the seventh. Many of the short cases deal with service systems, even in chapters where the text discussion may be manufacturing oriented. This is intended to provide a transfer of concepts that are more generally applicable.

The Role of Quantitative Methods

Although the text is managerially oriented, there is a clear recognition throughout that quantitative concepts are of great importance to managers in making the best decisions in operating systems. But it should be clear that the focus of the book is on the problems of P/OM. Thus, in Chapter 5, "Capacity Planning," we consider a decision tree analysis of capacity planning for new products and risky situations. We are not attempting to teach the subject of decision analysis, which is normally covered in another course, but are applying the analytical format of decision trees to capacity planning in a risky environment. Similarly, we use the distribution model of linear programming as a mode of analysis of distribution systems, warehouse location, and the dynamics of plant location. Again, we are not attempting to teach distribution methods of linear programming at that point, but are focusing on the relevant problems of P/OM. The same situation holds true for other analytical methods, such as linear programming, present values, waiting line models, and Monte Carlo Simulation.

If students have had previous courses that cover these analytical methods, instructors will probably not wish to assign the appendixes, which cover these methods, except as a review and source material. If the reverse is true for a particular situation, instructors can assign the appendixes at the points in their courses where they are needed.

I have retained the appendixes on analytical methods so that their contents can be assigned flexibly, depending on the emphasis that instructors may wish to give and the previous backgrounds of their students. I prefer that these materials be included in the appendixes for two reasons: (1) flexibility of assignment, and (2) because they do not interrupt the flow of the main topics of the text. Students should not be confused about which topics are at the core of P/OM and which are methodological in nature.

There are some important changes in the appendixes. For example, I have reworked Appendix B, "Linear Programming," providing an alternate explanation of the simplex method as an introduction to the tableau methodology, and have introduced a discussion of sensitivity analysis. Also, I have reworked Appendix D, "Waiting Lines," to provide more explanation of the interrelationships and their interpretation.

Throughout this edition I establish a closer linkage between the text chapters and supporting appendixes. This is accomplished by including some problems and cases that require a knowledge of one of the appendixes for appropriate analysis. In these instances, the need for the appendix is indicated.

Elwood S. Buffa
Pacific Palisades, California

ACKNOWLEDGMENTS

Materials in the book have been drawn from a wide variety of sources. Although I have made original contributions in specific areas of analysis and application and in the conceptual framework, the bulk of the material on which *Modern Production/Operations Management* is based comes from original work by scores of colleagues throughout the country. The sources of these materials are cited where the materials are discussed. I hope I have made no omissions.

Reviewers of the sixth edition provided reaction for the seventh edition manuscript development. Their comments were unusually helpful, suggesting new materials, reemphases, and clarifications that have been invaluable. I thank them for their time and generous efforts and for their contributions. They are: Michael P. Hottenstein of The Pennsylvania State University; Jill Kammermeyer of Middle Tennessee State University; W. J. Maddocks of the College of William and Mary; Bruce J. McLaren of Indiana State University; Henry B. Person of the University of Minnesota; Alan R. Raedels of Portland State University; Harold J. Steudel of the University of Wisconsin; Jesse S. Tarleton of the College of William and Mary; and Al Woerner of Fairleigh Dickinson University at Teaneck.

I have benefited greatly from reviews and comments on previous editions by professional colleagues such as Robert Albanese of Texas A & M University; Louis J. Allain of St. Johns University; Joseph D. Blackburn of Boston University; William H. Bolen of Georgia Southern College; Robert W. Boling of the University of Tennessee; John D. Burns of DePaul University; Y. S. Chang of Boston University; C. W. Dane of The University of Southern California; John P. Dory of New York University; Ronald J. Ebert of the University of Missouri-Columbia; Norbert L. Enrick of Kent State University; James A. Fitzsimmons of the University of Texas at Austin; George J. Gore of the University of Cincinnati; Gene K. Groff of Georgia State University; the late Stanley T. Hardy of Ohio State University; Warren Hausman of Stanford University; Thomas E. Hendrick of the University of Colorado; Roy Housewright of Western Illinois University; Michael P. Hottenstein of The Pennsylvania State University; Jarrett Hudnall, Jr., of Louisiana Tech University; Alan Krigline of the University of Akron; Terry Nels Lee of Brigham Young University; John P. Matthews of the University of Wisconsin; James L. McKenney of Harvard University; William T. Newell of the University of Washington; D. Roman of George Washington University; J. A. Sargeant of the University of Toronto; John E. Van Tassel, Jr., of Boston College; Richard J. Tersine of Old Dominion University; and Thomas E. Vollmann of INSEAD.

E. S. B.

CONTENTS

PART ONE

INTRODUCTION

CHAPTER 1

The Operations Function

WHY STUDY PRODUCTIVE SYSTEMS?

THE FIRST REASON TO STUDY PRODUCTIVE SYSTEMS AND LEARN about their effective management is that every enterprise, private or public, manufacturing or service, involves a productive system. There is an operations function in all enterprises. In manufacturing, the productive system is of great importance within the enterprise as a whole. In many service organizations the productive system and the product being offered are so completely bound up together that they are indistinguishable—what would McDonald's be without their unique delivery system? Therefore, to study productive systems, how they work, and how they are managed effectively, is to study an important function in organizations.

There is evidence that the United States is falling behind other countries such as Japan and West Germany in its ability to produce high quality products at reasonable costs. Finished steel has regularly been produced in these countries and delivered in the United States at prices that could not be met by domestic producers, including the transportation. While Japanese auto producers have increased their share of the U.S. auto market, Chrysler has been on the verge of bankruptcy, and Ford is seemingly not far behind.

It is interesting to observe that the average annual increase in productivity during recent years has been about 7 percent in Japan whereas it was only 1 to 2 percent in the United States. The unit labor cost increase during the same period was 7.5 percent for the United States, but only 3.4 percent for Japan. The productivity-labor cost connection is certainly a major factor in the diminished competitive position of U.S. industry. More recently, U.S. industrial productivity seems to have leveled off and even declined in the recession of 1980.

Although we have become less competitive during the past 10 to 15 years, the study of productive systems in schools of management and business administration has diminished. More recently, in articles on management education appearing in the popular press (*The Wall Street Journal* and *Time*), there has been a questioning of why business students have emphasized other functions rather than production, when the opportunities and salaries for jobs in production and operations seem to be among the very best. Perhaps one explanation for the diminished competitiveness of the United States lies in the fact that there are too few people interested in producing goods and services of high quality, low cost, when needed, and with the appropriate accompanying services. These are all good reasons to study productive systems, but in addition, the field is interesting and challenging.

PRODUCTIVE SYSTEMS OF SIGNIFICANCE

It was not long ago that the only productive systems thought to be significant were manufacturing systems. There seemed to be an insatiable demand for material goods, and it was in the production of goods that we learned the fundamentals of how to organize resources to produce something effectively. At the dawn of the Industrial Revolution, our attention was focused on the production of goods to satisfy our basic need and desire for material things. Resources were focused to develop manufacturing systems as the productive systems of significance.

In the short span of 200 to 300 years the industrial world developed from handicraft production systems to the highly efficient industrial machine of today. It was in this arena that much of today's knowledge of the *management* of productive systems was developed.

The fact that manufacturing systems were significant in society focused resources on the solution of problems. Some of the most capable managers focused on problems of production/operations management. Production problems attracted the attention of truly outstanding economists, mathematicians, engineers, sociologists, psychologists, and students of the managerial process itself. The result has been a relative abundance of physical goods at low cost, available in a fantastic range of items undreamed of by our ancestors. The result has also been a body of knowledge, experience, and technique dealing with forecasting, design, layout, job design, automation, scheduling models, inventory models, statistical quality control, computers, simulation, waiting line models, mathematical programming, and so on. There is also a sour note: The fantastic production machine also resulted in pollution and many more repetitive dull jobs.

SERVICE SYSTEMS BECOME SIGNIFICANT

Just as conditions in the past focused resources and attention on manufacturing systems, current conditions have focused attention and resources on new problems. In the past the operations phases of service activities, such as health care, education, transportation, and retailing, were carried on at almost the handicraft level. We suddenly realized that while our attention had been directed to the production of goods, very dramatic changes were developing. Health care and education had grown into huge systems and attracted attention (criticism) when their costs began to increase rapidly.

As the productivity of the economy increased, a reallocation of personal expenditures was taking place, indicated by Figure 1-1. Note that since about 1945 (the end of World War II), services have steadily increased from about 33 percent to 47 percent of personal consumption in 1980, largely at the expense of consumer nondurable goods. Consumer durable goods (dominated by automobiles and household equipment) have remained at an approximately level percentage of personal consumption expenditures since 1950. Of course, the absolute expenditures in all three categories have been increasing, but expenditures for services have been increasing much faster than those for goods.

The same general picture emerges for the United States economy as a whole. Services, as a percentage of Gross National Product (GNP), have increased from about 30 percent in 1948 to about 46 percent currently. The increase in the percentage for services relative to goods in GNP is due both to the reallocation taking place and to the inflated costs of services. The reasons for the cost increases are undoubtedly complex, but there is general agreement that productivity in the service sector has not increased as it has in manufacturing.

The Example of Medical Costs

Medical care is one area that has been the target of critics because of skyrocketing costs. The total U.S. health care bill has more than doubled during the last decade,

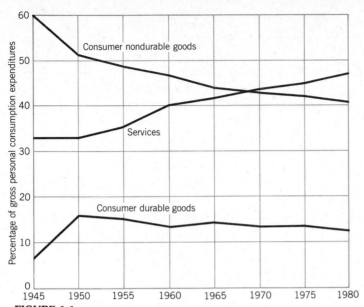

FIGURE 1-1
Relative importance of services and goods in personal consumption expenditures.
SOURCE: Economic Report of the President, 1981.

and in 1971 it stood at $70 billion per year (about $324 per person per year or about 7 percent of the GNP). These expenditures have increased at an average rate of almost 13 percent per year during the last decade.

Figure 1-2 confirms some of the reasons for concern. Since 1950 the price index for medical care has risen from 100 to 582, whereas the general index of consumer prices has risen to only 341. The price index of all services has far outstripped the general index, and medical care has been the price leader. Of course, during the period from 1950 to the present there have been substantial increases in productivity to help offset the effect of the general price increases, as is shown in Figure 1-2 (output per worker-hour increased from 100 to 173 between 1950 and 1979). Otherwise, the general price index would undoubtedly have increased faster than it did. In general, services have not benefited as much as manufacturing from productivity increases. Medical care cost increases are probably more complex because advancing medical technology has resulted in huge increases in overhead costs to finance expensive diagnostic and treatment equipment.

From the Corner Grocery Store to Significant Productive Systems

Other kinds of nonmanufacturing systems that were once regarded as simple, quaint, and insignificant have undergone great change. The corner grocery store was replaced by the supermarket, which has significant problems in such areas as forecasting, supply, inventory management, facility layout, and material handling. The individual hamburger joint is now a franchised mass food preparation service with operations problems that parallel those of some manufacturing systems.

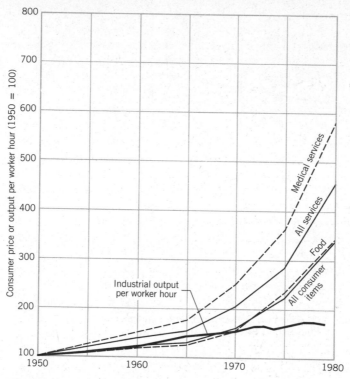

FIGURE 1-2
Comparative price indexes and industrial output per worker-hour index (1950 = 100).
SOURCE: *Economic Report of the President, 1981.*

Other franchised operations, such as motels, face significant operations problems that were not so important when every manager was an individual owner-entrepreneur. Banks have broadened their range of services with branch banking, becoming ardent users of computers and facing large-scale office operations. Other financial institutions, such as insurance companies, face mass information processing problems of a similar nature.

These kinds of organizations have significant productive systems because they are now significant in our society. Educational and medical systems are currently in high demand, soaking up huge resources. They deserve the attention of talented operations managers. Indeed, society demands that the service sector become as efficient as possible in converting its input resources to needed services, while still maintaining a certain quality of service. At any rate, these nonmanufacturing systems have taken their place as significant productive systems.

While we observe that the set of productive systems in the service sector differs in many ways from manufacturing, our thesis is that from the viewpoint of production/operations management the two systems are more alike than they are different. The possible transfer of concept, technique, and experience is certainly not on a one-to-one basis, but significant transfer is possible. We include them for study together with other well-known production systems.

Products Versus Services

Perhaps because the recognition of services as significant productive systems is recent, they are usually thought of as being rather separate and distinct enterprises. Products are tangible things that we can carry away with us, whereas services are intangible and perishable, being consumed in the process of their production. Products may be produced to inventory and made available "off-the-shelf," while availability of services means keeping the productive system that produces them in readiness to produce the service as needed. In addition, the person being served often participates in the productive process, providing part of the labor in self-serve systems. In product systems, there is very little if any contact with the users of the product—that is left to distribution and retailing during which customers purchase the item, or have it serviced. On the other hand, in service systems, there is a great deal of contact with the client or customer. Indeed, much of how individuals rate a service depends on how the service is given. Human contact is almost the essence of many service systems. The nature of products may result in processing to convert raw materials to physical products in a multitude of interrelated steps, but the processing required in services is usually simple, involving only a few steps.

Other important contrasts between products and services deal with the demand variability, markets, and the location of the productive system. The demand for products certainly varies with time. But that variability tends to be on a weekly, monthly, or seasonal basis. On the other hand, the demand for services is often extremely variable on a short-term basis; that is, weekly, daily, and even hourly variations are common. This extreme short-term variability of the demand for services means that the system must be able to expand and contract its capacity rapidly if it is to be cost efficient. Alternately, service systems can either absorb the costs of overcapacity by designing for peak load conditions, or absorb the costs of undercapacity (lost sales and customer dissatisfaction) if the system is designed for something less than peak loads.

Markets served by a productive system for products may be regional, national, or even international. Because of the size of potential markets for products, it is often possible to take advantage of the economies of scale through mechanization and automation. Thus, productivity in manufacturing has enjoyed very substantial increases over the years. Conversely, because services cannot be shipped to distant places, a productive unit must ordinarily serve a local market. Therefore, even though the total market may be national or international (e.g., the market for fast foods), the market served by a given productive unit is small, resulting in relatively small units that cannot take great advantage of economies of scale. The location of the productive system is then dictated by the location of local markets. If the service system is a nonprofit organization, then the location is dependent on the location of users, such as post offices, medical clinics, and so on.

The preceding contrasts between product and service systems are summarized in Table 1-1.

Services as a Part of the Product

If you examine the nature of the delivery system for physical products, the clean line between products and services is much less apparent. If you buy an automobile, you

TABLE 1-1   Characteristics of Systems to Produce Products *GOODS* versus Systems to Produce Services

~~Products~~ Goods	Services
Tangible	Intangible and perishable, consumed in the process of their production
Can be produced to inventory for "off-the-shelf" availability	Availability achieved by keeping the productive system open for service
Minimal contact with ultimate consumer	High contact with clients or customers
Complex and interrelated processing	Simple processing
Demand on system variable on weekly, monthly, and seasonal bases	Demand commonly variable on hourly, daily, and weekly bases
Markets served by productive system are regional, national, and international	Markets served by productive system are usually local
Large units that can take advantage of economies of scale	Relatively small units to serve local markets
Location of system is in relation to regional, national, and international markets	Location dependent on location of local customers, clients, and users

buy not only the product, but the guarantee and some servicing of the car. Almost all purchases of consumer products involve services as well as the product itself.

The services that extend beyond the manufacturer's guarantees and service are usually related to retailing operations. When producers buy products from other producers (raw materials and supplies), they may also be buying services in the form of credit, supply in relation to production schedules, technical advice and service, and so on.

Then, if you look inside the productive system for a product, you may find services needed to sustain the production process. For example, there will be machine maintenance, tool cribs to supply the required tools to mechanics, and others.

Finally, services may provide intangible social-psychological benefits that are not measured easily by the senses of touch, smell, sight, sound and taste. If buying an expensive sports car makes one feel better, can someone else make the judgment that "it isn't worth it" for that person?

Products as a Part of Services

Similarly, the clean line between products and services in a service-oriented system seems to fade. A fast-food operation delivers physical product along with the service. An auto repair service repairs the car, and provides the required parts as well. Hospital care involves medication, bandages, X-ray film, and so on.

Thus, although it may be valid to think of systems as primarily producing either products or services, it is better to think in terms of relative emphasis. Some manufacturing systems are predominately the producers of goods with very little service offered. Some service organizations, such as tax consultants, provide almost no physical product as a part of the service. But most productive systems provide a *bundle* of products and services (see Sasser et al., 1978), and appropriate analysis of the problems of production/operations management should recognize both aspects of the outputs of the system. The importance of both products and services should be apparent in the discussion of the BURGER case later in this chapter.

PRODUCTIVE SYSTEMS—A DEFINITION

We define productive systems as *the means by which we transform resource inputs to create useful goods and services.* The productive process is one of transformation or conversion, as shown in Figure 1-3. The resource inputs may take a wide variety of forms. In manufacturing operations, the inputs are various raw materials, energy, labor, machines, facilities, information, and technology. In service-oriented systems, the inputs are likely to be dominated by labor, but depending on the particular system, machines, facilities, information, and technology may also be important inputs (as in health care, for example). In food service systems, raw materials are an additional important input.

The conversion process itself involves not only the application of the technology, but also the adroit management of all the variables that can be controlled. This is where production/operations management is effective in designing and refining or redesigning the system and in planning and controlling operations as Figure 1-3 indicates.

The essence of effective production/operations management is to see the interrelationships of all the variables and to view the entire process as an integrated system, insofar as possible. When everything works properly, we have outputs of products and services that meet quantity, quality, and cost standards, which are available when needed. We will see the basic structure shown in Figure 1-3 emerge again and again as we develop the framework for addressing the problems of production/operations management.

THE MANAGEMENT OF PRODUCTIVE SYSTEMS

We pose three questions: What are the long-term strategic decisions in production/operations management that commit major resources and set the course for some time to come? How does one design a productive system in terms of jobs, the processing required, the physical flow and arrangement of facilities? What are the day-to-day, week-to-week, and month-to-month decisions that guide an ongoing operations system?

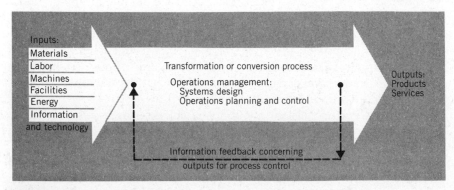

FIGURE 1-3
Productive systems as transformation or conversion processes.

Regardless of the nature of the service or product for which the productive system is designed, there is a general rationale. Let us illustrate by examining a well-known service with the above three questions in mind. The following case example covers production/operations management in a nutshell and sets a management framework for the entire book.

BURGER—A SERVICE SYSTEM EXAMPLE

Charles A. Berg has had the feeling that there is a very substantial market in his town for a good quality hamburger priced under $1.25. He feels that it can be delivered on demand, together with trimmings and a few limited options such as french fries and soft drinks at similar low prices. He thinks that the phrase "delivered on demand" should be translated to mean that a customer should be able to walk up to the window and place and receive an order within 1 minute. Even in peak hours, he feels that the customer's total wait in line and time at the window should not exceed 4 minutes. The quality should be consistently good, but gourmet quality is unnecessary. Berg feels that this bundle of products and services would appeal to many people.

Initial Design

After testing the idea informally on friends, Berg decides to set up a pilot operation for an initial experiment. At this stage, he is his own expert on everything and applies good common sense and the clichés of modern business. These include the use of his concept of production line methods and buying raw materials in quantities that seem to strike a balance between inventory costs, ordering costs, and quantity discounts. Berg's whole concept is geared to an attempt to match the output rate to the expected hourly demand rate. The hamburgers, french fries, and other items are produced at these rates and placed under infrared lamps to keep them warm. Any item not sold within 5 minutes is scrapped.

Everything seems to point to a successful experiment with some rough spots in day-to-day operations. Material costs are higher than anticipated, largely because of scrap. The variability of the demand pattern also affects the amount scrapped. Labor costs are higher than anticipated because the daily demand pattern has large peaks, and adequate peak-load staffing has resulted in considerable idle time during the off-peak periods. The main thing that Berg has been able to maintain, however, is his concept of quality and service. Because of this, the volume of business has been excellent. Figure 1-4 summarizes the initial design. Note that the outputs of the system include both products and services.

Berg has come to some conclusions about a workable size for such an operation and the kind of location that is most appropriate. He opens a branch across town in an excellent location and makes some modifications in the way he schedules labor. He also reduces the required labor input slightly by letting customers select their own items and simply pay the cashier. At this point, Berg establishes a new name for the enterprise—simply "BURGER"—which he has emblazoned high over his two units.

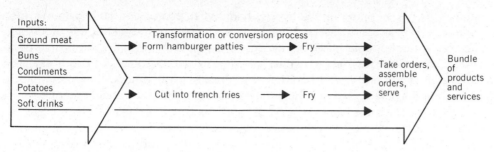

FIGURE 1-4
Initial BURGER system to produce a bundle of products and services.

Expansion Plans

The results at the branch are beyond expectations, and Berg is now planning for a large expansion, including possible franchising of the concept. Substantial capital is now available, as is the expertise to proceed. In addition, past experience has provided very important data (e.g., the characteristics of a good location, estimates of the optimal size of a branch, the expected product mix, the expected arrival rate of customers for each hour of the day, and some ideas about how to mechanize somewhat and otherwise improve the processing setup). Berg knows, however, that the current objectives take him well beyond the corner hamburger joint technology. He is now planning a system of BURGER joints, supported by advertising and image building with larger scale supply, storage, and control systems.

Now let us review the developments at BURGER to extract a rationale for the operations and for the system design. We started conceptually with attempts to make market predictions and long-range plans for the organization. We sharpened our notion of the business we were in, particularly the nature of the food service we provided and the cost and quality level of the food. We made broad studies of the size and location of markets and established a 5-year plan for sizes and locations of BURGER branches. These plans became important inputs for specifying the design characteristics of the service, which had an impact on the design of the productive system that we established. Theoretically, the design of the products and services is now fixed, but we will see. At this point, stop and think about how and why the design of BURGER products and services might change in the future.

We now concentrate our attention on the design of the complex system of jobs and processes because we plan to design a modular branch, and a system of branches. The inputs to the design of the system are from forecasts of demand, analysis of the product or service, technical requirements, and knowledge of human behavior. The forecasts provide data useful in determining a peak and average capacity in the general sense, but the output rates are affected by the processes used, the work flow layout, and the way we decide to manage the work teams.

The first design was based largely on our experience with the most recent branch, but preliminary cost figures suggest that both labor and material costs are too high. We relocate some processes to the central warehouse, because they can be done on a relatively large-scale basis involving some mechanization and automatic material

11

handling (e.g., chopping and extruding hamburger patties and cutting french fried potatoes). This also simplifies operations at each branch and allows the production line concept to be replaced by a rotating team approach to staffing branch systems. The latter concept was recommended after an expert in human behavior analyzed the present setup and found boredom and dissatisfaction among the young people who worked in the branches. The expert also stated that the rotating team concept had other important advantages because each person on the team learned all aspects of the processes. This broader job structure results in flexibility in case of absence or illness, and the work variety should relieve the boredom problem.

The basic work pattern seemed well developed now, but the work design expert quipped, "The only one idle during this process is the customer for an average of 2 minutes. What can we have him do that is useful?" An interesting question, but it was passed over for the moment, being kept in reserve. It did point up the fact, however, that we might change the service offered because of impact from the design and the job-process system. Because of the high material cost, another change in the product was considered but rejected: introducing a bit of cereal in the hamburger patty.

Another aspect of the system design centered on the material supply system from the central warehouse. There were two important parts of the supply system. One was concerned with the inventory levels to be maintained at the warehouse and at each branch to ensure continuous service to the customer. Storage adequate to ensure a full week's supply was provided at the warehouse plus 2 days' supply at each branch. A second problem was to determine an efficient supply routing to all branches each day.

The final overall system design, summarized in Figure 1-5, was rendered in terms of a design for the modular branch. Berg mused that the warehouse was now a manufacturing plant as well. He felt that his bundle of products and services seemed to have been valued in the marketplace. The components of the design included a work flow layout and architectural plans, a labor staffing plan that specified just how each operation was to be carried out, including labor time standards, a material flow plan, a customer flow plan and layout, the central warehouse design including storage layout and logistics supply system, the production operations layout, equipment specifications, a schedule for the acquisition of property and the building of branches, and a complete financial analysis.

Operating the Expanded System

In order to manage the ongoing operations of the expanded concept of BURGER, Berg recognized that a system of operating plans and controls was needed. These elements were necessary at the broad general level to chart the course for what was becoming a massive operation of a specialized type. Now, however, more detailed plans and controls were also needed to be sure that the details of the operation, which had been so finely tuned, were maintained within current objectives.

Berg felt that the heart of the BURGER empire (as it was now being called) was its superb service in a spotless place where one could get consistently good food at a low price. These characteristics of the quality of the food service offered by BURGER had to be maintained. This required a well-trained, highly motivated work force, and

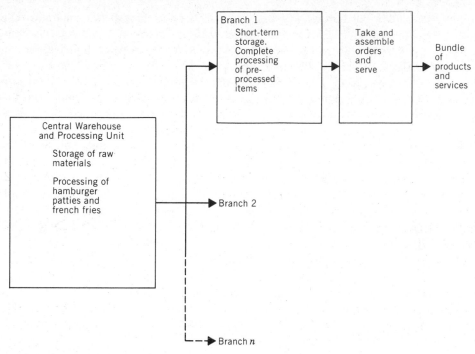

FIGURE 1-5
Expanded BURGER system to produce bundle of products and services.

reliable equipment. On the other hand, the massive supply problem required good planning, expert buying, close control over perishable products, and a distribution system which ensured that each branch had adequate supplies for sale. In addition, these broader plans had to take account of the rapid expansion in the number of both owned and franchised outlets.

At the outset, a forecasting system geared to the needs of day-to-day, week-to-week, and month-to-month operation was needed. Such a forecasting system had to reflect what was actually happening to the demand for BURGER's products, including trends and seasonal factors. The key forecasting factor, to which all other sales were tied, was the hamburger, so a statistical forecasting system was developed based on historical data. Each individual monthly forecast took account of current trends and seasonal factors. The forecast was the heart of the entire planning and control system because the other plans for aggregate levels of operation, materials control, and labor allocation were tied to the forecast of demand.

On the broad aggregate level, a measure of capacity and output was needed in order to make intermediate term plans and schedules in relation to demand. Such a measure was also needed to form the basis for orderly plans to bring new outlets into the operating system. Because virtually every customer order involved a hamburger, the basic unit of activity chosen was 100 pounds of hamburger sold. An average meal then involved a proportional amount of french fries, beverages, and so forth. Raw material ordering could be geared to this unit, as could other inputs such as labor. An aggregate planning and scheduling model was then constructed that was driven by forecasts of demand. The model yielded the best combination of regular

13

and overtime labor, and provided a basis for advance ordering of raw materials. The aggregate plan and schedule was then allocated to each branch. The aggregate plan was updated each month and presented for management approval and decision.

All raw material ordering was placed on a periodic inventory control system. Each week an order was placed for the amount sold the previous week plus or minus an adjustment for the anticipated sales in the upcoming week, based on data from the aggregate schedule. A buffer inventory of 1 week's supply was established as a minimum stock to absorb fluctuations in demand and variation in the supply lead time. Branch inventory was brought up to 2 days' supply each day with daily deliveries, based on forecasted sales rates. Throughout the inventory system, "first-in, first-out" rules were maintained to keep perishable materials as fresh as possible. The entire inventory management system was computerized and updated daily through the management information system (MIS). Each company-owned branch supervisor's performance was partially measured in terms of effective use of the raw materials provided.

Although the aggregate plan provided total values of approved regular and overtime work, a separate labor allocation was generated for the warehouse and owned branch outlets, based on branch forecasts and aggregate forecasts. Each supervisor was then given a monthly budget for regular and overtime labor to implement. This budget would allow the supervisor to hire or lay off personnel and use part-time and overtime work to meet the daily, weekly, and monthly fluctuations in labor needs. Each company-owned branch supervisor's performance was partially measured in terms of the effective use of labor.

Quality of product and service was a major concern, as noted previously. The main measures were consistent quality of food (hot items served hot, with meat still moist and bun not soggy, french fries hot and still crisp), customer and kitchen area cleaned continuously, and service times maintained within 1 minute for service and maximum customer waiting time of 4 minutes. With these measures of quality, an inspection team made regular rounds to all branches on a random call basis to measure service time and systematically rate the other aspects of quality on a rating form. The results were given to branch supervisors as well as to managers of franchised outlets, and were summarized in weekly reports generated through the management information system (MIS). Each company-owned branch supervisor's performance was partially measured in terms of the quality record. For franchise outlet managers, the quality measures were related to contract clauses, whereby a franchise could be revoked for consistently poor quality performance.

Maintenance of plant and equipment was also regarded as an important function. The cleanliness of the kitchen and customer areas was the responsibility of the individual supervisor. On the other hand, equipment and building maintenance was provided centrally. A regular preventive maintenance program on all equipment was maintained during the night shift, because the equipment was in use continuously every day. A small maintenance crew was used during the day to respond to emergency breakdowns.

Surveillance over the entire operation was conducted through the aggregate plan and a system of budgets and supervisory incentives. Profit performance was the key measure with individual components of material utilization, labor cost, and quality performance. Maintaining the delicate balance of operations involved the constant monitoring of the operating plans and control systems. Management must be sure that they represent current operations with accurate planning models and control reports, particularly because the situation is dynamic.

On a broader scale, there was the attempt to plan and control for the system as a whole through aggregate plans and schedules and the budgets and reports. Actual performance was compared with budget and was tied to a supervisor's and operating manager's incentive bonus plan.

Reassessment of Long-Term Goals

As the BURGER system grew, Berg periodically reviewed growth rates in relation to current capacity. His long-term strategy was to maintain a small but discernible gap between perceived future demand in marketing areas and system capacity. Financing new capacity was achieved through a combination of debt and retained earnings.

When new capacity was added, the new units were integrated into the existing systems. Periodically, Berg called for a review of existing systems because he felt that simply adding new units to existing systems could result in suboptimal operation.

PROBLEMS OF PRODUCTION/OPERATIONS MANAGEMENT

Reviewing the BURGER case example, and keeping in mind the three questions posed earlier, we can abstract a fairly typical list of operations management problems.

The key strategic planning decisions were as follows:

1. The selection and design of the particular bundle of products and services to be offered. It was finalized through assessment of interactions between the original concept, estimated costs of operation, equipment configurations, and alternate job or work crew designs.

2. Capacity planning decisions that also determined the locations for warehouses and branches and a growth plan.

3. A supply, storage, and logistics system.

The mature overall system design was rendered in terms of a design for the modular branch. The components of the design included a work flow layout and architectural plans, a labor staffing plan that specified just how each operation was to be carried out, including labor time standards, a material flow plan, a customer flow plan and layout, the central warehouse design including storage layout and logistics supply system, the production operations layout, equipment specifications, a schedule for the acquisition of property and the building of branches, and a complete financial analysis.

In reviewing what was done and how it was done, it appears that we employed an iterative design process, involving design and redesign to take account of various interactions. We employed long-range planning concepts, prediction and forecasting techniques, layout planning, equipment justification techniques, behavioral work concepts, product and service analyses, and waiting line methods and concepts. To be successful, the conception of the process and facilities design had to represent an integrated view of the conversion process for the system as a whole. In reviewing the longer term operations decisions which were made at BURGER, we must realize that they were very significant to the future of the organization. The decisions set the basic approach to supply, distribution, and operations for some time to come and committed the majority of the available capital of the enterprise.

The key decisions that set the design of the productive system were:

1. The design of the product/service bundle to be offered, finalized through an iterative process.
2. The selection of equipment and processes from among alternate technologies.
3. Job and work crew designs, including a crew schedule plan to take account of daily demand variations.
4. Detailed physical layout to accommodate work flow, equipment, and personnel, as well as the flow of customers.

The key problems and decisions in the day-to-day operations of BURGER were as follows:

1. Forecasting sales as a basis for planning and setting schedules.
2. Aggregate plans and schedules concerning how to allocate productive capacity consistent with demand.
3. Detailed scheduling of personnel and equipment in order to strike some balance between labor costs and the value of good service and scrap. Scheduling of work shifts and the assignment of personnel to the shifts so that the variable load was covered 7 days a week.
4. Inventory controls regarding the continuous supply of materials while maintaining reasonable costs of inventory and spoilage.
5. Quality control, setting permissible levels for unacceptable quality, as well as the definition of good quality for products and services. The adroit balance of these factors was regarded as crucial for BURGER.
6. Maintenance of the reliability of the system. With reference to maintenance effort, recognition of the random nature of equipment breakdowns and the fact that equipment downtime may be associated with important costs or loss of sales.
7. Cost control. Although many of the controls were meant to control costs, it is important to note that the control itself was on the activities that may generate cost, such as use of materials and labor to determine quality, and scrap. Cost control is then the derivative of activity control.

We have dealt with a service example in order to discuss the general nature of operations management problems, but we could just as well have used a manufacturing activity or a pure service activity. The relative importance of certain problems would have changed considerably with the nature of the system. For example, scheduling of workers and equipment would have been extremely important in a manufacturing system, as would the problem of equipment investment and maintenance.

Most service systems are labor intensive, resulting in emphasis on problems of maintaining quality and scheduling labor in work shifts for highly variable demand.

PERFORMANCE CRITERIA AND GOALS

The main criteria used by consumers of goods and services to evaluate the performance of productive systems is clearly understood. If one were to survey consumers, they would invariably express the degree of their satisfaction in terms of three dimensions: cost or price, availability (i.e., delivery time or waiting time), and quality. This does not mean that consumer behavior is simple, for there is ample evidence that it is very complex.

These three dimensions of consumer satisfaction then become the dominant bases for establishing criteria for the performance of productive systems. Although consumers' judgments may be relatively subjective, we must translate them into measures of performance that are as objective as possible. We must design a system to meet certain goals and to make operating decisions which maintain an appropriate balance between competing goals or improve that balance.

The criteria actually used are surrogates for consumers' judgments. While consumers are thinking of the cost to them, we must translate these into the labor costs, materials, and capital, and the appropriate balance between these cost components. We must think in terms of a larger system of interacting costs and cost trade-offs, as well as cost-price trade-offs. For example, the way that output is programmed for best cost performance may involve accumulating large inventories at considerable cost and risk in order to stabilize and reduce employment costs. Consumers' demand for time performance may be translated into the total time to serve them in a service operation, or delivery time for certain products, or off-the-shelf availability for certain other products. Consumers' demand for quality may translate into requirements in the design of products and the quality and consistency of workmanship. These characteristics, however, may finally be measured in such terms as chemical composition of raw materials, or tolerances maintained on critical dimensions of bearings.

To state these measures of performance suggests that the task is objective and perhaps even simple. It conveys the impression that to improve or even optimize the performance of a productive system, we simply put our efforts into the three areas of cost, on-time delivery or availability, and quality. Some of the reasons why the management of productive systems is neither as objective nor as simple as many would prefer are that the three dimensions of performance are not independent of each other. The time and quality factors can normally be improved with increased cost. Performance time may itself be a measure of quality as is true with many services. In some instances, extending performance time may improve quality. Therefore, in the decision process, it is the adroit balancing of the criteria that makes for the most effective decisions.

PRODUCTIVITY IN THE LONG TERM

We do not know who conceived the first productive systems. We do know that the great monuments of the ancient world required both technical know-how and a managerial system that organized resources, made grand plans, and executed those plans with excellent results. Examples are the Egyptian pyramids and sphinxes at Gizeh in about 2500 B.C., the Greek Parthenon in about 440 B.C., the Great Wall of China in about 214 B.C., and the construction marvels of the Roman world—aqueducts, public buildings, roads, and temples—which span a period including at least 400 to 100 B.C.

During and following the period of the building of the ancient monuments, a wide variety of products was produced through the handicraft system. Production/operations management began to develop with the Industrial Revolution, because it was during that period that the factory system evolved out of the handicraft system. A series of changes in industrial techniques, and in economic conditions made possible the development of larger productive units.

The Industrial Revolution

In 1764, James Watt made improvements on the steam engine that made it a practical power source. As a result, external energy sources began to replace muscle power in industry.

The sources of the productivity increases through 1920, shown in Figure 1-6, were probably dominated by the substitution of machine power and the application of division of labor. But late in this era, the seeds were being sown for dramatic changes.

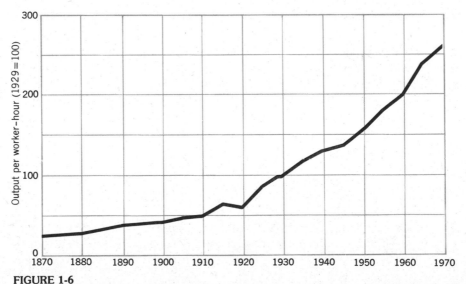

FIGURE 1-6
One hundred years of productivity growth. Output per worker-hour in United States manufacturing 1870–1972.
SOURCES: J. W. Kendick, Productivity Trends in the United States, Princeton University Press, Princeton, N. J., 1961, and the Bureau of Labor Statistics.

The Scientific Management Era

Just before the turn of the century, Frederick W. Taylor set in motion a managerial philosophy which he called "scientific management." The practice of the day was to allow workers to decide the means by which production would be achieved. They determined how to produce, according to their skills and past experience. The time required and the cost of production were guided by traditional methods.

Essentially, Taylor propounded a new philosophy which stated that the scientific method could and should be applied to all managerial problems. He urged that the methods by which work was accomplished should be determined by management through scientific investigation.

The science that Taylor envisioned was very slow to develop. The techniques, such as time study, production control boards, and wage incentive plans, came to be thought of as scientific management. To Taylor's chagrin, the broad general philosophy was often glossed over. The effects of the scientific management era can be seen in the dramatic rate of increase in productivity that developed during and after World War I (see Figure 1-6). Although the scientific management era produced great controversy, its results were to revolutionize managerial thought and practice.

Although Taylor was disappointed in the slow evolution of his science, important roots developed in the era that were a forecast of the modern era. These were the development and application of mathematical and probabilistic concepts. In 1915, F. W. Harris developed the first economic lot size model for a simple situation. In 1931, Walter Shewhart developed and introduced to industry statistical quality control concepts. Finally, in 1934, L. H. C. Tippett developed a sampling procedure to determine standards for work delays and work time called "work sampling." These early applications of mathematical and statistical technique foretold future events.

The Modern Era

The current rapid development of concept, theory, and technique began shortly after World War II. Research in war operations by the armed forces produced new mathematical and computational techniques that were applied to war operations problems. These problems seemed to parallel problems that occurred in productive systems, and the approach to war problems began to trickle into industrial use.

The original proposals for the applications of operations research to industry revolved around a broad systems approach to managerial problems. The techniques that were proposed for use were conceived of as modes of implementation. For a considerable period of time, however, the emphasis was put on the new and powerful analytical and computational techniques, and much of the broad systems view of problems became lost. Research and application became centered on such things as models of inventory control, mathematical programming, PERT/CPM, scheduling techniques, simulation, and waiting line models. The broad philosophical framework of systems analysis seemed to be something to talk about instead of something to do.

As with scientific management, there are probably good reasons why the current era has emphasized technique. It is much easier to work on a smaller problem of restricted scope than to grapple with the large-scale problems. The systems concept requires models that take account of higher-order interactions between organizational units. This is not only difficult to accomplish in a conceptual sense, but may approach the impossible in an organizational sense.

During the modern era, the field of production/operations management concentrated initially on quantitative methodology applied to productive systems. As these techniques become integrated into the field, however, production/operations management is again turning to the "management" in its apt title. Although models and techniques continue to be important, the emphasis is being placed on their managerial use, tradeoffs between quantitative and nonquantitative criteria, and on the relationships between problem areas.

The modern era is characterized by an acceleration of the substitution of machine power and the use of machines for computation and control. The specialization concept has been broadened and applied at all levels including work, specialization within organizations, and industry. However, the unique element in the modern era is science in management within the general framework of systems concepts. The average annual rate of productivity increase during the modern era is about 5 percent, although this average rate was not maintained during the 1973 to 1975 recession, nor in the period following.

THE PRODUCTIVITY CRISIS

Figure 1-6 presents a record for which any nation could be proud, but it ends in 1970; both Figure 1-6 and the proud record seem to end there. Following the 1973 to 1975 recession, U.S. productivity has seemed to flounder as shown by the leveling trend in Figure 1.2.

Table 1-2 provides a comparative record of productivity statistics for 6 countries during the recent period of 1960 to 1980. During that period, United States productivity averaged only 2.7 percent, ending with an actual decline in productivity in 1980 (−0.3 percent). During the same period, Japan had an average productivity

TABLE 1-2   Changes in Manufacturing Productivity, 1960-1980 (Annual changes in percent)

Year	United States	Canada	Japan	France	West Germany	United Kingdom
Output per year						
1960–80	2.7	3.8	9.4	5.6	5.4	3.6
1960–73	3.0	4.5	10.7	6.0	5.5	4.3
1973–80	1.7	2.2	6.8	4.9	4.8	1.9
1974	−2.4	1.6	2.4	3.5	6.0	0.8
1975	2.9	−2.6	3.9	3.1	4.8	−2.0
1976	4.4	4.9	9.4	8.2	6.3	4.0
1977	2.4	5.1	7.2	5.1	5.3	1.6
1978	0.9	3.1	7.9	5.3	3.8	3.2
1979	1.1	1.2	8.0	5.4	6.3	3.3
1980	−0.3	−1.4	6.2	0.6	−0.7	0.3

SOURCE. P. Capdevielle, and D. Alvarez, "International Comparisons of Trends in Productivity and Labor Costs," *Monthly Labor Review*, December 1981, pp. 14-20.

increase of 9.4 percent, and France and West Germany had productivity increases of 5.6 and 5.4 percent respectively.

Table 1-3 shows the effect of both productivity and hourly compensation on unit labor costs for the same six countries during the same 1960 to 1980 period. While the net cost effects were greater in Japan than in the United States during the earlier period of 1960 to 1973, the most recent period of 1973 to 1980 is of great concern, because unit costs increased by 7.5 percent in the U.S. versus only 3.4 percent in Japan, culminating in a 1980 increase of 11 percent versus only 0.8 percent in Japan. When these figures are expressed in U.S. dollars in the bottom half of Table 1-3, we see that the 1980 change in unit labor costs was 11 percent for the U.S. versus an actual decline in unit labor costs of 2.5 percent in Japan.

Both Japan and West Germany can deliver steel in the U.S. at prices which the U.S. producers cannot meet. Toyota has taken over a large share of the U.S. auto market while our domestic auto producers seem unable to compete not only on price, but also on the basis of the design of the product demanded and its quality. Managers know and understand what is happening to their competitive position.

TABLE 1-3   **Changes in Manufacturing Unit Labor Costs in 6 Countries, 1960–1980 (Annual changes in percent)**

Year	United States	Canada	Japan	France	West Germany	United Kingdom
Unit labor costs						
1960–80	3.8	4.7	5.3	5.9	4.7	8.8
1960–73	1.9	1.8	3.5	3.1	3.7	4.1
1973–80	7.5	9.5	3.4	9.9	4.7	17.2
1974	13.3	13.2	28.1	16.2	8.7	24.1
1975	8.8	17.8	12.6	16.1	7.5	32.5
1976	3.4	9.0	−2.5	5.6	0.9	12.7
1977	5.7	7.3	2.4	8.6	4.4	10.7
1978	7.3	4.3	−1.8	7.3	4.6	12.8
1979	8.6	8.6	−1.3	8.1	2.7	15.4
1980	11.0	10.9	0.8	14.3	8.7	23.3
Unit labor costs in U.S. dollars						
1960–80	3.8	4.4	8.0	6.5	9.3	6.6
1960–73	1.9	1.9	4.9	2.8	6.1	2.6
1973–80	7.5	6.4	8.3	10.9	11.2	15.3
1974	13.3	15.8	19.0	7.2	11.5	18.5
1975	8.8	13.3	10.7	30.3	13.1	25.8
1976	3.4	12.5	−2.4	−5.3	−1.6	−8.5
1977	5.7	−0.4	13.3	5.5	13.1	7.0
1978	7.3	−2.8	26.2	17.1	21.0	24.0
1979	8.6	5.7	−5.7	14.3	12.4	27.7
1980	11.0	11.1	−2.5	15.3	9.8	35.1

NOTE. Rates of change computed from the least squares trend of the logarithms of the index numbers.

SOURCE. P. Capdevielle, and D. Alvarez, "International Comparisons of Trends in Productivity and Labor Costs," *Monthly Labor Review,* December 1981, pp. 14–20.

The data in Tables 1-2 and 1-3 are alarming and are producing an inferiority complex among U.S. producers. Putting these data in perspective with comparative absolute productivity figures is valuable. These data represent productivity *changes* during the periods stated. However, on an absolute basis, U.S. productivity is by all odds the highest in the world by a substantial margin. If agriculture is included, the margin is even greater. Therefore, the concern is that the United States is losing its advantage and, of course, that it has already lost its lead in certain industries.

The reasons for the decline in United States productivity and ability to compete internationally are complex, involving socioeconomic factors in other cultures versus our own governmental policies, and many other factors. Certainly part of the cause is that we have made conscious social decisions that adversely affect productivity, but which improve air quality, noise levels, employee safety, and so on. Nations that ignore these factors may find that they will have to make similar social decisions at some point, tending to equalize this dimension of productivity change.

One fact seems clear: to reverse the decline in the U.S. position, we must place new emphasis on all the factors that contribute to productivity and quality improvement. We must train people in the art and science of managing productive systems. Professional managers of productive systems are at a premium today, for we now know that their skills are essential if we are to regain our competitive position with high quality and low cost products and services. What can these managers of productive systems do to produce better products at lower cost? Following is a sampler of the kinds of activities and decision areas. It involves strategy, technology, capacity, location, positioning policy, inventories, system dynamics, and planning. All these factors, which we discuss on the following pages, have productivity-quality implications.

THE OPERATING MANAGER AND STRATEGY

There are basically four functional types of managers in an enterprise: finance, marketing, operations, and personnel. There are strategic implications in all of these functions. The long-term financial viability of a firm can be affected by the financing mechanisms chosen. The labor and personnel policies can also have a bearing on the long-term viability: poor policies can "derail" an otherwise successful venture, and sound policies can build important aspects of human capital. Marketing can promote the fundamental values that exist and sense the directions that may be fruitful, showing the way for the future.

But the core of strategic planning is in operations—the other three only support the fundamental operations function of creating goods and services. The operating manager presides over the planning issues that set the course for quality, cost, dependability as a supplier, and flexibility/service. Operating managers must select an adroit combination of strategies involving processes and product designs for production.

The Productive System as a Competitive Weapon

Managers compete in part with their productive systems. Profitability is related to the price-cost gap, and the operations function has responsibility for the cost side of the equation. All costs of production and distribution are affected by the operations manager's decisions. Quality is a competitive weapon, whatever its target level. A reputation for dependability of supply is a strong competitive weapon, and the manager's strategic choice may have an important bearing on enterprise success. Finally, the manager's decision about whether or not to accommodate customer needs for variation in the product or service has an important bearing on the definition of the business.

Strategy and Technology

A strategy must be selected that joins the available producing technologies with the nature of the market. Choices can be made that emphasize low cost and availability of products or flexibility and quality. The traditional industrial image of low cost and high production volume can be precisely the wrong strategy for many situations, as Mr. Ford finally realized with his Model T. In selecting joint product/process strategies, single-minded drives toward extreme positions of strategy need careful consideration.

Successful operating managers may be rather contemplative, even academic, in their approaches to these strategic issues. High-technology, assembly line production systems are good images, but the manager's job is to assess the situation in relation to the market and retain an appropriate degree of flexibility.

Capacity and Location

The strategic implications of capacity and location planning are enormous. If you overbuild, you load costs of products and services with unneeded overhead. If you underbuild, you may miss market opportunities. If you build capacity in the wrong places, you increase distribution costs or miss market opportunities. Technological innovations in either products or processes can render physical facilities obsolete. Alternate strategies for adding capacity can have a marked effect on costs and flexibility of operation. Long planning and execution times can compound already fuzzy conclusions on the best strategies. But these strategic issues are a fascinating part of the operating manager's position.

Positioning Policy

One of the important decisions for managers of manufacturing operations is whether to adopt a to-stock or to-order positioning policy. In general, we assume that systems that produce high-volume standardized products will produce to stock, and systems that produce low-volume products with greater variety will produce to order. But there are exceptions to both of these situations.

The to-stock/to-order managerial decision rests on trade-offs between a number of conflicting advantages and disadvantages. There are market advantages to having products available off-the-shelf, but there are inventory risks. If the product is subject to obsolescence, the inventory risk may be substantial. There may be manufacturing cost reductions possible in manufacturing to stock, but are the risks worth it on balance?

Managing Inventories

Managers need to be aware of the nature of the production-distribution system in their particular industry, and the different functions that inventories perform in the system. First, inventories provide managers with flexibility. If there is an inventory of finished goods, for example, then the manager can deploy that inventory wherever the demand seems to be strong. Or, the manager with finished goods inventory can have options concerning the production plan for the upcoming period, rather than having to produce according to a "panic" schedule to meet high demand for a certain item.

Second, the astute manager who understands the virtues of each of the components of inventory can use them selectively to implement the corporate strategy in the marketplace. For example, in building inventory for a special promotion, a large part of the buildup must take place in the pipelines, resulting in time lags, and a larger than anticipated allocation of investment in inventories. Holding a portion of inventories as a buffer against random demand surges can help implement a "to-stock" policy. Seasonal inventories can be used to stabilize employment and to have ample products available in the market when a seasonal buying surge begins.

Managing System Dynamics

Finally, an understanding of the production-distribution system and its system dynamics is of considerable managerial importance. When demand changes, the structure of the system can produce amplified effects upstream in the system. Depending on the magnitude of time delays of information flows, an increase in consumer demand can result in an overreaction at the factory level resulting in hiring too many workers only to find that they were not needed and must be laid off. A large and sudden decrease in consumer demand could shut down the plant while the system feeds on the pipeline inventories. One common error is for managers to misinterpret pipeline filling during a demand increase as a part of a fundamental demand increase; the mistake results in gearing up for a greater increase than exists, usually resulting in too much inventory and too many workers than actually required.

Planning—The Manager's Weapon

The manager's weapon against the vagaries of the marketplace and the complexities of the production-distribution system is in planning. The planning process needs to raise the questions of possible misinterpretations of what is happening, and to make comprehensive plans that take all the data into account. It is in the planning process that the allocation of productive resources takes place for the upcoming production period. What is the most economical allocation of the short-term sources of capacity such as regular time, overtime, seasonal inventories, and outside capacity sources? Should new equipment purchases be considered? What will be the policy regarding hiring and layoff? What trade-off should be made between the most economical production plan and employee and community relations, if layoff is suggested by the economics of the situation?

THE FUTURE OF INDUSTRIALIZED SOCIETY

The modern era with its systems approach and powerful new tools of analysis will be tested severely in the future. Present trends of population growth, natural resource drain, and pollution are on a collision course with industrialized society. Some predict disaster for the existence of life on this planet. It is clear that world population is increasing at rates for which adequate support systems may reach limits, thus causing a reversal and decay of living standards. At the same time the effects of finite natural resource limits are being recognized, and indeed the methods of systems analysis have been used to analyze these complex problems and to predict the impact of alternatives.

No one doubts that the population-resource-pollution complex of problems is of great significance. The delivery systems for all kinds of products and services must be improved and must meet the requirements of a broader set of criteria if we hope to keep pace. This is the role of production/operations management in society.

From a quite different point of view, there will likely be changes in industrialized society. Some say that the postindustrial society has already arrived and that values are changing. There are forecasts that automation will take over, and that the industrial labor force will decline to the range of 2 to 10 percent of the total by the year 2000. A disturbing trend in industrial productivity suggests a leveling off in the late 1970s. The design of productive systems must find an appropriate role for humans and not treat them simply as links in a giant machine, unless total automation is achieved. Thus, even presuming that we survive pollution and gain control of population and limited natural resource problems, industrialized society seems destined for dramatic changes.

PLAN FOR THE BOOK

The main topics of the book divide according to the three basic questions raised in connection with the BURGER example: What are the strategic planning decisions? What decisions set the productive system design? What are the day-to-day decisions required to operate an ongoing productive system? But we are also interested in the interrelationships between topics.

The balance of the book deals with major groups of chapters that center on Strategic Planning in Part Two, including the system design, and Operations Planning and Control in Part Three.

There are also seven appendixes that supplement the main thrust of the text. These appendixes support particular topics in the main text and may be used either for review or to add more analytical substance. For example, the materials in Appendix A, Capital Costs and Investment Criteria, are useful at several points in the text where costs are analyzed. Appendixes B and C deal with linear programming and are useful where resource allocation is an issue or where transportation networks are being discussed. Appendix D, Waiting Lines, and Appendix E, Monte Carlo Simulation, are useful in dealing with certain aspects of service systems. Appendix F, Work Measurement, is an important adjunct to job and process design.

REVIEW QUESTIONS

1. Services have become relatively more important in our economy as indicated by Figure 1-1. It is also generally true that the dominant cost in services is labor.

What are the future prospects for continued rapid increases in productivity in the United States economy if the conversion to services continues?

2. The rise in medical costs seems to outstrip the price increases in other services, as well as the consumer price index in general. It also continues to rise very much faster than productivity (see Figure 1-2). From what you know of health care systems, what are the most promising areas for cost reduction and productivity increase?

3. If we define productive systems simply as "the means by which we transform resource inputs to useful goods and services," what do you envision as the problems of managing these kinds of processes?

4. Productivity in manufacturing has increased steadily since 1869, as shown by Figure 1-6, and has grown at an increasing rate since about 1920. Rationalize these increases in productivity. What were their sources? What role did operations management play?

5. Postulate an output per worker-hour curve for the service sector of our economy, similar to Figure 1-6. Rationalize the shape of the curve in a way similar to that shown in your answer to question 4.

6. The concept of division of labor has been broadly applied in our society. Give examples at the level of an individual job or task, within organizations, within industries, and within society in general.

7. What did the scientific management era contribute to useful concepts of operations management? How can we measure the value of these contributions?

8. Because both the modern era and the scientific management era profess to apply scientific methods to managerial problems, how can the modern era be distinguished from its predecessor? How can we measure the independent impact of the modern era?

9. Thinking in terms of the BURGER example, outline the problems of operations management. Which of the items in your list of problems do you feel are independent of other problems?

REFERENCES

Buffa, E. S., and J. S. Dyer, *Management Science/Operations Research: Model Formulation and Solution Methods* (2nd ed.), Wiley, New York, 1981.

Chase, R. B., and N. J. Aquilano, *Production and Operations Management: A Life Cycle Approach* (3rd ed.), Irwin, Homewood, Ill., 1981.

Fitzsimmons, J. A., and R. S. Sullivan, *Service Operations Management*, McGraw-Hill, New York, 1982.

Hayes, R. H., "Why Japanese Factories Work," *Harvard Business Review*, July–August 1981, pp. 56–66.

Sasser, W. E., R. P. Olson, and D. D. Wyckoff, *Management of Service Operations: Text, Cases, and Readings*, Allyn & Bacon, Boston, 1978.

Wheelwright, S. C., "Japan—Where Operations Really Are Strategic," *Harvard Business Review*, July–August 1981, pp. 67–74.

PART TWO

DECISIONS HAVING LONG-TERM SIGNIFICANCE

CHAPTER 2

Strategic Planning Decisions

THE CHAPTERS IN PART TWO ARE DIRECTED TOWARD LONG-TERM plans that have significance for the overall competitive strategy. The ultimate goal of the strategy of an enterprise is to integrate all the management functions such as marketing, operations, finance, human resources, and concern for the legal and social environment. However, the *competitive* strategy of the organization is represented primarily by its decisions with respect to its markets and its competitors.

The strategy naturally places certain demands on the production function, but a proactive stance can use policies for productive system design as a competitive weapon. What is the status of technology in both products and processes? Is technology likely to make either products or processes obsolete? How large should capacity be 5 or 10 years from now? Where should this capacity be located? Should the capacity be added in steady increments, or periodically in larger units? If the latter, will the initial slack capacity represent too large an overhead and risk? The capacity question is interrelated with the location of distribution points. Where should these distribution points be located? Should the system be tooled up for continuous output, or is a functional arrangement more in keeping with the risks? How will these decisions impact the design of the organization of work, jobs, and detailed physical design?

The preceding questions represent major managerial issues of long-term significance and their resolution should reflect the organization's overall competitive strategy. The decisions commit the organization in ways that are not easily changed without substantial loss. Such decisions commonly require major investments, often the largest of the enterprise assets.

PRODUCT-SERVICE STRATEGIES

At one extreme, we might have products or services that are custom in nature, where the product or service is especially designed to the specifications and needs of the customer or client. Examples are printing of advertising copy, a prototype spacecraft, many producer goods, or architectural services. A custom product is not available from inventory because it is one of a kind, and the nature of a service is such that it is not inventoriable whether custom or not. The emphasis in the custom product-service strategy is on uniqueness, dependability of delivery on time, quality, and flexibility to change the production process in accordance with changing customer preferences. Cost or price is a lesser consideration. If the enterprise is profit making, part of the strategy is to obtain the high profit margins that typically are available for custom designs.

At the other extreme, the product or service is highly standardized. Products of this type are available from inventory. They are "off-the-shelf" because each unit is identical and the nature of demand is such that availability and cost are important elements of competitive strategy. There is very little product differentiation, and there is a limited variety in the products. The most extreme examples are products that have virtually no variety such as standard steel and aluminum shapes, and commodities such as sugar or gasoline. Though not inventoriable, some services are available in highly standardized form such as social security, insurance, motor vehicle registration, and fast-food services. Important managerial concerns for highly standardized products or services are for dependability of supply and low cost.

Between the extremes of custom design and high standardization of product and services, we have mixed strategies that are sensitive to variety, some flexibility, to moderate cost, and dependability of supply. In these situations, quality of product or service is an important but not overwhelming criterion. In this middle ground, we have multiple products available, possibly from inventory, or on the basis of order, depending on enterprise strategy and the balance of costs. In the middle ground some of the products and services are available in fairly low volume, but some, such as automobiles, are available in high volume. The great majority of products available today are in the middle category. Most consumer products are available from inventory. Most producer goods are available by order and may be subject to some special design modifications to meet individual needs, though the basic designs are quite standard. Although services are not inventoriable, they may be available in basically standardized modules. For example, treatment of diseases follows standard practices though there are necessarily substantial variations in individual treatments.

The Product Life Cycle

The concept of the product life cycle unifies the previous discussion of product-service strategies. If we look at the possibilities shown in Figure 2-1 at an instant of time, we see the array of low-volume custom products and services, low-volume multiple model partially standardized products and services, high-volume partially standardized products and services, and high-volume highly standardized commodities. But if we traced the development of a product or service now available in high volume in highly standardized form from its original introduction, we would find that it had gone through phases. These phases are shown in Figure 2-1 as introduction at low volume and custom design, growth in sales during which variety became more limited, maturity during which the product variety is even more limited and it

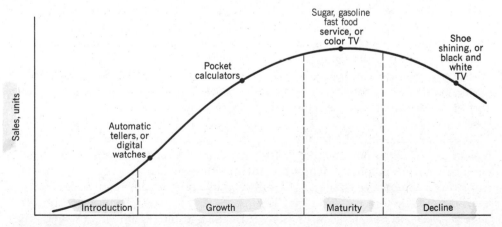

FIGURE 2-1
Typical S-curve of the introduction, growth, maturity, and decline in the life cycle of products or services.

becomes basically a commodity, and finally decline as substitutions become available that may be superior in terms of function, quality, cost, or availability.

The product life-cycle curve, often called the S-curve, is particularly important in marketing strategies for pricing and market penetration. Of course, one of the objectives in marketing strategy is to find ways to renew the life cycles of products that have matured or are in a state of decline. For example, there has been a market for calculators for a long time, satisfied by mechanical calculators for many years. But the mechanical calculator was replaced by the electromechanical calculator, the electronic calculator, and most recently by the pocket electronic calculator. Each generation of calculators has had a product life cycle that has followed the general S-curve development.

We should note that there are some custom products that are mature as custom products and that do not go through the phases that we have discussed. For example, there is a market for custom-built homes. Architects design such homes and contractors build them to specifications. The industry involved is mature in that it regularly produces custom designed homes and has refined a system, but if the custom home were produced in volume, it would no longer be a custom home.

PRODUCTIVE SYSTEM TYPES

The basic managerial strategies adopted for the productive system must be related to the product-service strategies. Obviously, it would be inappropriate to use a continuous process capable of producing millions of gallons of an experimental chemical. Again, we think in terms of alternate strategies for the extremes, as well as a middle ground.

Process-Focused Systems

A productive system for custom products or services must be flexible. It must have the ability to process according to the customer or client specifications. For example, an aerospace manufacturer must fabricate special component part designs. The equipment and personnel must be capable of meeting the individual component specifications and of assembling the components in the special configurations of the custom product.

The nature of the demand on the productive system results in intermittent demand for the use of the facilities, and each component flows from one process to the next intermittently. Physical facilities are organized around the nature of processes, and personnel are specialized by generic process type. For example, in a machine shop we might expect to find milling machine departments, lathe departments, drill departments, and so on. In a general hospital we find X-ray departments, laboratory, surgery, obstetric wards, and so on, as generic departments. The flow of the item being processed in intermittent systems is dictated by the individual product or service requirements, so the routes through the productive system are variable. Thus, the process-focused system with intermittent demand must be flexible as required by the custom product or service, and each generic department and its facilities are used intermittently as needed by the custom orders. Figure 2-2a and b show examples of

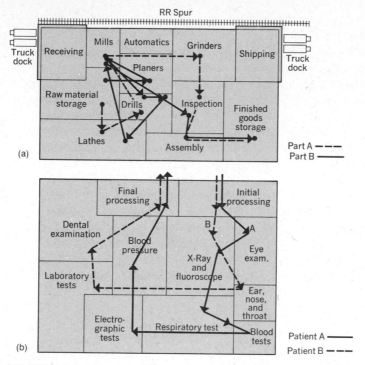

FIGURE 2-2
Common examples of process-focused systems (demand on system is intermittent); (*a*) machine shop, and (*b*) medical clinic.

process-focused systems with intermittent demand in a machine shop, and in a medical clinic.

Product-Focused Systems

By contrast, the nature of the demand on the productive system that produces highly standardized products or services results in continuous use. Also, the material flow may be continuous as in petroleum refining, or approaches continuous flow as with automobile fabrication and assembly. Because of the very high volume requirements of such systems, special processing equipment and entire producing systems can be justified as a productive system strategy. Processing is adapted completely to the product or service. Individual processes are physically arranged in the sequence required and the entire system is integrated for the single purpose, like a giant machine. Thus, continuous systems have a product focus. Under these extreme conditions of very high demand of highly standardized products the production process is integrated and makes use of mechanization and automation to achieve standardization and low cost. Inventories of standardized products may be an important element of production as well as marketing strategy.

We also find continuous use of facilities, and near continuous flow through productive systems in the service sector. Such mass processing systems are common in some government services such as social security. Also, fast-food services approach

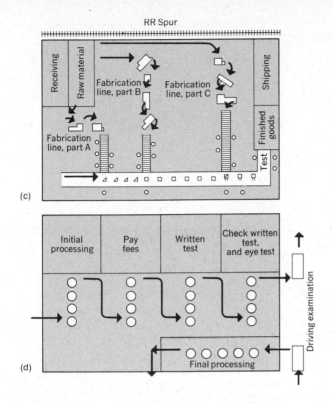

FIGURE 2-3
Common examples of product-focused systems (demand on system is continuous); (*a*) industrial fabrication and assembly lines, and (*b*) driver's license processing with serial flow.

continuous flow. Figures 2-3*a* and *b* show examples of product-focused systems where demand is continuous in manufacturing, and in driver's license processing.

Between the two extremes of intermittent demand (process focused) and continuous demand (product focused) systems we have a middle ground of productive systems that must deal with low-volume multiple products, and relatively high-volume multiple products. The low-volume multiple-product situation usually involves a process-focused system patterned after Figure 2-2, but products are produced in *batches*, thereby achieving certain economies of scale compared with the job shop system designed to deal with custom products.

The high-volume multiple-product situation is likely to employ a mixed production strategy that combines both the process-focused and product-focused systems of Figures 2-2 and 2-3. In manufacturing, it is often true that parts fabrication is organized on a batch-intermittent basis with final assembly organized on a line or continuous basis. Because parts fabrication output volume may be substantial but not large enough to justify continuous use of facilities, parts are produced in economical batches. The inventories resulting from batching again provide an important producing strategy. On the other hand, the nature of assembly makes possible continuous lines dedicated to certain products.

To summarize, we have two ways of classifying productive systems, by the nature of the demand on the system (intermittent or continuous), and whether or not

TABLE 2-1   **Two-way Classification of Productive Systems**

Type of productive system (nature of demand on system and focus)	Output is inventoriable	Output is noninventoriable (availability is defined as capability to produce)
Intermittent (process focus)	Batch processing	Jobbing printer Jobbing machine shop Large-scale projects General hospital Municipal offices

Continuous (product focus)	Commodity processing
	  Oil refining
	  Sugar refining
	  Auto production
	  Distribution systems
		Government services
		  Social Security
		  Mass food services
		  Transportation service

inventories are available as a strategy, as shown in Table 2-1. First, the nature of the demand on productive system, being intermittent or continuous, provides the basis for designing operations planning and control systems. If the system has intermittent demand, planning and control must be based on the individual production order, or its equivalent. We must be concerned with flexibility, variable routes through the system, general purpose equipment, and individual process and quality control. If the system has continuous demand, planning and control can be somewhat broader or aggregate in nature. The entire system becomes more interdependent and integrated. Failure at any stage within the integrated system may affect the system as a whole.

Whether or not the output is inventoriable is the second basis for classifying productive systems. In product systems, inventories can provide flexibility in the alternate producing strategies available. Just because inventories are an available strategy, however, does not mean that one would always choose to produce to stock rather than to order. That decision is more complex, depending on market and competitive factors and the broader positioning strategy chosen. By contrast, noninventoriable output systems hold their capability in readiness (in inventory), rather than the output itself. This is true of service systems as well as the custom product systems, and in that sense, the custom product system offers a service.

THE EXPERIENCE CURVE PHENOMENON

It is a well-established phenomenon in manufacturing that as experience is gained through production, unit costs are reduced. Originally, the cost improvement was attributed to a learning effect by workers, such as the division of labor effect noted by Adam Smith (the development of a skill or dexterity when a single task was performed repetitively). Now, however, the effect is recognized as resulting from a wide variety of additional sources, such as changes in production methods and tools, improved product design from the point of view of producibility, standardization, changes in layout and improved flow, economies of scale, and improvements in organization. Actually, the worker learning effect is one that usually occurs rather quickly.

The concepts of the experience curve (also called the learning curve) were first formalized in the aircraft industry during World War II, though there is currently a general recognition of its applicability and usefulness. Studies of production costs of military aircraft showed that with each doubling of *cumulative* total output of a model of an aircraft, the units costs were reduced by 20 percent of the unit cost before doubling. Thus, the second unit cost only 80 percent of the first, the fourth unit cost 80 percent of the second, the hundredth unit 80 percent of the fiftieth, and so on. This is formalized mathematically as

$$c_n = c_1 n^{-b} \qquad (1)$$

where

c_n = the cost for the nth item
c_1 = the cost of the first item
n = cumulative output in units
b = a parameter depending on the rate of unit cost decrease

The graph of Equation 1 for a specific example where $c_1 = \$10$ and $b = 0.322$ shows a nonlinear cost reduction curve in Figure 2-4. In practice, however, the more usual representation of the experience curve has been on log-log graph paper so that Equation 1 plots as a straight line. To see why, take the log of both sides of Equation 1, so we have

$$\log c_n = \log c_1 - b\,(\log n)$$

and,

$$b = \frac{\log c_1 - \log c_n}{\log n} \qquad (2)$$

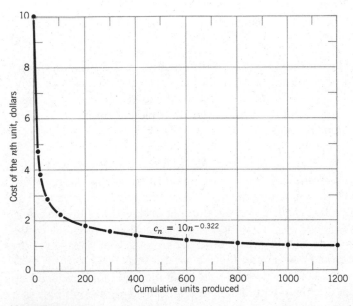

FIGURE 2-4
Form of 80 percent experience curve ($c_n = 10n^{-0.322}$) plotted with linear scales.

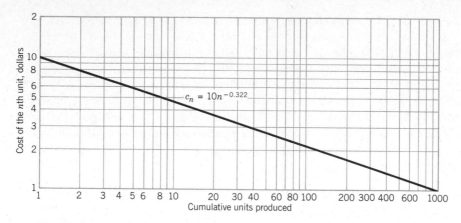

FIGURE 2-5
The experience curve, $c_n = 10n^{-0.322}$, plotted on log-log graph paper.

Noting that $\log 1 = 0$, and $\log 2 = 0.3010$, we can represent the first doubling of cumulative output, and derive a simple formula for computing the value of b for any experience curve:

$$b = \frac{\log 1 - \log (P/100)}{\log 2} = \frac{-\log (P/100)}{0.3010} \qquad (3)$$

where P is the unit cost percentage associated with the learning curve.

Taking a specific example where the first unit costs \$1, then the second unit would cost \$0.80 for an 80 percent experience curve. Substituting in Equation 3

$$b = \frac{-\log 80/100}{0.3010} = \frac{-\log 0.8}{0.3010} = \frac{0.0969}{0.3010} = 0.3220$$

Then, the 80 percent experience curve has the specific equation for our example of

$$c_n = c_1 n^{-0.322} \qquad (4)$$

To compute the cost of the nth unit one simply inserts the desired value of n, and the cost of the first unit, c_1, in either Equation 1 or 2, for a given value of b. The graph of the example where $c_1 = \$10$ for an 80 percent experience curve is shown in Figure 2-4 plotted with linear scales, and in Figure 2-5 plotted on log-log paper. The parameter b for experience curves with other percents of unit cost reduction for doubling cumulative output can be computed in a similar way.

Table 2-2 provides values of the parameter b for common values of experience curve percentages. The table also provides calculated values of the term n^{-b} in Equation 1 for various values of n, the cumulative number of units produced. The cost of the nth unit can then be calculated as the product of the cost of the first unit, c_1, and the corresponding table value. For example, for a 95 percent experience curve, the table value for n^{-b} for $n = 100,000$ is 0.4266. Therefore, if the first unit cost \$150, the 100,000th unit would cost $150 \times 0.4266 = \$63.99$.

The assumption of the experience curve that states that the unit cost is reduced by a constant percent for each doubling of cumulative output makes it easy to plot as a straight line on log-log paper without using the equations directly. For the example graphed in Figure 2-5, plot the cost for the first unit, $n = 1$, $c_1 = \$10$; then plot

TABLE 2-2   **Values of b, and n^{-b} for Common Experience Curve Percentages**

	Experience Curve Percentages						
	99	95	90	85	80	75	70
b	0.0145	0.0740	0.1520	0.2345	0.3220	0.4151	0.5146
n, Cumulative Output, Units				n^{-b}			
5	0.9769	0.8877	0.7830	0.6856	0.5956	0.5127	0.4368
10	0.9672	0.8433	0.7047	0.5828	0.4764	0.3845	0.3058
50	0.9449	0.7486	0.5518	0.3996	0.2837	0.1971	0.1336
100	0.9354	0.7112	0.4966	0.3396	0.2270	0.1478	0.0935
500	0.9138	0.6314	0.3888	0.2329	0.1352	0.0758	0.0408
1,000	0.9047	0.5998	0.3499	0.1979	0.1081	0.0568	0.0286
5,000	0.8838	0.5324	0.2740	0.1357	0.0644	0.0291	0.0125
10,000	0.8750	0.5058	0.2466	0.1153	0.0515	0.0219	0.0087
100,000	0.8563	0.4266	0.1738	0.0672	0.0245	0.0084	0.0027
1,000,000	0.8185	0.3597	0.1225	0.0392	0.0117	0.0032	0.0008

NOTE. Table values for n^{-b} can be used in Equation 1 to calculate unit costs for the nth item, c_n, given c_1. For example, for an 85 percent experience curve and $c_1 = \$150$, the cost of the 5,000th unit is $c_{5,000}$ = 150 × (Table value for 85 percent and $n = 5000$) = 150 × 0.1357 = \$20.36.

$n = 2$, $c_2 = 0.8 \times 10 = \$8$. These two points are sufficient to draw the straight line. Additional check points can be calculated, such as $n = 4$, $c_4 = 0.8 \times 8 = \$6.40$, and so on.

Strategic Implications of the Experience Curve

The experience curve is particularly important in the rapid developmental and mature phases of the product life cycle, and usually where the system is product-focused. Especially during these phases, an understanding of the effects of experience can be used effectively in strategic planning.

First, the firm that has the largest market share will have produced the largest number of units and will have the lowest cost, even if all firms are on the same percent experience curve. Second, if through process technology advantages a firm can establish itself on a lower percent experience curve than a competitor, it will have lower unit costs even if both firms have the same cumulative output. Third, a firm with greater experience can use aggressive price policy as a competitive weapon to gain even greater market share. Fourth, a firm can use aggressive process technology policy by allocating resources toward mechanization in earlier stages and automation in later stages of growth to maintain its position on the experience curve, or to improve the slope of its experience curve. This strategy is particularly important in the mature phase of the product life cycle where competition is focused on cost.

Limitations of the Experience Curve

Perhaps the greatest limitation of the experience curve is that the benefits finally run out simply because of product obsolescence, as indicated by the product life cycle curve of Figure 2-1. But even before maturity occurs, the cost reductions due to experience have been providing smaller and smaller returns. This is apparent from the shape of the curve in Figure 2-4; early experience provides large returns, but as the product matures, it becomes more difficult to obtain further cost reductions.

As the product goes through the stages of life-cycle development the productive system also matures through the stages of custom volume job shop (intermittent with process focus), low-volume (batch), high-volume (mixed intermittent-continuous), and very high-volume (continuous with product focus). Another way to view what is happening as the productive system evolves is to note that it is becoming much less flexible and more and more capital intensive. This evolution is a large part of what makes the experience curve work, but at the same time it makes the firm vulnerable to radical changes in consumer tastes and product obsolescence.

Experience Curve for Process-Focused Systems

In process-focused systems we do not have the opportunity to learn what comes from constant repetition of an activity. Also, the lower volume makes it less likely that there will be improvements that result from mechanization and automation, and flow improvements in layout.

Nevertheless, there is cost improvement in these kinds of systems. Process-focused systems learn how to serve their customers and clients better through order processing, better labor assignment and scheduling, better tool design, improved layout, and so on. The results of experience are more difficult to document because we do not have a specific product produced over a period of time for which we can accumulate cost data. Nevertheless, the cost-improvement phenomenon exists in process-focused systems, though the net effect is less dramatic than it is in product-focused systems.

Competing and the Operations Function

As we stated previously in this chapter, the competitive strategy of an organization is represented by its policies with respect to the marketplace and its competitors. What then are the key dimensions of this strategy insofar as the operations function is concerned? There are four dimensions that enterprises use effectively: cost, quality, dependability as a supplier, and flexibility/service.

Cost. Although the competitive weapon in the marketplace is price, profitability is related to the difference between price and cost, and cost is the variable that can allow lower prices which may be profitable. Therefore, to compete on the basis of price requires an operations function capable of producing at low cost. All costs, including the capital and distribution costs, are included. Therefore, the effects of the experience curve are included, as well as the effects of location, product design, equipment use and replacement, and so on.

Quality. An organization can compete on the basis of the quality of its products and services. Customers and clients will often be willing to pay more for superior products, or wait for delivery. Examples of such products are the Rolls Royce autos and IBM computers, or the services of Frank Lloyd Wright as an architect.

Dependability of Supply. A reputation for dependability of supply or even off-the-shelf availability is often a strong competitive weapon. Again, customers may trade off cost or even quality in order to obtain on-time delivery when they need an item.

Flexibility/Service. How standard is a product or service? If a customer wants a variation in the product or service, can it be accommodated? If you are producing a standardized item in large volume, it would probably not be worthwhile to offer this kind of flexibility. You would probably respond to a request for variation with, "I am not in that kind of business." Yet, there may be a substantial volume for that kind of business. So a competitor could offer flexibility as a way of competing effectively. In addition, what services go with the sale? Are spare parts as available as the original product? If something goes wrong, will the item be serviced quickly and effectively? Flexibility/service is then an important element in enterprise strategy that is provided by the operations function.

The strategy employed by a given organization may blend the foregoing four dimensions in unique ways that reflect their situation and their competencies.

PRODUCTIVE SYSTEM/PRODUCT-SERVICE JOINT STRATEGIES

When we examine the product-service and productive system types jointly, it is useful to think of the product-service volume as the independent variable and the productive system type as the dependent variable, as represented by Figure 2-6. As the product develops through its life cycle the productive system goes through a life cycle of its own from a job shop system (process-focused) when the product is in its initial stages through intermediate stages to a continuous system (product-focused) when the product is demanded in large volume.

These stages of product and process development are interdependent and feed on each other. There is the obvious dependence of the appropriate type of productive system on the volume of product that is sold. But in addition, the volume of product sold is dependent in part on costs, and the price-quality competitive position which is dependent on the use of the appropriate productive system. The experience curve is a reflection of all of the factors that operate in a productive system to reduce costs and is an important element in a manager's competitive strategy. The results of the experience curve can indeed be used as the basis for aggressive pricing that may in itself be an important factor in building market share, further building experience and a progression down the curve. For example, in anticipation of a lower cost per unit at larger volumes in future time periods, a calculator firm may price its products even lower than the initial cost of production. In such aggressive pricing, however, risks must be balanced with potential benefits.

But would a firm always follow the strategy implied by the diagonal line of Figure 2-6? As we noted in the previous discussion of productive system types, process-focused systems provide flexibility and are somewhat more adaptable to product variety and to high-quality production. Thus, where the manager's strategy is focused on providing service, high quality, and meeting customer's individual needs, combinations between product volume and productive system types that are below the line in Figure 2-6 may be more appropriate, probably combined with production "to order." On the other hand, if the manager's strategy is on price and off-the-shelf

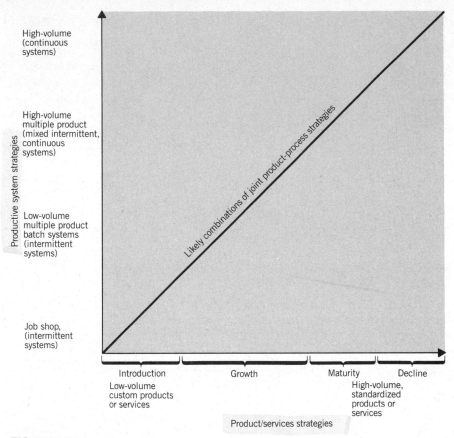

FIGURE 2-6
Relationship between product volume and the type of productive system used over a large range of volume occurring during the product life cycle.

availability, combinations above the line in Figure 2-6 may be more appropriate, combined with a production "to stock" system. Thus, we have a situation where Figure 2-6 may rovide a general relationship that should be observed, but actual strategies are better defined by a band or range as shown in Figure 2-7.

Competence in Operations

Some firms are very good at producing new products and bringing them to clients and customers, whereas others seem to have their greatest competence in refining the production of an item and producing it in large quantity, a strategy evident in many Japanese firms. This does not mean that one firm is more efficient than the other; it merely means that each has its own distinctive competence.

Perhaps one of the best prominent illustrations of how different firms operating in similar markets may take rather different joint strategies is the contrast between Texas Instruments (TI) and Hewlett Packard (HP). TI is an outstanding example of a firm that drives for high market share through aggressive pricing, depending on the experience curve to provide the long-run justification for the low prices of highly

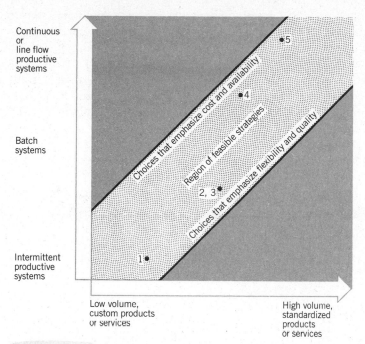

FIGURE 2-7
Mapping of productive system strategies in relation to product-service strategies. Feasible joint strategies occur in a region.

standardized products. HP, on the other hand, has followed a conscious policy of providing variety, innovative products, and high quality. HP intends to reap the higher unit profits that are the reward for innovation. When the field becomes crowded with competitors, HP moves on to the next innovation (see *Business Week*, June 9, 1975, pp. 50–58).

Given that there is a band of feasible strategies as indicated in Figure 2-7, one cannot say that there is a single correct strategy for a given situation. Rather there is a range of choices that may represent alternate joint strategies. Managers might choose a strategy that emphasizes cost and availability by choosing the combinations in the upper part of the band. Similarly, they could choose a strategy that emphasizes flexibility, choice, and quality by choosing combinations in the lower part of the band. In making these choices, managers need to take account of the distinctive competencies that their organization has developed. If they decide to fly in the face of these competencies and try to be something that they are not, they may be in for a long restaffing and learning period.

Examples of Joint Strategies. Hayes and Wheelwright [1979a] give specific examples of company strategy involving the Lynchburg Foundry, a wholly owned subsidiary of the Mead Corporation. Lynchburg has five plants in Virginia and surrounding states. The five plants represent different points in Figure 2-7. One plant is a job order shop making one-of-a-kind products, and the joint strategy is represented by point (1) in the lower left region of Figure 2-7. Two plants are organized to produce a variety of products in batches. These plants involve a strategy in the lower-middle range, where emphasis has been placed on the flexibility required by multiple products (points 2 and 3). A fourth plant is designed as a line-flow setup to produce only a few auto part castings. Thus, the joint strategy is represented by point (4) in the upper-middle range, and in the upper region where cost and availability are emphasized. Finally, the fifth plant is an automated pipe facility producing a highly standardized item in huge quantity on a continuous basis. The joint strategy for the fifth plant is therefore represented by point (5) in the upper region, to the left.

The Lynchburg examples indicate that an enterprise may need to employ different joint strategies for different product-process situations. The resulting planning and control policies and procedures need to be reflective of these quite different strategies; a uniform set of operations planning and control policies would be quite inappropriate.

It is unlikely that a strategy can remain static over long periods. As products or services mature in their life cycles, consumer preferences become known, designs become refined, volumes build, and the appropriate joint strategy must reflect these changes. Normally the progression involves a more capital intensive productive process that is more integrated, and there is necessarily a loss of flexibility [see Abernathy and Wayne, 1974].

Focus

An observation concerning the producing strategy of the Lynchburg Foundry is to note that each of the five plants has been specialized in some way. By specializing each plant, managers are given a more restricted scope that allows them to deal with more limited objectives, presumably making it possible for them to do their jobs more effectively. The advantages of specialization apply to managerial tasks as well as to other forms of work.

Skinner [1974] has referred to this concept of specialization by producing facility as "the focused factory." These concepts are closely linked with the overall enterprise strategy and indeed are an integral part of that strategy.

A factory that focuses on a narrow product mix for a particular market niche will outperform the conventional plant, which attempts a broader mission. Because its equipment, supporting systems, and procedures can concentrate on a limited task for one set of customers, its costs and especially its overheads are likely to be lower than those of the conventional plant. But, more important, such a plant can become a competitive weapon because its entire apparatus is focused to accompany the particular manufacturing task demanded by the company's overall strategy and marketing objective.

Thinking in terms of the five plants of the Lynchburg Foundry, each had been given a focus. The first was focused on one-of-a-kind products. Two plants were positioned to produce multiple products in batches. The fourth was focused on the production of a few auto part castings in high volume, and the fifth was a highly automated pipe factory which was focused entirely on that product. The managers of each facility were presented with a narrower range of customer types to supply that had unique requirements for quality, costs, and delivery. Although the Lynchburg Foundry is a large organization, the same general concepts can apply to individual product lines in a smaller organization.

The opposite producing strategy would have been to attempt to gain "economies of scale" by assembling all of these diverse objectives in one huge manufacturing facility managed centrally through common control systems. Presumably, the overhead per unit of output should be lower, but there is a trade-off in terms of meeting the diverse objectives of the several businesses that are involved.

Focus Versus Risk

As indicated earlier, there is risk of inflexibility that accompanies focus. The focused factory is a specialized facility that performs more limited tasks. Like highly specialized animals, a rapid change in the environment may lead to extinction. There is a loss of flexibility that results from more specialized equipment, systems, and even a managerial "hardening of the arteries," which makes the focused system vulnerable to change. Therefore, the concepts of focus should not be applied blindly. Rather, the manager's task is to provide the correct balance between specialization on the one hand and the risks of organizational obsolescence on the other. One of the most prominent examples of the potential dangers of focus is provided by the Ford Motor Company during the famous Model T era.

Figure 2-8 shows the price decline (in 1958 dollars) of the Model T during its long product life cycle. The price decline culminated in a costly conversion to the Model A, and finally, the price increases associated with the annual model changes began in about 1932.

Beginning in 1908, Henry Ford embarked on a conscious policy of price reduction that reduced the price from more than $5000 to nearly $3000. From that point on, the price decline was characterized by an 85 percent learning curve during the Model T era. Market share increased from 10.7 percent in 1910 to a peak of 55.4 percent in 1921. During this spectacular period of stable product design, innovations were largely process or production oriented:

The company accomplished savings by building modern plants, extracting higher volume from the existing plant, obtaining economies in purchased parts, and gaining efficiency through greater division of labor. By 1913 these efforts had reduced production throughput times from 21 days to 14. Later, production was speeded further through major process innovations like the moving assembly lines in motors and radiators, and branch assembly lines. At times, however, labor turnover reportedly ran as high as 40 percent per month.

Up to this point, Ford had achieved economies without greatly increasing the rate of capital intensity. To sustain the cost cuts, the company embarked on a policy of backward and further forward integration in order to reduce transportation and raw materials costs, improve reliability of supply sources, and control dealer performance. The rate of capital investment showed substantial increases after 1913, rising from 11 cents per sales dollar that year to 22 cents by 1921. The new facilities that were built or acquired included blast furnaces, logging operations, sawmills, a railroad, weaving mills, coke ovens, a paper mill, a glass plant, and a cement plant.

Throughput time was slashed to four days and the inventory level cut in half, despite the addition of large raw materials inventories. The labor hours required

43

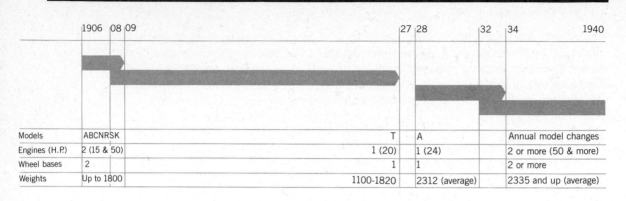

	1906 08 09	27 28	32 34 1940
Models	ABCNRSK	T	A	Annual model changes
Engines (H.P.)	2 (15 & 50)	1 (20)	1 (24)	2 or more (50 & more)
Wheel bases	2	1	1	2 or more
Weights	Up to 1800	1100-1820	2312 (average)	2335 and up (average)

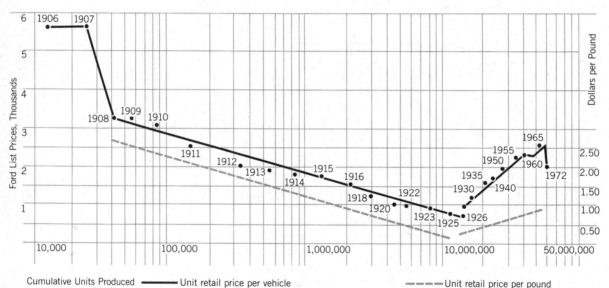

FIGURE 2-8

The Ford experience curve (in 1958 constant dollars). Source: W. J. Abernathy and K. Wayne, "Limits of the Learning Curve," *Harvard Business Review*, September–October 1974, pp. 109–119.

of unsalaried employees per 1000 pounds of vehicle delivered fell correspondingly some 60 percent during this period, in spite of the additions to the labor force resulting from the backward integration thrust and in spite of substantial use of Ford employees in factory construction.

Constant improvements in the production process made it more integrated, more mechanized, and increasingly paced by conveyors. Consequently, the company felt less need for management in planning and control activities. The percentage of salaried workers was cut from nearly 5 percent of total employment for 1913 to less than 2 percent by 1921; these reductions in Ford personnel enabled the company to hold in line the burgeoning fixed cost and overhead burden. [Abernathy and Wayne, 1974]

Beginning in the middle 1920s, however, General Motors successfully focused the competitive arena on product innovation. The Ford Company was so completely organized to produce a standardized product that the effects of the change in consumer demand nearly sunk the enterprise. While the company was a roaring success during the long period of stable consumer behavior, it had become a business "dinosaur," and could not adapt easily to the realities of the changed environment. Not only was the producing system inflexible, but so was management. A current observation concerning the inability of American auto manufacturers to adapt to consumer desire for smaller, more fuel-efficient cars suggests that Ford's ineffective strategy may have spread throughout the industry.

Positioning Strategy for Service Systems

Managers of service systems also have choices about how to match the nature of the productive system to the market situation. In the case of service systems, however, the productive system is intimately bound up with the marketing and service concept. The impression that the service system makes on clients and customers is affected by the way the service is given by personnel, and the way the system is designed.

The BURGER example in Chapter 1 involved choices by Charles Berg to design his service emphasizing low cost and availability with a limited menu. Initially, BURGER would have been positioned far above the diagonal line in Figure 2-6 at the low volume end of the horizontal axis. Berg's product-service strategy involved a continuous productive system and was rather risky. As the concept proved successful, Berg made cost improvements that stemmed from several sources, but perhaps the largest gains were due to the central processing, central purchasing, and the efficient distribution systems. So Berg's experience curve was paced largely by economies of scale in addition to smaller cost improvements in worker learning, better work methods and equipment, standardization, and so on. As the volume of business grew, Berg's position on Figure 2-6 moved almost horizontally toward the diagonal line, but throughout the growth period, he stayed above the line. Though the type of products and services is pointed toward a rather different market segment, the Benihana of Tokyo restaurant chain involves a similar positioning strategy.

But there are restaurant chains that replicate a module of traditional menus with large selection and individual service. The service system is more nearly like the low to high volume multiple product system, using a process-focused productive system. Such restaurant chains are emphasizing quality and service, but customers must wait for meals to be prepared, and cost is much less a criterion. These chains are below the diagonal in Figure 2-6, and move to the right as the overall volume develops, paced largely by the opening of new units. Again, the experience curve provides cost reductions from a variety of sources, but the dominant effect results from economies of scale.

There are many other contrasting examples where managers of service systems make choices concerning the position of their productive system in relation to the nature of the market. In health care, there is the general hospital versus the clinic, or specialized medical facilities. In package delivery, there is the Post Office versus the specialized services of UPS, Federal Express, and so on.

ORGANIZATION OF THE OPERATIONS FUNCTION

The nature of the organizational structure that an enterprise chooses for its operations function should be an outgrowth of its strategic choices for the productive system. As noted previously, the choice of productive system type is influenced by the balance of competitive factors of emphasis on quality, volume of output, flexibility, cost, and dependability of supply to its customers. If the choice based on these competitive factors results in an intermittent system with a process focus, then the organization must be structured to reflect these values, giving dominant support to product design flexibility, and quality. Conversely, if the choice of productive system type results in a continuous system with a product focus, then organizational structure must give dominant support to reliability of supply to its customers, and cost and price competitiveness. In either situation, we do not mean that the other factors are to be ignored, but that competitive priorities have been established.

Process-Focused Organizations

Figure 2-9 shows the general structure of a process-focused manufacturing organization (we show functions, because titles vary widely). The primary supervisory structure follows the physical departmentation. Primary supervisors also tend to be experts in the production technology they supervise, and must coordinate the utilization of people, machines, and material. Higher levels in the production organization involve a broader span of control by managers. The first aggregation of responsibility involves more producing departments, as with the manufacturing manager. But at the plant manager level, the functions that support production are added, such as

FIGURE 2-9
Process-focused organizational structure.

materials control, quality control, industrial engineering and plant maintenance, and purchasing. On the same level as the plant manager of a single plant operation there are the other functions of product engineering, finance and accounting, marketing, and personnel and industrial relations. In general, process-focused organizations have highly developed staff functions at higher levels in the organization, and cost and profit responsibility is also at a high level.

In larger organizations that may operate through multiple plants, the plant manager must necessarily incorporate an even larger span of control over other functions which usually include at least some aspects of personnel and industrial relations, accounting, and sometimes, depending on the nature of products and plant specialization, some aspects of product engineering and marketing. Thus, the production function is apt to be rather hierarchical in nature and include some functions other than strictly production at the higher levels. These higher level managers of production systems function as more general managers, and this may account for their generally high salaries.

Why does the process-focused structure give stronger support to the competitive priorities of product flexibility and quality? The product engineering function is separate and independent, and at a high level in the organization. Taking account of individual customer requirements in product design is heard by high-level managers, and is not compromised by trade-offs that might be made for strictly production objectives of standardization and low cost. Quality control is separate and independent from the production organization. The disadvantages of this structure are that management must provide a great deal of coordination between organizational units to make the system work, and that cost and supply time are not given high priority in the structure.

Product-Focused Organizations

Figure 2-10 shows the general structure for a product-focused manufacturing organization. Organization at the primary level is by product or product line. The first level supervisor is primarily responsible for execution of plans, but is supported by staff experts in production planning and scheduling, inventory control, and quality control who are responsible directly to the manager of the product department. In general, profit and cost responsibility is held in the product groups in product-focused organizations, and higher level staff provide coordination, but with much less direct influence over operating decisions.

In the product-focused organization, the close association of the control elements that bear on costs, on-time delivery, and quality makes the entire local organization tuned to perform effectively in achieving these goals. Authority is highly decentralized and this contributes to achieving the specialized objectives of the unit. Each manager of the production of a product line functions more nearly like an independent small organization with relatively little oversight and coordination from corporate levels.

The disadvantages of the product-focused organization are in the lack of flexibility of personnel who may have specialized to a high degree, and the inability of the organization to accommodate customer needs for variations in product design. Table 2-3 compares some of the major differences between process and product-focused organizations. [See Hayes and Schmenner, 1978.]

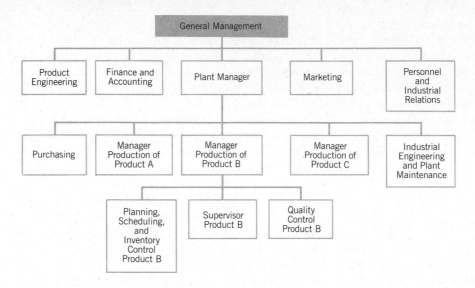

FIGURE 2-10
Product-focused organizational structure.

Organization of Service Systems

Service systems have some special characteristics that impact organization structure. First, the service itself cannot be inventoried. Secondly, we must remember that there is usually a product/service bundle that represents the output of the system, as we discussed in Chapter 1. Therefore, inventories of the product part of the bundle are as important as they would be in the delivery system of a product-oriented system. Third, service systems commonly are confronted with extremely variable demand on a short-term basis. For example, a fast-food outlet is very busy at mealtime hours, but experiences low demand during other hours; because of the day-end mailing practices of business, 40 to 60 percent of the letters brought to the post office plus that collected from local mail boxes is received between 4:00 and 8:00 P.M. Fourth, service operations are usually labor intensive, and fifth, the location of service operations is dictated by the location of users.

As with manufacturing organizations, there are process-focused, as well as product-focused, organizational structures, using the word *product* here in its more general sense to include services as a system output. Process-focused organizational structures are found in service situations where there is a process-focused physical system, such as in general hospitals or municipal offices. As with manufacturing systems, the organizational structure follows the physical departmentation. Thus, in a hospital, we might find departments of receiving, emergency, intensive-care, maternity, surgery, X-ray, cashier, and so on. The primary organizational structure follows the functional structure for the delivery of service.

In product-focused service systems such as motels, fast-food outlets, banks, and others, the service is usually made available in multiple locations so that each manager of a unit is in effect an operations manager with profit responsibility for that unit. Each unit manager has responsibility comparable with that of the manager of any

TABLE 2-3   **Differences Between Process- and Product-Focused Organizations**

	Process Focus	Product Focus
Profit or cost responsibility: where located	Central organization	Product groups
Size of corporate staff	Relatively large	Relatively small
Major functions of corporate staff	(a) Coordination with marketing (b) Facilities decisions (c) Personnel policies (d) Purchasing (e) Logistics-inventory management (f) Coordination of production schedules (g) Make versus buy, vertical integration decisions (h) Recruit future plant managers (i) Review plant performance	(a) Review of capital appropriation requests (b) Communicate corporate changes and requests (c) Act as clearing house for personnel information, management recruiting, purchasing, used equipment, management development programs (d) Evaluate and reward plant managers (e) Select plant managers and manage career paths—possibly across product group lines
Major responsibilities of plant organizations	(a) Use materials and facilities efficiently (b) Recruit production, clerical, and lower management workers (c) Training and development of future department and plant managers (d) Respond to special requests from marketing, within limited ranges	(a) Coordination with marketing (b) Facilities decisions (subject to marketing) (c) Purchasing and logistics (d) Production scheduling and inventory control (e) Make versus buy (f) Recruit management

SOURCE. R. H. Hayes, and R. W. Schmenner, "How Should You Organize Manufacturing," *Harvard Business Review*, January–February 1978, pp. 105–117.

small enterprise. In order to emphasize that responsibility and provide incentives, such unit operations are often established as profit centers. The corporate or central organization of these product-focused enterprises commonly provides financial and control functions to ensure that the quality and cost of the services provided by each unit manager are those intended. (See Sasser et al., 1978, Chapter 6, for a more general discussion of service firm organization.)

IMPLICATIONS FOR THE MANAGER

The positioning of the productive system in relation to the product/service system is of the greatest importance to managers. This positioning should be an integral part of the overall corporate strategy, and includes the decision of whether to produce "to stock" or "to order." The concept of the product life cycle provides a rationale for the growth, development, maturation and decline of products and services. Managers need to match the appropriate productive system type to their situation with respect to the product life cycle. Thus, in the general sense, managers would tend to follow the diagonal line of likely joint strategies in Figure 2-6.

However, application of the concept of joint product/productive system strategies recognizes that there is actually a band as shown in Figure 2-7 within which managers should operate, rather than a rigid solution for a given combination of volume and productive system type. Therefore, managers may choose to emphasize quality and diversity of multiple products as a way of gaining a competitive advantage. Alternately, a manager in the same basic situation might choose to compete on price and availability of a limited line. The success of enterprises which choose different bases for competing using their productive system as a weapon gives evidence that there is no one right answer to each situation.

The experience curve and its implications provide managers with a strategic competitive weapon. To gain market share is to gain operating experience that should result in lower costs, thereby providing either increased profits or lower prices which in turn can provide the basis for even greater market penetration. Thus, investment in improved process technology either by direct purchase or through allocations to research and development can maintain future costs on the experience curve. In dramatic breakthroughs of process technology a firm could even lower the slope of its experience curve, providing a very effective competitive weapon. A danger of the effects of the experience curve is the possibility of loss of flexibility that results from specialization, both in terms of the physical system as well as those who manage it.

It is well known that focus on a relatively narrow product line makes it possible for managers to outperform a comparable nonfocused situation. It is simply an application of the age-old principle of specialization. But there are dangers in focus applied blindly, and the real issue for managers responsible for designing organizations and productive systems is one of focus versus risk. Managers need to assess their particular situation, including their position in the product life cycle, the potential for product (and therefore process) obsolescence, their joint strategy for quality, availability, cost, and flexibility. Focus may be exactly what they need, but it is not always the answer. They need to think in terms of the balance between the advantages of focus and the risks that result from focus.

Finally, organizational structure should be chosen to give support to the joint strategy. In general, organizational structure follows the basic structure of the productive system. If the productive system is designed for process focus, then the organization should be process-focused, and vice versa.

IMPORTANT TERMS

Numbers in parentheses indicate page numbers

Experience curve (35)	Process-focused system (31)
Focus (42)	Product-focused organization (47)
Inventoriable product (34)	Product-focused system (32)
Learning curve (35)	Product life cycle (30)
Noninventoriable product (34)	S-curve (31)
Process-focused organization (46)	

REVIEW QUESTIONS AND PROBLEMS

1. Describe the concept of the product life cycle. Is it applicable to services as well as manufactured goods?

2. Where in their product life cycles would you place the following:
    a. word processing systems
    b. electric typewriters
    c. social security service
    d. sushi bars (Japanese raw fish)
    e. video dish players
    f. cassette tape decks
    g. reel to reel tape decks

3. Define the following terms:
    a. product-focused system
    b. process-focused system
    c. continuous system
    d. intermittent system

4. What is the experience curve phenomenon?

5. What is meant by the characterization of an experience curve as being a 90 percent curve?

6. If the first unit of an item cost $10, and the system follows a 90 percent experience curve, what is the equation for the cost of the nth unit, c_n? What is the cost of the 100th unit produced?

7. Another way of looking at the experience curve is in terms of the effects on productivity. If unit cost is decreasing, then productivity is increasing. Then the productivity of the nth unit, p_n could be expressed as

$$p_n = p_1 n^d$$

    where

    p_n = the productivity of the nth unit
    p_1 = the productivity of the first unit
    d = a parameter depending on the rate of productivity increase

51

Notice that the parameter *d* is positive, because we have an increasing productivity function instead of the decreasing cost function for the experience curve. If the productivity of the first unit were taken as 1.0 as an index of productivity, what would the productivity be for the 100th unit, if productivity increased 10 percent for each doubling of cumulative output?

8. How could a firm use the experience curve as a part of its competitive strategy?

9. Are there limitations to the benefits of the experience curve? Are there any dangers in its use?

10. What is meant by the productive system/product-service joint strategy?

11. How would you describe the productive system/product-service joint strategies of each of the following:

    a. Post Office

    b. United Parcel Service (UPS)

    c. Federal Express Company (FEC)

12. What is meant by the term *focus* in productive systems?

13. What are the risks of emphasizing focus in a managerial strategy?

14. What are the differences between process and product-focused organizations? Why do these differences occur?

15. What are the special characteristics of service organizations that may have impact on the way they are organized?

16. What are the parallels between organizational structures for service and manufacturing systems?

SITUATIONS

17. The Electronic Relay Company (*ERC*) came into being 5 years ago based on a new product innovation that involved micro-circuitry. The new "smart" relays could react much faster and time their action to coordinate with many special needs in complex equipment. Like many new products involving silicon chips, electronic relays had swept the industry and were in great demand because of their versatility and moderate cost.

    The relays were used in many types of equipment and the service requirements were quite variable, depending on the particular application. Although *ERC*'s output included 500 different models each year, they had developed a substantial demand for 10 popular models that seemed to find application in many different end-products. *ERC* was one of several firms in the field that had an excellent engineering staff that could design smart relays to individual customer needs. Sales had increased extremely rapidly, especially in the last 2 years when they had increased 40 percent each year. Longer-term sales forecasts indicated that a 30 percent annual increase was the best estimate for the next 5 years.

    The relays were produced in a flexible process-focused plant only on the basis of special order. The process departments were metal stamping, a small machine shop, electronics assembly, paint, final assembly, and an inspection and test. *ERC* had a minimum size order of ten, though some recent orders had been as large as 1000. Each order was first routed to engineering for design requirements and then to a cost estimating department for the construction of a bid price and estimated delivery commitment. If the customer accepted the terms, the materials required were ordered and a production order (*PO*) issued. The processes required were listed on the *PO* and the order was routed to the required departments in sequence, tested, and finally shipped to the customer. The typical time for production once the customer had accepted the terms was 6 weeks.

Because of the long-term forecasts, the president, Frank Moore, made strategic planning the subject of the next executive committee meeting. The views of the committee members were divergent, but summarized by those of the VP-manufacturing and VP marketing. The VP-manufacturing, Tom Hendrick, was strongly for standardizing on a relatively few high demand models and gearing up to produce them in quantity for a mass market.

"There are really only about ten different designs and models when you come right down to it. All the others are just minor variations of these ten. Right now, ten models account for 75 percent of orders. If we could just standardize on these, I could knock 50 percent of the cost out of them. In a couple of years the demand for just those ten would be such that we could automate a line and become the dominant producer in the industry. Let's take the cream of the business and let someone else wrestle with those small special orders."

Dick Lutz, the marketing VP, strongly disagreed.

"We will miss out on a lot of business if we don't give them what they need. They don't all have the same needs in their products. Our people are in touch with the market all the time, and we see some common needs as Tom says, but there are a lot of different situations out there. Sure an order for ten must drive Tom's people nuts, but we charge accordingly. We're making a lot of money from those small orders. Naturally we like the big orders too, and it's true that there is a natural tendency toward standardization because the customer can get a better price on one of our standard models. But let's not shove the market around, let's go with the market."

Vassily Rostopovich, the engineering VP, agreed with Dick Lutz, though not with great vigor. He said, "We are really good at designing the smart relay to meet individual needs. We have it down to a computer aided design process so we can produce a special design within a couple of days if we have to."

Frank said that he would think over what had been said and draft a position paper on *ERC*'s strategic plan for the next five years for discussion at the next executive committee meeting. What should Frank do? Outline a position paper that you would recommend to Frank.

18. Two firms are competing in the same market with products that are considered to be substitutes for each other. Firm *A* is the old established firm with a great deal of experience; cumulative production to date has been 100,000 units. Some years ago it produced its first unit at a cost of $c_1 = \$100$, and has been enjoying a 95 percent experience curve ever since. Firm *A* is the price leader, with current prices set at \$85 per unit, which other producers followed until

Firm *B* entered the market with a $40 price. The president of Firm *A* is astounded that Firm *B* is so foolish as to try to compete with them, since their experience is so great in the field.

Firm *B* has just entered the market after spending a great deal on research and development of new process technology. After setting up the initial highly automated plant, the cost of the first unit was $150. The news got around in the industry, and on hearing of it, the president of Firm *A* laughed and said, "another bust for automation." Since establishing the plant, Firm *B* has allocated funds generously to research and development of process technology and has made significant improvements on the original plant.

Firm *B* initially priced its product at the industry rate of $85 per unit, but soon dropped its price to its present $40. Their price policy has turned the industry upside down and business has been brisk indeed—they have already produced 5000 units. Having kept careful records on costs, the president of Firm *B* notes gleefully that they are on an 85 percent experience curve. He is particularly delighted because, having originally been a plant manager for Firm *A*, he is aware of their costs and experience curve data.

The president of Firm *A* is puzzled. "How can they undercut us? They must be losing money on every unit, they are actually pricing below our cost!"

How do you analyze this situation? Can Firm *A* possibly make out with its present price policy?

REFERENCES

Abernathy, W. J., and K. Wayne, "The Limits of the Learning Curve," *Harvard Business Review*, September–October 1974, pp. 109–119.

Baloff, N., "Startup Management," *IEEE Transactions in Engineering and Management*, Vol. EM-17, No. 4, November 1970.

Banks, R. L., and S. C. Wheelwright, "Operations vs. Strategy: Trading Tomorrow for Today," *Harvard Business Review*, May–June 1979, pp. 112–120.

Buzzell, R. D., B. T. Gale, and R. Sultan, "Market Share—A Key to Profitability," *Harvard Business Review*, January–February 1975.

Hayes, R. H., and R. W. Schmenner, "How Should You Organize for Manufacturing," *Harvard Business Review*, January–February 1978, pp. 105–118.

Hayes, R. H., and S. C. Wheelwright, "Link Manufacturing Process and Product Life Cycles," *Harvard Business Review*, January–February 1979.

Hayes, R. H., and S. C. Wheelwright, "The Dynamics of Process-Product Life Cycles," *Harvard Business Review*, March–April 1979a, pp. 127–136.

"Hewlett-Packard: Where Slower Growth Is Smarter Management," *Business Week*, June 9, 1975, pp. 50–58.

Sasser, W. E., R. P. Olson, and D. D. Wyckoff, *Management of Service Operations: Text, Cases, and Readings*, Allyn & Bacon, Boston, 1978.

Schoeffler, S., R. D. Buzzell, and D. F. Heany, "The Impact of Strategic Planning on Profit Performance," *Harvard Business Review*, March–April 1974.

Shapiro, B. P., "Can Marketing and Manufacturing Coexist?," *Harvard Business Review*, September–October 1977, pp. 104–114.

Skinner, W., *Manufacturing in the Corporate Strategy*, Wiley, New York, 1978.

Skinner, W., "Manufacturing—Missing Link in Corporate Strategy," *Harvard Business Review*, May–June 1969, p. 136.

Skinner, W., "The Focused Factory," *Harvard Business Review*, May–June 1974, p. 113.

Wheelwright, S. C., "Reflecting Corporate Strategy in Manufacturing Decisions," *Business Horizons*, February 1978, pp. 57–65.

CHAPTER 3

Demand Forecasting
for Operations

PLANNING AND CONTROL FOR OPERATIONS DEPENDS ON THE astute combination of intelligence about what is actually happening to demand and the forecasting of what we expect to happen. We need to make plans that range from a day-to-day to a year-to-year basis. The planning horizon depends on the particular application, but is relatively short. We need forecasting methods that are relatively inexpensive to install and maintain and that can be adapted to situations involving a large number of items to be forecast. This means that the data input and storage requirements should be modest and that computerized methods are a likely mechanism to update forecast data as needed.

The forecast is the single most useful and important data base for operations management decisions. Little if any strategic planning for future products, capacity, plant locations and distribution systems, and processes can be done without a forecast. In the "operating decisions" section of this book, we need forecasts for planning production and work force levels, for inventory replenishment, material control systems, and for scheduling machines and workers. Forecasting is covered early in this book so that we have information about how these important data are generated.

PREDICTING MARKETS FOR PRODUCTS AND SERVICES

Rational plans for products and services, including their productive systems, cannot be made without an estimate of the size of the market. This is true whether we are dealing with profit or nonprofit enterprises. If one is determining whether or not a new product or service should be launched, then the data on potential market size are crucial for the decision. If the basic decision has already been made to produce the product or service, then the information is just as crucial with regard to finalizing designs for both the product or service and the productive system.

When we are dealing with an ongoing situation, products and services may be in the growth or even saturation phase of their life cycles. In such instances, we are usually dealing with refinements of the product design and probably additions to physical capacity and/or a relocation or rebalancing of physical capacity. All of these kinds of plans are of a longer-term nature and often require the commitment of large investments. Therefore, insight into the future is required.

PREDICTION AND FORECASTING

We will use two different terms to describe methodologies for estimating future demand: "prediction" and "forecasting." Prediction as a term will have more of the flavor of the "crystal ball." When we predict, we are integrating a great deal of subjective and objective information to form our best estimate of the future. We use prediction methods when we have little experience on which to base estimates of the future. Forecasting, on the other hand, will be used to connote a statistical technique for *casting* the historical record *forward*. Forecasting depends on having enough historical data to be able to describe the record in statistical terms and on reasonably stable market generating factors. There is a place for both prediction and forecasting.

Table 3-1 summarizes some of the most pertinent and useful forecasting methods under three main headings. The time series models are applicable to shorter range forecasts for operations and are of particular value for inventory and production control. The causal methods are most appropriate for short- and medium-range forecasting, particularly as a basis for the aggregate planning methods that we discuss in Chapter 9. The predictive methods are appropriate for longer-range forecasts in connection with strategic decisions involving facilities planning, location, and product development.

TABLE 3-1   Methods of Prediction and Forecasting

Method	General Description	Applications	Relative Cost
Time series forecasting models:			
Moving averages	Forecast based on projection from time series data smoothed by a moving average, taking account of trends and seasonal variations. Requires at least two years of historical data.	Short-range forecasts for operations, such as inventory, scheduling, control, pricing, and timing special promotions.	Low
Exponential moving averages	Similar to moving averages, but averages weighted exponentially to give more recent data heavier weight. Well adapted to computer application and large numbers of items to be forecast. Requires at least two years of historical data.	Same as above.	Low
Fourier series least squares fit	Fits a finite Fourier series equation to empirical data, projecting trend and seasonal values. Requires at least two years of historical data. Computer required.	Same as above.	Low to medium
Causal forecasting methods:			
Regression analysis	Forecasts of demand related to economic and competitive factors that control or *cause* demand, through least squares regression equation.	Short- and medium-range forecasting of existing products and services. Marketing strategies, production and facility planning.	Medium
Econometric models	Based on a system of interdependent regression equations.	Same as above.	High
Predictive methods:			
Delphi	Expert panel answers a series of questionnaires where the answers of each questionnaire are summarized and made available to the panel to aid in answering the next questionnaire.	Long-range predictions, new products and product development, market strategies, pricing and facility planning.	Medium-high
Market surveys	Testing markets through questionnaires, panels, surveys, tests of trial products, analysis of time series.	Same as above.	High
Historical analogy and life cycle analysis	Prediction based on analysis of and comparison with growth and development of similar products. Forecasting new product growth based on the S-curve of introduction, growth, and market saturation.	Same as above.	Medium

Although good forecasting models have clearly shown their worth in business, industry, and government, there is an art to forecasting. The best results are seldom obtained through the mechanical application of a model. Subjective inputs from knowledgeable people can improve forecast accuracy. Two of the Situations at the end of the chapter provide information concerning actual experience in combining the inputs from more than one source, including subjective inputs.

REQUIREMENTS OF FORECASTS FOR OPERATIONS

The demand forecasting function serves many broad managerial purposes in both profit and nonprofit organizations. To be useful for operations planning and control, it is important that demand forecast data be available in a form that can be translated into demands for material, time in specific equipment classifications, and demands for specific labor skills. Therefore, forecasts of gross dollar demand, demand by customer or client classification, or demand by broad product or service classifications are of limited value for operations.

Planning and control for operations must necessarily take place at several different levels. Therefore, it is unlikely that one kind of forecast can serve at all levels. We require forecasts of different time spans to serve as the basis for operating plans developed for different *planning horizons*. These are (1) plans for current operations and for the immediate future, (2) intermediate-range plans to provide for the required capacities of personnel, materials, and equipment for the next 1 to 12 months, and (3) long-range plans for capacity, locations, changing product and service mix, and the exploitation of new products and services.

The required horizon of the forecast must be matched with the decision that it will affect. If the decision will depend on activities over the next 3 months, a 1-month forecast is valueless. On the other hand, it is unwise to select a forecasting model that has an acceptable 1-month error but has poor accuracy when projected 3 months ahead. Therefore, a major criterion for model selection is the match between decision time, forecast horizon, and forecasting accuracy.

COMPONENTS OF DEMAND

Figure 3-1 shows the 3-year record of the actual demand for a computing service. The company involved derives income from the use of its proprietary programs and the forecasting of usage can have an important bearing on many factors in planning operations. In general, the actual demand curve in Figure 3-1 shows an increasing demand for the service with considerable variation in demand; it is the types of variation that are of interest.

Some of the variation in demand can be explained by a statistical model and some cannot. The unexplainable variations we call "random" variations. In forecasting demand for operations, we would prefer not to respond to what we think might be simply random variations. Because many different customers are using the company's programs to suit their own schedules and needs, much of the seemingly odd increases or decreases from month to month come from this source. Company A using the programs may decide to initiate a new planning cycle that may have affected demand in August 1981, whereas company B may shut down for 2 weeks in August for vacations. The aggregation of all users' needs produces this kind of unexplained or random variation. Trying to determine why each month's demand was what it was is probably not worth the time and cost.

Although some of the variation in Figure 3-1 is not explainable, the aggregation of usage by all customers does produce a logical pattern. In spite of the random variations, there is some *average* demand for any particular period. For example, the average for the first quarter of 1981 is 21.51, for the first 6 months 22.03, and for the full year of 1981 it is 24.06. Each of these measures of average demand has some meaning, although they have limited usefulness in the form given.

It is obvious from Figure 3-1 that there is an upward *trend* in the demand for program usage, and the averages for the first quarter, first 6 months, and entire year verify an upward trend during 1981. The same conclusion is not quite so clear in 1982, however. The comparable figures for the first quarter, first 6 months, and full year of 1982 are: 29.72, 27.80, and 28.03. Each comparable figure indicates a growth in demand from year to year; however, both the graph and the 1982 figures indicate that demand may exhibit *seasonal* variation.

The components of demand that we must consider in forecasting models are then random, average levels, trend, and seasonal. Cyclic variations related to the business cycle are beyond our scope.

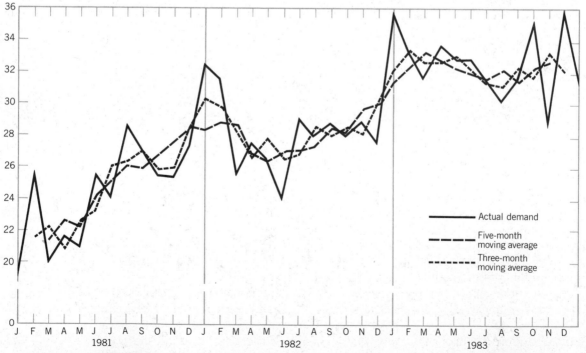

FIGURE 3-1
Monthly program usage with 3- and 5-month moving averages shown.

TIME SERIES FORECASTING METHODS

Moving Averages

The common way of smoothing the effects of random variations in demand is to estimate average demand by some kind of moving *average*. Table 3-2 gives some sample demand data taken from Figure 3-1 for the first 6 months.

A moving average is the average of *n* values centered on the period in question. For example, the first 3 months of actual demand in Table 3-2 are 19.36, 25.45, and 19.73, and the 3-month moving average is computed as (19.36 + 25.45 + 19.73)/3 = 21.51. Therefore, the estimate of February demand with random variations discounted by the averaging process is 21.51. When we estimate for March, we drop the January figure of 19.36 and add the April figure of 21.48. The new moving average centered on March is then (25.45 + 19.73 + 21.48)/3 = 22.22. If we were computing a 5-month moving average for March, the data would still be centered on that month. For example, the 5-month moving average for the first 5 months actual data from Table 3-2 is (19.36 + 25.45 + 19.73 + 21.48 + 20.77)/5 = 21.36.

Both Figure 3-1 and Table 3-2 show that actual demand is quite variable. The 3-month moving average is much more stable, however, because the demand for any 1 month receives only one-third weight. Extreme values are discounted; if they are simply random variations in demand, we are not strongly influenced by them when we gauge demand by the 3-month moving average.

Greater smoothing effect is obtained by averaging over a longer period, as is shown by the 5-month moving average in Table 3-2. Extreme values are discounted even more, because each period demand carries only a one-fifth weight in the moving average. Figure 3-1 shows 3- and 5-month moving averages plotted in comparison with actual demand for monthly program usage.

Note the smoothing effects and how the moving average lines reveal the trend and seasonal components in the data. The 5-month moving average produces greater smoothing effect, as we would expect. Here we note a conflict of objectives, however. The 5-month average discounts random effects more effectively, but the 3-month moving average gives more weight to the most recent data. Because the

TABLE 3-2		Actual Demand for Program Usage and Three- and Five-Month Moving Averages	
Date	Actuals	Three-Month Moving Average	Five-Month Moving Average
1981, Jan.	19.36	—	—
Feb.	25.45	21.51	—
Mar.	19.73	22.22	21.36
Apr.	21.48	20.66	22.57
May	20.77	22.56	22.24
June	25.42	23.33	23.96
July	23.79	25.85	25.03
Aug.	28.35	26.31	—
Sept.	26.80	—	—

program usage data in Figure 3-1 show both trend and seasonal components, we have a keen interest in emphasizing the most current data in the moving average.

Exponentially Weighted Moving Averages

One effective and convenient method for accomplishing differential weighting and smoothing is by exponentially weighted moving averages. The simplest exponential smoothing model estimates average smoothed demand for the current period S_t by adding or subtracting a fraction α (*alpha*) of the difference between actual current demand D_t and the last smoothed average S_{t-1}. The new smoothed average S_t is then

> New smoothed average = old smoothed average + α (new demand - old smoothed average)

Or stated symbolically

$$S_t = S_{t-1} + \alpha(D_t - S_{t-1}) \tag{1}$$

The smoothing constant, α, is between 0 and 1 with commonly used values of 0.01 to 0.30. Equation 1 can be rearranged as follows:

New smoothed average = α(new demand) + $(1 - \alpha)$ (old smoothed average),

or

$$S_t = \alpha D_t + (1 - \alpha)S_{t-1} \tag{2}$$

If $\alpha = 0.10$, then Equation 2 says that the smoothed average in the current period S_t will be determined by adding 10 percent of the new actual demand information D_t and 90 percent of the last smoothed average S_{t-1}. For example, if $\alpha = 0.1$, $D_t = 19.36$, and $S_{t-1} = 23.00$, then the new smoothed average is

$$S_t = 0.1 \times 19.36 + 0.9 \times 23.00 = 1.94 + 20.70 = 22.64$$

Because the new demand figure D_t includes possible random variations, we are discounting 90 percent of those variations. Obviously, small values of α will have a stronger smoothing effect than large values. Conversely, large values of α will react more quickly to real changes in actual demand (as well as to random variations). For example, if $\alpha = 0.4$ and the other data remain the same, the new smoothed average would be

$$S_t = 0.4 \times 19.36 + 0.6 \times 23.00 = 7.74 + 13.80 = 21.54$$

The components of D_t and S_{t-1} are now weighted quite differently, giving considerably more weight to current actual demand, D_t. The choice of α is normally guided by judgment, although studies could produce optimal values that minimize forecast errors.

Equation 2 actually gives weight to all past actual demand data. This occurs through the chain of periodic calculations to produce smoothed averages for each period. In Equation 2, for example, the term S_{t-1} was computed from

$$S_{t-1} = \alpha D_{t-1} + (1 - \alpha)S_{t-2}$$

which includes the previous actual demand D_{t-1}. The S_{t-2} term was calculated in a similar manner that included D_{t-2}, and so on, back to the beginning of the series.

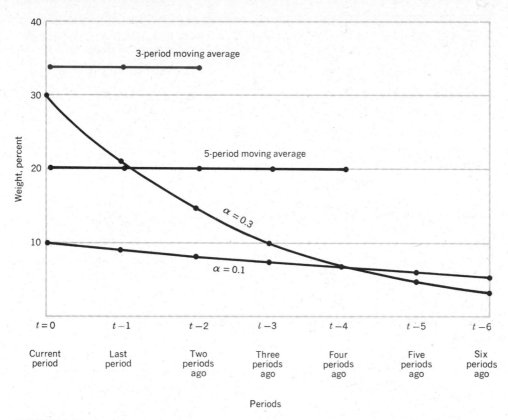

FIGURE 3-2
Comparative weightings given past data by 3- and 5-period moving averages, and by exponentially weighted moving averages with α = 0.1 and 0.3.

Therefore, the smoothed averages are based on a sequential process representing all previous actual demands.

Figure 3-2 shows comparative weightings given data by 3- and 5-period moving averages and by exponentially weighted moving averages with α = 0.1 and 0.3. Note the effectiveness of the exponentially weighted averages in placing heavier weight on the most recent data. Another factor implicit in Figure 3-2 is that exponentially weighted data give a weight to all prior actual demand data, although the effect of old data will be small.

It is important to place the time periods for S_t, D_t, and S_{t-1} in perspective and to recognize that the new smoothed average is not an extrapolation beyond known demand data. Instead, it is the most current smoothed average. It is not a forecast, but a statement of current demand.

It is also important to recognize that at least 1 year's historical data are required before confidence can be placed in the resulting forecasts. The initial assumed value of S_t has an impact on the early data, but due to the heavier weighting of recent data, the effects of errors in initial values becomes very small at the end of the initialization process.

Extrapolation and Forecast. Because no trend or seasonality is included in the

63

TABLE 3-3

Sample Computations for S_t and the Forecast, F_t, for the Simple Exponential Smoothing Model. Data for Actuals from Table 3-2. $\alpha = 0.2$.

Date	Actuals	Smoothed Average, S_t	Forecast, F_t
Initial	—	23.0	—
1981, Jan.	19.36	22.272	—
Feb.	25.45	22.908	22.27
Mar.	19.73	22.272	22.91
Apr.	21.48	22.114	22.27
May	20.77	21.845	22.11
June	25.42	22.560	21.85
July	—	—	22.56

model, direct extrapolation from S_t to infer a forecast is justified. Therefore, the forecast for the upcoming period F_{t+1} is taken directly as the computed value of S_t. Table 3-3 shows computations and forecasts for the first several months of the computer usage data.

Forecast Errors. Forecast errors are defined as

$$\text{Forecast error} = D_t - F_t$$

Forecast errors provide a measure of accuracy and a basis for comparing the performance of alternate models. Three error measures are commonly used:

1. Average error (AE)
2. Mean absolute deviation (MAD)
3. Mean squared error (MSE)

The average error should be near zero for a larger sample, otherwise the model exhibits *bias*. Bias indicates a systematic tendency for overforecasting or underforecasting. But AE obscures variability, because positive and negative errors cancel out.

The mean absolute deviation (MAD) provides additional information useful in selecting a forecasting model and its parameters. MAD is simply the sum of errors without regard to algebraic sign, divided by the number of observations.

The mean squared error provides information similar to MAD, but penalizes larger errors. MSE is computed by summing the squared individual errors and dividing by the number of observations.

Many forecasting computer programs automatically report all three error measures.

Trend Model. The apparent trend in the exponential smoothed averages is the difference between the successive values, $S_t - S_{t-1}$. If we attempted to compensate for trend using this raw measure, we would have a rather unstable correction, since random effects are still present. Sometimes we might record a negative trend, when in fact the general trend was positive. To minimize these irregular effects, we can stabilize the raw trend measure in the same way we stabilized actual demands, by applying exponential smoothing.

TABLE 3-4

Sample Computations for Trend Model
$\alpha = 0.2, \beta = 0.1$

Date	Actuals, D_t	S_t, Equation 3	T_t, Equation 4	F_t Equation 5
Initial	—	20.00	0	—
1981, Jan.	19.36	19.8720	– 0.0128	—
Feb.	25.45	20.9773	0.0990	19.86
Mar.	19.73	20.8070	0.0721	21.08
Apr.	21.48	20.9993	0.0841	20.88
May	20.77	21.0207	0.0778	21.08
June	25.42	21.9628	0.0164	21.10
July	23.79	—	—	22.13

We can smooth the $(S_t - S_{t-1})$ series with a smoothing constant, β (*beta*). The smoothing constant need not have the same value as α used in smoothing D_t.

Our computation of S_t must now reflect trend, so Equation 2 is modified by simply adding the old smoothed trend to the old smoothed average as follows:

$$S_t = \alpha D_t + (1 - \alpha)(S_{t-1} + T_{t-1}) \tag{3}$$

The updated value of T_t, the smoothed trend, is

$$T_t = \beta(S_t - S_{t-1}) + (1 - \beta) T_{t-1} \tag{4}$$

Equations 3 and 4 yield smoothed current values of demand and trend, so to forecast for the upcoming period, we extrapolate by adding T_t to the current smoothed average S_t as follows:

$$F_{t+1} = S_t + T_t \tag{5}$$

If we apply this trend model to the first several months of the computer usage data, using $\alpha = 0.2$ and $\beta = 0.1$ we have Table 3-4.

In applying the model, note that the current smoothed average S_t must be computed first by Equation 3, because this value is required to compute the current smoothed trend T_t by Equation 4. Using the data for March 1981 in Table 3-4, the forecast for April would be computed as follows:

$$S_{\text{Mar.}} = 0.2 \times 19.73 + 0.8 (20.9773 + 0.0990)$$
$$= 3.9460 + 16.8610 = 20.8070$$

$$T_{\text{Mar.}} = 0.1 (20.8070 - 20.9773) + 0.9 \times 0.0990$$
$$= - 0.0170 + 0.0891 = 0.0721$$

$$F_{\text{Apr.}} = 20.8070 + 0.0721 = 20.8791$$

The model using a direct estimation of trend is valuable when trend and random variation are present in the data. In addition, the concept is useful in some of the more complex models that combine estimates of average demand, trend, and seasonal components.

The simple exponentially smoothed forecast and the trend model forecast are plotted in relation to actual demand in Figure 3-3 for the program usage data. Because the raw data exhibit a trend, the simple model lags in its response. The trend

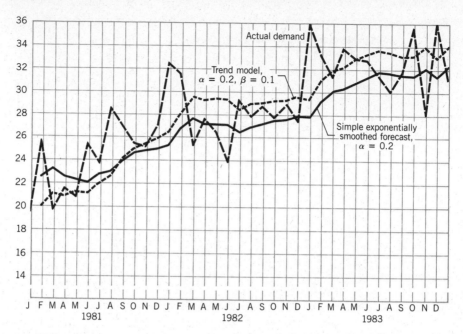

FIGURE 3-3

Forecasts of program usage by simple exponential smoothing and by the trend model.

model corrects for this lag and lies above the simple model forecast after initial conditions lose their effect.

For this model applied to the 3-year record of the computer usage data, with $\alpha =$ 0.2 and $\beta = 0.1$, AE = 0.33, MAD = 2.34, and MSE = 9.06. The choice of the two smoothing constants has an important influence on forecast errors. Holding $\alpha = 0.2$, the same computer usage data were run for values of $\beta = 0.01, 0.05, 0.1, 0.2, 0.3$. Subsamples yielded MAD = 2.23, 2.16, 2.34, 2.23, and 2.44, respectively. Because the objective in developing a forecasting system is to minimize forecast errors, testing the sensitivity of errors to parameter values is an important step in refining a system.

The initialization process requires a longer historical record for the trend model. There are two initially assumed values, S_t and T_t, and a 2-year history is normally assumed to be minimum.

Model for Seasonals. The basis for taking direct account of seasonal variations is to construct a seasonal index using the preceding year's data. For example, if we take the 1981 computer usage actual demands and divide each monthly demand by the annual average, we have a set of indexes. The average demand during 1981 was 24.07, so the index for January would be 19.36/24.07 = 0.804, and for February, 25.45/24.07 = 1.057. These initial indexes for 1981 are shown in Table 3-5, and are used only to initialize the process. A process for updating the indexes will be used in succeeding years so that they will reflect changes that may occur.

Given the initial indexes, we can normalize actual demand figures by dividing by the previous year's index in that period, I_{t-L} (L is the number of periods in one cycle—12 if data are by months, 4 if data are quarterly). Therefore, if actual demand for February 1982 is $D_t = 31.33$, we divide by the index for February in the previous

TABLE 3-5   **Sample Computations for Seasonal Model**
$\alpha = 0.1, \gamma = 0.3, L = 12$

Date	Actuals, D_t	S_t, Equation 6	I_t, Equation 7	F_t Equation 8
1981, Jan.	19.36		0.804	
Feb.	25.45		1.057	
Mar.	19.73		0.819	
Apr.	21.48		0.892	
May	20.77		0.863	
June	25.42		1.056	
July	23.79		0.988	
Aug.	28.35		1.178	
Sep.	26.80		1.113	
Oct.	25.32		1.052	
Nov.	25.22		1.048	
Dec.	27.14	30.00 (assumed)	1.128	—
1982, Jan.	32.52	31.0448	0.877	—
Feb.	31.33	30.9043	1.044	32.81
Mar.	25.32	30.9055	0.819	25.31
Apr.	27.53	30.9013	0.892	27.57
May	26.38	30.8679	0.860	26.67
June	23.72	30.0273	0.976	32.60
July	29.14	—	—	29.67

year, 1981, $I_{t-12} = 1.057$ to obtain $31.33/1.057 = 29.64$. The effect of this process is to deseasonalize by decreasing adjusted demand during high-demand periods and increasing it during low-demand periods. The deseasonalized smoothed average S_t is then

$$S_t = \alpha(D_t/I_{t-L}) + (1 - \alpha)S_{t-1} \tag{6}$$

However, the seasonal indexes for 1981 are reflective of only that year's experience. If the season cycle repeated itself accurately each year, using the 1981 indexes each year would be appropriate. Because random variations are a component, however, a single year's history as a basis for seasonal indexes is normally replaced by some averaging process, such as exponentially weighted averaging. Therefore, we use the following equation to update the seasonal indexes, where γ (*gamma*) is the smoothing constant for seasonal indexes:

$$I_t = \gamma(D_t/S_t) + (1 - \gamma)I_{t-L} \tag{7}$$

The actual demand D_t is divided by the new smoothed average S_t, computed by Equation 6 to reflect the amount by which D_t exceeds or falls short of the deseasonalized average. This variation from the deseasonalized average is weighted by the smoothing constant. The old seasonal index is last year's index and is weighted by $1 - \gamma$. The new index I_t is stored, to be used in computations for S_t and I_t next year.

The result, after the process has been in operation for several years, is that each seasonal index is based on seasonal variation that occurred L, $2L$, $3L$, and so on, periods ago. The most recent data are weighted more heavily depending on the value of the smoothing constant γ.

To forecast for the upcoming period, $t + 1$, we carry forward the most current smoothed average, S_t, but modify it by the seasonal index for the upcoming period,

I_{t-L+1}. Equation 8 has the effect of reseasonalizing the formerly deseasonalized smoothed average.

$$F_{t+1} = S_t I_{t-L+1} \tag{8}$$

Table 3-5 applies the seasonal model to the first several months of the computer usage data, using $\alpha = 0.1$ and $\gamma = 0.3$. In applying the model, the current smoothed average S_t is computed first by Equation 6, since this value is required to update the seasonal indexes by Equation 7 and to compute the forecast by Equation 8.

Using the data for April 1982 in Table 3-5, the forecast for May would be computed as follows:

$$S_{\text{Apr.}} = 0.1 \left(\frac{27.53}{0.892} \right) + 0.9 \times 30.9054$$

$$= 3.0863 + 27.8149 = 30.9012$$

$$I_{\text{Apr.}} = 0.3 \left(\frac{27.53}{30.9012} \right) + 0.7 \times 0.892$$

$$= 0.2673 + 0.6244 = 0.8917$$

$$F_{\text{May}} = 30.9012 \times 0.863 = 26.667$$

For the seasonal model applied to the 3-year record of the computer usage data, AE $= -0.15$, MAD $= 3.38$, and MSE $= 20.53$ ($\alpha = 0.1$, $\gamma = 0.3$).

Forecasting accuracy is not as good with the seasonal model. Why? First, it does not account for trend, which is a factor in the data. Second, an entire year of the data is consumed in order to initialize the seasonal indexes. The remaining 2-year sample may contain extreme values that carry larger weight in the smaller sample. Third, the seasonal cycles in the computer usage data may not be stable from year to year; the company was a new one with a short history.

As with the trend model, the choice of the smoothing constants affects forecasting errors. Subsamples used to compute MAD for several combinations of values of α and γ yield the following:

			γ		
α	0.01	0.05	0.10	0.20	0.30
0.1	3.67	3.60	3.54	3.44	3.38
0.2	3.65	3.75	3.73	3.60	3.37

Model for Trend and Seasonals. As might be expected, one can combine the trend model and the seasonal model. The equations to update smoothed trend and seasonals are the same, but the equation to compute the current value for the smoothed average, S_t, must reflect both the trend and seasonal variations.

$$S_t = \alpha(D_t/I_{t-L}) + (1 - \alpha)(S_{t-1} + T_{t-1}) \tag{9}$$

The trend, and seasonal index equations are

$$T_t = \beta(S_t - S_{t-1}) + (1 - \beta)T_{t-1} \tag{10}$$

TABLE 3-6 **Sample Computations for the Trend and Seasonal Model**
$\alpha = 0.2, \beta = 0.3, \gamma = 0.1,$ and $L = 12$

Date	Actuals D_t	S_t, Equation 9	T_t, Equation 10	I_t, Equation 11	F_t Equation 12
1981, Jan.	19.36			0.804	
Feb.	25.45			1.057	
Mar.	19.73			0.819	
Apr.	21.48			0.892	
May	20.77			0.863	
June	25.42			1.056	
July	23.79			0.988	
Aug.	28.35			1.178	
Sep.	26.80			1.113	
Oct.	25.32			1.052	
Nov.	25.22			1.048	
Dec.	27.14	30 (assumed)	1.0 (assumed)	1.128	—
1982, Jan.	32.52	32.8896	1.5669	0.823	—
Feb.	31.33	33.4932	1.2779	1.045	36.42
Mar.	25.32	34.0000	1.0465	0.812	28.48
Apr.	27.53	34.2099	0.7955	0.883	31.26
May	26.38	34.1179	0.5293	0.854	30.21
June	23.72	32.2102	−0.2017	1.024	36.59
July	29.14	—	—	0.982	31.62

$$I_t = \gamma(D_t/S_t) + (1 - \gamma)I_{t-L} \tag{11}$$

Finally, to forecast for the upcoming period, $t + 1$, we combine the elements of Equations 5 and 8,

$$F_{t+1} = (S_t + T_t)I_{t-L+1} \tag{12}$$

The value of S_t using Equation 9 must be computed first because it is used in Equations 10, 11, and 12. As before, computing the updated seasonal index produces an index to be stored for use a year hence.

Table 3-6 applies the trend and seasonal model to the first several months of the computer usage data, using smoothing constants of $\alpha = 0.2$, $\beta = 0.3$, and $\gamma = 0.1$. The initial seasonal indexes are those used to initialize the seasonal model in Table 3-5.

Using the data in Table 3-6 for May 1982 to forecast for June, sample computations are

$$S_{\text{May}} = 0.2(26.38/0.863) + 0.8(34.2099 + 0.7955)$$
$$= 6.1136 + 28.0043 = 34.1179$$

$$T_{\text{May}} = 0.3(34.1179 - 34.2099) + 0.7 \times 0.7955$$
$$= -0.0276 + 0.5569 = 0.5293$$

$$I_{\text{May}} = 0.1(26.38/34.1179) + 0.9 \times 0.863$$
$$= 0.0773 + 0.7767 = 0.8540$$

$$F_{\text{June}} = (34.1179 + 0.5293)1.056 = 36.5874$$

With three smoothing constants, the number of possible combinations increases substantially. Berry and Bliemel [1974] show how computer search methods can be used in selecting optimal combinations of the smoothing constants.

The initialization process is somewhat longer with the trend and seasonal model. One year of historical data is required just to initialize the seasonal indexes, plus the initialization of both S_t and T_t. Therefore, a 3-year historical record is normally required in order to place confidence in the results.

Adaptive Methods. As we have noted, it is common to use fairly small values of α in exponential smoothing systems in order to filter out random variations in demand. When actual demand rates increase or decrease gradually, such forecasting systems can track the changes rather well. If demand changes suddenly, however, a forecasting system using a small value of α will lag substantially behind the actual change. Thus, adaptive response systems have been proposed.

The basic idea of adaptive smoothing systems is to monitor the forecast error and, based on preset rules, to react to large errors by increasing the value of α. The effect of increasing α is to change the weights assigned to past data, increasing the weight placed on the most recent data. The forecast is then computed using the new weights. For example, if a step change in demand were to occur because of a radical change in the market, a large error would result. The large error signals that α should increase, giving greater weight to current demand. The forecast would then reflect the change in actual demand. When actual demand stabilizes at the new level, adaptive systems would reset the value of α to a lower level that filters out random variations effectively. A number of approaches to adaptive response systems have been proposed.

Although adaptive systems have an intuitively appealing rationale, at this writing their performance as compared with standard exponential smoothing forecast systems is in doubt. Two studies have produced conflicting results. Whybark [1972] tested six different forecasting models, four of which were adaptive. In general, the adaptive systems performed better than the simple exponential smoothing system.

A later study by Dancer and Gray [1977] compared the performance of a single exponential smoothing model, a double exponential smoothing model,* and one taking account of seasonal demand patterns, with the two adaptive systems that performed best in Whybark's study. Dancer and Gray found no significant differences in the performance of the adaptive systems compared with the standard models. These results are consistent with the results obtained by Church [1973] in developing a short-term forecasting system in connection with staff scheduling in a telephone business office. Additional research will be required to clarify the relative performance of adaptive models.

Dancer and Gray conclude that despite the fact that the adaptive model performed no better, there were two practical considerations which might cause inventory managers to switch to adaptive models. First, that adaptive models would be useful for new products for which little historical data were available—the adaptive models should correct and stabilize quickly. Second, a Trigg-Leach [1967] type adaptive model reduces manual intervention. These advantages must be traded off against the disadvantages of the greater historical data requirement, and the increased computer time requirements for adaptive systems compared with the simpler models.

---

* Double exponential smoothing is an alternate model that takes account of trend. It functions by processing the value of S_t computed by Equation 2 by smoothing it a second time, using Equation 2.

FOURIER SERIES FORECASTING METHODS

The speed, economy, and storage capacity of present-day computers have made it feasible to use fairly sophisticated mathematical models for forecasting. One such model is the least squares Fourier series forecasting model.

The mathematical background for this methodology was established by Joseph Fourier, a French physicist and mathematician. Fourier demonstrated that *any* periodic (i.e., seasonal) function which is finite, single-valued, and continuous over the period (season) may be represented by a mathematical series consisting of a constant term plus the sum of several sine and cosine terms.† The series is expressed as an infinite series, because in theory an infinite number of terms is required to duplicate mathematically the desired function with complete accuracy. As a practical matter, a finite number of terms in the range of 4 to 14 seems to produce excellent results in seasonal forecasting situations.

For example, when the six-term Fourier Series model was applied to the computer usage data, MAD = 1.86 was the result. Increasing the number of terms in the model will normally improve the fit to historical data; however, computer costs will increase. As a general rule the minimum number of model terms is equal to two times the number of peaks in a seasonal cycle plus 2. Looking at Figure 3-1 we would assume that the minimum number of terms for the computer usage example would be four. Figure 3-4 shows the output of the program when the number of terms is increased to 12. The variability of the forecast errors was reduced to MAD = 1.76 for the 12-term model, compared with 1.86 for the 6-term model. (Note that the decimal point has not been printed for the actual demand, forecast demand, and forecast error. The standard output for the program includes the histogram of errors, as well as the summary statistics on forecast errors.)

CAUSAL FORECASTING METHODS

When we have enough historical data and experience, it may be possible to relate forecasts to the factors in the economy that *cause* the trends, seasonals, and fluctuations. Thus, if we can *measure* the causal factors and we have determined their *relationships* to the product or service of interest, then we can compute forecasts of considerable accuracy.

The factors that enter causal models are of several types: disposable income, new

---

† The equation for the Fourier series is

$$F_t = a_1 + a_2 \sin wt + a_3 \cos wt + a_4 \sin wt + a_5 \cos wt + a_6 \sin wt + \ldots$$

where

$\quad\quad F_t$ = the numerical value of the series computed at time t

$\quad\quad a_1$ = a constant term

$\quad a_2, a_3, \cdot$ = coefficients defining the amplitude of the harmonics

$$w = \frac{2\pi}{T} = \frac{6.2832}{T}$$

$\quad\quad T$ = the length of the period (i.e., the number of forecast intervals per year, for example 4 quarters per year, or 12 months per year)

marriages, housing starts, inventories, cost-of-living indexes, as well as predictions of dynamic factors and/or disturbances, such as strikes, actions of competitors, and sales promotion campaigns. The causal forecasting model expresses mathematical relationships between the causal factors and the demand for the item being forecast.

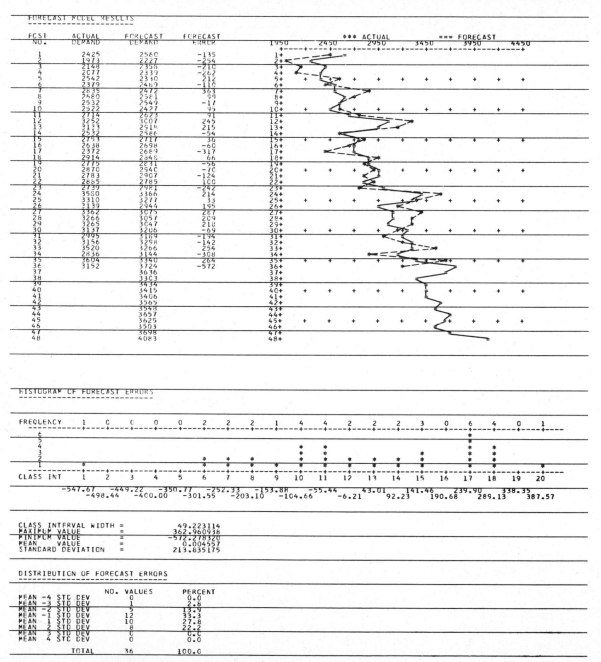

FIGURE 3-4
Computer output from 12-term Fourier series forecasting model.

As indicated in Table 3-1, there are two general types of causal models, and the costs range from medium to high for installation and operation.

Regression Analysis

Forecasting based on regression methods establishes a forecasting function called a *regression equation*. The regression equation expresses the series to be forecast in terms of other series which presumably control or cause the sales to increase or decrease. The rationale can be general or specific. For example, in furniture sales we might postulate that sales are related to disposable personal income: if disposable income is up, sales will increase, and if people have less money to spend, sales will be down. Establishing the empirical relationship is accomplished through the regression equation. To take additional factors, we might postulate that furniture sales are controlled to some extent by the number of new marriages and the number of new housing starts. These are both specific indicators of possible demand for furniture.

Table 3-7 gives data on these three independent variables—housing starts,

TABLE 3-7   **Data for 24 Years (1947–1970) Used in Performing Regression Analysis to Forecast 1971 Sales of Cherryoak Company**

Year	Housing Starts (H) (thousands)	Disposable Personal Income (I) ($ billions)	New Marriages (M) (thousands)	Company Sales (S) ($ millions)	Time (T)
1947	744	158.9	2291	92.920	1
1948	942	169.5	1991	122.440	2
1949	1033	188.3	1811	125.570	3
1950	1138	187.2	1580	110.460	4
1951	1549	205.8	1667	139.400	5
1952	1211	224.9	1595	154.020	6
1953	1251	235.0	1539	157.590	7
1954	1225	247.9	1546	152.230	8
1955	1354	254.4	1490	139.130	9
1956	1475	274.4	1531	156.330	10
1957	1240	292.9	1585	140.470	11
1958	1157	308.5	1518	128.240	12
1959	1341	318.8	1451	117.450	13
1960	1531	337.7	1494	132.640	14
1961	1274	350.0	1527	126.160	15
1962	1327	364.4	1547	116.990	16
1963	1469	385.3	1580	123.900	17
1964	1615	404.6	1654	141.320	18
1965	1538	436.6	1719	156.710	19
1966	1488	469.1	1789	171.930	20
1967	1173	505.3	1844	184.790	21
1968	1299	546.3	1913	202.700	22
1969	1524	590.0	2059	237.340	23
1970	1479	629.6	2132	254.930	24

Note. Company sales and disposable per-capita income have been adjusted for the effect of inflation and appear in constant 1959 dollars.

SOURCE. G. C. Parker and E. L. Segura, "How to Get a Better Forecast," *Harvard Business Review*, March–April 1971, based on data from *Statistical Abstract of the United States*, Bureau of the Census, Washington, D.C.

disposable income, and new marriages—and on sales of a hypothetical furniture company called the Cherryoak Company. We propose to build a relationship between the observed variables and company sales, where sales are dependent on, or caused by, the observed variables. Therefore, sales is termed the "dependent" variable and the observed variables are called the "independent" variables. The correlation coefficients between sales (S) and each of the independent variables are:

1. Disposable personal income (I)   0.805
2. Housing starts (H)   0.435
3. New marriages (M)   0.416

Because disposable income (I) correlates most strongly with company sales, let us start with it as an example. Using regression analysis we can determine the straight line that best fits the data expressing the relationship between sales (S) and disposable income (I). From statistics we know that the regression equation represents a straight line that minimizes the square of the deviations from it and sets the sum of the simple deviations to zero. The regression equation for the data of company sales (S) versus disposable income (I) is

$$S = 72.5 + 0.23\,I \tag{13}$$

where the coefficient, 72.5, is the y-axis intercept, and the slope of the straight line is 0.23. The form of the equation is the standard format of the equation of a straight line, $y = a + bx$, where y is the dependent variable, x the independent variable, a the y intercept, and b the slope. In regression analysis a and b are termed the *regression coefficients* and are the parameters that specify the equation.

The regression line is plotted in Figure 3-5, which shows some specific points for selected years. These points illustrate the kinds of forecast errors that would have resulted if one had used this equation to forecast Cherryoak furniture sales. To use the regression equation to forecast sales, one simply inserts the value of I and computes sales S. For example, if $I = 700$, then the forecaster could compute the value of S as $S = 72.5 + 0.23 \times 700 = \$233.5$ (million).

Reliability of Forecast. A number of statistical tests can be performed to help determine the accuracy of a regression equation as a forecasting device. Data resulting from these statistical tests are commonly generated automatically in standard regression analysis computer programs. Our particular interest is in the coefficients of determination and the standard error of estimate. In addition, there are important statistical tests concerning the significance of the regression coefficients that we will not discuss.

The coefficient of determination is simply r^2, the correlation coefficient squared. For our example, $r^2 = 0.805^2 = 0.65$. The coefficient of determination states the proportion of the variation in the regression equation that is explained by the independent variable. For our equation, 65 percent of the variation in sales is controlled by variation in I, and 35 percent is unexplained. Thus, we can expect large forecast errors if we use Equation 13. Apparently, other variables account for a substantial fraction of the changes in S that actually occur.

The standard error of estimate indicates the expected range of variation from the regression line of any forecast made. For example, the standard error of estimate for

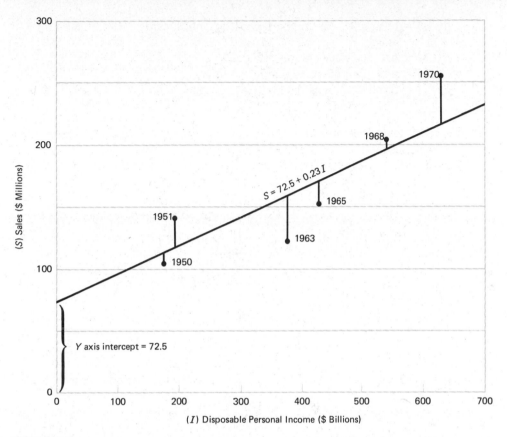

FIGURE 3-5
Simple regression line for sales dependent on disposable income. Data from Table 3-7.

our data and Equation 13 is 38.7. Because we assume a normal distribution of sales for each value of I, we can expect with some confidence that two-thirds of the time our estimate of S will be in the range of ±38.7. Therefore, if $I = 700$, then $S = 233.5$ as computed previously. However, with a standard error of estimate of 38.7, we are actually stating that two-thirds of the time we would expect the actual value of S to be in the range of 194.8 to 272.2, a rather broad range.

Obviously, we need to improve the forecasting ability of Equation 13, and we can accomplish this by including other causal factors in the regression equation.

Multiple Regression

The general concepts of simple regression analysis can be extended to include the effects of several causal factors through multiple regression analysis. For the data of Table 3-7, Parker and Segura [1971] show that the regression equation would be

$$S = 49.85 - 0.068M + 0.036H + 1.22I - 19.54T \tag{14}$$

where

S = gross sales per year

49.85 = base sales, or starting point from which other factors have an influence

M = new marriages during the year

H = new housing starts during the year

I = disposable personal income during the year

T = time trend ($T = 1, 2, 3, \ldots, n$)

and the coefficients that precede each of the causal factors represent the rate of influence on sales of changes in each of the causal factors M, H, I, and T.

The coefficient of determination for Equation 14 is 0.92, and the standard error of estimate is 11.9, indicating that the value of the equation as a forecasting mechanism has been increased substantially over Equation 13.

Equation 14 can be improved as a forecasting mechanism by making additional changes. The factor of new marriages is dropped, and last year's sales (S_{t-1}) is substituted in order to improve the overall forecasting accuracy. Also, last year's housing starts (H_{t-1}) is substituted for H, because this allows for the lag we would expect between construction time and the time home furnishing expenditures might be made. The revised equation is

$$S = -33.51 + 0.373\,S_{t-1} + 0.033 H_{t-1} + 0.672 I_t - 11.03T \qquad (15)$$

Forecasting accuracy has improved again with $r^2 = 0.95$, and the standard error of estimate = 9.7. Table 3-8 summarizes the record of actual versus forecasted sales and forecast errors for the entire 24-year period, and Figure 3-6 shows a comparative graph of actual versus forecasted sales.

When forecasts must be made for longer terms, as when new products and services are contemplated, or when new facility locations and capacities are being considered, multiple regression is a logical forecasting method. It requires considerable time and cost, because various hypotheses regarding the effect of variables may need to be tested. However, standard computing programs for multiple regression are now widely available which ease the burden and reduce the cost of application.

A considerable historical record is necessary for regression analysis to have validity. As a rule of thumb, Parker and Segura state that a 5-year record is needed for one independent variable, 8 years for two independent variables, and a longer history for three or more independent variables. These data requirements are often severe limitations to application.

Furthermore, there are four very important assumptions made in regression analysis that should be met. First, there is the assumption of linearity which states that the dependent variable is linearly related to the independent variables. Where the linear relationship does not hold, transformations can often be made that enable the requirements of this assumption to be met. The second basic assumption in regression analysis is that the variance of errors is constant. The third assumption is that errors from period to period are independent of each other, or not autocorrelated. Finally, regression analysis assumes that the errors are normally distributed. The nature and importance of these assumptions are covered in greater detail in Benton [1972], and Makridakis and Wheelwright [1978]. Obviously, considerable knowledge of statistical methods is required for the appropriate application of regression analysis.

Beyond possibly ignoring one or more of the important assumptions, one of the

TABLE 3-8

Differences in Actual Sales of Cherryoak Company, 1947–1970, and Sales Forecasted by Multiple Regression
(In millions of dollars)

Year	Actual Sales	Predicted Sales	Difference	Ratio of Actual Sales to Predicted Sales
1947	92.29	93.04	−0.75	0.99
1948	122.44	117.72	4.72	1.04
1949	125.57	136.91	−11.34	0.92
1950	110.46	129.33	−18.87	0.85
1951	139.40	128.65	10.75	1.08
1952	154.02	154.90	−0.88	0.99
1953	157.59	144.88	12.71	1.09
1954	152.23	145.17	7.06	1.05
1955	139.13	135.64	3.49	1.02
1956	156.33	137.44	18.89	1.13
1957	140.47	149.27	−8.80	0.94
1958	128.24	134.99	−6.75	0.95
1959	117.45	123.56	−6.11	0.95
1960	132.64	127.31	5.33	1.04
1961	126.16	136.52	−10.36	0.92
1962	116.99	124.20	−7.21	0.94
1963	123.90	125.56	−1.66	0.99
1964	141.32	134.79	6.53	1.05
1965	156.71	156.61	0.10	1.00
1966	171.93	170.59	1.34	1.01
1967	184.79	187.90	−3.11	0.98
1968	202.70	198.75	3.95	1.02
1969	237.34	227.95	9.39	1.04
1970	254.93	263.92	−8.99	0.96

SOURCE G C Parker and E. L. Segura, "How to Get a Better Forecast," *Harvard Business Review*, March–April 1971.

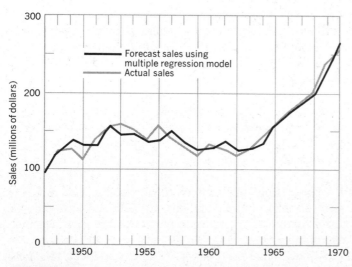

FIGURE 3-6
Forecast versus actual sales. Data plotted from Table 3-8.

great dangers in misapplying regression analysis is in assuming that a good fit to historical data guarantees that the regression equation will be a good forecasting device. The regression equation itself should be an expression of a good causal theory relating to factors in the regression model. In addition, we also need an understanding of the potential importance of factors that are not included in the model.

One of the differences, then, between time series forecasting models and causal methods is that time series accept increases or decreases in demand in an unbiased way, being rather mindless about the reasons for the increase or decrease. On the other hand, causal methods demand an explanation within the rationale of the forecasting system for demand changes that occur.

Econometric Forecasting Methods

In simplest terms, econometric forecasting methods are an extension of regression analysis and include a system of simultaneous regression equations. If, for example, in Equation 15 we attempted to include the effect of price and advertising, then there is the possibility of an interdependence, where our own sales can have an effect on these factors as well as vice versa.

For example, assume that sales is a function of GNP, price, and advertising. In regression terms we would assume that all three independent variables are exogenous to the system and thus are not influenced by the level of sales itself or by one another. This is a fair assumption as far as GNP is concerned. But if we consider price and advertising, the same assumption may not be valid. For example, if the per unit cost is of some quadratic form, a different level of sales will result in a different level of cost. Furthermore, advertising expenditures will influence the price of the product, because production and selling costs influence the per unit price. The price, in turn, is influenced by the magnitude of sales, which can also influence the level of advertising. All of this points to the interdependence of all four of the variables in our equation. When this interdependence is strong, regression analysis cannot be used. If we want to be accurate, we must express this sales relationship by developing a system of four simultaneous equations that can deal with the interdependence directly.

Thus in econometric form, we have

$$\begin{aligned} \text{Sales} &= f(\text{GNP, price, advertising}) \\ \text{Cost} &= f(\text{production and inventory levels}) \\ \text{Selling expenses} &= f(\text{advertising and other selling expenses}) \\ \text{Price} &= f(\text{cost} + \text{selling expenses}) \end{aligned}$$

Instead of one relationship, we now have four. As in regression analysis, we must (1) determine the functional form of each of the equations, (2) estimate in a simultaneous manner the values of their parameters, and (3) test for the statistical significance of the results and the validity of the assumptions.

To date econometric models have been used largely in connection with relatively mature products where a considerable historical record is available, and in industry and broad economic forecasts. For example, the Corning Glass Works developed econometric models to forecast television tube sales [Chambers et al., 1971]. These models were used to forecast future sales 6 months to 2 years to spot turning points sufficiently in advance to assist decisions for production and employment planning.

Industry econometric models have been developed to forecast activity in the forest products industry. Also, the economic forecasting models developed at UCLA and the Wharton School are econometric models.

PREDICTIVE METHODS

In this age of management science and computers, why must we resort to qualitative methods to make some of the most important predictions of future demand for products and services—predictions on which hinge the greatest risks involving large investments in facilities, as well as risks in market development? The answer is that where we have no historical record, statistical methods have no validity. What people think, samplings of how they react to market tests, knowledge of consumer behavior, and analogy with similar situations may be the best we can do. Given this situation the most scientific approach is to bring as much order as possible to these kinds of judgments. We cannot create hard demand data that do not exist. The qualitative methods are of considerable significance then, because they provide a basis for some important decisions.

Delphi Methods

Technological forecasting is a term used in connection with the longest-term predictions, and the Delphi technique is the methodology often used as a vehicle. The objective of the Delphi technique is to probe into the future in the hope of anticipating new products and processes in the rapidly changing environment of today's culture and economy. In the shortest range of such predictions, it can also be used to estimate market sizes and timing.

The technique draws on a panel of experts in a way that eliminates the possible dominance of the most prestigious, the most verbal, and the best salespeople. The object is to gain the benefit of expert opinion in the form of a consensus instead of a compromise. The result is pooled judgment with both the range of expert opinion and the reasons for differences of opinion shown.

The Delphi technique was first developed by the RAND Corporation as a means of achieving these kinds of results, in comparison with conferences and panels where the individuals are in direct communication, thus eliminating the undesirable effects of group interaction.

The panel of experts can be constructed in various ways and often includes individuals from both inside and outside the organization. It may be true that each panel member is an expert on some aspect of the problem, but that no one is an expert on the entire problem. In general, the procedure involves the following.

1. Each expert in the group makes independent predictions in the form of brief statements.
2. The coordinator edits and clarifies these statements.

3. The coordinator provides a series of written questions to the experts that combine the feedback supplied by the other experts.

4. Steps 1 to 3 are repeated for several rounds. Convergence is usually obtained with a small number of rounds in practice.

One of the most extensive probes into the technological future was reported by TRW, Inc. [North and Pyke, 1969]. The project involved the coordination of 15 different panels corresponding to 15 categories of technologies and systems that were believed to have an effect on the company's future. Anonymity of panel members was maintained to stimulate unconventional thinking. A Delphi method was then used to question and requestion the experts as follows:

Round one. The experts were asked to list probable technical events in their categories that could have a significant impact on the company. Each event was weighted on the basis of desirability, feasibility, and timing. After duplications were edited and eliminated, a total of 1186 predictions resulted.

Round two. Each panel member received a composite list of the edited predictions contributed by the panel in his/her category, plus those from other panels that were related to that member's category. Each panelist was asked to evaluate all events on the basis of the same three factors of desirability, feasibility, and timing.

Round three. Wide differences of opinion concerning events and dates were eliminated by discussing predictions individually with the panelists involved. The result was a composite rating of each event on the basis of its desirability, its feasibility, the probability that the event would occur, and the probability estimates of the timing of occurrence. The extensive results then were formed into logic networks.

Market Surveys

Market surveys and the analysis of consumer behavior have become quite sophisticated, and the data that result become extremely valuable inputs to predicting market demand. In general, the methods involve the use of questionnaires, consumer panels, and tests of new products and services. The field is a specialty in itself and beyond our scope.

There is considerable literature dealing with the estimation of new product performance based on consumer panels [Ahl, 1970), using analytical approaches [Bass, 1969; Claycamp and Liddy, 1969], as well as simulation and other techniques [Bass, King, and Pessemeier, 1968]. Proposed products and services may be compared with the products and known plans of competitors, and new market segments may be exploited with variations of product designs and quality levels. In such instances, comparisons can be made with data on existing products. These kinds of data are often the best available to refine the designs of products and facilities for new ventures.

Historical Analogy and Life-Cycle Analysis

Market research studies can sometimes be supplemented by reference to the performance of an ancestor of the product or service under consideration, applying an analysis of the product life-cycle curve discussed in Chapter 2. For example, the assumption was made that color television would follow the general sales pattern experienced with black and white television, but that it would take twice as long to reach a steady state [Chambers, Mullick, and Smith, 1971]. Such comparisons provide guidelines during the initial planning phases and may be supplemented by other kinds of analyses and studies as initial actual demand becomes known. Chase and Aquilano [1977] focus their attention on the life cycle of products in studying the problems of production management.

IMPLICATIONS FOR THE MANAGER

If there is a single, most important set of data for managers, it is forecast data. Virtually every important decision in operations depends in some measure on a forecast of demand. For example, the broad aggregate decisions concerning hiring and layoff of personnel, use of facilities, overtime, and the accumulation of seasonal inventories are developed in relation to a forecast of expected demand. In service industries, such as hospitals or telephone exchange offices, it is necessary to provide service 24 hours per day, 7 days per week. Scheduling personnel to perform these services (who normally work only 40 hours per week) depends on the demand for service. Inventories of raw materials, work in process, and finished goods are of great importance to manufacturing systems. Inventories of supply items are important to the smooth functioning of most service systems. Constructing rational inventory policies depends on forecasts of usage.

Managers are keenly aware of their dependence on forecasts. Indeed, a great deal of executive time is spent in concern over trends in economic and political affairs and how events will affect demand for their products or services. An issue is the relative value of executive opinion versus quantitative forecasting methods.

Executives are perhaps most sensitive to events that may have a significant impact on demand. Quantitative techniques are probably least effective in "calling the turn" that may result in sharply higher or lower demand, because quantitative methods depend on historical data.

Management science has attempted to automate sensitivity to sharp changes in demand through adaptive systems and through causal models. As we noted in our discussion of adaptive forecasting systems, success has been elusive, and it is not clear that the performance of adaptive systems is superior. Causal models suffer least from sluggishness, since they are constructed to reflect the effects on demand which are caused by indicators in an industry or in the economy.

The manager's choice of forecasting models must take account of the forecasting range required, accuracy requirements, and cost. The exponential smoothing methods are particularly adaptable to short-range forecasting and are inexpensive to install. The annual cost of maintaining such systems increases as the forecasting range is shortened, simply because the system must be updated more often.

Exponential smoothing forecasts are particularly adaptable to computer systems, because a minimum number of data items need to be stored for each item to be forecast. The data storage requirements increase as one moves from the simple to the more complex models that take account of trend and seasonal variations.

Whether or not the additional complexity is justified depends on the balance between the forecasting accuracy needed and cost. The fact that exponential smoothing systems are adaptable to electronic computing makes them particularly attractive for forecasting large numbers of items, as is often required for inventory controls.

When the forecasting horizon requirement is somewhat longer, and the need for accuracy is greater, causal methods should be favored by management. These conditions are common when managers must make broad-level plans for the allocation of capacity sources that may involve the expansion or contraction of short-term capacity. These aggregate plans are discussed in Chapter 9 and may involve hiring or layoff of personnel, use of overtime, the accumulation of seasonal inventories, the use of back-ordering or lost sales, or the use of subcontracting. These are important managerial decisions, and forecasting accuracy requirements may justify the costs of causal methods.

Box and Jenkins [1970] have developed a highly sophisticated forecasting methodology in which a general class of forecasting methods is postulated for a particular situation. In stage one, a specific model is tentatively identified as the forecasting method best suited to that situation. The forecasting models may range from moving averages through exponential and adaptive methods to regression analysis. In stage two, the postulated model is fit to the available historical data, and a check is run to determine whether or not the postulated model is adequate. Various statistical tests are involved. If the postulated model is rejected, stage two is used to identify an alternate model, which is then tested. The process is repeated until a satisfactory model has been identified.

These more sophisticated forecasting systems are costly, but may be justified to reduce the risk involved in important managerial decisions.

IMPORTANT TERMS

Numbers in parentheses indicate page numbers

Adaptive forecasting (70)

Average error (64)

Bias in forecasting (64)

Causal factors (71)

Causal forecasting methods (71)

Coefficient of determination (74)

Delphi methods (79)

Double exponential smoothing (70)

Econometric forecasting (78)

Exponentially weighted moving average (62)

Forecast error (64)

Fourier series forecasting (71)

Life-cycle analysis (80)

Market surveys (80)

Mean absolute deviation, MAD (64)

Mean squared error, MSE (64)

Moving average (61)

Multiple regression (75)

Prediction (57)

Regression analysis (73)

Reliability of forecast (74)

Seasonal variation (60,66)

Smoothed average (62)

Smoothing constants, α, β, γ (62,65,67)   Time series forecasting (61)

Standard error of estimate (74)   Trend (60,64)

REVIEW QUESTIONS AND PROBLEMS

1. What common components of demand do we wish to take into account in a forecasting system for operations?

2. What are the general smoothing effects of a small number of periods in a moving average (perhaps three to five periods)? What are the effects on the ability of a moving average to track a rapidly changing demand?

3. What are the general smoothing effects of values of α in the 0.01 to 0.20 range in exponential forecasting systems? How do systems with low values of α track rapidly changing demand?

4. Show that exponential forecasting systems actually give weight to all past data.

5. How can one rationalize the fact that to extrapolate or forecast using the basic model of Equation 2, we simply use the most current smoothed average, S_t, and phase it forward by one period?

6. If one uses a no-trend model to forecast demand where a trend actually exists, what is the nature of the error that results?

7. Figure 3-7 is a graph of 5.5 years of the monthly average number of patients in a large hospital. Table 3-9 gives the corresponding data.

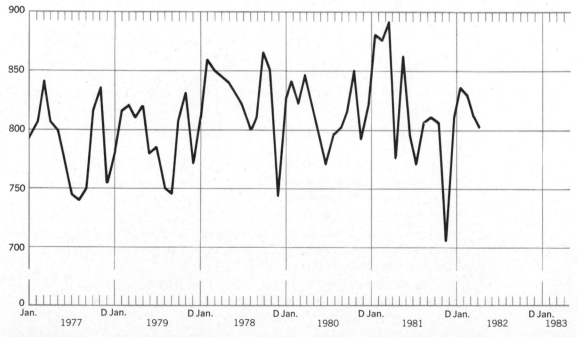

FIGURE 3-7
Monthly average inpatients at a large hospital.

TABLE 3-9   **Monthly Average Number of Inpatients at a Large Hospital**

Month	Year					
	1977	1978	1979	1980	1981	1982
January	795	780	815	830	820	820
February	810	820	865	840	880	835
March	840	825	850	825	875	830
April	820	815	845	845	890	815
May	800	825	840	830	775	800
June	765	780	825	810	865	
July	745	785	820	770	795	
August	740	750	800	795	770	
September	750	745	810	805	805	
October	820	830	870	815	810	
November	840	810	850	850	805	
December	755	770	745	790	705	

a. Compute 3- and 5-month moving averages for the first year and plot the results as forecasts of F_{t+1} on a graph in comparison with the actual values. How do you evaluate the results as forecasts of inpatient census?

b. Compute exponentially smoothed forecasts for the first 2 years of data using Equation 2, assuming a smoothing constant of $\alpha = 0.10$ (remember that the forecasts to be plotted are F_{t+1}). How do you evaluate the results as forecasts?

c. If the Fourier series program is available, compute forecasts using 6 and 14 terms.

8. What is the raw measure of trend used in the trend model? Why do we smooth it?

9. Using the data in Table 3-9, compute forecasts for February and March 1977. Assume that initial values of S_{t-1} and T_{t-1} are 800 and 0.0, respectively, and $\alpha = 0.2$, $\beta = 0.1$.

10. Recognizing that for the trend model, $F_{t+1} = S_t + T_t$, how can Equation 3 be simplified?

11. Using the data for 1977 in Table 3-9, construct an *initial* set of monthly seasonal indexes. Why do we smooth these indexes for subsequent years, rather than simply using the initial values?

12. Using the data for 1978 in Table 3-9, and the initial monthly seasonal indexes generated in the preceding exercise, compute the forecasts for February and March 1978, using the seasonal model. Assume that the initial values of $S_{t-1} = 820$, $\alpha = 0.2$, and $\gamma = 0.3$.

13. Using the data for 1978 in Table 3-9, and the 1977 initial seasonal indexes generated previously, compute the forecasts for February and March, 1978 using the trend *and* seasonal model. $S_{t-1} = 820$, $T_{t-1} = -1.0$, $\alpha = 0.2$, $\beta = 0.1$, and $\gamma = 0.3$.

14. What is the general structure of adaptive forecasting systems?

15.   What is the rationale behind the Fourier series forecasting methodology?

16.   Distinguish the statistical methodology of causal methods of forecasting from time-series methods.

17.   As in the Cherryoak Company example used in the text, if we find a regression equation that fits historical data accurately, why not assume that it will be a good forecasting device? Why have a theory to explain why the equation fits the data?

18.   Define the coefficient of determination and the standard error of estimate as measures of forecast reliability in regression analysis.

19.   What are the assumptions made in regression analysis?

20.   How is econometric forecasting different from regression analysis?

21.   Using the final regression model of Equation 15 developed by Parker and Segura for the Cherryoak Company, and the data in Table 3-7, compute the sales forecast for 1970. Check your answer with the forecasts given in Table 3-8.

22.   The standard error of estimate for Equation 15 was given as 9.7. Interpreting the significance of the forecast of 227.95 for 1969 given in Table 3-8, what is the probability of actual sales as low as $227.95 - 9.7 = \$218.25$ million?

23.   Contrast the meaning of the terms *prediction* and *forecasting*, as they are used in this book.

24.   How does the Delphi method gain the benefit of expert opinion in the form of consensus rather than compromise?

25.   What kinds of values to the planning base of TRW resulted from the type of Delphi study reported?

26.   What kinds of data useful in planning product and productive system designs result from market surveys? From historical analogy and life-cycle analysis?

SITUATIONS

27.   The hospital for which data are given in Table 3-9 and plotted in Figure 3-7 is attempting to improve its nurse scheduling system. Initially, it is concentrating on broad planning for the aggregate levels of nursing personnel needed.

   In the past, the number of nursing personnel had been determined from the peak demand expected through the year. With the heavy pressure to reduce costs, the hospital administrator was now considering alternatives that took account of shorter-term variations in the patient load. Therefore, the initial effort was to improve forecasting. An exponential smoothing model was applied to the 5.5-year historical record, using a smoothing constant of $\alpha = 0.2$. These studies of the historical record resulted in forecasting error measurements of MAD = 31.9 for the simple exponential smoothing model. The hospital administrator felt that the errors were too large, stating that he could do almost as well based on his knowledge of fluctuations. For example, he expected a relatively small number of patients in December because those with "elective" medical problems avoided the holiday season; these elective cases usually came in the spring.

85

The administrator was contemplating the use of more sophisticated forecasting models and wondered whether a model that accounted for trends and seasonals would result in greater forecasting accuracy. He also wanted advice concerning the possible use of a regression model.

Finally, the hospital administrator was deeply concerned about the 1981 data. The hospital had a record average of 890 patients in April of that year, but a record low of only 705 in December. He felt that the situation was explainable by the fact that the load had built up because of the increase in population in the community and that the low in December reflected the opening of enlarged facilities by the nearby county hospital. He wondered, however, what plans he should make for the balance of 1982 and for 1983.

What recommendations would you submit to the hospital administrator?

28. Berry, Mabert, and Marcus [1975] report a study of forecasting teller window demand at the Purdue National Bank. Exponential smoothing using the equivalent of seasonal factors that reflected special day effects were the unique part of the forecasting model. Trend was not included in the model, because no appreciable trend was observed in the historical data.

Causes of Demand Variation

Analysis of historical data included substantial variation in the number of "cash slips" processed per day by tellers. There were significant differences in cash slip volume depending on the day of the week, as follows:

Day	Daily Average	Standard Deviation
Monday	422	113
Tuesday	293	113
Wednesday	385	100
Thursday	305	135
Friday	508	169

The average load on Tuesday, for example, was only 58 percent of the average Friday load. Part of this variation was random or unpredictable as a result of individuals' particular reasons for going to the bank on a particular day, to the weather, and so forth. In addition to the random variation, however, a substantial amount of the variation could be attributed to weekly, biweekly, and monthly payments. Taking Monday as an example, when the Mondays that involved known reasons for demand variation were removed from the historical data, average demand dropped from 422 to 407 cash slips, but even more significantly, the standard deviation dropped from 113 to only 65. In other words, Monday's demand becomes somewhat more predictable when special days are taken into account.

Eight different kinds of special days were isolated that had a significant effect on the teller window demand,

1.   Regular days

2.   Academic paydays

3.   Fiscal year paydays (monthly)

4.   Days on which both an academic and fiscal year paydays occurred

5.   Day following an academic payday

6.   Day following a fiscal year payday

7.   Days that followed a fiscal year payday and which occurred on an academic payday

8.   Biweekly paydays (Wednesday)

Forecasting Model

From the data regarding the effect of special days on demand, a set of seasonal type indexes was constructed and taken into account in computations by the following three equations:

$$S_t = \alpha(D_t/F'_m) + (1 - \alpha)S_{t-1} \tag{16}$$

$$F'_m = \gamma(D_t/S_t) + (1 - \gamma)F_m \tag{17}$$

$$F_{t+1} = S_t \times F'_m \tag{18}$$

where I_m = special day factor for day m

F'_m = updated special day factor for day m

Note that the equations are very nearly the same as our seasonal model represented by Equations 6, 7, and 8. The differences are in the seasonal indexes (special day factors). The special day factor for day m, F'_m, is constructed from the historical data depending on the code of eight types of special days and combinations of days listed previously. F'_m is used in Equation 16 to compute the smoothed average S_t at the end of each day, based on the cash slip count for the day D_t. These factors deflate actual demand in computing S_t. The special day factor F'_m is then updated by current data in Equation 17 and used to reflate S_t for the forecast computation in Equation 18. Because the bank's special day schedule is dominated by a single large employer (Purdue University), special day factors could be computed for long periods in advance, making long-range forecasts possible. Equation 18 makes it possible to forecast n periods in advance by inserting the updated special day factor for the future day.

Comparative Models

A remaining question was, what is the incremental gain in adding successive refinement to the computation of special day factors in the model? Five models were constructed that progressively took account of additional causes of demand variation, and were tested on the historical data. In each instance, experiments were run to determine the parameter values, α and γ, that minimized forecast error. The results for the optimal values of the parameters are shown in Table 3-10.

TABLE 3-10   **Purdue National Bank Forecasting Study. Forecast Error Standard Deviation for Optimal Parameters α and γ**

Model Accounts for Special Day Variations Listed	Monday	Tuesday	Wednesday	Thursday	Friday
Basic model, no special days	102.2	144.8	160.0	76.0	166.2
Paydays	93.0	97.9	94.1	71.5	83.3
Paydays, and day following	83.3	60.7	79.2	66.1	81.8
Academic paydays, fiscal year paydays, days on which both types of paydays occurred, day following any payday, academic payday that follows a fiscal year payday	65.3	57.5	79.3	61.2	61.1
All of the above plus biweekly paydays (Wed. only)	—	—	67.3	—	—

SOURCE. W. L. Berry, V. A. Mabert, and M. Marcus, "Forecasting Teller Window Demand with Exponential Smoothing," *Institute for Research in the Behavioral, Economic, and Management Sciences,* Purdue University, Paper No. 536, November 1975.

How do you evaluate the results? What effect do you think results from the fact that the special day factors are static, that is, not time dependent as in the seasonal model represented by Equations 6, 7, and 8? Because the model isolates causes of variation, is it a causal model? If you were the manager of the Purdue National Bank, which of the forecasting models, if any, would you install?

One of the results of the model indicates that the teller staffing requirements for Mondays, for example, varies between four and nine tellers, depending on the particular special day factor. How could you staff these extreme variations in load?

(29.) A study by Reisman et al. [1976] was conducted in a manufacturing company, after experience with an existing forecasting system during the 1974 recession. The company produced residential and light commercial air conditioners and heating units. The recession had resulted in a 25 to 30 percent decline in housing starts, a major factor in the company's sales. The company forecasting system was producing grossly optimistic forecasts. A revised forecasting system was established that combined two kinds of objective forecasts plus a subjective forecast from the field, as shown in Figure 3-8.

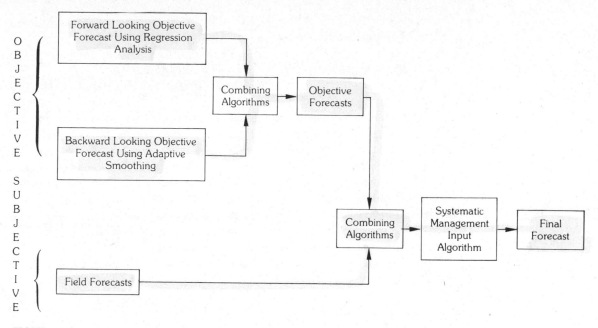

FIGURE 3-8
Forecasting system combining objective and subjective forecasts.
Source: A. Reisman, K. Gudapati, R. Chandrasekaran, P. Darukhanavala, and D. Morrison, "Forecasting Short-Term Demand, *Industrial Engineering, 8*(5), May 1976, pp. 38–45.

Objective Forecasts

Two different objective forecasts were used, adaptive exponential smoothing and regression analysis. Because the company had been caught in a downturn, both objective forecasts were designed to react to rapid changes in market indicators.

The adaptive exponential smoothing model used historical data for computing projections and was regarded as "backward looking." Adaptive smoothing techniques incorporate mechanisms for sensing rapid changes in demand, even though the basic parameter value may be set to a relatively small value in order to filter out random fluctuations in demand. The model used also incorporated adjustments for seasonality. The system was tested against a moving average by subjecting both to a 50 percent increase in demand over a 6-month period. The adaptive smoothing model sensed the change of trend after about 2 to 3 months and quickly adapted itself to the new level. On the other hand, the moving average forecast was quite sluggish in responding to the rapid increase in demand.

The forecast based on regression analysis was regarded as "forward looking" because it involved projections of variables known to be associated with the company's demand through previous regression analyses. For example, the regression equation for cooling units involved the variables gross private domestic investment ($PDIC$), private housing starts (HST), and government

89

purchases of goods and services (*GVTC*). The resulting regression equation ($r^2 = 0.762$) for cooling units was

$$\text{Deseasonalized cooling units} = -57{,}725.5 + 292.058(PDIC) + \\ 7822.676(HST) + 216.536(GVTC) \quad (19)$$

The result of the regression equation was reseasonalized in quoting forecasts. For the forecast to be forward looking, we must remember that forecast values of the three variables must be inserted in the regression equation in order to obtain an estimate of future sales units. The real value of the regression forecast was in its behavior with respect to sharp upturns and downturns. The response of the regression model was very similar to that of the adaptive smoothing model, the main difference being that there was no lag, because the projections of regression variables that cause demand produced immediate forecast changes in response to changes in the causal variables.

The two objective forecasts were combined into a final objective forecast in proportion to their error contributions. This was accomplished by taking the weighted sum of the two forecasts, with weights that were inversely proportional to the MAD of the two forecasting techniques.

Field Forecasts

The field forecasts were subjective and involved the sensitivity of field managers to what was happening in their regions. The field forecasts were submitted in a systematic way so that the results from 28 districts could be combined and merged with the objective forecasts. Systematic procedures were used for tracking and modifying field forecasts in order to improve their accuracy and determine their contributions in the final forecasts. Correction factors were computed for each region and each month by dividing actual demand by the field forecast, resulting in a correction ratio. The correction ratios were then smoothed by taking a 3-month moving average. The correction factors were applied to field forecasts, and the final field forecast was then the sum of corrected field forecasts.

Combining Objective and Subjective Forecasts

The final objective forecast was then combined with the final field forecast by weighting the two in proportion to their error contributions, following the same procedure for combining the two objective forecasts.

How do you evaluate the new forecasting system? Of what value are the field forecasts in relation to the objective forecasts? Will the field forecasts become more accurate by virtue of the information feedback concerning their errors? Because the forward-looking forecast is only as accurate as the projections of economic indicators used in the regression equation, do we have a forecast or "crystal ball gazing"? If you were president of the company, would you install this forecasting system? Would you modify the system? If so, how?

TABLE 3-11   **Comparative Results of Company Forecasts and Three Models**

| Technique | MAD (percent) | Hours Required for | | | Compute Time Required for development and run (seconds) | Time Elapsed Before Forecast Produced (days) |
		Model Development	Forecasting	Total		
Company	15.9	—	103.0	103.0	—	27
Exponential smoothing	15.1	7.1	4.9	12.0	2.19	2
Harmonic	14.1	6.9	4.3	11.2	1.21	2
Box-Jenkins	14.0	11.6	5.9	17.5	2.31	2.5

SOURCE. V. A. Mabert, "Statistical Versus Sales Force-Executive Opinion: A Time Series Analysis Case Study," *Decision Sciences,* 7(2), April 1976, pp. 310–318.

30. Mabert [1976] reports a comparative study of the performance of a sales force-execution opinion approach to forecasting single-item demand over a 5-year period with three statistical techniques. The study was carried out in the Duncan Manufacturing Company and dealt with one of their main products.

The company used a judgmental approach in preparing annual forecasts of demand. Each fall, sales personnel submitted estimates of customer needs for the coming year. The process involved managerial review of these estimates and the determination of a final demand forecast by period. The results of the judgmental approach were compared with three statistical forecasting methods: an exponential smoothing model taking account of seasonal factors similar to the one presented in the chapter, a harmonic model similar to the Fourier series methodology presented in the chapter, and the Box-Jenkins methodology.

Twelve years of historical data on actual demand and company forecasts were available for analysis. The first 7 years of data were used to identify and estimate the appropriate statistical models and their parameters used for comparison. The models were then used to forecast the last 5 years with comparative performance data, as shown in Table 3-11.

Statistical analysis showed that the Box-Jenkins and Fourier series model forecast errors were significantly different from the company's errors, but showed no significant difference among the three statistical procedures. The company forecasts required at least six times the hours of the next lowest technique. The 103 hours for the company forecasts included the time of the sales staff, district managers, and the vice-presidents involved.

Based on the comparative data, how do you evaluate statistical forecasting versus sales force-executive opinion? Wherein lies the advantage of each? Based on the comparative studies, if you were president of the Duncan Company, would you replace the company procedures with one of the statistical forecasting techniques? Why?

31. The following is an article, "Incorporating Judgments in Sales Forecasts;

Application of the Delphi Method at American Hoist & Derrick," by Shankar Basu and Roger G. Schroeder, reprinted from a 1977 issue of *Interfaces*, Volume 7, No. 3, May 1977, and is reprinted here with permission.

Read the article with the following questions in mind: The forecasts for the American Hoist & Derrick Company were for 5 years in advance. How much faith do you think should be put in these forecasts? Would you be willing to make plans that involved large investments in plant and equipment based on the forecasts? How do you evaluate the forecast methodology used for longer-term forecasts?

INCORPORATING JUDGMENTS IN SALES FORECASTS: APPLICATION OF THE DELPHI METHOD AT AMERICAN HOIST & DERRICK‡

*Shankar Basu**
and
Roger G. Schroeder†

ABSTRACT

In many organizations complete reliance on historical data is not an adequate basis for forecasting future sales. Since underlying conditions or assumptions may be changing, a means of incorporating management judgment in sales forecasts is needed. This paper reports on the development and application of a Delphi method ("opinion methodology") for sales forecasting at the American Hoist & Derrick Company. Although the Delphi method has only been in use for one year, the sales forecast error for 1975 was reduced to less than 1 percent, whereas sales forecast errors for the previous ten years were significantly higher.

Introduction

American Hoist & Derrick is a well-known manufacturer of construction equipment, with annual sales of several hundred million dollars. Their sales forecast is an actual planning figure—not merely a goal—since it is used to develop the master production schedule, cash flow projections, and work force plans. Consequently, the top management personnel at American Hoist & Derrick are extremely concerned with predicting sales as accurately as possible. Due to this concern, management is reluctant to rely on any single forecasting method. Thus, while the Delphi method of sales forecasting is emphasized in this paper, the 1975 sales forecast was developed using a number of methods [Chambers et al., 1971].

In the past, American Hoist & Derrick sold everything they could make. Sales

* Manager, Marketing Analysis, American Hoist & Derrick Co., St. Paul, Minnesota.
† Professor of Management Science, Graduate School of Business Administration, University of Minnesota, Minneapolis, Minnesota.
‡ Reprinted with permission from *Interfaces*, 7(3), May 1977.

forecasts were derived by a few key individuals, who utilized various methods to analyze the data from plant managers and sales personnel, but relied principally upon selective judgment. Over the past ten years, these subjective forecasts have been in significant error and this has caused a great deal of concern in top management.

Beginning with the 1975 sales forecast, top management wanted to assess the sales potential accurately, in order to determine just how fast the production capacity should be expanded. Such an estimate could not be based solely upon historical sales, since these only reflected previous production constraints. Additionally, rapidly changing economic conditions made the past a relatively poor predictor of the future—for production costs as well as expected sales. Consequently, the managers decided to temper historical data with informed judgment by utilizing the Delphi method to develop a five-year sales forecast. However, alternate forecasts were also prepared, using regression analysis and exponential smoothing, in order to avoid undue reliance on any single method and to provide a bench mark with which the other results could be compared.

Due to space limitations, only the Delphi method is discussed in this paper. The next section describes the actual use of the Delphi method at American Hoist & Derrick; the following section summarizes the results and conclusions of its use. The last section, an Appendix, details the general Delphi technique with particular emphasis on developing sales forecasts, for those unfamiliar with the basic method. (The Appendix is not included in this reprint.)

Delphi Method Use at American Hoist & Derrick

Formulating the Delphi Study. *The well-known Delphi method consists of: (1) a panel of experts, (2) a series of rounds, and (3) a questionnaire for each round. Each member of the panel responds anonymously to the questionnaire on each round and the summarized responses of the panel are fed into the next round. At AH & D it was decided to use three rounds for the Delphi study.*

In constructing the panel a total of 23 key individuals were selected. The panel selection was based on the following criteria:

- Personnel who had been doing these forecasts intuitively.
- Personnel who were responsible for using these sales forecasts.
- Personnel whose activities were affected by these forecasts.
- Personnel who had a strong knowledge of market place and corporate sales.

Care was taken to include knowledgeable personnel from different functional areas of the corporation.

In the case of sales forecasting the Delphi questionnaire should request not only sales estimates of interest, but also such information as an industry projection and a business indicator. This additional information will provide a check against the sales figure through correlation and it also helps the respondents develop their process of estimation. A close look at the corporate revenue for American Hoist & Derrick over the last five years revealed that the construction equipment group generated approximately 60 percent of the total revenue. The most logical industry that total company sales would correlate with is, therefore, the construction equipment industry. A graphical and analytical check demonstrated that these two time series were indeed correlated. Next, leading, roughly coincident, and lagging indicators were tried for best fit with the construction equipment industry. The closest fit was obtained with GNP in current dollar series and GNP was therefore determined to be the business indicator of interest.

The questionnaire then requested the following four estimates on each of the three rounds:

- Gross National Product, current dollars.
- Construction equipment industry shipments, current dollars.
- American Hoist & Derrick construction equipment group shipments, dollars.
- American Hoist & Derrick, corporate value of shipments, current dollars.

The First Round. To help obtain a realistic median on the first round, all four estimates which were being requested had data input. The data input were actual figures for the past five to seven years. Compound growth rate and graphical representation of each series were included. Opinion on percent increase expected for the next five years was requested. Figure 3-9 is a part of the first round questionnaire for

Construction Industry Estimate

The following figures and graph show historical sales figures for power cranes, shovels, walking draglines and walking cranes for the last seven years. Please indicate your estimate for each of the next six years. (% increase expected and graphically).

Year	% Increase	Industry Sales Mil $	Calendar Year	% Increase Expected
1967		511	1974	-----
1968	2.5	524	1975	-----
1969	9.7	575	1976	-----
1970	0.4	598	1977	-----
1971	6.5	637	1978	-----
1972	12.8	719	1979	-----
1973	35.4	974		

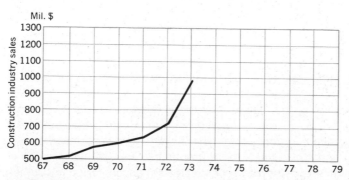

FIGURE 3-9
Sample: Partial first round request for information.

the construction industry estimate. A similar page was included for each of the other three estimates requested.

The responses on the first round were collected and summarized. A standard statistical analysis of the responses was conducted which generated for each of the four series—number of observations, largest observation, smallest observation, range of observations, mean, confidence limits, standard deviation and median.

The Second Round. *The second round questionnaire included feedback on actual responses together with the above standard statistical analysis. Each panel member's response was indicated and his revised estimate was requested in the second round. (See Table 3-12 for a sample of the data feedback for the construction industry estimate.) On the second round all members of the panel were asked for*

TABLE 3-12 **Sample: Partial Second Round Feedback of Estimates**

You Are	Construction Equipment Industry Annual % Increase in Shipments					
	1974	1975	1976	1977	1978	1979
1	5.0	7.0	7.0	6.0	6.0	6.0
2	25.0	20.0	15.0	20.0	20.0	15.0
3	6.5	5.4	7.6	8.2	10.0	10.0
4	15.0	10.0	8.0	0.0	2.0	5.0
5	20.0	20.0	8.0	8.0	6.0	7.0
6						
7						
8	15.0	3.0	7.0	6.0	6.5	4.0
9						
10	20.0	10.0	5.0	10.0	10.0	10.0
11	7.0	8.0	5.0	5.0	6.0	
12	20.0	4.0	5.0	16.0	2.2	4.0
13	13.0	5.0	4.5	8.5	8.8	10.2
14	25.0	2.0	3.0	6.0	7.0	8.0
15	20.0	10.0	5.0	5.0	5.0	7.0
16	35.0	0.0	7.0	9.0	0.0	(10.0)
17						
18	30.0	5.0	6.0	6.0	6.0	6.0
19	(20.0)	5.0	9.0	3.0	3.0	3.0
20	10.0	5.0	7.0	10.0	8.0	10.0
21						
22	20.0	10.0	20.0	35.0	25.0	15.0
23						
High	35.0	20.0	20.0	35.0	25.0	15.0
Low	(20.0)	0.0	3.0	0.0	0.0	(10.0)
Range	55.0	20.0	17.0	35.0	25.0	25.0
Mean	15.7	7.6	7.6	9.5	7.7	7.1
Std. Dev.	12.3	5.5	4.1	8.0	6.3	5.7
95% Confidence	9.3/22.0	4.7/10.4	5.4/9.7	5.4/13.6	4.5/10.0	4.0/10.2
Your Revised Estimate Explanation	. . . .		. . . .		. . . .	

explanations of their responses, irrespective of whether their responses fell in the top, bottom or interquartile range. The logic behind including the entire population was that the explanations of any person might be important and meaningful for the total population.

The response to the second round was of a "brain storming" nature. There was an outpouring of explanations from the panel members. The individual reasons for estimates were collected, summarized and listed under separate headings of GNP, CE Industry, AH & D Construction Equipment group and AH & D total shipments. All these explanations were then categorized into positive and negative factors for each of the four estimates. Relevant published data and opinion of well-known economists were also collected and prepared for input into the third round.

The Third Round. The third and final questionnaire was designed with extreme care. The format for this round was:

- Restatement of the initial question.
- Feedback of a respondent's first and second estimates.
- Second round response, standard statistical analysis.
- Factors that were considered important by the respondents in reaching their estimate in the second round.
- Related facts, figures and views of external experts.
- A request for the respondent's revised estimate.
- A request for comments or opinions.

Table 3-13 shows that portion of the third round questionnaire applicable to sales in the entire construction equipment industry; similar formats were used for Gross National Product (GNP) sales in the AH & D construction equipment group, and total sales for American Hoist & Derrick.

Statistical analysis on the third round was considered as the final forecast by the panel. The standard deviation and 95 percent confidence band had narrowed sufficiently to consider this forecast a reasonable consensus of the panel.

Results and Conclusions

Sales Forecast Accuracy. The use of the Delphi method had a direct and definite impact on the American Hoist & Derrick sales projection. Top management was presented three forecasts: one developed using the Delphi method; another used regression analysis; and a third forecast developed using exponential smoothing. The Delphi forecast was considered most credible by top management because it incorporated the experienced judgment of 23 key corporate individuals. This confidence was subsequently justified, as indicated in Table 3-14. The 1975 Delphi sales forecast was within $1.1 million of the actual 1975 sales, that is, the sales forecast error was reduced to less than one-third of one percent. Due to an extensive management reorganization and reassignment of key individuals in 1976, the Delphi method was not used to develop a new five-year sales forecast or update the previous one. In spite of this, the 1976 sales forecast—corresponding to the second year of the

TABLE 3-13   Sample: Partial Third Round Input of Data and Request for Final Estimate

Construction Equipment Industry

1.	*Question:* *Restated*	Estimate percent increase in CE industry shipments in current dollars for calendar years.				

		1975	1976	1977	1978	1979
2.	*Your first est.:*					
	Your second est.:					
3.	Second Round Response:					
	High	10.0	10.0	10.0	10.0	10.0
	Low	4.0	5.0	6.0	5.0	6.0
	Range	6.0	5.0	4.0	5.0	4.0
	Mean	7.14	7.56	7.92	6.7	7.75
	Std. Dev.	2.29	1.34	1.79	1.51	1.51
	95% Conf.	5.5/8.8	6.6/8.5	6.6/9.2	5.6/7.8	6.6/8.8

4. *Factors that were considered by the respondents:*

Negative
— Long delivery time
— Slow recovery in industry from recession
— Interest rate, financial control over expansion, repair and maintenance of current equipment
— Continued slowdown in housing
— Environmental factors causing project delays
— Drying up of federal funds
— Downtrend in backlogs

Positive
— Price increases
— Accelerated export business, continued worldwide demand of machinery for energy related projects

5. *Related figures for your consideration:* (Source: F. W. Dodge)

Construction contract awards in April and May were 32% above the depressed 1st quarter average. First quarter capital appropriation jumped 66% to 16.9 billion. This follows a 104% increase between the third and fourth quarters of 1974.

6.	*Your revised estimate:*					
		1975	1976	1977	1978	1979
	Percent increase expected:					

7. *Comments, other facts and figures you would like to see or show:*

TABLE 3-14

Actual Versus Forecast Sales (American Hoist & Derrick)

	1975	1976
Actual sales (millions)	$359.1	$410
Forecast sales (millions) Using Delphi method	$360.2	$397
Forecast error	+0.3%	−3.3%

original five-year projection—was within $13 million of actual 1976 sales, resulting in a forecast error of less than four percent. This was considerable improvement over the previous forecast errors of plus or minus 20 percent. Additionally, the Delphi forecasts were more accurate than the forecasts developed using regression analysis or exponential smoothing. The forecasts developed using these latter techniques were incorrect by $30–50 million, indicating a forecast error on the order of 10–15 percent.

One negative aspect of the study is the time period required to develop the forecast: approximately three months to complete all three rounds, evaluate the results, and produce a final consensus. However, the authors estimate that the next Delphi sales forecast, to be developed in late 1977, will be completed in only four to six weeks. This improved response time is expected to result from a Delphi education-training program and the use of precoded input forms in conjunction with a General Electric Statistical analysis system for data analysis.

Uniform Sales Estimates. Apart from the improvement in forecast accuracy, the next most beneficial aspect of the Delphi study was that it provided a reasonably uniform estimate of sales among different managers. The managers on the panel were presented with accurate past and present economic conditions and data on the business environment. Through successive rounds of Delphi, they developed a congruence in outlook on business conditions and corporate sales. Table 3-15 indicates the median, standard deviation, and range of the responses for each of the three rounds for estimates of the GNP and total sales in the construction equipment industry. The tendency toward consensus is indicated by the reduction in the range, standard deviation, and in the 95% confidence interval from one round to the next. All numerical estimates exhibited this type of reduction in variance.

This tendency toward congruence resulted in a relatively uniform base for future decision making among the participants in the study. Managers reacted very favorably to involvement in the forecast, and exhibited interest by requesting the results of

TABLE 3-15

Convergence of Some Estimates

			GNP Estimates 1978 % Growth		
	High	Low	Range	Standard Deviation	Median
Round 1	12.0	0.0	12.0	2.9	6.5
2	10.0	0.0	10.0	2.6	6.0
3	8.5	5.0	3.5	1.5	5.9

			Construction Equipment Industry Estimates 1978 % Growth		
	High	Low	Range	Standard Deviation	Median
Round 1	25.0	0.0	25.0	6.3	5.9
2	15.0	0.0	15.0	3.9	6.0
3	13.0	5.0	8.0	2.4	6.3

the study. Particular enthusiasm was shown in the second round, when each manager was asked for the reasons behind his/her forecasts. A great many corporations lack this uniformity of outlook, and quite divergent assumptions are made about sales potential. Even if there is a published forecast for sales, it probably will not have been internalized by managers to the extent that occurs from participation in a Delphi study. At American Hoist & Derrick there was a very marked divergence in sales estimates among managers in the first round; this divergence was greatly reduced upon completion of the third round.

Conclusions

The following conclusions were arrived at by the authors in conducting the Delphi study for sales forecasting:

1. Delphi has definite utility as an analytical tool for predicting sales of a corporation. As the forecasts incorporate anticipation of the future by experienced and qualified individuals, the results seem to be meaningful and realistic. Though the results can be used singularly, it is suggested that they be used in conjunction with other quantitative approaches to sales forecasting.

2. Apart from its analytical value, a Delphi study has an inherent educational value. The corporate officers are presented with past and present economic conditions and status. As a result, there is the development of a congruence in outlook on business conditions and corporate sales volume. This provides for a more uniform singular base for decision making by the different managers involved in the study.

REFERENCES

Ahl, D. H., "New Product Forecasting Using Consumer Panels," *Journal of Marketing Research*, 7(2), May 1970, pp. 159–167.

Armstrong, J. S., and M. C. Grohman, "A Comparative Study of Methods for Long-Range Market Forecasting," *Management Science*, 16(5), January 1969.

Bass, F. M., "A New Product Growth Model for Consumer Durables," *Management Science*, 16(5), January 1969.

Bass, F. M., C. W. King, and E. A. Pessemeier, *Applications of the Sciences in Marketing Management,* Wiley, New York, 1968.

Basu, S., and R. G. Schroeder, "Incorporating Judgments in Sales Forecasts: Application of the Delphi Method at American Hoist & Derrick," *Interfaces*, 7(3), May 1977, pp. 18–27.

Benton, W. K., *Forecasting for Management,* Addison-Wesley, Reading, Mass., 1972.

Berry, W. L., and F. W. Bliemel, "Selecting Exponential Smoothing Constants: An Application of Pattern Search," *International Journal of Production Research*, 12(4), July 1974, pp. 483–500.

Berry, W. L., V. A. Mabert, and M. Marcus, "Forecasting Teller Window Demand

With Exponential Smoothing," *Journal of the Academy of Management, 22*(1), March 1979, pp. 129–137.

Box, G. E. P., and G. M. Jenkins, *Time Series Analysis, Forecasting, and Control,* Holden-Day, San Francisco, 1970.

Brown, R. G., *Smoothing, Forecasting and Prediction,* Prentice-Hall, Englewood Cliffs, N.J., 1963.

Buffa, E. S., and J. G. Miller, *Production-Inventory Systems: Planning and Control* (3rd ed.), Irwin, Homewood, Ill., 1979.

Chambers, J. C., S. K. Mullick, and D. D. Smith, *An Executive's Guide to Forecasting.* Wiley, New York, 1974.

Chambers, J. C., S. K. Mullick, and D. D. Smith, "How to Choose the Right Forecasting Technique," *Harvard Business Review*, July–August 1971, pp. 45–74.

Chase, R. B., and N. J. Aquilano, *Production and Operations Management* (rev. ed.), Irwin, Homewood, Ill., 1977.

Church, J. G., "Sure Staf: A Computerized Scheduling System for Telephone Business Offices," *Management Science, 20*(4), December 1973, Part II, pp. 708–720.

Claycamp, H. J., and L. E. Liddy, "Prediction of New Product Performance: An Analytical Approach," *Journal of Marketing, 6*(4), November 1969, pp. 414–421.

Dalkey, N. C., and O. Helmer, "An Experimental Application of the Delphi Method to the Use of Experts," *Management Science, 9*(6), April 1963.

Dancer, R., and C. Gray, "An Empirical Evaluation of Constant and Adaptive Computer Forecasting Models for Inventory Control," *Decision Sciences, 8*(1), January 1977, pp. 228–238.

English, J. M., and G. L. Kernan, "The Prediction of Air Travel and Aircraft Technology to the Year 2000 Using the Delphi Method," *Transportation Research, 10,* 1976, pp. 1–8.

Groff, G. K., "Empirical Comparison of Models for Short Range Forecasting," *Management Science, 20*(1), September 1973, pp. 22–31.

Mabert, V. A., "Statistical Versus Sales Force-Executive Opinion Short Range Forecasts: A Time Series Analysis Case Study," *Decision Sciences, 7*(2), April 1976, pp. 310–318.

Makridakis, S., A. Hodgsdon, and S. C. Wheelwright, "An Interactive Forecasting System," *The American Statistician, 28*(4), November 1974, pp. 153–158.

Makridakis, S., and S. C. Wheelwright, *Forecasting Methods and Applications,* Wiley, New York, 1978.

Milkovich, G. T. et al., "The Use of the Delphi Procedures in Manpower Forecasting," *Management Science, 19*(3), October 1972, pp. 211–221.

North, H. Q., and D. L. Pyke, "Probes of the Technological Future," *Harvard Business Review*, May–June 1969.

Parker, G. G. C., and E. L. Segura, "How to Get a Better Forecast," *Harvard Business Review*, March–April 1971, pp. 99–109.

Reisman, A., K. Gudapati, R. Chandrasekaran, P. Darukhanavala, and D. Morrison, "Forecasting Short-term Demand," *Industrial Engineering, 8*(5), May 1976, pp. 38–45.

Trigg, D. W., and A. G. Leach, "Exponential Smoothing with an Adaptive Response Rate," *Operational Research Quarterly, 18*(1), March 1967, pp. 53–59.

Whybark, D. C., "A Comparison of Adaptive Forecasting Techniques," *The Logistics and Transportation Review*, *8*(3), 1972, pp. 13–26.

Winters, P. R., "Forecasting Sales by Exponentially Weighted Moving Averages," *Management Science*, *6*(3), April 1960, pp. 324–342.

CHAPTER 4

Technology and the Design of Products and Services

THE STRATEGIC IMPLICATIONS OF MANAGING TECHNOLOGY EF-
fectively are shown clearly by the success of firms such as Eastman Kodak,
IBM, and DuPont. These firms have allocated a larger-than-average proportion of their budgets to research and development (R & D). Their emphasis
on R & D provides them with new product and process innovations that help them
remain in leading positions within their industries. Product innovations are those resulting in new or improved products, such as the video recorder as a consumer
product, or the silicon chip used in various electronic products. Process innovations
are those that affect the technology for producing products that may result in lower
costs or better quality, or otherwise affect the ability of the enterprise to produce
more effectively.

The competitiveness and profitability of a firm depend in part on the design and
quality of the products and services that it produces, and on the cost of production.
Therefore, the relationship of product innovation to process technology and process
innovation is of considerable interest. Predicting the nature and impact of innovation
can place one firm in a more competitive position than a firm that does not anticipate
these events.

The design of the productive system depends in large part on the design of the
products and services to be produced. A product or service designed one way may
be costly to produce, but may be somewhat less costly when designed another way.
Finally, the mix of products to be offered is important not only to the marketing
program, but to the production program. One mix of products may utilize available
equipment quite well and result in low costs. However, another mix of products may
violate capacity constraints and require large capacity additions to be effective.

TECHNOLOGICAL INNOVATION

In simplest terms we tend to think of the conversion of scientific discovery to application in products, services, and processes as a chain of events: scientific discovery,
invention, development, innovation, and application. There are commonly long time
lags in this chain, as enabling conditions pace developments. For example, processes
for shale oil extraction were known for some time, but economic factors did not
justify their costly development. Cheaper sources of crude oil and other energy forms
were used first. Given the shortage of conventional energy sources, however, and
the resulting price increase, the application of shale oil processes may become a
more viable possibility. As another example, all the electronic circuitry required for
portable radios was available for many years; however, a true miniature radio was
not possible until the development of the transistor. Finally, to take a service item, all
the technology necessary for a mass food preparation service has been available for
many years. Yet enterprises such as BURGER (discussed in Chapter 1) were not
possible until our culture had developed a willingness to make trade-offs between
time, food quality, and price.

The chain-event model does not help to explain the driving forces that produce
the innovations near the end of the chain. Does the process flow from scientific
discovery to application rather naturally as a river flows from higher to lower elevation,

or is the process somewhat more complex? Do new product innovations stimulate innovations in productive processes, or is that also too simple a concept?

Abernathy and Townsend [1975] suggest that product innovation, process innovation, and changes within a segment of industry appear to feed on each other. "No single external force, such as market factors or technological factors, is dominant in stimulating technological innovation. Sources of stimulation that arise within a productive segment are more frequently the critical factor that sparks technological innovation." They further state, "Historical patterns of development in several productive segments suggest that the efforts of engineers and managers in improving production processes themselves may be a key factor in stimulating technological innovation."

TECHNOLOGICAL INNOVATION IN THE COMPUTER INDUSTRY

It has been commonly held that most innovations are market stimulated and usually applied to new products rather than to production processes. The results of one study in the computer industry are shown in Table 4-1. Note that the largest stimulation source of innovations is in the market and that the greatest application impact is on products.

However, when the same data are analyzed taking into account the vertical integration structure within the industry their results are suggestive of a startlingly different conclusion. Figure 4-1 shows the flow of innovations allocated to three levels of industrial integration for the computer industry, based on the data from Table 4-1. The dotted lines with arrows in Figure 4-1 show the source of innovation stimulation, and the solid lines emerging from the "innovation boxes" indicate the frequency and area of application impact. Note that "market factors" represent the primary source

TABLE 4-1

Source and Impact of Successful Innovations in the Computer Industry

	Components and Supply Manufacturers	Computer Manufacturers
Stimulation source		
Market	47 (61%)	28 (31%)
Production	17 (22%)	32 (36%)
Technical	10 (13%)	20 (22%)
Administrative	3 (4%)	10 (11%)
	77	90
Application impact		
Product	60 (78%)	49 (54%)
Component	10 (13%)	28 (31%)
Process	7 (7%)	13 (14%)
	77	90

SOURCE. S. Meyers and D. Marquis, *Successful Industrial Innovations*, National Science Foundation, Washington, D.C., 1969, pp. 69–70.

of stimulation for 61 percent of the innovations produced by the computer components and supply manufacturers. However, market factors in that industrial segment
are the same as the process equipment needs of the two higher processes in the
chain of vertical integration, the computer manufacturers and the computer users.
The greatest impact of innovation is upstream.

Abernathy and Townsend note that:

*most innovations in the lower levels of the vertical integration chain are product
innovations. These are at the same time process innovations for processes at
higher levels of vertical integration and as such have direct productivity implications. In fact, from a strict perspective of the process at the highest level of
vertical integration (computer users), all of the innovations considered here are
process innovations and all have implications for process productivity.*

For example, wide-bodied aircraft were product innovations for aircraft manufacturers, but were process innovations to the airlines with very important productivity
implications.

Note that the industrial structure culminates in a service industry, that of providing
computing service to users. Thus, we see an example of the interlinking between a
service industry and manufacturing industries that provide equipment for the

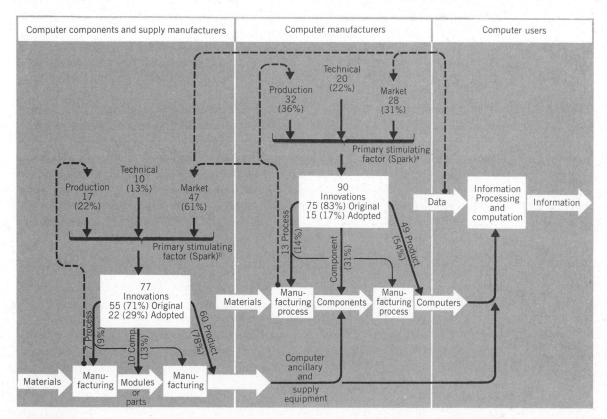

FIGURE 4-1
Technological innovation in the computer industry.
SOURCE: *W. J. Abernathy, and P. L. Townsend, "Technology, Productivity and Process Change,"*
Technological Forecasts and Social Change, 7(2), January 1975. Data from Meyers and Marquis. 1969.

processes. Figure 4-1 represents a closed loop system for innovation in the industry, where market stimulation means to be stimulated by an opportunity to serve process needs of an organization higher in the integration structure. A comparable analysis of the transportation industry was also performed, which also culminates in a service, with similar results.

INTERACTION BETWEEN PRODUCT AND PROCESS INNOVATION

We have already alluded to the iterative process between product design and productive system design. Each has an impact on the other in determining the designs of both. This iterative process apparently also takes place on a macro level within industries, as is shown by Figure 4-1, and the concept includes the design of services as well as that of the manufactured product. The nature of services offered is affected by the productive process and vice versa, and so on back through the chain.

A MODEL OF PROCESS AND PRODUCT INNOVATION

Utterback and Abernathy [1975] developed a dynamic model of process and product innovation in firms and tested it on empirical data. The model relates the product and process innovations to three stages of development.

Stage 1

The first stage begins early in the life of products and services and of processes; initially, the innovations are stimulated by needs in the marketplace. Process innovations also are stimulated by the need to increase output rate (see Figure 4-2). In terms of innovation rate, product innovation is high and the initial emphasis is on product performance maximization. There may be an anticipation that new capabilities will, in turn, expand requirements in the marketplace.

Although we may think largely in terms of physical products, service innovations are quite comparable; for example, the initial introduction of innovative services such as social security, no-fault auto insurance, comprehensive health services (e.g., Kaiser Permanente), fast-food services, and so on.

Utterback and Abernathy call the first phase "performance maximization" for products and services and "uncoordinated" for processes. High product innovation rates increase the likelihood that product diversity will be extensive. As a result, the productive process is composed largely of unstandardized and manual operations, or operations that rely on general purpose equipment. The productive system is likely to be of the process focused type, but the characterization—uncoordinated—is probably justified in most instances because the relationships between the required operations are still not clear.

Stage 2

Price competition becomes more intense in the second stage as the industry or product and service group begins to reach maturity. Productive system design emphasizes

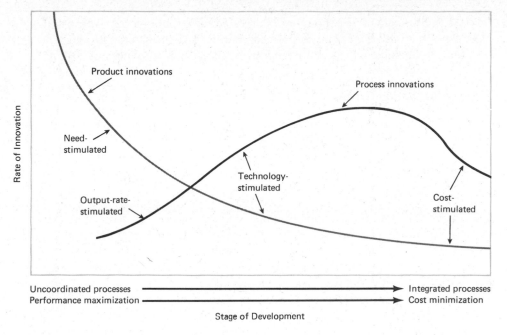

FIGURE 4-2
Relationships of product and process innovations in a dynamic model.
SOURCE: *J. M. Utterback, and W. J. Abernathy, "A Dynamic Model of Process and Product Innovation by Firms,"* Omega, 1975.

cost minimization as competition in the marketplace begins to emphasize price. The productive process becomes more capital-intensive and more tightly integrated through production planning and control.

At this stage, the production process often is segmented in nature. This is true partly because integration is taking place at a broader level through managerial control systems and partly because the dominant system type is the process-focused system. As shown in Figure 4-2, process innovations dominate; however, both process and product innovations are stimulated by technology.

Stage 3

Finally, as the entire system reaches maturity and saturation, innovations tend to be largely cost stimulated, as indicated in Figure 4-2. Further price competition puts increasing emphasis on cost minimizing strategies, and the production process becomes even more capital intensive and product focused.

The productive process becomes more highly structured and integrated, as illustrated by automative assembly lines, continuous chemical processes, and such highly automated, large-scale service systems as social security. The productive process becomes so highly integrated that it is difficult to make changes because any change at all creates significant interactions with other operations in the process.

The model of innovation indicates the close relationship between the design and development of products and services and the productive system design. In fact, during the third, or cost-minimizing, stage, the effects of innovation on product cost follow a surprisingly clear pattern. In addition, however, the model demonstrates the close tie-in between the nature of innovation at various times in the product life cycle and the positioning strategy of the enterprise regarding its productive system.

Plotting Innovation Cycles

Even in a period of stable product designs, there appears to be an innovation cycle. Figure 4-3 shows a plot of product and process innovations, and technological transfers over a 38-year period at the Ford Motor Company. Ford-initiated innovations were rated on a scale of 1 to 5 by four independent industry experts. The innovations ranged from the introduction of the plastic steering wheel (average rating 1) in 1921 to the power-driven final assembly line (average rating 5) in 1914. Figure 4-3 shows that new product applications occurred in clusters associated with new models, followed by a decline as the new designs became standardized. Process innovations peaked after the product innovations, presumably to integrate the processes with existing operations and to reduce costs. Technological transfers plotted in Figure 4-3 refer to the transfer of process technology to or from associated industries. These transfers increased as Ford undertook vertical integration.

Managing Technological Change

One of the results of the Ford study was that the need was recognized for balance between a cost-reducing strategy and new product innovations, which were at odds. "The ability to switch to a different strategy seems to depend on the extent to which

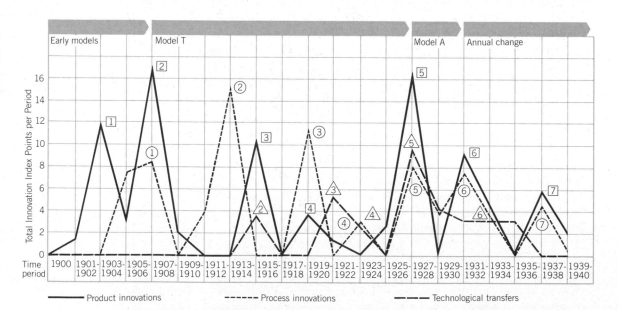

FIGURE 4-3
Innovation and process change at Ford.
SOURCE: W. J. Abernathy, and K. Wayne, "Limits of the Learning Curve," Harvard Business Review, September–October 1974, pp. 109–119.

the organization has become specialized in following one strategy and on the magnitude of change it must face. An extreme in either factor can spell trouble" [Abernathy and Wayne, 1974].

This balance can be achieved by periodically inaugurating major product innovations, stressing cost reduction along the experience curve between model changes. An alternate mode of achieving balance is to decentralize within the corporate structure; that is, to have separate organizations follow different strategies within the same general product line. One organization might follow the Ford Model T strategy of cost reduction and volume expansion. Another might develop innovative products or processes which, when developed, might follow the cost reduction strategy, perhaps finally displacing the former products.

INTERACTION BETWEEN PRODUCT-SERVICE DESIGN AND PRODUCTIVE SYSTEM DESIGN

On the macro level we saw that innovation in products at lower levels of the vertical integration chain fed into process innovations (productive system design) at higher levels of vertical integration within an industry. At this broad industry-wide level, there is an interaction between product-service design and the design of the productive system. Both the designs of services and products may be involved, for example, in both the computer and transportation industries the industry culminates in services rendered instead of a physical product.

A similar process takes place within an enterprise where the design of products and services is partially dependent on the productive system design, and vice versa. The concept is so well-recognized in the mechanical industries that a name has been coined for the process of designing products from the point of view of producibility—*production design.*

Production Design

The producibility and minimum possible production cost of a product are originally established by the product designer. The most clever production engineer cannot change this situation; he or she can only work within the limitations of the product design. Therefore, the obvious time to start thinking about basic modes of production for products is while they are still in the design stage. This conscious effort to design for producibility and low manufacturing cost is referred to as "production design," as distinct from functional design. To be sure, the product designer's first responsibility is to create something that functionally meets requirements. But once functional requirements are met, there are ordinarily alternate designs, all of which meet functional requirements. Which of these alternatives will minimize production costs? A well-conceived design has already narrowed the available alternatives and specified, for example, a sand casting, if that is appropriate in view of both function and cost considerations.

Given the design, process planning for manufacture must be carried out to specify in careful detail the processes required and their sequence. Production design first sets the minimum possible cost that can be achieved through such factors as the specifications of materials, tolerances, basic configurations, and the methods of join-ing parts. Final process planning then attempts to achieve that minimum through the specification of processes and their sequence which meet the exacting requirements of the design. Here, process planners may work under the limitations of available equipment. If the volume is great or the design stable, or both, however, process planners may be able to consider special-purpose equipment including semiauto-matic and automatic processes and special purpose layout. In performing their functions, process planners set the basic design of the productive system.

The thesis of a production design philosophy is that alternatives of design that still meet functional requirements nearly always exist. For the projected volume of the product, then, what differences in cost would result? Here we must broaden our thinking, because the possible areas of cost that can be affected by design are likely to be more pervasive than we imagine. There are the obvious cost components of direct labor and materials. But perhaps not so obvious are the effects on equipment costs, tooling costs, indirect labor costs, and the nonmanufacturing costs of en-gineering.

Indirect costs tend to be hidden, but suppose one design required 30 different parts, whereas another required only 15 (e.g., the reciprocating automobile engine versus the rotary engine). There are differences in indirect costs as a result of greater paper work and the cost of ordering, storing, and controlling 30 parts instead of 15 for each completed item.

Interchangeable Parts. Designs for component parts need to be specified carefully so that any part from a lot will fit. This is accomplished by establishing tolerances for part dimensions that take into account the manufacturing tolerances of mating parts. The result of design for interchangeable parts is interchangeable assembly. Assembly costs are then much lower than they would be if workers had to select combinations of mating parts that fit.

Standardization. Custom products are bound to be more costly than standardized products, but managers must attempt a balance that clients and customers will ac-cept. The Ford Model-T example in Chapter 2 is an excellent example of what can happen when this balance is ignored. But given the appropriate balance, there are many economic benefits to standardization. The cost items affected are raw materials inventory, in-process inventory, lower setup costs, longer production runs, improved quality controls with fewer items, opportunities for mechanization and automation, more advantageous purchasing, better labor utilization, lower training costs, and so on. Indeed, all the benefits that result from the experience curve discussed in Chap-ter 2 are appropriate for product standardization.

Simplification. When two or more parts are finally assembled rigidly together, perhaps the unit can be designed as one piece, thus eliminating an assembly opera-tion. This is often feasible when a single material will meet service requirements for all surfaces and cross sections of the part. Another example is the substitution of a plastic snap-on cap instead of a screw-on cap for some applications. The cost of the materials and labor for the snap-on cap is very much less. Simplifying the design of services offered has similar implications.

Modular Designs. If the same component or subassembly can be used in a variety of products, or in a product family, production costs can be reduced. Thus modular design is one way to offer product variety while holding the number of components and subassemblies to some reasonable level. For the modular components, we can have the advantages that result from volume and the experience curve, while offering product variety in the marketplace.

Design and Redesign

The design process is an iterative one. In a sense, it is never done. New information feeds in from users, and we find ways to improve designs that reduce production costs, although the quality criterion is often an objective as well.

As an example of production design and redesign, Bright [1958] describes the development of electric light bulb manufacturing during the period from 1908 to 1955. Initially, a batch process was used involving manual operations and simple equipment. The conversion from batch to continuous operation was achieved by adopting systematic layout, standardizing operations, and effecting operation sequence changes. Then, however, the light bulb itself was redesigned a number of times to facilitate process changes and permit mechanical handling. Finally, an evolution took place in which individual standardized manual operations were replaced by mechanical operations, and these operations were in turn integrated to produce a fully automated process.

Also, in manufacturing there are numerous examples that reflect redesign of products from the viewpoints of processes and materials used, methods of joining parts, tolerances, design simplification, and techniques for reducing the amount of processing.

AUTOMATION AND CAD/CAM

Although automation is new in the sense that the principles have only been applied relatively recently to mechanical and assembly types of processes, the basic ideas are not new. Such processes as thermostatic control of room temperature have been used for many years. The common float valve used in toilets automatically fills the tank to a given level and then shuts off. The process industries have used the principles of automation for some time to control chemical processes. But, the coupling of computer aided design (CAD) and computer aided manufacturing (CAM) is quite new and has considerable significance for potential productivity increases in industry.

The economics of industrial mechanization began with the tasks where mechanization could be justified and where machines could perform tasks that could not be accomplished manually. As labor has become more expensive relative to machines, a continuous process of substitution has taken place. The substitution of machines to perform the *control* functions of the human operator had to wait until the present when labor rates are very high. The ultimate development in this trend is a completely integrated automatic sequence of operations, without human labor or control other than to program the system once it is designed and installed.

Although the "automatic factory" does not exist today, there are portions of factories that are indeed automatic. For example, Seiko has developed a system for the automatic assembly of watches, in which no human input to the assembly process is required. A West Coast facility of General Motors manufactures auto wheels

111

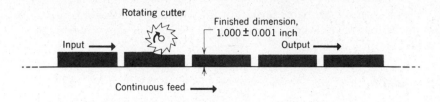

FIGURE 4-4
Open loop automation setup for milling a part to a standard dimension.

automatically, without manual assistance. The raw material enters at one end as strip steel and coiled bar, is automatically rolled, cut, formed, welded, punched, assembled, painted, and dried. The wheel emerges at the opposite end as a completely finished product.*

Open Loop Automation

There are two main approaches to controlling automation, open and closed loop systems. Open loop automation involves essentially the automatic handling of parts between operations in such a way that the part is indexed and placed in the exact position to be processed by the subsequent operation or machine. The whole sequence is coordinated carefully so that the several operations in the sequence go through their cycles at just the right instant when all parts have been indexed in position. What we have then is one giant machine, coordinated to work as a unit.

The possible types of processes that can be included in such a sequence are limited only by economics and the imagination of the process design engineers. Most types of metal machining, gauging, and inspection processes have been incorporated, as well as some assembly or joining operations. These types of process designs are typical of large-volume, standardized products such as automobiles. Figure 4-4 shows one station of what could be considered a series of operations. Parts are fixed to the transfer device which moves them past cutting tools such as the one shown. Other operations in the sequence might be sidecuts, slots, induction hardening, grinding, lapping, and gauging. All of the tools, including the one shown, are preset to yield the desired dimensions on the part. Once set, operations proceed automatically. Direct labor would be required only to load parts into the beginning process, unload at the end, and to start and stop the process. Depending on the part design and the relative economic advantage, the loading and unloading operations could also be mechanized.

Obviously, given the automated process, the system is largely determined, including the design of jobs.

Closed Loop Automation

Figure 4-5 shows what is necessary to close the loop. Closing the loop is accomplished by feedback of information about measurements made on the output. In the

* D. B. Dallas, "The Advent of the Automatic Factory," *Manufacturing Engineering* November 1980, pp. 66–76.

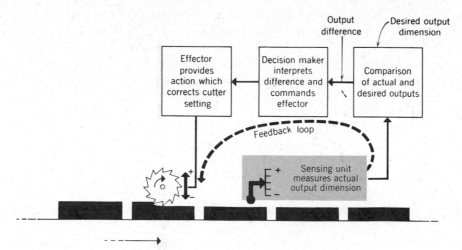

FIGURE 4-5
Closed loop automation setup for milling a part to a standard dimension.

feedback loop, we need a *sensing* unit, to measure and record characteristics of the output (in the example, a dimension), and a means of *comparison* of the actual output with the desired output. The difference, which may be either positive or negative, is then fed to a *decision maker* which interprets the error information and commands the *effector* to make a correction in the proper direction and magnitude so the output will meet standards.

Numerically Controlled Processes

When positions or paths of cutter tools are under the control of a digital computer, we have numerical control. The feedback paths in this case do not emanate from a measurement taken on the workpiece itself, but from the basic positioning controls of the tools or work tables that determine the position of cutters relative to the work. The feedback loops continually compare actual position with programmed position and apply correction when necessary.

When two dimensions are controlled, we have *position control,* illustrated by the drilling of holes that must be positioned accurately. The drill tool can be moved in two dimensions to accomplish the desired position, after which the tool advances into the work to produce the hole. Such a system could be programmed to drill a series of holes accurately positioned on the work. Obviously, such a closed loop drilling operation could be included as one of the operations in an open loop automation system.

When the ideas of position control are carried one step further, by controlling three dimensions, we have *contour control.* Not only is position controlled, but also the actual path of the cutter. This involves a much more complex programming problem because complex curves and surfaces must often be specified. Contour control systems have great flexibility in terms of part shapes that can be produced, as well as in change of shapes from job to job. Instead of the part being processed through a sequence of machines or machine centers, it is often possible to perform all the required operations with a single setup, because the cutter can be programmed to make cuts in any path needed to produce the required configuration. Very complex parts can be produced with a single setup.

One of the great advantages of numerically controlled systems is that the machine tool is not tied up for long periods during setup, because practically all preparation time is in programming, which does not involve the machine tool. In addition, repeat orders require virtually no setup time, other than inserting the part program in the machine for processing. Thus, the field of applicability includes parts that are produced in low volumes. Therefore, automation is having an important impact on process and job designs for both high-volume standardized types of products, and low-volume products through numerically controlled processes (even custom designs).

The computer controlled manufacturing system has been coupled with computer controlled product design systems to produce a powerful combination. The acronym used in industry for this type of design and manufacture is CAD/CAM (Computer Aided Design/Computer Aided Manufacturing). Finally, because the information regarding design and manufacture is available on computer files, it has been possible to use the data together with other information for production planning and control purposes, thus achieving an integration that has great significance for the present and the future.

Robotics

One of industrial America's exports has been the concept of robotics. Although the idea was developed in the United States, the Japanese are way ahead in the application of robots. Robots are essentially mechanized arms and hands that are capable of performing many operations ranging from machining to assembly. Robots are not in widespread use, even in Japan, but because of the productivity crisis in the United States, the media has focused considerable attention on them. Table 4-2 shows the number of robots in use in Japan, the U.S., Western Europe, and in General Motors. Note that while GM had only 4.2 percent of the world total in 1981, they forecast that they will have 14 percent of the world total by 1990. Obviously, GM intends to press automation as a mechanism for increasing productivity.

Robots are in use in a number of other U.S. companies such as Chrysler, International Harvester, and Xerox. It seems likely that their use will increase as they become economical substitutes for labor.

TABLE 4-2   **Utilization of Industrial Robots**

	'80	'81	'82	'83	'84	'85	'90
World	16,000	24,000					100,000
Japan	8,500	14,000					
U.S.	3,200	4,300					
W. Europe	2,800	4,100					
Other	1,500	1,600					
GM	425	1,000					14,000

SOURCE. General Motors Research Laboratories.

GROUP TECHNOLOGY—A PROCESS INNOVATION

Group technology is a concept for organizing manufacturing resources to increase productivity in process-focused situations involving parts and products that are similar, perhaps different sizes or types of the same product. The idea is to group similar machines as in a process-focused system, but to arrange the flow of the family of products in line fashion. Because the sequence of operations is similar, machines can be arranged in functional groups, but these groupings of equipment can be arranged in a sequence that fits the various sizes and types fairly well.

An excellent example of group technology is actually quite old. The Simmonds Saw Company probably did not think in terms of the current buzz word when they arranged their physical layout, shown in Figure 4-6, but the result has the advantage that many of their saws require approximately the same kinds of processes. Therefore, they reaped the benefits of process-focused and product-focused systems simultaneously. Note that the basic physical layout is process-focused, with departments such as forging and welding, grinding, and so on. But, each of the products flow through the process departments in about the same sequence as in a product-focused system.

Group technology concepts include the physical arrangement, but in addition involve a classification and coding system that is computerized. The coding system exploits the commonalities in the family of parts and products, and in more

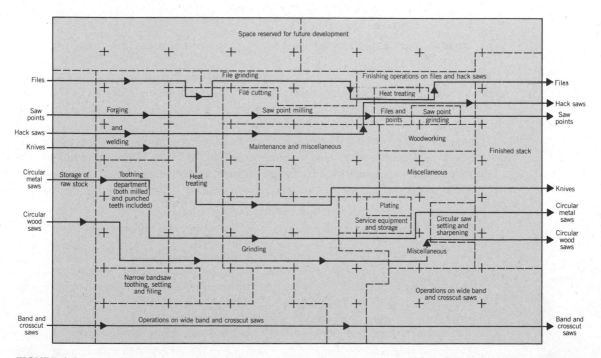

FIGURE 4-6
Simmonds Saw Company arrangement for group technology.
SOURCE: *F. E. Folts.* Introduction to Industrial Management, *McGraw-Hill Book Company, New York, 1963.*

advanced systems couples to computer aided design and manufacturing systems (CAD/CAM).

DESIGN OF SERVICES OFFERED

Although no term has been coined to describe it, a process similar to production design occurs and represents the interaction between the design of services to be offered and the productive system design. The motivation for altering the service offered may be accommodations to cost factors and service quality as measured by time performance and other dimensions. Some of the kinds of accommodation in the nature of services offered are as follows:

1. Transfer some of the activity involving the service to the client or customer. This has been one of the most common techniques for lowering costs. In hospitals, supermarkets, and mass-food services, the patient or customer performs some of the activities that were formerly a part of the service. The result is usually a lower labor cost and the elimination of some activities performed by the productive system.
2. Eliminate some aspects of service entirely.
3. Change the mix of services offered.
4. Change the reaction time for service; that is, give poorer service by applying fewer resources to the operation.
5. Change other aspects of service quality, perhaps the range of services offered.

Table 4-3 indicates some of the interactions between the design of services offered and the productive system design for several well-known types of systems. The kinds of accommodations listed for both services and productive systems are not intended to be exhaustive.

Unfortunately, there seems to be a consensus that the quality of all kinds of services has deteriorated. The reasons are probably that most service operations are labor intensive, and labor-saving devices are uncommon in service operations. The result is that rising wage costs are not compensated for by increases in productivity.

An Example [Yourdon, 1970]

A simulation study of computing service provides an example. Four different mixes of computing service offered by a service bureau were considered: 100 percent time sharing, 100 percent batch processing, and two alternatives that provided a mix of time sharing and batch processing according to given schedules.

A computer program was written to simulate operations under the four types of service mixes, taking into account assumptions on sales generation, revenue, capacities, and costs of all types. The program calculated profit and loss statements, the time needed to break even, and profitability. Although only one equipment configuration was used, the same program could easily be used to make similar calculations for three or more basic machines, for example, the IBM

TABLE 4-3   **Interactions Between the Design of Services Offered and the Productive System Design for Several Types of Services**

Types of Service	Types of Alteration of Service Offered to Accommodate Needs of Productive System	Types of Alteration of Productive System to Accommodate Needs of Service Offered
Nursing care in hospitals	Specialization by levels to reduce costs (e.g., nurses aides).	Changes of layout and activity scheduling.
Food markets	Self-service to reduce cost.	Change in layout and flow. Balance of numbers of check-out stands to maintain waiting time standards.
Postal service	Reduction of services to reduce costs (e.g., number of deliveries per day).	Introduction of some semiautomatic equipment for sorting. System improvement, etc., to improve overall delivery time.
Food service	Elimination of waiters and waitresses to reduce cost, as in cafeterias, and to reduce waiting time and cost in mass food outlets.	Change of layout and flow.
Computing service (e.g., in service bureaus)	Change mix of types of services offered (e.g., time share, batch processing, etc.)	Change mix of equipment (e.g., basic machine and peripheral equipment).
Fire protection	Increase or decrease time to react and provide service.	Relocate stations and/or add or delete stations to maintain a reaction time standard.
Police protection	Increase or decrease time to react and provide service.	Increase or decrease size of police staff. Reallocate staff based on changing crime patterns.
Emergency medical service	Increase or decrease time to react and provide service. Change mix of services available on an emergency basis.	Relocate ambulance stations and/or add or delete stations to maintain a reaction time standard. Change equipment and/or level of training of paraprofessional medical personnel.
Airline cabin service	Change average ratio of passengers to flight attendants. Eliminate services and reduce quality of services offered to reduce cost.	Increase public relations efforts through the media.

360/50, the GE-265, and the XDS-940. The three machines have different capacities and software availabilities and widely varying monthly lease costs. The end result of such a study combines the market estimates and projections, design of the service to be offered, and the interaction with the equipment configuration (productive system design in our terms). The combination yielding maximum profit would presumably be selected.

THE PRODUCT MIX PROBLEM

We have recognized that the product and productive system design decisions require trade-offs in order to jointly optimize them. Now, what are the prime decision areas, and what decision processes support them? The decision points are focused on the approval of specific designs and product mixes and required alterations to the productive system. There is often the drive to gain advantages through modularity of design and standardization.

Thus, managers are again forced to look at any product-service design decision within a systems context. How will a new or redesigned product or service be received? What impact will it have on the existing product line? What is the best new product mix? What is the impact on the productive system, its design, and its capacities? How will the new design affect operating schedules? And, of course, what are the effects on revenue, costs, and profits? Some of these effects are reflected in forecasts and estimates of incremental revenues and costs, but the manager must make judgmental trade-offs.

One way of expressing the system of problems surrounding product design is to ask, "What happens to the optimum mix of products when a new product or product line is introduced?"

The product mix problem is a general one throughout industry, and solutions should reflect the most economical allocation of capacity to demand. For example, in oil refining, there are interdependencies in the quantities of different products to be produced. If more of one product is to be produced, such as heating oil, then less of some other products will be produced. The profitability of various products may be different, and there are limits to the markets for each. The result is a complex programming problem to determine the best product mix to produce. The interdependencies always exist in oil refining because the basic raw material, crude oil, can be processed into many different products. An increase or decrease in one always means a change in the quantities of some other products.

In the mechanical industries, the product mix problem is not so obvious. Nevertheless, the mix problem can be acute if we are operating near capacity with time-shared facilities. At this point the interdependencies become critical, and increases or decreases in the amount of one product produced can mean changes in the amounts of other products produced. These problems have been approached through mathematical programming.

The analysis of adding (or deleting) a product can be important in the managerial decision process. In the linear programming format, it focuses managerial attention on the system of products and overall impact on contribution and the impact on the productive system and its capacities. Through sensitivity analysis, the linear programming decision format focuses managerial attention on possible opportunities for selectively enlarging capacity. See Appendix B for coverage of linear programming methods.

IMPLICATIONS FOR THE MANAGER

The design of products and services is of strategic interest for the manager of operations because the nature of the product or service has great impact on the design of the system to produce it, and vice versa. The manager can often obtain lower costs by exploiting the relationship between the product or service and the productive system.

Innovation is the generator of new products and services. Studies of innovation within industries indicate that a majority of innovations may be classified as product innovations. When we look at the vertical integration structure of an industry, however, we find that product innovations at lower levels in the hierarchy are, in fact, process innovations for the higher levels in the structure. Thus, there is an interaction between product design and productive system design even in these macro terms.

The term *production design* is used in industry to connote the important interaction between product and system design. Some of the common interactions involve accommodation in the product design to processes and materials, methods of joining parts, tolerances, design simplifications, and reduced amount of processing.

With the developing lack of competitiveness of U.S. industry, managers will look to automation to help meet the productivity crisis. The concepts are no longer theoretical, but can be applied in a broad spectrum of business and industry. The greatest benefits come with the integration of the design of products with the manufacturing methods. Computer aided design and manufacturing (CAD/CAM) is a powerful tool when used appropriately. Small lot production of families of products can be approached through group technology, coupled with CAD/CAM concepts.

The accommodations by the design of services offered are most often to cost considerations and may result in the client or customer doing part of the activity. The result is that the client or customer gets less service or a different mix of services or waits longer to obtain service. Managers of service operations need to be sensitive to the nature of their clientele in order to maintain an appropriate definition of the service offered in relation to the cost of providing the service. Unfortunately, improvements in productivity in service operations are less common, and cost reduction objectives are most likely to be achieved through changes in the nature of the service offered. The details of product design, system location, and productive system design all flow from predictions and forecasts of markets.

IMPORTANT TERMS

Numbers in parentheses indicate page numbers

Automation (111)	Position control (113)
CAD/CAM (111)	Process innovation (103)
Closed loop automation (112)	Product innovation (103)
Contour control (113)	Production design (109)
Group technology (115)	Product mix (118)
Numerically controlled process (113)	Robotics (114)
Open loop automation (112)	Technological innovation (103)

REVIEW QUESTIONS

1. How does the analysis of the vertical integration structure of an industry affect one's views of the nature and source of innovations?

2. Develop an analysis of the flow of innovations through the vertical integration structure, such as Figure 4-1, for another industry. The emphasis here is on the structure, not the innovation data.

3. Discuss the relationship of functional design and production design in determining a product design that meets functional requirements, cost considerations, and the limitations of available processes.

4. Discuss the nature of costs that can be affected by alternate product designs.

5. What feedback loops provide information for the redesign of products and the productive system?

6. What is the difference between open and closed loop automation? What is required to close the loop?

7. Define these terms: position control, contour control.

8. What is the meaning of the term, CAD/CAM?

9. What kinds of accommodation in the nature of services offered may result from cost and quality pressures?

10. What kinds of interactions between the design of services offered and the productive system design are likely to occur for fire protection, police protection, emergency medical service, and airline cabin service?

11. What are the criteria and values that enter the decision process for determining whether or not a new product design should be approved?

12. What kinds of data might result from an analysis of product mix when we are considering the addition or deletion of a product or service? How might these data be of value in making the product decision?

SITUATIONS

13. Nels Jensen started his grocery business 35 years ago in the Lake Tahoe resort community. The combination of good management and a market among well-to-do patrons produced an independent supermarket of unsurpassed quality. One of the hallmarks of the Jensen success model was his emphasis on and definition of the service aspects of his store. Those service aspects were: 10 hours of operation every day and minimum customer hassle and waiting time to obtain the desired purchases and get checked out.

   A study of some of the major changes that occurred over the years revealed that both the nature and quality of service and the system design successively affected each other. When the store was small, employees were stationed in areas to help customers select items, check out, bag, and transfer purchases to the parking lot. Later, with a much larger volume of customers, the system transferred virtually all the selection process to the customer, and the system design focused on the check-out stand.

By controlling the number of check-out counters in operation, Jensen set a service standard that he tried to maintain. The standard was set in terms of the time the customer had to wait before being served. Jensen felt that for his clientele, a waiting time of 1.5 minutes was about as long as would be tolerated without complaint. In fact, however, he tried to control waiting time by keeping an eye on the size of the waiting lines. Anytime the lines had two or more people waiting, he would open another check-out counter, even if he had to operate it himself. He then tried to schedule checker shifts to provide capacity for the peak shopping hours. He also trained some of the checkers to do other work, such as pricing and storing stock on display shelves, to provide flexibility in the number of checkers available when peak loads occurred.

Jensen tried several variations of the check-out system. Originally, employees helped unload carts to the checkers, but as labor costs increased, this activity was transferred to the customer. Customer complaints resulted. Then, having changed the design of the check-out stand, Jensen tried a system in which the checkers worked directly from the cart. However, the checkers complained of backaches from constantly having to lean over to obtain items from the carts.

Jensen then modified the system with a new cart and check-out stand design system. This still enabled the checker to work directly from the cart, but did not require leaning over to obtain items. The new cart–check-out stand system raised the working level. The cart had a hinged end, which the checker opened, thus placing the bottom of the cart at the check-out stand working level. In this way, all aspects of service could remain the same in terms of waiting time—what the customer had to do to obtain service, and the check-out time.

The next cycle of system design involved what is called *front-end automation*. Measurements made in a survey by Jensen indicated that the average time for a customer in the check-out process was 5.5 minutes, including 1.5 minutes of waiting time. The 4.0 minutes for actual check out included 2.5 minutes for ringing up the sale and placing the purchases in bags. The balance was payment, which often involved check cashing, as well as some chitchat and other miscellaneous activities. With the advent of item scanning systems, Jensen saw the possibility of improving overall service time by reducing the check-out time itself and possibly simultaneously reducing labor costs.

The scanning systems required that a universal code be placed on products (the bar-pattern codes now commonly used on product packages) that would be read by the scanners. A customer's entire order could then be moved rapidly over the scanner. The system required the customer to load purchases on a belt that fed the purchases to the checker, who repositioned them to move past the scanning eye. The scanner read and transmitted the information to a computer, which translated the information into prices and a total bill, including sales tax. The checkers' activities were thus confined to scanning, bagging, collecting, and making change.

Although the scanning system had other operating advantages, Jensen was most interested in a possible service improvement, assuming that a productivity increase might justify the scanner's installation on a reasonable basis. The system was installed partially, as a test. Measured results indicated that check-out time, exclusive of waiting time prior to check out, was reduced to an average of 2.4 minutes. In addition, checker productivity increased from an average of $252 of sales per hour to $500, and check-out errors were reduced by 65 percent. Checkers were paid $4.50 per hour.

Jensen could install the scanning system to cover the present 12 check-out stands for a lease cost of $7000 per month. Even though only an average of 6 check-out stands were in use (current system), if he should decide to install the scanners, he would want the entire system to be automated. His concern was that service would be improved, in the sense that the customers' time in a system would be reduced. On the other hand, the scanner system represented a step backward, in that the customers would have to unload their carts and load the conveyor belt. He was not sure how his type of customers would react.

Should Jensen install the scanner system? Why?

14. History records that the electronic pocket calculator had a product ancestor known as the mechanical desk calculator—first hand powered and later electrically powered. It was a mechanical marvel, prized by those whose jobs required accurate computations and by organizations that needed both accuracy and relatively high productivity in computations not justified for programming on computers.

Calculatron, Inc., was a major manufacturer of desk calculators and had enjoyed long-term profitability. It had a loyal work force of semiskilled and some highly skilled employees. Although product improvements had continued through the years, the basic design of Calculatron's product line was stable during the previous 15 years, and product design changes were carefully implemented to take account of the existing production lines. The market for desk calculators had been an expanding one, and with the advantage of a relatively stable product design, Calculatron had been able to specialize production methods, making continuous improvements in productivity through investments in labor-saving equipment. The productivity increases had helped secure the firm's market position through competitive pricing and produced profitability and security for both the enterprise and its employees. Employees enjoyed high wages and salaries and excellent pension and other benefits. Employees were organized and affiliated with the AFL-CIO and union-management relationships had been generally very good.

Enter electronic minicircuitry, with microcircuitry and the "chip" on the horizon. The first electronic desk calculator had just been announced by a competitor. Calculatron was not far behind. It had employed a staff of electronic engineers 2 years previously and assigned them the task of producing a revolutionary redesign of the product line. The prototypes had already been tested, and the product and production engineers were at work in the production design phase simultaneously developing preliminary designs of the productive system required to produce the new electronic product line.

Market forecasts indicated a conversion of the former mechanical calculator volume to the electronic, with a "kicker," because a large replacement market was available for the faster, quieter, and more capable electronic machines.

TABLE 4-4   **Worker-Hour Requirements and Capacities for Refrigerators and Air Conditioners**

	Worker-Hours per Unit		Capacities (Worker-Hours per Month)
	Refrigerators	Air Conditioners	
Air conditioner Assembly line	0	3	6000
Refrigerator Assembly line	2.9	0	8000
Machine shop	2.0	2.5	7500
Unit department	1.5	1.3	5000

The one sour note in the market was the prediction that soon a pocket-sized calculator would be possible if the research and development on microcircuits were to materialize. Reports concerning startling technological innovations in microcircuitry indicated that the probability of a breakthrough was high.

The production engineers are ready to develop final designs of the productive system for the new electronic calculator line. A meeting of the executive committee has been convened to examine preliminary plans for production in relation to short- and longer-term market forecasts and predictions.

a. What kinds of guidelines for the productive system design should the executive committee establish for the production engineers?

b. What plans should Calculatron make for the introduction of the new product line?

c. What kinds of longer-term plans should Calculatron make for future product and process innovation in the calculator field?

*15. A company produces refrigerators and is contemplating the addition of air conditioners to the product line. They are currently producing 2000 refrigerators per month. There is idle capacity in the assembly line, as well as in the machine shop and the refrigeration unit departments.

Planners have estimated that the air conditioners could use the same facilities in the production of parts in the machine shop and refrigeration unit departments and that the only manufacturing facility which would need to be added is a final assembly line for the air conditioners. The capacity estimates and worker-hour requirements for both products are summarized in Table 4-4. The planners also estimate that the contributions to profit and overhead for the two products will be $50 for the air conditioners and $38 for the refrigerators. Note that any additional labor required by the air conditioners has been deducted as a variable cost from the gross revenue per air conditioner to obtain the $50 contribution.

The planners then solve a linear programming problem for the optimum product mix and obtain the schedule of 1250 refrigerators and 2000 air conditioners per month. See the computer solution and sensitivity analysis in Figure 4-7.

* This situation requires the application of concepts in appendix B, Linear Programming.

```
ENTER THE NAME OF THIS PROJECT:   REF AND AIR COND
MAXIMIZE OR MINIMIZE:   MAXIMIZE
OBJECTIVE FUNCTION:   Z = 50AIR + 38REF
CONSTRAINT EQUATIONS:
(1) 3AIR ≤ 6000
(2) 2.9REF ≤ 8000
(3) 2.5AIR + 2REF ≤ 7500
(4) 1.3AIR + 1.5REF ≤ 5000
```

```
    LPRUN
```

REF AND AIR COND

THE OPTIMAL VALUE OF THE OBJECTIVE FUNCTION IS: 147,500.000

THE VARIABLES IN THE SOLUTION ARE

VARIABLE		AT LEVEL	
	AIR		2.0000E3
	REF		1.2500E3
	SLK2		4.3750E3
	SLK4		5.2500E2

DO YOU WISH SENSITIVITY ANALYSIS?   YES

		SHADOW	LB	CURRENT	UB
CONSTRAINT	1	8.3333E-1	3.2609E3	6.0000E3	9.0000E3
	2	0.0000E0	3.6250E3	8.0000E3	7.2370E75
	3	1.9000E1	5.0000E3	7.5000E3	8.2000E3
	4	0.0000E0	4.4750E3	5.0000E3	7.2370E75
Price	AIR		4.7500E1	5.0000E1	7.2370E75
	REF		0.0000E0	3.8000E1	4.0000E1

—END—

FIGURE 4-7
Refrigerator-air-conditioner computer solution and sensitivity analysis for Situation 15.

At the executive committee meeting, where the planners make a presentation of their analysis and recommendations, strong opposition is encountered from the vice-president in charge of marketing. She objects to the fact that the proposal calls for a reduction in the output of refrigerators from 2000 to only 1250 per month. "Why should we give away part of our market? Why not produce for the full market demand of 2000 refrigerators per month? We have the capacity."

a. Examine the profitability of alternate proposals for including the air conditioners in the product line.

b. In the linear programming solutions schedule, the machine shop is fully utilized. How much additional machine shop capacity would be required if refrigerator output were maintained at 2000 per month? Would the capacities of any other departments be affected?

c. What should the company do?

REFERENCES

Abernathy, W. J., and P. L. Townsend, "Technology, Productivity and Process Change," *Technological Forecasting and Social Change*, 7(4) 1975.

Abernathy, W. J., and K. P. Wayne, "Limits of the Learning Curve," *Harvard Business Review*, September–October 1974, pp. 109–119.

Bass, F. M., "A New Product Growth Model for Consumer Durables," *Management Science, 16*(5), January 1969.

Boyer, C. H., "Lockheed Links Design and Manufacturing," *Industrial Engineering, 9*(1), January 1977, pp. 14–21.

Bright, J. R., *Automation and Management,* Graduate School of Business Administration, Harvard University, Boston, 1958.

Gerstenfeld, A., "Technological Forecasting," *Journal of Business, 44*(1), January 1971, pp. 10–18.

Hudson, R. G., J. C. Chambers, and R. G. Johnston, "New Product Planning Decisions Under Uncertainty," *Interfaces, 8*(1) Part 2, November 1977, pp. 82–96.

Meyers, S., and D. Marquis, *Successful Industrial Innovations,* National Science Foundation, Washington, D.C., 1969, pp. 69–70.

Utterback, J. M., and W. J. Abernathy, "A Dynamic Model of Process and Product Innovation by Firms," *Omega*, 1975.

Yourdon, E., "CALL/360 Costs," *Datamation*, November 1970, pp. 22–28.

CHAPTER 5

Capacity Planning

THE LONG-RANGE OPERATIONS STRATEGY OF AN ORGANIZA-
tion is expressed to a considerable extent by capacity plans. It is in connection with capacity planning that the following issues must be considered.
What are the market trends, both in terms of market size and location, and
technological innovations? How accurately can these factors be predicted? Is there a
technological innovation on the horizon that will have an impact on product or service
designs? How will capacity needs be affected by the new products? Are there process
innovations on the horizon that may affect production methods? Is a more continuous
productive system justified in the near future? How are capacity needs affected by
process innovations? Will it be profitable to integrate vertically during the planning
horizon? In planning new capacity, should existing policies for using overtime and
multiple shifts be reviewed? In planning new capacity, should we expand existing
facilities or build new plants? What is the optimal plant size? Should a series of smaller
units be added as needed, or should larger capacity units be added periodically?
Should the policy be to provide capacity so that some lost sales may be incurred, or is
demand to be met?

The foregoing strategic issues must be resolved as a part of capacity planning. In
assessing alternatives, the revenues, capital costs, and operating costs may be compared, but managers may need to trade off the possible effects of the strategic issues
against economic advantages and disadvantages.

Definition of Capacity

*Capacity is the limiting capability of a productive unit to produce within a stated time
period, normally expressed in terms of output units per unit of time.* But capacity is
an illusive concept, because it must be related to the intensiveness with which a
facility is used. For example, it may be the policy to work a plant 5 days per week,
one shift per day, producing a maximum of 1000 units per week. On this basis, one
might rate the regular capacity as 1000 output units per week. But this limit can be
increased by working overtime, resulting in a capacity limit with overtime of 1150
units. By adding a second shift, however, the capacity can be pushed to perhaps
1800 units per week.

Another way of increasing a capacity limit is to engage in subcontracting when it is
feasible. Thus, changing policies with respect to the intensiveness with which facilities
are used can change capacities without actually building new capacity. These alternate sources of capacity can provide managers with important flexibility in making
capacity plans.

Measures of Capacity

When the output units are relatively homogeneous, the capacity units are rather
obvious. For example, an auto plant uses numbers of autos, a beer plant uses cases
of beer, and a nuclear power plant uses megawatts of electricity.

When the units of output are more diverse, it is common to use a measure of the
availability of the limiting resource as the capacity measure. For example, the airlines
use available seat miles (ASMs) as a measure. They do not use "number of seats,"

TABLE 5-1   **Measure of Capacity for Different Types of Organizations**

Type of Organizations	Capacity Measure
Auto plant	Number of autos
Steel plant	Tons of steel
Beer plant	Cases of beer
Nuclear power plant	Megawatts of electricity
Airline	Available seat miles (ASMs)
Hospital	Available bed-days
Movie theater	Available seat-performances
Restaurant	Available seat-turns
Jobbing machine shop	Available labor-hours
School of Business Administration	Available semester or quarter sections

because such a measure does not provide an indication of the potential intensiveness of use of the seats. Similarly a restaurant would not use seats as a measure because it does not indicate how many "turns" they can accommodate. Thus, available seat-turns would be an appropriate measure for a restaurant.

Finally, a jobbing machine shop has many different types of equipment performing a wide variety of machining operations, and the outputs may be unique parts that are never repeated. The value of the labor and material of the outputs could vary widely. Therefore, the capacity of the shop is normally stated as the capacity of the limiting resource, the availability of labor hours. Labor hours are used rather than machine hours, because there is usually a ratio of two or three times as many machine hours available as labor hours; that is, the skilled machinist is the limiting resource.

Table 5-1 shows common capacity measures for a number of different types of organizations.

PROCESS FOR CAPACITY PLANNING

The process of capacity planning may be summarized as follows:

1. Predict future demands, including the possible impact of technology, competition, and other events.
2. Translate predictions into physical capacity requirements.
3. Generate alternate capacity plans related to requirements.
4. Analyze economic effects of alternate plans.
5. Identify risks and strategic effects of alternate plans.
6. Decide on a plan for implementation.

PREDICTING FUTURE CAPACITY REQUIREMENTS

Long-range forecasts of demand are difficult. There are always contingencies that can have important effects, such as recessions, wars, oil embargos, or sweeping technological innovations. Therefore, predicting demand also requires an assessment of contingencies. The contingencies are apt to be rather different, depending on the situation. Mature products are more likely to have stable and predictable growth, whereas the markets for new products may be quite uncertain.

Mature Products with Stable Demand Growth

Many products and services enjoy mature, stable markets. Examples of products and commodities are steel, aluminum, fertilizer, cement, and automobiles. Examples of services are airline travel and health care. In Chapter 3, Table 3-2 summarized prediction and forecasting methods that have value for the longer term. Recall that the predictive methods were Delphi, market surveys, and historical and life-cycle analyses. The causal forecasting methods were regression and econometric models. In addition to these formal predictive methods, executive opinion and extrapolation are common methods for estimating future demand.

For mature stable products, causal models are often appropriate. In a comparative study, Armstrong and Grohman [1972] showed that an econometric model was superior to subjective methods in forecasting the U.S. air travel market. Also, Basu and Schroeder [1977] showed that long-range forecasts based on executive opinion could be improved by incorporating the Delphi method at the American Hoist & Derrick Company.

Given long-range predictions of demand, we must generate capacity requirements. It is unlikely that these capacity needs will be uniform throughout the productive system. A balance of capacities of subunits exists that reflects the discrete nature of capacity. For example, the existing receiving, shipping, and factory warehouse area may accommodate a 50 percent increase in output, but the assembly line may already be operating at full capacity and the machine shop at 90 percent of capacity. The capacity gaps can then be related to future capacity requirements, as shown in Table 5-2.

In Table 5-2, predicted capacity requirements are shown for an enterprise through 1993. The presumption is that these predicted requirements are the expected values that take into account contingencies for the situation, and involve a growth rate of approximately 10 percent per year. Optimistic and pessimistic predictions of requirements could also be made.

TABLE 5-2   Predicted Requirements, Current Capacities, and Projected Capacity Differences

	Capacity, Units per Year			
	Current, 1983	1985	1988	1993
Predicted capacity requirements	10,000	12,000	15,000	20,000
Machine shop capacity	11,000	—	—	—
Capacity (gap) or slack	1,000	(1,000)	(4,000)	(9,000)
Assembly capacity	10,000	—	—	—
Capacity (gap) or slack	—	(2,000)	(5,000)	(10,000)
Receiving, shipping, and factory warehouse capacity	15,000	—	—	—
Capacity (gap) or slack	5,000	3,000	—	(5,000)

In Table 5-2 the projected gaps are shown in parentheses. Currently there is slack capacity in the machine shop and in the receiving, shipping, and warehouse areas. In 2 years, however, both the machine shop and assembly line will need additional capacity. These capacity gaps will grow as shown for 1988 and 1993. On the other hand, the receiving, shipping, and factory warehouse capacities will be adequate through 1988.

Identifying the size and timing of projected capacity gaps provides an input to the generation of alternate plans. We may plan to meet demand either by providing the expected required capacity or partially by utilizing alternate sources, or we may absorb some lost sales. We can provide the needed capacity in smaller increments as needed or in larger increments that may involve initial slack capacity. We may enlarge existing facilities, establish new producing locations for the additional capacity, or relocate the entire operation.

New Products and Risky Situations

It is difficult to predict capacity requirements for new products initially or in the rapid developmental phase of product life cycles. There are also situations involving mature, stable products, such as oil, where the capacity planning environment is risky owing to unstable political factors. The prediction of capacity requirements in these kinds of situations needs to place greater emphasis on the distribution of expected demand. Optimistic and pessimistic predictions can have a profound effect on capacity requirements.

For example, suppose that the product represented in Table 5-2 is in the rapid developmental stage of its life cycle. There may be considerable uncertainty about the future market because of economic factors and developing competition.

Table 5-3 includes optimistic and pessimistic capacity predictions that affect capacity requirements drastically. The optimistic requirement schedule assumes approximately a 20 percent per year compound growth rate in demand, and the pessimistic schedule only a 5 percent compound growth rate. A 20 percent growth rate might be justified given favorable economic conditions and a slight gain in market share in spite of competition. A 5 percent growth rate might be justified given the success of foreign competition and a smaller market share even though the market as a whole is assumed to expand.

Tables 5-4 and 5-5 show the widely differing capacity needs for the optimistic and pessimistic predictions. If we assume the optimistic schedule, we need large capacity

TABLE 5-3   **Expected, Optimistic, and Pessimistic Predictions of Requirements**

	Capacity, Units per Year			
	Current, 1983	1985	1988	1993
Expected capacity requirements[a]	10,000	12,000	15,000	20,000
Optimistic requirements	10,000	14,500	25,000	62,000
Pessimistic requirements	10,000	11,000	12,800	16,000

[a] From Table 5-2.

TABLE 5-4   **Predicted Requirements, Current Capacities, and Projected Capacity Differences for the Optimistic Prediction**

| | Capacity, Units per Year | | | |
	Current, 1983	1985	1988	1993
Predicted optimistic capacity requirements	10,000	14,500	25,000	62,000
Machine shop capacity	11,000	—	—	—
Capacity (gap) or slack	1,000	(3,500)	(14,000)	(51,000)
Assembly capacity	10,000	—	—	—
Capacity (gap) or slack	—	(4,500)	(15,000)	(52,000)
Receiving, shipping, and factory warehouse capacity	15,000	—	—	—
Capacity (gap) or slack	5,000	500	(10,000)	(47,000)

TABLE 5-5   **Predicted Requirements, Current Capacities, and Projected Capacity Differences for the Pessimistic Prediction**

| | Capacity, Units per Year | | | |
	Current, 1983	1985	1988	1993
Predicted pessimistic capacity requirements	10,000	11,000	12,800	16,000
Machine shop capacity	11,000	—	—	—
Capacity (gap) or slack	1,000	—	(1,800)	(5,000)
Assembly capacity	10,000	—	—	—
Capacity (gap) or slack	—	(1,000)	(2,800)	(6,000)
Receiving, shipping, and factory warehouse capacity	15,000	—	—	—
Capacity (gap) or slack	5,000	4,000	2,200	(1,000)

additions quickly and huge capacity additions within 10 years. If we fail to provide the capacity, we may miss the market, and lost sales could be an important opportunity cost. On the other hand, if we assume the pessimistic schedule, we need only modest amounts of capacity within 5 years that might be provided by multiple shifts and overtime. Even the 10-year capacity gaps seem relatively modest. How do we make capacity plans under such uncertain conditions?

The capacity planning problem may be set in either of the two demand prediction situations just discussed, or between them. In either the stable or uncertain demand situations, we need to consider the effect of contingencies. A formal methodology for considering these contingencies is the Delphi method. The dominant informal methodology is executive opinion of what will happen.

GENERATION OF ALTERNATE CAPACITY PLANS

When capacity gaps have been identified, alternate plans can be considered. These alternatives may involve the size and timing of added capacity, the use of overtime

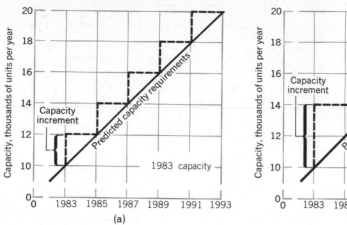
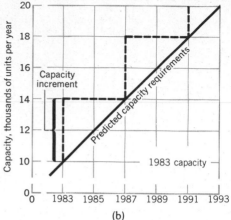

FIGURE 5-1
Capacity increments to meet requirements, (a) through 2000-unit increments each two years, and (b) through 4000-unit increments each four years.

and multiple shifts, outside capacity sources, absorption of lost sales, and the location of new capacity.

Large or Small Capacity Increments

When an enterprise enjoys stable demand growth, the issues are centered on how and when to provide the capacity, rather than *if* capacity should be added. Taking the data for expected capacity requirements from Table 5-2, there is a linear growth in capacity requirements of 1000 units per year. One issue is whether capacity should be added more often in smaller increments to keep up with demand (Figure 5-1a) or in a larger increments by a slower schedule (Figure 5-1b).

Both Figures 5-1a and 5-1b assume that demand will be met through production, so that there will be slack capacity immediately after an addition. The slack capacity declines as requirements increase and falls to zero when the next increment to capacity is installed, if timing is perfect. Whether smaller or larger increments of capacity will be more economical depends on the balance of incremental capital and operating costs for a particular organization and whether or not economies of scale exist. A unit of capacity added now may cost less than a unit added later, and yet the slack capacity must be carried as additional overhead until it is actually productive.

Alternate Sources of Capacity

Another issue in generating capacity plans is whether or not alternate capacity sources can be used near a capacity limit. Figure 5-1 assumes that demand is met through regular productive capacity. Figure 5-2 assumes that the timing of increments to capacity makes it necessary to use overtime, multiple shifts, and subcontracting where it is feasible. The cost effects of using alternate sources of capacity are to trade off some of the costs of carrying slack capacity against the costs of overtime and multiple shift premium, productivity losses resulting from pushing capacity be-

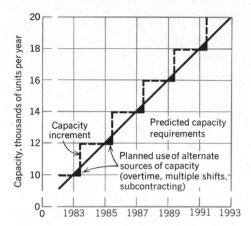

FIGURE 5-2
Capacity increments timed to use alternate sources of capacity to meet requirements.

yond normal limits, and the extra costs of subcontracting units of output. Again, whether or not the use of alternate sources of capacity will be more economical for a particular organization depends on the balance of incremental capital and operating costs.

Lost Sales

Another alternative to meeting demand through regular productive capacity, or alternate capacity sources, is to absorb some lost sales. This is a risky strategy, because it is possible that market share could be lost permanently. On the other hand, near capacity limits, contributions decline because of overtime and shift premium and productivity losses. Thus, absorbing lost sales could be more economical in some situations, yet managers hesitate to risk losing market share. They may be forced into absorbing lost sales at capacity limits, but would resist the idea of planning to absorb lost sales as a part of a capacity planning strategy.

The question of the location of new capacity is strategically important, involving an assessment of market location, system distribution costs, and other factors. We shall defer discussion of location until the next chapter.

Cost Behavior in Relation to Volume

Figure 5-3 shows a general picture of what happens to costs as volume increases. We are particularly interested in cost behavior at capacity limits of first and second shifts, because these are the conditions that prevail when capacity is added. Near capacity limits, variable costs increase as a result of increased use of overtime and subcontracting and because of congestion when facilities are maximally utilized.

On the other hand, when new capacity is first installed, it is not fully utilized unless the expansion is long overdue. Therefore, variable costs for the new capacity are likely to be relatively high, reflecting poor utilization of labor and other resources. But the new capacity relieves the stress on existing facilities, making it possible to eliminate overtime and/or multiple shifts.

133

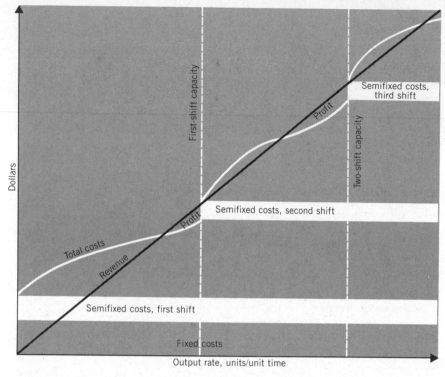

FIGURE 5-3
General structure of costs over a wide range of volume.
SOURCE: *E. S. Buffa, and W. H. Taubert, "Evaluation of Direct Computer Search Methods for the Aggregate Planning Problem,"* Industrial Management Review, *Fall 1967.*

The combination of new and existing capacity then reflects a variable cost structure that will improve as the new capacity becomes loaded. The fixed costs of existing capacity are spread over a larger and larger number of units as the volume is driven through capacity limits to second and even third shift levels. Thus, the fixed cost per unit declines as existing facilities become more fully utilized. New capacity that is relatively poorly utilized will have high fixed costs per unit.

Economies of Scale

The nature of cost structures just discussed suggests that for a given facility there should be an optimum output that minimizes fixed plus variable costs. Figure 5-4 shows unit variable and fixed cost data for a simulated manufacturing enterprise that was driven through an operating range which included the use of a second shift. Variable costs per unit were computed and are plotted as data points. Unit costs vary, depending on the amount of overtime used for the direct and indirect work force and the costs incurred by management decisions to expand or contract the work force. In general, overtime was used increasingly as production exceeded 450 units per month, and a second shift was required above 550 units per month. The fixed cost per unit curve in Figure 5-4 is simply the $30,000 fixed cost divided by the

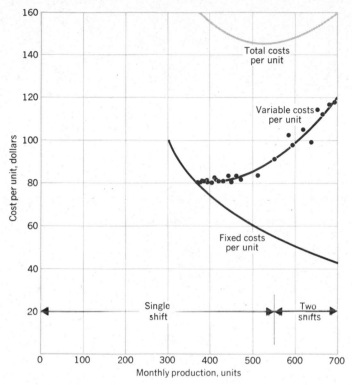

FIGURE 5-4
Unit variable, fixed, and total costs for a plant in relation to volume. Normal capacity without overtime is 450 units per month, and *minimum unit cost* capacity is 525 units per month.

number of units produced. The total unit cost curve is the sum of the variable plus fixed costs and exhibits an optimum unit cost at about 525 units per month. In this case the second shift may be economical, depending on demand, expansion possibilities, and so on.

We can characterize the plant represented by the costs of Figure 5-4 as a 525 units per month plant; that is its minimum unit cost capacity, given the first and second shift capacities. Another way to characterize that plant is in terms of its normal (no overtime) capacity of 450 units per month. Because optimal plant operating points are usually not known, it is common to state normal capacities. In these terms, the minimum unit cost capacity for the plant of Figure 5-4 is (525/450) × 100 = 117 percent of normal.

Usually there are economies of scale that may come from two basic sources: lower fixed cost per unit and/or lower variable costs per unit. The lower fixed costs accrue because plant and equipment costs of larger plants are less than proportional to capacity. Larger plants are likely to have better balance of subunits with less slack capacity in subunits. Lower variable costs may also accrue to the larger plant because larger volume may justify more mechanization and automation. The result is that minimum unit costs could be substantially less for larger plants, as shown in Figure 5-5.

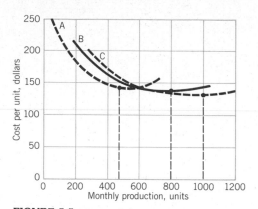

FIGURE 5-5
Economies of scale illustrated by three successively larger plants. *Minimum unit cost* plant sizes are $A = 525$ units per month, $B = 800$ units per month, and $C = 1000$ units per month.

ECONOMIC EVALUATION OF CAPACITY PLANS

Capacity plan alternatives may involve various size units that may differ in their productivity, reflecting economies of scale. As shown in Figures 5-1 and 5-2, the timing of investments in new capacity can be quite different for alternate plans. Timing of investments depends on the choice of the size of capacity increments and on the use of alternate sources of capacity. If plans involve lost sales, then lost contribution becomes a future opportunity cost. Because all of these costs are future costs, and the time spans may be long, a discounted cash flow analysis is appropriate for comparing alternatives. In the following two examples we shall compute net present values as a criterion.

Mature Products with Stable Demand Growth

An Example. As an example, assume the situation described by Figures 5-1 and 5-2. In order to simplify the analysis, we shall consider only the first four years. We shall compute for four basic alternatives:

1. Capacity added January 1, 1983 and 1985 in increments of 2000 units.
2. Capacity of 4000 units added January 1, 1983.
3. Capacity added as of July 1, 1983 and 1985 in increments of 2000 units, depending on overtime and multiple shifts to meet requirements during the first 6 months of 1983 and 1985.
4. Capacity of 4000 units added January 1, 1984, depending on overtime and multiple shifts to meet requirements during 1983.

Costs. There are economies of scale in the larger plant of 4000 units that are reflected both in the original investment and in the operating costs. Also, units produced using overtime and multiple shifts cost an additional $1.00 per unit. The investment and operating costs are summarized in Table 5-6. In the analysis we shall assume that the cost of capital for the enterprise is 15 percent. Operating costs for

TABLE 5-6   **Original Investment Requirements and Operating Costs**

Plant Size, Units per Year	Original Investment	Operating Costs per Unit	Operating Costs per Unit When Using Alternate Sources of Capacity
2000	$1,000,000	$10	$11
4000	1,800,000	9	10

the existing capacity are $10 per unit, but increase to $11 per unit when using alternate sources of capacity.

Alternative 1. Figure 5-6 summarizes the structure of cash flows that must be considered in determining the net present value for Alternative 1. The first investment of $1 million is already at present value. The second investment must be discounted to present value by the present value factor of a single payment 2 years hence at 15 percent, $PV_{sp} = 0.756$. The present value factors are available from Table G-1 in Appendix G or may be computed from $PV_{sp} = 1/(1 + i)^n$, where $i =$ annual interest rate in decimals, and $n =$ number of years. For this example, $1/(1 + 0.15)^2 = 0.756$.

The incremental operating costs are related to the actual product produced using the new capacity. When the new capacity comes "on-stream" at the beginning of 1983, it will be entirely slack capacity. Requirements increase linearly as in Figure 5-1a, and during the first year 500 units will be produced by the new capacity. During the second year 1500 units will be produced, and at the end of the second year the first expansion will be fully utilized.

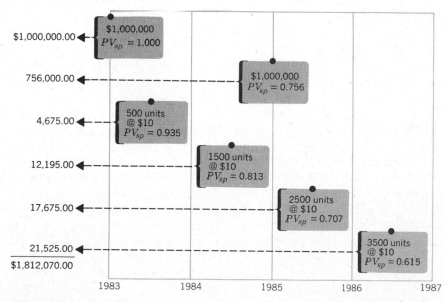

FIGURE 5-6
Present values for Alternative 1.

137

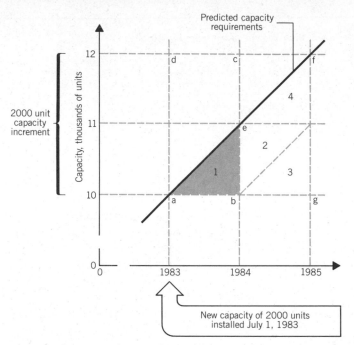

FIGURE 5-7
Geometric representation of units produced in 1983 and 1984 for Alternative 1.

The fact that only 500 units will be produced on the new capacity during the first year, and 1500 units during 1984, may be seen by the geometry of Figure 5-7. The production *rate* is increasing linearly to match the requirements, and at the end of the first year the production rate has increased to 11,000 units. Only one quarter of the 2000 unit capacity of the new facility is used during the first year. The full capacity is represented by the area of the rectangle *abcd*. The number of units produced in 1983, however, is represented by the right triangle 1, defined by *abe*, which is one quarter of the area of the rectangle. To verify that 1500 units are produced on the new facility in 1984, note that the trapizoidal area *befg* may be divided into three right triangles, 2, 3, and 4, that are congruent to triangle 1; that is, they are each identical to triangle 1, and represent a total area equivalent to 1500 units.

In 1985, the second 2000 units of capacity will be added to the first expansion, and the pattern repeats. The 500 units produced by the second expansion are added to the 2000 units produced by the first expansion. Then, during 1985 the units produced by new capacity are 2000 on expansion number 1 plus 500 units on expansion number 2. In 1986, 2000 units will be produced by the first expansion plus 1500 units by the second expansion. At the end of 1986 the second expansion will be fully utilized.

In reducing the operating costs to present values we assume that the costs for the 500 units produced by the new plant during 1983 are centered in the middle of the year. Centering these values is a simplification to reduce calculations for this example. The value, $PV_{sp} = 0.935$ was obtained from Table G-1 by linear interpolation. The interpolated values vary slightly from the formula which yields $PV_{sp} = 0.933$. The present value for the production costs in 1983 is, then, $500 \times 10 \times 0.935 =$

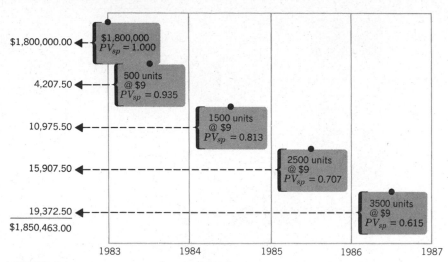

FIGURE 5-8
Present values for Alternative 2.

$4675.00. Similarly, the production costs from added capacity of succeeding years are assumed to be centered during the year. The present value factors used are the interpolated values.

Figure 5-6 shows the total present value of the investment and operating costs for two cycles of capacity additions to be $1,812,070. This value will be compared with the values derived by similar methods for the other three alternatives.

Alternative 2. Figure 5-8 summarizes the cash flows for Alternative 2. The only investment required is in 1983. The production costs from the new capacity are less than those for Alternative 1 because of the economy of scale effect. The economies of scale in capital and operating costs are not sufficient to counterbalance the advantage of Alternative 1, which delays part of the investment in capacity until 1985. Still, Alternative 2 has a strategic advantage of greater slack capacity during the 4-year period.

Alternative 3. Alternative 3 is similar to 1 except that each investment in capacity can be delayed 6 months by depending on overtime and multiple shifts to meet requirements during that time interval. Recall that using alternate capacity sources results in an incremental cost of $1.00 per unit. See Figure 5-9 for the structure of present values.

The production cost must now reflect the timing and extra cost of the output produced by alternate sources. In 1983, 125 units are produced on the existing capacity during the first 6 months at $11 per unit (note that the new capacity is not yet available). In this case, the costs are the same as for the new capacity. We have centered these costs at the end of the third month in 1983, and the present value factor of $PV_{sp} = 0.968$ is interpolated from Table G-1. Production costs for the balance of 1983 are centered at the end of the ninth month. Production costs in 1985 are handled in a similar manner. The total present value figure for Alternative 3 shows a net advantage from delaying the investments and obtaining fuller utilization of the new capacity.

Figure 5-10 shows a geometric representation of the number of units produced on

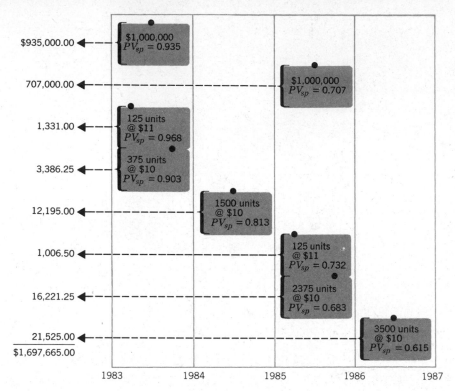

FIGURE 5-9
Present values for Alternative 3.

alternate capacity sources, and after the installation of the new capacity of 2000 units on July 1, 1983. Triangle 1 has an area that is one-fourth the area of the large triangle *abc*. The area of the large triangle represents the 500 units that must be produced in 1983 to meet increasing requirements through alternate capacity sources plus new capacity. Therefore, the area of triangle 1 representing production on alternate capacity sources represents 500/4 = 125 units. The sum of the areas of triangles 2, 3, and 4 represents the production on the new capacity installed July 1, or 3 × 125 = 375 units.

Alternative 4. This alternative is similar to Alternative 2, but uses the investment delay concept of Alternative 3. The large plant is installed in 1984, and the 500-unit capacity requirement in 1983 is met through overtime and multiple shifts. (See Figure 5-11.)

The present values for the four alternatives are:

1. $1,812,070   3. $1,697,665
2. $1,850,463   4. $1,616,931

The cost structures in this example favor the use of alternate capacity sources in order to delay capital investments for either the small or large plants. Delaying the investment has the advantage of obtaining better utilization of the new capacity when it is installed. Alternative 4, involving the larger plant with economies of scale, has the

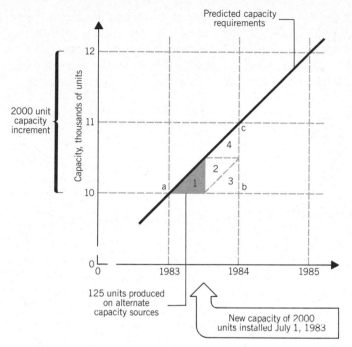

FIGURE 5-10
Geometric representation of units produced in 1983 for Alternative 3. The area of triangle 1 represents the 125 units produced on alternate capacity sources. The sum of the areas of triangles 2, 3, and 4 represents the 375 units produced on the 2000 unit capacity increment installed July 1, 1983.

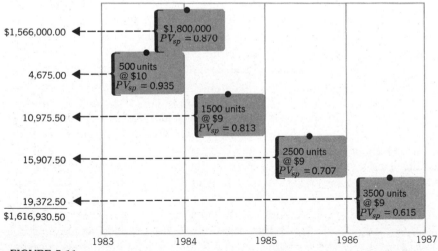

FIGURE 5-11
Present values for Alternative 4.

minimum present value cost. Alternative 4 also has the strategic advantage over Alternative 3 of providing greater slack capacity during the 4 years. This slack capacity could be put to use at no incremental investment cost if demand should be greater than expected.

Note that without the use of alternate capacity sources in Alternatives 1 and 2, the economy of scale effect in Alternative 2 is not great enough to counterbalance the large initial investment. Another way of looking at the cost difference between Alternatives 1 and 2 is that Alternative 2 results in poor utilization of the larger plant. The poor utilization results in relatively large capital costs per unit which counterbalance the economy of scale advantage.

Variations. The basic methodology illustrated by the example can be applied to a host of variations in capacity expansion strategy by expanding the alternatives list. For example, added alternatives could involve different locations coupled with expansion, answering the question of whether or not relocation is justified at this time. Erlenkotter's [1973] dynamic programming models of expansion consider expansion and location as joint decisions. Vertical integration proposals can be included as alternatives, if equivalent raw materials and other affected costs are accounted for in all alternatives. Other possibilities include the capacity effects of new products or process innovations.

Inflation in both investment requirements and operating costs can be taken into account by the present value methodology without difficulty. Also, assumptions regarding the centering of operating expenses made in the example can be relaxed by constructing a more detailed model.

New Products and Risky Situations

When the color TV market began to develop rapidly, the need for new capacity was apparent, but how fast would the market develop? Could existing facilities for black and white TV be converted? Would market shares remain stable? Would color TV repeat the growth pattern of black and white? Similar uncertainties occurred in other new products such as pocket calculators and microwave ovens.

Market uncertainties might also occur in mature products that have enjoyed stable growth, because of impending technological innovations or political uncertainties. Imagine the market uncertainties in the mechanical calculator field when solid state electronics became practical. The design of an electronic desk calculator became an obvious objective. What would an electronic desk calculator cost? Would the mechanical calculator become completely obsolete or would the electronic model be expensive, leaving a market for mechanicals? Suppose a shipping company regularly did a substantial business from the U.S. West Coast to the East Coast and Europe. What effect would the closing of the Panama Canal have on operations and capacity needs?

If demands are uncertain, lead times can be important. It may take considerable time for planning, for obtaining government permits that currently involve environmental impact studies, and for construction. The length of these lead times becomes of even greater importance when planning for products with uncertain demand. Events can occur within the lead times that change the logical alternatives.

Capacity planning in these situations requires an assessment of the risks. The effect of the probability that risky events will occur needs to be accounted for. If the market is uncertain, a probabilistic prediction of the market provides basic data.

An Example. Suppose that we are planning future capacity for a product which is in the rapid developmental phase. Present annual capacity is 20,000 units. New competition is becoming very aggressive, but the enterprise expects to retain its market share. The sales department feels that market share could be increased with aggressive promotion. Estimates of the total market vary, some feeling that growth might be explosive in the next 4 to 5 years. On the other hand, there is the additional uncertainty concerning continuing technological innovation that could stunt the growth of the current line. Thus, expected, optimistic, and pessimistic market predictions are made and assigned probabilities that each might occur. The predictions are converted to capacity requirements per year as follows:

	1983, Current	1984	1985	1986	1987
Optimistic ($p = 0.25$)	17,000	24,000	34,000	48,000	66,000
Expected ($p = 0.50$)	17,000	20,000	24,000	29,000	35,000
Pessimistic ($p = 0.25$)	17,000	19,000	21,000	23,000	25,000

The optimistic requirements are based on the assumption of a 40 percent annual growth; the expected, a 20 percent annual growth; and the pessimistic, only a 10 percent annual growth (capacities rounded).

Strategies. Three alternate strategies are developed, each designed with the three market assumptions in mind. The variable costs of production are the same as for the present capacity because no new process technology is involved. The three alternatives are:

1. Install new capacity in 1985, 1986, and 1987 in increments of 15,000 units.
2. Install new capacity in 1985, 1986, and 1987 in increments of 5000 units.
3. No capacity additions.

The 15,000-unit capacity additions require an investment of $800,000 each, and the 5000-unit additions require an investment of $300,000 each, reflecting an investment economy for the larger units. *The operating costs per unit are the same for both sizes of capacity additions.* Given each of the three strategies, the outcomes will depend on which requirements schedules actually occur. When requirements exceed capacity, sales are lost, so the cost of lost contribution of $50 per unit must be taken into account in evaluating the alternatives.

For each of the three strategies, any of the three market assumptions could occur with the stated probabilities. Figure 5-12 is a decision tree representing the strategies and events. In order to evaluate the three alternate strategies, we must compute the present value of each of the nine possible outcomes.

Present Values of Outcomes. The present values for each of the three outcomes given each of the three basic strategies are shown in Tables 5-7, 5-8, and 5-9. The calculations for Alternative 1 in Table 5-7 are typical. In Alternative 1a of Table 5-7, the optimistic requirements in relation to the proposed capacity with additions provide the basis for computing lost sales. Because there are no operating cost economies of scale between the large- and small-capacity additions, the operating cost differences between alternatives are measured by the lost sales.

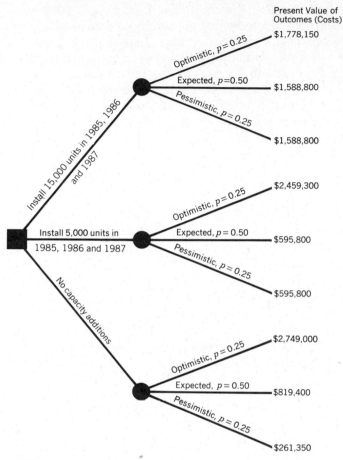

Present Value of Outcomes (Costs)

Optimistic, $p = 0.25$ — $1,778,150

Expected, $p = 0.50$ — $1,588,800

Pessimistic, $p = 0.25$ — $1,588,800

Install 15,000 units in 1985, 1986 and 1987

Install 5,000 units in 1985, 1986 and 1987

Optimistic, $p = 0.25$ — $2,459,300

Expected, $p = 0.50$ — $595,800

Pessimistic, $p = 0.25$ — $595,800

No capacity additions

Optimistic, $p = 0.25$ — $2,749,000

Expected, $p = 0.50$ — $819,400

Pessimistic, $p = 0.25$ — $261,350

FIGURE 5-12
Decision tree for the risky market example.

The present value calculations reduce all future net cash flows in the 4-year planning horizon to the planning base period of 1983, at the interest rate of 15 percent. The capacity additions occur 2, 3, and 4 years hence, and each is reduced to present value. The lost sales are assumed to be centered within the year that they occur, and the present value factors are interpolated from Table G-1. The present value of the investments and lost sales costs of $1,778,150 for Alternative 1 is the outcome for that alternative shown in the decision tree of Figure 5-12. All the cost outcomes shown in Figure 5-12 are computed similarly in Tables 5-7, 5-8, and 5-9.

Expected Values of Alternate Strategies. In order to evaluate the three strategies, we compute their expected values by "rolling back" the decision tree. We multiply the present value of the cost outcome by the probability of its occurrence and add the three probability weighted values to obtain the expected value for the strategy. This is done for all three strategies in Table 5-10.

Alternative 2, involving the installation of the three 5000-unit-capacity additions, produces the lowest expected present value costs. Note that Alternative 2 incurs lost

TABLE 5-7   **Alternative 1: New Capacity in 1985, 1986, and 1987 in Increments of 15,000 Units at a Cost of $800,000 Each (interest rate = 15%)**

		1983, Current	1984	1985	1986	1987
1a.	Optimistic Requirements	—	24,000	34,000	48,000	66,000
	Proposed additions to capacity	—	—	15,000	15,000	15,000
	Proposed capacity	20,000	20,000	35,000	50,000	65,000
	Lost sales	—	4,000	0	0	1,000
	Present values:					
	New capacity, 1985, 800,000 × 0.756 =			$604,800		
	New capacity, 1986, 800,000 × 0.658 =			526,400		
	New capacity, 1987, 800,000 × 0.572 =			457,600		
	Lost sales, 1984, 4,000 × 50 × 0.813 =			162,600		
	Lost sales, 1987, 1,000 × 50 × 0.535 =			26,750		
	Total			$1,778,150		
1b.	Expected requirements	—	20,000	24,000	29,000	35,000
	Proposed additions to capacity	—	—	15,000	15,000	15,000
	Proposed capacity	20,000	20,000	35,000	50,000	65,000
	Lost sales	—	0	0	0	0
	Present values:					
	New capacity, 1985, 800,000 × 0.756 =			$604,800		
	New capacity, 1986, 800,000 × 0.658 =			526,400		
	New capacity, 1987, 800,000 × 0.572 =			457,600		
	Total			$1,588,800		
1c.	Pessimistic requirements	—	19,000	21,000	23,000	25,000
	Proposed additions to capacity	—	—	15,000	15,000	15,000
	Proposed capacity	20,000	20,000	35,000	50,000	65,000
	Lost sales	—	0	0	0	0
	Present values:					
	Same as for 1b.			$1,588,800		

sales only if the optimistic prediction actually materializes, but it requires much smaller capital investment than Alternative 1. Alternative 3 requires no capital investments, but incurs large costs of lost sales even for the pessimistic requirements prediction. On balance, Alternative 2 is the most economical capacity plan, given the probabilities of obtaining each of the requirement's predictions.

Recall, however, that it is not the expected value of costs which will actually materialize. The actual costs will depend on the actual capacity requirements. If, in fact, the optimistic prediction materializes, the present value of costs under Alternative 2 would be $2,459,300, which is $681,150 greater than if the 15,000 unit additions had been installed. How would managers respond to the situation if by mid-1984 (with the first 5000-unit-capacity addition under construction) it appeared that the optimistic prediction was valid? Of course, they would adjust plans, presumably through a new set of predictions and alternatives. There would be no logic in following through with the original decision by installing the two remaining small-capacity additions (see Magee [1964]).

The example is relatively simple in the alternatives selected and in the cost structure represented. With large future costs being involved, managers would probably consider more alternatives and perhaps more than three probabilistic predictions. Also, a more complex cost structure might represent the situation more accurately. But these are straightforward extensions of the same methodology.

TABLE 5-8   **Alternative 2: New Capacity in 1985, 1986, and 1987 in Increments of 5000 Units at a Cost of $300,000 Each (interest rate = 15%)**

	1983, Current	1984	1985	1986	1987
2a. Optimistic requirements	—	24,000	34,000	48,000	66,000
Proposed additions to capacity	—	—	5,000	5,000	5,000
Proposed capacity	20,000	20,000	25,000	30,000	35,000
Lost sales	—	4,000	9,000	18,000	31,000

Present values:

New capacity, 1985,	$300,000 \times 0.756 =$	$226,800
New capacity, 1986,	$300,000 \times 0.658 =$	197,400
New capacity, 1987,	$300,000 \times 0.572 =$	171,600
Lost sales, 1984,	$4,000 \times 50 \times 0.813 =$	162,600
Lost sales, 1985,	$9,000 \times 50 \times 0.707 =$	318,150
Lost sales, 1986,	$18,000 \times 50 \times 0.615 =$	553,500
Lost sales, 1987,	$31,000 \times 50 \times 0.535 =$	829,250
Total		$2,459,300

	1983, Current	1984	1985	1986	1987
2b. Expected requirements	—	20,000	24,000	29,000	35,000
Proposed additions to capacity	—	—	5,000	5,000	5,000
Proposed capacity	20,000	20,000	25,000	30,000	35,000
Lost sales	—	0	0	0	0

Present values:

New capacity, 1985,	$300,000 \times 0.756 =$	$226,800
New capacity, 1986,	$300,000 \times 0.658 =$	197,400
New capacity, 1987,	$300,000 \times 0.572 =$	171,600
Total		$595,800

	1983, Current	1984	1985	1986	1987
2c. Pessimistic requirements	—	19,000	21,000	23,000	25,000
Proposed additions to capacity	—	—	5,000	5,000	5,000
Proposed capacity	20,000	20,000	25,000	30,000	35,000
Lost sales	—	0	0	0	0

Present values:

Same as for 2b.	$595,800

RISKS AND STRATEGIC EFFECTS

Many important effects of alternate capacity plans can be represented in an expanded decision tree. For example, if a technological breakthrough can be assigned a probability of perhaps $p = 0.30$, then a branch in the tree can be structured for "no breakthrough" ($p = 0.70$) and "breakthrough" ($p = 0.30$). Other risks can be handled similarly in the formal decision-tree analysis.

Many strategic effects, however, must be evaluated through managerial trade-off. If the most economical plan involves lost sales and possibly a decline in market share, the manager must weigh the lower expected cost against the loss of market share. Specific capacity plans might have an impact on competition, flexibility of operations, market locations, labor policies, market share, and so on.

IMPLICATIONS FOR THE MANAGER

Capacity planning involves top managers in decisions that have important strategic implications. These decisions often have an impact on and are affected by other

TABLE 5-9   **Alternative 3: No Capacity Additions (interest rate = 15%)**

		1983, Current	1984	1985	1986	1987
3a.	Optimistic requirements	—	24,000	34,000	48,000	66,000
	Proposed capacity	20,000	20,000	20,000	20,000	20,000
	Lost sales	—	4,000	14,000	28,000	46,000
	Present values:					
	Lost sales, 1984,	$4,000 \times 50 \times 0.813 =$		$162,600		
	Lost sales, 1985,	$14,000 \times 50 \times 0.707 =$		494,900		
	Lost sales, 1986,	$28,000 \times 50 \times 0.615 =$		861,000		
	Lost sales, 1987,	$46,000 \times 50 \times 0.535 =$		1,230,500		
	Total			$2,749,000		
3b.	Expected requirements	—	20,000	24,000	29,000	35,000
	Proposed capacity	20,000	20,000	20,000	20,000	20,000
	Lost sales	—	0	4,000	9,000	15,000
	Present values:					
	Lost sales, 1985,	$4,000 \times 50 \times 0.707 =$		$141,400		
	Lost sales, 1986,	$9,000 \times 50 \times 0.615 =$		276,750		
	Lost sales, 1987,	$15,000 \times 50 \times 0.535 =$		401,250		
	Total			$819,400		
3c.	Pessimistic requirements	—	19,000	21,000	23,000	25,000
	Proposed capacity	20,000	20,000	20,000	20,000	20,000
	Lost sales	—	0	1,000	3,000	5,000
	Present values:					
	Lost sales, 1985,	$1,000 \times 50 \times 0.707 =$		$35,350		
	Lost sales, 1986,	$3,000 \times 50 \times 0.615 =$		92,250		
	Lost sales, 1987,	$5,000 \times 50 \times 0.535 =$		133,750		
	Total			$261,350		

TABLE 5-10 **Expected Values of Three Alternate Strategies**

Alternative 1: $0.25 \times 1,778,150 + 0.50 \times 1,588,800 + 0.25 \times 1,588,800 = \$1,636,137$
Alternative 2: $0.25 \times 2,459,300 + 0.50 \times 595,800 \ \ + 0.25 \times 595,800 \ \ = \$1,061,675$
Alternative 3: $0.25 \times 2,749,000 + 0.50 \times 819,400 \ \ + 0.25 \times 261,350 \ \ = \$1,162,288$

enterprise functions in addition to operations. They interface with the marketing function in terms of product strategies and market predictions. They interface with engineering and technology in terms of both product and process innovations. Capacity decisions may commit resources that commonly represent the major assets of a firm, requiring financing by debt or equity instruments. Finally, capacity decisions may also set directions for the philosophy governing the productive system design. Will the design emphasize cost and availability, suggesting a product-focused system, or flexibility and quality, suggesting a process-focused system?

Predicting long-range market trends is difficult because events that may cause major demand shifts are unpredictable. Nevertheless, there are many commodities and mature products whose demand seems caused by basic trends in population, industrialization, urbanization, and so forth. Causal forecasting models have been shown to be useful for these types of products. Even in these stable product situations, however, economic and political events can have an impact on capacity needs to an extent not foreseen by historical data-based models. Executive opinion, possibly formalized through the Delphi method, may be the basis for these long-range predictions. New product predictions are most often based on these latter methods, often in combination with market surveys and reference to product life-cycle analyses.

Given market predictions, the capacity planning options available to managers involve frequent smaller capacity additions versus less frequent larger units and the use of other sources of capacity, either marginally or as a part of an ongoing capacity philosophy. There is no single right answer to these options. Rather, the answer is in the appropriate analysis that provides logical alternatives and evaluation methods. Each situation has its unique growth and cost structure characteristics. In general, deterministic methods are adequate in mature product situations, but probabilistic methods are needed when market predictions are risky.

Although formal economic evaluation is extremely important because of the capital commitments, the results must be regarded as one important input to the decision process. Strategic factors must be weighed and may be the basis for a final choice. With the economic analysis of alternatives available, and an identification of the strategic effects of each alternative, managers can make trade-offs. In effect, the trade-off process allows a pricing of strategic effects.

IMPORTANT TERMS

Numbers in parentheses indicate page numbers

Alternate capacity source (132)	Lost sales (133)
Capacity gap (129)	Mature product (129, 136)
Capacity limit (134)	Strategic effects (146)
Economies of scale (134)	

REVIEW QUESTIONS AND PROBLEMS

1. Review the six-step process for capacity planning. Now think in terms of proposals that you know about or have heard about for expanding electric utility capacity through nuclear power plants.

   Do you think all of the steps were followed? Which steps involved the most time? Identify the risks and strategic effects to the company.

2. What are the appropriate methods for predicting future requirements for:

   a. Electric power

   b. Oil tankers

   c. Hula-hoops

3. Why might there be imbalances in the existing capacities of departments in a hospital such as x-ray, laboratory, intensive care, and the like?

4. A fertilizer company is reviewing its future capacity needs. The company has concluded that its share of the market demand will expand at the rate of 20 percent per year for the next 5 years. Production is highly capital intensive, and transportation costs for distribution are also important.

   What kinds of alternatives do you think should be considered?

5. Using the cost-volume relationship shown in Figure 5-3 as a background:

   a. Under what conditions would you expect minimum unit cost plant size (output) to include a second shift?

   b. What are the factors that might result in a larger plant being more cost effective than a smaller one?

6. Define the following terms: regular capacity, optimal capacity, and maximum capacity.

7. Home computers are now coming on the market. They are quite powerful, involving keyboard input, video output, and very substantial memory capacities, and are designed to use rather capable languages such as BASIC. Prices range from $600 to $1500 and are declining.

   If you were tooling up to produce such a product, how would you go about assessing the market for the next 5 years? What kinds of capacity strategies would you generate? What decision methodology would you use?

8. Referring to question 7, what strategic factors should be weighed and traded off against objective cost-profit results in your strategies?

*9. New alternatives are made available for the example of economic analysis of a mature product given in the text. The present value calculations for the text example are given in Figures 5-6, 8, 9, and 11.

   A radically new process technology, that has generated tremendous enthusiasm has been developed by the company engineers. The process has been automated so that capital and material costs dominate; labor costs have been almost eliminated. Therefore, operating costs have been drastically reduced. The result is that two new alternatives have been added to the four given in the text. The two new alternatives involve the possibility of expansion including the automated processes and costs as follows:

   a. Capacity added January 1, 1983 and 1985 in increments of 2000 units.

   b. Capacity of 4000 units added January 1, 1983.

   These plants would be designed for 24-hour operation because of their capital intensive nature. Therefore, other plans involving alternate sources of capacity are not feasible.

   There is an economy of scale in the investment cost of the larger plant. The operating costs of the two plant sizes are the same, however, by the nature of the new process. The investment and operating costs are shown in Table 5-11.

   Compute present values for the two alternatives and compare the results

* This problem requires the application of present value concepts in Appendix A, "Capital Costs and Investment Criteria."

TABLE 5-11

Investment and Operating Costs for Problem 9

Plant Size, Units per Year	Original Investment	Operating Costs per Unit
2000	$1,300,000	$1
4000	2,000,000	1

with the four alternatives computed in the text. What decisions should be made? Why?

*10. This problem is an extension of the text example for the economic evaluation of a product in its rapid development phase. The decision-tree structure is given in Figure 5-12.

A technological breakthrough in an automated production process is now available that can be incorporated with new capital additions. The result would be a dramatic cost decrease of $30 per unit. On the other hand, it is estimated that plant investment costs would increase to $900,000 each for the 15,000-unit plant, and $375,000 each for the 5000-unit plant.

The optimistic, expected, and pessimistic requirements schedules, as well as the probability estimates, remain the same as in the text example. The internal rate of return is 15 percent.

a. What are the present values of each of the nine possible outcomes?

b. What are the expected values of the three alternatives?

c. Which alternative would you choose? Why?

SITUATIONS

11. SITCOM is a producer of electronic home appliances including VHS (Video Home System) television recorders located in northern California. The packaged product weighs about 75 pounds. SITCOM was not the innovator of the system. Rather, they sat back and let RCA and others develop the market and are currently producing under license agreements. SITCOM has a conscious strategy of being a follower with new product innovations. They do not have the financial resources to be a leader in research and development.

SITCOM's strategy is to establish themselves in the market as it develops with a quality product, waiting for the surge in sales in the product life cycle associated with the rapid developmental phase. They intend to be ready with the capacity to capitalize on the market surge. SITCOM has proved their competence in marketing and in assembly type production. The production strategy places great emphasis on parts procurement, quality control of vendors, and on materials management in general. This strategy results in the comparatively low capacity costs associated with an assembly operation.

SITCOM's present opportunity is indicated by the fact that industry sales of VHS recorders has increased 30 percent per year for the past 2 years, and

---

* This problem requires the application of present value concepts in Appendix A, "Capital Costs and Investment Criteria."

TABLE 5-12   **Forecasted Requirements and Capacity Needs for SITCOM**

	Year					
	Current Year					
	0	1	2	3	4	5
Forecast, 1000 units	100	140	195	270	350	450
Capacity (Gap), or Slack, 1000 units	5	(35)	(90)	(165)	(245)	(345)

forecasts for the next year and 2 years hence are even more enticing. SITCOM has established a 10 percent market share position and feels that they can at least maintain this position if they have the needed capacity, and possibly improve their market share if competitors fail to provide capacity at the time it is needed.

The forecasts and capacity gaps are indicated in Table 5-12. SITCOM regards the first-year forecast as being quite solid based on their present market share and a compilation of several industry forecasts from different sources. They are less sure about forecasts in future years, but they are basing these forecasts on patterns for both black and white and color TV sales during their product life cycles.

SITCOM's VHS model has a factory price of $600. Variable costs are 70 percent of the price. Inventory carrying costs are 20 percent of inventory value, 15 percent of which represents the cost of capital. SITCOM's facility planners estimate that a 40,000 unit plant can be built for $5 million and a 100,000 unit plant for $10 million. Land and labor are available in the area, and either size plant can be built within a year.

1. What capacity plans do you think SITCOM should make for next year? Why?

2. What longer-term capacity plans should SITCOM make? Why?

3. What are the implications of these plans for marketing, distribution, and production?

*12. CHEMCO is a chemical manufacturing company that has been successful in research and development. It has built its reputation by exploiting its excellent research staff's ability to develop new and useful products. The firm has been able to capitalize on being an innovator, reaping the high profits that result from being first with a product and facing little initial competition. The company has promoted new products strongly, obtaining an identification with them that has carried over into longer-term market dominance in many cases. A recent new product PRIMEBEEF seemed to have remarkable effects as a cattle feed additive. It resulted in a higher proportion of high-grade beef.

Having been involved in many new product introductions, CHEMCO has learned to deal with the market uncertainties of new products. Therefore, when initial market tests for PRIMEBEEF were successful, capacity planning became

* This situation requires the application of present value concepts in Appendix A, "Capital Costs and Investment Criteria."

an issue. CHEMCO developed flexible capacity plans that took account of contingencies. The potential market was large, but not certain. It was known that competitors were already attempting imitations. Therefore, part of the strategy was to expand output as soon as possible to establish their market position. The capacity planning issues were centered in plant size and expandability of a small plant, should that be the decision. After making market estimates, CHEMCO decided on a 10-year planning horizon.

Market Scenarios

Marketing predictions could be framed in several scenarios that were structured as follows with probability estimates:

a. Demand would be high initially, product identification successful, and demand would remain high. Probability = 0.60.

b. Demand would be high in the initial 2 years, but competition would be so keen that demand would be low thereafter (third through tenth years). Probability = 0.10.

c. Demand would be initially low and remain low. The product would never be very successful. Probability = 0.30.

From the above three scenarios, they noted that the probability of an initial (first 2 years) high demand was $p = 0.70$, which formed the basis for a capacity strategy that would start with a small plant that could be expanded after 2 years if in fact demand was high during the initial period.

Alternatives

Two basic capacity strategies were based on the market predictions: Alternative 1—build a large plant, cost, $3 million; Alternative 2—build a small but expandable plant initially, cost $1,300,000. If initial demand is high, decide within 2 years whether or not to expand it at a cost of $2,200,000. This decision involved risks also, because even if initial demand were high ($p = 0.70$), the probability was only $p = 0.60$ that it would be high thereafter. Therefore, the conditional probability that demand would be high following a decision to expand was $p = 0.60/0.70 = 0.86$.

Revenue Patterns. Estimates of annual income were made under the assumptions of each alternate demand pattern as follows:

1. A large plant with high volume would yield $1 million annually in cash flow.

2. A large plant with low volume would yield only $100,000 annually because of high fixed costs and inefficiencies.

3. A small plant with low demand would be economical and would yield annual cash income of $300,000.

4. A small plant, during an initial period of high demand, would yield $450,000 per year, but this yield would drop to $400,000 yearly in the long run because of competition. (The market would be larger than under number 3, but would be divided up among competitors.)

5. If the small plant were expanded to meet sustained high demand, it would yield

$700,000 cash flow annually and would be less efficient than a large plant built initially.

6. If the small plant were expanded but high demand was not sustained, estimated annual cash flow would be $50,000.

Analysis and Decision. CHEMCO decided that the capacity planning program was definitely risky and that a careful analysis should be made before attempting a decision. The president of the company stated that he wished to preserve CHEMCO's historical record of maintaining an 18 percent before tax return on investments. He also raised the questions of whether or not they had all the information they needed and whether there were other strategies that should be considered.

What analysis should be made? What should CHEMCO do?

REFERENCES

Armstrong, J. S., and M. C. Grohman, "A Comparative Study of Methods for Long-Range Market Forecasting," *Management Science, 19*(2), October 1972, pp. 211–221.

Basu, S., and R. G. Schroeder, "Incorporating Judgments in Sales Forecasts: Application of the Delphi Method at American Hoist & Derrick," *Interfaces, 7*(3), May 1977, pp. 18–27.

Buffa, E. S., and J. S. Dyer, *Management Science/Operations Research: Model Formulation and Solution Methods.* (Second Edition) Wiley, New York, 1981, chapter 14.

Buffa, E. S., and W. H. Taubert, "Evaluation of Direct Computer Search Methods for the Aggregate Planning Problem," *Industrial Management Review*, Fall 1967, pp. 19–36.

Erlenkotter, D., "Sequencing Expansion Projects," *Operations Research, 21,* 1973, pp. 542–553.

Huettner, D., *Plant Size, Technological Change, and Investment Requirements*, Praeger Publishers, New York, 1974.

Magee, J. F., "Decision Trees for Decision Making," *Harvard Business Review,* July–August, 1964.

Manne, A. S. (editor), *Investments for Capacity Expansion: Size, Location, and Time Phasing.* MIT Press, Cambridge, Mass, 1967.

Manne, A. S., "Waiting for the Breeder," *Review of Economic Studies, 41* (Supplement), 1974, pp. 47–65.

Marshall, P. W., et al., *Operations Management: Text and Cases.* Irwin, Homewood, Ill., 1975, pp. 312–322.

Morris, W. T., *The Capacity Decision System.* Irwin, Homewood, Ill., 1967.

Nord, O. C., *Growth of a New Product—Effects of Capacity Expansion Policies.* MIT Press, Cambridge, Mass., 1963.

Petersen, E. R., "A Dynamic Programming Model for the Expansion of Electric Power Systems," *Management Science, 20*(4) Part II, December 1973, pp. 656–664.

Skinner, W., *Manufacturing in the Corporate Strategy.* Wiley, New York, 1978.

CHAPTER 6

Location and Distribution

THE STRATEGIC SIGNIFICANCE OF FACILITY LOCATION IS CON-
nected with capacity decisions. Indeed, the issue of capacity expansion immediately raises the companion issue of where to expand in order to tie in
effectively with the distribution network. We have separated the materials
into two chapters because the approaches to the subproblems are quite different,
and to divide the materials into manageable units.

The location of facilities involves a commitment of resources to a long-range plan.
Thus the predictions of the size and location of markets are of great significance.
Given these predictions we establish facilities for production and distribution that
require large financial outlays. In manufacturing organizations these capital assets
have enormous value, and even in service organizations the commitment of resources may be very large. Location and distribution take on even greater significance, because these plans represent the basic strategy for accessing markets and
may have significant impact on revenue, costs, and service levels to customers and
clients.

It is not immediately obvious that location is a dominant factor in the success or
failure of an enterprise. Indeed, it is not uniformly important for all kinds of enterprises. Decentralization within industries must mean that many good locations exist
or that the location methods used could not discriminate between alternate locations.

General technological constraints will commonly eliminate most of the possible
locations. Or, to take the opposite point of view, a technological requirement may
dominate and that activity is then oriented toward the technical requirement. For
example, mining is raw material oriented, beer is water oriented, aluminum reduction
is energy oriented, and service activities including sales are consumer or client
oriented. If some technological requirement, such as raw material location, water, or
energy, does not dominate, then manufacturing industries are often transportation
oriented.

The criterion for choice of location is intended to be profit maximization for economic activities. If the prices of products are uniform in all locations, then the criterion becomes one of minimizing relevant costs.

If the costs of all inputs are independent of location but product prices vary, then
the criterion for locational choice becomes maximum revenue. In such instances,
locations will gravitate to the location of consumers, and the general effect will be to
disperse or decentralize facilities.

If all prices and costs are independent of location, then choice will be guided by
proximity to potential customers or clients, to similar and competing organizations,
and to centers of economic activity in general.

INDUSTRIAL PLANT LOCATIONS

In most plant location models, the objective is to minimize the sum of all costs affected by location. Some items of cost, such as freight, may be higher for city A and
lower for city B, but power costs, for example, may have the reverse pattern. We are
seeking the location that minimizes costs on balance.

In attempting to minimize costs, however, we are thinking not only of today's
costs, but of long-run costs as well. Therefore, we must be interested in predicting

155

the influence of some of the intangible factors that may affect future costs. Thus, factors such as the attitude of city officials and townspeople toward a new factory site in their city may be an indication of future tax assessments. Poor local transportation facilities may mean future company expenditures to counterbalance this disadvantage. A short labor supply may cause labor rates to be bid up beyond rates measured during a location survey. The type of labor available may indicate future training expenditures. Thus, although a comparative cost analysis of various locations may point toward one community, an appraisal of intangible factors may be the basis of a decision to select another. The result is an excellent example of a managerial decision with multiple criteria, where trade-offs must be made between the various values and criteria.

The general problem indicating the nature of trade-offs required is illustrated by Table 6-1. In Table 6-1a we see the results of comparative cost analyses for six alternate sites, and site 1 has the lowest projected monthly cost of $28,237. In Table 6-1b, however, there are listed 14 subjective factors that management felt were important in this particular location study. The relative importance of these factors is not immediately obvious, nor is it obvious how they should be related to the objective costs. A formal methodology is needed to provide the basis for managerial decisions.

TABLE 6-1   (a) Objective Factor Costs and (b) Subjective Factors for Six Sites

Site	Material	Marketing	Utilities	Labor	Building	Taxes	Total Objective Factor Cost (OFC)
1	$1079	$1316	$ 9,460	$12,773	$514	$3095	$28,237
2	945	1485	11,563	11,249	563	3470	29,275
3	490	1467	12,768	10,422	539	3580	29,266
4	979	1600	10,548	12,159	490	3755	29,531
5	925	1263	10,898	12,333	612	3701	29,732
6	1507	1950	11,628	12,244	612	3393	31,334

(a)

Availability of transportation	Union activities	Community services	Competition
Industrial sites	Recreation facilities	Employee transportation facilities	Complementary industries
Climate	Housing	Cost of living	Availability of labor
Educational facilities	Future growth		

(b)

SOURCE. Adapted from P. A. Brown, and D. F. Gibson, "A Quantified Model for Facility Site Selection–Application to a Multiplant Location Problem," *AIIE Transactions,* 4(1), March 1972, pp. 1–10. Copyright American Institute of Industrial Engineers; reprinted with permission.

A PLANT LOCATION MODEL

Know concepts

A model that attempts to deal with the multidimensional location problem was developed by Brown and Gibson [1972]. This model classifies criteria affecting location according to the model structure, quantifies the criteria, and achieves the balancing or trade-off among criteria.

Classification of Criteria

The model deals with any list of criteria set by management, but classifies them as follows.

1. *Critical*—criteria are critical if their nature may preclude the location of a plant at a particular site, regardless of other conditions that might exist. For example, a water-oriented enterprise, such as a brewery, would not consider a site where a water shortage was a possibility. An energy-oriented enterprise, such as an aluminum smelting plant, would not consider sites where low-cost and plentiful electrical energy was not available. Critical factors have the effect of eliminating sites from consideration.

2. *Objective*—criteria that can be evaluated in monetary terms, such as labor, raw material, utilities, and taxes, are considered objective. A factor can be both objective and critical; for example, the adequacy of labor would be a critical factor, whereas labor cost would be an objective factor.

3. *Subjective*—criteria characterized by a qualitative type of measurement. For example, the nature of union relationships and activity may be evaluated, but its monetary equivalent cannot be established. Again, criteria can be classified as both critical and subjective.

Model Structure

For each site i, a location measure LM_i is defined that reflects the relative values for each criterion.

$$LM_i = CFM_i \times [X \times OFM_i + (1 - X) \times SFM_i] \qquad (1)$$

where CFM_i = the critical factor measure for site i
$\quad$ ($CFM_i = 0$ or 1).

$\quad OFM_i$ = the objective factor measure for site i
$\quad\quad$ ($0 \leqslant OFM_i \leqslant 1$, and $\Sigma_i\, OFM_i = 1$)

$\quad SFM_i$ = the subjective factor measure for site i
$\quad\quad$ ($0 \leqslant SFM_i \leqslant 1$, and $\Sigma_i\, SFM_i = 1$)

$\quad\quad X$ = the objective factor decision weight ($0 \leqslant X \leqslant 1$)

The critical factor measure CFM_i is the product of the individual critical factor indexes for site i with respect to critical factor j. The critical factor index for each site is either 0 or 1 depending on whether the site has an adequacy of the factor or not. If any critical factor index is 0, then CFM_i and the overall location measure LM_i are also 0. Site i would therefore be eliminated from consideration.

157

The objective criteria are converted to dimensionless indices in order to establish comparability between objective and subjective criteria. The objective factor measure for site i, OFM_i, in terms of the objective factor costs, OFC_i, is defined as follows.

$$OFM_i = [OFC_i \times \Sigma_i \, (1/OFC_i)]^{-1} \tag{2}$$

The effect of Equation 2 is that the site with the minimum cost will have the largest OFM_i, the relationships of total costs between sites are retained, and the sum of the objective factor measures is one. This is accomplished through the weighting of the OFCs by the sum of the reciprocals of the OFCs summed over all sites; raising the result to the power -1 converts the OFMs to proportions, with large values representing relatively more desirable results than small values.

The subjective factor measure for each site is influenced by the relative weight of each subjective factor and the weight of site i relative to all other sites for each of the subjective factors. This results in the following statement:

$$SFM_i = \Sigma_k \, (SFW_k \times SW_{ik}) \tag{3}$$

where SFW_k = the weight of subjective factor k relative to all subjective factors, and
SW_{ik} = the weight of site i relative to all potential sites for subjective factor k

Preference theory is used to assign weights to subjective factors in a consistent and systematic manner. The procedure involves comparing subjective factors two at a time. If the first factor is preferred over the second, then the numerical value of 1 is assigned to the first factor and 0 to the second, and vice versa for the opposite result. If one is indifferent regarding the two factors, a rating of 1 is given both factors. Procedures are also included for higher-order rankings. As with objective factors, the ratings are normalized, so that the sum of subjective weightings for a given site adds to 1.

Finally, the objective factor decision weight, X, must be determined. This factor establishes the relative importance of the objective and subjective factors in the overall location problem. The decision is commonly based on action by a management committee, reflecting policies, past data, and an integration of a wide variety of subjective factors. The determination of X could logically be subjected to a Delphi process (see Chapter 3).

With all the data inputs, equation 1 can be used to compute the location measure, LM_i, for each site, and the site that receives the largest LM_i is selected. Brown and Gibson [1972] extend the model to multiplant location and present a computed example of the evaluation of six sites, involving capacity constraints. Sensitivity analyses are shown to indicate how decisions would change when the objective factor decision weight, X, is varied from 0 to 1.0. The entire procedure has been programmed for electronic computing using a 0-1 programming algorithm capable of treating problems as large as 150 variables and 50 constraints.

Table 6-1 supplies the general data on objective costs and subjective factors for the Brown and Gibson example. Table 6-2 summarizes the objective, subjective, and overall location measures for the six sites for $X = 0.8$. Site 1 produces the largest overall location measure. Note, however, the sensitivity analysis shown in Figure 6-1.

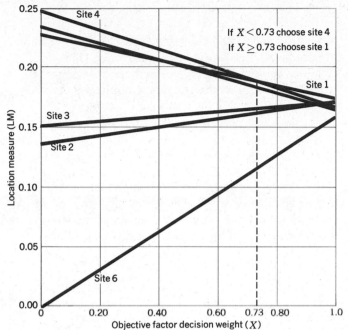

FIGURE 6-1
Sensitivity of location measures to changes in objective factor decision weight.
SOURCE: *P. A. Brown, and D. F. Gibson. "A Qualified Model for Facility Site Selection—Application to a Multiplant Location Problem,"* AIIE Transactions, 4 (1), March 1972, pp. 1–10. Copyright © American Institute of Industrial Engineers; reprinted with permission.

Site 1 is indicated for values of X of 0.73 or more, whereas site 4 would be the choice for values of X less than 0.73. Management is therefore in a position to evaluate the limited range of choices that have finally resulted from the study.

TABLE 6-2

Objective and Subjective Factor Measures and Location Measures for Six Sites ($X = 0.8$)

Site	Objective Factor Measure	Subjective Factor Measure	Location Measure
1	0.17433	0.22839	0.18514
2	0.16814	0.13638	0.16179
3	0.16819	0.15257	0.16507
4	0.16669	0.24880	0.18311
5	0.16556	0.23386	0.17922
6	0.15709	0.00000	0.12568

SOURCE. P. A. Brown, and D. F. Gibson, "A Quantified Model for Facility Site Selection–Application to a Multiplant Location Problem," *AIIE Transactions,* 4(1), March 1972, pp. 1–10. Copyright American Institute of Industrial Engineers; reprinted with permission.

COMPETITION AS A CRITICAL LOCATION FACTOR

The location of competition, and the anticipated competitive reaction to a locational choice can be of extreme importance. The example of the Brown-Gibson model includes competition as a suggested *subjective* factor, and perhaps it belongs there in many situations. But, listed there among 13 other factors it appears to take on a benign status, its effects to be traded off routinely among the other factors.

In many situations, however, competition and competitive reaction may be a critical or dominant factor in locational choice. It can operate within the Brown-Gibson framework as a critical factor and eliminate locations from further consideration, or it can become a dominant criterion that dictates a locational choice. This can happen when one location seems to be clearly the best from the point of view of competition, even though there may be advantages in objective and subjective criteria for other locations. Perhaps this is why managers may trust a location model only for more routine problems, but override a model for important location decisions.

CAPITAL EXPENDITURE—VOLUME EFFECTS

Another important variable between alternate locations is the relationship between fixed and variable expenses. The fixed investment costs can differ considerably, depending on local construction and land costs and variations in the particular site selected. Therefore, the concept of break-even analysis could be used to contrast the objective cost factors of individual locations. Such a break-even analysis is valid only for volumes near the design or break-even capacity, because large changes in volume would entail differences in capital investment as well as possible differences in variable costs.

MULTIPLANT LOCATION

Multiplant location is influenced by existing locations as well as the kinds of economic factors that we have already discussed. Each location considered must be placed in economic perspective with the existing plants and market areas. The objective factor measures focus on the minimizing of total production-distribution costs. This aim is somewhat different from the location analysis for a single plant, because each alternate location requires a different allocation of capacity to markets in order to minimize overall costs. The formal problem can be placed in a linear programming framework and solved in a distribution table. See Appendix C for a review of linear programming-distribution methods.

An Example

The Pet Food Company has experienced increasing demand for its dog food and cat food products, particularly in the South and Southwest. (The Pet Food Company is used as an example in Appendix C in discussing linear programming concepts in

TABLE 6-3
Production and Distribution Costs, Plant Capacities, and Market Demands for the Pet Food Company, Existing and Proposed Plants

	Distribution Costs per 1000 Cases to These Markets Centers					Normal Plant Capacity, 1000 Cases per Week	Production Cost per 1000 Cases
	Atlanta (V)	Buffalo (W)	Cleveland (X)	Denver (Y)	Los Angeles (Z)		
Existing plants							
Chicago (A)	18	16	12	28	54	46	270
Houston (B)	24	40	36	30	42	20	265
New York (C)	22	12	16	48	44	34	275
Proposed plants							
Denver (D)	40	40	35	2	31	20	262
Los Angeles (E)	57	70	64	31	3	20	270
Salt Lake (F)	50	50	46	14	19	20	260
Market demand, 1000 cases per week	30	18	20	15	37		

distribution.) As a result of this market expansion, the company is now considering the construction of a new plant with a capacity of 20,000 cases per week.

Surveys have narrowed the choice to three general locations: Denver, Los Angeles, and Salt Lake City. Because of differences in local wage rates and other costs, the estimated production costs per thousand cases are different, as indicated in Table 6-3. The distribution costs from each of the proposed plants to the five distribution points and the new estimated market demands in each area are also shown in Table 6-3. The production costs in the existing plants at Chicago, Houston, and New York are $270, $265, and $275 per thousand cases, respectively.

These data are summarized in the three distribution tables shown in Figure 6-2, one for each of the three possible configurations that include the new plant at Denver, Los Angeles, or Salt Lake City. Because production costs vary in the alternate locations, we must minimize the sum of the production plus distribution costs. For example, the typical item of cost represented by the Chicago-Atlanta square in Figure 6-2 is made up of the production cost at Chicago of $270 plus the distribution cost from Chicago to Atlanta of $18 from Table 6-3, or $270 + $18 = $288 per week. Similarly, for the proposed plant at Salt Lake City, the cost shown in square Salt Lake City-Buffalo in Figure 6-2 is the production cost at Salt Lake City of $260 plus the Salt Lake City-to-Buffalo distribution costs of $50, or $260 + $50 = $310 per week.

The important question now is: Which location will yield the lowest production plus distribution costs for the system of plants and distribution centers?

To answer this question, we solve the three linear programming distribution problems, one for each combination. Figure 6-2 shows the optimum solutions for each configuration. In this instance, the objective cost factors favor the Los Angeles location. The Los Angeles location results in the lowest production plus distribution cost of $34,411 per week. The Los Angeles location is $439 per week (almost $23,000 per year) less costly than the Salt Lake City location and $464 per week (more than

161

(a) New plant at Denver

To Distr. Points / From Factories	Atlanta (V)	Buffalo (W)	Cleveland (X)	Denver (Y)	Los Angeles (Z)	Available from factories, 1000's
Chicago (A)	288 (30)	286	282 (16)	298	324	46
Houston (B)	289	305	301	295	307 (20)	20
New York (C)	297	287 (18)	291 (4)	323	319 (12)	34
New Plant at Denver	302	302	297	264 (15)	293 (5)	20
Required at distribution points, 1000's	30	18	20	15	37	120

Production cost = $32,310
Distribution cost = 2,565
Total $34,875
(a)

(b) New plant at Los Angeles

To Distr. Points / From Factories	Atlanta (V)	Buffalo (W)	Cleveland (X)	Denver (Y)	Los Angeles (Z)	Available from factories, 1000's
Chicago (A)	288 (26)	286	282 (20)	298	324	46
Houston (B)	289	305	301	295 (15)	307 (5)	20
New York (C)	297 (4)	287 (18)	291	323	319 (11)	34
New Plant at Los Angeles	327	340	334	301	273 (20)	20
Required at distribution points, 1000's	30	18	20	15	37	120

Production cost = $32,470
Distribution cost = 1,941
Total $34,411
(b)

(c) New plant at Salt Lake City

To Distr. Points / From Factories	Atlanta (V)	Buffalo (W)	Cleveland (X)	Denver (Y)	Los Angeles (Z)	Available from factories, 1000's
Chicago (A)	288 (30)	286	282 (16)	298	324	46
Houston (B)	289	305	301	295 (15)	307 (5)	20
New York (C)	297	287 (18)	291 (4)	323	319 (12)	34
New Plant at Salt Lake City	310	310	306	274	279 (20)	20
Required at distribution points, 1000's	30	18	20	15	37	120

Production cost = $32,270
Distribution cost = 2,580
Total $34,850
(c)

FIGURE 6-2

Optimum production-distribution solutions for three proposed locations for the additional Pet Food Company plant. (a) New plant at Denver, (b) new plant at Los Angeles, and (c) new plant at Salt Lake City.

$24,000 per year) less costly than the Denver location. The Los Angeles location is less costly because the lower distribution costs more than compensate for the higher production costs, as compared with the other two alternatives.

The combined production-distribution analysis then provides input concerning the objective factor costs (OFC) in the Brown-Gibson location model discussed previously. The subjective factors would be evaluated as before and a final decision would be based on both objective and subjective factors and the relative weights placed on them.

LOCATIONAL DYNAMICS FOR MULTIPLANTS

Suppose that the Pet Food Company decides to build the Los Angeles plant. The balance of cost factors that produced the solution shown in Figure 6-2b could change, however. Then, the allocation of capacity to markets should also change in order to minimize relevant costs. Thus, location analysis is a continuous consideration rather than a one-shot analysis performed only at the time of expansion.

Let us assume that after the Los Angeles plant was built, the Pet Food Company experienced a net decline in demand because of the entry of aggressive new competitors in the market. Instead of a total demand of 120,000 cases per week as projected in the original location analysis, only 105,000 cases are required.

The result is that any three of the plants can meet the demand by using overtime capacity. The company is now faced with comparing the objective and subjective factors of five production-location alternatives. The five alternatives are: operate all plants at partial capacity, plus four additional alternatives that each involve shutting down one of the plants and meeting requirements using the other three plants operating on overtime schedules.

In order to compare the alternatives, five different linear programming distribution tables would be developed. In order to keep the alternatives involving overtime capacity within the linear programming framework, the overtime capacity would be regarded as a separate source of supply. In actual shipment, units produced on overtime would not be segregated; overtime capacity would simply reflect higher costs of production. Five optimal production-distribution tables would be generated and the variable plus fixed costs of operation compared for the five alternatives. The alternative with the lowest cost would be the one favored on the basis of objective factor costs. The final decision would necessarily be influenced by both objective and subjective factors, because a plant shutdown has a number of important effects on employee and community relationships.

OFF-SHORE LOCATIONS

The lure usually held out to manufacturers to locate off-shore in foreign countries has been the relatively cheap labor available in some areas. Although rapidly increasing wages in many foreign countries have changed this situation in recent years, this argument still can be made in many foreign areas.

For a particular manufacturer, the important question is: *Is a net advantage*

163

available in a foreign location? There are several important reasons why there may not be. Wage levels themselves are not the important parameter; rather, *labor costs* will determine the advantage or disadvantage. Wages can be high and labor costs can be simultaneously low. The equating factor is *productivity.* Although the American worker is paid a relatively large wage rate, the relatively large capital investment per worker multiplies his or her efforts through special tools, mechanization, and automation.

Of course, the temptation is to assume that we can couple the advantage in lower wages with high productivity by using the same levels of mechanization and managerial practice abroad. The difference in basic production economics in these two contrasting situations must be noted. Because labor is inexpensive relative to capital in some foreign locations, we may find it wise to use relatively more labor and less expensive machinery in these situations. The resulting productivity and final labor costs thus would be more in line with those usually achieved in the foreign environment. The most economical manufacturing methods and techniques are not necessarily those with the greatest possible mechanization, but those that, for a given situation, strike a balance between the costs of labor and capital costs.

There are many costs in addition to labor to consider. If there is a net labor cost advantage, will it be counterbalanced by higher costs of materials, fuel and power, equipment, credit, and so on?

Studies of production costs in the United States and abroad, involving companies with both domestic and foreign operations, have indicated considerable variability in the relative advantage or disadvantage of foreign locations. Apparently, there are some products, industries, or companies that are favored by the structure of foreign costs; however, these same conditions are unfavorable to others. Products in the industries that have a relatively high labor content seemed to have lower costs abroad. On the other hand, industries whose cost structure is dominated by materials, energy, and capital had higher costs abroad.

WAREHOUSE LOCATION

Whereas industrial plant location is often oriented toward dominant factors, such as raw material sources or even personal preferences of owners, warehouse location is definitely distribution oriented. Although the particular site choice will be affected by subjective factors, such as those included in the Brown and Gibson model, the focus of interest in the warehouse location problem is on minimizing distribution cost. One reason why warehouse location is interesting is that the problem occurs more frequently than plant location and can be evaluated by objective criteria.

Earlier efforts in logistics and distribution management attempted to define the most appropriate customer zones for existing warehouses. These graphical approaches centered on the determination of lines of constant delivery costs. Since the 1950s, however, there has been a variety of attempts to deal with warehouse location as a variable to be determined, using mathematical programming, heuristic and simulation approaches, and branch and bound methods.

The general nature of the problem is to determine warehouse location within the constraints of demand in customer zones in such a way that distribution cost is minimized for a given customer service level. Warehouse capacity is determined as a part of the solution. Customer service is defined in terms of delivery days, thus limiting the number of warehouses that can service a given zone. Distribution costs are the sum of transportation cost, customer service cost, and warehouse operating costs. The warehouse operating costs break down into costs that vary with volume, fixed costs of leasing or depreciation, fixed payroll, and fixed indirect costs.

First, let us dispose of the possibility of calculating the distribution costs of all warehouse-customer zone combinations and simply selecting the combination that has the minimum cost property. The impracticality of this enumeration approach is discussed by Khumawala and Whybark [1971].

Consider the following characteristics of a medium-sized manufacturing firm that distributes only in the United States:

1. *5000 customers or demand centers.*
2. *100 potential warehouse locations.*
3. *5 producing plants.*
4. *15 products.*
5. *4 shipping classes.*
6. *100 transportation rate variables involving direction of shipment, product, geographical area, minimum costs, rate breaks, and so forth.*

One single evaluation can be made by making an assignment of customers to warehouses for each of the product lines and then using the computer to search the minimum freight rates for that assignment. That would determine the total cost of that particular warehouse location alternative. Each other assignment would be evaluated the same way until all were complete and the least cost alternative found. Although this seems feasible, the company described above has over 12 million alternate distribution systems. Even if the evaluation of each alternative could be performed in just 3 seconds, the evaluation of all alternatives would take over 1 year of computer time at 24 hours per day.

Since the "brute force" approach is impractical, we must consider techniques that make some trade-off with reality through simplifying assumptions. We will discuss three practical approaches that have been used in large-scale applications.

Esso—The Branch and Bound Technique

Effroymson and Ray [1966] developed a model that involves a procedure using branch and bound methods and linear programming to produce optimal solutions with reasonable computing time. The location system was applied in the Esso Company to several location problems involving 4 plants, 50 warehouses, and 200 customer zones. The procedure involves the application of rules for including or excluding warehouse locations, depending on whether or not their competitive savings cover their fixed costs of operation. Linear programming is used at points in the procedure to compute lower bound costs. By following out the branches, computing upper and lower bound costs, warehouse locations can be either definitely included in the optimum solution or excluded, leading to the final optimum solution. An example of the procedure together with a case history is given in Atkins and Shriver [1968].

Hunt-Wesson Foods, Inc.—An Application of Mathematical Programming

Hunt-Wesson Foods, Inc. produces several hundred distinguishable commodities at 14 locations and distributes nationally through 12 distribution centers. The company decided to undertake a study of its distribution system, particularly the location of distribution warehouses. Five changes in location were indicated involving the movement of existing distribution centers as well as the opening of new ones. The cost reductions resulting from the study were estimated to be in the low seven figures.

Geoffrion and Graves [1974] formulated the Hunt-Wesson distribution problem in such a way that the multicommodity linear programming subproblem decomposes into as many independent classical transportation problems as there are commodities. The resulting problem structure included 17 commodity classes, 14 plants, 45 possible distribution center sites, and 121 customer zones. Thus, three levels of distribution were accounted for—plants, distribution centers or warehouses, and customer zones.

Demand for each commodity at each customer zone was known. Demand was satisfied by shipping via regional distribution centers (warehouses), with each customer zone being assigned exclusively to a warehouse. Upper and lower limits were set on the annual capacity of each warehouse. Warehouse location sites were selected to minimize total distribution costs, which were composed of fixed plus variable cost components.

The Hunt-Wesson warehouse location study indicates that the cost reductions possible are of great significance and justify careful study. Geoffrion and Graves state that similar results were obtained in an application for a major manufacturer of hospital supplies with 5 commodity classes, 3 plants, 67 possible warehouse locations, and 127 customer zones.

Ralston Purina—An Application of Simulation

Markland [1973] applied a computer simulation methodology in evaluating field warehouse location configurations and inventory levels for the Ralston Purina Company.

The basic structure of product flow is a multilevel, multiproduct distribution system involving plant warehouses, field warehouses, wholesalers, and finally retail grocers. Shipments from the five warehouses may go to other plant warehouses, to field warehouses, or to wholesalers. Inventories are maintained at the plant warehouse, field warehouse, and wholesaler levels. Also, shipments may go from any of the five field warehouses to any of the 29 demand analyses areas representing the wholesale level or to any of the other field warehouses.

Model Structure. Markland modeled the distribution system in the basic format of system dynamics as a dynamic feedback control system where product flow is the main control variable. Product flow and inventory level equations were written to represent all flow combinations and inventory levels at plant and field warehouses. Constraints on maximum inventory levels at plant and field warehouses were established, as well as constraints on maximum plant production capacity.

Sample Results. The system was simulated for six different field warehouse configurations and for different inventory service levels. The number of field warehouses was varied from zero to the existing five. Thirty-two field warehouse location patterns

166

were tested involving combinations of warehouses, using a procedure of dropping warehouses from the existing pattern. In the example given, Ralston Purina saved $132,000 per year by consolidating field warehouses from five to three. The proposed elimination of intermediate warehouses as a policy would have increased costs by $240,000 per year compared with the optimal policy of using only three field warehouses. In addition to the preceding result, it was found that an 85 percent inventory service level minimized distribution cost.

The three warehouse location methodologies discussed are apparently all quite powerful and capable of dealing with problems of practical size. The real advantage of the simulation methodology is that nonlinear costs can be represented easily and that the other features, such as inventory policy, can be included. The advantage of the Hunt-Wesson application is in its capability for handling extremely large-scale systems and in representing the storage in transit costs that are important for firms such as Hunt-Wesson and Ralston Purina. Finally, the branch and bound procedure is efficient in computing time.

LOCATION OF REGIONAL HEALTH SERVICES

Whereas industrial plant and warehouse location is influenced strongly by distribution costs, the location of services is oriented toward the location of users. Retail outlets will seek out locations that can maximize their revenue. Medical facilities need to be placed within the reach of those who are ill. Fire stations and ambulance services should be located to provide a certain minimum response time. Thus, the services location problem, as well as the techniques used, is somewhat different from the industrial plant and warehouse location problems.

The objective of health care planners is often stated as allocating facilities to locations such that primary health care demanded by the population is maximized. Implementing such an objective, however, depends on how one weights and trades off several criteria. In order to make rational location plans, demographic data are needed that characterize aspects of user behavior. Abernathy and Hershey [1972] developed a location model that provides optimum locations within a region for different criteria so that decision makers have a basis for trade-off analysis in determining actual locations.

Model Description

The model assumes a defined medical service area, such as that shown in Figure 6-3, where the numbered geographic areas represent census blocks. The xy axes provide a grid for specifying the location of populations and health care facilities. Three cities are located within the area of Figure 6-3, and demographic data are available concerning the behavior of the population regarding the use of medical facilities. The demographic data are divided into strata that exhibit relatively homogeneous patterns of medical facility use. The key variables measure the extent to which the propensity to seek care decreases as distance to a health facility increases.

Based on the stratified data, equations are developed that describe the utilization

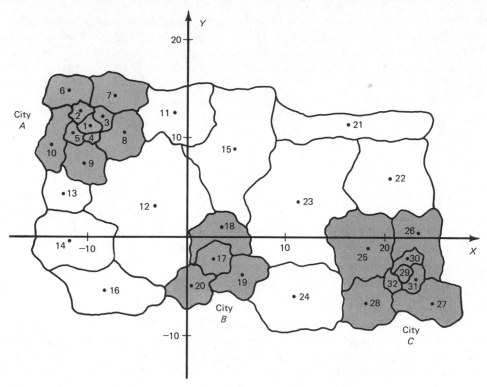

FIGURE 6-3
A hypothetical medical service area with 32 census blocks and three cities. City populations are (approximately) $A = 17,000$, $B = 9000$, and $C = 13,000$. Distances on xy axes are in miles.
SOURCE: *W. J. Abernathy, and J. C. Hershey. "A Spatial-Allocation Model for Regional Health-Services Planning," Operations Research, 20, May–June 1972, pp. 629–642.*

of a facility in relation to distance and the probability of choosing a particular center relative to the distance to the nearest center. Total demand is determined by summing the demand over all centers, strata, and census blocks. The model determines the (xy) coordinates for health centers in such a way that some criterion is optimized. In the example problem, four criteria were used.

1. *Maximum utilization:* maximize the total number of visits to centers.

2. *Minimum distance per capita:* minimize the average distance per capita to the closest center.

3. *Minimum distance per visit:* minimize the average per visit travel distance to the nearest center.

4. *Minimum percent degradation in utilization:* minimize the average reduction in the number of visits individuals in the community make as a percentage of the visits made if they were in immediate proximity to a center.

The system was optimized by a computer search methodology that searches a multidimensional criterion surface to find the optimum point. Any of the preceding criteria could be used, as well as others.

An Example

Abernathy and Hershey provide the results of a study for the medical service region of Figure 6-3. Data were given for the key variables in four strata, together with the coordinate locations of population centers by stratum. Optimum locations were generated using a computer search routine for one, two, three, and four centers for each of three criteria independently. Table 6-4 shows the coordinate locations of centers for the three different criteria. Figure 6-4 shows the locations of one center in relation to the grid and the three cities for the three criteria.

If there were only one health center for the region, its optimum location would depend on which criterion is used, because different geographic areas have different behavior patterns, as shown in Figure 6-4. When criterion 1 (maximize utilization) is used, the center is located near the center of city C. This is because this area contains a large number of individuals for whom distance is a strong barrier. But this location choice tends to increase overall distance per capita. Individuals whose use is curtailed most by long travel distance are favored by this criterion; however, it shifts the transportation costs to those who are less sensitive to distance. Criterion 2 (minimum distance per capita) results in a location near the population—distance centroid for

TABLE 6-4 **Location Coordinates in Miles for Three Criteria and Different Numbers of Centers** (see Figures 6-3 and 6-4 for locations of coordinates)

	Criterion					
	(1) Maximize Utilization		(2) Minimize Distance per Capita		(3) Minimize Distance per Encounter	
Center Number	x	y	x	y	x	y
I With 1 center						
1	21.00	−3.00	0.64	1.20	−8.70	10.00
II With 2 centers						
1	21.4	−3.7	17.6	−3.30	18.50	−3.30
2	−9.89	10.4	9.89	10.4	−9.90	10.40
III With 3 centers						
1	22.40	−3.1	21.52	−2.78	22.30	−3.20
2	−10.16	10.40	−10.20	10.40	−10.20	10.40
3	3.63	−2.75	3.60	−2.80	3.60	−2.80
IV With 4 centers						
1	22.40	−3.14	22.00	−3.50	21.23	−3.08
2	−10.20	10.40	−10.10	10.30	−9.80	10.40
3	3.59	−2.78	2.69	−4.80	3.61	−2.70
4	11.32	−2.25	3.76	3.04	−11.35	3.00
V With 5 centers[a]						
1	22.40	−3.10				
2	−9.72	10.61				
3	3.24	−3.19				
4	−11.62	3.24				
5	11.04	−2.00				

[a] Determined only for the first criterion.

SOURCE. W. J. Abernathy, and J. C. Hershey, "A Spatial-Allocation Model for Regional Health-Services Planning," *Operations Research*, 20 (3), May–June 1972, pp. 629–642.

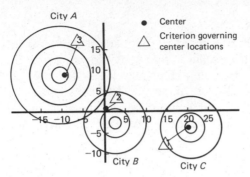

FIGURE 6-4
Location of one center based on three different criteria.
SOURCE: W. J. Abernathy, and J. C. Hershey, "A Spatial-Allocation Model for Regional Health-Services Planning," Operations Research, 20, May–June 1972, pp. 629–642.

the region, near city B. Criterion 3 (minimum distance per visit) results in a location near the center of the largest city, city A.

LOCATION OF EMERGENCY UNITS

The location of emergency units, such as ambulances, fire stations, and police services, has a dynamic character. The nature of demand for service and response time requirements creates the need for adaptation as units are called or dispatched to perform service, leaving their previous locations unprotected. Because personnel costs constitute as much as 90 to 98 percent for emergency services, fixed locations are less justified.

In general, fire stations are usually at fixed locations when they are dispatched, whereas ambulances and police cars are more mobile and may be dispatched from any location. The distinction between fixed and mobile locations breaks down in periods of high demand, because the units may be dispatched directly from one incident to the next.

The location problem for emergency units might be more correctly termed an "allocation" or "deployment" problem. It is the strategy by which the services meet some standard of performance, such as reaction time. Therefore, bound up within the location problem we have: the total capacity of the system, the location or patrol patterns, priorities for different kinds of calls, which units are actually dispatched in response to a call, and the circumstances under which relocation or redeployment takes place. The major objective of the design of an emergency system is to reduce to a low level the possibility that a true emergency call will need to be backlogged.

Design of Response Areas

The location problem is tied closely to the area for which the emergency unit has primary responsibility. Several objectives may be involved in the actual design of these response areas: minimum response time, work load balancing, demographic homogeneity, and administrative requirements. Rules of thumb have used square or circular patterns to minimize travel time to the scene of an emergency. Speed may depend on specific streets used. If travel time rather than distance is taken as the criterion, a "square" travel time response area would have its longer dimension correspond with the higher-speed streets. Closely related to the design of response areas are site selection for new and changed facilities and the dynamic problems of prepositioning and repositioning to change locations as load develops.

Location of Fire Units

In the case of fire units, prepositioning means determining the location of the fixed-position fire stations themselves. The fire station location problem can be divided into two main classes. First are those where the call rate is high relative to fire protection capacity, such as in New York City or Chicago. In these situations, queuing analysis and stochastic simulation are appropriate, and the concepts of prepositioning and repositioning represent important strategies. Where the call-capacity ratio is relatively low, as in Denver, a static approach may be justified.

Relocation of Fire Units

Kolesar and Walker [1974] designed a fire company relocation algorithm for use in New York City. The New York problem is typical of large cities, where more than one serious fire may be in progress simultaneously. They state that, on the average, 10 such problems occur daily in New York. A five-alarm fire in Manhattan could deplete the area of half of its fire-fighting units, resulting in a sharp degradation of fire protection. Under such circumstances, it is common practice to relocate the remaining units in selected "empty" firehouses to anticipate further alarms. The fire department developed a computer-based system to relocate in such a way that minimum total expected response times result.

Referring to Figure 6-5, suppose that two fires have simultaneously required the services of the seven fire companies shown; one region is uncovered. The problem is how to redeploy in order to minimize expected response time. The model assumes that the call rate will be random. The "square root law" is applied to approximate the expected response distance. This law states that the expected response distance is proportional to the square root of the area served by a fire company.

The algorithm for relocation performs with the following main steps:

1. Determine the need for relocation. An uncovered response area is detected by a program called "trigger." This program comes into play whenever a fire requires the use of at least three engines and two ladders. An uncovered area is one that falls below the minimum standard of having at least one company within x minutes of every alarm box.
2. Determine which of the empty firehouses should be filled. A heuristic rule is used to select the firehouse associated with the largest number of uncovered response areas.
3. Determine the available companies to relocate. A heuristic rule chooses available companies with the lowest relocation costs. A feasibility check is made to be sure that no area becomes uncovered as a result of a potential relocation.

171

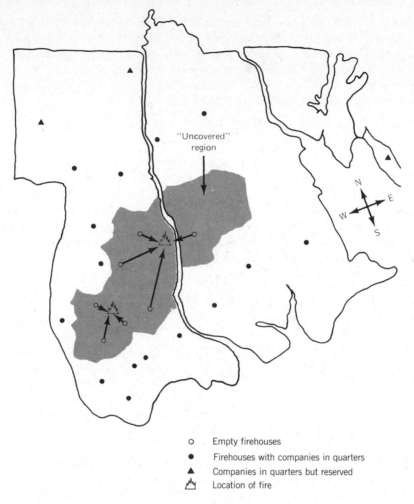

○   Empty firehouses

●   Firehouses with companies in quarters

▲   Companies in quarters but reserved

🔥   Location of fire

FIGURE 6-5
A sample relocation problem.
SOURCE: *P. Kolesar, and W. E. Walker. "An Algorithm for the Dynamic Relocation of Fire Companies,"* Operations Research, 22, March–April 1974, pp. 249–274.

4. Solve a linear programming assignment problem to minimize total relocation distance.

Now we return to Figure 6-5, which shows the locations of two fires, the locations of the seven ladder companies working at the fires, and the region left uncovered. In step 1, it was found that there were nine uncovered response areas.

Step 2 indicated that there were two solutions, each considering four of the seven empty firehouses that provide a minimum coverage.

In step 3, the program selects the companies to relocate. The least cost assignment is indicated by the dashed arrows in Figure 6-6.

The least travel distance solution produced by step 4 is shown by the solid arrows.

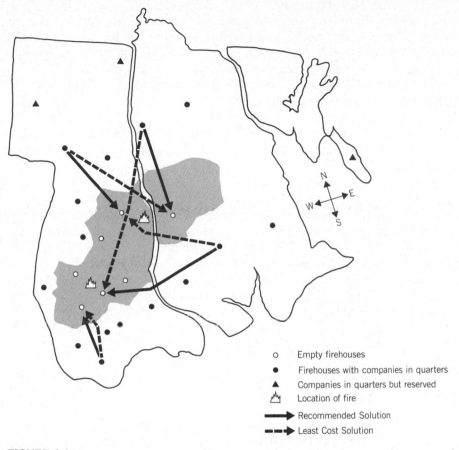

o Empty firehouses

● Firehouses with companies in quarters

▲ Companies in quarters but reserved

🔥 Location of fire

➡ Recommended Solution

╌╌▶ Least Cost Solution

FIGURE 6-6
Solutions to the sample relocation problem.
SOURCE: *P. Kolesar, and W. E. Walker. "An Algorithm for the Dynamic Relocation of Fire Companies,"* Operations Research, 22, March–April 1974, pp. 249–274.

The solution produced by step 4 results in a 22 percent reduction in travel distance and only a 9 percent increase in cost.

Location of Ambulances

The ambulance location problem is similar in general terms to the fire station location problem. The response time depends on the state of the system at the time a call for service occurs. However, an ambulance normally responds with only one unit and is usually occupied with that call for only a relatively short service time. The number and location of hospitals will have an effect on the time that an ambulance is tied up. The longer the ambulance is tied up giving service, the more likely another call will be received while the unit is busy. The mean call rate is typically a function of the time of day, so that the size of the ambulance fleet in service also varies during the day. In Los Angeles, typical response times are 3.5 minutes and ambulance service time are 17 minutes.

Fitzsimmons [1973] developed a simulator for an emergency medical system and validated it both in comparison with analytical models and data from the Los Angeles Ambulance System. In the model, travel time is computed as the sum of x and y distance-times to correspond to the usual urban rectangular layout plan. Although each vehicle had a home base, the simulator was designed to include a mobile system (where ambulances can be dispatched en route). The simulator included capability for both ambulances and helicopters.

Given the validated simulation model, we have an effective vehicle for the evaluation of alternatives in terms of numbers and locations of both ambulances and hospitals and for the evaluation of alternate policies. The alternatives were evaluated mainly in terms of response time.

Number and Location of Ambulances. The effect on response time of having 1 to 10 ambulances in the system was evaluated for single and dispersed home stations. The single home stations were at a hospital. In general, the response time for a single station levels off at about three ambulances in the system, as shown in Figure 6-7; however, response time for dispersed deployment continues to decline. Waiting time for the single station falls to near zero with three ambulances in the system.

A series of 20 runs evaluated hypotheses concerning location deployment patterns, and dispersed deployment dominated the single station alternative for all criteria. Furthermore, optimal locations improved mean travel time to the scene by about 12 percent, as compared with existing locations. Finally, it was found that optimal deployment was a function of load.

Number and Location of Hospitals. A series of simulation runs was made in which the number of hospitals was varied from one to four, using a single ambulance located centrally. Mean time to the hospital was reduced with the addition of hospitals to the system, but response time and waiting time were only slightly reduced, and ambulance utilization declined about 2 percent, as shown in Figure 6-8. Mean travel time to the scene actually increased slightly. Locating hospitals optimally reduced mean waiting time only slightly because of reduced ambulance utilization.

Control Policies. Alternate dispatch policies were evaluated involving no radio communication, radio dispatch but without mobile transmitters on ambulances, and two-way radio communication. These alternate policies were evaluated under loads varying from call rates of 15 to 45 per day. Simulated response time was reduced by 7 to 8 percent with radio dispatch; however, the two-way radio dispatch system was little better than the basic system. Nevertheless, the two-way system was recommended, since it effected some improvement.

Even though ambulance systems may be physically dispersed, simulation experiments showed a definite advantage of pooling ambulances into one central dispatch command. Of course, this result would be predicted from queuing theory (see Appendix D).

Alternate ambulance deployment policies were also evaluated, indicating an advantage for an adaptive system. The adaptive system allows repositioning of vehicles as load builds up, instead of having each vehicle return to its home base at the end of an incident.

Fitzsimmons [1970] developed a computer program named "Computerized Ambulance Location Logic" (CALL) to determine optimum ambulance deployment. Based on evaluations for particular ambulance locations, the computer routine

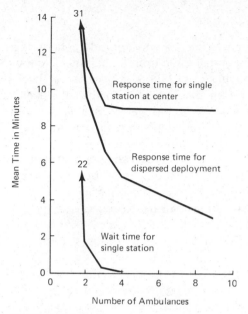

FIGURE 6-7
Response times for single ambulance station and dispersed locations for uniform distribution of calls within the geographical area.
SOURCE: J. A. Fitzsimmons, "Emergency Medical Systems: A Simulation Study and Computerized Method of Deployment of Ambulances," Ph.D. dissertation, University of California, Los Angeles, 1970.

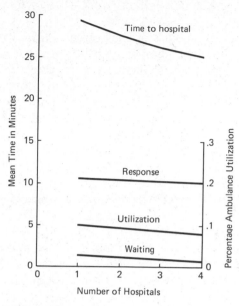

FIGURE 6-8
Effect of the number of hospitals in the system on response time.
SOURCE: J. A. Fitzsimmons, "Emergency Medical Systems: A Simulation Study and Computerized Method for Deployment of Ambulances," Ph.D. dissertation, University of California, Los Angeles, 1970.

directs changes in the ambulances' locations to decrease the system's mean response time.

Results. The CALL model was applied to the problem of establishing locations for 14 ambulances in Los Angeles. The ambulance system in Los Angeles is under the jurisdiction of the fire department, and the problem was to select 14 out of 34 sites that could house an ambulance unit. The fire department had made preliminary decisions on location with the object of locating an ambulance within 2.5 miles of every point in the city, or a 5-minute response time at 30 miles per hour. Application of CALL resulted in the relocation of nine ambulances. The relocations produced an almost 9 percent reduction in mean response time and a 33 percent reduction in the probability of a response time greater than 6 minutes. An important side effect of the new deployment was a more balanced work load as a result of shorter response times.

It was found that ambulances had a 10 percent average utilization rate. As in all productive systems having large demand variation, good service is achieved with a large fraction of server idle time, so that an ambulance unit is likely to be available when an emergency occurs.

175

LOCATION OF RETAIL OUTLETS

Early models of retail outlet location were based on the gravity model. The models involved the hypothesis that two cities attract retail trade from an intermediate town approximately in direct proportion to the populations of the two cities and in inverse proportion to the square of the distances from the two cities to the intermediate town. While the gravity model had severe limitations, the gravity or attraction concepts have carried over into models that are nearly as simple, but inject some aspects of consumer behavior.

Huff [1962] developed a model in which the *utility* of a given shopping center is directly proportional to the ratio S/T^λ, the ratio of the size of the shopping center to the travel time. Size is measured in terms of square footage of selling space. The travel time is modified by λ which is estimated empirically to reflect the effect of travel time on various kinds of shopping trips. Huff cites empirical evidence that these two factors exert an influence on a consumer's choice of a shopping center and may be the only variables needed to predict such behavior.

Based on the utilities calculated for all centers, one computes the probability of a consumer at a given origin traveling to a given shopping center. When this probability is multiplied by the number of consumers in a defined area, we have an approximation of the expected number of consumers who are likely to travel to a given shopping center for a given type of shopping trip. The basic statement of the model is then

$$E_{ij} = P_{ij}C_i = \frac{\dfrac{S_j}{T_{ij}^\lambda}}{\displaystyle\sum_{j=1}^{n} \dfrac{S_j}{T_{ij}^\lambda}} \cdot C_i \tag{4}$$

where E_{ij} = the expected number of consumers at i that are likely to travel to shopping center j

$\quad C_i$ = the number of consumers at i

$\quad P_{ij}$ = the probability of a consumer at a given point of origin i traveling to a given shopping center j

$\quad S_j$ = the size of a shopping center j

$\quad T_{ij}$ = the travel time involved in getting from a consumer's travel base i to shopping center j

$\quad \lambda$ = a parameter which is to be estimated empirically to reflect the effect of travel time on various kinds of shopping trips.

Empirical Validation

A suburban community was selected within the metropolitan Los Angeles area that had within it three rather distinct neighborhoods. These neighborhoods were the points of consumer origin. Data were gathered by questionnaires from householders in the three neighborhoods regarding which shopping center they had last patronized, which center they normally patronized for several kinds of purchases, and information on family income. Information was also gathered on 14 shopping centers

TABLE 6-5

Sizes and Proximity of Neighborhoods to Selected Shopping Centers

Shopping Center (j)	Gross Size [Sq. Ft. of Selling Area] (S_j)	Travel Time [Minutes] from Neighborhood 1 (T_{1j})	Travel Time [Minutes] from Neighborhood 2 (T_{2j})	Travel Time [Minutes] from Neighborhood 3 (T_{3j})
J_1	239,000	2.8	3.6	4.2
J_2	236,000	11.1	6.8	8.6
J_3	326,000	13.3	17.0	14.3
J_4	97,000	15.0	14.7	8.6
J_5	1,250,000	15.4	16.1	20.5
J_6	281,000	14.0	17.8	15.2
J_7	228,000	17.8	17.4	11.5
J_8	326,000	21.7	21.4	15.5
J_9	203,000	22.9	22.7	27.0
J_{10}	222,000	20.0	17.8	27.1
J_{11}	502,000	15.7	19.2	17.4
J_{12}	425,000	27.6	27.7	25.8
J_{13}	134,000	10.8	7.7	5.2
J_{14}	121,000	10.4	9.4	16.1

SOURCE. D. L. Huff, *Determination of Intra-Urban Retail Trade Areas*, Graduate School of Management, UCLA, 1962.

within a 20-mile radius from each of the neighborhoods. Table 6-5 indicates the data on gross size of the 14 shopping centers and the travel times to each of the shopping centers from each of the three neighborhoods, respectively. Estimates of the value of λ were also obtained for each of the different kinds of shopping trips.

Comparisons of observed and expected numbers of consumers going to each of the 14 shopping centers were then generated. Table 6-6 is an example of one of these involving furniture purchases. The correlation coefficient between observed and expected values for each of the three neighborhoods is quite high.

Use of the Model

Based on the model, one can estimate the number of consumers coming to a given shopping area for a given type of purchase. Then, by determining from survey data average household income in the area and the average family budget figures for various kinds of purchases, the annual sales potential for a shopping center is determined (multiply each of the budget figures by the expected number of consumers for that type of purchase). Thus the model produces data concerning the sales potential for alternate locations. One would choose a location that would maximize potential revenue. Given the location in a shopping center, the problem then becomes one of finding a suitable site, based on a host of intangible criteria and values.

IMPLICATIONS FOR THE MANAGER

The emphasis in industrial plant location is to minimize costs; however, we are speaking of longer run costs, and many intangible factors may influence future costs. Thus, a manager is faced with making trade-offs between tangible costs in the present

TABLE 6-6   **Comparison of Observed and Expected Number of Consumers from Each of the Three Neighborhoods Who Last Made a Furniture Purchase at One of the Specified Shopping Centers,[a] Undifferentiated for Age or Income[b] (Distance measured in travel time minutes)**

Shopping Center	Neighborhood 1		Neighborhood 2		Neighborhood 3	
	Obs.	Exp.	Obs.	Exp.	Obs.	Exp.
J_1	51	51.66	68	65.83	80	78.21
J_2	0	1.50	4	16.72	1	7.43
J_3	0	1.30	0	3.27	1	1.95
J_4	0	0.00	0	1.33	0	3.05
J_5	3	3.43	24	14.06	11	2.30
J_6	6	0.98	6	2.55	12	1.38
J_7	0	0.00	3	2.17	3	2.78
J_8	0	0.00	1	2.00	0	15.0
J_9	0	0.00	0	1.10	0	0.00
J_{10}	2	0.00	16	2.02	4	0.00
J_{11}	0	0.00	0	3.88	1	1.58
J_{12}	0	1.31	0	1.50	1	0.00
J_{13}	0	0.91	0	7.28	8	21.82
J_{14}	0	0.91	6	4.29	0	0.00
Total	62	62.00	128	128.00	122	122.00

[a]$r =$	.99	.94	.96
$\lambda =$	2.542	2.115	3.247
[b]Avg. adult age	37.15	35.52	38.10
Avg. stated income	6130	7246	6611

SOURCE. D. L. Huff, *Determination of Intra-Urban Retail Trade Areas,* Graduate School of Management, UCLA, 1962.

and a myriad of subjective factors that may influence future costs. The Brown-Gibson model provides a framework for the integration of objective and subjective factors using preference theory to assign weights to factors in a consistent manner.

Multiplant location is influenced by existing locations, because each location considered must be placed in economic perspective with the existing plants and market areas. Each alternate location considered results in a different allocation of capacity to markets, and the manager's objective is to minimize costs for the system as a whole. The concept of locational dynamics provides the manager with a basis for balancing costs among producing plants as demand shifts in different market areas. In some instances, an appropriate economic decision might be to close a plant, and enlarge capacity in the remaining plants through the use of overtime.

Although it is often true that plant location (particularly the location of individual versus multiple plants) is dominated by the owner's or manager's personal preference for location, warehouse location is dominated by the cost criterion. Here, the managerial objective of minimizing distribution cost can be enhanced considerably through the use of well-developed computer assisted distribution planning systems.

The very nature of service operations requires a manager to seek locations based on an analysis of the location of users. Thus, whereas warehouses and many industrial plant locations are distribution oriented, the location of service operations is user oriented. Service facilities must be decentralized and relatively local in nature in order to bring the service rendered to the users. The basis on which locations in relation to users is chosen depends largely on the nature of the system.

The managers of health service facilities are faced with complex criteria in attempting to provide locations that give the best public service. The Abernathy-Hershey study indicated the need for trading off criteria of maximum utilization, minimum distance per capita, and minimum distance per encounter.

The managers of emergency systems such as ambulances, fire protection, and police protection are faced with the need for rapid response. The random nature of the timing and frequency of calls for service, in combination with varying time for response and service, place the problem within the general framework of a waiting line situation. But the managers of such systems would have to provide an extremely large and expensive capacity in order to meet the response standards imposed if facilities were provided for peak demand. These facilities would necessarily be idle most of the time. Since queuing of calls to any great extent is not acceptable, deployment strategies have been used to provide service at reasonable cost. Thus, locations become mobile for ambulances and police protection through two-way communication systems. Instead of always returning to a home base, ambulances and patrol cars may be redeployed in transit. In fire protection systems, units may be relocated (redeployed) when a major fire occurs in order to minimize expected response time if another major fire were to break out.

Managers of retail stores focus on maximizing revenue in determining locations. The basic model developed by Huff involves the hypothesis that two cities attract retail trade from an intermediate town approximately in direct proportion to the population of the two cities and in inverse proportion to the square of the distances of the two cities to the intermediate town, modified by some aspects of consumer behavior.

IMPORTANT TERMS

Numbers in parentheses indicate page numbers

Branch and bound (165)

Critical factor measure (157)

Locational dynamics (163)

Objective factor decision weight (158)

Objective factor measure (157)

Preference theory (158)

Response areas (170)

Subjective factor measure (157)

REVIEW QUESTIONS AND PROBLEMS

1. In the concepts of locational choice, what is meant by a location oriented toward a technical requirement? Give examples.

2. In locational choice, under what conditions must the criterion be maximum profit? Maximum revenue? Minimum relevant costs?

3. In the Brown-Gibson location model, how is a critical factor weighted? An objective factor?

4. In the Brown-Gibson location model, what is the rationale for weighting subjective factors?

5. In the Brown-Gibson location model, how are the relative weights between objective and subjective factors determined in the overall location problem? Are location choices sensitive to this relative weighting?

6. How can differences in capital expenditure requirements between locations be traded off against differences in variable costs?

7. How is the problem of locating a single plant different from that of locating an additional plant in an existing system of producing facilities?

8. Define the warehouse location problem.

9. Under what conditions might the location of emergency units, such as fire stations, be regarded as a dynamic relocation and redeployment problem? A static location problem?

10. Kolesar and Blum developed a relocation algorithm for fire units. Suppose two fires break out simultaneously. How would the algorithm function in relocating the remaining units?

11. In the model for locating retail outlets, what factors are used to predict consumer behavior?

12. In the model used for locating retail outlets, how is the probability that a given customer will travel to a given shopping center calculated? What aspects of consumer behavior are implied by this calculation?

13. Assume the data given in the example for the location of regional health services. Figure 6-4 shows the location of one center based on the *independent* optimization of each of the three criteria: (1) maximum utilization, (2) minimum distance per capita, and (3) minimum distance per visit. Criterion (1) favors a location near the center of city C, criterion (2) favors a location near city B, and criterion (3) a location near the center of city A.

    Assume that only one center will be financed, so that we must decide on a single location that best satisfies our trade-off among the three criteria. We know, however, that the three criteria are not independent of each other.

    How much weight do you think should be given each of the three criteria in the final location of the health center? Where do you think the center should be located in Figure 6-4?

SITUATIONS

*14. A company supplies its products from three factories and five distribution warehouses. The company has been expanding its sales efforts westward and in the South and Southwest. It has been supplying these markets from existing distribution centers, but current volume in the new locations has raised the question of the advisability of a new warehouse location.

    Three possible locations are suggested because of market concentrations: Denver, Houston, and New Orleans. Data concerning capacities, demands, and costs are given in Table 6-7.

---

* This situation requires the application of concepts in Appendix C, Linear Programming—Distribution Methods.

TABLE 6-7
Production Costs, Distribution Costs, Plant Capacities, and Market Demands for Situation 14

| From plants | Distribution Costs per Pair, Handling, Warehousing, and Freight | | | | | | | | Normal Weekly Capacity Pairs | Unit Production Cost |
| | Existing Warehouses | | | | | Proposed New Warehouses | | | | |
	Atlanta	Buffalo	Cincinnati	Cleveland	Milwaukee	Denver	Houston	New Orleans		
Atlanta	$0.27	$0.46	$0.43	$0.45	$0.48	$0.65	$0.58	$0.55	25,000	$2.62
Chicago	0.49	0.48	0.42	0.44	0.32	0.50	0.54	0.60	20,000	2.68
Detroit	0.50	0.38	0.41	0.36	0.42	0.55	0.60	0.65	27,000	2.70
Forecast, Weekly Market Demand, Pairs	8000	15,000	11,000	13,000	9000	16,000	16,000	16,000		

Based on these data, which warehouse location should be chosen? What additional criteria might be invoked to help make a choice? How should management decide whether or not to build the new warehouse or continue to supply from the existing warehouses? *Hint:* Three linear programming distribution tables must be formulated, solved, and compared.

*15. A company has three plants located in Detroit; Hammond, Indiana; and Mobile, Alabama that distribute to five distribution centers located at Milwaukee; Cleveland; Cincinnati; Erie, Pennsylvania; and Mobile, Alabama. Table 6-8 shows distribution costs per unit, together with data on production costs at regular and overtime, fixed costs when the plants are operating and when shut down, plant capacities at regular time and the additional output available at overtime, and market demands.

The problem facing the company is that the demand for their products has fallen somewhat owing to an economic recession. The forecasts indicate that the company cannot expect rapid recovery from the demand levels shown in Table 6-8. They are considering the possibility of closing a plant, but are also quite sensitive to the impact of such an action on employee, union, and community relationships. The nature of their products requires semiskilled personnel for a substantial fraction of the labor force in each plant.

    a. What configuration of production plants operating and product distribution system would be most economical?

    b. How do you, as the manager of this operation, trade off the economic advantages of minimum cost operation for the recession period against the subjective factors? What decision should you make, as manager?

    Hint: Four linear programming distribution tables must be formulated, solved, and compared, one with all plants operating, and one each with one of the plants shut down and capacity being met with the other two through overtime, if necessary.

---

* This situation requires the application of concepts in Appendix C, Linear Programming—Distribution Methods.

TABLE 6-8
Distribution Costs, Production Costs, Fixed Costs, Plant Capacities, and Market Demands for Situation 15

From Plants	Distribution Costs per Unit					Normal Weekly Capacity, Units	Unit Produc- tion Cost	Fixed Costs	
	Milwau- kee	Cleve- land	Cincin- nati	Erie	Mobile			When Operating	When Shut Down
Detroit—Reg.	$0.50	$0.44	$0.49	$0.46	$0.56	27,000	$2.80	$14,000	$6,000
Detroit—OT						7,000	3.52		
Hammond—Reg.	0.40	0.52	0.50	0.56	0.57	20,000	2.78	12,000	5,000
Hammond—OT						5,000	3.48		
Mobile—Reg.	0.56	0.53	0.51	0.54	0.35	25,000	2.72	15,000	7,500
Mobile—OT						6,000	3.42		
Forecast Weekly Market Demand, Units	9000	13,000	11,000	15,000	8000				

16. The Woods Furniture Company of Grand Rapids is an old-line producer of quality wood furniture. They are still located at the original plant site in a complex of buildings and additions to buildings. The plant is bursting at the seams again and is in need of further expansion. There is no room left for expansion on the old site, so a variety of alternatives has been considered in and around Grand Rapids. The final alternatives include the removal of all rough mill operations to a second site in town and the building of an entirely new plant on available property about 5 miles outside of town.

At that point, the treasurer comes to the president with a deal she has uncovered through a contact with a North Carolina wood supplier. The town of Lancaster, North Carolina, is anxious to bring in new industry and is willing to make location there very attractive. After considerable discussion, it is agreed that Woods should at least listen to a proposal. It turns out that the inducements are substantial. They include a free site large enough for Woods' operations, plus options to buy adjacent land for expansion at an attractive price within 5 years, no city taxes for 5 years, the building of an access road to the property, and the provision of all utilities to the site at no cost.

After hearing the proposal, Woods' officers retire to an executive committee meeting. In a burst of enthusiasm, the treasurer moves that the proposal be accepted.

a. What additional information should Woods obtain in order to evaluate the proposal?

b. How should the Woods Company make the location decision?

c. Should Woods accept the proposal from the town of Lancaster, North Carolina?

17. The Pumpo Pump Company is currently located in the industrial district of a large city, and several problems have led to the decision to relocate. First and most important, the present site is old and inefficient, and there is no room left for easy expansion. A contributing factor is high labor rates, which translate almost directly into high labor costs in the products.

TABLE 6-9   (a) Objective Factor Costs, Millions of Dollars per Year, and (b) Subjective Factors, for Four Sites, for the Pumpo Pump Company

	Labor	Trans-porta-tion	Real Estate Taxes	Fuel	State Taxes	Electric Power	Water	Total Objective Factor Costs
City A	1.50	0.60	0.03	0.04	0.02	0.04	0.02	2.25
City B	1.60	0.70	0.05	0.06	0.04	0.07	0.03	2.55
City C	1.85	0.60	0.06	0.06	0.05	0.05	0.03	2.70
City D	3.45	0.50	0.10	0.06	0.08	0.06	0.05	4.30

(a)

	Subjective Factor						
	Labor Supply	Type of Labor	Attitude	Appear-ance	Transpor-tation	Recreation	Union Activity
City A	Adequate	Good	Good	Fair	Good	Good	Significant
City B	Plentiful	Excellent	Very good	Good	Very good	Very good	Negligible
City C	Plentiful	Excellent	Very good	Good	Good	Very good	Negligible
City D	Plentiful	Excellent	Good	Good	Very good	Very good	Active

(b)

The company has been able to operate with an independent union, and the president feels that relationships have been excellent. Recently, there has been a great deal of pressure for the union to affiliate with the Teamsters. Although this is not the major reason for moving, the president hopes that a carefully planned move may avoid future labor problems, which he feels would have an adverse effect on the company. As the search for a new site continues, the president seems to place more emphasis on this labor relations factor.

The search has finally narrowed to four cities, and comparative data are shown in Table 6-9. Objective factor costs that can be measured and seem to be affected by alternate locations are shown in Table 6-9a. The president is surprised by the range in these costs, city D having costs 1.9 times those of city A.

Seven subjective factors have been isolated as having importance, and the search staff has made a preliminary rating of each factor (see Table 6-9b). The first six factors were rated on a scale of "excellent, plentiful, very good, good, adequate, or fair." The seventh factor, union activity, was rated "active, significant, moderate, or negligible."

When the summary data were presented to the president, he was impressed, but expressed concern about how to equate the various objective and subjective factors and requested further study. The search staff has decided to use the Brown-Gibson location model.

a.   Compute the objective factor measure (OFM) using Equation 2.

b.   Compute the subjective factor decision weights (SFW_k), the *relative weights* to be assigned to each subjective factor. In order to do this, compare factors two at a time and conclude for each paired comparison which factor, in your judgment, is more important. Assign the more important factor a value of 1 and the less important a value of 0. If you feel that the two factors are of equal value, assign a 1 to both.

If the process is carried out by a group, develop a table on a chalkboard with the factors in a column at the left and the comparisons to be made across the top. When all combinations of comparisons have been made, total the 1's in each row representing the sum of the preference values for that factor. The factor weight is then the factor sum divided by the total preference values for all factors. As a check on work, the sum of all factor weights, should equal 1.0.

If the process is done individually, place the name of each factor on a separate piece of paper. Make the two-by-two comparisons, tallying the values on the backs of the pieces of paper that identify the factors. Sum and compute weights as indicated previously.

c. Determine site weights (SW) for each factor. The determination of site weights for each factor follows a similar procedure. Comparisons of each site for each subjective factor must be made, one factor at a time. The data rating each factor for each site given in Table 6-9b serve as a guide for the weighting process.

A separate table of comparisons is required for each factor. For example, using the factor of labor supply, develop a comparison table with the four sites in a column at the left and the six comparisons to be made across the top. Insert 1's and 0's in the table, representing the results of comparison. Total the 1's in each row representing the sum of preference values for that site, and compute site weights. The site weights for the factor, labor supply, are $A = 0.0, B = 0.3333, C = 0.3333, D = 0.3333$, as a checkpoint for this development.

The result of this step is a table that gives the site weights for each subjective factor; that is, a 7×4 table of 28 site weights.

d. Compute the subjective factor measure (SFM) for each of the four sites, using Equation 3. For each site, SFM is the sum of the successive multiplication of the factor weights determined previously by the site weights, for each factor. For each site, there are seven such multiplications that produce the SFM for that site. As a check, the sum of the SFMs for the four sites should be 1.0.

e. Compute the final location measures (LM) for each site. In order to do this, you must decide on the proportion of the decision weight that you wish to place on objective factors. This is a judgmental process, but you should be able to justify why you have chosen a given objective factor decision weight, X. Given the selection of a value of X, the final location measures are calculated using Equation 1. As a final check, the total of the location measures for all four sites should be 1.0.

f. How sensitive is the final decision as indicated by the LMs to variation in the objective factor decision weight, X? If the value you have selected for

X were to change slightly, would the location selected by the model change?

g.   Given the results of the Brown-Gibson model for Pumpo Pump Company, what decision do you think should be made? Are you satisfied that the model has allowed you to make the necessary trade-offs between objective and subjective factors and that your values (the decision maker's) have been properly and effectively represented in the trade-off process?

18.   CERAMCO, a Newark, New Jersey, based company specializing in ceramic products, is considering the location of a new plant for its successful product GAMMATRON. This product is a specially treated ceramic wool material that has remarkable insulating properties for homes.

GAMMATROM is CERAMCO's success story, having developed the product and established a market for it. The demand has developed rapidly in the past 5 years, and new producers have entered the market with essentially equivalent products. Competition has been intense more recently and has resulted in price deterioration in some market areas. There are four firms that market products with similar characteristics, but the maximum market share of any of them is 21 percent. CERAMCO has 38 percent of the market currently. One competitor is located on the West Coast, two in the East, and one in the greater Cleveland area.

Industry sales have been increasing at the rate of 15 percent per year, and this rate of increase is expected to continue at least for the next 2 or 3 years. CERAMCO's president stated that he expected at least a 10 percent annual increase for the next 10 years. He feels that CERAMCO should be able to maintain their market share and possibly improve it if they do some of the right things.

The plant location problem has been turned over to Steve Lippman, a staff assistant to the president. Steve has an MBA degree and is considered to be a bright, analytically oriented person. Early in the project Steve had identified the Brown-Gibson location model as being just what he needed. Steve had isolated three alternatives, each of which would accommodate a 10,000 ton per year plant.

Steve used six objective cost factors (building, labor, market, materials, taxes, and utilities), and eight subjective factors (availability of labor, availability of transportation, community services, competition, cost of living, future growth, housing, and union activities). The results of Steve's Brown-Gibson model analysis are shown in Table 6-10 for an objective factor decision weight of $X = 0.80$.

Newark Plant Expansion. This alternative required the smallest investment ($4 million) since the property was already owned, and had other advantages of close proximity to the corporate offices. Organizationally, it was the simplest also, because the basic organization was already in place, but needed to be expanded. The difficulty with this alternative was that the product was bulky, and shipping costs were high to some market areas. CERAMCO's policy had been to absorb a portion of shipping charges in market areas where a competitor

185

TABLE 6-10   **CERAMCO Objective and Subjective Factor Measures and Location Measures for Three Sites ($X = 0.80$)**

Site	Objective Factor Measures	Subjective Factor Measures	Location Measures
1. Newark	0.15022	0.22814	0.16580
2. Hammond	0.15410	0.23415	0.17011
3. Omaha	0.15552	0.23301	0.17102

had a plant and therefore, a competitive advantage. Two of CERAMCO's competitors had plants within 100 miles of the Newark plant.

Hammond, Indiana. Investment requirements were estimated as $6 million. It would be necessary to develop a complete production organization, and with two plants, CERAMCO anticipated coordination problems, particularly regarding marketing areas to be served by each plant. The Midwest was regarded as a very large potential market that was being served by CERAMCO and the Cleveland competitor, with CERAMCO meeting competition with generous freight allowances. Labor and other costs were relatively high for this location, but these costs were counterbalanced somewhat by the reduction in freight allowances that would result. These cost differences were reflected in the Objective Factor Costs of the Brown-Gibson model analysis.

Omaha, Nebraska. Investment requirements were $6.5 million. The rationale for this location was that a competitor was located there, and the market center in Omaha was pretty much the property of this competitor. Although population statistics showed a lower density in the plains states, Steve was impressed by comments made by the president that he would sure like to "go head to head" with the competitor and not simply leave the large market area with no competition. His idea was that with plants in Newark and Omaha, the more dense population in the Midwest could be served. Labor and other costs were more moderate, and current freight allowances were small in the aggregate simply because CERAMCO did very little business in the area. It was recognized that a substantial part of the investment requirements were in market development. As with the Hammond plant, it would be necessary to develop a complete production organization, together with similar coordination problems.

The president has called a meeting of the Executive Committee to consider the question of the location of the new plant. Steve will present his results and recommendations. He has decided to recommend the Omaha location.

How do you analyze the situation? What would you recommend?

REFERENCES

Abernathy, W. J., and J. C. Hershey, "A Spatial-Allocation Model for Regional Health-Services Planning," *Operations Research, 20,* May–June 1972, pp. 629–642.

Atkins, R. J., and R. H. Shriver, "New Approach to Facilities Location," *Harvard Business Review,* May–June 1968, pp. 70–79.

Beckman, M., *Location Theory.* Random House, New York, 1968.

Brown, P. A., and D. F. Gibson, "A Quantified Model for Facility Site Selection—Application to a Multiplant Location Problem," *AIIE Transactions, 4,* March 1972, pp. 1–10.

Buffa, E. S., and J. S. Dyer, *Management Science/Operations Research: Model Formulation and Solution Methods.* (Second edition), Wiley, New York, 1981.

Chaiken, J. M., and R. C. Larson, "Methods for Allocation Urban Emergency Units: A Survey," *Management Science, 19,* Part 2, December 1972, pp. 110–130.

Effroymson, M. A., and T. A. Ray, "A Branch-Bound Algorithm for Plant Location," *Operations Research, 14,* May–June 1966, pp. 361–368.

Fitzsimmons, J. A., "Emergency Medical Systems: A Simulation Study and Computerized Method for Deployment of Ambulances." Ph.D. dissertation, UCLA, 1970.

Fitzsimmons, J. A., "A Methodology for Emergency Ambulance Deployment," *Management Science, 19,* February 1973, pp. 627–636.

Geoffrion, A. M., and G. W. Graves, "Multicommodity Distribution System Design by Benders Decomposition," *Management Science, 20*(5), January 1974, pp. 822–844.

Huff, D. L., "Determination of Intra-Urban Retail Trade Areas," UCLA, Graduate School of Management, 1962.

Khumawala, B. M., and D. C. Whybark, "A Comparison of Some Recent Warehouse Location Techniques," *The Logistics Review, 7,* 1971.

Kolesar, P., and W. E. Walker, "An Algorithm for the Dynamic Relocation of Fire Companies," *Operations Research, 22,* March–April 1974, pp. 249–274.

Markland, R. E., "Analyzing Geographically Discrete Warehouse Networks by Computer Simulation," *Decision Sciences, 4,* April 1973, pp. 216–236.

Whitman, E. S., and W. J. Schmidt, *Plant Relocation: A Case History of a Move.* American Management Association, New York, 1966.

CHAPTER 7

Processes, Jobs, and Facility Layout

THERE ARE STRATEGIC DECISIONS INVOLVING THE DESIGN OF products/services, the capacity, and a location for the system, that are an integral part of the productive system design. The core of that productive system, however, is the complex of technology and people. The entire design process is interdependent and the products%services and locations are also partially influenced by the productive process, and vice versa. We will concentrate our attention in this chapter on the blending of technology and people as components of a productive system. Because productive systems are such a blend, they are often called "sociotechnical systems." We will also consider some of the special design problems encountered in integrating the process-job systems into a physical design.

The result of this process is to develop a rationale for the organization of the work to be done and to relate it to machines and technology. The physical integration of these factors is the facility layout. Whether or not the layout permits an effective design from points of view other than work flow and physical efficiency depends on how technology and people are molded into a system.

We must consider the alternatives of division of labor versus broad spectrum jobs. In the past, process planning (i.e., technology and layout) has been thought of as the independent variable and people and job designs as the dependent variables. In that framework, job designs were results of process or technology planning. Currently developing concepts and practices consider the two components jointly to produce designs that satisfy the needs of both.

PRODUCTIVE SYSTEM DESIGN AS A STRATEGIC DECISION

Figure 7-1 is a diagram that relates the major elements of long-term strategic decisions to the productive system design. The process diagrammed should be thought of as being dynamic. It must take account of changing consumer preferences; changing demand quantity, mix, and location; changing technological innovations in products *and* processes; and changing social and cultural values of employees.

A good design will be one in which a balance is achieved between the competing criteria and values. Some of the criteria are economic, related to markets and demand, some are behavioral, related to consumer behavior and to job satisfaction, and some are technological, involving products and processes.

BURGER—A Service System Example

Assume we are starting with a new idea for a useful product or service, as we did in Chapter 1 in discussing the BURGER enterprise. We started with an attempt to make market predictions and long-range plans (blocks 1 and 2) for an organization to provide a service of certain defined characteristics in the food service market (block 3). This concept of the business also involved a definite focus for the productive system. As we sharpened our concept of the business (particularly the nature of the food service provided and the food quality), we made broad studies of the size and location of markets and the size and location of branches. These plans became important inputs to blocks 3 and 4, which involve the design of the food service and its impact on the design of facilities.

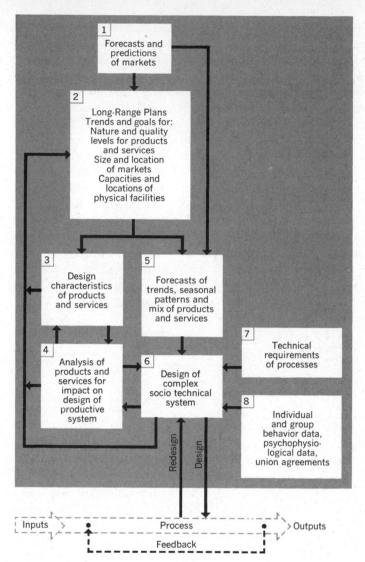

FIGURE 7-1
Process and facilities design module.

Recall that at one point in the evolution of BURGER, plans were made to design a modular branch as well as a system of branches. The inputs to the design of the productive system were from blocks 4, 5, 7, and 8. The forecasts (block 5) provided data useful in determining a peak and average capacity, but the output rates were affected by the processes used, the work flow layout (block 7), and the way we decided to put the work teams together (block 8).

The first design was based largely on experience with the most recent branch, but preliminary cost figures suggested that both labor and material costs were too high. The first alternatives were to relocate some processes at the central warehouse, because they could be done on a larger scale for all branches, with greater mechanization and automatic material handling. This change simplified operations at each branch and resulted in the dropping of the production line concept and the adoption of a rotating team approach to staffing the branches. Alternatives were considered that involved the possible alteration of the service offered in order to accommodate some of the needs of the productive system (the interaction between blocks 4 and 6). All of these developments represented cost improvements that helped BURGER on its way down an experience curve, thereby making it more competitive in the fast-foods industry.

Using systems concepts, we see feedback loops in Figure 7-1. The productive system design process involves a feedback of information to an analysis and design of the service offered and to the long-range plans that in turn affect capacities and location. In an ongoing situation, there is a continuing information feedback and interaction between all the elements according to the structure of Figure 7-1. The process is dynamic and interactive. The changes are often small ones, but on occasion there may be massive changes, for example, radical product design changes or the abandonment of old facilities and the planning of new ones.

CRITERIA AND VALUES

From the time of the Industrial Revolution to the present, the main pressures influencing the design of processes and jobs have been productivity improvement and economic optimization. Adam Smith stated the advantages of division of labor as the guiding principle, and managers have applied this principle progressively over time. The specialization principle has been applied throughout industry and is currently being applied in service and nonmanufacturing systems.

The specific technology involved limits the extent to which division of labor *can* be pursued and market size limits how far it *will* be pursued. But within these limits, managers usually have a wide range of choices of job and process design involving different degrees of labor specialization. Present-day technology and enormous markets for many products and services have indeed fostered specialization. In short, from the time of Adam Smith to the present, the dominant criterion has been the economic one. It was assumed that finely divided jobs were better because they would increase productivity and that other factors were correlated with productivity. Incentive pay schemes were used to maintain workers' motivation.

Beginning in the early 1930s, however, another criterion was proposed as a counterbalance—job satisfaction. Studies indicated that workers responded to other factors in the work situation. In the late 1940s, the value of the job satisfaction criterion developed from a morale-building program at IBM. The term *job enlargement* was coined to describe the process of reversing the trend toward specialization. Practical applications of job enlargement were written up in the literature, describing improvements in productivity and quality levels resulting from jobs of broader scope.

PROCESS-JOB CONCEPTS

There are constraints imposed by technology that limit the possible arrangements of processes and jobs, and there are constraints imposed by job satisfaction and social

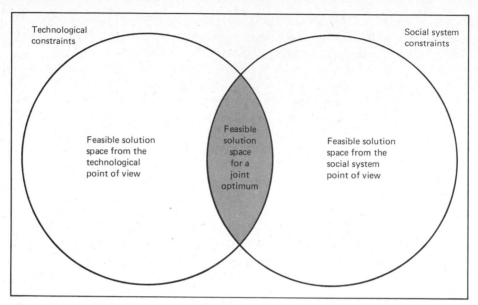

FIGURE 7-2
Feasible solution spaces for technological and social systems, and joint solution space.

system needs. The circle marked "technological constraints" in Figure 7-2 indicates that all job designs within the circle represent feasible solutions from a technological point of view, and all points outside the circle are infeasible. Similarly, the circle marked "social system constraints" indicates that all job designs within that circle represent feasible solutions from the socio-job satisfaction point of view. Within the shaded area of overlap between the two circles, we have a solution space that meets the constraints of both technology and the social system. The shaded area defines the only solutions that can be considered as feasible in joint terms. Our objective, then, is to consider jointly the economic and social system variables, and find the best solution. Because optimization is an unclear process in job design, we seek solutions that are acceptable.

Managers' Model of Job Breadth

Looking within the joint feasible solution space, Scoville [1972] developed models that examine job breadth from the points of view of managers and workers. Figure 7-3 shows a graphic form of the managers' model.

The tasks and duties required can be shuffled in many ways to form the continuum of narrow versus broad job designs. For example, in auto assembly, jobs can be finely divided as with conventional auto assembly lines, or at the opposite extreme, one worker or a team could assemble the entire vehicle. This kind of job enlargement can be termed *horizontal*. Ultimately, a vertical enlargement could be envisioned where jobs incorporate varying degrees of quality control, maintenance, repair, supply, and even supervisory functions.

The curves in Figure 7-3 are rationalized as follows (Scoville argues for the shape of the curves rather than for any specific numerical solution):

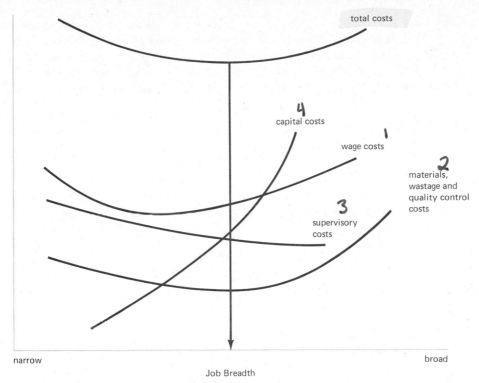

FIGURE 7-3
Manager's model of job breadth.
SOURCE: *J. G. Scoville, "A Theory of Jobs and Training,"* Industrial Relations, 9, *1969, pp. 36–53.*

1. The wage costs curve reflects low productivity for both very narrow and very broad jobs, with a minimum wage cost (maximum productivity) somewhere in the middle range. Training costs go up as the scope of jobs increase, whereas turnover costs are most important for narrow jobs. Thus the wage costs curve declines to a minimum and increases thereafter as job breadth increases.

2. Material, scrap, and quality control costs are high with narrow jobs owing to lack of motivation. Penalties are also high for broad jobs because the advantages of division of labor are lost. The advantages of division of labor are the development of a skill or dexterity when a single task is performed repetitively, a saving of time normally lost in changing from one activity to the next, and the invention of machines or tools that seem normally to follow when workers perform specialized tasks of restricted scope. In addition, there is the advantage of division of labor stemming from payment for limiting skills; that is, if the work is organized so that each person performs the entire sequence of operations, the wage paid would be dictated by the most difficult or rarest skill required by the entire sequence. Thus, the enterprise would pay for the highest or most limiting skill, even when the workers were performing routine tasks. With division of labor, however, just the amount of skill needed could be purchased.

3. Supervisory costs decline with broader jobs because that function is progressively incorporated with lower level jobs through job enlargement.

193

4. Capital costs per worker rise on the assumption that capital-labor cost ratios and inventory cost of goods in process both increase. The capital-labor ratio for narrow jobs is low, reflecting the use of simple tools. The capital per worker for skilled broader jobs, however, reflects the worker's capability to use several machines as needed, e.g., an X-ray technician may use different machines for different types of X-rays.

The total cost curve in Figure 7-3 is the sum of the individual cost component curves and reflects an optimum where managers would choose to operate. As with all cost allocation problems where each extreme strategy involves a cost, the joint optimum must be somewhere between the extremes. The pure strategies cannot represent the optimum, because the low cost solution necessarily results from a balance of costs.

Workers' Model of Job Breadth

Scoville's model of job breadth from the workers' viewpoint is shown graphically in Figure 7-4. The wage-productivity and employment probability curves are multiplied to produce the discounted expected earnings curve. If one then subtracts the worker-borne training costs, a net economic benefits curve (not shown) may be obtained, which has a maximum near the broad end of the spectrum.

Thus, Scoville's models indicate that there are optimum job designs from an economic point of view. However, because the factors that enter the two points of view are different, it is unlikely that managers and workers could agree on how work should be organized.

We have a rationale for process and job design in an equilibrium model, where the balance of forces between labor and management is likely to produce an organization of work somewhere within the joint feasible region.

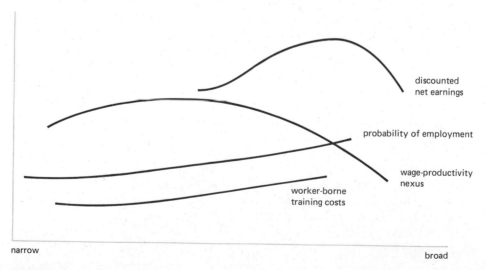

narrow

broad

FIGURE 7-4
Worker's model of job breadth.
SOURCE: J. G. Scoville, "A Theory of Jobs and Training," Industrial Relations, 9, 1969, pp. 36–53.

194

TECHNOLOGICAL VIEW OF PROCESS PLANNING AND JOB DESIGN

Although the general methods we will describe were developed in manufacturing systems, they have been adapted and widely used in many other institutions, such as offices, banks, and hospitals.

Figure 7-5 shows the overall development of process plans in a manufacturing situation. Process planning takes as its input the drawings or other specifications that

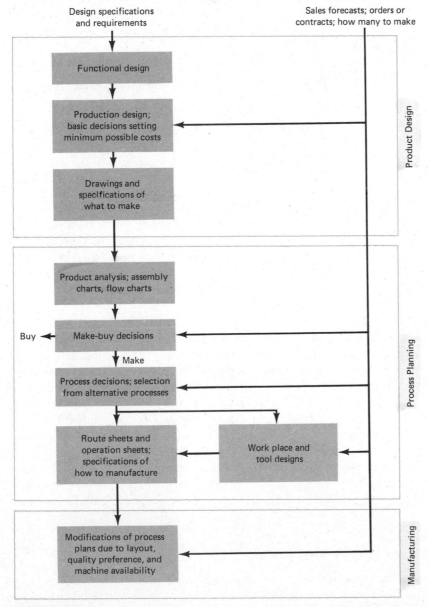

FIGURE 7-5
Development of processing plans.

indicate *what* is to be made and the forecasts, orders, or contracts that indicate the *quantity* to be made. The drawings are then analyzed to determine the overall scope of the project. If it is a complex assembled product, considerable effort may go into "exploding" the final product into its implied component parts and subassemblies. This overall planning may take the form of special drawings that show the relationship of parts, cutaway models, and assembly drawings. Preliminary decisions are made concerning some assembly groupings to determine which parts to make and buy, as well as the general level of tooling expenditures. Then for each part, a detailed routing through the system is developed. Technical knowledge is required concerning processes, machines and their capabilities, costs, and production economics. Ordinarily, a range of processing alternatives is available. The selection may be influenced strongly by the projected volume and stability of product design.

Product Analysis

SKIP
↓

The product to be manufactured is first analyzed primarily from a technological point of view to determine the processes required.

Assembly Charts. Schematic and graphic models are commonly developed to help visualize the flow of material and the relationship of parts. The assembly chart can be useful in making preliminary plans regarding subassemblies, where purchased parts are used in the assembly sequence, and appropriate general methods of manufacture. The assembly chart is often called a "Gozinto" chart, for the words, "goes into." For example, where in the process might production lines be appropriate? Figure 7-6 is an assembly chart for a simple capacitor. Notice how clearly the chart shows the relationship of the parts, the sequence of assembly, and which groups of parts make up subassemblies. The chart is a schematic model of the entire manufacturing process at one level of detail.

Operation Process Charts. Assuming that the product is already engineered, we have complete drawings and specifications of the parts, their dimensions and tolerances, and materials to be used. The engineering drawings specify locations, sizes, and tolerances for holes to be drilled and surfaces to be finished for each part. With this information, the most economical equipment, processes, and sequences of processes can be specified. Figure 7-7 is an example of an operation process chart for the same capacitor for which the assembly chart of Figure 7-6 was prepared.

An operation process chart is a summary of all required operations and inspections. It is a general plan for manufacture. Although the focus of such charts is on the technological processing required, it is obvious that the jobs to be performed by humans have also been specified. Some discretion in the makeup of jobs still exists, especially in the assembly phase; however, it is clear that "technology is in the saddle."

Analysis of Human-Machine Relationships

Given the product analysis and the required technological processing, individual job designs become the focus. Concepts and methods used have developed over a long period beginning with the scientific management era. The professional designers of processes and jobs have been industrial engineers in industry. In the post-World War

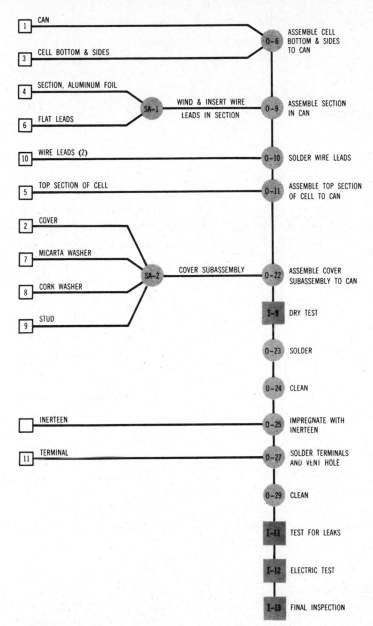

FIGURE 7-6
Assembly or "Gozinto" chart for a simple capacitor.

II period, psychologists and physiologists have contributed concepts and methods concerning the role of humans in productive systems, thus broadening the technological view.

Humans and Machines. In the technologists' view, humans have certain physiological, psychological, and sociological characteristics that define their capabilities and limitations in the work situation. These characteristics are thought of not as fixed quantities, but as distributions that reflect individual variation.

197

In performing work, human functions are envisioned in three general classifications:

1. Receiving information through the various sense organs.

2. Making decisions based on information received and information stored in the memory of an individual.

3. Taking action based on decisions. In some instances the decision phase may be virtually automatic because of learned responses, as in a highly repetitive task. In others, the decisions may involve extensive reasoning and the result may be complex.

Note that the general structure of a closed loop automated system, discussed in Chapter 4, includes similar functions. Wherein lies the difference? Are automated machines like humans? Yes, in this model of humans in the system, machines and humans are alike in certain important respects. Both have sensors, stored information, comparators, decision makers, effectors, and feedback loops. The difference is

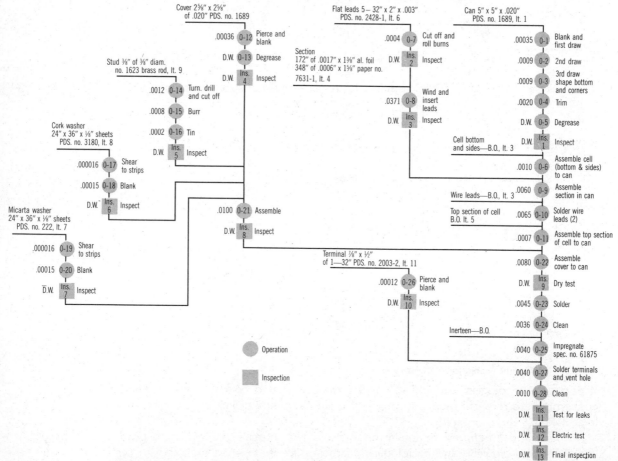

FIGURE 7-7
Operation process chart for a simple capacitor. (Courtesy Westinghouse Electric Corporation.)

in the humans' tremendous range of capabilities and in the limitations imposed by physiological and sociological characteristics. Thus, machines are much more specialized in the kinds and ranges of tasks they can perform. Machines perform tasks as faithful servants reacting mainly to physical factors. Humans, however, react to their psychological and sociological environments as well as to the physical environment.

Although there are few guides to the allocation of tasks to humans and machines on other than an economic basis, a subjective list of the kinds of tasks most appropriate for humans and for machines is given by McCormick [1970].

Conceptual Framework for Human-Machine Systems

We have noted that humans and machines can be thought of as performing in similar functions in work tasks, although they each have comparative advantages. The functions they perform are represented in Figure 7-8.

Information is received by the *sensing function*. Sensing by humans is accomplished through the sense organs. Machine sensing can parallel human sensing through electronic or mechanical devices. Machine sensing is usually much more specific or single purpose in nature than the broadly capable human senses.

Information storage for humans is provided by memory or by access to records. Machine information storage can be obtained by magnetic tape or disk, punched cards, and cams and templates.

The function of *information processing and decision making* is to take sensed and stored information and produce a decision. The processing could be as simple as a choice between two alternatives, depending on input data, or very complex, involving deduction, analysis, or computing to produce a decision for which a command is issued to the effector.

The effector or *action function* occurs as a result of decisions and command, and may involve the triggering of control mechanisms by humans or machines or a communication of decisions. Control mechanisms would, in turn, cause something physical to happen, such as moving the hands or arms, starting a motor, or increasing or decreasing the depth of a cut on a machine tool.

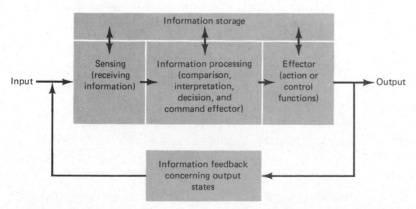

FIGURE 7-8
Functions performed by worker or machine components of worker-machine systems.

Skip ↓

Input and output are related to the raw material or the thing being processed. The output represents some transformation of the input in line with our previous discussions of systems. The processes themselves may be of any type: chemical, processes to change shape or form, assembly, transport, or clerical.

Information feedback concerning the output states is an essential ingredient, because it provides the basis for control. Feedback operates to control the simplest hand motion through the senses and the nervous system. For machines, feedback concerning the output states provides the basis for machine adjustment. Automatic machines couple the feedback information directly so that adjustments are automatic (closed loop automation). When machine adjustments are only periodic, based on information feedback, the loop is still closed, but not on a continuous and automatic basis.

Obviously, automation is the ultimate of the technological view of job design, for the principles of automation, as discussed in Chapter 4, are applied to the fullest extent possible when technologists design jobs.

go ↓

THE SOCIOTECHNICAL VIEW OF PROCESS PLANNING AND JOB DESIGN

In the sociotechnical view, the concepts and methods of the technological view are mechanistic, with humans thought of as machines or, worse, as just links in machines. This view states that, without question, the central focus of the technological approach is technology itself and that technology is taken as given without exploring the full range of the possible alternatives.

Briefly, sociotechnical theory rests on two essential premises. The first is that there is a joint system operating, a sociotechnical system, and that joint optimization of social and technological considerations is appropriate. The second premise is that every sociotechnical system is embedded in an environment. The environment is influenced by a culture and its values and by a set of generally accepted practices, where there are certain roles for organizations, groups, and people.

Englestad [1972] developed a set of psychological job requirements. These requirements are an interpretation of empirical evidence which suggests that workers prefer tasks of a substantial degree of wholeness, where the individual has control over the materials and the processes involved:

1. The need for the content of a job to be reasonably demanding in terms other than sheer endurance, yet provide at least a minimum of variety (not necessarily novelty).
2. The need for being able to learn on the job (which implies standards and knowledge of results) and to go on learning. Again, there is a question of neither too much nor too little.
3. The need for some minimum area of decision.
4. The need for some minimum degree of social support and recognition in the work place.

5. The need to be able to relate what one does and what one produces to one's social life.

6. The need to feel that the job leads to some sort of desirable future.

Thus the principles of process and job design may be summarized as the application of the concept of joint optimization between technology and social system values and the ideal of wholeness and self-control. These are the principles that would guide the organization of work in specific situations, resulting in the establishment of job content. The determination of job methods in the sociotechnical view results from a concept of the semiautonomous work group that, by and large, creates its own work methods.

PROCESS-JOB DESIGN IN RELATION TO LAYOUT

As discussed in Chapter 2, there are two basic types of physical systems, process focused and product focused systems. Although many actual systems are combinations of these two extremes, the two types illustrate the nature of jobs that result. Figure 7-9 shows the general layout patterns.

Recall the mapping of productive system strategies in relation to product strategies introduced in Chapter 2 as Figure 2-7. At one extreme, where product volumes are low and variety, flexibility, and quality are the prime strategies, the economical production system will be a functional layout such as Figure 7-9a. Such a solution to the layout of physical facilities results in relatively good utilization of equipment by time sharing it for various jobs requiring a certain production technology.

At the other extreme, for products that are standardized and produced in high volume, there is little if any difference in process requirements from unit to unit. Specialization in the form of line or product layout is economically justified, as shown in Figure 7-9b. Between the extremes, we find mixed types of layout.

The appropriateness of a given layout type in supporting the competitive strategy depends on the economics of alternate solutions. For example, if plant, equipment, and other resources were costless, we would set up separate product-focused facilities for each product. Each product would have its own production line. Because these factors of production are not free, we must have sufficient utilization of facilities to justify "single-product" lines. For an oil refinery or a steel mill, a very high utilization is important because of the immense capital requirements. For a fast-food operation, perhaps 50 percent utilization is sufficient.

One of the ways that managers can position their production facilities to take advantage of product layout in what would otherwise seem to be a functional layout situation is to exploit product families. Product families have similarities between parts, materials, assembly structures, and so on. Each individual product may have relatively low volume, so that product lines would not be economically justified. But if the line of products can be designed, or redesigned, to standardized common parts, it may be possible to specialize layout. For example, the FMC-Crane & Cable Company redesigned its product line from this viewpoint. Frames and other parts were standardized so that a production line could be used up to the final stages of

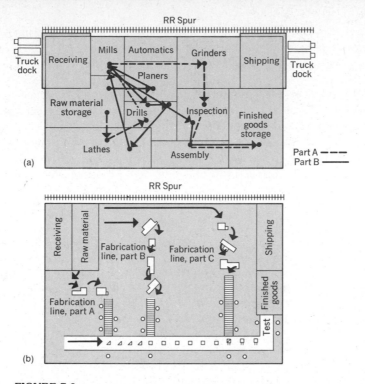

FIGURE 7-9
(a) Functional layout pattern for process focus, and (b), product or line layout for product focus.

assembly, where the uniqueness of individual products required separate handling. The firm was repositioning itself on the product-process matrix shown in Figure 2-7.

Finally, the choice of layout type is closely related to a choice of job and organization design. If one chooses a functional layout, then a process-focused organizational design is associated with it. A line layout design brings with it the characteristics of a product-focused organizational design. The two forms of the basic organization of the work to be done have rather far-reaching implications for the design of jobs, their breadth and satisfaction to workers.

Job Breadth Versus System Type

Process focused systems are associated with a functional layout pattern, as shown in Figure 7-9a. With functional layout, departments are generic in type, with all the operations of a given type being done within that department. For example, Figure 7-9a represents a machine shop, and the grinding department performs all kinds of metal work involving grinding. The department has a range of grinding equipment so it has relatively broad capability within the skill category. There are many examples of other systems where functional layout is employed, for example, hospitals, municipal offices, and so on.

The job designs that are associated with functionally laid out systems tend to be relatively broad, though specialized. For example, mechanics in the grinding depart-

202

ment can usually perform a wide variety of such work. Normally they are trained to operate several machines, because this breadth offers flexibility. Similarly, an X-ray department in a hospital does a broad range of X-ray work. The variety of work in both situations stems both from the more general nature of operations in the departments and from the fact that each job order received may be slightly different. Such functional systems require employees who can perform within a skill category. They are specialized, but their skills are more closely related to craft specialties. There is repetition in the work in the sense that an experienced X-ray technician has probably performed all the common types of X-rays previously, but there is a continuing mix of job orders that lends variety to the work.

Product-focused systems are associated with line-type operations, as illustrated by Figure 7-9b. The flow is organized entirely around the product being produced. Each operation being performed must fit into the flow in a highly integrated manner. The operations are highly repetitive. Each employee performs just a few elements of the work that in themselves may seem unrelated because of the "balance" among operations required to obtain smooth flow. The balance among operations is critical to making the system function as an efficient high output system. The higher the output requirements, and the more work stations along the line, the greater the likelihood the system will be balanced with a short, repetitive cycle that restricts the content of each individual job.

LINE LAYOUT FOR PRODUCT-FOCUSED SYSTEMS

The jobs that result from the line balance process are likely to contain small work elements which are difficult to relate to end products. To appreciate the situation, the process of assembly line balancing needs to be understood. Actual line balancing processes are rather sophisticated, but a simple example will show how jobs are constructed from the work required to assemble a simple toy automobile.

Line Balance Concepts

Figure 7-10 shows a wooden toy car, the parts of which are named and numbered. By examining the toy car, we can see the sequence restrictions that must be observed in its assembly. For example, the hubcaps must be installed on the wheels prior to subsequent assembly steps to ensure that the wood axle is not broken as a result of impact. Finally, the wheels cannot be assembled until the axle has been inserted in the car body.

These sequences must be observed, because the toy car cannot be assembled correctly in any other way. On the other hand, it makes no difference whether the headlights are assembled before or after the wheels are assembled. Similarly, it makes no difference whether the front or rear wheels are assembled first.

These task sequence restrictions are summarized in Table 7-1. In general, the assembly tasks listed in the table are broken down into the smallest whole activity. For each task, we note in the right-hand column the task or tasks that must immediately precede it. Tasks *a* and *e* can take any sequence because no tasks need precede them. However, task *b* (install right headlight) must be preceded by task *a*

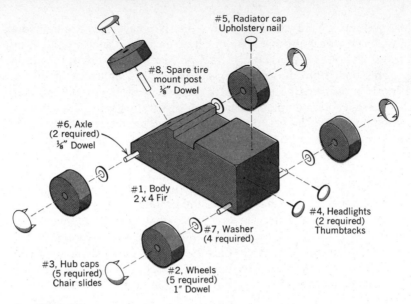

FIGURE 7-10
Toy car with parts and assembly details.

TABLE 7-1   **List of Assembly Tasks Showing Performance Times and Sequence Restrictions for the Toy Car Assembly**

Task	Task Description	Performance Time, Seconds	Task Must Follow Task Listed Below
a	Position body to conveyor	2	—
b	Install right headlight	3	a
c	Install left headlight	3	a
d	Install radiator cap	3	a
e-1	Install hubcap on spare tire	4	—
e-2	Install hubcap on wheel	4	—
e-3	Install hubcap on wheel	4	—
e-4	Install hubcap on wheel	4	—
e-5	Install hubcap on wheel	4	—
f	Assemble spare tire post on spare tire	2	e-1
g	Assemble spare tire subassembly to body	2	a,f
h-1	Press axle on wheel	2	e-2
h-2	Press axle on wheel	2	e-3
i-1	Assemble washer to wheel-axle subassembly	1	h-1
i-2	Assemble washer to wheel-axle subassembly	1	h-2
j-1	Assemble front wheel-axle-washer subassembly to body	2	a, i-1
j-2	Assemble back wheel-axle-washer subassembly to body	2	a, i-2
k-1	Assemble washer to front axle	1	j-1
k-2	Assemble washer to back axle	1	j-2
l-1	Press second wheel on front axle	2	e-4, k-1
l-2	Press second wheel on back axle	2	e-5, k-2
m	"Drive" car off conveyor	2	b,c,d,g,l

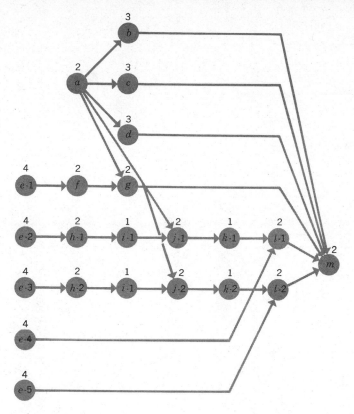

FIGURE 7-11
Precedence diagram representing the sequence requirements shown in Table 7-1, for the toy car assembly example. Numbers indicate the task performance times.

(position body to conveyor). Only the immediate predecessor tasks are listed to avoid redundancy.

The precedence restrictions in Table 7-1 are summarized in the diagram in Figure 7-11. Now we can proceed with the grouping of tasks to obtain balance. But balance at what rate of output? What is to be the capacity of the line? This is an important point and one that makes the line balance problem difficult. If there were no capacity restrictions, the problem would be simple; one could take the lowest common multiple approach. For example, if we had three operations that required 3.2, 2.0, and 4.0 minutes respectively, we could provide eight work places for the first, five for the second, and ten for the third.* The capacity of the line would be 150 units per hour at each of the operations, and the cycle time would be 0.4 minutes. But capacity would then be specified by balance rather than by market considerations.

For illustrative purposes, assume that we must balance the line for an 11-second cycle. A completed unit would be produced by the line every 11 seconds. To meet this capacity requirement, no station could be assigned more than 11 seconds of work on the tasks shown in Figure 7-11. The total of all task times is 53 seconds. Therefore, with an 11-second cycle, five stations is the minimum possible. Any solu-

* The task times may be determined through a process known as work measurement. Appendix F, "Work Measurement," provides a review of the methods of this process.

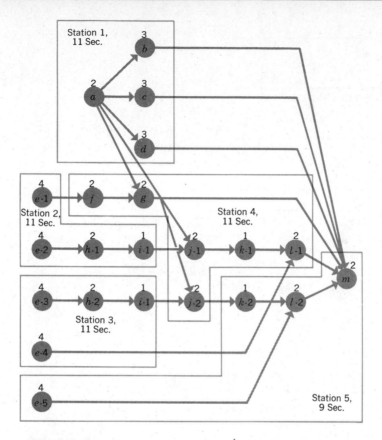

FIGURE 7-12
A solution to the toy car assembly line balancing example. Cycle time = 11 seconds; idle time = 2 seconds in Station 5.

tion that required more than five stations would increase direct labor costs. Figure 7-12 shows a solution that assumes five stations.

Although this example is simple, it illustrates the concepts of assembly line balancing. As the product becomes more complex, the relationships between tasks that end up within jobs may be more disjointed. As the enterprise is rewarded for its success by public acceptance of its product, volume increases and lines are rebalanced for smaller cycle times to achieve higher output rates, further restricting the content of jobs.

The supplement to this chapter provides a discussion of techniques applicable to practical line balancing problems. These techniques have been computerized.

Decision to Organize Facilities by Product

The managerial decision to organize the work on a product or line basis is a significant one. Some important requirements should be met, and there are some consequences affecting the work force that should be weighed carefully before implementing the decision.

If we are to organize as a product focused system, the following conditions should be met:

1. Volume adequate for reasonable equipment utilization.
2. Reasonably stable product demand.
3. Product standardization.
4. Part interchangeability.
5. Continuous supply of material.

Continuous system concepts have found their greatest field of application in assembly rather than in fabrication. A moment's reflection makes it obvious why this is true. Machine tools commonly have fixed machine cycles; this factor makes it difficult to achieve balance between successive operations. The result is poor equipment utilization and relatively high costs. In assembly operations where the work is more likely to be manual, balance is much easier to obtain because the total job can be divided into smaller elements. If station 10 is too short whereas 16 is too long, part of the work of station 16 probably can be transferred to 10 (perhaps the tightening of a single bolt). Because very little equipment is involved at each station anyway, utilization of equipment may not be of great importance.

When the conditions for product-focused systems are met, significant economic advantages can result. The production cycle is speeded up because materials approach continuous movement. Because very little manual handling is required, the cost of material handling is low. In-process inventories are lower compared with batch processing because of the relatively fast manufacturing cycle. Because aisles are not used for material movement and in-process storage space is minimized, less total floor space is commonly required than for an equivalent functional system, even though more individual pieces of equipment may be required. Finally, the control of the flow of work (production control) is greatly simplified for product-focused systems because routes become direct and mechanical. No detailed scheduling of work to individual work places and machines is required, since each operation is an integral part of the line. Scheduling the line as a whole automatically schedules the component operations.

Given the decision for designing a product-focused system, the major problems are (1) deciding on a production rate or cycle time, and (2) subdividing the work so that smooth flow can result. The subdivided activities need to be balanced so that each operation has an equivalent capacity, that is, the line balance problem discussed previously.

Production Line Design and Job Satisfaction

As noted earlier, the production line concept epitomizes division of labor and specialization, and is the target of considerable criticism. The general line balance techniques do not seem to leave a door open for discussion of job design alternatives. The process starts with the determination of a cycle time that meets the output rate needs and progresses toward the generation of stations (jobs) made up of tasks which meet the needs of the cycle and do not violate technological constraints. Job

207

satisfaction as a criterion seems to have no role in this process. The issue is: Are there alternatives that allow us to address the question of the degree of fractionation of jobs while retaining the production line concept?

Multiple Stations and Parallel Lines. Given a capacity or production rate requirement, we can meet that requirement by a single line with cycle time c, or two parallel lines with cycle time $2c$, or three parallel lines with cycle time $3c$, and so forth. Line balance programs have been developed that enable us to use multiple parallel lines. As the number of parallel lines increases, the scope of jobs increases, and finally, we have complete horizontal job enlargement. The point is that the alternatives do exist, even with the line organization of work.

In addition to increasing job scope, there are a number of advantages resulting from the parallel line-multiple station concept. First, from the line balance point of view, balance may be easier to achieve because the larger cycle time offers a greater likelihood of attaining a good fit with low residual idle time. This is particularly true when some of the task times are nearly equal to the single-line cycle time. Furthermore, a multiple line design increases flexibility of operations enormously. Output gradations are available; that is, one can have one, two, three, or more, lines operating or not operating; and one can work overtime or undertime with all the line combinations. There are fewer dependent operations; for example, if there is a difficulty with an operation in line 1, it may not affect line 2. A machine breakdown in line 1 need not stop the operation of line 2.

From a human organization viewpoint, the parallel line-multiple station concept has all the advantages of horizontal job enlargement. Work groups can be smaller and more cohesive. A team spirit may be engendered by competition between line teams on the bases of output, quality, safety, and other dimensions. On the other hand, capital investment is likely to increase with parallel line designs because of the duplication of equipment.

FUNCTIONAL LAYOUT FOR PROCESS-FOCUSED SYSTEMS

In functional layout, processing units are organized by function on the assumption that certain skills and expertise are available in that service facility. Therefore, an X-ray department of a hospital normally offers such a broad range of skills and knowledge that a physician can call for virtually any kind of X-ray.

Many examples of process focused systems can be found in practice, for instance, in manufacturing, hospital and medical clinics, large offices, municipal services, and libraries. In every situation, the work is organized according to the function performed. The machine shop is one of the most common examples, and the name and much of our knowledge of process-focused systems results from the study of such manufacturing systems. Table 7-2 summarizes typical departments or service centers that occur in several generic types of process-focused systems.

In all the generic types of process-focused systems, the item being processed (part, product, information, person) normally goes through a processing sequence, but the work to be done and the sequence of processing vary. At each service center, the specification of what is to be accomplished determines the details of processing and the time required. For each service center, we have the general conditions of a

TABLE 7-2

Typical Departments or Service Centers for Various Generic Types of Process-Focused Systems

Generic System	Typical Departments or Service Centers
Machine shop	Receive, Stores, Drill, Lathe, Mill, Grind, Heat-Treat, Inspection, Assembly, Ship
Hospital	Receiving, Emergency, Wards, Intensive-Care, Maternity, Surgery, Laboratory, X-ray, Administration, Cashier, etc.
Medical clinic	Initial Processing, External Examination, Eye, Ear, Nose and Throat, X-ray and Fluoroscope, Blood Tests, Electrocardiagraph and Electroencephalograph, Laboratory, Dental, Final Processing.
Engineering office	Filing, Blueprint, Product Support, Structural Design, Electrical Design, Hydraulic Design, Production Liaison, Detailing and Checking, Secretarial Pool.
Municipal offices	Police Dept., Jail, Court, Judge's Chambers, License Bureau, Treasurer's Office, Welfare Office, Health Dept., Public Works and Sanitation, Engineer's Office, Recreation Dept., Mayor's Office, Town Council Chambers.

waiting line (queuing) system, with random arrivals of work and random processing rates. When we view a process-focused system as a whole, we can visualize it as a network of queues with variable paths or routes through the system, depending on the details of processing requirements. An important problem in the design of such systems is the relative location of the service centers or departments.

Decision to Organize Facilities by Process

To obtain reasonable utilization of personnel and equipment in process-focused flow situations, we assemble the skills and machines to perform a given function in one place, and then route the items being processed to the functional centers. If we tried to specialize according to the processing requirements of each type of order in production-line fashion, we would have to duplicate many kinds of expensive skills and equipment. The utilization for each order might be very low unless the volume for that type were very large. Thus, when flexibility is the basic system requirement, a functional arrangement is likely to be the most economical. The flexibility required may be of several types: flexibility of routes through the system; flexibility in the volume of each order; and flexibility in the processing requirements of the item being processed.

Other advantages of the functional design become apparent when it is compared with the continuous flow or production line concept. The jobs that result from a process-focused organization are likely to be broader in scope and require more job knowledge. Laborers are expert in some field of work, whether it is heat-treating, medical laboratory work, structural design, or city welfare. Even though the func-

TABLE 7-3

Criteria for Determining the Relative Location of Facilities in Process-Focused Systems

Generic System	Criterion
Manufacturing	Interdepartment material handling cost
Hospital	Personnel walking cost between departments
Medical clinic	Walking time of patients between departments
Offices	Personnel walking cost between areas and equipment, or face-to-face contacts between individuals

tional mode implies a degree of specialization, it is specialization within a generic field of activity, and the variety within that field can be considerable. A pride in workmanship has been traditional in this form of organization of work by trades, crafts, and relatively broad specialties. Job satisfaction criteria seem easier to meet in these situations than when specialization results in highly repetitive activities.

Relative Location of Facilities Problem. Once we decide to organize productive facilities on a functional basis, the central design problem is where to locate the individual functional units. In a machine shop, should the lathe department be located adjacent to the mill department? In a hospital, should the emergency room be located adjacent to intensive care? In an engineering office, should product support be located adjacent to electrical design? In municipal offices, should the welfare and health department offices be adjacent to each other? The locations will depend on the need for one facility to be adjacent relative to the need for other pairs of facilities to be adjacent. We must allocate locations based on relative gains and losses for alternatives and seek to minimize some measure of the cost of having facilities nonadjacent.

Criteria. We always are attempting to measure the interdepartmental interactions required by the nature of the system. How much business is carried on between departments, and how do we measure it? In manufacturing systems, material must be handled from department to department; in offices, people walk between locations to do business and communicate; and in hospitals, patients must be moved and nurses and other personnel must walk from one location to another. Table 7-3 summarizes criteria for four systems.

By their very nature, functional systems have no fixed path of work flow. We must aggregate for all paths and seek a combination of relative locations that optimizes the criterion. Although this location combination may be poor for some paths through the system, in the aggregate it will be the best arrangement of locations.

Complexity of the Relative Location Problem. Figure 7-13 shows, in schematic form, six process areas arranged on a grid. If any of the six departments can be located in any of the six alternate locations, there are $6! = 720$ possible arrangements, of which 90 are different in terms of their effects on the cost of inter-

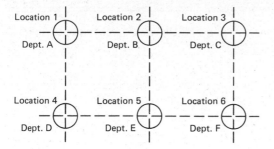

FIGURE 7-13
There are 6! = 720 arrangements of the six process areas in the six locations of the grid.

departmental transactions. For this trivial problem, we could consider enumerating all the different location combinations, comparing aggregate costs, and selecting the combination with minimum cost. However, the number of combinations to evaluate increases rapidly as we increase the number of departments. For just 9 departments on a 3 × 3 grid, we have more than 45,000 combinations. For 20 departments arranged on a 4 × 5 grid, we have 608 × 10¹⁵ combinations. Therefore, we must rule out enumeration as a practical approach.

Operation Sequence Analysis

An early graphical approach to the problem led to a powerful computerized model, which we will also examine. Operation sequence analysis maintains close contact with the nature of the problem and is useful for relatively small problems.

For example, a private industrial clinic performs services under contract to a number of business and industrial firms. These services include medical examinations for new employees, as well as annual physical examinations for all employees. The clinic performs eight types of examination sequences, depending on the details of the individual contracts. Many people who have been examined complained about excessive walking because of the clinic layout. The director of the clinic wants to know what a good solution would look like.

Table 7-4 represents a 1-month sample of the flow between the 11 departments, aggregating over all types of examinations. Table 7-4 is called a load summary and summarizes the flow among all combinations of departments.

The graphical approach to finding a solution places the information contained in the load summary in an equivalent schematic diagram, in which circles represent the functional service centers. Connecting lines are labeled to indicate the intensity of travel or transactions between centers, in either direction. Figure 7-14 is a first solution and is obtained merely by placing the work centers on a grid, following the logic of the pattern indicated by Table 7-4. The initial solution may be improved by inspecting the effect of changes in location. When an advantageous change is found, the diagram is altered. For example, in Figure 7-14 work center 4 has a total of 300 trips to or from work centers that are not adjacent, that is, 2 and 6. If work center 4 is moved to the location between 2 and 6, all loads to and from 4 become adjacent.

Further inspection shows that 200 nonadjacent trips occur between work centers 6 and 8. Is an advantageous shift possible? Yes: By moving 9 down and placing 8 in

TABLE 7-4   **Load Summary: Sample of Number of Trips per Month Between All Combinations of Departments for an Industrial Medical Clinic**

From Departments		1 Initial Processing	2 Eye Examination	3 Ear, Nose, and Throat	4 X-ray and Fluoroscope	5 Blood Tests	6 Blood Pressure Check	7 Respiratory Check	8 Electrographic	9 Laboratory	10 Dental Examination	11 Final Processing
Initial processing	1		600									
Eye examination	2			400	100			100				
Ear, nose, and throat	3				350	50						
X-ray and fluoroscope	4						100	450				
Blood tests	5							50				
Blood pressure check	6				100					150	100	
Respiratory check	7						50		450	100		
Electrographic	8						200			250		
Laboratory	9										500	
Dental examination	10											600
Final processing	11											

the position vacated by 9, the number of nonadjacent trips is reduced from 200 to 100. Figure 7-15 shows the diagram with these changes incorporated.

Further inspection reveals no further obvious advantageous shifts in location. Figure 7-15 has a trip-distance rating of $2 \times 100 = 200$, that is 100 trips $\times$ 2 units of grid distance. For larger problems, the grid distance becomes an important part of the measure of effectiveness, because frequently used work centers might be separated by many grid units. Figure 7-15 represents a good solution because most of the work centers are adjacent to the other work centers involving interdepartmental flow.

The Block Diagram. The block diagram is developed by substituting estimated areas for the small circles in the schematic diagram. Initially, this can be done with block templates to find an arrangement that is compatible with both the flow pattern of the schematic diagram and the various size requirements for departments. Figure 7-16 shows such an initial block diagram. Although the essential character of the schematic diagram is retained, Figure 7-16 obviously does not yet represent a practical solution. A slight variation of the shapes of departments will enable us to fit the system into a rectangular configuration and meet possible shape and dimension re-

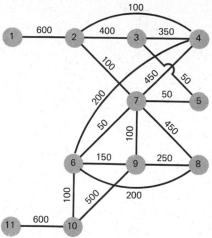

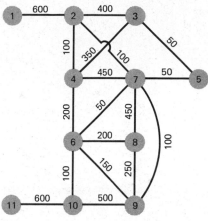

FIGURE 7-14
Initial graphic solution developed from load summary of Table 7-4.
SOURCE: *Figures 7-14 to 7-17 are from E. S. Buffa, "Sequence Analysis for Functional Layouts,"* Journal of Industrial Engineering, *6(2), March–April 1955.*

FIGURE 7-15
Schematic diagram incorporating changes suggested by Figure 7-14.

strictions that may be imposed by the site, an existing building, or the desired configuration of a new building. Figure 7-17 shows such a block diagram.

The final block diagram represented by Figure 7-17 becomes an input to detailed layout. The detailed layout phase would undoubtedly require minor shifts in space allocation and shape, but the basic relationships would be retained.

CRAFT (Computerized Relative Allocation of Facilities)

The graphical approach to the determination of the relative location of departments has obvious limitations. Its effectiveness depends on the individual analyst's insight, and as the number of activity centers increases, the technique breaks down rapidly. Practical problems in facility location often involve 20 or more activity centers, and this number is already at the limit for feasible use of the operation sequence analysis technique. To overcome this limitation, a computerized relative allocation of facilities technique (CRAFT) was developed, which easily handles up to 40 activity centers and has other important advantages.

The CRAFT Program. The CRAFT program takes as input data matrices of interdepartmental flow and interdepartmental unit transaction cost, together with a representation of a block layout. The block layout that is fed in may be the existing layout or any arbitrary starting solution if a new facility is being developed. The program calculates geographic department centers and an estimate of total interaction cost for the input layout. The governing heuristic algorithm then asks: What change in interaction cost would result if locations of departments were exchanged? Within the computer, the locations of the activity centers are exchanged, and the interaction costs are recomputed. Whether the result is an increase or a decrease, the difference

213

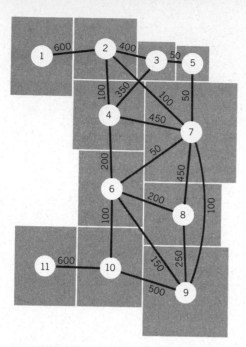

FIGURE 7-16
Initial block diagram. Estimated areas are substituted for circles in the schematic diagram of Figure 7-15.

is recorded in the computer's memory. The program then asks the same question for other combinations of departments, and again records cost differences. It proceeds in this way through all combinations of exchanges. The present algorithm involves either two- or three-way exchanges.

When the cost differences for all such combinations have been computed, the program selects the exchange that would result in the largest reduction, makes the exchange in locations on the block diagram, and then prints out the new block layout, the new total interaction cost, the cost reduction just effected, and the departments involved in the exchange. The basic procedure is then repeated, generating a second and a third improved block layout, and so on. Finally, when the procedure indicates that no further cost-reducing location exchanges can be made, the final block layout is printed out. This becomes the basis for a detailed template layout of the facility.

The program has the capacity for handling 40 activity centers. Any departmental location can be held fixed simply by specifying in the instructions that the department (or departments) is not a candidate for exchange. This feature has great practical importance, because existing layouts cannot be completely rearranged. Fixed locations may develop when costly heavy equipment has been installed, or the location of receiving or shipping facilities may be determined by the location of roads or railroad spurs. Finally, the locations of some work groups often make it desirable to treat them as fixed points in the layout. A new development also enables it to include relocation costs as well as interaction costs in the computer program for relayout [Hicks and Cowan, 1976].

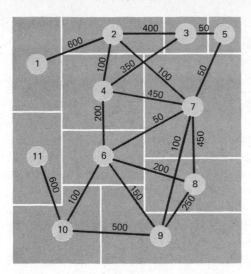

FIGURE 7-17
Block diagram that takes account of rectangular building shape.

A three-dimensional version of CRAFT has been developed by Roger Johnson [1982] which makes it possible to deal with large-scale problems associated with space allocation and layout of office space in multistory office buildings, as well as manufacturing facilities.

Project Systems and Fixed-Position Assembly

Large-scale projects are common in today's economy. In terms of facility utilization, they are intermittent systems, and their physical layout deserves a special comment. Examples of familiar large-scale projects are huge aerospace projects such as the Polaris missile, aircraft assembly, ship building, or large construction projects. Some of these kinds of projects involve basically conventional manufacturing systems to produce components that go into the project itself. The systems that manufacture these components will be typical of either intermittent or continuous manufacturing systems.

The heart of the project concept, however, lies in the assembly process, which is usually done on a fixed-position basis, either by necessity (as with buildings, dams, and bridges) or for reasons of economy (as with missiles, aircraft, ships, and other very large projects). In these fixed-position assembly situations, the equivalent of functional centers are commonly arranged around the unit being constructed in "staging areas." Some of the staging areas will be storage locations where the material or components will remain until needed in the process. Other areas may involve some degree of fabrication or prefabrication before final assembly on the major unit.

Proximity of staging areas to the major unit may depend on frequency of use and travel time between the staging area and the unit. For example, in constructing a skyscraper, the heating and air conditioning unit need only be installed once; however, forming lumber and reinforcing steel will be used continuously throughout the rough construction stages. The general concept of the computer location algorithms

215

apply to project systems as well as to the kinds of situations already discussed. Because the project is commonly a one-time system, however, formal location procedures have not been used in practice, although the potential for use is valid.

IMPLICATIONS FOR THE MANAGER

Managers need to recognize that the basic design of the productive system is an important element of strategic planning. The system design should help implement the broader enterprise strategy, considering changing demand, changing customer preferences for product mix and quality, and changing social and cultural values of employees.

Many of the problems of the operations manager stem from employees' dissatisfaction with the nature of their jobs. Labor disputes erupt over issues referred to as working conditions and require endless hours of negotiations and grievance hearings for settlement. Even when the issues are not stated in terms of job design, job satisfaction, and dehumanization at the work place, it is often felt that these are the real issues. If the structure of processes, jobs, and layout took account of the worker's model of job breadth, psychological job requirements, and job enrichment principles, perhaps the operations manager would face fewer labor disputes resulting from these causes.

Although alterations in the process and job design structures can be made in existing organizations, managers have the greatest opportunity for innovation when new facilities are being planned. It is during these opportune times that fundamental alternatives to the organization of work can be considered most easily.

The manager needs to know about the results of studies of alternate job design structures, the fundamental conflict between the managers' and the workers' models of job breadth, psychological job requirements, and the success of semiautonomous work groups in designing their own work methods. If the process and job design structure and the physical layout have conflict built into them, the resulting operating problems may be severe. The moral, "ye shall reap as ye have sown," will be of little consolation.

A manager needs to have a clear understanding of the appropriateness of different layout flow patterns. Aside from the job design aspects, product or line flow layout is appropriate only under certain conditions. The volume of activity necessary to justify specialized line operations is relatively large and requires a standardized product or service—variations are difficult to incorporate into line systems. The conflict between job specialization and job satisfaction is a difficult one for managers. Specialization has many benefits to society and to an individual enterprise. There seems to be little question that specialized line-type operations are easier to plan for, easier to schedule, easier to control, require less space per unit of capacity, and so on. Yet specialized jobs create a work environment that raises social responsibility issues for managers.

It seems unlikely that large-scale productive systems can or should be converted from line operations. On the other hand, managers need to raise questions about feasible alternatives that may exist within the joint sociotechnical solution space. Experience has shown that there are often solutions to process-job design problems which satisfy both sets of criteria if there is a genuine effort to find them.

In choosing the appropriate type of layout, managers should carefully relate the problem to the job design question. Functional layout allows somewhat broader jobs, though there is specialization within general areas. Product layout is likely to produce narrowly designed jobs. But the choice of productive system type also has a great impact on the enterprise strategy in relation to its chosen markets. If the nature of the products and markets and/or the manager's choices within the market dictate flexibility of product design, quality, and service, then a functional design is likely to be better. If the nature of products and markets emphasizes cost and off-the-shelf availability, then product layout is a likely choice.

IMPORTANT TERMS

Numbers in parentheses indicate page numbers

Assembly chart (197)	Job satisfaction (191)
CRAFT (213)	Line balance (203)
Fixed-position assembly (215)	Line layout (203)
Functional layout (208)	Operation process chart (196, 198)
Gozinto chart (197)	Operations sequence analysis (211)
Job breadth (192)	Sociotechnical system (200)
Job enlargement (191)	

REVIEW QUESTIONS

1. What are the factors that limit the extent of division of labor in practice?
2. Using an assembly line as an example, what are the factors that determine the nature and content of jobs that could be designed?
3. What is the sociotechnical systems approach to job design?
4. What is the nature of the manager's model of job breadth? Of the worker's model of job breadth? Do they result in the same kinds of job design?
5. What is the technological view of process planning and job designs?
6. What are the tools of product analysis? How are job designs affected by their use?
7. In the technologist's view, what are humans' functions in performing work? In which kinds of functions do humans have superiority over machines and vice versa?
8. What is the sociotechnologist's view of process planning and job design?

TABLE 7-5

Tasks, Performance Times, and Precedence Requirements for Problem 18

Task	Performance Time, Minutes	Task Must Follow Task Listed Below
a	4	—
b	3	a
c	5	b
d	2	—
e	4	c
f	6	d
g	2	—
h	3	dg
j	5	h
k	2	—
l	3	k
m	4	l

9. What are Englestad's psychological job requirements? Are they compatible with the technological view of job design?

10. Define the terms *functional layout* and *line layout*.

11. Under what conditions would functional layout be appropriate?

12. What is the relative location of facilities problem?

13. Table 7-3 summarizes types of criteria that might be used to determine the relative location of facilities in functional systems. Where would criteria other than those listed be important?

14. In the decision to organize for a product focus, why is each of the following factors a condition that should be met?

   a. Volume adequate for reasonable equipment utilization.

   b. Reasonably stable product demand.

   c. Product standardization

   d. Part interchangeability.

   e. Continuous supply of material.

15. Define the nature of the line balance problem.

16. Describe the line balance problem as a queuing situation. What simplifications are made in the deterministic form of line balancing?

17. How is it possible to introduce the question of appropriate job breadth into the process for designing and balancing production lines?

18. Table 7-5 shows a list of assembly tasks with sequence restrictions and performance times. Construct a precedence diagram for the assembly. Balance the line for an output rate of 10 units per hour.

19. Consider the schematic diagram shown in Figure 7-15. Can you improve it?

20. A manufacturing concern has four departments and the flow between combinations of departments is as follows:

From	To			
	A	B	C	D
A		2		2
B	2		4	
C		3		1
D	2		1	

a. Using the Operations Sequence Analysis technique, how should the departments be arranged?

b. Now suppose that the area requirements are as follows:
   Department A—3600 square feet
   Department B—2400 square feet
   Department C—2400 square feet
   Department D—1600 square feet
Sketch the block diagram based on your answer in a.

c. Now assume that the four departments are located in two separate buildings which are 100 feet apart. The two buildings have floor areas of 60 × 100 = 6000 square feet housing Departments A and C, and 40 × 100 = 4,000 square feet housing Departments B and D, respectively. What should be the space allocation to the four departments if the material handling costs are as follows:

From	To			
	A	B	C	D
A		1	1	2
B	1		1	2
C	1	1		2
D	2	2	2	

21. An organization does job machining and assembly, and wishes to relayout its production facilities so that the relative location of departments reflects somewhat better the average flow of parts through the plant. In Table 7-6 we show an operation sequence summary for a sample of seven parts, with approximate area requirements for each of the 13 machine or work centers. The numbers in the columns headed by each of the parts indicate the number of the work center to which the part goes next. Just below the sequence summary is shown a summary of production per month and the number of pieces handled at one time through the shop for each part.

   a. Develop a load summary showing the number of loads per month going between all combinations of work centers.

   b. Develop an idealized schematic layout that minimizes nonadjacent loads.

   c. Develop a block diagram that reflects the approximate area requirements, and which results in an overall rectangular shape.

TABLE 7-6   **Operations Sequence Summary for Problem 21**

Machine or Work Center	Area, Square Feet	Work Center Number	Part						
			A	B	C	D	E	F	G
Saw	50	1		2	2				2
Centering	100	2		4	3				3
Milling machines	500	3	5	9	5	5		4	4
Lathes	600	4		5,7	7		5	10	5
Drills	300	5	8	3	4	11	7		6
Arbor press	100	6					11		7
Grinders	200	7		12	12		6		8
Shapers	200	8	9			3			9
Heat treat	150	9	11	4					10
Paint	100	10						11	11
Assembly bench	100	11	12	13	13	13	13	13	12
Inspection	50	12	13	11	11				13
Pack	100	13							
Production Summary									
Pieces per month			500	500	1600	1200	400	800	400
Pieces per load			2	100	40	40	100	100	2
Loads per month			250	5	40	30	4	8	200

22. A layout study was made in the engineering office of a large aerospace manufacturer. Initially the study focused on the flow of work through the system, but it was difficult to generate meaningful cost data on this basis.

The search for realistic measures of effectiveness finally narrowed down to the relative location of people in the organization as required by their face-to-face contacts with others in the organization. It was decided to collect data on face-to-face contacts initiated by each person for a 1-month period, and to accumulate this data in the form of the matrix of Table 7-7. The entire department was divided into ten groups or areas as indicated in Table 7-7. Each cell value indicates the number of face-to-face contacts initiated by that group; for example, 15 from A to B. Table 7-8 summarizes the area requirements for each group as well as the average hourly wage paid in each group. Figure 7-18 shows the present block layout.

Prepare a new block layout within the constraints of the overall size of the layout shown in Figure 7-18.

SITUATIONS

23. Figure 7-1 relates the major elements of long-term strategic decisions to the productive system design. In the text, this diagram was discussed in terms of the development of BURGER, from its inception as an enterprise.

Now, think in terms of an existing product in its rapid developmental stage. The product is currently manufactured in five models, with two of the models accounting for 75 percent of the total output. Demand forecasts include a 20

TABLE 7-7   **Number of Face-to-Face Contacts per Month in an Engineering Office for Problem 22**

From	(A) Filing	(B) Supervision	(C) Blueprint	(D) Product Support	(E) Structural Design	(F) Electrical Design	(G) Hydraulic Design	(H) Production	(I) Detailing and Checking	(J) Secretarial Pool
A Filing		15				5		10		15
B Supervision	20		25	40	100	90	80	160	85	60
C Blueprint										
D Product Support	10	15					20	280		10
E Structural Design	50	20	600			40			340	50
F Electrical Design			475					160	270	60
G Hydraulic Design	10		460	20				140	320	45
H Production Liaison	20			200	160	190	240			680
I Detailing and Checking		210	690	40	190	240	80			20
J Secretarial Pool		25						15		

percent increase each year for the next 6 years. The existing manufacturing facilities are in New England, but the market is national, with a small export market. The present plant is expansible, with enough surrounding property to accommodate an ultimate tripling of volume. Hourly workers bargain collectively and are represented by an industrial union affiliated with the AFL. Labor relations are generally harmonious. The average weight of the product is 20 pounds, including packaging.

TABLE 7-8   **Area Requirements and Average Wage Rates for Ten Groups in a Large Engineering Office**

	Group	Area	Average Hourly Wage
A	Filing	20 × 15 = 300 sq. ft.	$2.25
B	Supervision	30 × 15 = 450 sq. ft.	5.00
C	Blueprinting	40 × 15 = 600 sq. ft.	2.10
D	Product support	25 × 20 = 500 sq. ft.	2.70
E	Structural design	65 × 25 = 1625 sq. ft.	4.50
F	Electrical design	25 × 35 = 875 sq. ft.	4.50
G	Hydraulic design	45 × 30 = 1350 sq. ft.	4.50
H	Production liaison	20 × 70 = 1400 sq. ft.	2.70
I	Detailing and checking	70 × 25 = 1750 sq. ft.	3.60
J	Secretarial pool	70 × 15 = 1050 sq. ft.	2.40
		90 × 110 = 9900 sq. ft.	

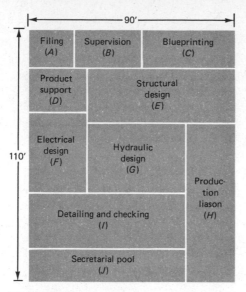

FIGURE 7-18
Existing block layout for ten groups within a large engineering office.

Management is considering scenarios for expansion and has asked a consulting firm for general proposals. Outline three scenarios that the company might use as a basis for planning. What are the advantages of each of your scenarios? What are the disadvantages and risks?

24. Following is a situation that occurred in the Hovey and Beard Company, as reported by J. V. Clark.*

This company manufactured a line of wooden toys. One part of the process involved spray painting partially assembled toys, after which the toys were hung on moving hooks that carried them through a drying oven. The operation, staffed entirely by women, was plagued with absenteeism, high turnover, and low morale. Each woman at her paint booth would take a toy from the tray beside her, position it in a fixture, and spray on the color according to the required pattern. She then would release the toy and hang it on the conveyor hook. The rate at which the hooks moved had been calculated so that each woman, once fully trained, would be able to hang a painted toy on each hook before it passed beyond her reach.

The women who worked in the paint room were on a group incentive plan that tied their earnings to the production of the entire group. Since the operation was new, they received a learning allowance that decreased by regular amounts each month. The learning allowance was scheduled to fall to zero in six months, since it was expected that the women could meet standard output or more by that time. By the second month of the training period, trouble had developed. The women had progressed more slowly than had been anticipated, and it appeared that their production level would stabilize somewhat

* From J. V. Clark, "A Healthy Organization," *California Management Review, 4,* 1962.

*below the planned level. Some women complained about the speed that was
expected of them, and a few of them quit. There was evidence of resistance to
the new situation.*

*Through the counsel of a consultant, the supervisor finally decided to bring
the women together for more general discussions of working conditions. After
two meetings in which relations between the work group and the supervisor
were somewhat improved, a third meeting produced the suggestion that control of the conveyor speed be turned over to the work group. The women
explained that they felt that they could keep up with the speed of the conveyor
but that they could not work at that pace all day long. They wished to be able
to adjust the speed of the belt, depending on how they felt.*

*After consultation, the supervisor had a control marked, "low, medium, and
fast" installed at the booth of the group leader, who could adjust the speed of
the conveyor anywhere between the lower and upper limits that had been set.
The women were delighted and spent many lunch hours deciding how the
speed should be varied from hour to hour throughout the day. Within a week,
a pattern had emerged: the first half-hour of the shift was run on what the
women called "medium speed" (a dial setting slightly above the point marked
"medium"). The next two and one-half hours were run at high speed, and the
half-hour before lunch and the half-hour after lunch were run at low speed.
The rest of the afternoon was run at high speed, with the exception of the last
45 minutes of the shift, which were run at medium speed.*

*In view of the women's report of satisfaction and ease in their work, it is
interesting to note that the original speed was slightly below medium on the
dial of the new control. The average speed at which the women were running
the belt was on the high side of the dial. Few, if any, empty hooks entered the
drying oven, and inspection showed no increase of rejects from the paint room.
Production increased, and within three weeks the women were operating at 30
to 50 percent above the level that had been expected according to the original
design.*

Evaluate the experience of the Hovey and Beard Company as it reflects on
job design, human relationships, and the supervisor's role. How would you
react as the supervisor to the situation where workers determine how the work
will be performed? If you were designing the spray painting setup, would you
design it differently?

25. The following situation is drawn from an article by G. Woolsey.*

*A Canadian manufacturer of heavy equipment had installed an automated
warehouse as a base for worldwide supply of spare parts for their equipment.
The automated system involved filling orders for spare parts that would ultimately be packed and shipped. Orders were coded by a clerk, indicating the
item and its location, using a keyboard and a cathode ray tube (CRT) information display. In the warehouse, forklift operators also had a small CRT on the
truck that listed the necessary items and locations to complete an order.*

The trucks were routed to the correct position in the warehouse by a com-

* From G. Woolsey, "Two Digressions on Systems Analysis: Optimum Warehousing and Disappearing
Orange Juice," *Interfaces,* 7 (2), February 1977, pp. 17–20.

puter, the trucks being guided by wires in the floor. On arrival at the correct location, the truck raised the operator automatically to the proper level, so that the item could be picked out of the bin. The truck operator then pressed a button to indicate that the particular item had been obtained. The computer then routed the truck and operator to the next station to pick another item. When all the items for an order had been filled, the computer routed the truck back to the packing and shipping location. The process was then repeated for the next order.

The only control that operators had over their trucks was a "kill" button that could stop them in case of an impending collision. This never happened, since the computer program knew the position of all trucks and programmed them around each other. If the operator stepped off the truck, a "dead man" control stopped the truck.

The automated system had replaced a conventional order picking system in which forklift truck operators performed essentially the same process manually.

On installation, the automated system ran smoothly with virtually zero errors in picking items. Then, however, errors increased to new record levels, absenteeism became a problem, and there were some examples of what appeared to be sabotage. The warehouse supervisor was particularly outraged because the company had agreed to a massive across-the-board pay increase for operators in order to get the union to accept the new computer system. The union had argued that the operators now worked with a computer and that the job was more complex.

What is the problem? Should the multimillion dollar automated system be scrapped? Should the jobs be redesigned? What do you propose?

26. Read the following excerpt from an article with these questions in mind:

    a. Is there a rational explanation for the situation described in the article? Should the system be redesigned to broaden jobs? Why? If you were a consultant to the owner-manager of the enterprise described, what would you recommend?

    b. If you were a worker in this kind of factory, what kinds of satisfaction would you be able to obtain from your work? Do you think that these kinds of satisfactions are adequate for the average industrial worker? How pervasive do you think the situation described is in American industry?

WORKING IN A SOUTHERN SWEATSHOP: A REPORT
*Mimi Conway**

Until the mid-1970s when I made the voluntary transition from professional-class suburbanite to piece-work employee in a Southern garment factory, a second was almost a meaningless unit of time. It was soon to become a very meaningful measure of my economic health and welfare.

I had been an investigative reporter of 10 years before I became dissatisfied with

* Reprinted with permission from: *Los Angeles Times* Opinion Section, Sunday, September 2, 1979.

the limitations of journalistic probings into the human condition. I wanted to write fiction, which is, to me, emotional truth. The novel I had in mind necessitated my capturing the rhythms of life on an American assembly line, the sort of life that this Labor Day weekend commemorates. For this purpose, and to earn a living while I wrote, I applied for factory work.

A small apparel factory hired me. When I walked into the windowless corrugated metal building in the industrial park on the outskirts of town—the workplace equivalent to the trailer camps that many of the apparel workers lived in—I began learning about working in America in a way new to me.

I began working as a "legger," simultaneously operating three hissing presses that put the permanent-press crease into military pants. "Making production" meant making perfect creases in 650 pant legs a day, 81 legs each hour, one leg every 42 seconds. In exchange for this I received $2.10 an hour, then the minimum wage.

I had not expected that the more experienced leggers would be generous and sharing with what they had learned about working optimally. The cooperative spirit among these workers surprised me. After all, I was an outsider and a Northerner.

On the other hand, I had not expected to find physical work so demanding. Clipboard and stop watch in hand, the absentee factory owner's relative would often pause by my presses suggesting how to save a few seconds in the way I smoothed the cloth before releasing the press hoods. Satisfied that I was working at my physical limit, he moved on to the next worker, and the next.

My goal was to work as fast as I could without either making mistakes or getting hurt. The hot metal hoods had no safety catches, and they sometimes crashed without warning. Like other leggers, I had mild burns on my fingers and arms. The knowledge that burned or bandaged hands made reaching my production quota impossible and the fear of being seriously hurt kept me alert. I did not want to be maimed as had leggers before me.

To get through the day, I learned to accept the pressure—a kind of numbed attentiveness—of working with dangerous equipment. And I became inured to the particular kind of sharp leg pains that come from standing on cement for eight and nine hours a day. I even joined the other workers in bolting down lunch in order to steal 10 minutes of our half-hour break back at the machines in order to fill our daily quota.

I had much more trouble accepting the fact that production levels were set by the fastest worker, although that is illegal. It was standard practice for the efficiency expert to revise the quota upward when too many workers were able to make it.

Nor did I get used to the fact that our employer guaranteed neither a steady paycheck nor fixed hours. When, for example, equipment broke down further up the line or insufficient material had not been prepared for the end-production workers to process, we were sent home in the middle of the day, without pay. More frequently, we were required to work overtime. What rankled was not being told about extra work until just before clock-out time, when the parking lot was already filled with waiting cars of cranky children and husbands needing to get to other factories for second-shift work. Most Friday afternoons we were told we had to work at least a half day on Saturday.

On the last line of production, where the temperature was constantly over 100 degrees, my fellow production workers, sweating women in sleeveless shirts, the "oven girl," the "bundle girls," the leggers and the "toppers"—were the youngest, strongest women in the plant. At the other end of the long room, where it was not suffocatingly hot, mostly older women bent over sewing machines, making pockets, button holes, zippers, belt loops, every component of military pants.

The factory was filled with long rows of toiling grandmothers, and daughters, sisters-in-law and cousins, all women except for the boss, the efficiency expert, the mechanics and some of the inspectors. In this small Southern factory, operating under a U.S. government contract, everyone was white except for two Asians and a single black woman.

The women I worked with had an attitude of strength and unity. Several times the best legger walked off her presses when one of the hoods thudded down unexpectedly; it gave others the courage to do the same. Another legger quit after getting a severe shock from the steam gun we used to remove imperfect creases. After that, we repeatedly complained to the plant manager about the condition of the equipment until it was repaired properly.

Much of what I learned in the apparel factory was from the women with whom I worked. But I never learned why all of us worked so hard. We knew that when our machines were broken, the allowances for "lost time" were insufficient. We knew we were making only the minimum wage. Yet we worked harder and harder, the only visible reward being the job well done, the satisfaction of making production, and, of course, the bottom line: keeping our jobs in a region and at a time when work was scarce. As best I could figure it, the women I worked with were courageous in trying to fight what they could and were silent in the face of what they were powerless to change alone.

At the time, I did not know that textiles are the bedrock of the Southern economy. The industry's $16 billion to $18 billion in sales annually is 30 percent to 50 percent higher than the volume of Southern agricultural sales. Textiles account for one-quarter of the jobs in five Southern states.

Nor did I know that textile manufacturers pay the lowest industrial wages in the nation. Mill workers earn $75 a week less than the average American factory worker. And textiles is the only major U.S. industry that is not unionized.

REFERENCES

Arcus, A. L., "COMSOAL: A Computer Method for Sequencing Operations for Assembly Lines," *International Journal of Production Research,* 4(4), 1966.

Armour, G. C., and E. S. Buffa, "A Heuristic Algorithm and Simulation Approach to Relative Location of Facilities," *Management Science,* 9(1), 1963, pp. 294–309.

Buffa, E. S., G. C. Armour, and T. E. Vollmann, "Allocating Facilities with CRAFT," *Harvard Business Review,* 42(2), March–April 1964, pp. 136–159.

Buxey, G. M., "Assembly Line Balancing with Multiple Stations," *Management Science,* 20(6), February 1974, pp. 1010–1021.

Chapanis, A., *Man-Machine Engineering.* Wadsworth, Belmont, Calif., 1965.

Davis, L. E., and J. C. Taylor, eds., *Design of Jobs.* Penguin Books, Middlesex, England, 1972.

Dar-El, E. M. (Mansoor), "MALB—A Heuristic Technique for Balancing Large Scale Single-Model Assembly Lines," *AIIE Transactions, 5*(4), December 1973.

Englestad, P. H., "Socio-Technical Approach to Problems of Process Control," in *Design of Jobs*, L. E. Davis, and J. C. Taylor, eds., Penguin Books, Middlesex, England, 1972.

Francis, R. L., and J. A. White, *Facility Layout and Location: An Analytical Approach.* Prentice-Hall, Englewood Cliffs, N.J., 1974.

Hicks, P. E., and T. E. Cowan, "CRAFT-M for Layout Rearrangement," *Industrial Engineering, 8,* May 1976, pp. 30–35.

Johnson, R., "Spacecraft for Multi-floor Layout Planning," *Management Science, 28*(4), April 1982.

Lee, R. C., and J. M. Moore, "COORELAP-Computerized Relationship Layout Planning," *Journal of Industrial Engineering, 18*(3), March 1967, pp. 195–200.

Lew, P., and P. M. Brown, "Evaluation and Modification of CRAFT for an Architectural Methodology," in *Emerging Methods in Environmental Design and Planning,* edited by G. T. Moore. MIT Press, Cambridge, Mass., 1970.

McCormick, E. J., *Human Factors Engineering* (3rd ed.). McGraw-Hill, New York, 1970.

Mansoor, E. M. (Dar-El), "Assembly Line Balancing—An Improvement on the Ranked Positional Weight Technique," *Journal of Industrial Engineering, 15*(5), March–April 1964.

Nugent, C. E., T. E. Vollmann, and J. Ruml, "An Experimental Comparison of Techniques for the Assignment of Facilities to Locations," *Operations Research, 16*(1), January–February 1968, pp. 150–173.

Ritzman, L. P., "The Efficiency of Computer Algorithms for Plant Layout," *Management Science, 18*(5), January 1972, pp. 240–248.

Scoville, J. G., "A Theory of Jobs and Training," *Industrial Relations, 9,* 1969, pp. 36–53. Also in L. E. Davis, and J. C. Taylor, eds. *Design of Jobs.* Penguin Books, Middlesex, England, 1972.

Vollmann, T. E., and E. S. Buffa, "The Facilities Layout Problem in Perspective," *Management Science, 12*(10), June 1966, pp. 450–468.

SUPPLEMENT

On Assembly Line Balancing

This supplement on assembly line balancing provides insight into the kinds of techniques used for balancing large assembly lines. To be useful for these large-scale problems, the techniques need to be computerized so that optimal solutions for such problems can be generated in a relatively short time.

There are many such techniques; however, we will present the basic COMSOAL, developed by Arcus [1966], and the basic Ranked Positional Weight Technique, followed by an improvement on that technique called MALB that has been computerized. The improvement by Mansoor [1964] went relatively unnoticed until it was computerized for large scale problems by Dar-El [1973]. (Dar-El and Mansoor

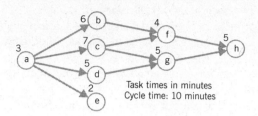

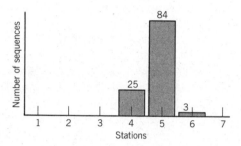

FIGURE 7-19

(*a*) Eight task precedence diagram, and (*b*) histogram of 112 feasible solutions for a 10-minute cycle time.
SOURCE: A. L. Arcus, "COMSOAL: A Computer Method for Sequencing Operations for Assembly Lines," International Journal for Production Research, Vol. 4, No. 4, 1966.

are the same person.) The computerized version appears to perform extremely well in comparison with the best previously known line balance methods. MALB is most easily explained by first presenting the basic Ranked Positional Weight Technique, including the method by which it has been improved.

COMSOAL

The basic methodology of COMSOAL developed by A. L. Arcus [1966], is based on the generation of a fairly large number of feasible solutions to the line balance problem by biased sampling. Alternate solutions to the particular line balance problem are then based on the best solutions generated. The sampling universe is all of the feasible solutions to the particular problem, there being a finite probability that optimal solutions will be generated, a slightly larger probability of "next best solutions," and so on. Of course, the sample size governs the probability of generating excellent solutions and the economic feasibility of the technique is in the process of generating feasible solutions rapidly, and biasing the generation of these solutions toward the better ones.

The simple example shown in Figure 7-19 illustrates the theory behind COMSOAL. Figure 7-19*a* shows a precedence diagram for an 8-task assembly job which is to be balanced for a 10-minute cycle time.* Arcus manually enumerated all of the

* The task times may be determined through a process known as work measurement. Appendix F, *"Work Measurement,"* provides a review of the methods of this process.

112 feasible combinations of the tasks which involved 4, 5, or 6 stations and Figure 7-19a shows the histogram of results. There were 25 solutions that used 4 stations, 84 that used 5 stations, and only 3 that used 6 stations. Obviously there are additional feasible solutions involving 7 and 8 stations, but they are not very interesting.

COMSOAL generates feasible solutions by the following general procedure:

Skip ↓

Step I

First, by scanning precedence information, list A is formed which tabulates the total number of tasks that immediately precede each given task. For the example of Figure 7-19a we have

List A Task	Total Number of Immediately Preceding Tasks
a	0
b	1
c	1
d	1
e	1
f	2
g	2
h	2

Step II

The computing routine then scans list A to identify all tasks that have no preceding tasks and places them in list B, the "available list." For our simple example, only task a meets these requirements so that list B is

(Available) List B	Task
	a

Step III

The available list B is then partitioned by placing in list C those tasks which have times no greater than the time left available at the station being assigned work. List C is called the "fit list" because only elements that fit the time left to be assigned within a station are listed. In our example, the available time at station 1 is 10 because no assignments have yet been made, and the time for task a in the list B is only three, so it is transferred to list C

(Fit) List C	Task
	a

Step IV

In the simplest form of COMSOAL, assignment is now made by selecting at ran-

229

Skip
↓

dom from the fit list a task to be assigned to station 1. Because only task *a* is in the fit list at this point, it is selected and assigned to station 1.

Step V

Eliminate task *a* from lists B and C (leaving them empty).

Step VI

Update list A by scanning the immediate followers of task *a* and deduct 1 from the tally of the "total number of preceding tasks" as follows:

List A Task	Total Number of Immediately Preceding Tasks
a	0
b	$1 - 1 = 0$
c	$1 - 1 = 0$
d	$1 - 1 = 0$
e	$1 - 1 = 0$
f	2
g	2
h	2

Step VII

Update the tasks available in list B by transferring from list A all tasks now listed as having no preceding tasks. List B becomes:

(Available) List B	Task
	b
	c
	d
	e

Step VIII

Transfer from list B to list C those tasks that fit the remaining time to be assigned to station 1, or $10 - 3 = 7$. Because in this instance all of the task times in list B are 7 or less, the fit list becomes

(Fit) List C	Task
	b
	c
	d
	e

Step IX

Select at random from list C a task to assign to station 1.

Step X

Eliminate the selected task from lists B and C. Repeat Steps VI through X until station 1 has been as fully assigned as it can be, and continue the procedure, station by station, until all elements are assigned.

As a solution is completed its station count is compared with the station count of the previous best sequence. If there is an improvement, the new solution is stored and the old one discarded. The result is that the computer memory holds no more than two solutions at any one time.

The COMSOAL procedure just outlined was simplified to facilitate the explanation. Actually, instead of selecting a task at random from the fit list, C, as mentioned in both steps IV and IX, the program biases the selection of the element by weighting the tasks in the fit list. A second variation from the procedure outlined provides for aborting a solution as soon as it becomes apparent that the accumulated idle time of the incomplete solution exceeds the total idle time of the previous best solution, because the solution being generated cannot be an improvement. The result of the aborting procedure is to save computer time and have that time spent in examining potentially better solutions.

The weighting procedure for biasing the selection of tasks from the fit list developed by Arcus is a product of the weights computed by the following five rules:

Rule 1

Weight tasks that fit in proportion to task time. The effect of this weighting is to give large tasks a greater probability of being assigned than small ones.

Rule 2

Weight tasks that fit by $1/X'$, where X' is equal to the total number of unassigned tasks minus 1, less the number of all of the tasks that follow the task being considered. The effect of Rule 2 is to give those tasks that have a large number of followers a greater probability of being assigned than tasks with a small number of followers.

Rule 3

Weight tasks that fit by the total number of all following tasks plus 1. The effect of this rule is to prefer tasks which, when selected, will be replaced and therefore expand the available list.

Rule 4

Weight tasks that fit by the times of the task and of all following tasks. The effect of this rule is to combine the advantages of Rules 1 and 3 by selecting large tasks early at each station in the entire sequence or, alternatively, by preferring tasks which, although small, tend to expand the available list.

Rule 5

Weight tasks that fit by the total number of following tasks plus 1, divided by the

231

number of levels that those following tasks occupy plus 1. The effect of this weight is to give tasks in the longest chains the greatest probability of being assigned first.

Results

The computer program designed to operate in the form just described, with the weighting and aborting procedures, is described by Arcus as being applicable to the sequencing and assembly line balance problem in simple form. Arcus applied the program to a 45-task example and produced optimal assignments. Arcus also applied the program to a 70-task example (22 stations) and to a 111-task industrial example (27 stations).

COMSOAL for the Balance Problem in Complex Form

Having found a computing procedure that produced optimal or near optimal solutions for basic line balance problems, Arcus proceeded to provide for a series of other more realistic constraints on the program. In essence, these constraints affect the fit list which must satisfy the new constraints in addition to those stated earlier. We shall not attempt to describe these additional constraints in detail, but the following list should serve to describe their general nature:

1. Tasks larger than the cycle time.
2. Tasks that require two workers.
3. Tasks fixed in location.
4. Space for parts.
5. Time to obtain a tool.
6. Time for the worker to change position.
7. Time to change the position of a unit. (Orientation of the unit being worked on.)
8. Grouping tasks by criteria.
9. Wages related to tasks.
10. Worker movement between units being assembled.
11. Mixed production on the same line.
12. Stochastic task performance times.

Arcus states that the earlier model of COMSOAL was implemented by Chrysler Corporation. Also, a hypothetical line with 1000 tasks and a known optimum of 200 stations with zero idle time has been run. In addition, a sequence requiring 203 stations resulting in 1.48 percent idle time was computed in about 2 minutes of IBM 7094 time, and, a line has been run with 111 tasks, 5 mixed products, and all of the complexities just listed.

One of the obvious advantages of a program such as COMSOAL for the production scheduling function in an enterprise is the rapidity with which we can call for alternate balance solutions in an attempt to provide the best possible way to adjust to changes in the employment level called for by aggregate plans. COMSOAL can also help in building the cost model required for the aggregate plan. It can evaluate the realistic cost effects of decisions for different production levels. Because the employment levels are not a continuous function of production rate, we need the actual number of employees required so we can determine the actual hiring and layoff costs that would be associated with decisions to change levels.

RANKED POSITIONAL WEIGHT TECHNIQUE

The basis for the assignment of tasks to stations for this rule is to determine weightings for each task based on the sum of the time to perform that task plus the performance times of all the tasks which follow it in the precedence chart. The tasks are then listed in descending order of the weights, together with corresponding immediate predecessor tasks. Tasks with the largest weights are then assigned to station 1, taking account of precedence constraints. When station 1 has assignments that fill the cycle time, then assignments are made to station 2 in the same way, and so on. Successive iterations may be made to determine the minimum cycle time for a given number of stations. This solution will give the most even distribution of work across stations.

An example will serve to explain the basic Ranked Positional Weight Technique, and the nature of the MALB improvement. Let us assume the balance problem posed by the precedence diagram of Figure 7-20. The numbers inside the circles are the task numbers, and those outside are the task performance times in seconds. Below the diagram we have calculated the positional weights, taking advantage of the fact that the weight for a task is its own task time plus the positional weight of the tasks which follow and are dependent on it. (Any duplications are eliminated.) Therefore, hand computing time is reduced by computing positional weights from right to left in the precedence diagram. Table 7-9 shows the positional weights in rank order with immediate predecessors indicated.

Next, consider the range of possible solutions. Note that the largest task time is $t = 45$ seconds for task No. 3, and the sum of all task times is 185 seconds. Therefore, the maximum number of stations that we wish to consider is $185/45 = 4.1$, or 4. We

TABLE 7-9	Tasks in Rank Order of Positional Weight, with Immediate Predecessors Indicated		
Task Number	Time Required, Seconds	Positional Weight	Immediate Predecessors
2	38	136	—
3	45	79	—
1	4	78	—
4	12	74	1, 2
5	10	68	2
6	8	62	4
7	12	58	5
8	10	54	6
9	2	46	7
10	10	44	8, 9
11	34	34	3, 10

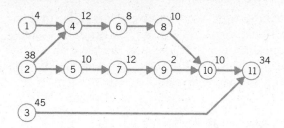

Task Number	Task Time	Plus Positional Weight of Task Number	Positional Weight
11	34	—	34
10	10	11	44
9	2	10	46
7	12	9	58
5	10	7	68
8	10	10	54
6	8	8	62
4	12	6	74
1	4	4	78
2	38	4, 5 (less times for Tasks 10 and 11)	136
3	45	11	79
	185 seconds		

FIGURE 7-20

Precedence diagram showing tasks required (circles with numbers), and technological sequence require-ments. Numbers outside circles are task times in seconds. Positional weights are calculated below the diagram as the sum of the task times plus the positional weights of the tasks that immediately follow (less any adjustments for duplications). For example, the times for tasks 10 and 11 are duplicated in the positional weights of tasks 4 and 5, therefore, in computing the positional weight for task 2 we have: 38 + 74 + 68 − (10 + 34) = 136.

could have, then 4, 3, 2, or 1 stations. Figure 7-21 shows the balance delay graphs for 4, 3, and 2 stations. Balance delay, *d,* is defined as

$$d = \frac{100(nc - \Sigma t_i)}{nc} \tag{1}$$

where $n =$ number of stations on the line
   $c =$ cycle time
   $t_i =$ task times

and *n, c,* and the t_i are integer numbers.

Note that the minimum possible balance delays in Figure 7-21 are 1.6, 0.5, and 0.5 percent for 4, 3, and 2 stations, respectively. Assume that output requirements are for approximately 40 units per hour; therefore, a cycle time in the range of 60 to 70 seconds would provide the needed capacity. From Figure 7-21, we see that a cycle time of 62 seconds will in fact produce a minimum balance delay with 3 stations. We will therefore determine balance for 3 stations with a minimum cycle time.

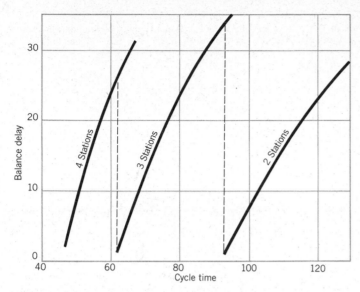

FIGURE 7-21
Balance delay graphs for the balance problem of Figure 7-19.

The basic procedure is then as follows:

1. Select the work time with the highest positional weight and assign it to the first work station.

2. Calculate the unassigned time for the work station by calculating the cumulative time for all tasks assigned to the station and subtract this sum from the cycle time.

3. Select the work unit with the next highest positional weight and attempt to assign it to the work station after making the following checks:

   a. Check the list of already assigned units. If the "immediate predecessor" tasks have been assigned, precedence will not be violated; proceed to step 3b. If the immediate predecessor tasks have not been assigned, proceed to step 4.

   b. Compare the task time with the unassigned time. If the task time is less than the station unassigned time, assign the task and recalculate unassigned time. If the task time is greater than the unassigned time, proceed to step 4.

4. Continue to select, check, and assign if possible until one of the two conditions has been met:

   a. All tasks have been assigned.

   b. No unassigned work unit remains that can satisfy both the precedence requirements and the "less than the unassigned time" requirement.

5. Assign the unassigned task with the highest positional weight to the second work station, and continue through the preceding steps in the same manner.

TABLE 7-10   **Assignments of Tasks to Stations by Rank Positional Weight Technique, for Three Stations, and a Cycle Time of $c = 64$ Seconds. Slack Time is $S = 7$ Seconds**

Task Number	Weight	Predecessors	Time	Cumulative Station Time	Unassigned Time	Remarks
			Assignments to Station 1			
2	136	None	38	38	26	Assigned
3	~~79~~	~~None~~	~~45~~	~~83~~		$> c$
1	78	None	4	42	22	Assigned
4	74	1, 2	12	54	10	Assigned
5	68	2	10	64	0	Assigned
			Assignments to Station 2			
3	79	None	45	45	19	Assigned
6	62	4	8	53	11	Assigned
7	~~58~~	~~5~~	~~12~~	~~69~~		$> c$
8	54	6	10	63	1	Assigned
			Assignments to Station 3			
7	58	5	12	12	52	Assigned
9	46	7	2	14	50	Assigned
10	44	8, 9	10	24	40	Assigned
11	34	3, 10	34	58	6	Assigned

6. Continue assigning tasks to stations until all tasks have been assigned. Using these assignment rules, we generate Table 7-10 as a solution to the problem. This is the best solution possible with these assignment rules. If one attempts solution at $c = 63$ seconds by the assignment rules, it is impossible to assign all tasks to only 3 stations. Referring to Figure 7-21, this solution for $c = 64$ seconds has a balance delay of 3.5 percent and slack units not assigned of $s = 7$ seconds.

MALB Assignment Rules

Dar El (Mansoor) improves on the solution presented in Table 7-10 by allowing backtracking after the initial assignments have been made to test other combinations of task times to see if they yield improvement. Dar-El's modified rules are as follows:

1. Begin by selecting the lowest cycle time corresponding to each of the number of work stations possible, for example, by reference to the balance delay graphs. Record the slack units available.

2. Select the task with the highest positional weight and assign it to the first work station.

3. Calculate the unassigned time for the station by calculating the cumulative time for all tasks assigned to the station and subtract this sum from the cycle time.

4. Select the task with the next highest positional weight and attempt to assign it to the station after making the following checks:

    a. Check the list of already assigned tasks. If the immediate predecessor tasks

Skip (to end)

TABLE 7-11   **Assignment of Tasks to Stations Resulting from Application of Dar-El's Rules, c = 62 seconds, S = 1 second in station 2**

Station 1		Station 2		Station 3	
Task Number	Time, Seconds	Task Number	Time, Seconds	Task Number	Time, Seconds
2	38	3	45	6	8
5	10	1	4	8	10
7	12	4	12	10	10
9	2		—	11	34
Totals	62		61		62

TABLE 7-12   **Comparative Results between Basic and MALB Assignment Rules for the Sample Problem in Figure 7-20**

	Basic Positional Weight Rules			MALB Assignment Rules		
	Number of Stations			Number of Stations		
	2	3	4	2	3	4
Minimum cycle time, seconds	97	64	52	94	62	48
Balance delay, percent	4.5	3.5	11	1.5	0.5	3.5
Unassigned slack time, seconds	9	7	23	3	1	7

have been assigned, precedence will not be violated; proceed to step 4b. If the immediate predecessor tasks have not been assigned, proceed to step 5.

b. Compare the task time with the unassigned time. If the task time is less than the station unassigned time, assign the task and recalculate unassigned time. If the task time is greater than the unassigned time, proceed to step 5.

5. Continue to select, check, and assign if possible until one of the two following conditions is met:

a. A combination is obtained where the remaining unassigned time is less than, or equals the slack units available (proceed to step 8).

b. No unassigned task remains that can satisfy both the precedence and the unassigned time requirements (proceed to step 6).

6. Cancel each assigned task in turn, starting with the one having the lowest positional weight (the last one assigned) and eventually working back, go through steps 4 and 5 until either:

a. A combination is obtained where the remaining unassigned time is less than or equals the slack units available (proceed to step 8).

b. All combinations possible have unassigned times in excess of the slack units available so that no solution is possible (proceed to step 7).

7. Select a cycle time having one more unit and start again with step 2.

8. Assign the unassigned task with the highest positional weight to the second station and proceed through the preceding steps in the same manner.

9. Continue assigning tasks to stations until all tasks have been assigned.

Note that rules 2, 3, 4, 5, 8, and 9 are the same as the rules for the basic procedure with a minor modification to rule 4. The important modifications are in rules 1, 6, and 7. Applying these rules to the same problem, Dar-El produces the solution shown in Table 7-11 with a cycle time of $c = 62$ seconds with one slack unit unassigned and a balance delay of only 0.5 percent. Dar-El shows similar results for 4 stations and 2 stations. The comparative results are shown in Table 7-12.

QUESTIONS AND PROBLEMS

1. In the COMSOAL model, what are the functions of lists A, B, and C?

2. In the most basic COMSOAL procedure, how are tasks selected from the fit list to assign to a station?

3. In the problem section of the chapter, Table 7-5 summarizes a list of tasks, performance times, and sequence restrictions for the assembly of a product. Assuming that the maximum station time is 10 minutes, develop the following: Lists A, B, and C for the initial assignments to station 1.

   a. Which tasks would be initially assigned to station 1, assuming that weights are assigned to tasks as the product of the five rules?

   b. Given whatever assignments to station 1 were made in (a), update Lists B and C. Can any additional assignments be made to station 1, using the same weighting procedure?

   c. When the line balance problem is stated in complex form, taking account of the 12 kinds of additional constraints, how is the basic COMSOAL procedure affected?

4. Using the basic Ranked Positional Weight Technique and the same data specified in Problem 3,

   a. Balance the line for a 10-minute cycle time. How many stations are required, and what balance delay results?

   b. Balance the line for a 9-minute cycle time. How many stations are required, and what balance delay results?

   c. Balance the line for a cycle time of 8 minutes. How many stations are required, and what balance delay results?

5. Using the solution for Problem 4(a) involving a cycle time of 10 minutes, can improvements be made using the MALB assignment rules?

PART
THREE

OPERATING DECISIONS

CHAPTER 8

Operations Planning and Control

WE NOW TURN OUR ATTENTION TO THE SHORTER-TERM, DAY-to-day, month-to-month kinds of decisions that bear on operations planning and control. Given the strategy, capacities, distribution system, and physical system, what kinds of plans are necessary for effective operation, what kinds of controls are necessary, and what are the criteria by which we select from among alternate plans and controls?

Part Three is concerned with such questions as: What should be our positioning policy: manufacture to stock, or to order? For a service organization, should the service be available on demand, or only on order? What policies and procedures will guide us in setting basic activity rates? Should we hire or lay off personnel, and in what numbers? When is using overtime justified instead of increasing the size of the work force? When should we take the risk of accumulating seasonal inventories to stabilize employment? How big should inventories be to sustain the production and distribution system? What policies and procedures are appropriate for controlling inventories and reordering materials? What policies and procedures are necessary to schedule workers and equipment for effective operations? Should the utilization of workers and machines be maximized, or is there a value to idleness? How do we maintain the reliability of the productive system so that specified quantity and quality are produced? When is a preventative maintenance policy justified? What policies and procedures can be effective in controlling labor and other costs? Is it possible to control costs, or is it actually the activities that must be controlled?

In this chapter we introduce some of the basic concepts of operations planning and control.

POSITIONING POLICY

We return to the topic of system classification discussed in Chapter 2. Recall that we classified systems as either process focused, or product focused. This classification is largely a function of the process technology and the way it is organized to achieve goals with respect to chosen markets.

Recall that we used a process-focused system when demand on individual processes was intermittent, that is, when the demand for the use of the process for any particular item would not be continuous, therefore, not justifying the dedication of that process to that item. In order to have reasonable utilization of the process, we routed all items requiring the process to it, so that the process becomes a functional unit or department in the productive system, and the physical layout is termed *functional*. Common examples are lathe, milling, and inspection departments in a machine shop; or X-ray, laboratory, surgery, and intensive care wards in a general hospital.

When demand on processes by a product is continuous, we can organize facilities for a product focus, resulting in an in-line sequence of operations, all dedicated to the particular product. Recall that the physical layout is then termed a *line or product* layout.

In Chapter 2, we then developed Table 2-1, showing examples of systems for each situation (demand on facilities is either intermittent or continuous) and for another set of conditions depending on whether or not the output of the system was inventoriable. The latter classification in that instance reflected a physical ability to inventory the output or not. That is, one cannot produce custom parts, large-scale projects, cured patients, or social security service to stock.

Now, let us consider only those products that *could* be produced to stock; that is, a decision is possible. In such situations, managers may decide to produce only to order for a variety of important reasons, even though it would be possible to produce to stock. The possible reasons for a to-order policy might be to offer product design flexibility to customers, to minimize the risk associated with carrying inventories, to control quality more closely, and so on. On the other hand, managers might decide to adopt a to-stock policy for the same type of product for good and compelling reasons; for example, to offer better service in terms of availability, to reduce variable costs, and to increase market share by making items available off-the-shelf when customers have the urge to buy.

The choice between a to-order or to-stock production policy is not necessarily made by whether or not a product- or process-focused physical system has been adopted. For example, one might think that the auto industry, which has adopted a product-focused system, would certainly be a to-stock producer. But this has not been the case uniformly. Until the auto inventory crisis in the late 1970s, Chrysler produced to-stock, but G.M. and some others produced to-order. It may be easy to envision how Chrysler could produce to stock, because there is obviously a great deal of product standardization. It may be more difficult to envision how G.M. could produce only to order, since although standardized, there are a great many options to choose from: color, style, engine size, and so on. But G.M. and some others produce each car to a specific order, depending on computer-based information systems to match production with orders. Dealers may place orders for cars that they have not yet sold, of course, but they would then own that inventory—the producer would not take the inventory risk.

To summarize, then, we have the possibility of two types of systems, product or process focused, in combination with two possible positioning policies, to-stock or to-order, as shown in Table 8-1, together with examples.

TABLE 8-1   **Positioning Policy versus Type of System**

Type of System	Positioning Policy	
	Make To-Stock	Make To-Order
Product Focused	*Product-Focused/To-Stock* Office copiers TV sets Calculators Gasoline Wholesalers Distributors	*Product-Focused/To-Order* Construction equipment Buses, trucks Experimental chemicals Textiles Wire and cable Electronic components
Process Focused	*Process-Focused/To-Stock* Medical instruments Test equipment Electronic components Some steel products Molded plastic parts Spare parts	*Process-Focused/To-Order* Machine tools Nuclear pressure vessels Electronic components Space shuttle Ships Construction projects

A reason for emphasizing the to-stock/to-order positioning policy at this point is that the management systems for planning and controlling production, scheduling, and inventory policy are very different, depending on the positioning decision. A to-stock policy results in each item being indistinguished from the others, so planning and controls can deal with all like items in the same way. A to-order policy means that each order must be controlled separately in a much more complex way; we must be able to respond to individual customers concerning the progress of an order, to quote delivery dates, and control the progress of each order through the plant.

In practice, the positioning policy allows a combination of both to-stock and to-order operations, because many organizations actually engage in a mixture of product-market situations. Consequently, it is important for managers to realize that even though outputs may appear similar on the surface, very different management procedures are usually necessary because of the different policy contexts in which the products are produced.

NATURE OF THE PRODUCTION-DISTRIBUTION SYSTEM

In order to understand scheduling and control problems, we need to understand the overall flow and appreciate the importance of system inventories, and the system dynamics. Figure 8-1 represents the production-distribution system for an inventori-

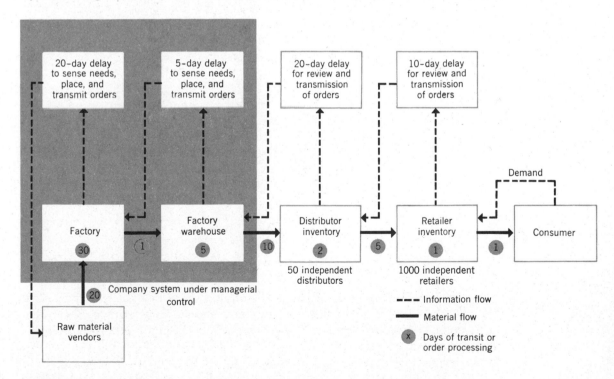

FIGURE 8-1
Production-distribution system for high-volume continuous system showing broad flow of materials and information, transit times, and order processing delays. (System flow rate averages 4000 units per week.)   243

able item such as a small appliance. The flow and major functions performed are shown, together with information flow required for the replenishment of inventories. There are 1000 independent retailers, 50 independent distributors, and a single factory in the system. Each of the distribution steps involves a stock point for the finished product. Therefore, one way of looking at the distribution system downstream from the factory is to envision it as a *multistage* finished goods inventory system.

We assume that each retailer replenishes inventory *periodically* and has a replenishment cycle that involves the review of demand and inventory status, transmission of orders to the supplying distributor, and the filling and shipping of orders by the distributor. Similarly, each distributor has a similar periodic replenishment cycle, based on the assessment of demand from retailers, the transmission of orders to the factory warehouse, followed by the filling and shipping of the orders. Similar periodic cycles are required for the factory warehouse in ordering from the factory and for the factory itself in ordering raw materials from vendors.

In a sense, inventories make possible a rational to-stock productive system. Without them we could not achieve smooth flow, obtain reasonable utilization of facilities, or expect to give reasonable service in terms of off-the-shelf availability. At each stage of both manufacturing and distribution, inventories *decouple* the various operations in the sequence. By providing a buffer, or cushion, between each pair of activities, inventories make the required operations sufficiently independent of each other so that low cost operations can be carried out. For example, with inventories the warehousing operation can proceed relatively independently of manufacturing. Similarly, the existence of inventories at the retail level makes it possible to carry on that function relatively independently; replenishment stocks can be ordered only periodically.

Thus, when raw materials are ordered, a supply is ordered that is large enough to justify the out-of-pocket cost of putting through the order and transporting it to the plant. When production orders to manufacture parts and products are released, they are made large enough to justify the cost of writing the orders and setting up machines. Running parts through the system continuously (or in batches) tends to reduce handling costs. Similarly, in distributing finished products to warehouses and other stock points, freight and handling costs per unit are lower if we ship in quantity. Therefore, although inventories are costly, they are vital to low cost manufacture and distribution.

SYSTEM INVENTORIES

Using Figure 8-1, let us examine the kinds of inventories that occur in the system. Our concern will be mainly with the physical flow and the information system related to inventory replenishment. Some inventory will be required just to fill the flow pipelines of the system, another component to take account of the periodic nature of the ordering cycles, and a third component to absorb random fluctuations in demand. Depending on the nature of the policies for factory scheduling, additional seasonal inventories might also be required.

TABLE 8-2   **Summary of Pipeline Inventory Requirements for Finished Goods**
(average system flow rate is 4000 units per week)

	Average Transit Delay Time, Days	Average Pipeline Inventory, Units (4000 × Days/7)
Factory to factory warehouse	1	571
Delays at factory warehouse	5	2,857
Warehouse to distributors	10	5,714
Delays at distributors	2	1,143
Distributors to retailers	5	2,857
Delays at retailers	1	571
Retailers to customers	1	571
Totals	25	14,284

Pipeline Inventories

If the average system flow rate is 4000 units per week and it takes 1 day to transport the products from the factory to the warehouse, then there are an average of 4000/7 = 571 units per day in motion in the factory to warehouse pipeline at all times. If the order processing delay due to handling at the factory warehouse is another 5 days (from Figure 8-1), then there are an average of 4000 (5/7) = 2857 units tied up in the warehouse segment of the pipeline at all times because of the delay.

Table 8-2 summarizes the pipeline inventory requirements for finished goods at each stage in the system, indicating an average of 14,284 units required just to fill the pipelines. These inventories cannot be reduced, unless transit times, delays, or handling times can be reduced. Pipeline inventories are proportional to the system flow rate and the physical flow time. If the system flow rate increases, pipeline inventories must increase to keep the system functioning.

Cycle Inventories

We will assume that inventory replenishment is periodic, that is, a decision is made once each period (weekly, biweekly, monthly, etc.) to determine how much to order. The average order size is then set by the ordering frequency and requirements at each stage. (We will consider alternate ordering methods in Chapter 10.)

The average retailer orders once every 2 weeks following a review of sales. Note that once an order is placed the information and physical flow cycle follows that shown in Figure 8-1. The ordering cycle, however, is on a regular 2-week basis and is not altered by the delays shown. Therefore, when a retailer orders, it must be for a 2-week supply, just to meet average demand.

The average retailer sells 4000/1000 = 4 units per week, or 8 units during the 2-week ordering cycle. No less than 8 units must be on hand to service sales during the replenishment period, and the *average* inventory for this purpose is half this amount, or $\bar{I} = 4$ units, as shown in Figure 8-2. The cycle inventory for the system of 1000 retailers is then $4 \times 1000 = 4000$ units. (Details for these concepts will be discussed in Chapter 10.) Table 8-3 summarizes the cycle inventory requirements of

TABLE 8-3   **Summary of Cycle Inventory Requirements for Finished Goods**
(average system flow rate is 4000 units per week)

	Reorder Cycle Time, Weeks	Average Cycle Inventory, Units
1000 Retailers	2	4,000
50 Distributors	4	8,000
Factory warehouse	6	12,000
Total		24,000

the system, showing that an average of 24,000 units is required in inventory because of the periodic nature of ordering.

Buffer Inventories

Buffer inventories are designed to absorb random fluctuations in final customer demand, thereby decoupling supply operations from the effects of demand variability. The size of these inventories depends on the nature of the demand distribution and the established service levels. The buffer stock needed to cushion the effects of greater than expected demand is the difference between the maximum reasonable demand and the average demand during the supply lead time.

Suppose, for example, that management wants to limit the chance of stock-out to 5 percent, and that from the demand distribution for the average retailer, the probability of a demand of 18 units or less is 95 percent during the 17-day supply lead time. Therefore, the maximum reasonable demand during the supply lead time is $D_{max} = 18$ units. This is consistent with management's willingness to run out of stock 5 percent of the time. Because the average demand during the supply lead time is $\bar{D} = 9.7$ units, the required buffer stock would then be $B = 18 - 9.7 = 8.3$ units, as shown in Figure 8-3. (Details for these concepts will be discussed in Chapter 10.) The average system buffer stock for 1000 retailers is then $8.3 \times 1000 = 8300$ units. Table 8-4 shows the computation of buffer stocks for finished goods for the system as a whole, 20,229 units.

TABLE 8-4   **Summary of Buffer Inventory Requirements for Finished Goods**
(average system flow rate is 4000 units)

	Average Demand per Week, $\bar{D}$	Lead Time, Days	Average Demand During Lead Time, $(\bar{D}/7) \times LT$	Maximum Demand During Lead Time	Average System Buffer Stock, Units
1000 Retailers	4	17	9.7	18	8,300
50 Distributors	80	35	400.0	550	7,500
Factory warehouse	4000	36	20,571.4	25,000	4,429
Total					20,229

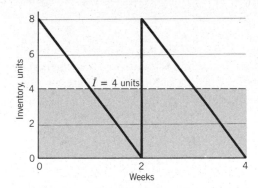

FIGURE 8-2
Average retailer's cycle stock.

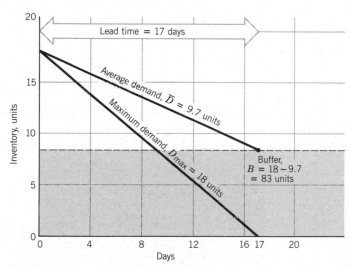

FIGURE 8-3
Average retailer's buffer stock.

System Finished Goods Inventories

Summarizing, the finished goods inventories for the system as a whole needed to accommodate all three functions are as follows:

1. Pipeline inventories   14,284
2. Cycle inventories   24,000
3. Buffer inventories   20,229
    Total   58,513

These inventories are required by the assumed structure of the system and the ordering rules and service levels used. They represent the minimum possible amounts necessary to operate the system. Inventories might be larger than this

minimum if controls were not effective or if seasonal inventories were also accumulated in the system.

The impact of inventories on the problem of scheduling the factory is emphasized
when one notes that ordinarily management has control over only approximately
one-third of the total system inventories, the balance being in the distribution system
under the control of independent wholesalers and retailers.

SYSTEM DYNAMICS

What is the impact of activities downstream in the production-distribution system on
factory scheduling? To answer this question, we focus our attention again on the
multistage system diagrammed in Figure 8-1.

Suppose that consumer demand falls by 10 percent from its previous rate. During
the next inventory review the retailer reflects this 10 percent decrease in orders for
replenishment sent to the distributor, but 10 days have elapsed. Similarly, the
distributor reflects the decrease in the next orders to the factory warehouse for replenishment, but an additional 20 days have elapsed before the factory warehouse
will be aware of the impact of the fall in sales. Adding up all the time delays in the
information system, the factory will not learn of the 10 percent fall in demand until
35 days have passed. Meanwhile, the factory has been producing $1.00/0.90 = 1.11$
times the new consumer requirement (111 percent). An excess of 11 percent would
have accumulated each day in inventory at the various stock points. The system
inventory will have increased to $11 \times 35 = 385$ percent of the usual normal day's
supply.

In order to react to the change, retailers, distributors, and the factory warehouse
decrease the quantities ordered. To take account of the excess inventory, the factory
will now have to cut back by substantially more than 10 percent. The effect of the
information time lags in the system is to amplify the original 10 percent change at the
consumer level. The change in production levels is much greater than would have
seemed justified by immediate feedback of the simple 10 percent decrease in consumer demand, and inventories have increased instead of decreased. A more rapid
communication of changes in demand can reduce the magnitude of this amplification
and eliminate the boom-to-bust swings in factory activity.

Figure 8-4 is identical to Figure 8-1 with the exception that a more direct information feedback loop has been added in the form of a system for assessing actual
demand and forecasting demand for the upcoming period. The 10-day delay in
communicating the actual demand and forecasting information reduces the total
delay by 25 days. A 10 percent decrease in sales under this system would mean an
excess inventory of only $11 \times 10 = 110$ percent of the normal levels would accumulate before the factory was aware of the demand change. The more rapid feedback thus stabilizes the levels of inventories and factory activity.

COMPREHENSIVE PLANNING FOR PRODUCTION

In addition to the more direct information feedback of forecast information as shown
in Figure 8-4, there are planning actions that managers take to react appropriately to

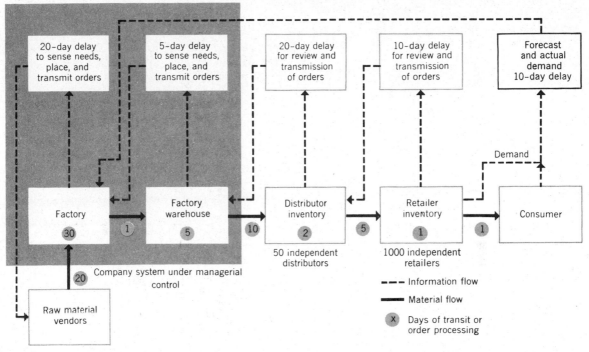

FIGURE 8-4
Production-distribution system with information feedback loop provided by forecasts and up-to-date information concerning actual consumer demand.

the market demands. First, how do the forecasts translate into aggregate schedules of production activity, and numbers of workers required? What is the most appropriate use of the sources of short-term capacity such as regular time, overtime, seasonal inventories, and possible outside capacity sources, such as subcontracting? Given these kinds of decisions, a *master schedule* of what is to be produced and when must be developed. The master schedule then becomes the basis for other plans that must be carefully coordinated, such as material procurement, plans to hire or lay off workers, and detailed schedules for staffing. The broad outlines of this process are shown in Figure 8-5 for the same production-distribution system we have been using as an example.

Operations Planning and Control Systems

Figure 8-6 presents the broad relationships of the plans and controls for the operations phase of a productive activity. Physically, the productive process is a transformation or conversion process, as shown in Chapter 1. Above the productive process shown in Figure 8-6, we have outlined the planning processes in block form. The basis for planning centers in forecasts is covered in Chapter 3.

Based on forecasts, we must make aggregate plans and schedules. These aggregate plans set the basic activity and personnel levels in the short term—they represent short-term capacity decisions. Such decisions involve determining whether to

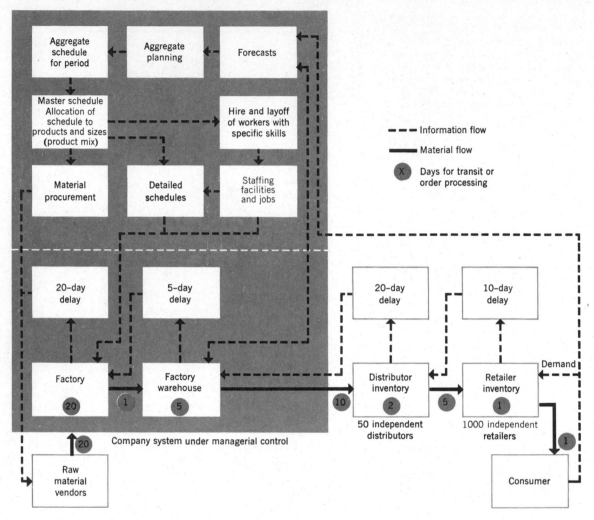

FIGURE 8-5
Relationship of forecasts, aggregate scheduling, and detailed scheduling to a production-distribution system.

enlarge or contract the size of the labor force, how much to use overtime capacity, and if we are dealing with a to-stock product, whether to build or draw down inventories. Aggregate plans (see Chapter 9) become the basis for other plans, such as raw material ordering and inventories, equipment, and detailed personnel schedules.

Below the productive process in Figure 8-6 are the systems for controlling the quality, quantity, and costs for the plans made. As in all kinds of control processes, we need a way of monitoring the aspects over which we wish to establish control, and we need standards for comparison. The control system makes comparisons, interprets results, and takes action to readjust processes to conform to standards. Management attempts to achieve a system optimum by means of various types of controls. Inventories are significant in many systems, and Chapter 10 considers the

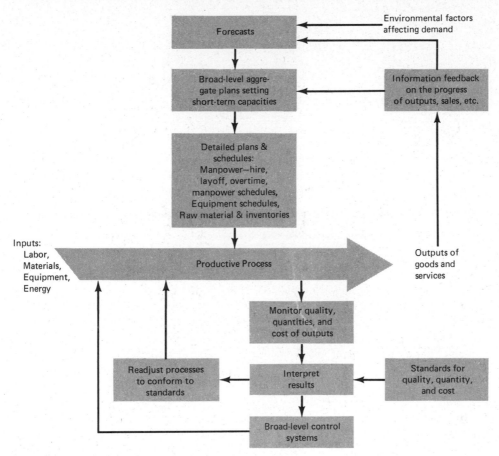

FIGURE 8-6
Operations planning and control systems.

functions and control models for inventories. Industrial planning, scheduling, and control systems are the subject of Chapters 11 and 12, and Chapter 13 discusses project planning and control. Some of the special problems of service systems are covered in Chapter 14, and finally, the concepts and methods for maintaining system reliability are discussed in Chapter 15.

THE MATERIALS MANAGER—AN EMERGING ORGANIZATIONAL CONCEPT

In the traditional manufacturing organizational form, we would expect to find the main functions of purchasing, manufacturing, marketing, personnel, and finance on a level with each other, as in Figure 8-7. Then, production planning and inventory control would report to the manufacturing function, and distribution and traffic would report to marketing. Of course, there have been wide variations in this general organizational form in practice. Functionally, this traditional form makes a great deal of sense. After the product is produced, it is turned over to the marketing function for distribution. Purchasing is seen as a separate function in this structure.

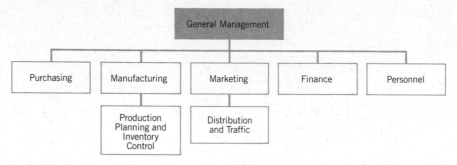

FIGURE 8-7
Traditional organizational structure.
SOURCE: *Adapted from: J. G. Miller, and P. Gilmour, "Materials Managers: Who Needs Them,"* Harvard Business Review, *July–August 1979.*

Beginning perhaps in the early 1960s, the concept of the materials manager developed. The concept was that one person should control all of the activities that dealt with the physical flow of materials. The theory behind the concept was that purchasing, production, and distribution were not actually separate activities, but three aspects of the same broad activity. The experiences that triggered this development were the problems with excess inventory, especially during times of changing demand (see our preceding comments on systems dynamics), meeting customer promised delivery dates, and so on. In the traditional structure, there were coordination slips between the separate functions. The structure illustrated by Figure 8-8 was created in an attempt to integrate the activities involved with material flow, and the materials manager position was born. In this integrated form of the materials management structure, the materials manager has co-equal status with the other main functions, and has overall responsibility for purchasing, production planning and inventory control, and distribution and traffic.

In a survey conducted by Miller and Gilmour [1979], over 50 percent of the organizations now have a materials manager in some form. This is in contrast to a survey taken in 1967, where only 3 percent reported the use of materials managers

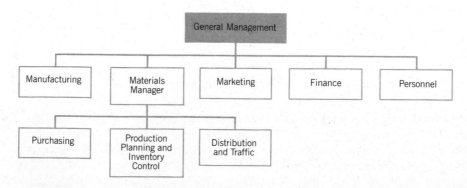

FIGURE 8-8
Integrated materials management structure.
SOURCE: *Adapted from: J. G. Miller, and P. Gilmour, "Materials Managers: Who Needs Them,"* Harvard Business Review, *July–August 1979.*

in their organizations. The integrated form accounted for 31 percent of the reporting companies where a materials manager existed. Miller and Gilmour found not only the integrated form of the concept of Figure 8-8, but variations that gave particular organizational emphasis to distribution, supply, or manufacturing.

Distribution Emphasis

Organizations that gave a distribution emphasis had materials managers whose span of control included production planning and inventory control, and distribution and traffic. With the materials managers being able to integrate these two functions, they were closer to and more sensitive to markets than sources of supply. Organizations with the distribution emphasis accounted for 23 percent of the companies with materials managers.

Supply Emphasis

Organizations that emphasized raw material and other supplies had materials managers in a structure that integrated purchasing with the production planning and inventory control as being closest to the supply sources, with distribution reporting elsewhere. This structure accounted for 18 percent of the companies with materials managers.

Manufacturing Emphasis

Manufacturing is in the middle of the materials flow, so this structure integrated production planning and control with the manufacturing function, and accounted for 28 percent of the materials managers in the survey.

There are controversial aspects to the materials manager concept. Marketing managers often resist implementation of the concept on the grounds that it places too much power and influence in one person's hands. The counter argument should not be one of the balance of power and influence, but the appropriate choice of an organizational structure for operations and other functions consistent with the external environment of the organization and its chosen strategies.

OPERATIONS/MARKETING INTERFACE

The major decisions in the production/operations function almost invariably have impact on the marketing function in some way. If production plans call for layoffs, reducing overtime allocations, and the drawing down of seasonal inventories, the marketing function may find that their customer promises cannot be met, that delivery times are inordinately long, or that products are available off-the-shelf, but they are the wrong products in the mix.

Taking the other point of view, the marketing forecasts are often wide of the mark, both in terms of the aggregate, but particularly for individual products in the mix. To provide good delivery service on a wide variety of items requires large inventories, under these conditions. We have the basis for conflict between the two functions,

253

and mechanisms for cooperation need to be established. The areas of potential conflict also extend into quality control, cost control, new product introduction, and adjunct services as indicated in Table 8-5.

The explanation for why the conflicts should develop are several. There are different reward and incentive structures for managers in the two functions. There is inherent complexity resulting from two different functions being involved, and there is a lack of exposure of managers in each function to the real problems of the other; normally marketing managers have developed without manufacturing experience, and vice versa.

There should be neither a sales dominance nor a manufacturing dominance. The firm has profit motives that are not normally achieved through maximizing sales at the expense of high cost, nor minimizing costs at the expense of revenue, but achieving a balance.

Both functions need to be a part of the generation of the overall strategy of the firm as we discussed in Chapter 2. What is the joint strategy? Is it to provide limited variety at low cost, available off-the-shelf, or is it to provide customers with options in

---

TABLE 8-5 **Areas of Operations/Marketing Interface Requiring Cooperation with Potential Conflict**

Problem Area	Typical Marketing Comment	Typical Manufacturing Comment
1. Capacity planning and long-range.	"Why don't we have enough capacity?"	"Why don't we have accurate sale forecasts?"
2. Production scheduling and short-range sales forecasting.	"We need faster response. Our lead times are ridiculous."	"We need realistic customer commitments and sales forecasts that don't change like wind direction."
3. Delivery and physical distribution.	"Why don't we ever have the right merchandise in inventory?"	"We can't keep everything in inventory."
4. Quality assurance.	"Why can't we have reasonable quality at reasonable cost?"	"Why must we always offer options that are too hard to manufacture and that offer little customer utility?"
5. Breadth of product.	"Our customers demand variety."	"The product line is too broad—all we get are short uneconomical runs."
6. Cost control.	"Our costs are so high that we are not competitive in the marketplace."	"We can't provide fast delivery, broad variety, rapid response to change, and high quality at low cost."
7. New product introduction.	"New products are our life blood."	"Unnecessary design changes are prohibitively expensive."
8. Adjunct services such as spare parts inventory support, installation, and repair.	"Field service costs are too high."	"Products are being used in ways for which they weren't designed."

SOURCE. B. P. Shapiro, "Can Marketing and Manufacturing Coexist?" *Harvard Business Review,* September–October 1977, pp. 104–114. Reprinted by permission of the *Harvard Business Review.* Copyright © 1977 by the President and Fellows of Harvard College; all rights reserved.

product design with flexibility and service? Is competition focused in low cost and availability, or in innovation and flexibility? What is the production function really good at? What is the marketing function really good at? Do the competencies of each fit in with the corporate strategy? Top managers need to strive for cooperation between the two functions, in part by including both in strategy generation. If both functions are involved in the generation of the strategy, then there will at least be an understanding about goals that should form the basis for cooperation.

SERVICES, UNIQUE FEATURES FOR PLANNING AND CONTROL

The special characteristics of service and nonmanufacturing operations that need to be taken into account in problems of planning and scheduling are as follows:

1. The output cannot be inventoried.
2. Extremely variable demand on a short-term basis, but often weekly and seasonal variations as well. Backlogging and/or smoothing of demand is often difficult or impossible.
3. Operations are usually labor intensive.
4. The location of service operations is dictated by the location of users.

Problems Resulting from a Noninventoriable Output

Unlike physical products, services are consumed in the process of their production. In manufacturing systems, the decoupling function of inventories allows us to carry on each set of activities relatively independently. We use buffer inventories to decouple demand variations from operations and to provide good delivery service. We use seasonal inventories to buffer the effects of seasonal variations in demand on employment levels and to minimize peak physical capacity requirements.

Therefore, in service systems, one of the most important strategies for manipulating short-term capacity in aggregate planning and scheduling is absent. The strategic alternatives that remain in aggregate planning are: hiring and layoff of personnel, use of part-time employees, overtime, and in some instances actually scheduling demand to conform to resources by using a reservation system. With no inventory buffering, it is likely that the full impact of demand variations is transmitted to the operating system.

Problems Resulting from Demand Variability

In the telephone industry, it is not uncommon for calls made during the busiest hour of each week within a year to vary by a factor of 1.38 to 1 (peak to valley); the Saturday and Sunday call load constitutes only about 55 percent of that of the typical weekday; and the peak-to-valley variation during a typical day varies by a factor of 128 to 1. The demand for fire protection in New York City on an average day reveals that the peak is 7.7 times the minimum fire alarm rate. The demand for emergency medical service in Los Angeles has been shown to vary from a low of 0.5 calls per hour at 6 A.M. to a peak of 3.5 calls per hour at 5:30 P.M., a ratio of 7 to 1. As a result of day-end mailing practices by business, 40 to 60 percent of letters brought to the post office plus that collected from local mail boxes is received between 4:00 and 8:00 P.M.

The previous examples represent some of the most extreme cases. Unlike most manufacturing systems, however, inventories cannot buffer variation in demand for service from the service producing system. Therefore, one of the significant problems for service system managers is to devise buffering systems. In many medical service systems, this may be accomplished through scheduling office appointments and by treatment priority systems. In hospitals, scheduled admissions can be manipulated to smooth occupancy level. In most instances, however, the dominant available strategies used to cope with demand variability are queuing, when possible, personnel scheduling, and more careful control of product price and promotion.

Problems Resulting from Labor Intensiveness

Traditionally, manufacturing has enjoyed a continuous increase in productivity, stemming from the substitution of other forms of energy for human energy and from mechanization and automation. By contrast, education, medical service, the postal service, and most other labor intensive service activities have recorded very small productivity increases. For example, during the period of 1956 to 1967, productivity in U.S. industry increased 34 percent, whereas productivity in the U.S. Postal Service increased only 4 percent. Wage increases in service operations translate almost directly into increased costs and prices.

Although the overall demand for services has increased tremendously, service systems can expand only by hiring more labor. The result has often been massive problems of scheduling an army of individual workers. There have been few economies of scale, nor is there a likelihood that there will be future economies of scale. Mechanization and automation are unlikely mechanisms for reducing the strains imposed by greater and greater demands for services. Some of the logical alternatives are more efficient use of personnel through scheduling and other management techniques.

Problems Resulting from System Location

The very nature of service and nonmanufacturing operations is such that they must be decentralized and geographically dispersed to be available to users. This means that each unit is relatively small in scale, and so suffers all the economic consequences of small-scale operations. One of these consequences has been that the aggregate and detailed scheduling techniques used have often been those appropriate for handicraft industries.

The result of the situation for service organizations is that managers are much more restricted in what can be done to plan and control operations effectively. The fact that the output cannot be inventoried removes the option of using inventory as a short-term source of capacity. When this factor is combined with extreme demand variation and labor intensive operations, the most effective technique to plan and control operations may be simply personnel scheduling. The fact that markets are local in nature prevents the development of large, efficient units, and the use of more sophisticated planning and control methods.

IMPLICATIONS FOR THE MANAGER

Positioning Policy. One of the really important decisions for managers of manufacturing operations is whether to adopt a to-stock or to-order positioning policy. In general, we assume that systems that produce high-volume standardized products will produce to stock, and systems that produce low-volume products with greater variety will produce to order. But there are exceptions to both of these situations. For example, many segments of the steel industry produce to order, and producers of lower volume products often specialize in a segment of the industry to gain a competitive edge in that segment by offering off-the-shelf availability and lower price. In addition, between the extremes, there is the bulk of products produced in batches. Here, the issue is whether to produce the batch to-stock, or to accumulate orders until an economical batch can be produced.

The to-stock/to-order managerial decision rests on trade-offs between a number of conflicting advantages and disadvantages. There are market advantages to having products available off-the-shelf, but there are inventory risks. If the product is subject to obsolescence, the inventory risk may be substantial. There may be manufacturing cost reductions possible in manufacturing to stock, but are the risks worth it on balance? The production planning and control procedures are much more complex for a to-order system. How does this fact enter the system of trade-offs?

The Production-Distribution System. Managers need to be aware of the nature of the production-distribution system in their particular industry, and the different functions that inventories perform in the system. First, the decoupling function is of considerable managerial significance, because of the flexibility that it provides managers.

Second, the astute manager who understands the virtues of each of the components of inventory—pipeline, cycle, buffer, seasonal—can use them selectively to implement the corporate strategy in the marketplace. For example, in building inventory for a special promotion, a large part of the buildup must take place in the pipelines, resulting in time lags between production and final sales, and a larger than anticipated allocation of investment in inventories. Cycle stock may make economical operations possible. Buffer stock can be used to be more sure that random demand surges do not deplete inventories resulting in poor service, when the intention of a to-stock policy was to make the product available off-the-shelf. Seasonal inventories can be used to level employment and to ensure ample inventory when a seasonal buying surge begins.

Finally, an understanding of the production-distribution system *and* its system dynamics is of considerable managerial importance. When demand changes, the structure of the system can produce amplified effects upstream in the system. Depending on the magnitude of time delays, a 10 percent increase in consumer demand can result in an overreaction at the factory level resulting in hiring too many workers, only to find later that they were not necessary and must be laid off. A large and sudden decrease in consumer demand could shut down the plant while the system feeds on the pipeline inventories. One common error is for managers to misinterpret pipeline filling during a demand increase as a part of a fundamental demand increase; the mistake results in gearing up for a greater increase than exists, usually resulting in too much inventory and too many workers for the actual need.

Comprehensive Planning. The manager's weapon against the vagaries of the marketplace and the complexities of the production-distribution system is in planning. The planning process needs to raise the questions of possible misinterpretations of what is happening, and to make comprehensive plans that take all the data into account. The aggregate planning and scheduling process is of fundamental importance to managers, for it is here that the allocation of productive resources takes place for the upcoming planning period. What is the most economical allocation of the short-term sources of capacity such as regular time, overtime, seasonal inventories, and outside capacity sources? Should new equipment purchases be considered? What will be the policy regarding hiring and layoff? What trade-off should be made between the most economical production plan and employee and community relations, if layoff is suggested by the economics of the situation?

The Materials Manager and Organization. The emerging organizational concept of the materials manager is one that will be engaging the time and interest of managers. There are benefits to be gained by integrating the subfunctions that relate to smooth materials flows. The traditional organizational structure depends on interorganizational coordination to be sure that materials move smoothly from raw materials, through production, and on to distribution. The materials management concept sees all these subfunctions as a part of the same process, and proposes to achieve a better coordination through intraorganizational coordination. The fact that such a large proportion of companies has chosen to implement the materials management concept only partially, resulting in an emphasis for supply, production, or distribution should not go unnoticed, for this means essentially that they felt that they could implement their corporate strategy more effectively in their chosen mode.

Service Managers. The nature of service organizations shifts the emphasis of operations planning and control as compared with manufacturing. The highly variable demand on a short-term basis with no finished goods inventory as a buffer puts the emphasis for short-term capacity planning on personnel scheduling. If the manager allocates too little labor, service will be poor and there may be lost sales. Yet, peak capacity needs may be for only a relatively short period. Again, the manager is faced with trade-offs between costs of excess capacity and foregone service, and in emergency service systems this trade-off can be a very cruel one involving human life.

IMPORTANT TERMS

Numbers in parentheses indicate page numbers

REVIEW QUESTIONS AND PROBLEMS

1. What is meant by a to-stock/to-order positioning policy? How is it different from the positioning strategy discussed in Chapter 2?

2. What is the nature of the production planning and control system that must be used if the decision has been made to manufacture to order? To stock?

3. What is the function of cycle inventories at each of the following stages in a production-distribution system?

    a. Raw material storage.

    b. Within a factory.

    c. Finished goods at a factory warehouse.

    d. Distributor warehouse.

    e. Retailers.

4. A production-distribution system for dry dog food is made up of a factory, a factory warehouse, 10 regional distribution warehouses, and 10,000 retailers. The average handling, delay, processing, and transit times are as follows:

    2 days—production process
    1 day —transit to factory warehouse
    2 days—handling delays at factory warehouse
    7 days—transit to distributor
    4 days—handling and delays at distributor
    4 days—transit to retailers
    2 days—handling and delays at retailers

    The average retailer's flow rate is 200 pounds per day, and all other stages are geared to this aggregate flow.
    Compute the system finished goods pipeline inventory.

5. The finished goods inventory replenishment process for the system described in Problem 4 follows. Compute the average system cycle inventory:

    a. The production process is continuous with output flowing continuously to the factory warehouse.

    b. The 10 regional distributors order every 2 weeks to cover needs.

    c. The 10,000 retailers order weekly to cover their needs.

6. Buffer stocks are held at each of the major stock points in the system described by Problems 4 and 5. The factory warehouse has set D_{max} during the 5-day replenishment time from the factory at 6000 tons.
    The average supply time from the factory warehouse to distributors is 10 days, and distributors feel that the maximum reasonable demand during this exposure time is $D_{max} = 1200$ tons.
    The average retailer supply time from distributors is 6 days, and retailers feel that the maximum reasonable demand they will experience during the 6-day supply time is $D_{max} = 1500$ pounds.
    Compute the system buffer stock.

7. Compute the total system finished goods inventories for the dog food company described in Problems 4, 5, and 6.

8. Suppose that for the production-distribution system of Figure 8-1, retail demand suddenly increases 20 percent. Explain what happens to inventory levels for distributors and at the factory warehouse.

9. What is aggregate planning and scheduling? What decisions are made as a result of these plans?

10. Explain the organizational concept of the materials manager.

11. What are the special characteristics of service and nonmanufacturing operations that need to be taken into account in problems of planning and control?

SITUATIONS

12. The Aircraft Maintenance Company (AMCO), performs jet engine maintenance on contract for airlines in five branch locations. The company maintains branch inventories at each of the maintenance locations. At its national warehouse, the company obtains the required parts from manufacturers and maintains an inventory of these parts, using a periodic inventory reorder control system (periodic systems place orders by a regular time cycle, e.g., once each four weeks). Also at the national warehouse, parts are assembled into kits for each type of engine maintained, and an inventory of kits is retained. The national warehouse kit inventory is also controlled using a periodic inventory reorder system.

Each branch maintains an inventory of kits, and reorders weekly from the national warehouse, based on usage. Thus, there are two levels of inventories; parts and kits at the national warehouse, and kits at the branches. The general physical and information flow is shown in Figure 8-9.

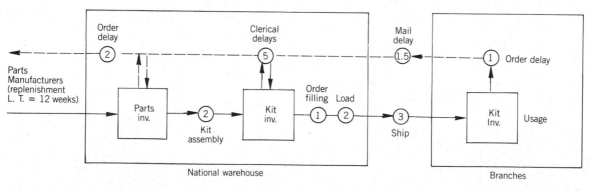

FIGURE 8-9
Aircraft Maintenance Company, information and physical flow.

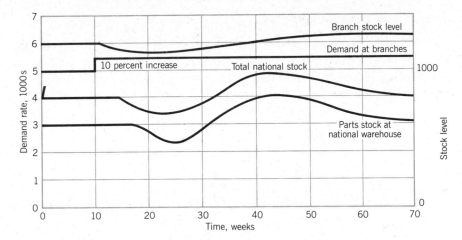

FIGURE 8-10
Aircraft Maintenance Company, simulated response to a 10 percent increase in demand.

The nature of engine maintenance operations requires fast turnaround time and contracts include a penalty for each hour beyond standard that an engine spends in the maintenance operation. Thus, kit availability is very important to profitable operations. On the other hand, aircraft engine parts represent high value, and controlling inventory levels is also important.

The company has been studying its inventory system, and has simulated the basic elements of the multistage structure. Figure 8-10 shows the simulated response of the system to a 10 percent increase in usage at branches. Management was surprised by the volatile reaction of inventories to the 10 percent increase in demand, particularly those at the central warehouse. Management felt that they should be able to smooth out the response somewhat.

What changes in policies or structure do you recommend?

13. The vice-president in charge of manufacturing of the Wash-N-Dry Appliance Co. is pondering his problems of employment and production scheduling. He has been receiving criticism from the union because historically, employment levels have fluctuated considerably. He has replied that sales also fluctuate, so why should the union expect that employment should be stable? The union president maintains that employment levels actually fluctuate more than sales, and charges that the reason is bad management. The company board of directors has just held its bimonthly meeting.

Among the reports presented to the board were status reports concerning operations, a portion of which are shown in Table 8-6. The board was upset over the rapid growth in finished goods inventories which had increased by almost 43 percent in the last 8 weeks and was even 11 percent higher than it was a year ago. The comparison with the figures for the previous year at this time was particularly unsettling because sales levels were actually lower than they were a year ago. The board chairman instructed the president to take action immediately to reduce finished goods inventories. The president defended himself by pointing to the fact that employees were already being laid

TABLE 8-6   **Abstract from Operations Report to Board of Directors, Wash-N-Dry Company**

	Current 80th Week	8 Weeks Ago	52 Weeks Ago
Order backlog, aggregate units	5,200	5.300	5,400
Finished goods inventory, units	2,500	1,750	2,250
Finished goods inventory, dollar value	$37,500	$26,250	$33,750
Number of employees	750	1,010	625

off at a rapid rate, the employment level currently being almost 26 percent below the level only 8 weeks ago. He also said, "inventories are never the problem, they are only symptoms."

Immediately after the board meeting, the president met with the VP-manufacturing and "raised hell," using other colorful language not normally included in textbooks. The essence of his comments where that finished goods inventory had to be slashed drastically even if it meant a plant shutdown. "After all, that was how the auto industry reduced its inventories in the 1974–75 depression." The union president walked in at that point, having heard the president's order and the justification. The discussions that followed were also censored, but involved strike and boycott threats.

Working late that evening, the VP-manufacturing resolved that he must "get a handle on this problem" (or he might lose his position). He assumed that he could muddle through the current crisis, but that he would probably not survive if it happened again. The next morning, he put his staff to work gathering statistics that he hoped might help shed light on the basic problem. Some of these data he plotted as shown in Figure 8-11.

He knew he had been operating by moving from one crisis to the next, but even he was startled by Figure 8-11. The union president was correct, em-

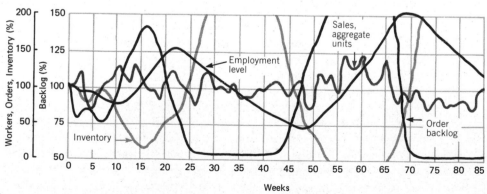

FIGURE 8-11
Indexes of sales, inventory, and employment for the Wash-N-Dry Company.

ployment levels seemed to fluctuate more than sales. But the inventory and backlog curves went off the chart.

a.   What is the basic problem?

b.   Should the VP-manufacturing take as his goal to minimize finished goods inventory? Why?

c.   Should the VP-manufacturing take as his goal to stabilize employment? Why?

14.   The manager of a large branch bank is under heavy pressure from central headquarters to reduce costs of operation. On surveying the items of cost that are under her control, she identifies labor, and materials and supplies as the two main cost components. After examining the materials and supplies costs, however, she finds that virtually all of the forms and other supplies used are specified by headquarters as a part of the system. While she could institute a "save paper and pencils" campaign, she is convinced that it would yield very little in terms of tangible cost reduction. She is left with labor cost as the one cost component that may yield cost reductions.

The labor force is made up of tellers and clerical personnel who provide support to the branch officers. The clerical personnel are kept fairly busy, and the manager is certain that it would not be feasible to operate with one less person, even though she observes some idle time.

The manager has been aware through casual observation that the load at the tellers' windows varies during the day, and from day to day during the week. Her service philosophy has always been to staff the tellers' windows so that bank customers do not have to wait. Perhaps this excellent service policy will have to be sacrificed a bit during times of peak load. As luck would have it, one teller resigns for personal reasons, and another receives a request of transfer to another branch in a preferred location. Therefore, the manager has the opportunity to experiment with a lower level of teller staffing without the distasteful aspects of dismissals or other actions to reduce the size of the teller force.

After the first week of operation, the manager has received many complaints from tellers about the workload, and from customers about the poor service. Yet, she has still observed periods where the workload has been light and the tellers relatively idle. She hires one new teller, and ponders her problem of controlling teller labor costs.

How can the branch manager gain control over teller labor costs? What information does she need? What are possible solutions to her problem?

15.   An appliance manufacturer is attempting to deal with the range of inventory problems he confronts. He produces a line of small household appliances that are sold in the $20 to $75 range, and the demand patterns are seasonal in nature. The raw materials are approximately 10 percent of the manufacturing cost, and labor is approximately 60 percent. Labor is semiskilled and can usually be trained to be normally productive within 3 months. Although not paternalistic toward his employees, the owner feels a strong social responsibility about providing good working conditions and stable employment. Labor turn-

over, however, has been high in spite of labor being paid higher than average wages for similar work.

The production cycle is relatively short, being approximately 2 weeks for the average item, and the owner has taken advantage of this fact by keeping finished goods inventories to no more than 1 month's supply for any time during the seasonal demand pattern. He accomplishes this control by keeping in close touch with market trends and seasonals through a well-conceived forecasting system.

The owner has commissioned a study by an outside consultant and has focused attention on minimizing his inventories throughout the process, that is, raw material, work-in-process, and finished goods inventories. The consultant has manipulated the owner, however, into agreeing that the first phase of the study should be a report which defines the scope and objectives of the study. Draft a statement of the portion of the consultant's phase I report which defines the statement of the problem and what the scope and objectives of the study should be.

REFERENCES

Buffa, E. S., and J. G. Miller, *Production-Inventory Systems: Planning and Control* (3rd ed.). Richard D. Irwin, Homewood, Ill. 1979.

Magee, J. F., and D. M. Boodman, *Production Planning and Inventory Control* (2nd ed.). McGraw-Hill, New York, 1967.

Miller, J. G., and P. Gilmour, "Materials Managers: Who Needs Them," *Harvard Business Review*, July–August 1979.

Monden, Y., "What Makes the Toyota Production System Really Tick?" *Industrial Engineering, 13*(1), January 1981, pp. 36–46.

Moore, F. G., and R. Jablonsky, *Production Control* (3rd ed.). McGraw-Hill, New York, 1969.

Peterson, R., and E. A. Silver, *Decision Systems for Inventory Management and Production Planning*, John Wiley & Sons, New York, 1979.

Plossl, G., and O. Wight, *Production and Inventory Control: Principles and Techniques*, Prentice-Hall, Englewood Cliffs, N.J., 1967.

CHAPTER 9

Planning Aggregate Production, Work Force, and Inventory Levels

"I F DEMAND WERE ONLY CONSTANT, MANAGING PRODUCTIVE systems sure would be a lot easier." The sage who made that statement prefers to remain anonymous, because he knows that although it is so true, only a dreamer dares to think about an ideal world. And, the sage is not a dreamer, but a vice-president of manufacturing who works in the real world of random demand variations, and seasonality. He must be concerned with the utilization of facilities and work force, and about the level of inventories. "When inventories seem too large, the president complains about the investment tied up, and the cost of carrying them. When inventories are low, the marketing vice-president complains about poor service to customers. When I have to lay off workers during a sales slump, the union president complains and sometimes makes threats, and I have even had visitations from the town mayor pleading for whatever employment stabilization measures that are possible."

This manufacturing VP has the responsibility of producing high quality products, at low cost, timed to be available when the market wants them. But, in addition, the VP must consider trade-offs between cost and employment stabilization, cost and market timing, and market timing and employment stabilization. When product demand is seasonal, the problems of achieving the needed balance between these factors is much more difficult.

MANAGERS POLICIES FOR DEALING WITH LOAD LEVELING

Managers use a number of policies to cope with the problems that result from seasonality; among them are the adoption of counter-seasonal products, influencing demand, some interesting organizational adaptations, legal coordination with other organizations, and aggregate planning. We will discuss the first four policies at this point, reserving the balance of the chapter for the important topic of aggregate planning.

Counter-seasonal Products

One of the most common managerial stategies to obtain good utilization of facilities and work force, and to stabilize employment, is to acquire and integrate into the system counter-seasonal products. The strategy is to find product lines that use the same production technology, but have a demand pattern that complements the existing lines. The classic example is lawn mowers and snow blowers.

Figure 9-1 shows a situation where the original plant load built up to a peak during the summer, resulting in large hiring and layoff costs, and investment in physical capacity for the peak. By adding the proposed product line, the total plant load would be much more level throughout the year. The costs of labor fluctuations are eliminated, the basis for improved labor relations is established, and both labor and facilities utilization are improved. The peak physical capacity requires only a 50 percent increase, assuming that temporary measures such as overtime can be used for the late summer mini-peak. But, physical production should be approximately double. Assuming the same revenue per unit of load, total revenue would double, in addition to the other advantages.

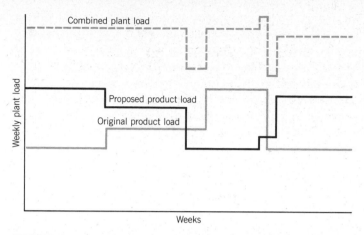

FIGURE 9-1
Load leveling effect of adding a seasonally complementary product line to an existing product line.

Obviously, the adoption of a new product line is a decision that is made at high levels in any organization. The decision involves all the major functional units, but its impact on the production function is very important indeed. Vergin [1966] found in his analysis of eight manufacturing organizations that the counter-seasonal product was the dominant managerial strategy, almost to the exclusion of other very attractive alternatives, such as aggregate planning.

Influencing Demand

This well-known managerial practice is illustrated by post-Christmas sales, and the airlines' offerings of special prices during the off-season and during the night. But the pricing practice has ramifications beyond simply increasing sales. Managers can also influence demand by compensatory allocation of promotion budgets. By stimulating demand during the off-season, managers can help level plant load, having important effects on costs, capacities, and employment stabilization. As we will see later in this chapter, formal models of aggregate planning have been constructed that make the production and marketing decisions jointly in order to approach a system optimum.

Organization Adaptations

Managers make fundamental adaptations of their organizations in an attempt to smooth demand in relation to resources that are often fixed. For example, in one of the early applications of aggregate planning in a chocolate factory, the firm changed its location to a rural area in order to take advantage of the farm labor available in the fall and winter season. Thus, a hiring and layoff smoothing strategy became compatible with seasonal production. The guaranteed annual wage in the meat-packing industry makes it possible to vary the length of the work week without substantial wage variations. Of course, the adoption of counter-seasonal products is also an adaptive response.

An interesting organizational adaptation that has implications for seasonal operations is Blackburn College.* Every student must work 15 hours per week, regardless of his or her financial position. Besides certain educational and operational cost values to such a program, the cost of labor force fluctuation between summers and the academic year is zero. According to the treasurer, "We have a highly intelligent work staff that retires every four years, without pension."

Coordination with Other Organizations

One of the common managerial strategies has been to subcontract needs above certain capacity limits when possible. Such a managerial strategy involves coordination between two usually different firms in the marketplace. A larger integrated firm may make subcontracting arrangements with smaller, more flexible firms operating in the same field. Galbraith [1969] quotes examples in the coal and oil-refining industries.

In other situations, managerial strategy may involve coordination between producers and customers in which the producer may be able to increase lot sizes, split lots, or delay or speed up deliveries in order to smooth the work load. In return the customer receives preferential supply treatment.

Finally, it may be possible for some organizations to form a coalition that can have the effect of smoothing work loads. For example, electric utilities join together in networks of supply that enable them to meet peak demands for the network system as a whole. If each individual utility had to meet its individual peak demands, higher plant investment would be required in the aggregate and for each organization. The airlines have found that by sharing equipment when route structures are noncompetitive and counter-seasonal, the organizations involved can achieve somewhat better equipment utilization.

NATURE OF AGGREGATE PLANNING

Most managers want to plan and control operations at the broadest level through some kind of aggregate planning that bypasses details of individual products and the detailed scheduling of facilities and personnel. This fact is a good illustration of how managerial behavior actually employs system concepts by starting with the whole. Management would rather deal with the basic relevant decisions of programming the use of resources. This is accomplished by reviewing projected employment levels and by setting activity rates that can be varied within a given employment level by varying hours worked (working overtime or undertime). Once these basic decisions have been made for the upcoming period, master and detailed scheduling can proceed at a lower level within the constraints of the broad plan. Finally, last-minute changes in activity levels need to be made with the realization of their possible effects on the cost of changing production levels and on inventory costs.

What is needed first for aggregate plans is to develop some logical overall unit of measuring output, for example, gallons of paint in the paint industry, cases in the beer industry, perhaps equivalent machine hours in mechanical industries, beds occupied in hospitals, or pieces of mail in a post office.

* "The School That Works," *Time*, May 18, 1981, p. 77.

Second, management must be able to forecast for some reasonable planning period, perhaps up to a year, in these aggregate terms. Finally, management must be able to isolate and measure the relevant costs. These costs may be reconstructed in the form of a model that will permit near optimal decisions for the sequence of planning periods in the planning horizon.

The sequential nature of the decisions should be kept in mind. A decision on employment levels and activity rates made for an upcoming period cannot be termed either right or wrong, good or bad. Decisions will also be made two periods hence based on the decisions just made, on new information about the actual progress of sales, and on the forecasts for the balance of the planning horizon. The result is that all decisions are right or wrong only in terms of the sequence of decisions over an extended period of time.

Most of our discussion deals with systems that produce inventoriable items, where the existence of finished goods inventories can make possible a trade-off for the costs of changes in employment level. However, systems that cannot store their output are discussed in Chapter 13, "Large-Scale Projects," and Chapter 14, "Service Systems."

Aggregate planning increases the range of alternatives for capacity use that can be considered by management. The concepts raise such broad basic questions as: To what extent should inventory be used to absorb the fluctuations in demand that will occur over the next 6 to 12 months? Why not absorb these fluctuations by simply varying the size of the work force? Why not maintain a fairly stable work force size and absorb fluctuations by changing activity rates through varying work hours? Why not maintain a fairly stable work force and activity rate and let subcontractors wrestle with the problem of fluctuating order rates? Should the firm purposely not meet all demands? Each of the preceding policies may be termed *pure strategies*, because only one policy is used to smooth production activity.

In most instances, it is probably true that any one of these pure strategies would not be as effective as a balance among them. Each strategy has associated costs, and we seek an astute combination of the pure strategies, called a *mixed strategy*.

COSTS

The basic picture of costs is shown in Figure 5-3, in Chapter 5. The same basic structure is appropriate for manufacturing concerns, hospitals, the postal service, and many other service organizations. For some kinds of governmental operations, the revenue line could be substantially different, depending on the basis for obtaining budget to cover expenses.

What happens to total costs as volume increases? This cost behavior is of the greatest interest, especially near or at the sharp changes in the reorganization of resources that occurs with the addition or deletion of second and third shifts. Multiple shifts are common in manufacturing, hospitals, and the postal service; however, a single-shift operation would have a structure similar to that shown for the first shift in Figure 5-3. Following the conventional accounting definition of fixed, semifixed, and variable costs, the interesting factors that dominate the shape taken by the total cost curve are in the semifixed and variable cost categories.

To put on a second shift would require a reorganization of the supervisory structure and other managerial functions, causing a quantum increase in costs. In addition, some physical changes in the reorganization of facilities may be required to maintain a two-shift operation. Thus, we observe the discontinuities in the total cost curve at the limits of one- and two-shift capacity.

But why should we not expect the variable costs to be linear? There are a variety of reasons, and we illustrate some of them in Figure 9-2. First, it is important to look at the system as something dynamic, changing in response to changes in demand, product or service mix, technology, and changing organizational and social patterns. To regard the enterprise as being static is to overlook the entire flavor and character of the problems of operations management.

In Figure 9-2a the payroll costs may be close to being linear, although even this assumption could be attacked on the basis of the supply and demand for labor, as

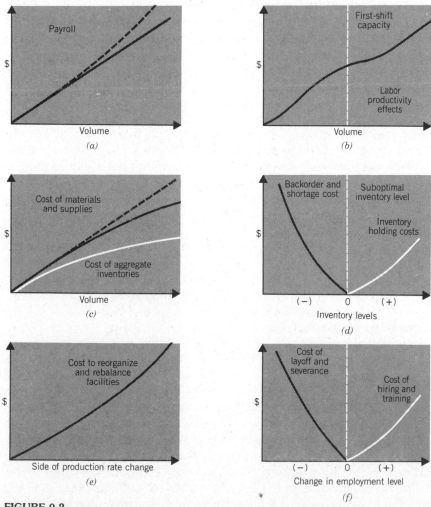

FIGURE 9-2
Selected cost behavior patterns.

indicated by the dashed line in Figure 9-2a. In any case, the productivity of labor in relation to volume of activities shown in Figure 9-2b makes the labor cost per unit a nonlinear function. Viewing labor in the aggregate and not considering substantial changes in basic technology, we would expect the toe of the productivity curve to exhibit start-up difficulties that would be reflected in low output per worker-hour. In the middle range of one-shift operations, the curve may be approximately linear. But as we approach the limits of one-shift capacity, productivity falls off because of increased congestion, cramped quarters, interference, and delays. There is a logical tendency to try to achieve the increased output near the limits of one-shift capacity through the use of overtime with the existing work force and its higher cost of marginal productivity. Changes in technology might change the level and contour of the curve, but the general nonlinearities would remain.

In Figure 9-2c we see two cost components related to material. We assume that the cost of materials could be linear with volume (dashed line), but quantity discounts and an aggressive procurement staff should produce economies at higher volumes (solid line). As volume goes up, the size of the aggregate inventory necessary to maintain the production-distribution process increases also, but not in direct proportion.

In Figure 9-2d we examine the relative cost of holding either too much or too little inventory. This presupposes that there exists, for each level of operation, some ideal aggregate inventory to sustain the productive process. Inventories, however, might vary from this ideal amount for two possible reasons. First, they might be different from the ideal levels because of the capriciousness of consumer demand. If demand were less than expected, we would incur extra inventories and the cost of holding them. If demand were greater than expected, we would incur backorder or shortage costs and the possible opportunity costs of lost sales or volume of activity. A second basic reason why aggregate inventories might differ from ideal levels is as a result of conscious managerial design. Management might consciously accumulate extra inventories in a slack demand season to reduce the costs of hiring, layoff, and overtime. These costs of holding too much or too little inventory are probably not linear for larger ranges.

Finally, in Figures 9-2e and 9-2f, we have included two items of cost associated with changes in output and employment levels. When output rates are changed, there are some costs in reorganizing and replanning for the new level and in rebalancing crews and facilities.

Cost-volume patterns will not be linear for many of the reasons discussed, and therefore, profit appears in a "pocket" beyond a break-even point. If the total cost curve lies entirely above the revenue line, then losses will be less in the upper region. Profit increases to a point where the diseconomies discussed become effective. At that point profit is reduced as volume continues to increase and may disappear as we approach the limits of one-shift capacity.

The reasons for the relative increases in costs and decline in profits are related to the behavior of some of the cost components, but the profit decline generally is associated with the decline of labor productivity, use of overtime, and the relative inefficiency of newly hired labor. These cost increases normally are somewhat greater than the savings in material and inventory costs, when operating near a capacity limit. When the decision to add a second shift is made, there will be increased semifixed costs in order to put on the second shift. As we progress into the second shift volume range, labor productivity will be relatively low, reflecting start-up conditions, and a pattern similar to the first shift will be repeated.

In some of the analyses of operations management problems, we assume linear approximations to nonlinear cost functions in order to simplify problems and to conceptualize models. In many instances, the assumption of linearity is an excellent one, but near a capacity limit it may be dangerous.

Many costs affected by aggregate planning and scheduling decisions are difficult to measure and are not segregated in accounting records. Some, such as interest costs on inventory investment, are opportunity costs. Other costs are not measureable, such as those associated with public relations and public image. However, all the costs are real and bear on aggregate planning decisions.

PROBLEM STRUCTURE

The simplest structure of the aggregate planning problem is represented by the single-stage system shown in Figure 9-3. In Figure 9-3 the planning horizon is only one period ahead; therefore, we call Figure 9-3 a "single-stage" system. The state of the system at the end of the last period is defined by W_0, P_0, and I_0, the aggregate work force size, production or activity rate, and inventory level, respectively. The ending state conditions become the initial conditions for the upcoming period. We have a forecast of the requirements for the upcoming period; through some process, decisions are made that set the size of the work force and production rate for the upcoming period. Projected ending inventory is then, $I_1 = I_0 + P_1 - F_1$, where F_1 is forecasted sales.

The decisions made may call for hiring or laying off personnel, thus expanding or contracting the effective capacity of the productive system. The work force size, to-

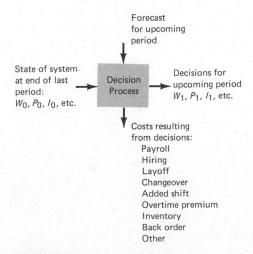

FIGURE 9-3
Single-stage aggregate planning decision system where planning horizon is only one period. W = size of work force, P = production or activity rate, and I = inventory level.

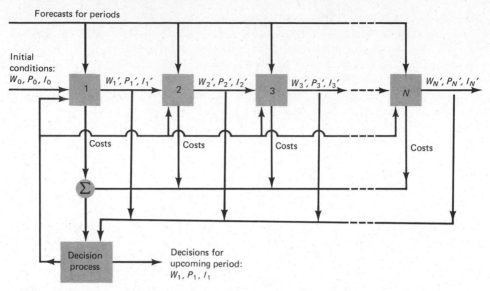

FIGURE 9-4
Multistage aggregate planning decision system for planning horizon of N periods.

gether with the decision on activity rate during the period, then determines the required amount of overtime, inventory levels, or back-ordering, whether or not a shift must be added or deleted, and other possible changes in operating procedure. The comparative costs that result from alternate decisions on work force size and production rate are of great interest in judging the effectiveness of the decisions made and the decision process used. The comparative cost of a sequence of such alternate decisions is also of interest in judging the applicability of the single-stage model.

Let us suppose that we make a sequence of independent decisions by the structure of the single-stage model of Figure 9-3. If the forecasts for each period for the first four periods are progressively decreasing, our decision process responds by decreasing both the work force size and the activity rate in some combination, incurring layoff and changeover costs. Then, for the fifth through tenth periods, we find the period forecasts are progressively increasing, and each period the decision process calls for hiring personnel and increased activity rates, incurring more hiring and changeover costs. The single-period planning horizon has made each independent decision seem internally logical, but has resulted in the laying off of workers only to hire them back again.

If we had been able to look ahead for several periods with an appropriate decision process, we might have decided to stabilize the work force size, at least to some extent, and absorb the fluctuations in demand in some other way. For example, we could have changed activity rate through the use of overtime and undertime or by carrying extra inventories through the trough in the demand curve. Broadening the planning horizon can improve the effectiveness of the aggregate planning system.

Figure 9-4 shows a multistage aggregate planning system where the horizon has been expanded with forecasts for each period. Our objective is the same as before: to make decisions concerning the work force size and production rate for the upcoming period. In doing so, however, we consider the sequence of projected decisions in relation to forecasts and their cost effects. The decision for the upcoming period is to be affected by the future period forecasts, and the decision process must consider the cost effects of the sequence of decisions. The connecting links between the several stages are the W, P, and I values that are at the end of one period and the beginning of the next. The feedback loop from the decision process may involve some iterative or trial-and-error procedure to obtain a solution.

DECISION PROCESSES FOR AGGREGATE PLANNING

Given the structure of Figure 9-4, our interest is drawn to the decision processes. There are several, classified as graphic, mathematical, heuristic, and computer search methods. We classify them further as static versus dynamic as well as single-stage versus multistage models. We discuss the graphic, mathematical, and computer search methods.

Graphic Methods

Table 9-1 shows a forecast of expected production requirements in column 4, by months; these data are cumulated by months in column 5. The ratio of peak to valley in the requirements schedule is 11,000 in July to 4,000 in February and March, or $11,000/4,000 = 2.75$.

Note, however, that the number of working days per month varies considerably. Column 2 shows that the number of working days varies from 23 in March and

TABLE 9-1
Forecast of Production Requirements and Buffer Inventories: Cumulative Requirements, Average Buffer Inventories,[a] and Cumulative Maximum Production Requirements

(1) Month	(2) Production Days	(3) Cumulative Production Days	(4) Expected Production Requirements	(5) Cumulative Production Requirements Col. 4 Cumulated	(6) Required Buffer Inventories	(7) Cumulative Maximum Production Requirements. Col. 5 + Col. 6	(8) Col. 2 × Col. 6	(9) Production Requirements per Production Day. Col. 4 ÷ Col. 2
January	22	22	5,000	5,000	2,800	7,800	61,600	227.3
February	20	42	4,000	9,000	2,500	11,500	50,000	200.0
March	23	65	4,000	13,000	2,500	15,500	57,500	173.9
April	19	84	5,000	18,000	2,800	20,800	53,200	263.2
May	22	106	7,000	25,000	3,200	28,200	70,400	318.2
June	22	128	9,000	34,000	3,500	37,500	77,000	409.1
July	20	148	11,000	45,000	4,100	49,100	82,000	550.0
August	23	171	9,000	54,000	3,500	57,500	80,500	391.3
September	11	182	6,500	60,500	3,000	63,500	33,000	590.9
October	22	204	6,000	66,500	3,000	69,500	66,000	272.7
November	22	226	5,000	71,500	2,800	74,300	61,600	227.3
December	18	244	5,000	76,500	2,800	79,300	50,400	277.8
							743,200	

[a] Average buffer inventory = 743,200/244 = 3045.9 units.

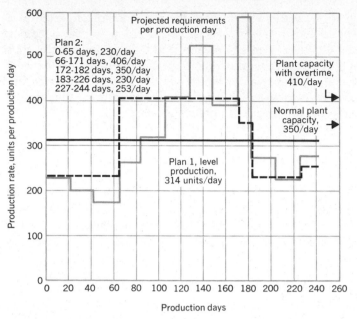

FIGURE 9-5
Comparison of two production plans that meet requirements.

August to only 11 in September. (The plant closes for 2 weeks in September owing to vacations scheduled to coincide with required plant maintenance.) Therefore, the swing in production requirements per production day (see column 9 of Table 9-1) varies from 6500/11 = 591 in September to only 4000/23 = 174 in March, or a ratio of 591/174 = 3.40. This substantial variation in daily production requirements is shown by the graph of requirements in Figure 9-5. Developing aggregate schedules that meet these seasonal requirements is part of the problem. Developing schedules that minimize the incremental costs associated with meeting requirements is the challenge.

Assume that normal plant capacity is 350 units per day. Additional capacity can be obtained by employing labor at overtime to a maximum capacity of 410 units per day. The *additional* cost per unit is $10 for units produced during overtime hours.

Buffer Inventories and Maximum Requirements. Column 6 of Table 9-1 shows buffer inventories stated as minimum stocks. These buffer stocks were determined by a judgmental process. Their purpose is to provide for the possibility that market requirements could be greater than expected. When we add these buffer inventories in each month to the cumulative production requirements in column 5, we have cumulative maximum requirements, as shown in column 7. Column 8 provides the basis for weighting the buffer inventory by production days and for computing the average buffer inventory of 3045.9 units, at the bottom of the table.

Alternate Plans

Plan 1, Level Production. The simplest production plan is to establish an average output level that meets annual requirements. The total annual requirements are shown as the last figure in the cumulated requirements schedule in column 5 of Table 9-1—76,500 units. Because there are 244 working days, an average daily output of 76,500/244 = 314 units should cover requirements. We may find problems with such a schedule because of timing, but we shall see what to do about these problems later. Our strategy is simple: accumulate seasonal inventory during the slack requirements months to be used during peak requirements months. The level production plan is shown in relation to the production requirements per day in Figure 9-5 as Plan 1.

The inventory requirements for Plan 1 are calculated in Table 9-2. The production in each month is computed in column 3 and accumulated in column 4 to produce a schedule of units available each month, starting with a beginning inventory of 2800 units, the required buffer inventory in January. Then, by comparing the units available in column 4 with the cumulative maximum requirements schedule in column 5, we generate the schedule of seasonal inventories in column 6.

Looking at the seasonal inventories for Plan 1 in column 6, they vary from a maximum of 8376 units in April to a minimum of −3552 in September. The significance of the negative seasonal inventories is that the plan calls for dipping into buffer stocks. In August, we propose to use 1006 out of the planned buffer of 3500 units, but in September, we actually exceed the planned buffer by 552 units. In other words, the plan would actually require back-ordering or the expected loss of the sale of 552 units in September. The plan recovers in subsequent months and meets aggregate requirements, but incurs total shortages for the year of 7738 units.

We decide not to plan to use the buffer inventory, since the buffer was designed to

TABLE 9-2
Calculation of Seasonal Inventory Requirements for Plan 1

(1)	(2)	(3)	(4) Cumulative Units Available. Cumulative Production + Beginning Inv. (2800)	(5) Cumulative Maximum Requirements, from Col. 7 of Table 9-1	(6) Seasonal Inventory[a] = Col. 4 − Col. 5	(7) Col. 1 × Col. 6
Production Days	Production Rate, Units, per Day	Production in Month, Units, Col. 1 × Col. 2				
22	314	6,908	9,708	7,800	1,908	41,976
20	314	6,280	15,988	11,500	4,488	89,760
23	314	7,222	23,210	15,500	7,710	177,330
19	314	5,966	29,176	20,800	8,376	159,144
22	314	6,908	36,084	28,200	7,884	173,448
22	314	6,908	42,992	37,500	5,492	120,824
20	314	6,280	49,272	49,100	172	3,440
23	314	7,222	56,494	57,500	−1,006	−23,138
11	314	3,454	59,948	63,500	−3,552	−39,072
22	314	6,908	66,856	69,500	−2,644	−58,168
22	314	6,908	73,764	74,300	− 536	−11,792
18	314	5,652	79,416	79,300	116	2,088
244						

[a] Average seasonal inventory (positive values in column 7/days) = 780,010/244 = 3147.6 units.

absorb unexpected sales increases. (If we plan to use them, they lose their buffering function.) How do we adjust the plan to take the negative seasonal inventories into account? All we need to do is increase the beginning inventory by the most negative seasonal inventory balance, −3552 units in September. This new beginning inventory level has the effect of increasing the entire schedule of cumulative units available in column 4 of Table 9-2 by 3552 units. Then, average seasonal inventories will also be increased by 3552 units.

The seasonal inventories for Plan 1 are calculated in Table 9-2 as 3147.6 units, weighted by production days, assuming that we use buffer stocks and record shortages as indicated in column 6. If we revise the plan so that the buffer inventories are not used, the average seasonal inventory would be 3147.6 + 3552 = 6699.6 units.

Assuming that inventory holding costs are $50 per unit per year and that shortage costs are $25 per unit short, we can now compute the relative cost of the variants of Plan 1. If beginning inventories are only 2800 units, the annual inventory cost is 50 × 3147.6 = $157,380, and the shortage cost is 25 × 7738 = $193,450. The total incremental cost is then $350,830.

By comparison, if we decide not to use up buffer inventory, the average seasonal inventories are 6699.6 units at a cost of $50 × 6699.6 = $334,980, the total incremental cost for comparison. Obviously, for these costs of holding inventories and incurring shortages, it is more economical to plan on larger inventories. In other situations, the reverse might be true. If the cost of shortages is only $20 per unit, it would be slightly more economical to take the risk. Or alternately, if the cost of holding inventories were $62 per unit per year and shortage cost were $25 per unit, then the balance of costs would also favor taking the risk of incurring shortages. Of course, there are other factors that enter the decision of whether or not to risk incurring shortages, such as the potential of losing market share permanently.

Plan 1 has significant advantages. First, it does not require the hiring or layoff of personnel. It provides stable employment to workers and would be favored by organized labor. Also, scheduling is simple—314 units per day. From an incremental production cost viewpoint, however, it fails to consider whether or not there is an economic advantage in trading off the large seasonal inventory and shortage costs for overtime costs and/or costs incurred in hiring or laying off personnel to meet seasonal variations in requirements.

Plan 2, Using Hiring, Layoff, and Overtime. Note from Figure 9-5 that normal plant capacity allows an output of 350 units per day and that an additional 60 units per day can be obtained through overtime work. Units produced on overtime cost an additional $10 per unit in this example.

Up to the normal capacity of 350 units per day, we can increase or decrease output by hiring or laying off labor. A worker hired or laid off affects the net output rate by 1 unit per day. The cost of changing output levels in this way is $200 per worker hired or laid off, owing to hiring, training, severance, and other associated costs.

Plan 2 takes advantage of the additional options of changing basic output rates and using overtime for peak requirements. Plan 2 is shown in Figure 9-5 and involves two basic employment levels: labor to produce at normal output rates of 230 and 350 units per day. Additional variations are achieved through the use of overtime when needed. The plan has the following schedule:

TABLE 9-3 **Calculation of Incremental Costs for Plan 2**

(1) Production Days	(2) Production Rate/Day	(3) Units of Production Rate Change	(4) Units Produced at Overtime Production Rates Greater Than 350 or 230 × Col. 1
22	230	−0−	−0−
20	230	−0−	−0−
23	230	−0−	−0−
19	406	120	1,064
22	406	−0−	1,232
22	406	−0−	1,232
20	406	−0−	1,120
23	406	−0−	1,288
11	350	−0−	−0−
22	230	120	−0−
22	230	−0−	−0−
18	253	−0−	414
		240	6,350

Production rate change costs = 240 × 200 = $48,000
  (A change in the basic rate of one
  unit requires the hiring or layoff of
  one worker at $200 each)
Overtime costs at $10 extra per unit = 10 × 6,350 =   63,500
Seasonal inventory cost (2356.4 units at $50
per unit per year) = 50 × 2356.4 =   117,820

　　　Total incremental cost = $229,320

0 to 65 days—produce at 230 units per day.

66 to 171 days—produce at 406 units per day (66 units per day at overtime rates; hire 120 workers to increase basic rate without overtime from 230 to 350 units per day).

172 to 182 days—produce at 350 units per day (no overtime).

183 to 226 days—produce at 230 units per day (lay off 120 workers to reduce basic rate from 350 to 230 units per day again).

227 to 244 days—produce at 253 units per day (23 units per day at overtime rates).

The calculations of the seasonal inventory requirements for Plan 2 are similar to those for Plan 1. The seasonal inventory for Plan 2 has been reduced to only 2356 units, 75 percent of Plan 1 with shortages and 35 percent of Plan 1 without shortages.

To counterbalance the inventory reduction, we must hire 120 workers in April and lay off an equal number in October. Also, we have produced a significant number of units at overtime rates from April to September and in December. The costs of Plan 2 are summarized in Table 9-3. The total incremental costs of Plan 2 are $229,320, 65 percent of Plan 1 with shortages and 68 percent of Plan 1 without shortages.

The trade-offs produce a somewhat more economical plan, but require substantial fluctuations in the size of the work force. Whether the social and employee relations' consequences are to be tolerated is a matter for managerial judgment. If the employment fluctuation is greater than management feels can be tolerated, other alternatives involving a smaller employment fluctuation can be computed. Perhaps some of the variations can be absorbed by more overtime work, and in some kinds of industries, subcontracting can be used to meet the most severe peak requirements.

Plan 3, Adding Subcontracting as a Source. Assume that management wishes to consider a third alternative that involves smaller work force fluctuation, using overtime, seasonal inventories, and subcontracting to absorb the balance of requirements fluctuations. Plan 3 has the following schedule:

0 to 84 days—produce at 250 units per day.

85 to 128 days—produce at 350 units per day (hire 100 workers to increase the basic rate from 250 to 350 units per day).

129 to 148 days—produce at 410 units per day (60 units per day produced on overtime, plus 1700 units subcontracted).

149 to 171 days—produce at 370 units per day (20 units per day produced on overtime).

172 to 182 days—produce at 410 units per day (60 units per day produced on overtime, plus 1380 units subcontracted).

183 to 204 days—produce at 273 units per day (23 units per day produced on overtime; lay off 100 workers to reduce employment level from basic rate of 350 to 250 units per day).

205 to 244 days—produce at 250 units per day.

Plan 3 reduces seasonal inventories still further to an average of only 1301 units. Employment fluctuation is more modest, involving the hiring and laying off of 100 workers. Only 4066 units are produced at overtime rates, but a total of 3080 units is subcontracted at an additional cost of $15 per unit.

Table 9-4 summarizes the costs for all three plans. For the particular example, Plan 3 is the most economical, being 83.7 percent as costly as Plan 2 and only 65.4 percent as costly as Plan 1 with shortages. The buffer inventories are nearly the same for all plans, so their costs are not included as incremental costs.

Even though Plan 3 involves less employment fluctuation than Plan 2, it may be felt to be too severe. Other plans involving less fluctuation could be developed and their incremental costs determined in the same way.

Cumulative Graphs. Although Figure 9-5 shows the effects of the production rate changes quite clearly, it is actually somewhat easier to work with cumulative curves, as shown in Figure 9-6. The procedure is to plot first the cumulative production requirements. The cumulative maximum requirements curve is then simply the former curve with the required buffer inventories added for each period. The cumulative graph of maximum requirements can then be used as a basis for generating alternate program proposals. Any production program that is feasible, in the sense that it meets requirements while providing the desired buffer stock protection,

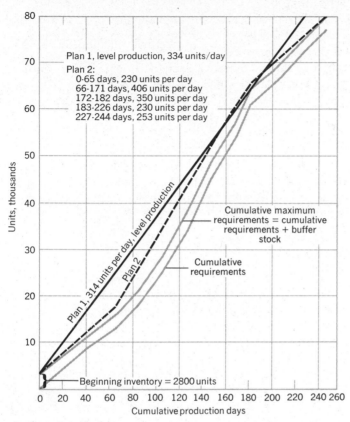

FIGURE 9-6
Cumulative graphs of requirements and alternate production programs.

TABLE 9-4	**Comparison of Costs of Alternate Production Plans**			

| | Plan 1 | | | |
| | With Shortages | Without Shortages | Plan 2 | Plan 3 |
Costs				
Shortages[a]	$193,450	—	—	—
Seasonal Inventory[b]	157,380	$334,980	$117,820	$ 65,070
Labor Turnover[c]	—	—	48,000	40,000
Overtime[d]	—	—	63,500	40,660
Subcontracting[e]	—	—	—	46,200
Totals	$350,830	$334,980	$229,320	$191,930

[a] Shortages cost $25 per unit.

[b] Inventory carrying costs are $50 per unit per year.

[c] An increase or decrease in the basic production rate of one unit requires the hiring or layoff of one employee at a hiring and training, or severance, cost of $200 each.

[d] Units produced at overtime rates cost an additional $10 per unit.

[e] Units subcontracted cost an additional $15 per unit.

must fall entirely above the cumulative maximum requirements line. The vertical distances between the program proposal curves and the cumulative maximum requirements curve represent seasonal inventory accumulation for each plan.

Graphic methods are simple and have the advantage of visualizing alternate programs over a broad planning horizon. The difficulties with graphic methods, however, are the static nature of the graphic model and the fact that the process is in no sense cost or profit optimizing. In addition, the process does not generate good programs itself, but simply compares proposals made.

The alternate plan proposals used in connection with the graphic methods indicate the sensitivity in alternate plans to the use of various sources of short-term capacity: seasonal inventories, shortages, use of overtime capacity, and subcontracting. Mathematical and computer search models attempt to find optimal combinations of these sources of short-term capacity.

Mathematical Optimization Methods

We will discuss two mathematical optimization methods: the Linear Decision Rule, and linear programming. Both have a basis for optimizing the model developed, so our interest is in appraising how closely the two models represent reality.

The Linear Decision Rule. The Linear Decision Rule (LDR) was developed in 1955 by Holt, Modigliani, Muth, and Simon [1955, 1956, 1960] as a quadratic programming approach for making aggregate employment and production rate decisions. The LDR is based on the development of a quadratic cost function for the company in question with cost components of (1) regular payroll, (2) hiring and layoff, (3) overtime, and (4) inventory holding, back-ordering, and machine setup costs. The quadratic cost function is then used to derive two linear decision rules for computing work force level and production rate for the upcoming period based on forecasts of aggregate sales for a preset planning horizon. The two linear decision rules are optimum for the model.

Figure 9-7 shows the form of the four components of the cost function. The work force size is adjusted in the model once per period with the implied commitment to pay employees at least their regular time wages for that period. This is indicated in Figure 9-7a. Hiring and layoff costs are shown in Figure 9-7b; the LDR model approximates these costs with a quadratic function as shown. If the work force size is held constant for the period in question, then changes in production rate can be absorbed by the use of overtime and undertime. Undertime is the cost of idle labor at regular payroll rates. The overtime cost depends on the size of the work force, W, and on the aggregate production rate, P.

The form of the overtime-undertime cost function in relation to production rate is shown in Figure 9-7c, being approximated by a quadratic function. Whether overtime or undertime costs will occur for a given decision depends on the balance of costs defined by the horizon time. For example, in responding to the need for increased output, the costs of hiring and training must be balanced against the overtime costs. Or conversely, the response to a decreased production rate would require the balancing of layoff costs against the costs of undertime.

The general shape of the net inventory cost curve is shown in Figure 9-7d. When inventories deviate from ideal levels, either extra inventory carrying costs must be

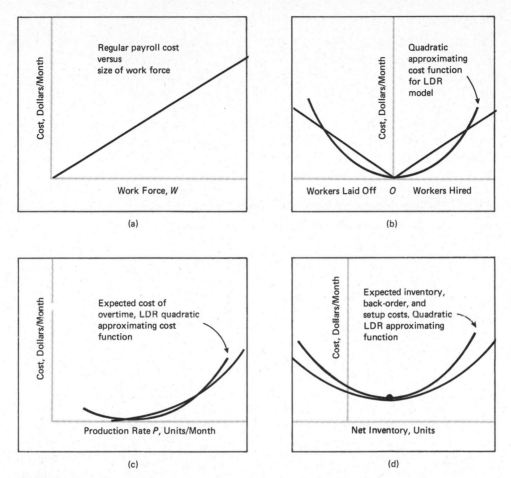

FIGURE 9-7
Approximating linear and quadratic cost functions used by the Linear Decision Rule (LDR) model.

absorbed if inventory levels are too high, or costs of back-ordering or lost sales will occur if inventory levels are too low. Again, these costs are approximated by a quadratic function in the LDR model.

The total incremental cost function is then the sum of the four component cost functions for a particular example. The mathematical problem is to minimize the sum of the monthly combined cost function over the planning horizon time of N periods. The result of this mathematical development is the specification of two linear decision rules to be used to compute the aggregate size of the work force and the production rate for the upcoming period. These two rules require as inputs the forecast for each period of the planning horizon in aggregate terms, the ending size of work force, and inventory level in the last period. Once the two rules have been developed for a specific application, the computations needed to produce the decisions recommended by the model require only 10 to 15 minutes by manual methods.*

---

* The equations for the Linear Decision Rule Model are given in the supplement to this chapter.

An Example

An LDR model was developed for a paint company and applied to a 6-year record of known decisions in the company. Two kinds of forecasts were used as inputs: a perfect forecast and a moving average forecast. The actual order pattern was extremely variable, involving both the 1949 recession and the Korean War. The graphical record of actual factory performance compared with the simulated performance of the LDR is shown in Figures 9-8 and 9-9 for production rates and work force levels. Costs were reconstructed for the 6-year period of actual operation and projected for the decision rules based on the nonquadratic cost structure originally estimated from paint company data. The cost difference between the actual company performance and performance with the LDR with the moving average forecast was $173,000 per year in favor of the LDR.

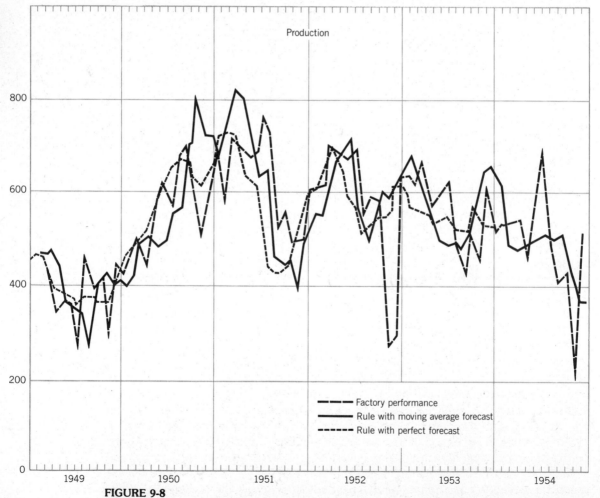

FIGURE 9-8
Comparative performance of the Linear Decision Rule (LDR) with actual factory performance for production rates.
SOURCE: *C. C. Holt, F. Modigliani, and H. A. Simon. "A Linear Decision Rule for Employment Scheduling,"* Management Science, *2(2), October 1955.*

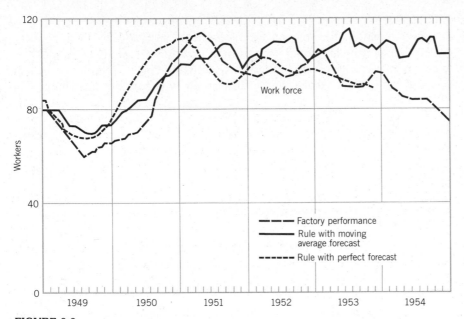

FIGURE 9-9
Comparative performance of the Linear Decision Rule (LDR) with actual factory performance for work-
force size.
SOURCE: *C. C. Holt, F. Modigliani, and H. A. Simon. "A Linear Decision Rule for Production and
Employment Scheduling,"* Management Science, 2(2), October 1955.

LDR has many important advantages. First, the model is optimizing, and the two
decision rules, once derived, are simple to apply. In addition, the model is dynamic
and representative of the multistage kind of system that we discussed in connection
with Figure 9-4. On the other hand, the quadratic cost structure may have severe
limitations and probably does not adequately represent the cost structure of any
organization.

Linear Programming Methods. The aggregate planning problem has been developed in the context of distribution models, as well as more general formulations of
linear programming. Distribution methods of linear programming have some limitations when applied to the aggregate planning problem. The distribution model does
not account for production change costs, such as hiring and layoff of personnel. Thus,
resulting programs may call for changes in production levels in one period, requiring
an expanded work force, only to call for the layoff of these workers in the future
periods. Also the linearity requirement often is too severe. Still, the model has considerable flexibility to include a variety of costs, and is relatively simple to formulate and
use. A detailed formulation and example of the distribution model for aggregate
planning, and a discussion of extensions and applications are included in the supplement at the end of this chapter.

The more general linear programming formulation makes it possible to include
production level change costs in the model. Hanssmann and Hess [1960] developed
a linear optimization model that is entirely parallel with the Linear Decision Rule in
terms of using work force and production rate as independent decision variables and
in terms of the components of the cost model. The main difference between the

285

Hanssmann-Hess (H-H) and LDR models is that all cost functions must be linear and that linear programming is the solution technique in the H-H model. One's preference between the two models would depend on a preference for either the linear or quadratic cost model in a given application. A generalized linear optimization model for aggregate planning is formulated in the supplement at the end of this chapter.

There have been many applications of linear programming to the aggregate planning problem. Also, Lee and Moore [1974] have applied the general goal programming format to the aggregate planning problem. Goal programming is an extension of linear programming that uses the slack variables to free the user from the usual unidimensional objective function. Managerial goals are identified and placed in priority order.

Search Decision Rule (SDR)

A computer optimum-seeking procedure may be used to evaluate systematically a cost or profit criterion function at trial points. In the procedure it is hoped that an optimum value will be found eventually, but there is no guarantee. In direct search methods of computer optimum seeking, the cost criterion function is evaluated at a point, the result compared with previous trial results, and a move determined on the basis of a set of heuristics ("rules of thumb"). The new point is then evaluated, and the procedure repeated until either a better solution resulting in an improved value of the objective function cannot be found or the predetermined computer time limit is exceeded. Taubert [1968, 1968a] experimented with computer search methods, using the paint company data as a vehicle.

The costs to be minimized are expressed as a function of production rates and work force levels in each period of the planning horizon. Therefore, each period included in the planning horizon requires the addition of two dimensions to the criterion function, one for production rate and one for work force size for each period in the planning horizon.

Table 9-5 shows a sample of the computer output for the first month of factory operation of the paint company. The computer output gives the first month's decision as well as an entire program for the planning horizon of 10 months. In the lower half of the table the program prints out for the entire planning horizon the component costs of payroll, hiring and layoff, overtime, inventory, and the total of these costs. Thus a manager is provided not only with the immediate decisions for the upcoming month, but also with the projected decisions based on monthly forecasts for the planning horizon time and the economic consequences of each month's decisions. Of course, the more distant projections lose much of their significance. The projections are updated with each monthly decision based on the most recent forecast and cost inputs. The total cost of the SDR program exceeds the LDR total by only $806 or 0.11 percent. This difference may be accounted for by the fact that the SDR used a planning horizon of only 10 months as compared with the 12-month horizon used by the LDR.

With the encouraging results in virtually duplicating the performance of LDR for the paint company, it was decided to test SDR in more demanding situations. Thus, models were developed for three rather different applications: (1) the Search Company (Buffa and Taubert, [1967]), a hypothetical organization involving a much

TABLE 9-5   **SDR Output for the First Month of Factory Operation (Perfect Forecast)**

A. SDR Decisions and Projections

Month	Sales (gallons)	Production (gallons)	Inventory (gallons)	Work Force (men)
0			263.00	81.00
1	430	471.89	304.89	77.60
2	447	444.85	302.74	74.10
3	440	416.79	279.54	70.60
4	316	380.90	344.44	67.32
5	397	374.64	322.08	64.51
6	375	363.67	310.75	62.07
7	292	348.79	367.54	60.22
8	458	345.63	268.17	58.68
9	400	329.83	198.00	57.05
10	350	270.60	118.60	55.75

B. Cost Analysis of Decisions and Projections (dollars)

Month	Payroll	Hiring and Layoff	Overtime	Inventory	Total
1	26,384.04	743.25	2558.82	18.33	29,704.94
2	25,195.60	785.62	2074.76	24.57	28,080.54
3	24,004.00	789.79	1555.68	135.06	26,484.53
4	22,888.86	691.69	585.21	49.27	24,215.03
5	21,932.79	508.43	1070.48	0.36	23,512.06
6	21,102.86	383.13	1206.90	7.06	22,699.93
7	20,473.22	220.51	948.13	186.43	21,828.29
8	19,950.99	151.70	2007.33	221.64	22,331.66
9	19,395.30	171.76	865.74	1227.99	21,660.79
10	18,954.76	107.95	−1395.80	3346.46	21,012.37
					241,530.14

SOURCE. W. H. Taubert, "Search Decision Rule for the Aggregate Scheduling Problem," *Management Science, 14* (6), February 1968, pp. 343–359.

more complex cost model including the possibility of using a second shift when needed; (2) the Search Mill (Redwine, [1971]), based on disguised data obtained from a major American integrated steel mill; and (3) the Search Laboratory (Taubert [1968a]), a fictitious name for a division of a large aerospace research and development laboratory. All three situations represent significant extensions beyond the paint company application with highly complex cost models and other factors to challenge the SDR methodology. Results from the Search Laboratory application are discussed in Situation 21.

Flowers and Preston [1977] applied the SDR methodology to work force planning in one department of a tank trailer manufacturer. The department had a work force ranging from 14 to 23 employees, and the company employed a total of 250 to 350 persons. Because the department worked almost exclusively from a backlog of firm orders, the assumption of perfect forecasts was logical and was accepted by management as representing reality. The simplicity of the situation made it possible to restrict decisions to the single variable of work force size. SDR decisions were about 3 percent less costly than actual decisions. This saving was regarded as significant by management and led to their desire to extend the model to include the entire work force.

COMPARATIVE PERFORMANCE
OF AGGREGATE PLANNING
DECISION PROCESSES

Because the LDR is optimal for the model, it has commonly been used as a standard for comparison by proposers of new decision processes for aggregate planning. The availability of a standard for comparison has been particularly valuable for decision processes that are not mathematically optimal. By substantially duplicating LDR performance on standard problems, such as the paint company, the general validity of new methods has been established. Such comparisons, however, fall short of validating the performance of any decision process in real environments. LDR assumes that cost structures are quadratic in form, when in fact cost functions may take a variety of mathematical forms. Thus, the best evaluation of the comparative performance of alternate decision processes is in the real world, where we are attempting to optimize the costs (or profits) actually found, instead of a restrictive model of cost behavior.

Lee and Khumawala [1974] report a comparative study carried out in the environment of a firm in the capital goods industry having annual sales of approximately $11 million. The plant was a typical closed job-shop manufacturing facility in which parts were produced for inventory and then assembled into finished products either for inventory or for customer order. A model of the firm was developed that simulated the aggregate operation of the firm. Simulated demand forecasting in the model provided an option to use either a perfect or imperfect forecast, and four alternate aggregate planning decision processes were used to plan production and work force size.

The four decision processes were LDR, SDR, Parametric Production Planning, and the Management Coefficients model. Parametric Production Planning is a decision process proposed by Jones [1967] that uses a coarse grid search procedure to evaluate four possible parameters associated with minimum cost performance in the firm's cost structure. The cost structure is developed for the particular firm and is free of constraints on mathematical form. The four parameters are then inserted in decision rules for work force size and production rate. There is no guarantee of optimality.

The Management Coefficients model was proposed by Bowman [1963] and establishes the *form* of decision rules through rigorous analysis, but determines the *coefficients* for the decision rules through statistical analysis of management's own past decisions. The theory behind Bowman's rules is rooted in the assumption that management is actually sensitive to the same behavior used in analytical models and that management behavior tends to be highly variable rather than consistently above or below optimum performance.

The assumption in the Management Coefficients model then is that management's performance can be improved considerably simply by applying the derived decision rules more consistently. In terms of the usual dish-shaped cost function, inconsistency in applying decision rules is more costly than being slightly above or below optimum decisions, but being consistent, because such functions are commonly quite flat near the optimum.

TABLE 9-6

Comparative Profit Performance

	Imperfect Forecast	Perfect Forecast
Company decisions	$4,420,000	—
Linear Decision Rule	$4,821,000	$5,078,000
Management Coefficients model	$4,607,000	$5,000,000
Parametric Production Planning	$4,900,000	$4,989,000
Search Decision Rule	$5,021,000	$5,140,000

SOURCE. W. B. Lee and B. M. Khumawala, "Simulation Testing of Aggregate Production Planning Models in an Implementation Methodology," *Management Science*, 20 (6), February 1974, pp. 903–911.

Results

Table 9-6 summarizes comparative profit performance for actual company decisions and the four test decision models. When the imperfect forecast available to the management of the firm is used, all four decision models result in increased profits. The minimum mean profit increase compared with company decisions is $187,000 (4 percent) using the Management Coefficients model. The maximum mean increase is $601,000 (14 percent) using SDR. The contrast between the profit figures for the perfect and imperfect forecast gives a measure of the value of forecast information. Although perfect forecasts increase profits ($119,000 for SDR), forecast accuracy is less significant than the decision process ($601,000 difference between SDR and company decisions, and $414,000 difference between SDR and Management Coefficients).

JOINT DECISIONS AMONG OPERATIONS, MARKETING, AND FINANCE

The entire thrust of aggregate planning and scheduling methods is to employ systems concepts in making the key decisions for operations. The results of coordinating decisions concerning activity levels, work force size, use of overtime, and inventory levels amply illustrate that these kinds of decisions should be made jointly rather than independently. To make them independently is to suboptimize. But why stop with the operations function? Would even better results be obtained if some of the key operational decisions were made jointly with other key decisions in marketing and finance?

Tuite [1968] proposed merging marketing strategy selection and production scheduling. Holloway [1969] proposed price as an independent variable coupled with allocations of compensatory promotion budgets. Bergstrom and Smith [1970] proposed estimating revenue versus sales curves for each product in each time period, the amount to be sold considered as a decision variable dependent upon price and possibly other parameters. Finally, Damon and Schramm [1972] proposed to make decisions jointly in production, marketing, and finance. In their model, marketing sector decisions are made with respect to price and promotion expenditures, and the finance sector decisions are made with respect to investment in marketable securities and short-term debt incurred or retired. The solution technique was a computer search methodology similar to SDR.

AGGREGATE PLANNING FOR NONMANUFACTURING SYSTEMS

The general nature of aggregate planning and scheduling problems in nonmanufacturing settings is basically similar in that we are attempting to build a cost or profit model in terms of the key decision variables for short-term capacity. The degrees of freedom in adjusting short-term capacity in nonmanufacturing settings are likely to be fewer, however, because of the absence of inventories and subcontractors as sources of capacity. The result is that the manager is more likely to attempt to control demand through techniques like reservations, or to absorb fluctuations in demand rather directly by varying work force size, hours worked, and overtime.

We will not attempt any detailed discussion of aggregate planning in nonmanufacturing here, because separate chapters that follow deal with operations planning and control in large-scale projects and in service systems. These chapters will include the special problems of both aggregate and detailed schedules in such systems.

IMPLICATIONS FOR THE MANAGER

The aggregate planning problem is one of the most important to managers, because it is through these plans that major resources are deployed. Through the mechanisms of aggregate planning, management's interest is focused on the most important aspects of this deployment process; basic employment levels and activity rates are set, and where inventories are available as a part of the strategy, their levels are also set. Given managerial approval of these broad level plans, detailed planning and scheduling of operations can proceed within operating constraints stated by the aggregate planning model.

We have discussed the structure of the aggregate planning problem and a number of alternate decision processes. At this point the graphic methods are probably most frequently used. Mathematical and computer search methods have been developed in an effort to improve on the traditional methods by making the process dynamic, optimum seeking, and representative of the multistage nature of the problem. Several models have been of value mainly as stepping stones to more useful models that represent reality more accurately. The most important single stepping stone has been the LDR; however, its original advantage in requiring only simple computations has been largely offset by the computer.

Presently, the computer search methods seem to offer the most promise. Although some of the analytical methods do produce optimum solutions, we must remember that it is the model which is being optimized. The real-world counterpart of the model is also optimized only if the mathematical model duplicates reality. The computer search methods are only optimum seeking by their nature, but do not suffer from the need to adhere to strict mathematical forms in the model and can therefore more nearly duplicate reality in cost and profit models.

The extension of aggregate planning models to make joint decisions among the production, marketing, and finance functions is most encouraging and demonstrates progress in our ability to employ systems concepts.

Perhaps the greatest single contribution of formal models to aggregate planning is that they provide insight for the manager into the nature of the resource problem faced. Managers need to understand that good solutions ordinarily involve a mixed strategy which uses more than one of the available options of hiring–layoff, overtime, inventories, outside processing, and so forth. The particular balance for a given organization will depend on the balance of costs in that organization. Even if formal models are not used for decision making, they may be useful as managerial learning devices concerning the short-term capacity economics of their enterprise. Their judgment about the most advantageous combination of strategies at any particular point in the seasonal cycle can be developed through a gaming process.

The manager must be concerned not only with the direct economic factors that enter the aggregate planning problem, but also with the human and social effects of alternate plans. These kinds of variables are not included in formal models; however, by considering a range of alternate plans that meet the human and social requirements in varying degrees, managers can make trade-offs between costs and the subjective values. Thus, the formal models can help managers generate aggregate plans that are acceptable on the basis of broadly based criteria.

Inventories are not available to absorb demand fluctuations in service and non-manufacturing situations. Although this variable is not available as a managerial strategy, the aggregate planning problem in such organizations is conceptually similar. Thus, managers must focus their strategies on hiring and layoff, the astute use of normal labor turnover, and the allocation of overtime and undertime. In service-oriented situations, the use of part-time workers is often an effective strategy.

IMPORTANT TERMS

Numbers in parentheses indicate page numbers

Counterseasonal product (267)

Goal programming (286)

Graphic method of aggregate planning (275)

Heuristic (286)

Linear Decision Rule, LDR (282)

Load leveling (267)

Management coefficients model (288)

Master production schedule (269)

Mixed strategy (270)

Organizational adaptation (268)

Parametric production planning (288)

Pure strategy (270)

Search Decision Rule, SDR (286)

Subcontracting (280)

REVIEW QUESTIONS AND PROBLEMS

1. What is the meaning of the term *aggregate plan*? What are the objectives of aggregate plans? What are the inputs and the nature of outputs?

2. Place aggregate planning in context with the term *planning horizon*. What is the appropriate planning horizon for aggregate planning?

3. Discuss the relevant cost components involved in aggregate planning decisions.

4. Under what conditions would a single-stage aggregate planning decision system be appropriate?

5. In what ways does a multistage aggregate planning system take account of realities that in fact would affect decisions for production rates and work force size?

6. Appraise graphic methods of aggregate planning.

7. Compare the Linear Decision Rule with the multistage aggregate planning decision system discussed and summarized by Figure 9-4. What compromises with reality, if any, have been made by the LDR model?

8. Compare the Hanssmann-Hess linear programming model of aggregate planning with the multistage decision process discussed and summarized by Figure 9-4. What compromises with reality have been made, if any, in the linear programming model?

9. As a decision system, contrast the SDR with the LDR. What are the advantages and disadvantages of each?

10. Referring to Figure 9-7:

    a. Rationalize why the cost of overtime should increase at an increasing rate as production rate increases.

    b. If inventory varies from the optimal level (minimum cost level), why would the incremental costs increase at an increasing rate as represented in Figure 9-7*d*?

11. Criticize the usefulness and validity of the strict aggregate planning concept, that is, making decisions solely in aggregate terms of work force size and production rate.

12. What is the meaning of the term *capacity* in aggregate planning models? How does a decision to hire, lay off, or subcontract affect capacity? How does physical or limiting capacity affect these decisions?

13. Cost comparisons between the result of actual managerial decisions and those produced by solving decision rule models are typically made by running both sets of decisions through the cost model and then comparing the results. Does this methodology seem valid? If not, what other approach might be followed?

14. Account for the difference in performance of the several aggregate planning decision systems in the study summarized by Table 9-6.

15. What values are gained by expanding aggregate planning decision systems to produce joint decisions among operations, marketing, and finance? Are there any disadvantages?

TABLE 9-7

Projected Production and Inventory Requirements

Month	Production Requirements	Required Buffer Stocks	Production Days
Jan.	3000	600	22
Feb.	2500	500	18
Mar.	4000	800	22
Apr.	6000	1200	21
May	8000	1600	22
June	12,000	2400	21
July	15,000	3000	21
Aug.	12,000	2400	13
Sept.	10,000	2000	20
Oct.	8000	1600	23
Nov.	4000	800	21
Dec.	3000	600	20
	87,500	17,500	244

16. Table 9-7 gives data that show projected requirements for the production of a medium-priced camera, together with buffer stock requirements and available production days in each month. Develop a chart of cumulative requirements and cumulative maximum requirements for the year, plotting cumulative production days on the horizontal axis and cumulative requirements in units on the vertical axis.

17. Using the data of Table 9-7, compare the total incremental costs involved in a level production plan, in a plan that follows maximum requirements quite closely, and in some intermediate plan. Normal plant capacity is 400 units per working day. An additional 20 percent can be obtained through overtime, but at an additional cost of $10 per unit. Inventory carrying cost is $30 per unit per year. Changes in production level cost $5000 per 10 units in production rate. Extra capacity may be obtained through subcontracting certain parts at an extra cost of $15 per unit. Beginning inventory is 600 units, or must be determined for some plans.

18. Given the data in Table 9-4:

    a. What value of inventory carrying cost would make Plans 1 and 2 equally desirable?

    b. What hiring-layoff cost makes Plans 1 and 2 equally desirable?

    c. What subcontracting cost makes Plans 2 and 3 equal?

SITUATIONS

19. Schwarz and Johnson [1978] have reevaluated the empirical performance of the paint company application of the LDR. The results of the paint company applications of LDR compared with company performance are summarized in Table 9-8. The inventory related costs (inventory plus back-order costs = 361 + 1566 = 1927) account for 1927 × 100/4085 = 47.2 percent of the total

TABLE 9-8   **Comparative Costs in Thousands for the Paint Company, 1949–1953**

		Decision Rule	
Type of Cost	Company Performance	Moving Average Forecast	Perfect Forecast
Regular payroll	$1,940	$1,834	$1,888
Overtime	196	296	167
Inventory	361	451	454
Backorders	1,566	616	400
Hiring and layoffs	22	25	20
Total cost	$4,085(139%)	$3,222(110%)	$2,929(100%)

SOURCE. C. C. Holt, F. Modigliani, and H. A. Simon, "A Linear-Decision Rule for Production and Employment Scheduling," *Management Science, 2* (2), October 1955.

company performance costs. On the other hand, these costs account for only $(451 + 616 = 1067) \times 100/3222 = 33.1$ percent of LDR total costs with the moving average forecast, and $(454 + 400 = 854) \times 100/2929 = 29.2$ percent of LDR costs with the perfect forecast.

Schwarz and Johnson focus attention on the source of cost reductions in Table 9-8. They point out that inventory-related cost reductions by themselves account for nearly all the cost reduction achieved, as shown in Table 9-9. They then state the following hypothesis:

The LDR (substitute any other aggregate planning model you like) has not been implemented because, despite its conceptual elegance, most of the cost savings of the LDR may be achieved by improved aggregate inventory management alone.

The authors argue that if company management had begun with an initial gross inventory of 380 units (corresponding to the LDR's ideal *net* inventory of 320 units) as the LDR did, total company costs would have been only $3,228,000. This is approximately the same total cost achieved by LDR using the moving average forecast. In addition, they state, "More important, *any* initial gross inventory between 380 and 700 would have resulted in total com-

TABLE 9-9   **Source of Major Cost Reductions for the LDR Application in the Paint Company**

	LDR (Moving Average Forecast) versus Company Performance	LDR (Perfect Forecast) versus Company Performance
Total cost reduction	4085 − 3222 = 863	4085 − 2929 = 1156
Inventory related cost reduction	1927 − 1067 = 860	1927 − 854 = 1073
Percent, inventory to total cost reduction	99.7%	92.8%

pany costs *lower* than the LDR with moving average forecasts." Schwarz and Johnson state further:

> *Please note that we do* not *claim that the paint company management was following the 'wrong' inventory policy, although given the firm's 'true' back-order and holding costs it would appear that it was. We also do not claim that management could be expected to have made exactly the same sequence of monthly production and work force decisions as they did before, given a higher buffer inventory. We* do *claim the following: virtually all of the LDR's cost savings could have been obtained without recourse to any aggregate planning model. All that was necessary was a different inventory management policy: in this case a significantly higher buffer inventory.*

Given the empirical findings by Schwarz and Johnson, do you feel that a company should ignore aggregate planning concepts and simply focus on aggregate inventory management, as implied in the authors' hypothesis? Would the results have been the same in another organization where the inventory costs were twice what they were in the paint company? Ten times what they were in the paint company? In relation to the preceding two questions, how do you interpret the statement by Schwarz and Johnson: "Please note that we do *not* claim that the paint company management was following the 'wrong' inventory policy, although given the firm's true backorder and holding costs it would appear that it was"? If we accept the Schwarz-Johnson implied conclusion, that only inventory management is needed, what recommendations regarding aggregate planning would you make to organizations that produce no inventoriable product?

20. The hospital admissions system is used as an overall mechanism for planning and scheduling the use of hospital facilities. The basic unit of capacity is the hospital bed, and bed occupancy level is the variable under management control. Bed occupancy level, in turn, opens up revenue flow from the broadly based health care services of the hospital. The utilization and resulting revenue from these hospital services depend, in turn, on patient mix selection that affects length of stay of patients. The demand on other hospital services, such as X-ray and other laboratories, then flows from patient mix.

The problem of operations management is not simply to maximize bed occupancy level, because emergency demands must be met and because the cost of such services incurred when bed occupancy levels are too high increases rapidly. Thus, an aggregate planning and scheduling model must take account of scheduling the flow of elective arrivals and the patient mix therefrom, as shown in Figure 9-10. This flow can be regulated to some substantial degree, because the actual admission date for such cases can be scheduled, and this represents the hospital manager's buffer against the seeming capriciousness of demand. The flow of emergency cases, however, is on a random arrival basis and compounds the problem greatly. The cost-effectiveness of the entire hospital admissions system is dependent on variables that follow probabilistic distributions. Most costs are fixed in nature (rooms, beds, laboratory facilities, basic staff), comprising up to 75 percent of total hospital costs. Yet the demand on these services is highly variable in nature.

Do you feel that aggregate planning is a useful concept in hospitals? What form should it take, that is, should it be a cost-minimizing approach, an attempt merely to find feasible solutions, a methodology designed to maximize service to patients, or what? Do you feel that any of the formal models discussed in the chapter can be applied?

21. Taubert [1968] developed an aggregate planning cost model for the Search Laboratory, a hypothetical name for a real company. The laboratory is housed in a 100,000 square foot facility employing a staff of 400. Approximately 300 members of the staff are classified as direct technical employees, and the balance are indirect administrative support for the operations of the laboratory.

The laboratory offers a capability through its scientific staff and facilities, and widely fluctuating employment could severely impair this capability. The research programs of the laboratory are funded by both the government and the corporation, and an important part of the operating environment is wide fluctuations in government sales and rapid shifts in technology. Thus the operations planning problem is defined by the need for employment stability on the one hand and wide fluctuations in government sales on the other.

Specifically, the operations planning problem is centered in a monthly decision by the director to determine the size of the scientific staff and administrative staff as well as the allocation of the scientific staff to government contracts, corporate research programs, and overhead. Overhead charges arise when there are no contracts or corporate research programs available for scientists. This charge is in addition to the charges normally made to overhead for the usual indirect costs. In effect, then, overhead is used as a buffer to absorb fluctuations in the demand for scientific personnel. The four independent decision variables incorporated in the aggregate planning model are as follows:

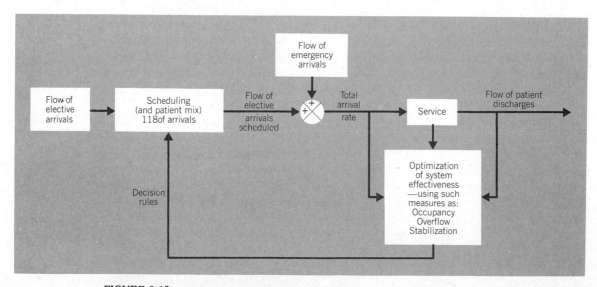

FIGURE 9-10
An overview view of the hospital admissions process.
SOURCE: J. H. Milsum, E. Turban, and I. Vertinsky. "Hospital Admissions Systems: Their Evaluation and Management," Management Science, 19(6), February 1973, p. 655.

1. The size of the scientific staff:

   WG_t = personnel allocated to government contracts
   WR_t = personnel allocated to corporate research programs
   WO_t = personnel allocated to overhead

2. WI_t = size of the indirect administrative support staff.

Cost Model

Figure 9-11 shows the 12 cost relations that form the components for the cost model of the Search Laboratory. Note that a variety of mathematical relationships are included, such as linear, piecewise linear, constraints, and nonlinear forms. Taubert also built into the model a complete set of equations representing the overhead cost structure used to compute the overhead rate for any given set of decision variables. The resulting overhead rate is then used to compute the monthly government sales volume, which in turn is compared with a cumulative sales target.

The inputs to the decision system are monthly forecasts of contract personnel, research personnel, overhead personnel, and a cumulative sales target that represents the financial plan of the laboratory. The total personnel forecast must be met, and it is a part of the director's operations planning problem to determine the best combination of decision variables that will accomplish the objective. Failure to meet the personnel requirements increases costs, and this effect is also implemented in the cost model.

Results

Taubert validated the cost model against the financial record of the laboratory over a $5\frac{1}{2}$-year period. Following the validation, the decision system was operated for each month in the $5\frac{1}{2}$-year test period. A 6-month planning horizon was used that required SDR to optimize a 24-dimensional response surface (four decisions per month for a 6-month planning horizon). Figure 9-12 summarizes the comparative results. Figure 9-12a shows the contrast between SDR decisions on contract and research personnel compared with forecasts; Figure 9-12b shows a similar comparison of actual management decisions compared with forecasts. Note that the SDR decisions responded much more smoothly to fluctuating personnel forecasts than did actual management decisions.

The costs resulting from SDR decisions compared with actual management decisions indicated that SDR would have produced cost savings. Over the $5\frac{1}{2}$-year test period, the SDR advantage ranged from a high of 19.7 percent to a low of 5.2 percent, averaging 11.9 percent over the entire test period. The SDR decisions produced lower overhead rates and significant cost reductions in direct payroll, research program staffing, sales target penalties and rewards, and direct hiring costs. It achieved these results largely through the more extensive use of overtime.

If you were the manager of the Search Laboratory, would the aggregate planning system developed be helpful in making decisions? If so, what kinds of decisions? The Search Laboratory is a system without inventories. With inven-

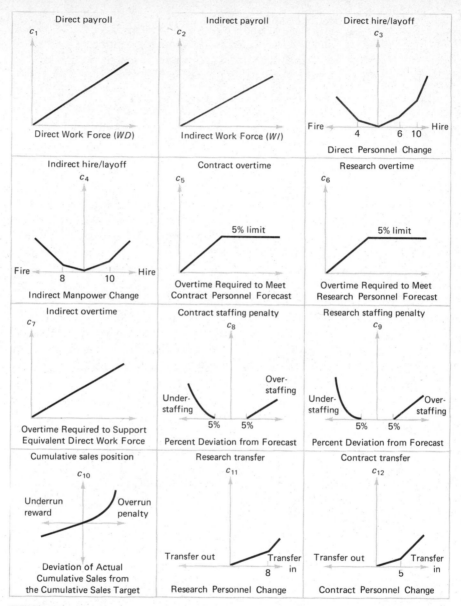

FIGURE 9-11
The 12 cost relationships for the Search Laboratory cost model.
SOURCE: *W. H. Taubert. "The Search Decision Rule Approach to Operations Planning," Unpublished PhD dissertation, UCLA, 1968.*

tories not available as a trade-off, are the manager's hands tied? Is there any flexibility left for him or her?

22. As a follow-up on the Search Laboratory model discussed in Situation 21, Taubert [1968] subsequently disaggregated the decision variables for the size of the scientific staff into six departments. In effect, each department was con-

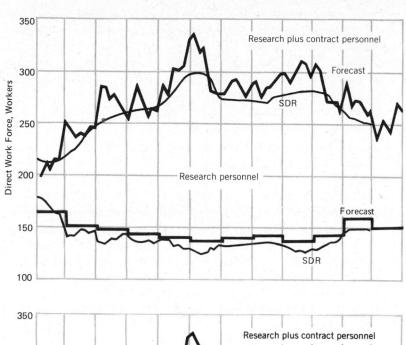

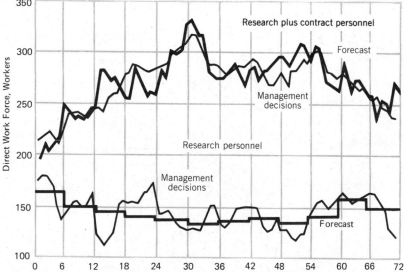

FIGURE 9-12
Results of SDR decisions for Search Laboratory I compared with forecasts and actual management decisions.
SOURCE: *W. H. Taubert. "The Search Decision Rule Approach to Operations Planning," Unpublished PhD disseration, UCLA, 1968.*

sidered a miniature laboratory with its own contract and research manpower forecast as a sales target. Thus, the allocation of research personnel had to be made in each of the six departments. Although some transferring of personnel was allowed, this practice was limited because of the fact that, in general, scientists are not interchangeable and cannot readily be shifted from one department or technical expertise to another simply to meet fluctuating personnel needs. Residual departmental personnel adjustments then had to be handled by hiring and layoff decisions.

The SDR decisions followed the forecasts with a smooth response, carrying members of the scientific staff in overhead for short periods of time when faced with downturns in the personnel forecasts.

How do you evaluate the disaggregate planning system? Would the additional detail be useful, or simply excess baggage?

23. Geoffrion, Dyer, and Feinberg [1972] developed an aggregate planning model for a school of management and applied it at the Graduate School of Management at UCLA. The faculty of the school may be viewed as engaging in three primary activities: formal teaching, school service (e.g., administration and curriculum development), and activities such as research and student counseling. The formal teaching occurs at three levels: graduate, lower-division undergraduate, and upper-division undergraduate. The basic planning unit of output is the equivalent course section and all activities are related to that equivalence. Thus, "course releases" are given for such items as administrative activities, curriculum development, and research, so that the overall allocation of faculty effort can be planned in terms of equivalent course section capacity.

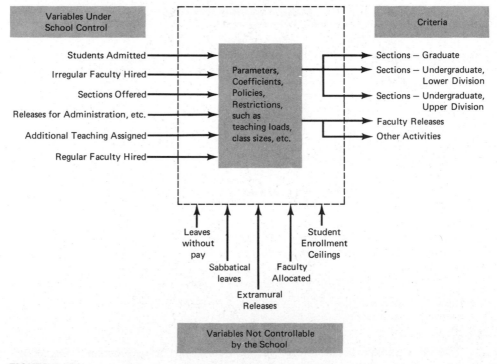

FIGURE 9-13

Aggregate planning model for a school of management.

SOURCE: *Adapted from A. M. Geoffrion, J. S. Dyer, and A. Feinberg. "An Interactive Approach for Multi-criterion Optimization, with an Application to the Operation of an Academic Department,"* Management Science, 19(4), December 1972, pp. 357–368.

Figure 9-13 summarizes an aggregate planning and scheduling model for such a school. The major features of the model are the identification of the variables under school control, those not controllable by the school (such as policies, procedures, and restrictions), and the multiple criteria and output by which resulting aggregate schedules are judged. The capacity to carry on the various activities is complicated by the differing roles of the various kinds of faculty. For example, lecturers provide only teaching service, being assigned eight quarter courses per academic year, but no administrative, committee, or other assignments. Regular faculty teach five quarter courses per year, but carry on many other activities, such as counseling, committee service, and research. Teaching assistants assist in courses and sometimes teach sections of courses in the ratio of one full-time assistant for six equivalent course sections. University rules permit only faculty with certain qualifications to teach graduate level courses, upper-division undergraduate courses, and so on.

Thus, administrators are forced to think in terms of various decision alternatives in filling vacancies in the faculty, as well as in deciding on the other variables under control. The number of students admitted can be controlled, the aggregate number of course sections can be varied, and the amount of equivalent nonteaching activities can be varied.

The central university administration determines certain upper limits of capacity through its budget allocations for faculty and student enrollments, and leaves of absence and extramural releases reduce the capacity available in the planning period.

The criteria and output listed on the right of Figure 9-13 are in fact the unique conception of the school model. As outputs, they represent the aggregate schedule for courses of different levels to be offered, plus faculty time spent in other ways. However, they are also the dimensions of a multiple criterion problem, on which the decision-maker's preference for a given mix of activities is defined.

The decision model is actually interactive between the decision maker and a computational model in which the decision maker estimates weights for his or her preference for each of the outputs. Given these weights, a mathematical programming algorithm allocates available faculty time to courses at the several levels, releases, research, and additional activities. The computer output of the results is then examined, and the weights are altered if necessary. The weights, in fact, are expressive of the decision-maker's preference for the relative emphasis between criteria. They are estimates of marginal substitution rates between each pair of criteria, for example, how many sections of lower-division courses the decision maker is willing to give up for an additional graduate section. This approach to the problem is an attempt to incorporate within the quantitative model dimensions of the multiple criteria for decisions. Given the broad allocations of faculty effort in the aggregate schedule, detailed schedules for actual faculty course assignments must be made, as well as correlated classroom and other facility schedules.

How do you evaluate the school of management aggregate planning system? Would it be really useful to administrators, or would it fall into disuse? What is the criterion in the model?

24. Krajewski and Thompson [1975] developed an aggregate employment planning model for public utilities and applied it in the specific setting of a telephone company. The model has important implications both for management and for the public. The implications for management are for improving resource management and taking advantage of the infrastructure of costs to maximize returns. The implications for the public are in the allowable prices (rates) they must pay.

In the specific setting of a telephone company, the model covered the plant personnel required to install, remove, relocate, repair, and maintain all equipment used for telephones. This equipment ranges from the telephone itself to cable and wires necessary for cross-country transmission. Four classes of employees are involved: PBX repairmen, installer-repairmen, cable splicers, and linemen. In general, the four work groups are regarded as crafts, with the only interchangeability being that linemen can also make telephone connections.

The demand for service is subject to some seasonality for installation and removal of phones (summer peak), and weather conditions can produce seasonal demands for service and cable installation and splicing. On the other hand, telephone repair service is closely related to the number of phones in service. The result of the seasonal nature of the aggregate demand is that the size and timing of hirings, layoffs, and use of overtime work and part-time employees are important decisions. The adroit use of the flexibility available in the employment decisions is a buffer available to management to deal with seasonality, because the output of the system cannot be stored. Two additional variables are under managerial control to deal with demand variations, but both of them interact with the employment decisions: they can vary the level of service and for construction work they can subcontract.

Krajewski and Thompson developed a linear programming model designed to minimize aggregate employment related costs over a planning horizon. The costs were full- and part-time wage costs for regular and overtime work, hiring costs, layoff costs, and subcontracting costs. Within the model, hiring costs were segregated for replacement, a rehire of one laid off, and a hire for expansion. The latter requires additional capital investment, which in turn has rate base implications. The model also contains constraints on employment, production, overtime, and backlog or service delay.

The managerial use of the employment planning model is to prepare annual budgets for the plant department and to determine the monthly operating guidelines for hiring, layoff, overtime by labor class, and for subcontracting.

Some of the results of the study are in the service delay versus cost relationships and the rate of return versus cost to public relationships. For an illustrative simplified example, they showed that the service delay-cost curve was quite shallow; that is, the annual cost difference between zero and a 5-day delay was only $11,200. The reason is found in the model structure, because the service delay-cost trade-off is only through overtime and hiring costs, which are a small fraction of total employment costs.

Expansion of the work force to accommodate demand increases requires supporting capital investment, and this investment goes into the *rate base* on which the company is allowed to earn a return. Therefore, Krajewski and

Thompson defined an additional cost to expand, involving equity rate of return and depreciation. This cost then enters into the balance of costs for employment planning and leads to an incentive to expand work force in the capital intensive work groups, such as linemen. The result here is that for a demand growth of 10 percent in their example, the model with rate of return yields a 31 percent larger lineman work force for the same service, compared with the results if the capital cost is excluded. The net result is a greater total cost of $5300 to be passed on to the consumer for the same service level.

How do you evaluate the aggregate employment planning system developed for the telephone company? How would you as a manager use the results of the system in monthly planning? Is there an incentive for the telephone company to expand the lineman work force and use less overtime and subcontracting in order to optimize its rate base?

REFERENCES

Bergstrom, G. L., and B. E. Smith, "Multi-item Production Planning—An Extension of the HMMS Rules," *Management Science*, *16*(10), June 1970, pp. 614–629.

Bowman, E. H., "Consistency and Optimality in Managerial Decision Making," *Management Science, 9*(2), January 1963, pp. 310–321.

Buffa, E. S., "Aggregate Planning for Production," *Business Horizons,* Fall 1967.

Buffa, E. S., and J. G. Miller, *Production-Inventory Systems: Planning and Control* (3rd ed.). Irwin, Homewood, Ill. 1979.

Buffa, E. S., and W. H. Taubert, "Evaluation of Direct Computer Search Methods for the Aggregate Planning Problem," *Industrial Management Review*, Fall 1967.

Connel, B. C., E. E. Adam, Jr., and A. N. Moore, "Aggregate Planning and Scheduling in Food Service Systems With Varying Technologies," forthcoming.

Damon, W. W., and R. Schramm, "A Simultaneous Decision Model for Production, Marketing, and Finance," *Management Science, 19*(2), October 1972, pp. 161–172.

Flowers, A. D., D. L. Dukes, and W. D. Curtiss, "A Dynamic Programming Approach to Workforce Scheduling," Private communication, November 1977.

Flowers, A. D., and S. E. Preston, "Workforce Scheduling with the Search Decision Rule," *Omega, 5*(4), 1977.

Galbraith, J. R., "Solving Production Smoothing Problems," *Management Science, 15*(12), August 1969, pp. 665–674.

Geoffrion, A. M., J. S. Dyer, and A. Feinberg, "An Interactive Approach for Multi-criterion Optimization, with an Application to the Operation of an Academic Department," *Management Science, 19*(4), December 1972, pp. 357–368.

Hanssmann, F., and S. W. Hess, "A Linear Programming Approach to Production and Employment Scheduling," *Management Technology, 1,* January 1960, pp. 46–52.

Holloway, C. A., "A Mathematical Programming Approach to Identification and Optimization of Complex Operational Systems with the Aggregate Planning Problem as an Example." Unpublished PhD dissertation, UCLA, 1969.

Holt, C. C., F. Modigliani, and J. F. Muth, "Derivation of a Linear Decision Rule for

Production and Employment," *Management Science, 2*(2), January 1956, pp. 159–177.

Holt, C. C., F. Modigliani, J. F. Muth, and H. A. Simon, *Planning, Production, Inventories and Work Force.* Prentice-Hall, Englewood Cliffs, N. J., 1960.

Holt, C. C., F. Modigliani, and H. A. Simon, "A Linear Decision Rule for Production and Employment Scheduling," *Management Science, 2*(2), October 1955, pp. 1–30.

Jones, C. H., "Parametric Production Planning," *Management Science, 13*(11), July 1967, pp. 843–866.

Krajewski, L. J., and H. E. Thompson, "Efficient Employment Planning in Public Utilities," *Bell Journal of Economics and Management Science,* Spring 1975.

Lee, S. M., and L. J. Moore, "A Practical Approach to Production Scheduling," *Production and Inventory Management*, 1st Quarter, 1974, pp. 79–92.

Lee, W. B., and B. M. Khumawala, "Simulation Testing of Aggregate Production Planning Models in an Implementation Methodology," *Management Science, 20*(6), February 1974, pp. 903–911.

Monden, Y., Two-Part Series on Toyota's Production Smoothing: Part One, "Smoothed Production Lets Toyota Adapt to Demand Changes and Reduce Inventory," *Industrial Engineering,* Vol. 13, No. 8, August 1981, pp. 42–51; Part Two, "How Toyota Shortened Supply Lot Production Time, Waiting Time and Conveyance Time," *Industrial Engineering,* Vol. 13, No. 9, September 1981, pp. 22–30.

Redwine, C. N., "A Mathematical Programming Approach to Production Scheduling in a Steel Mill," Unpublished PhD dissertation, UCLA, 1971.

Schwarz, L. B., and R. E. Johnson, "An Appraisal of the Empirical Performance of the Linear Decision Rule," *Management Science, 24*(8), April 1978, pp. 844–849.

Taubert, W. H., "Search Decision Rule for the Aggregate Scheduling Problem," *Management Science, 14*(6), February 1968, pp. 343–359.

Taubert, W. H., "The Search Decision Rule Approach to Operations Planning," Unpublished PhD dissertation, UCLA, 1968a.

Tuite, M. F., "Merging Market Strategy Selection and Production Scheduling," *Journal of Industrial Engineering, 19*(2), February 1968, pp. 76–84.

Vergin, R. C., "Production Scheduling Under Seasonal Demand," *Journal of Industrial Engineering, 17*(5), May 1966.

SUPPLEMENT
Linear Decision Rule Model, and
Linear Programming Methods of
Aggregate Planning

LINEAR DECISION RULE MODEL

The objective function is the sum of all costs over the planning horizon, as indicated in Equation 1. These costs are represented by the four cost functions segregated in Equation 2 as regular payroll, hiring and layoff, overtime, and inventory-connected costs.

The problem is then to minimize costs over N periods, or

$$C_N = \sum_{t=1}^{N} C_t \qquad (1)$$

and

$$C_t = [(c_1 W_t) \qquad \text{Regular payroll costs}$$

$$+ c_2 (W_t - W_{t-1})^2 \qquad \text{Hiring and layoff costs} \qquad (2)$$

$$+ c_3 (P_t - c_4 W_t)^2 + c_5 P_t - c_6 W_t \qquad \text{Overtime costs}$$

$$+ c_7 (I_t - c_8 - c_9 S_t)^2] \qquad \text{Inventory-connected costs}$$

subject to restraints,

$$I_{t-1} + P_t - F_t = I_t \qquad t = 1, 2, \ldots N \qquad (3)$$

The total cost for N periods is given by Equation 1 and the monthly cost, C_t, is given by Equation 2. Equation 3 states the relationship between beginning inventory, production, and sales during the month, and ending inventory.

Equations 1, 2, and 3 are general and applicable to a broad range of situations. By estimating the values of the c's a specific factory cost structure can be specified. For a paint factory, Equation 4 is the result:

$$C_N = \sum_{t=1}^{N} \{[340 W_t] + [64.3(W_t - W_{t-1})^2]$$

$$+ [0.20(P_t - 5.67 W_t)^2 + 51.2 P_t - 281 W_t] \qquad (4)$$

$$+ [0.0825(I_t - 320)^2]\}$$

OPTIMAL DECISION RULES FOR THE PAINT FACTORY

A solution to Equation 4 was obtained by differentiating with respect to each decision variable. The result for the paint factory is contained in Equation 5 and 6:

$$P_t = \begin{Bmatrix} +0.463\,S_t \\ +0.234\,S_{t+1} \\ +0.111\,S_{t+2} \\ +0.046\,S_{t+3} \\ +0.013\,S_{t+4} \\ -0.002\,S_{t+5} \\ -0.008\,S_{t+6} \\ -0.010\,S_{t+7} \\ -0.009\,S_{t+8} \\ -0.008\,S_{t+9} \\ -0.007\,S_{t+10} \\ -0.005\,S_{t+11} \end{Bmatrix} + 0.993\,W_{t-1} + 153 - 0.464 I_{t-1} \tag{5}$$

$$W_t = 0.743\,W_{t-1} + 2.09 - 0.010 I_{t-1} + \begin{Bmatrix} +0.0101\,S_t \\ +0.0088\,S_{t+1} \\ +0.0071\,S_{t+2} \\ +0.0054\,S_{t+3} \\ +0.0042\,S_{t+4} \\ +0.0031\,S_{t+5} \\ +0.0023\,S_{t+6} \\ +0.0016\,S_{t+7} \\ +0.0012\,S_{t+8} \\ +0.0009\,S_{t+9} \\ +0.0006\,S_{t+10} \\ +0.0005\,S_{t+11} \end{Bmatrix} \tag{6}$$

where P_t = the number of units of product that should be produced during the forthcoming month t.

W_{t-1} = the number of employees in the work force at the beginning of the month (end of the previous month).

I_{t-1} = the number of units of inventory minus the number of units on back order at the beginning of the month.

W_t = the number of employees that will be required for the current month t. The number of employees that should be hired is therefore $W_t - W_{t-1}$.

S_t = a forecast of number of units of product that will be ordered for shipment during the current month t.

Equations 5 and 6 would be used at the beginning of each month. Equation 5 determines the aggregate production rate and Equation 6, the aggregate size of the work force.

LINEAR PROGRAMMING METHODS OF AGGREGATE PLANNING

The Distribution Model

The distribution model of linear programming was originally proposed for aggregate planning by Bowman.* In the context of the distribution model, "sources" are the capacity sources, and "destinations" are the sales periods to which output will be assigned. The objective function of the model minimizes production plus storage costs. The constraints are available capacity, and sales demand which must be met. The model assigns units of capacity to minimize costs within the capacity and sales constraints. See Appendix C, Linear Programming—Distribution Methods for formulation and solution methods.

Table 9-10 shows the generalized matrix of costs and the rim conditions. For example, the capacities rim conditions are represented by the "total capacities" column on the far right; and the sales requirements rim conditions are represented by the "total requirements" row at the bottom of the table. The computation of the cost elements for each cell is as indicated. There are n periods in the planning horizon. We will discuss the construction of the costs and rim conditions.

The sources of capacity are initial inventory, I_0, regular time production capacity in period i, R_i, and overtime capacity in period i, O_i. Note in Table 9-10 that following the initial inventory, there is a regular production capacity, and an overtime capacity for each period in the far right column under "Total Capacities."

The sales requirements rim conditions are indicated by the S_i, the forecasted sales in each period. The ending inventory is I_n, and both I_0 and I_n must be specified.

The cell elements are the costs associated with each period, and include both production and storage costs, as appropriate. For example, reading across the initial inventory row, Inventory (0), the costs have the following significance: initial inventory held for assignment to sales period 2 will have accumulated storage costs of C_I; that is, one period's storage costs. Initial inventory held for assignment to sales period 3 will have accumulated two periods of storage cost or $2C_I$, and so on for n periods, where initial inventory will have accumulated storage costs of $(n - 1)C_I$. Initial inventory held to the end of the nth period, that is, ending inventory will have accumulated storage costs of nC_I.

Similarly, the row, "Regular (1)" costs indicate that regular production assigned and used in period 1 will have accumulated only the cost of production, C_R. However, that amount assigned to be produced in period 1 and sold in period 2 will have accumulated one period's storage cost for a period 2 cost of $C_R + C_I$, and that amount assigned for sale in period 3 will have accumulated two periods' storage cost for a period 3 cost of $C_R + 2C_I$, and so on.

Some of the cell elements indicate a cost M, an overwhelmingly large cost, in order to forestall the possibility of assignment of production for sale in those periods. Such assignments would have the significance of production in one period for sale in the previous period, which obviously is not feasible in this formulation. Note the costs for the nth column, rows R (2) and O (2) have the factor $(n - 2)$. This is because the sales periods 1 and 2 are not included in the computation of inventory

* E. H. Bowman. "Production Scheduling by the Transportation Method of Linear Programming," *Operations Research*, 4 (1), 1956.

TABLE 9-10
Unit Costs for Distribution Table Representation of Aggregate Planning

| Production Periods (Source) | Sales Periods (Destination) | | | | | | | Total Capacities |
	(1)	(2)	(3)		(n)	Inventory (n)	Slack	
Inventory (0)	0	C_I	$2C_I$	... ...	$(n-1)C_I$	nC_I	0	I_0
Regular (1)	C_R	$C_R + C_I$	$C_R + 2C_I$	... ...	$C_R + (n-1)C_I$	$C_R + nC_I$	0	R_1
Overtime (1)	C_O	$C_O + C_1$	$C_O + 2C_1$	... ...	$C_O + (n-1)C_I$	$C_O + nC_I$	0	O_1
Regular (2)	M	C_R	$C_R + C_I$	... ...	$C_R + (n-2)C_I$	$C_R + (n-1)C_I$	0	R_2
Overtime (2)	M	C_O	$C_O + C_I$	... ...	$C_O + (n-2)C_I$	$C_O + (n-1)C_I$	0	O_2
Regular (3)	M	M	C_R	... ...	$C_R + (n-3)C_I$	$C_R + (n-2)C_I$	0	R_3
Overtime (3)	M	M	C_O	... ...	$C_O + (n-3)C_I$	$C_O + (n-2)C_I$	0	O_3
...	...	...	...	... ...	...	...	...	...
...	...	...	...	... ...	...	...	...	...
Regular (n)	M	M	M	... ...	C_R	$C_R + C_I$	0	R_n
Overtime (n)	M	M	M	... ...	C_O	$C_O + C_I$	0	O_n
Total Requirements	S_1	S_2	S_3	... ...	S_n	I_n	*	

Notation:

I_i = Inventory at the end of the ith period.
R_i = Maximum number of units that can be produced during the ith time period on regular time.
O_i = Maximum number of units that can be produced during the ith time period on overtime.
S_i = Number of units of finished product to be sold (delivered) during the ith time period.
C_R = Cost of production per unit on regular time.
C_O = Cost of production per unit on overtime.
C_I = Cost of storage per unit per time period.

* Slack total = $I_0 + \Sigma R + \Sigma O - \Sigma S - I_n$

SOURCE: From E. H. Bowman, "Production Scheduling by the Transportation Method of Linear Programming," *Operations Research*, 4(1), 1956.

cost because sales period 1 represents an infeasible assignment, and period 2 is the period in which production takes place. Therefore, no inventory cost is incurred for either of these two periods. A similar logic holds for the $(n-3)$ factors in rows R (3) and O (3).

An Example

Table 9-11 provides sales requirements, production rates by period, and cost data for a small-appliance manufacturer. The regular production rate is 30 units per day, so that in a 21-day period, the maximum regular capacity would be $21 \times 30 = 630$ units. An additional 6 units per day can be produced on overtime, resulting in an additional capacity of $21 \times 6 = 126$ units, as indicated in Table 9-11.

Table 9-12 shows the distribution table required to determine the optimum production program for the data in Table 9-11. The typical cost elements follow the format of Table 9-10. When the distribution table is solved by the methods discussed in Appendix C, Linear Programming—Distribution Methods, the optimum production program shown in Table 9-13 results.

Interpretation. The initial seasonal inventory of 1000 units was used in periods 1, 2, 3, and 4 to provide for the requirements peak that occurs in periods 2 and 3 (see the requirements schedule in Table 9-11). The regular production in period 1 was

TABLE 9-11   **Production Requirements, Production Rates, and Cost and Inventory Data for a Small-Appliance Manufacturer**

			Maximum per Period	
Periods	Days in Period	Requirements, Units	Regular Time	Overtime
1	21	700	630	126
2	21	1000	630	126
3	21	1000	630	126
4	21	900	630	126
5	20	600	600	120
6	20	600	600	120
7	20	500	600	120
8	20	600	600	120
9	20	300	600	120
10	20	300	600	120
11	20	300	600	120
12	20	400	600	120
	244	7200	7320	1464

Cost of production per unit, regular time, $C_R =$ $40
Cost of production per unit, overtime, $C_O =$ $60
Cost of storage per unit per time period, $C_I =$ $20
Beginning inventory, units, $I_0 =$ 1000
Ending inventory, units, $I_n =$ 700

used in that period to satisfy some of the period 1 requirements, and no overtime was necessary in that period, and so on.

There are several cells with zero evaluations, indicating that alternate optimal solutions exist. For example, we can satisfy more of the period 1 requirement from initial inventory and hold the production in that period to satisfy some of the period 2

TABLE 9-12   **Distribution Table for Production Program. Data From Table 9-11**

Production Periods (Source)	Sales Periods (Destinations)					Inventory	Slack	Total Capacities by Period, Units
	(1)	(2)	(3)		(12)	(12)		
Inventory (0)	0	20	40	... ...	220	240	0	1000
Regular (1)	40	60	80	... ...	260	280	0	630
Overtime (1)	60	80	100	... ...	280	300	0	126
Regular (2)	M	40	60	... ...	240	260	0	630
Overtime (2)	M	60	80	... ...	260	280	0	126
Regular (3)	M	M	40	... ...	220	240	0	630
Overtime (3)	M	M	60	... ...	240	260	0	126
...	...	...	...	... ...	...	...	...	...
...	...	...	...	... ...	...	...	...	...
Regular (12)	M	M	M	... ...	40	60	0	600
Overtime (12)	M	M	M	... ...	60	80	0	126
Total Requirements	700	1000	1000	... ...	400	700	1884	9784

TABLE 9-13
Optimum Production Program to Minimize Production and Inventory Costs

Production Periods (Source)	(1)	(2)	(3)	(4)	(5)	(6)	(7)	(8)	(9)	(10)	(11)	(12)	(12)	Slack	Total Capacities by Periods
							Sales Periods (Destination)								
Inv. (0)	700	126	126	48											1000
R (1)		630													630
O (1)														126	126
R (2)		244	386												630
O (2)														126	126
R (3)			488	142											630
O (3)														126	126
R (4)				630											630
O (4)				80										46	126
R (5)					600										600
O (5)														120	120
R (6)						600									600
O (6)														120	120
R (7)							500							100	600
O (7)														120	120
R (8)								600							600
O (8)														120	120
R (9)									300					300	600
O (9)														120	120
R (10)										300				300	600
O (10)														120	120
R (11)											300		300		600
O (11)													80	40	120
R (12)												400	200		600
O (12)													120		120
Total Reqr.	700	1000	1000	900	600	600	500	600	300	300	300	400	700	1884	9784

requirement. But because the costs are the same if we hold 630 units of initial inventory one more period as compared with holding the 630 regular units produced one more period, we are completely indifferent to which units are held.

The requirements peak at the beginning of the year is met almost entirely through regular production and inventory; overtime production is used only in the fourth period when the beginning seasonal inventory is almost used up. Overtime production is used again in the 11th and 12th periods to build up the ending inventory requirements specified as 700 units.

There is adequate capacity to meet the requirements peak near the beginning of the year *if* the beginning inventory is set at 1000 units. On the other hand, if beginning inventory had been set as low as 500 units, regular and overtime capacity could not have met the sales requirements. It would have been necessary either to obtain outside capacity, to back order, or to lose some sales.

In evaluating the use of the distribution model in this example, we note that work force size changes would have been necessary, or very large idle time costs would have been incurred in the 7th through 11th periods. Also, the program calls for an increase in regular time production (presumably through hiring) between the 7th and 8th periods (from 500 to 600 units), although the 9th period production is immediately cut to 300 units. If production change costs had been explicitly considered in the model, it probably would have been less costly to meet the 8th period increase in requirements through overtime production rather than by expanding the regular work force size and incurring the costs of hiring and layoff.

Extensions of the Distribution Model*

Multiple Products. The basic table can be extended to more than one product by establishing a separate column in each period for each product, but labeling of the rows and the number of rows remain the same, because we assume that the available capacity will be time-shared by the set of products. The unit product and storage costs need not be identical for all periods, even though this is not made explicit in the notation.

Backlogging Demand. In Table 9-12, the cells with an "M" cost are infeasible. However, if we decided that backlogged demand was a feasible alternative in the system, we could meet period 1 demand through production in period 2, for example. We could extend the backlogging time by meeting period 1 demand in periods 3, 4, 5, and so on. If the cost to backlog was $10 per unit per period backlogged, then the regular time cost for Table 9-12 to meet period 1 demand in period 2 would be $40 + $10 = $50 per unit. The cell cost for meeting period 1 demand by overtime in period 2 would be $60 + $10 = $70 per unit. To meet period 1 demand by regular production in period 3 would cost $40 + $20 = $60 per unit, and by overtime, $60 + $20 = $80, and so on.

Lost Sales. If stockouts are allowed in the system, then a portion of demand is not met. The distribution table can be modified by adding a lost sales row for each period. The cell cost would be the unit cost of a lost sale, presumably the lost contribution.

Perishability. If the product has a limited shelf life and cannot be sold after being in inventory for a stated time, then assignments beyond that life are infeasible. To take account of this factor, the cell costs beyond the shelf life would be replaced by the M cost to eliminate them from the solution. For example, in Table 9-12, for a 3-month shelf life, the production on either regular or overtime in period 1 could be held through period 4. Beyond period 4 in those two rows, the costs would be replaced by M, including the 12th period inventory column.

Subcontracting. Capacity can be expanded by adding subcontracting as a source; that is, adding a subcontracting row for each production period. The cell costs are the subcontracting cost per unit plus any accumulated inventory cost, depending on how long the units are held before they are used to satisfy demand, as in our example.

Experience Curve Effects. These effects are to increase capacity and to lower unit costs. Therefore, the capacity rim conditions would need to be adjusted to reflect the capacity changes in future periods. Similarly, the cell costs for regular and overtime would be adjusted to reflect the appropriate unit production costs for a given period.

---

* See K. Singhal, "A Generalized Model for Production Scheduling by Transportation Method of LP," *Industrial Management, 19* (5), September–October 1977, pp. 1–6.

Minimize

$$Z = \sum_{t=1}^{T} (c_t X_t + \ell_t W_t + \ell_t' O_t + h_t I_t^+ + \pi_t I_t^- + e_t w_t^+ + e_t' w_t^-) \qquad (7)$$

subject to, for $t = 1, 2, \ldots, T$

$$+ I_t = I_{t-1} + X_t - S_t$$
$$I_t = I_t^+ - I_t^- \qquad (8)$$
$$+ W_t = W_{t-1} + w_t^+ - w_t^- \qquad (9)$$
$$Q_t - U_t = m X_t - W_t \qquad (10)$$
$$\qquad (11)$$

$X_t, I_t^+, I_t^-, W_t, w_t^+, w_t^-, O_t, U_t \text{ all} \geq 0$

Where:

$S_t =$ Demand in period t (in units of product).
$W_t =$ Work force level in period t, measured in regular time hours.
$w_t^+ =$ Increase in work force level from period $t - 1$ to t (in hours).
$w_t^- =$ Decrease in work force level from period $t - 1$ to t (in hours).
$O_t =$ Overtime scheduled in period t (in hours).
$U_t =$ Undertime (unused regular time capacity) scheduled in period t (in hours).
$X_t =$ Production scheduled for period t (in units of product).
$I_t^+ =$ On-hand inventory at the end of period t
$I_t^- =$ Back order position at the end of period t.
$m =$ Number of hours required to produce one unit of product.
$\ell_t =$ Cost of an hour's worth of labor on regular time in period t.
$\ell_t' =$ Cost of an hour's worth of labor on overtime in period t.
$e_t =$ Cost to increase the work force level by one hour in period t.
$e_t' =$ Cost to decrease the work force level by one hour in period t.
$h_t =$ Inventory carrying cost, per unit held from period t to $t + 1$.
$\pi_t =$ Back order cost, per unit carried from period t to $t + 1$.
$c_t =$ Unit variable production cost in period t (excluding labor).

FIGURE 9-14
Generalized linear optimization model for aggregate planning.

Generalized Linear Optimization Model for Aggregate Planning

The distribution model of linear programming has disadvantages compared with later linear programming models developed. The most serious disadvantage is that it does not include the costs of changing production capacity levels. The distribution model assumes that the capacity levels have already been determined by another process.

A minor disadvantage of the distribution model is that it does not deal directly with the decision variable of work force size, and the number of workers to be hired or laid off. These values must be computed outside the model to reflect the need for more or fewer workers depending on the capacity levels set.

In the time since Bowman developed the distribution model for aggregate planning, a number of linear programming formulations have been developed that overcome these disadvantages. Most of these models can be viewed as variations on the generalized information shown in Figure 9-14 (Equations 7–11).* See Appendix B for linear programming methods.

* See E. S. Buffa and J. G. Miller, *Production-Inventory Systems: Planning and Control*, 3rd edition, Richard D. Irwin, Inc., Homewood, Ill., 1979.

The objective function (Equation 7) minimizes, over the entire planning horizon of T periods, the sum of regular production costs, regular and overtime labor costs, inventory and backlogging costs, and work force change costs.

Constraint Equation 8 merely states that the ending inventory I_t, equals the beginning inventory plus the production during the period minus demand during the period.

Constraint Equation 9 states a further restriction on ending inventory, I_t, to take account of the balance between inventory on hand and back orders.

Constraint Equation 10 states that the work force level in period t, W_t, measured in regular time hours, is equal to the previous period level, W_{t-1}, plus any additions or decreases due to hiring or layoff.

Constraint Equation 11 states a required balance between the sum of overtime hours scheduled less undertime or unused capacity in period t, and the hours used to produce the number of units scheduled, X_t, less the work force size in hours available. This equation ensures that all production occurs on regular time or overtime. The undertime variable, U_t, is a slack variable, to take account of the fact that the work force may not always be fully utilized.

Finally, all the variables are restricted to be nonnegative.

CHAPTER 10

Inventory Replenishment Policies

I N THE PRECEDING CHAPTER ON AGGREGATE PLANNING, INVEN-
tories were viewed as a source of short-term capacity. In this role, managers
can use inventories as a trade-off against other sources of short-term capacity.
Now, however, we wish to focus on inventories themselves and consider
policies for their control, item by item. In this chapter we discuss replenishment
policies for independent demand inventory items, where demand for the item is
based on statistical variation. In Chapter 12, we discuss policies for dependent demand items, where demand is determined by production schedules of end-products.

STOCK POINTS IN A PRODUCTION-DISTRIBUTION SYSTEM

Figure 10-1 identifies the main stock points that occur in a production-distribution
system from raw materials and ordering of supplies through the productive process,
culminating in availability for use. At the head of the system, we must have raw
materials and supplies in order to carry out the productive process. If we are to be
able to produce at minimum cost and by the required schedule, these materials and
supplies need to be available. Therefore, we need to develop policies for deciding
when to replenish these inventories and how much to order at one time. These
issues are compounded by price discounts and by the need to ensure that delays in
supply time and temporary increases in requirements will not disrupt operations.

As a part of the conversion process within the productive system we have in-
process inventories, which are converted to finished goods inventories. The finished
goods inventory levels depend on the policies used for deciding on the production
lot sizes and their timing and on the usage rates determined by distributors' orders.
High volume items would justify different policies for production and inventory replenishment than medium- or low-volume items. The production lot size decisions
and their timing are very important in relation to the economical use of personnel
and equipment and may justify continuous production of a high-volume item. On
the other hand, low-volume items will be produced only periodically in economic
lots. Again, we will need policy guidelines to determine the size of buffer inventories
to absorb the effects of production delays and random variations in demand by
distributors.

The functions of distributors and retailers are those of inventorying products to
make them available. Distributors and retailers often carry a wide range of items, and
they need replenishment policies that take into account this kind of complexity. They
commonly place routine orders periodically, ordering a variety of items from each
supplier. Price discounts are often an additional factor to consider.

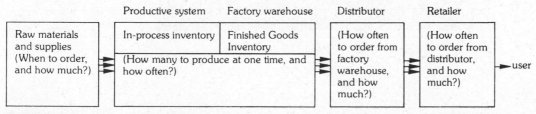

FIGURE 10-1
Main stock points in a production-distribution system.

Although the details of problems may differ at each level in the production-distribution system, note that at each level the basic policy issues are in the inventory replenishment process, focused on the order quantity and when to order. We have a general class of problems for which the concepts of economic order quantities (*EOQ*) provide important insights. We will first develop the concepts within the framework of the size of purchase orders, and later we will see how the concepts may be adapted for the inventory problems downstream in the system.

SIZE OF PURCHASE ORDERS

Figure 10-2 is a diagram of what happens to inventory levels for a particular item of raw material used in our system. Assume an annual requirement of $R = 2000 \times 52 = 104,000$ units, or an average of 2000 units per week. The inventory levels would fluctuate, as in Figure 10-2a, if we were to order in lots $Q = 10,000$ units. The

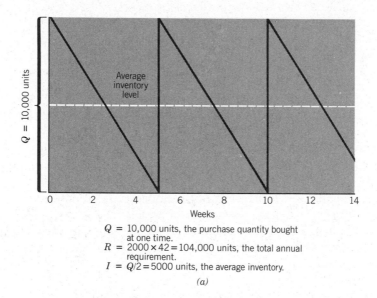

Q = 10,000 units, the purchase quantity bought
at one time.
R = 2000 × 42 = 104,000 units, the total annual
requirement.
I = $Q/2$ = 5000 units, the average inventory.

(a)

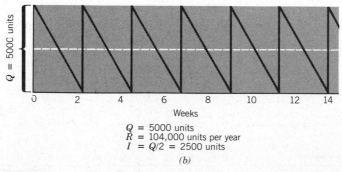

Q = 5000 units
R = 104,000 units per year
I = $Q/2$ = 2500 units

(b)

FIGURE 10-2
Simplified model of the effect of lot size on inventory levels.

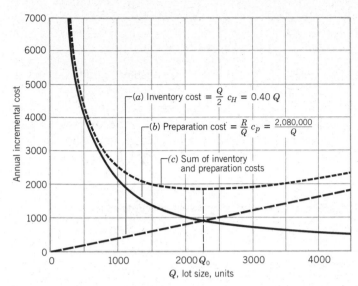

FIGURE 10-3
Graphical model of a simple inventory problem.

average inventory level for the idealized situation is one-half the number ordered at one time or $Q/2 = 5000$ units.

If the item is ordered more often in smaller quantities, as shown in Figure 10-2b, the inventory level will fall in proportion to the number of units ordered at one time. Inventory level will affect the incremental costs of holding inventory, and therefore these inventory carrying costs will be proportional to the lot size Q, the number ordered at one time.

From Figure 10-2 we see also that the total annual cost of placing orders for the order pattern of Figure 10-2b will be twice as large as for the order pattern of Figure 10-2a, because we order twice as often for the same annual requirement. Therefore, we have isolated two types of incremental costs that represent the quantitative criteria for the inventory system. They are the costs associated with inventory level, *holding costs,* and those associated with the number of orders placed, *preparation costs.*

In further defining the system, let us construct a graph that shows the general relation between Q (lot size) and the incremental costs that we have isolated. We noted in Figure 10-2 that if Q were doubled, average inventory level was doubled. It costs perhaps $c_H = 80$ cents per year to carry a unit of inventory. (Costs include such items as interest, insurance, and taxes.) Because the average inventory level is $Q/2$, and $c_H = 80$ cents, then the annual incremental costs associated with inventory are

$$\frac{Q}{2}(c_H) = \frac{Q}{2}(0.80) = 0.40Q \tag{1}$$

Substituting different values for Q, we can plot the result as in Figure 10-3, curve *a.*

The costs of ordering can be plotted in a similar way. The number of orders placed per year to satisfy requirements is $R/Q = 104,000/Q$. If the costs for preparing and following up an order are $c_P = \$20$, then the total annual incremental costs due to ordering are

$$\frac{R}{Q}(c_P) = \frac{104{,}000}{Q}(20) = \frac{2{,}080{,}000}{Q} \tag{2}$$

Therefore, as Q increases, the annual incremental costs due to ordering decrease. This relationship is plotted in Figure 10-3, curve (b), by substituting different values of Q in Equation 2.

Figure 10-3, curve c, shows the resulting total incremental cost curve, determined simply by adding the two previous curves. We have a model that expresses the total incremental cost as a function of the variables that define the system. The equation for the total cost curve is also determined by adding Equations 1 and 2 for the two separate cost functions.

$$TIC \quad = \quad \frac{Q}{2} \quad\quad c_H \quad\quad + \quad\quad \frac{R}{Q} \quad\quad c_P$$

$$\tag{3}$$

$$\begin{array}{c}\text{Total}\\\text{incremental}\\\text{cost}\end{array} = \left(\begin{array}{c}\text{Average}\\\text{inventory}\end{array}\right)\left(\begin{array}{c}\text{Unit inventory}\\\text{cost per year}\end{array}\right) + \left(\begin{array}{c}\text{Number}\\\text{of orders}\\\text{per year}\end{array}\right)\left(\begin{array}{c}\text{Cost}\\\text{of an}\\\text{order}\end{array}\right)$$

The controllable variable in Equation 3 that can be manipulated by management is Q (lot size). Uncontrollable variables are requirements related to such factors as consumer demand, taxes, and insurance rates. For our example, uncontrollable variables are c_H (inventory costs per unit), R (demand or requirements), and c_P (order preparation costs).

A General Solution

For our simplified model we can select the optimum policy as the minimum point on the total incremental cost curve of Figure 10-3, or $EOQ = 2280$ (the symbol EOQ denotes the optimal value of Q). This is a solution to the specific problem with the given values for c_H, R, and c_P. From Equation 3 for the total incremental cost, we may derive a formula for the minimum point on the curve by use of differential calculus. The formula that represents the general solution for the model is

$$EOQ = \sqrt{\frac{2Rc_P}{c_H}} \tag{4}$$

This formula gives directly the value EOQ, that yields the minimum total incremental cost for the model. Substituting for the values in our example, we have

$$EOQ = \sqrt{\frac{2 \times 104{,}000 \times 20}{0.80}} = \sqrt{5{,}200{,}000} = 2280.35 \text{ units}$$

In using Equation 4, if it is desired to express economic quantity in dollars, the requirements must also be expressed in dollars. Similarly, if the requirements are expressed in monthly rates, the inventory cost must be expressed as a monthly rate. These and other changes in the units lead to modifications of the formula used in practice. Also, in practice, charts, graphs, and tables based on the formula are often used to minimize computations, or more currently, computing systems automatically issue purchase orders for the quantities computed by the formula.

The incremental cost of the optimal solution, TIC_0, is also simple:

$$TIC_0 = \sqrt{2c_P c_H R} \qquad (5)$$

Substituting the values from our example gives

$$TIC_0 = \sqrt{2 \times 20 \times 0.8 \times 104{,}000} = \sqrt{3{,}328{,}000} = \$1824.28$$

Important Assumptions

The *EOQ* model is intuitively attractive because it minimizes the obvious incremental costs associated with an inventory replenishment. In applying the model, however, there are three important assumptions:

1. Average demand is continuous and constant, represented by a distribution that does not change with time. Therefore, if there is significant trend or seasonality in the average annual requirements, R in Equation 4, the resulting costs will not be optimal, and there may be other control problems as well.

2. Supply lead time is constant. Although this assumption may be reasonable in many situations, supply lead times are often quite variable. The result of variable lead time is that the timing of the receipt of the order quantity produces excess inventories when lead times are shorter than expected and produces shortages when lead times are longer than expected. The resulting costs would not be optimal.

3. Independence between inventory items. The *EOQ* model assumes that the replenishment of an inventory item has no effect on the replenishment of any other inventory item. This assumption is valid in many instances, but breaks down when a set of supply items is coupled together by a common production plan.

There are various ways of dealing with the effects of these three assumptions. Indeed, much of the research on inventory models that followed the development of Equation 4 has centered on concepts and techniques for dealing with situations where one or more of the assumptions is not valid in practice.

The Effect of Quantity Discounts

The basic economic order quantity formula assumes a fixed purchase price. When quantity discounts enter the picture, the total incremental cost equation is no longer a continuous function of order quantity, but becomes a step function with components of annual inventory cost, ordering cost, and material cost involving the price discount schedule. The total incremental cost equation becomes

$$TIC = c_H Q/2 + c_P R/Q + p_i R \qquad (6)$$

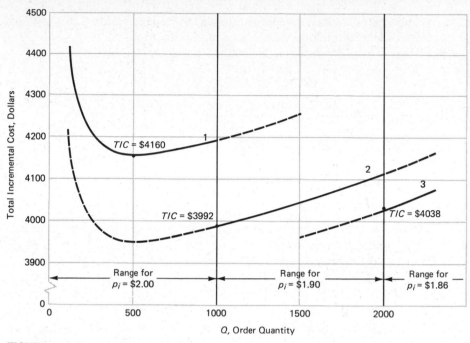

FIGURE 10-4
Total incremental cost curves for inventory model with three price breaks. $R = 2000$ units per year, $c_P = \$20$, $F_H = 0.16$.

where p_i is the price per unit for the ith price break, and $c_H = p_i F_H$, where F_H is the fraction of inventory value. The procedure is then one of calculating to determine if there is a net advantage in annual ordering plus material costs to counterbalance the increased annual inventory costs.

As an illustration, assume that a manufacturer's requirement for an item is 2000 per year. The purchase price is quoted as $2 per unit in quantities below 1000, $1.90 per unit in quantities between 1000 and 1999, and $1.86 in quantities above 2000. Ordering costs are $20 per order, and inventory costs are 16 percent per year per unit of average inventory value, or $0.32 per unit per year at the $2 unit price. Equation 4 indicates that the economic order quantity is

$$Q_0 = \sqrt{\frac{2 \times 20 \times 2{,}000}{0.32}} = \sqrt{250{,}000} = 500 \text{ units}$$

Using the preceding data and Equation 6, we can compute TIC for each of the three price ranges, as shown in Figure 10-4 (the solid line curves indicate the relationships for valid price ranges):

1. Note that for the $2 price that applies for Q *less than* 1000, $EOQ = 500$ units produces the lowest cost of $4,160 (Curve 1).

2. However, between order quantities of 1000 and 1999, the price of $1.90 per

TABLE 10-1   **Incremental Cost Analysis to Determine Net Advantage or Disadvantage When Price Discounts Are Offered**

	Lots of 500 Units Price = $2.00 per Unit	Lots of 1000 Units Price = $1.90 per Unit	Lots of 2000 Units Price = $1.86 per Unit
Purchase of a year's supply ($p_i \times 2000$)	$4000	$3800	$3720
Ordering cost ($20 \times 2000/Q$)	80	40	20
Inventory cost (average inventory $\times$ unit price $\times$ 0.16)	80	152	298
Total	$4160	$3992	$4038

unit applies, and when $Q = 1000$, $TIC = \$3992$—a cost saving of $168 per year, compared with ordering in lots of 500 units (Curve 2).

3. Finally, at Q *greater than or equal to* 2000, the price of $1.86 per unit applies, and $TIC = \$4,038$ at $Q = 2000$ units (Curve 3).

The lowest cost ordering policy is to take advantage of the first price break, but not the second and to order in lots of $Q = 1000$ units. Summary calculations are shown in Table 10-1.

With other numerical values, it is possible for Curve 2 to have its optimum occur within the middle price range or for Curve 3 to have its optimum occur in the upper price range. Therefore, a general procedure is needed as follows:

1. Calculate the *EOQ* for each price.
2. Eliminate *EOQ*s that fall outside of valid price ranges.
3. Calculate *TIC*s for valid *EOQ*s and at price breaks.
4. Select lot size associated with the lowest *TIC*.

DEALING WITH VARIABILITY OF DEMAND

In the simple inventory models we assumed that both demand and supply lead times were constant. Yet variability of demand and supply lead time is an element of reality that can be very important. It imposes two-sided risks.

We can cushion the effects of demand and supply lead time variation by absorbing risks in carrying larger inventories, called *buffer stocks*. The larger we make these buffer stocks, the greater our risk, in terms of the funds tied up in inventories, the possibility of obsolescence, and so on. However, we tend to minimize the risk of running out of stock.

On the other hand, although the inventory risk can be minimized by reducing buffer inventories, the risks associated with poor inventory service increase, including

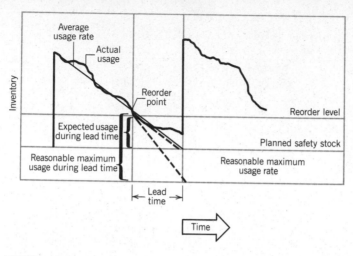

FIGURE 10-5
Structure of inventory balance for a fixed reorder quantity system.

the costs of back-ordering, lost sales, disruptions of production, and so on. Our objective, then, is to find a rational model for balancing these risks.

Service Levels and Buffer Stocks (Constant Lead Time)

Figure 10-5 shows the general structure of inventory balance when a fixed quantity Q is ordered at one time. When inventory falls to a preset reorder point P, an order for the quantity Q is placed. The reorder point P is set to take account of the supply lead time L, so that if we experience normal usage rates during L, inventory is reduced to the planned buffer stock when the order for Q units is received. But demand may not occur at a constant rate, and inventories may decline to the reorder point P earlier or later than expected. If demand during lead time is greater than expected values, inventory levels may decline below the planned buffer stock level. In the limiting situation, if we experience maximum reasonable demand during lead time (as shown in Figure 10-5), inventory levels will decline to zero by the time the order for Q units is received. The size of the needed buffer stock, B, is the difference between the expected or average demand $\overline{D}$ and the maximum reasonable demand during the supply lead time D_{max}, or $B = D_{max} - \overline{D}$. The issue concerns how we define D_{max}.

Defining D_{max}. Maximum reasonable demand is not a fixed number that we can simply abstract from a distribution of demand; instead it depends on an analysis of the risks. Assume the record for the distribution of demand that exceeds a given level, shown in Figure 10-6. This figure represents only the random variations; if there were other effects, such as trend and seasonals, they have been removed by standard statistical techniques. Note that average monthly demand was $\overline{D} = 460$ units.

Because the average monthly usage rate is 460 units, and if we assume a lead time of $L = 1$ month, we could be 90 percent sure of not running out of stock by having 620 units on hand when the replenishment order is placed (see Figure 10-6

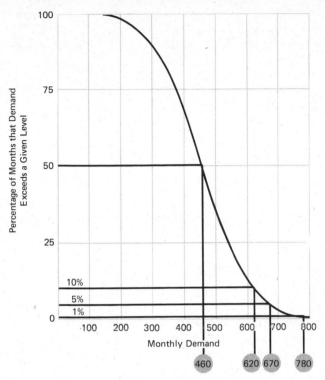

FIGURE 10-6
Distribution showing the percentage of months that demand exceeded a given level.

for the demand rate associated with 10 percent). The buffer stock required for this 90 percent service level is $B = 620 - 460 = 160$ units. Similarly, if we wish to be 95 percent sure of not running out of stock, then $B = 670 - 460 = 210$ units. For a 99 percent service level (1 percent risk of stockout), the buffer stock level must be increased to $B = 780 - 460 = 320$ units.

From the shape of the demand curve, it is clear that required buffer stock goes up rapidly as we increase service level, and therefore, the inventory carrying cost of providing this assurance goes up. These effects are shown by the calculations in Table 10-2, in which we have assumed the demand curve of Figure 10-6, assigning a value of $100 to the item and inventory holding costs of 25 percent of inventory value. The average inventory required to cover maximum reasonable usage rates during the 1-month lead time is calculated for the three service levels shown. To offer service at the 95 percent level instead of the 90 percent level requires an incremental $1250 per year, but to move to the 99 percent level of service from the 95 percent level requires an additional $2750 in inventory cost. Note that these inventory costs are increasing at an increasing rate per additional percent of service level.

Management could define D_{max} at any of the three levels of demand by setting a service level policy. Given the service level policy, the buffer stock required to implement that policy is, simply, $B = D_{max} - \bar{D}$. The value for D_{max} sets the order point P which allows for the needed buffer stock B.

323

TABLE 10-2

Cost of Providing Three Levels of Service in Figure 10-5 (Item is valued at $100 each and inventory holding costs are 25 percent)

	Service Level		
	90%	95%	99%
Expected maximum usage for one month replenishment time	620	670	780
Buffer stock required, $B = D_{max} - 460$	160	210	320
Value of buffer stock, $100 \times B$	$16,000	$21,000	$32,000
Inventory holding cost at 25 percent	$ 4,000	$ 5,250	$ 8,000

Practical Methods for Determining Buffer Stocks

The general methodology that we have discussed for setting buffer stocks is too cumbersome for practical use in systems that may involve large numbers of items. Computations are simplified considerably if we can justify the assumption that the demand distribution follows some particular mathematical function, such as the normal, Poisson, or negative exponential distributions.

First, let us recall the general statement for buffer stocks:

$$B = D_{max} - \bar{D} \qquad (7)$$

Note, however, that $D_{max} = \bar{D} + n\sigma_D$; that is, the defined maximum reasonable demand is the average demand $\bar{D}$, plus some number of standard deviation units n that is associated with the probability of occurrence of that demand (in practice, n is often called the safety factor). Substituting this statement of D_{max} in our general definition of B (Equation 7), we have

$$B = D_{max} - \bar{D} = (\bar{D} + n\sigma_D) - \bar{D} \qquad (8)$$
$$= n\sigma_D$$

This simple statement allows us to determine easily those buffer stocks that meet risk requirements when we know the mathematical form of the demand distribution. The procedure is as follows:

1. Determine whether the normal, Poisson, or negative exponential distribution approximately describes demand during lead time for the case under consideration. This determination is critically important, involving well-known statistical methodology.

2. Set a service level based on (a) managerial policy, (b) an assessment of the balance of incremental inventory and stockout costs, or (c) an assessment of the manager's trade-off between service level and inventory cost when stockout costs are not known.

3. Using the service level, define D_{max} during lead time in terms of the appropriate distribution.

4. Compute the required buffer stock from Equation 8, where n is termed the safety factor and σ_D is the standard deviation for the demand distribution.

We will illustrate the methodology in the context of the normal distribution.

Buffer Stocks for the Normal Distribution

The normal distribution has been found to describe many demand functions adequately, particularly at the factory level of the supply-production-distribution system [Buchan and Koenigsberg, 1963]. Given the assumption of normality and a service level of, perhaps, 95 percent, we can determine B by referring to the normal distribution tables, a small part of which has been reproduced as Table 10-3. The normal distribution is a two-parameter distribution, which is described completely by its mean value $\bar{D}$ and the standard deviation σ_D. Implementing a service level of 95 percent means that we are willing to accept a 5 percent risk of running out of stock. Table 10-3 shows that demand exceeds $\bar{D} + (n\sigma_D)$ with a probability of 0.05, or 5 percent of the time, when $n = 1.645$; therefore, this policy is implemented when $B = 1.645 \, \sigma_D$. As an example, if the estimate of σ_D is $s = 300$ units, and $\bar{D} = 1500$

TABLE 10-3

Area Under the Right Tail of the Normal Distribution (showing the probability that demand exceeds $\bar{D} + n\sigma_D$ for selected values of n)

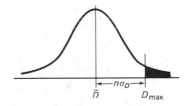

$D_{max} = \bar{D} + n\sigma_D$	Probability
$\bar{D} + 3.090\sigma_D$	0.001
$\bar{D} + 2.576\sigma_D$	.005
$\bar{D} + 2.326\sigma_D$	.010
$\bar{D} + 1.960\sigma_D$	.025
$\bar{D} + 1.645\sigma_D$	.050
$\bar{D} + 1.282\sigma_D$	0.100
$\bar{D} + 1.036\sigma_D$	.150
$\bar{D} + 0.842\sigma_D$	.200
$\bar{D} + 0.674\sigma_D$	.250
$\bar{D} + 0.524\sigma_D$	.300
$\bar{D} + 0.385\sigma_D$	0.350
$\bar{D} + 0.253\sigma_D$	.400
$\bar{D} + 0.126\sigma_D$	.450
$\bar{D}$	.500

95%
90%
80%
70%
60%
50%   325

units, assuming a normal distribution, a buffer stock to implement a 95 percent service level would be $B = 1.645 \times 300 = 494$ units. Such a policy would protect against the occurrence of demands up to $D_{max} = 1500 + 494 = 1994$ units during lead time. Obviously, any other service level policy could be implemented in a similar way. However, because the cost of carrying buffer stocks increases at an increasing rate, it should be evident that a 100 percent service level is usually prohibitively expensive in practice.

Buffer Stocks When Both Demand and Lead Time Are Variable

The problem of determining buffer stocks when both demand and lead time vary is somewhat more complex. When both lead time and demand vary, we have an interaction between the fluctuating demand and the fluctuating lead time, similar to the situation shown in Figure 10-7.

In such situations, a Monte Carlo simulation may determine buffer stocks. To carry out the simulation, we need data describing both the demand and the lead time distributions. Then we can develop buffer stock requirements for the various risk levels of stockout. We can implement whatever risk level we choose by selecting the corresponding buffer stock. The methodology and computed examples are developed in Buffa and Miller [1979] and in McMillan and Gonzalez [1973].

DETERMINING SERVICE LEVELS

The service level states the probability that all orders can be filled directly from inventory during a reorder cycle. As we have stated, the buffer inventory that is de-

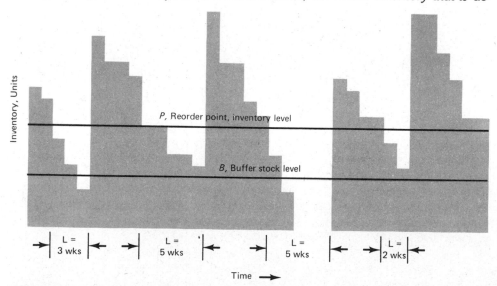

FIGURE 10-7
Inventory balance when both demand and lead time vary. When inventory falls to the reorder point P, the quantity Q is ordered. Inventory falls below the buffer stock level B twice, and a stockout occurs during the third cycle.

signed to provide for the risk of stockout is $B = n\sigma_D$. Assuming a normal distribution and a service level of 95 percent (chance of a stockout is 0.05), then from Table 10-3 the safety factor is $n = 1.645$.

Now let us examine more closely the meaning of this service level statement of policy. It means that there is 1 chance in 20 that demand during lead time will exceed the buffer stock *when there is exposure to risk;* that is, when inventories approach the ordering time. It does not mean that 5 percent of the demand is unsatisfied, but rather that demand during lead time can be expected to exceed buffer stock for 5 percent of the replenishment orders. In other words, the chance that demand will exceed the buffer stock for any given replenishment order is 5 percent.

Effect of Order Size

This interpretation of service level immediately shows us that the expected quantity short over a period of time is proportional to the number of times we order, because we are exposed to shortages only once for each reordering cycle. For our example with buffer stocks designed for a chance of stockout of 0.05, if we ordered Q units 20 times per year, we would expect shortages to occur an average of only once per year. If we ordered in quantities of $2Q$ only 10 times per year, we would expect stockouts to occur only once every other year, on the average. Larger orders provide exposure to risk less often and will result in lower annual expected quantities short for the same service level.

Expected Quantities Short

For a given safety factor and distribution of demand during lead time, we can compute the expected quantity short. Assuming a normal distribution of $\bar{D} = 50$ units during lead time and $\sigma_D = 10$ units, let us determine the expected quantity short for service levels of 80, 90, 95, and 99 percent. Based on the safety factors for the stated service levels (Table 10-3), the computed buffer stocks are

$$B_1 = 0.842 \times 10 = 8.42, \text{ or }9 \text{ units } (80 \text{ percent service level})$$
$$B_2 = 1.282 \times 10 = 12.82, \text{ or } 13 \text{ units } (90 \text{ percent service level})$$
$$B_3 = 1.645 \times 10 = 16.45, \text{ or } 17 \text{ units } (95 \text{ percent service level})$$
$$B_4 = 2.326 \times 10 = 23.26, \text{ or } 24 \text{ units } (99 \text{ percent service level})$$

The values of n approximate the safety factors for the stated service levels, so $B = n\sigma_D$ gives slightly better service because of rounding upwards to integer units.

Brown [1963] has shown that the expected quantity short *per order* is the product of σ_D and $E(k)$, where $E(k)$ is the partial expectation for a normal distribution with unit standard deviation. The partial expectation is the expected value of demands beyond some specified level. Brown [1967] developed tables of partial expectations for the normal distribution, a small part of which is reproduced in Table 10-4. Estimates of the expected quantity short per order can be obtained from Table 10-4 for a given safety factor which, in turn, is associated with a given service level. Reading from Table 10-4, the expected quantities short per order for our example and the four service levels are:

Service Level, Percentage	Expected Quantity Short per Order, Units = $E(k) \times \sigma_D$ (rounded to two decimals)
80	$0.11156 \times 10 = 1.12$
90	$0.04730 \times 10 = 0.47$
95	$0.02089 \times 10 = 0.21$
99	$0.00441 \times 10 = 0.04$

For each of the service levels indicated, the expected quantity short for each order is as given, and these expected shortages are rather startlingly small. The effect of a given service policy may be misleading unless it is translated into its equivalent expected quantity short per order. Although a 90 percent service policy may seem relatively loose, it holds fairly tight control in terms of the expected shortages on each ordering cycle.

Optimal Service Levels, Shortage Costs Known

Now that we have methods for estimating the expected quantity short per order, we can determine the optimal service level if we know the relevant costs. Let us slightly

TABLE 10-4   **Expected Quantity Short per Order for Values of the Safety Factor n**

Safety Factor, n	Service Level, Percent	$E(k)$, Expected Quantity Short/σ_D
3.090	99.9	0.00028
2.576	99.5	0.00158
2.326	99.0	0.00441
1.960	97.5	0.00945
1.645	95.0	0.02089
1.282	90.0	0.04730
1.036	85.0	0.07776
0.842	80.0	0.11156
0.674	75.0	0.14928
0.524	70.0	0.19050
0.385	65.0	0.23565
0.253	60.0	0.28515
0.126	55.0	0.33911
0.0	50.0	0.39894

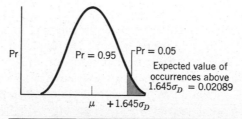

SOURCE. R. G. Brown, *Decision Rules for Inventory Management*. Holt, Rinehart & Winston, New York, 1967.

amplify the example that we have been using. Suppose that annual requirements for the example item are $R = 3000$ units per year; inventory holding costs are $c_H = \$20$ per unit per year; ordering costs are $c_P = \$25$ per order; and shortage costs are $c_S = \$100$ per unit short. If the order quantity were $Q = 500$ units, six orders per year would be required.

Let us examine the annual buffer inventory and shortage costs for the four different service levels. We already computed the buffer inventory and expected quantities short per order. Because there are six orders per year, the *annual* expected quantity short is $6\sigma_D E(k)$. These values and the relevant costs are summarized in Table 10-5. The service policy that minimizes relevant costs for these data is the 95 percent policy which involves maintaining a buffer of $B = 17$ units. This policy results in an annual expected quantity short of $6 \times 0.21 = 1.26$ units and a minimum total relevant cost of \$466 per year. What would be the optimal service policy if the cost of shortages was only $c_S = \$40$?

Optimal Service Levels, Shortage Costs Unknown

It is frequently true that we do not know the value of c_S with any degree of confidence. Many factors in a given situation may affect the true cost of shortages. Some of these factors may be reasonably objective, but difficult to measure. For example, although part shortages in assembly processes create costly disruptions and delays, measuring these costs is quite another matter. Also, when shortages occur, it may be necessary to back-order or to expedite them with special handling and extra costs. These incremental costs are real, but they are not segregated in cost records. Thus, making realistic estimates of their value would be costly in itself, and these data-

---

TABLE 10-5

Annual Buffer Inventory and Shortage Costs for Four Service Levels ($\bar{D} = 50$ units during lead time, $\sigma_D = 10$ units, $c_H = \$20$ per unit per year, $c_S = \$100$ per unit short, $R = 3000$ units per year, and $Q = 500$ units per order)

	Approximate Service Level, Percentage			
	80	90	95	99
Buffer inventory[a].				
$B = n\sigma_D = 10 \times n$	9	13	17	24
Expected quantity short per order[b]				
$\sigma_D E(k) = 10 \times E(k)$	1.12	0.47	0.21	0.04
Annual quantity short	6.72	2.82	1.26	0.24
Buffer inventory cost.				
$c_H B = 20 \times B$	\$180	\$260	\$340	\$480
Shortage cost, $c_S(R/Q) \times$ (expected quantity short per order) $= 100 \times 6 \times$ (expected quantity short per order)	\$672	\$282	\$126	\$24
Total incremental costs	\$852	\$542	\$466	\$504

[a] Values of n from Table 10-3 for given service level.
Values of B rounded to next highest integer.
[b] $E(K)$ from Table 10-4.

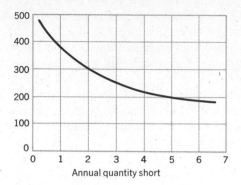

FIGURE 10-8

Annual buffer inventory costs versus annual quantity short for a system where: $D = 50$ units during lead time, $\sigma_D = 10$ units, $c_H = \$20$ per unit per year, $R = 3000$ units per year, and $Q = 500$ units per order.

gathering costs could exceed the value of the information. If a shortage definitely results in a lost sale, we can impute a shortage cost equal to the lost contribution. But do we know whether the sale is lost for certain, or must we merely estimate the probability of a lost sale? Finally, the loss may be intangible, such as the loss of goodwill of a valued customer who receives poor service.

For all the preceding reasons, we may not be able to estimate values of c_S with sufficient precision to justify an analysis similar to that given in Table 10-5 as a basis for selecting an optimum service level policy. Nevertheless, in the absence of known shortage costs, we still have valuable data from Table 10-5. We have objective annual buffer inventory costs for various service level policies, and we have the expected annual quantities short that would result from each service level policy. The graphical relationship between buffer inventory cost and annual quantities short is shown in Figure 10-8. These data provide the basis for the manager's subjective choice of inventory policy trade-offs that must be made.

FIXED REORDER QUANTITY SYSTEM

The structure of the fixed reorder quantity system was illustrated by Figure 10-5. A reorder level has been set by the point P, which allows the inventory level to be drawn down to the buffer stock level within the lead time if average usage rates are experienced. Replenishment orders are placed in a fixed, predetermined amount (in practice, not necessarily the EOQ) that is timed to be received at the end of the supply lead time. The expected maximum inventory level becomes the order quantity Q plus the buffer stock B. The average inventory, then, is $B + Q/2$. Usage rates are reviewed periodically in an attempt to react to seasonal or long-term trends in requirements. At the time of the periodic reviews, the order quantities and buffer stock levels may be changed to reflect the new conditions. Buffer stock levels are set based on determinations of the appropriate service level policy. This policy reflects the balancing of buffer inventory costs and shortage costs, or the manager's trade-off between buffer inventory cost and the expected quantity short. But buffer stocks are actually allowed for by setting the reorder point P, because $P = D_{max}$.

The parameters that define a fixed reorder quantity system are Q, the fixed number ordered at one time, and the reorder point P.

Fixed reorder quantity systems are common where a perpetual inventory record is kept or where the inventory level is under sufficiently continuous surveillance that notice can be given when the reorder point has been reached. One of the simplest methods for maintaining this close watch on inventory level is the use of the "two-bin" system. In this system, the inventory is physically (or conceptually) separated into two bins, one of which contains an amount equal to the reorder inventory level, P. The balance of the stock on hand is placed in the other bin, and day-to-day needs are drawn from it until it is empty. At this point, it is obvious that the reorder level has been reached, and a stock requisition is issued. Then stock is drawn from the second bin, which contains an amount equal to the average use during the lead time plus a buffer stock. The stock is replenished when the order is received, and the physical segregation into two bins is made again; the cycle then is repeated.

Fixed reorder quantity systems are common with low-valued items, such as nuts and bolts, and where close surveillance over inventory levels is not necessary.

PERIODIC REORDER SYSTEM

A common alternate system of control fixes the reorder cycle instead of the reorder quantity. In such systems, the inventory status is reviewed on a periodic basis, and an order is placed for an amount that replenishes inventories to a planned maximum

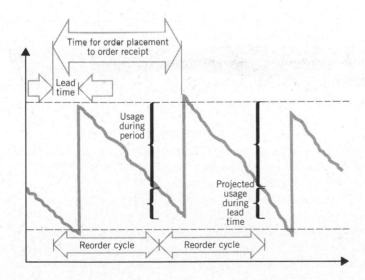

FIGURE 10-9

Periodic reorder system of control. An order is placed at regular intervals of variable size Q. In each instance, Q = usage during the past period + projected usage during lead time.

based on usage, as shown in Figure 10-9. The reorder quantity is variable in size, covering anticipated normal usage during the supply lead time, plus usage since the last review. A maximum planned inventory level, I_{max}, is indicated in Figure 10-9.

An economic reorder cycle can be approximated by computing EOQ; the economic reorder cycle would then be Q_0/R, where R is the annual requirement. For example, if $Q_0 = 7500$ units and annual requirements were $R = 100,000$ units, then the economic cycle would be $7500/100,000 = 0.075$ years, or 3.9 weeks. This value would probably be rounded to 4 weeks.

The periodic reorder system has some advantages in production cycling, where high valued items require close control, in the control of items that may deteriorate with time, and where a number of items may be ordered from the same supplier. In the latter situation, it may be possible to gain shipping cost advantages by grouping orders normally sent to a common supplier. In addition, the periodic system makes possible operating efficiencies by reviewing the status of all items at the same time. Because of these advantages, the review cycle is commonly set by considerations other than just the individual item economic reorder cycle.

Perhaps the single most important advantage of the periodic reorder system is that the periodic review of inventory and usage levels provides the basis for adjustments to take account of demand changes. This is particularly advantageous with seasonal items. If demand increases, order sizes increase; if demand decreases, order sizes decrease. Therefore, as actually used, the periodic system does not assume constant demand, as in the EOQ system.

OPTIONAL REPLENISHMENT SYSTEM

Control systems that combine regular review cycles and order points are also used (called s, S systems in the literature). In such systems, stock levels are reviewed on a periodic basis, but orders are placed only when inventories have fallen to a predetermined reorder level, $P_{(s)}$. Then, an order is placed to replenish inventories to a maximum level denoted by $I_{max(S)}$, which is sufficient for buffer stocks plus expected needs for one cycle, as in the periodic system.

Such systems have the advantage of the close control associated with the periodic reorder system, resulting in minimum buffer stocks. On the other hand, because replenishment orders are placed only when the reorder point has been reached, fewer orders are placed on the average. Therefore, ordering costs are comparable with those associated with fixed reorder quantity systems.

ABC CLASSIFICATION OF INVENTORY ITEMS

Equal control effort for all items is not ordinarily justified. First, the differing value of inventory items suggests that we concentrate our attention on higher valued items and be less concerned about low valued items. For example, Figure 10-10 shows a fairly typical relationship between the percentage of inventory items and the percentage of total dollar inventory value. Twenty percent of the items account for 60 percent of the total dollar inventory value in Figure 10-10. The second 20 percent of

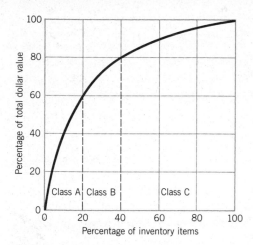

FIGURE 10-10
ABC classification of inventory items versus dollar volume.

items account for 20 percent of the value, and finally, the greatest percentage of items (60 percent) accounts for only 20 percent of total inventory value. Because inventory costs are associated directly with inventory value, the potential cost saving from closer control is greater among the first group, which accounts for most of the inventory value.

Second, even though an item may in itself be of low value, it is possible that the cost of a stockout could be considerable. For example, the shortage of a seemingly minor raw material item could cause idle labor costs and loss of production on an entire assembly line. Therefore, for both of the preceding reasons, a classification of inventory items by the degree of control needed allows managers to place their efforts where the returns can be most important.

Controls for Class A Items

Close control is required for inventory items that have high stockout costs, plus those items in Figure 10-10 that account for a large fraction of the total inventory value. The closest control might be reserved for raw materials used continuously in extremely high volume. Purchasing agents may arrange contracts with vendors for the continuous supply of these materials at rates that match usage rates. In such instances, the purchase of raw materials is not guided by either economical quantities or cycles. Changes in the rate of flow are made periodically as demand and inventory position changes. Minimum supplies are maintained to guard against demand fluctuations and possible interruptions of supply.

For the balance of Class A items, periodic ordering, perhaps on a weekly basis, provides the needed close surveillance over inventory levels. Variations in usage rates are absorbed quickly by the size of each weekly order, according to the periodic, or optional systems discussed previously. Also, because of the close surveillance, the risk of a prolonged stockout is small. Nevertheless, buffer stocks that provide excellent service levels will be justified for items having large stockout costs.

Controls for Class B Items

Periodic ordering once or perhaps twice per month could be sufficient for Class B items, again applying the periodic, or optional replenishment systems. Stockout costs for Class B items should be moderate to low, and buffer stocks should provide adequate control of stockout, even though the ordering occurs less often.

Controls for Class C Items

Class C items account for the great bulk of inventory items, and carefully designed but routine controls should be adequate. A reorder point system will ordinarily suffice. For each item, action is triggered when inventories fall to the reorder point. If usage changes, orders will be triggered earlier or later than average, providing the needed compensation. Semiannual or annual reviews of the system parameters should be performed to update usage rates, estimates of supply lead times, and costs, resulting in possible changes in *EOQ*.

The development of the concepts of *EOQ*, buffer stocks, and common managerial control systems has been in the context of raw materials and supplies. Recall from Figure 10-1, however, that there are stock points downstream in the process where similar decisions of inventory replenishment are required. The concepts and control systems are transferable with modification to the production phase and to the other stock points.

PRODUCTION ORDER QUANTITIES AND PRODUCTION CYCLING

In the process-focused model of productive systems, where demand is independent, as with spare parts, and production is carried out in batches, management must decide how large these batches should be. The concept of *EOQ* represented by Equation 4 can be applied directly, recognizing that preparation costs are the incremental costs of writing production orders, controlling the flow of orders through the system, and setting up machines for the batch; inventory costs are associated with holding in-process inventory.

However, the assumption that the order is received and placed into inventory all at one time is often not true in manufacturing. Equation 4 assumes the general inventory pattern shown in Figure 10-11a, where the entire order quantity Q is instantaneously received into inventory. The inventory is then drawn down at the usage rate, subsequent orders being placed with sufficient lead time so that their receipt coincides with the minimum inventory level.

For many manufacturing situations the production of the total order quantity takes place over a period of time, and the parts go into inventory in smaller quantities as production continues. This results in an inventory pattern similar to Figure 10-11b. The maximum and average inventory levels are reduced, and the optimum cost quantity formula becomes

$$Q_p = \sqrt{\frac{2Rc_p}{c_H\left(1 - \dfrac{r}{p}\right)}} \qquad (9)$$

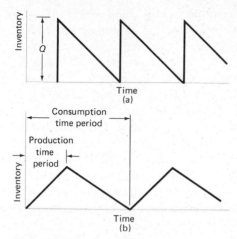

FIGURE 10-11

Comparison of inventory balance: (a) when the order quantity, Q, is received all at one time, and (b) when Q is received over a period of time.

where r = requirements or usage rate (short term, perhaps daily or weekly)

p = production rate (on same time base as for r)

c_P = ordering and setup cost

c_H = unit inventory cost

Q_p = minimum cost production order quantity

R = annual requirements

The Q_p that results is larger than that which would result from Equation 4. Average inventory is smaller for a given Q_p and balance between setup costs and inventory costs takes place at a higher value of the order quantity Q. The number of production cycles per year is R/Q_p.

The total incremental cost of the optimal production order quantity is

$$TIC_0 = \sqrt{2c_P c_H R\left(1 - \frac{r}{p}\right)} \qquad (10)$$

There are additional problems related to production cycling that we will cover in Chapter 11. Also, the demand for parts and components is dependent on the demand for the primary product and more specifically on its production schedule. Because of the "lumpy" nature of demand for dependent items, the concepts of requirements planning are important to production lot size policies. Requirements planning will be covered in Chapter 12.

ORDERS FOR REPLENISHMENT OF FINISHED GOODS BY WAREHOUSES, DISTRIBUTORS, AND RETAILERS

Let us consider the factory warehouse first. It is often true that no orders for replenishment would be placed by the factory warehouse, because the factory and its warehouse may be considered a single unit in terms of stock points for finished

335

goods. In such situations, products go directly to the factory warehouse for finished goods storage. When the sales organization controls inventories, sometimes orders to the factory for replenishment of types and sizes may occur. Such orders could be on the basis of fixed order quantities, those ordered when inventories fall below the order point, or periodically based on the quantities needed to replenish inventory to some preset level, as in the periodic reorder system. The normal distribution is commonly used as a basis for the design of buffer stocks at this level in the system.

For distributors and retailers, however, orders for replenishment are more likely to be placed periodically, ordering all needed items from a given supplier. By combining orders for all items from a given supplier, it may be possible to effect freight cost advantages. Although we can derive an individual "economic order cycle time," EOQ/R, for each item, it may not be worthwhile, as noted previously. Setting different optimal cycle times for different products loses the advantage of reviewing needs for a group of items at one time and possibly loses freight advantages as well. The result is that economic order cycle times are seldom used, the cycle being set by these other considerations.

The negative exponential distribution has been found to describe demand at the distributor level, and the Poisson and negative exponential distributions have been useful descriptions of demand at the retail level. These distributions then provide a basis for the design of buffer stocks.

IMPLICATIONS FOR THE MANAGER

It is not uncommon for inventories to represent 20 to 30 percent of the total assets of a manufacturing organization. Even in nonmanufacturing organizations, inventories of materials and supplies can represent a significant investment. Therefore, inventory replenishment policies are an important aspect of day-to-day managerial control.

The simple concepts of EOQ provide the basis for balancing the costs affected by inventory replenishment decisions. Note that the typical total incremental cost curve shown in Figure 10-3 was shallow near the optimum. Thus, managers need to be more sensitive to operating in the optimum range rather than slavishly following an EOQ based policy. In following an EOQ policy, it is important to recognize that the assumption of constant demand is crucial. This assumption is often not true in practice. Seasonal variations and dependent demand in production lot size decisions may favor periodic ordering and other policies coupled with inventory planning.

The concepts underlying the design of buffer stocks and service levels should be of concern to managers. Defining a maximum reasonable demand, D_{max}, requires a managerial trade-off of buffer inventory cost versus service level, unless good estimates of shortage costs are available. Recognizing the relationship between service level and the expected quantity short is important if managers are to be able to make good judgments about appropriate service levels. Also, recognizing the effect of order size on the expected quantity short, for the same service level, helps managers make appropriate service level decisions.

Most inventory replenishment systems for the Class C low-valued items can be automated through computing systems. On the other hand, Class A and sometimes

Class B items may need the attention of a responsible executive, because the decisions can be of crucial significance to operating success.

Inventory replenishment for finished goods, particularly at the distributor and retail levels, can be accomplished by either an order point or periodic reorder system. However, there are often important advantages for the periodic system. The advantages stem from the possible grouping of orders to a given supplier in order to minimize freight costs and from the close surveillance over inventory and demand levels that is possible in such systems.

IMPORTANT TERMS

Numbers in parentheses indicate page numbers

ABC classification of inventories (332)	Optimal service level (329)
Buffer stocks (321)	Optional replenishment system (332)
Economic order quantity, EOQ (318)	Periodic reorder system (331)
Economic reorder cycle (332)	Poisson distribution (324)
Expected quantity short (327)	Preparation costs (317)
Fixed reorder quantity system (330)	Production cycling (334)
Holding costs (317)	Production order quantity (334)
Incremental costs (317)	Quantity discounts (319)
Lead time (322)	s, S system (332)
Maximum reasonable demand, D_{max} (322)	Service levels (327)
Negative exponential distribution (324)	Shortage cost (329)
Normal distribution (324)	Variability of demand (321)

REVIEW QUESTIONS AND PROBLEMS

1. What are the relevant costs that management should try to balance in deciding on the size of purchase orders? How do they vary with order size?

2. What is the total incremental cost equation involving
    a. Ordering and inventory costs?
    b. Price discounts?
    c. Shortage costs?

3. Explain the rationale for the derivation of Equation 4.

4. We have the following data for an item that we purchase regularly: annual requirements, $R = 10,000$ units; order preparation cost, $c_P = \$25$ per order; inventory holding cost, $c_H = \$10$ per unit per year.

a.   Compute the economic order quantity, EOQ.

b.   Compute the number of orders that must be placed each year and the annual cost of placing the orders.

c.   Compute the average inventory if EOQ units are ordered at one time, and compute the annual cost of the inventory.

5.   Suppose that the estimate of c_P in question 4 was in error, being only $20 per order. What is the value of EOQ? What is the percentage change in EOQ for the 20 percent decrease in c_P?

6.   Suppose that the estimate of c_H in question 4 was in error, being actually $15 per unit per year. What is the value of EOQ? What is the percentage change in EOQ for the 50 percent increase in c_H?

7.   A price discount schedule is offered for an item that we purchase as follows: $1 per unit in quantities below 800, $0.98 per unit in quantities of 800 to 1599, and $0.97 per unit in quantities of 1600 or more. Other data are $R = 1600$ units per year, $c_P = \$5$ per order, and inventory holding costs are 10 percent per year of average inventory value, or $0.10 per unit per year at the $1 per unit price. The value of EOQ using Equation 4, is 400 units. What should be the size of the purchase quantities in order to take advantage of the price discounts?

8.   What are the assumptions involved in the simple EOQ formula, Equation 4?

9.   Define the following terms:

a.   Order point

b.   Lead time

c.   Reorder level

d.   Maximum demand

e.   Safety factor

f.   Service level

10.   If the average demand during lead time is $\bar{D} = 200$ units, and the buffer stock is $B = 125$ units, what is D_{max}? What managerial judgment is required to determine D_{max}?

11.   Under what conditions can service level be determined objectively?

12.   If demand during lead time follows a normal distribution, and we wish to maintain a 95 percent service level, what is the safety factor? If the standard deviation is $\sigma = 100$ units, what is the buffer stock required to implement the 95 percent service level?

13.   If we were attempting to decide between an order size policy of $Q = 500$, or $Q = 1000$, which would we choose if our only concern were to minimize the risk of stockouts? Why?

14.   Explain the concepts of "expected quantity short per order" and "annual expected quantity short."

15.   What happens to the annual expected quantity short if

a.   The buffer stock is increased?

    b. The order size is increased?

    c. Annual requirements double, same order size?

    d. Through a policy change, service level is increased?

    e. Annual requirements double, *EOQ* policy?

    f. Variability of demand increases?

16. What "triggers" a replenishment order in each of the following managerial control systems?

    a. Fixed reorder quantity system

    b. Periodic reorder system

    c. Optional replenishment system

17. Explain the concept of the "two bin" system.

18. Under what conditions would one use the fixed reorder quantity system in preference to the periodic reorder system, and vice versa?

19. As time passes, any inventory control system may become dated as demand, costs, and competitive pressures change. Thus, periodic review of system parameters is important. What are the parameters that should be reviewed for the fixed reorder quantity and periodic reorder systems?

20. What are likely to be the most appropriate replenishment policies for distributors and retailers?

21. Define an economic reorder cycle time. Why is it that organizations which use a periodic reorder policy may not actually use the economic cycle time?

22. Weekly demand for a product, exclusive of seasonal and trend variations, is represented by the empirical distribution shown in Figure 10-12. What safety or

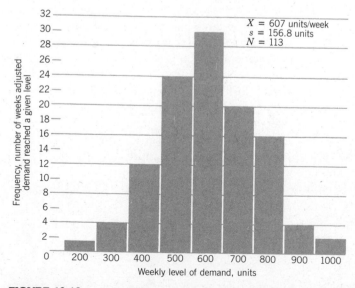

FIGURE 10-12

Distribution representing random variation in weekly sales, exclusive of seasonal and trend variations.

buffer stock would be required for the item to ensure that one would not run out of stock more than 15 percent of the time? 5 percent of the time? 1 percent of the time? (Assumed lead time is 1 week.)

23. If the demand distribution is normal with $\bar{D} = 1000$ units per week and the standard deviation is estimated as $s = 200$ units,

    a. What is the buffer stock required for the 90, 95, and 99 percent service levels?

    b. What is the expected quantity short per order for each service level?

    c. If inventory holding costs are $c_H = \$10$ per unit per year, and $c_S = \$15$ per unit short, which of the three service levels is most economical if 32 orders per year are placed? ($Q = 1612$, or approximately 32 orders per year, i.e., $52{,}000/1612 = 32.25$.)

    d. If order size is reduced to $Q = 1000$ units, how is service policy affected?

    e. If order size is increased to $Q = 2600$ units, how is service policy affected?

24. A manufacturer is attempting to set the production lot size to use for a particular item that is manufactured only periodically. The incremental cost of writing manufacturing orders is approximately $10. The aggregate cost of setting up machines for the production run is $40. The inventory holding cost is $1 per unit per year.

    The annual requirements for the item are 52,000, and the production rate is 5000 units per week.

    a. What is the most economical manufacturing lot size?

    b. How many production runs are needed per year to satisfy requirements?

    c. What considerations should influence your choice of the actual lot size selected?

25. In arid and semiarid climates, permanently installed lawn sprinkler systems are used. Automating the control of such systems has been a common procedure for parks and golf courses. More recently, systems have been designed that are low enough in cost so that homeowners can be relieved of the bother of the watering cycle.

    One such system was designed with the homeowner in mind. The user can set the watering cycle to come on every 1, 2, or 4 days and so on, and set the amount of time that the sprinklers run, for example, 3, 11, 22, 45, 60, or 90 minutes and so on. In addition, there is a moisture sensor that is implanted in the lawn. If when the cycle is ready to trigger, the moisture sensor indicates that the soil is still moist enough, the cycle will be skipped.

    Relate the sprinkler control system to one of the inventory control systems discussed in the text.

SITUATIONS

26. The Mixing and Bagging Company produces a line of commercial animal feeds in 10 mixes. The production process itself is rather simple, as the company

name implies. There is a variety of basic grain and filler ingredients that is mixed in batches. The mixed product is fed to an intermediate storage hopper, from which it is conveyed to a bagging operation. The bags of feed are then loaded on pallets and moved to the nearby warehouse for storage.

The operations are supervised by a foreman. Direct labor is provided by a full-time worker who operates the mixing and blending equipment, plus four full-time and 10 part-time workers. The foreman is paid $15,000 per year, the mixer-operator $5 per hour, the other full-time workers $4 per hour, and the 10 part-time workers are paid $3 per hour.

The usual routine in making a production run is as follows: The foreman receives job tickets from the office indicating the quantities to be run and the formula. The job tickets are placed in the order in which they are to be processed. At the end of a run, the foreman purges the mixing system and ducts of the previous product. This takes 20 minutes.

Meanwhile, the foreman has directed the mixer-operator and the four full-time employees to obtain the required ingredients for the next product from the storeroom. When the mixing equipment has been purged, the mixer-operator loads the first batch of materials according to the formula in the mixer and gets it started. This takes about 10 minutes. The total time spent by the mixer-operator in obtaining materials and loading the mixer is 30 minutes. The four full-time employees devote the 30 minutes to obtaining materials.

During the previous activities, the foreman has turned his attention to the bagger line, which requires minor changeover for the bag size and the product identifying label sewed on the top edge of the bag as it is sewed closed.

While the foreman was purging the system, the 10 part-time employees have transferred what is left of the last run to the warehouse, which requires about 15 minutes. They are then idle until the bagging operation is ready to start again.

The inventory in the finished goods warehouse is valued according to the sale price of the item, which is about $5 per 100 pounds. The cost of placing the material in the warehouse has been calculated as approximately $0.25 per 100 pounds, based on the time required for one of the part-time workers to truck it to the warehouse and place it in the proper location. The front office has calculated that the storage space in the owned warehouse was worth about $10 per square foot per year, but because the bags were palletized and stacked 12 feet high, this cost reduced to only $0.20 per 100 pounds per year. The product mixes were stable, and there was very little risk of obsolescence. There was some loss because uninvited guests (rats, etc.) came to dine. The total storage and obsolescence costs were estimated as 5 percent of inventory value.

The Mixing and Bagging Company has a factory overhead rate that it applied to materials and direct labor. This overhead rate is currently 100 percent and is applied to the average material cost of $1.87 per 100 pounds, plus the direct labor costs of $0.13 per 100 pounds. The company earns 8 percent after tax and can borrow at the local bank for an interest rate of 9 percent.

The factory manager is currently reviewing the basis for deciding on the length of production runs for products. He figures that operations are currently at about 85 percent of capacity. He has heard of *EOQ* as a basis for setting the length of production runs. What values should he assign to c_P and c_H for his operations?

27.   Mr. Winston DeBay, president of the Ronald S. Woods Publishing Company, has called in a consultant to help him reconsider his reordering policies and practices. Woods publishes textbooks in business and economics, and once a book is published, a recurring problem is keeping it in stock in order to meet demand. For each book, there is a set of film masters for each page. A reprint order would be placed with a printer who performs all the manufacturing operations and delivers printed books to the publisher's warehouse.

The costs of reordering involve a minimum or fixed charge to cover machine setup and related one-time costs, plus a per unit variable cost to cover paper, ink, book covers, and the like. The typical fixed costs are in the range of $500 to $2000, and the per unit variable costs are in the range of $1 to $3, depending on the particular book.

Mr. DeBay's practice had been to spend about 3 days twice per year reviewing the status of each book on the list to decide if a reprint order should be released and if so, the order size.

Mr. DeBay described his present policies as follows: "We get two peaks per year, the big one in July, and usually a second one in December. These peaks correspond to the fall ordering by bookstores for schools on both the semester and quarter systems, and the second smaller peak covers needs for the second semester and winter quarters. There are somewhat smaller orderings to cover the spring quarter and summer sessions, but these do not bother us much. Our fiscal year begins March 1, in order to key in with the sales year.

"In May, I order what I think I will need for the fall, and I order again in October for what I think we will need for the balance of the academic year. I keep a minimum stock unless I know a book is being revised, or going out of print. Then I cut it closer, and try to just about use up the minimum stock to coincide with the receipt of the new order."

The consultant asked, "How do you forecast your needs?" DeBay stated, "I watch the progress of sales and adoptions, and take into account the age of the edition. If the book is in the second or third year, used books will cut into sales rather sharply, and I take it into account."

The consultant produced a copy of Figure 10-13, stating, "Here is a forecast of one of your typical books, using a computer program—would forecasts of this nature help you in making decisions regarding the number of copies to reorder?" (Figure 10-13 was produced by the Fourier Series Forecasting Program described in Chapter 3.) DeBay responded that he probably could use such a forecast. "It picks out the peaks and valleys pretty well, but it couldn't take the other things into account. It (the program) doesn't know what I know."

The consultant said that he had looked into the costs for book reordering in order to compute an economical order quantity that balances the cost of reordering against the inventory holding costs. Assuming that $R = 12{,}000$ units per year, $c_P = \$1500$ per reorder, and $c_H = \$0.63$ per unit per year, then $EOQ = 7559$ units for the example book. In other words, an order for EOQ lasts for an average of $7559/12{,}000 = 0.63$ years, or 7.6 months. "What do you think of simply ordering *EOQ* whenever inventory drops to a reorder point that we would set? The reorder point would be that inventory level sufficient to cover sales during the supply lead time, plus a minimum stock."

DeBay responded, "I don't like that idea. To match with our type of business, the reorder point would have to change all the time, depending on the time of year. If we were floating into our July–August peak without a great big inventory, we would be clobbered and lose sales. On the other hand, if we hit the reorder point during slack months, I would not get very excited."

Next, the consultant raised the possibility of setting up a periodic cycle for reordering, perhaps every 3, 6, or 12 months. "Then you would order enough to cover sales since the last reordering, plus projected usage during the lead time. We call that a periodic reorder system. Based on your costs, I figure that an optimum cycle would be $EOQ/R = 7559/12{,}000 = 0.63$ years, or 7.6 months. Perhaps we could set an eight-month cycle—would you like that better?"

DeBay responded, "No, I don't like that idea either. A cycle as short as three months would kill us—you said yourself that the reordering costs were signifi-

```
* * * LEAST SQUARES FOURIER SERIES FORECAST MODEL * * *


FORECAST MODEL RESULTS
----------------------
```

FCST NO.	ACTUAL DEMAND	FORECAST DEMAND	FORECAST ERROR
1	444	561	-117
2	235	402	-167
3	854	711	143
4	391	503	-112
5	3259	3208	51
6	2163	2029	134
7	1055	712	343
8	486	439	47
9	751	969	-218
10	422	1500	-1078
11	622	617	5
12	1098	687	411
13	715	611	104
14	490	300	190
15	553	644	-91
16	556	419	137
17	3187	3222	-35
18	1787	1981	-194
19	466	663	-137
20	263	319	-56
21	906	919	-13
22	2193	1452	741
23	793	496	297
24	876	639	237
25	574	561	13
26	229	252	-23
27	615	667	-52
28	274	299	-25
29	3156	3172	-16
30	2064	2004	60
31	684	830	-146
32	280	271	9
33	1389	1158	231
34	1669	1332	337
35	505	806	-301
36	-201	446	-647
37		440	
38		-12	
39		617	
40		34	
41		3627	
42		1165	
43		1140	
44		-136	
45		1468	
46		924	
47		685	
48		38	

```
                                                    ------ *** ACTUAL      ---- === FORECAST
                                            0    1000      2000      3000      4000
                                            +----+----+----+----+----+----+----+----+----
                                     M   1+
1976-                                    2+
                                     JA  3+
                                         4+
                                         5+
                                         6+
                                         7+
                                         8+
                                         9+
                                     DJ 10+
                                        11+
1977-                                   12+
                                        13+
                                        14+
                                     JA 15+
                                        16+
                                        17+
                                        18+
                                        19+
                                     DJ 20+
                                        21+
1978-                                   22+
                                        23+
                                        24+
                                        25+
                                        26+
                                     JA 27+
                                        28+
                                        29+
                                        30+
                                     DJ 31+
                                        32+
1979-                                   33+
                                        34+
                                        35+
                                        36+*
                                     JA 37+
                                        38+
                                        39+
                                        40+
                                        41+
                                        42+
                                     DJ 43+
                                        44+
                                        45+
                                        46+
                                        47+
                                        48+
```

FIGURE 10-13
Least squares Fourier Series forecast model.

cant. I would rather carry some inventory costs. Besides, I won't lose sales if I have stock on hand. Frankly, I don't like any of the regular cycles you suggest. As I said, the business comes in July–August and in December–January. I can't help that, it's the way it is, and I'm not going to experiment with changing the way the business comes to us. Maybe you can help a little with the forecasting, but I don't like your *EOQ*s and your regular cycles. Those things are for somebody else's business that goes by the book. The book business doesn't go by the book!"

Given this encounter, what should the consultant recommend? Would a fixed quantity or a periodic system be appropriate? Why, or why not?

28. The following article is a case study of the installation of "An Integrated Inventory Control System," by Michael J. Lawrence.*

AN INTEGRATED INVENTORY CONTROL SYSTEM
Michael J. Lawrence

Introduction

Inventory control is one of the earliest yet consistently fruitful application areas for the techniques of management science. Rarely are the cash benefits exceptional such as one might experience with management science applications in strategic decision-making areas. However, it is also rare if a well developed and properly used statistically based inventory control system does not enable inventories to be significantly reduced while maintaining or improving the level of customer service. This paper presents a case study of the development of an inventory control system designed to serve the needs of a division of a large U.S. based chemical company.

The usual objective of an inventory control system can be summarized as providing an agreed level of customer service for the cheapest price. There are three fundamental and interrelated aspects in an inventory control system: forecasting future demand, deciding when and how much to re-order and deciding where stocks should be held. The case presented in this paper illustrates the use that can be made of a computer based statistical forecasting system to aid short term sales forecasting. Practical experience has shown that computer aided forecasting which includes routine management review and adjustment provides a better, more reliable and more consistent forecast than either a statistical or a subjective forecast alone. When coupled with a tracking procedure to report original and revised forecasting errors it provides a feedback loop enabling continuous monitoring of the error and measured improvement in forecasting skills. The case also illustrates the inventory reduction possible through the use of a two-stage inventory system comprising a central warehouse feeding smaller branch warehouses.

The Company

The inventory control system was designed for a division whose sales were in excess of $120 million per annum achieved with a product line of about 1,500

* Published originally in *Interfaces*, 7(2), February 1977, Copyright © 1977, The Institute of Management Sciences, reprinted with permission.

specialty chemical products sold through eight branches principally to the textile industry. Two U.S. based and two European based affiliated manufacturing facilities supplied the products which were all initially inventoried in a national warehouse in New Jersey. From there the products were, if necessary, blended and mixed, and supplied on requisition to the eight branches, which serviced customers in their area.

Customer service was a very important aspect of the business. Customers generally maintained no inventories to speak of, and expected that orders placed one day would be delivered the following morning. As the product line was largely duplicated by competition, customer service was recognized as the key to maintaining market share.

When products were ranked on the basis of sales volume it was observed that the top 5 percent of products accounted for 35 percent of sales volume, whereas the top 20 percent of products accounted for 85 percent of sales. The inventory level was on an average of $4\frac{1}{4}$ months' supply. With the products partitioned into three groups based on sales volume, the slower moving products and faster moving products had 25 percent above average inventory with the medium selling products below average inventory.

The Earlier Inventory Control System

Before discussing the new inventory control system which was developed, some comments are made on the earlier system and its performance to provide a point of reference and to illustrate the problems being experienced.

Sales forecasting was perceived as the biggest problem with the existing system. Firm manufacturing commitments for overseas supplied goods had to be entered into six months prior to receipt of goods. For the locally manufactured goods the lead time commitment was four months. The long manufacturing lead times were necessitated by production considerations and could not reasonably be reduced. Product sales, depending as they did on the tastes of the fashion business, were quite erratic and marketing management, who manually updated a six month rolling forecast every month, tended to build in a generous factor of safety. The forecasts were developed on a branch basis and consolidated nationally at the head office. Together with the current inventory and order position, this gave the necessary data for generating new manufacturing orders. The short end of the branch level forecasts were used by the branches in conjunction with maintaining their inventories through re-orders on the national warehouse. The inventory replenishment parameters (re-order point and re-order quantity) had been developed and used for some years for manufacturing re-orders but had not been maintained for branch re-orders.

As mentioned, the total inventory level was about $4\frac{1}{4}$ months' supply. This represented an average safety stock level of about 2.6 months' supply, of which 2.35 months was in the branches and 0.25 months in the national warehouse. The term safety stock is used to refer to the amount of stock on hand when a new shipment arrives.

The national/branch inventory balance was not as planned. Management was constantly attempting to reduce the branch inventory level and increase the national warehouse stock. The situation defied change and appeared to be a result of hoarding by branches as a result of poor service by the national warehouse. While it was *believed at the time that this was a very disadvantageous situation, we shall see later in this report that its economic significance was not considerable.*

The service level experienced was defined in the study as the ratio of quantity supplied out of stock to quantity ordered. Historically the customers had received a service level of 99 percent. This was accomplished despite a branch/customer service level of 89 percent by referring 5 percent of orders to nearby branches for delivery and 5 percent of orders to other than nearby branches or to the manufacturing plants for air freighting. Needless to say, referring orders involved an additional transportation cost premium, as well as taking additional clerical time. However, the national warehouse/branch warehouse service level was 60 percent, reflecting the lack of inventory at the national warehouse. Hence, a branch re-order on average was 60 percent filled out of stock and 40 percent backordered.

The order cycle lead time for the branch re-orders depended on two factors:

- *whether the product was sold in the as-manufactured condition or required blending,*

- *whether the product was in stock.*

The following table gives the lead time in calendar days:

	In Stock	Out of Stock
Sold as manufactured	8–20 days	34–44 days
Sold blended	11–26 days	41–58 days

The distribution of the lead time appeared due to uncontrollable factors and approximated a uniform distribution.

The head office computer based information system contained the inventory status for each product at each location. The national warehouse stock records were satisfactory as they were updated concurrently with receipts or shipments. However, because the branches received orders and shipped goods days before the central computer received this data and because of inadequate controls on the recording of interbranch transfers, the central computer data of branch stock levels was not accurate. The branches maintained their own accurate stock card files manually.

A project was underway at the time to develop a real time order entry system tied into each branch by visual display units and teleprinters for producing packing slips, shipping documents, etc. The new system would have the capability to maintain accurately all stock records at the head office. Completion was planned for one year after the planned completion of the inventory control project. It was decided to design both systems with all necessary links to facilitate later integration but not to delay the implementation of the inventory control system.

Features of the Inventory Control System Adopted

Forecasting. As sales forecasting was a recognized problem area and since a dependable forecasting approach is vital to a sound inventory control system, much effort was expended on studying the forecasting requirements and exploring alternate solutions. After this analysis it was determined that the right solution should give consideration to the following points:

(a)   Divisional management wanted the branch level marketing management to be in control of the forecasting, as their customer and product knowledge was indispensable.

(b)   Forecasting trials on a sample of two years of actual sales data revealed that the triple exponential smoothing* forecasting technique was 25 percent more accurate than previous manual forecasts on a branch/product basis (accuracy measured by standard deviation of forecast error).

(c)   Despite firm marketing conviction that the product line was seasonally affected, no seasonal component could be statistically detected.

(d)   About 10 percent of the sales volume was so called referral orders. These are orders referred to another branch because of lack of stock availability. The system would need to record these sales against the "home" branch.

(e)   With roughly 9,000 forecasts to be prepared each month, computational speed would be an important consideration in selecting a forecasting technique.

(f)   Forecasting trials on national sales data revealed greater accuracy than that obtained by summing the forecasted branch sales.

The forecasting solution adopted was to develop a branch/product level forecast for the next six months using the triple exponential smoothing technique. The appropriate set of forecasted products was sent to each branch for approval or amendment. If the statistical forecast was amended, the salesman would indicate by means of a code why the change was made. Codes covered, for instance, such conditions as new key customer, loss of key customer to competition, fashion change, expected marketing plan impact, etc. The branch adjusted forecasts were consolidated on the computer at the head office by key punching the amendments. The computer program then compared the consolidated branch level forecasts with a separately prepared national level forecast and any deviations greather than a predetermined percentage were printed out for management reconciliation. This would be done bearing in mind the greater accuracy of the national level forecast. The purpose for coding the reason for amending the statistical forecast was to develop a tabulated feedback for marketing management indicating which types of amendments on average improved forecasting accuracy and which types led to a less accurate forecast. The feedback loop created a continuous learning environment for improving forecasting skills with an established reference basis of the exponential smoothing technique to measure progress.

Re-order Points. The minimum safety stock sufficient to achieve a given level of

---

* Triple exponential smoothing assumes a quadratic trend. For methods, see R. G. Brown, *Smoothing, Forecasting and Prediction.* Prentice-Hall, Englewood Cliffs, N.J., 1963, pp. 136–144.

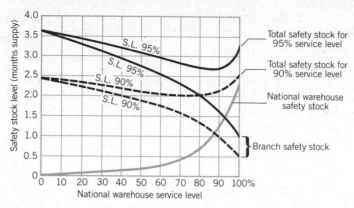

FIGURE 10-14

Safety stocks required at branch and national (central) warehouse level to achieve given customer service.

branch service to customers needs to be jointly calculated for both the national and the branch warehouses. The factors entering the decision include forecast accuracy, customer service level desired, distribution of lead time for manufacturing re-orders and distribution of lead time for branch re-orders. All these factors are product dependent.

An approximate analytical solution was obtained to indicate the level of safety stock required at branch and national warehouses in order to achieve various levels of branch customer service. The solutions were then checked by running a series of computer simulations. The results are presented graphically (see Figure 10-14), showing, for a customer service level, the safety stock levels expressed in months supply plotted against the national warehouse service level.

The safety stock level for both the branch and the national warehouse is plotted together with the total safety stock in the system. The general shape of the curves is as expected. If the national warehouse service to the branches is increased by raising the stock level in the national warehouse, the branch inventory level can be reduced while still maintaining the same customer service.

For a 90 percent service level the balance of inventories between national and branch warehouses is not very critical. The national warehouse service level can be anywhere from 60 to 90 percent with no real impact on the total level of safety stock. The minimum is achieved by a national warehouse service level of 75 percent and a total safety stock equal to two months' supply. The service level of the national warehouse had historically been about 60 percent with the branch service level at 89 percent, which from this graph is satisfactory.

The goal was to increase the branch service level to 95 percent and so reduce the number of orders referred out of the region. The graph pertaining to this branch service level reveals that the national warehouse service level is now more critical. Operating it at a 60 percent service level would involve a total safety stock of 2.95 months while at the optimum of 85 percent service level the total safety stock is 2.7 months; that is, a saving of one week's inventory. The graphs are not included here, but for higher branch service levels the national warehouse service level is still more critical.

The graphs reveal the value in total safety stock terms of having a two-stage distribution system of a national warehouse and branches. Obviously there are other reasons for having a national warehouse than reduction of safety stock. For instance, in this case study all blending and mixing of the products from the various plants needed to be carried out centrally. On the other hand, a national warehouse does involve more transportation cost in a multiplant environment. As the broad structure of the distribution system was not in the terms of reference of the study this question was not explored.

For a branch level of 90 percent the use of a national warehouse saves in this case about $1\frac{1}{2}$ weeks of safety stock, while for a 95 percent branch service level about three weeks of safety stock are saved. The value of the national warehouse would be greater were the national/branch order lead times less. The graphs are based on the national/branch lead times presented earlier which range from 8–26 days if the product is in stock, to 34–53 days in the case of the product not being in stock. The impact on safety stock of reducing this lead time and its variability was not explored in the project, though it was believed to be high. In addition, consideration was given to not holding national inventories of some imported products which were always sold in the as-manufactured condition. Freight savings could be realized by shipping direct but were not of sufficient magnitude to offset the increased inventory costs.

Consolidation on a regional basis of slower moving stock was investigated and was found to have some attractive benefits. Safety stock reduction was in the vicinity of 40 percent due mainly to lowering of forecasting error. Order processing savings coupled with average inventory level reduction (excluding safety stock) promised at least an additional $60,000 per year savings.

To summarize, the safety stock allocation adopted was based on providing a branch service level of 95 percent with a national warehouse service level of 85 percent. This resulted, on average, in one month's safety stock in the national warehouse and $1\frac{3}{4}$ month's safety stock in the branch warehouse. For any given product, its safety stock depended on its forecast accuracy, where manufactured, and whether sold in the as-manufactured or blended condition. Additionally, the desired customer service was product dependent, determined by a service level code associated with each product. These factors were used in the computer based model to arrive at the appropriate national and branch warehouse re-order points for each product in terms of months supply.

The re-order quantity was calculated on an approximate basis using the simple EOQ model. While it was recognized that this approach would lead theoretically to a too low re-order quantity when compared to an "exact" solution, the lack of accuracy of the re-order cost estimate made a more refined computational procedure seem a waste of time.

Implementation of System

The initial implementation of the inventory control system (see Figure 10-15) allowed for:

(i)   Statistical forecasts on a branch level of the high and medium volume products. This comprised 40 percent of the 1,500 products and included more than 90 percent of the sales volume. On a national basis all products were forecasted.

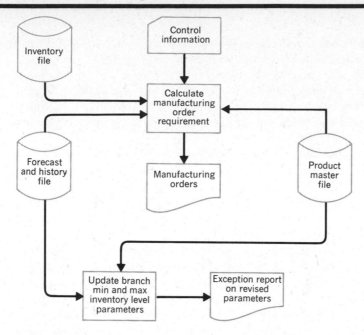

FIGURE 10-15
Inventory control system.

Each branch amended, where necessary, its statistical forecast based on its marketing, product and customer experience and knowledge.

(ii)   Branch control of its inventory and re-ordering from the national warehouse, by application of the product specific re-order level and re-order quantity parameters. These values were initially supplied to all branches and then updated quarterly on an exception basis.

(iii)   Head office control of reconciling the consolidated branch level forecasts and the national forecast.

(iv)   Computer prepared manufacturing re-orders, on an automatic basis once each month.

(v)   Gradual shift in the level and balance of inventories to approach the calculated optimum levels while avoiding disruptions.

At the time of implementation the national warehouse inventory levels were reliably contained in the EDP inventory file. While branch inventory levels were on the EDP file they were out of date by a week or more. The only reliable up-to-date inventory file sufficient for branch inventory maintenance was a manual system in the branch. This gave a valuable opportunity to allow the branch logistics personnel to control their end of the system and utilize the computer prepared re-order parameters and so gain experience and confidence in the system. It was planned that when the new real time computer order entry system was installed, up-to-date reli-

able inventory status data would be available and branch re-ordering could then be handled automatically, along the same lines as had been followed manually.

Benefits

Benefits from the implementation of the project, which incidentally took place about 12 months after project inception, arose from three main areas:

(i)   Stock reduction from improvement of forecasting accuracy;

(ii)   Stock reduction from improvement of inventory re-order point and re-order quantity calculations; and

(iii)   By increasing branch service level to 95 percent, a reduction of additional costs incurred in referring orders to other branches or back to manufacturing after taking into account the increased inventory at the branch warehouses.

In addition, considerable benefits flowed from the computer forecasting in the reduction of clerical work load on the sales force and also in the head office where previously the manually prepared forecasts had been consolidated.

Direct measurement of project benefits was not considered possible because of the number of changes introduced. For instance, raising the level of customer service provided by the branch had the combined effect of increasing branch inventory, reducing referred orders together with their attendant additional costs, and providing the customer with better service.

The bulk of the cost benefits were provided by the improved forecasting approach which provided a two week stock usage reduction. The benefits gained by the improved re-order point, re-order quantity parameters were estimated at about one week's usage. In total, this inventory reduction amounted to a little over 10 percent of average operating inventory, to save the company in the order of $300,000 per annum at the 20 percent inventory cost used. Additionally, raising the branch service level was expected to save $50,000 per annum after allowing for the increased inventory. The consolidation of slow moving items into regional warehouses was planned for later implementation and promised a saving of at least $100,000 per annum. In total, savings were believed to be in excess of $450,000 or 15 percent of the inventory carrying cost.

QUESTIONS

a.   What are the advantages and disadvantages of the new forecasting system?

b.   How do you reconcile the fact that the simulation shows that branch safety stock actually declines rapidly as National Warehouse service level increases? Why would not the reverse policy of keeping Branch safety stock high and National safety stock low be even better?

c.   What further improvements do you feel could be made in the recommended system?

d. Do you agree that the basis for inventory replenishment should be *EOQ*? Throughout the system? For all items?

e. What is your evaluation of the installed system as a whole? As a manager, would you install it or ask for restudy and possible changes? If the latter, what changes?

REFERENCES

Austin, L. M., "Project *EOQ*: A Success Story in Implementing Academic Research," *Interfaces, 7*(4), August 1977, pp. 1–12.

Brown, R. G., *Decision Rules for Inventory Management.* Holt, Rinehart and Winston, New York, 1967.

Buchan, J., and E. Koenigsberg, *Scientific Inventory Control.* Prentice-Hall, Englewood Cliffs, N.J., 1963.

Buffa, E. S., and J. G. Miller, *Production-Inventory Systems: Planning and Control* (3rd ed.). Irwin, Homewood, Ill., 1979.

Lewis, C. D., *Demand Analysis and Inventory Control.* Lexington Books, London, 1975.

Magee, J. F., and D. M. Boodman, *Production Planning and Inventory Control* (2nd ed.). McGraw-Hill, New York, 1967.

McMillan, C., and R. F. Gonzalez, *Systems Analysis: A Computer Approach to Decision Models* (3rd ed.). Irwin, Homewood, Ill., 1973.

Peterson, R., and E. A. Silver, *Decision Systems for Inventory Management and Production Planning.* Wiley, New York, 1979.

CHAPTER 11

Industrial Scheduling Systems

I N CHAPTER 9 WE WERE CONCERNED WITH THE DEVELOPMENT OF comprehensive plans that involved scheduling production levels, work force requirements, and resulting inventory levels in aggregate terms. In this chapter, we use to agregate plan as a constraint within which we must develop more detailed master schedules for individual end-products, and schedules for facilities and personnel.

Scheduling for high volume continuous systems is focused more in the aggregate plan, and translating and implementing the plan, because the entire system operates more as a giant machine. Scheduling process-focused systems requires more detailed planning, because individual orders must be handled in batches.

SCHEDULING AND AGGREGATE PLANNING

The broad outline of the scheduling process for the multistage production-distribution system is shown in Figure 11-1. Forecasts are produced for the planning horizon as an input to the aggregate planning process. Basic decisions on production rate and work force levels for the upcoming period are then produced by the aggregate plan. We can either compute the overtime, subcontracting required, and the projected end-of-period inventory, or these data will be produced as a part of the aggregate planning procedure, depending on the model used. Translating these

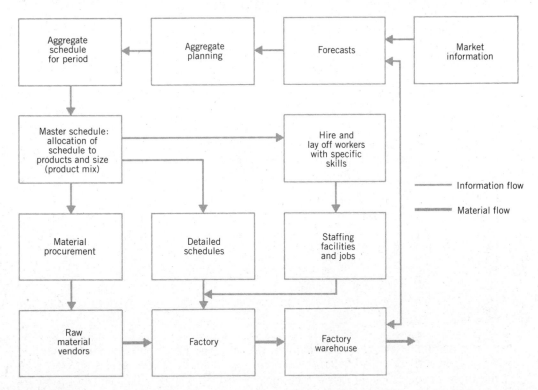

FIGURE 11-1
Relationships between aggregate planning and master and detailed plans and schedules.

aggregate plans into master schedules and detailed work schedules is the next task. The master schedule becomes the basis for raw material procurement, the specific plans for hiring or layoff of workers, and detailed schedules for facilities and workers.

Master Schedules and Product Mix

Aggregate scheduling produces a set of constraints within which we must operate. These broad level decisions are important in setting the basic production strategy for the best use of resources. Master schedules are stated more specifically in terms of the quantities of each individual product to be produced and the time periods for production. For example, the aggregate schedule might call for 1000 units in planning period 1, where the planning period might be a month or perhaps a 4-week period. If there were three products, the more detailed master schedule would indicate the quantities of each of the three products to be produced in each week of the planning period, consistent with the aggregate schedule.

As an example, assume the aggregate schedule calls for a level production rate during the three-period planning horizon. The periods of planning horizons are often months or 4-week periods. The latter is particularly convenient, because it breaks the year into $52/4 = 13$ periods of equal size. The weekly master schedule then conveniently fits most work schedules in our society. In our example we will assume three 4-week periods in the planning horizon.

The aggregate plan may have produced the following:

Aggregate Plan				
Period (4 weeks)	Initial	1	2	3
Aggregate forecast	—	1200	1100	800
Production	—	1000	1000	1000
Aggregate inventories	800	600	500	700

Now we must disaggregate the forecasts on a weekly basis for the three products. Suppose that the composition of the forecasts is as follows:

Forecasts for Three Products													
Period		1				2				3			
Week	1	2	3	4	5	6	7	8	9	10	11	12	Total
Product 1	100	100	100	100	100	80	75	75	75	75	65	50	995
Product 2	150	125	125	100	75	75	75	65	65	65	60	50	1030
Product 3	75	75	75	75	100	120	125	135	135	60	50	50	1075
Total	325	300	300	275	275	275	275	275	275	200	175	150	3100
Period total		1200				1100				800			3100

The aggregate schedule by planning periods was to be level at 1000 units per 4-week period. The aggregate forecasts are declining, but the forecasts by weeks for the three products follow different patterns. Products 1 and 2 decline, but product 3 increases during the second 4-week period, although declining rapidly in the third 4-week period.

TABLE 11-1a
Master Schedule for Three Products Consistent with Forecasts and Aggregate Production Plan

Period		1				2				3		
Week	0	1	2	3	4	5	6	7	8	9	10	11	12
Product 1, production	—	—	250	—	—	125	—	125	—	250	—	—
Product 2, production	—	250	—	250	—	125	—	125	—	—	250	—
Product 3, production	250	—	—	—	250	—	250	—	250	—	—	250
Total production	250	250	250	250	250	250	250	250	250	250	250	250
Capacity, aggregate plan	250	250	250	250	250	250	250	250	250	250	250	250
Deviation	0	0	0	0	0	0	0	0	0	0	0	0

TABLE 11-1b
Product End of Week Inventory Profiles Associated with Master Schedule

Period		1				2				3		
Week	0	1	2	3	4	5	6	7	8	9	10	11	12
Product 1, inventory	400	300	200	350	250	150	195	120	170	95	270	205	155
Product 2, inventory	250	100	225	100	250	175	225	150	210	145	80	270	220
Product 3, inventory	150	325	250	175	100	250	130	255	120	235	175	125	325
Total inventory	800	725	675	625	600	575	550	525	500	475	525	600	700
Inventory, aggregate plan	800	600	600	600	600	500	500	500	500	700	700	700	700
Deviation	0	125	75	25	0	75	50	25	0	(225)	(175)	(100)	0

The master scheduling problem requires the construction of schedules for each of the products, consistent with the aggregate plan, the forecasts, and planned inventories. Table 11-1 shows a master schedule that fits these requirements. The production plan in Table 11-1a indicates an initial cycling between the three products, where productive capacity is allocated each week to one of the products. In the fifth week, the strategy changes to cycle product 3 every other week, to take account of the high forecast requirements of that product during the fifth through ninth weeks. In the tenth week, the plan returns to a 3-week cycling of the three products.

The individual product inventory profiles that would result from the master schedule are shown in Table 11-1b. Note that the individual inventory balances, I_t, are end-of-week figures that result from the simple accounting equation, $I_t = I_{t-1} - F_t + P_t$, where F_t is the forecast and P_t the production during the week. For example, in Table 11-1b, the initial inventory for product 3 is $I_0 = 150$ units, requirements were forecast as $F_1 = 75$ units and production is scheduled as $P_1 = 250$ units. Therefore, the projected inventory at the end of week 1 is $I_1 = 150 - 75 + 250 = 325$ units as indicated in Table 11-1 for product 3. The total end-of-week inventory is simply the sum of the inventories for the three products. The inventory called for by the aggregate plan was an end-of-period (4-week) figure, so there are deviations from plan in the first 3 weeks of each 4-week period, but the deviation is zero in the last week of each 4-week planning period.

The master scheduling methods indicated by this discussion follow from the simple logic of the disaggregation of aggregate plans. In more complex situations, problems might have occurred because of conflicts in forecast requirements, production capacities, and inventory position, resulting in stockout. Alternate plans could be tried to see if the problem could be solved. It may be necessary to cycle back to a reevaluation of the aggregate plan, with possible changes.

In the master schedule of Table 11-1, no attempt was made to consider the balance of setup and inventory costs. These questions will be considered later in the chapter. Optimizing methods for master scheduling are developed by Hax and Meal [1975] in a hierarchical product planning system.

The master schedule provides a basis for detailed plans of materials flow, equipment, and personnel schedules. These plans are likely to be different for product- versus process-focused productive systems. Obviously all materials, components, and subassemblies need to be coordinated with the master schedule, and this is the subject of Chapter 12 on "Material Requirements Planning."

DETAILED SCHEDULING FOR PRODUCT-FOCUSED SYSTEMS

A result of the allocation to types and sizes gives basic information for detailed scheduling, detailed hiring and layoff instructions, and material procurement schedules, as shown in Figure 11-1. Conflicts in detailed schedules may occur at this point because of capacity limitations for either labor or facilities.

In setting the individual type and size production rates and personnel schedules, the scheduler may be faced with either great rigidity or reasonable flexibility, depending on the nature of the processes and the productive system design. For example, the output rates of production lines are at a fairly fixed hourly rate.

What flexibility does the scheduler have to obtain a certain target weekly or monthly rate of output? There are basically two alternatives. The work force on the line can be scheduled to work shorter or longer hours (including overtime or undertime), or the entire line can be rebalanced with more or fewer work stations to achieve a somewhat higher or lower hourly rate of output. The latter would be used to achieve more drastic changes in output rate, because it involves hiring or laying off personnel. Here, however, the scheduler will be following the basic instructions given by the aggregate plan and master schedule, which presumably have taken into account the relative costliness of changing production rates through changing hours, using overtime, and rebalancing (hiring and laying off).

The aggregate plan establishes the constraints under which the scheduler must perform. Thus we see that assembly line balance is a subject for concern not only for the original design of productive systems, but also for continued operation. For example, the use of rebalancing to achieve different hourly rates of output is common in automotive assembly lines.

If the line is completely rigid in design, being mechanically paced, then the scheduler can change total output for the period only by changing the number of hours worked or by changing the line speed. The rigid system is, of course, often used.

The main problems of detailed scheduling are to devise ways of following out the aggregate plan and master schedule as far as possible, since the broadly based optimization has already taken place. Following the allocation of aggregate production to product types and sizes, an iterative process begins that develops a tentative plan and checks back to see if the details of the plan fit the constraints.

The first question raised in the schematic diagram of Figure 11-2 involves possible changes in employment levels called for by the aggregate plan and master schedule. These changes will require rebalancing of personnel to facilities. In many instances, alternate staffing plans may exist for various output rates, based on previous careful studies. The result of rebalancing will be to hire or lay off personnel in specific skill categories, checking to see if the result is within the aggregate plan. If the aggregate planning model has been carefully constructed to reflect the relationship between productivity and personnel, it should be possible to adjust personnel assignments within the constraints of the plan. Balance solutions must deal with assignment of whole worker units, so that costs and capacity increase or decrease in step fashion rather than in a continuous relationship to work force size.

When the hiring-layoff question has been answered with resultant rebalancing, this information is an input to the initial attempt to generate a detailed schedule of products to facilities. The scheduler then generates a detailed assignment of product items to facilities by production days, as well as assignments to subcontractors, if that is appropriate. The result is then checked in an iterative fashion to see if assigned levels of overtime, subcontracting, and inventories meet the requirements of the aggregate plan and master schedule. Other constraints must also be observed, such as maintenance schedules and agreed company-union work rules.

In a parallel way the existing schedules are reviewed for possible modification based on new information dealing with the progress of actual sales versus forecast sales. The schedules of production commitments are then updated by adding the newest information and dropping off the oldest period.

Based on the resultant information the scheduler may then develop full schedules for two or three time spans, such as those shown at the bottom of Figure 11-2. For some specific company situations most of the process could possibly be computerized.

HIERARCHICAL PLANNING FOR HIGH-VOLUME CONTINUOUS SYSTEMS

Hierarchical planning is a methodology by which decisions at aggregate levels provide constraints that more detailed levels must meet, and the execution of plans at the detailed levels provide useful feedback that may generate change in higher-level, more aggregated decisions. The result is that hierarchical planning systems are responsive to the organizational structure of the firm and serve to define a framework for the partitioning and linking of the planning activities. Hax and Meal [1975] report an application of such a plan in a process manufacturing firm stated as being analogous to a chemical plant or steel mill. They point out that it is difficult to construct general purpose hierarchical planning systems that could be applied to any kind of industry. Instead, the planning effort must be tailored to a specific organization and its idiosyncrasies.

The example firm is a multiplant, multiproduct operation with three distinct seasonal demand patterns. There is a strong incentive to maintain a nearly level manufacturing rate for the following reasons.

1. The capital cost of equipment is very high compared with the cost of shift premium for labor, and the plants normally operate three shifts 5 days a week with occasional weekend work.

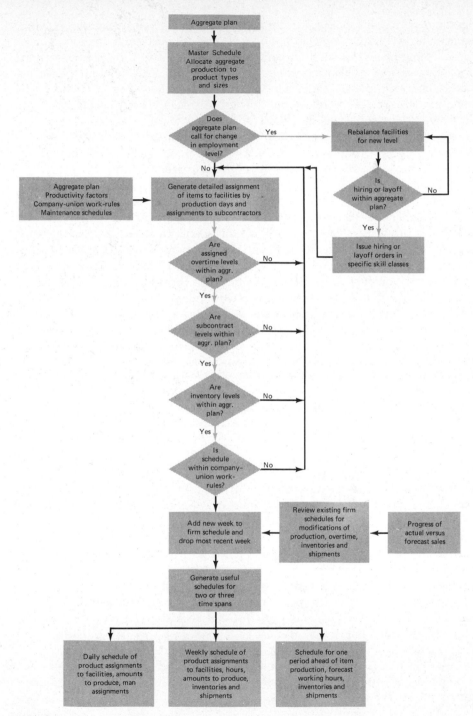

FIGURE 11-2
Flow diagram of operations scheduling for product-focused systems.

2.   The labor union is very strong and exerts pressure to maintain constant production levels throughout the year for employment stabilization.

At the beginning of the study the symptoms of problems were poor customer service, excessive inventory, and high production costs. The high inventory in the face of poor customer service was caused by excessive seasonal stock accumulation for some items and shortages for others. High production costs were due primarily to runs that were uneconomically short, with consequent high setup cost and low productivity. These in turn resulted from the high stockout rate and the consequent need to produce a small amount of each of many items in order to satisfy backorders. Hax and Meal state the problem to be solved as:

. . . planning aggregate production levels, particularly in allocating available production capacity among several product types with differing seasonal demand patterns, and in the subsequent detailed scheduling of each item belonging to a product type.

System Structure

The first step in the development of the planning and control system to help solve the stated problem was to define levels of aggregation for the various items produced. This was done by examining the extent to which sets of decisions regarding production were interdependent. If two sets of decisions were found to be independent, they were totally separated in the hierarchy of decisions.

Beginning at the most detailed level, items sharing a major setup cost were grouped into "families." Thus, scheduling decisions for items in a family were very dependent, whereas the opposite was true for items in different families. It was also found that decisions for a family in one time period were strongly tied to decisions for the same family in other time periods. This time dependence resulted from the need to accumulate seasonal inventories in both product families.

Product families were aggregated into "types," if they shared a common seasonal pattern and production rate. This facilitated seasonal planning, because only the aggregate for all families in the type group needed to be considered in developing the plan.

The next step in the process was the development of a hierarchy of decisions based on the relationships developed in the aggregation process. The following steps were developed.

1.   Assignment of families to plants
2.   Seasonal planning
3.   Scheduling of families
4.   Scheduling of items

In addition to the preceding steps, basic inventory methods were used to establish minimum run lengths and overstock limits. The complete decision sequence is shown in Figure 11-3. A brief description of the several submodels and the nature of their interaction follows.

Plant/Product Assignment Subsystem (PAS). The *PAS* determines the plant locations at which each family should be manufactured. The model balances the cost of interterritory transportation against incremental capital investment cost required to manufacture the product family in question. The model is run annually to take account of new products and changes in variable manufacturing cost and demand patterns.

Seasonal Planning Subsystem (SPS). The *SPS* is the aggregate planning subsystem, and it determines the production requirements and seasonal stock accumulations by product type for each plant. The objective is to minimize total regular and overtime production costs plus inventory holding costs, subject to constraints on available regular and overtime labor, meeting demand, and safety stock requirements. The labor force size was not included as a decision variable, because employment stability was assumed. Linear programming was used as the solution technique.

Family Scheduling Subsystem (FSS). The *FSS* is used to schedule enough production for the families in a product type to use the time allocated to the type by the seasonal planning subsystem. This includes the accumulation of the necessary seasonal stock.

Item Scheduling Subsystem (ISS). The *ISS* determines the production quantities for each item within the constraints of the family schedules determined by the family

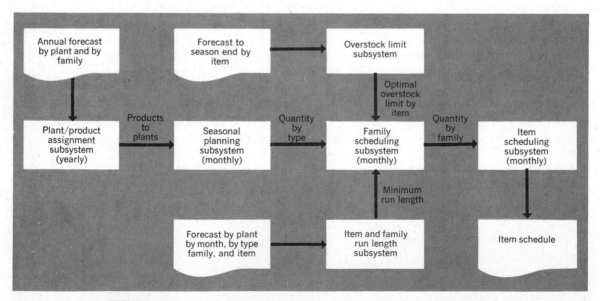

FIGURE 11-3
Decision sequence in planning and scheduling.
SOURCE: A. C. Hax, and H. C. Meal. "Hierarchical Integration of Production Planning and Scheduling," in *Studies in Management Sciences, Vol. I, Logistics,* edited by M. A. Geisler, North Holland-American Elsevier, Amsterdam, 1975.

scheduling subsystem. As in *FSS,* overstock limits are observed, and an attempt is made to maximize customer service. In order to carry out this task, Hax and Meal developed heuristics that equalize the expected runout times for the items in the family.

Results

Hax and Meal report a total development cost in the range of $150,000 to $200,000. Although exact benefits were not reported, they stated that cost reductions from smoother production, fewer emergency interruptions, and reduced inventory carrying costs were expected to be more than $200,000 per year in each plant.

BATCH PRODUCTION FOR PROCESS-FOCUSED SYSTEMS

As discussed in Chapter 2, most often it is not possible to produce continuously because the quantities needed do not justify the full use of facilities. In order to obtain fuller utilization of machines and personnel a variety of parts and sizes may be produced on the same equipment. Machines are grouped by generic type as shown in Figure 2-2a and b, and individual orders or jobs are processed in batches. In such systems, the basis for planning and control is the individual job order. The use of facilities is intermittent, and orders may follow different paths through the system, depending on the individual processing requirements of the product or part.

Capacity Versus Lot Size

Many batch processing systems have very limited choice of the order size or lot size. These kinds of systems are normally those that produce a noninventoriable or a custom output. The lot size is dictated by the customer order in such instances, and because the item is custom in design, there is little or no opportunity to group orders for more efficient processing.

An extremely common type of system is one in which the output is inventoriable and produced in substantial volume, even though the volume may not justify continuous production. In these situations, the manager must determine the lot size to be produced at one time. For example, average annual requirements may be $R = 12,000$ units, but production time for this quantity might require only 160 hours. Therefore, there are many options available.

Suppose that once machines are set up for our example, the variable or "run time" is only 0.80 minutes per unit, but 5 hours are required to set up machines for the lot. If lots of $Q = 1000$ units were scheduled, then 12 setups are required totaling $5 \times 12 = 60$ hours. The total run time is $0.8 \times 12,000 = 9600$ minutes, or 160 hours. The total setup and run time is then $60 + 160 = 220$ hours, and the average production rate including setup is $12,000/220 = 54.5$ units per hour. Then, for different lot sizes, output in units per hour including setup, and total hours for 12,000 units is as follows:

Q, Units per Lot	Units per Hour, Including Setup	Total Hours for 12,000 Units
1000	54.5	220.0
2000	63.2	190.0
5000	69.8	172.0
12,000	72.7	165.0

The total machine and worker time requirements for the lot of 1000 units are 33.3 percent greater than the lot of 12,000 units.

On the other hand, when setup time is somewhat smaller in relation to run time, perhaps only 60 minutes per setup, comparable calculations indicate the following:

Q, Units per Lot	Units per Hour, Including Setup	Total Hours for 12,000 Units
1000	69.8	172.0
2000	72.3	166.0
5000	73.9	162.4
12,000	74.5	161.0

In this instance, total machine and worker time requirements for the lot of 1000 units are only 6.8 percent greater than for the lot of 12,000 units. When setup times are large in relation to run times, system capacity is very sensitive to the lot size chosen, and capacity is diluted when scheduling small lots. Conversely, for the same lot size, if setup times can be reduced, capacity increases. However, setup times are not usually the decision variable. Instead, lot size is the decision variable under managerial control. Of course, our example deals only with one item in showing the capacity-lot size relation. It is lot size policy that we must be concerned about, where the cumulative effects of large or small lots affect capacity and the cost of providing capacity.

Independent *EOQ* Scheduling

Why not determine lot sizes economically, according to the *EOQ* Equations 4 or 9 from Chapter 10? *EOQ*s would be computed independently for each item and processed through the system as a lot. Sometimes this decision may be a good one, but quite often Equations 4 or 9 are oversimplifications of the true situations, and improved decision policies can be used. Some of the complexities that commonly intrude on the simplicity of Equations 4 and 9 are as follows:

1. Because of differing requirements, setup costs, and inventory carrying costs for each job, inventories that result from *EOQ* lots may not last through a complete cycle. Because of stockouts, special orders of smaller size may then be needed, resulting in capacity dilution.
2. When operating near capacity limits, competition for machine and/or worker time may cause scheduling interference. In order to maintain scheduled commitments, lots may be split. Again, a side effect is to reduce capacity.

TABLE 11-2
Requirements, Costs, and Production Data for Ten Products Run on the Same Equipment

(1) Product Number	(2) Annual Requirements, R_i	(3) Sales per Production Day (250 days per year), Col. 2/250, r_i	(4) Daily Production Rate, p_i	(5) Production Days Required, Col. 2/Col. 4	(6) Inventory Holding Cost per Unit per Year, c_{H_i}	(7) Machine Setup Cost per Run, c_{P_i}	(8) EOQ, Equation 9 from Chapter 10	(9) Number OF Runs per Year, Col. 2/Col. 8	(10) Production Days per Lot, Col. 8/Col. 4	(11) TIC_0, Equation 10 from Chapter 10
1	9,000	36	225	40	$0.10	$40	2928	3.1	13.0	$245.93
2	20,000	80	500	40	0.20	25	2440	8.2	4.9	409.88
3	6,000	24	200	30	0.15	50	2132	2.8	10.7	281.42
4	12,000	48	600	20	0.10	40	3230	3.7	5.4	297.19
5	16,000	64	500	32	0.02	50	9578	1.7	19.2	167.04
6	15,000	60	500	30	0.50	40	1651	9.1	3.3	726.64
7	8,000	32	1000	8	0.35	30	1190	6.7	1.2	403.27
8	9,000	36	900	10	0.05	60	4743	1.9	5.3	227.68
9	2,000	8	125	16	0.55	25	441	4.5	3.5	226.89
10	3,000	12	200	15	0.20	20	799	3.8	4.0	150.20
				241		$380			70.5	$3136.14

3. Rush jobs may require the running of special orders of nonoptimal size.

4. Sometimes there is a "bottleneck" machine or process through which all or most jobs must be sequenced. The limited capacity may exert pressure toward smaller lot sizes, diluting capacity in order to meet scheduled commitments on at least a part of job orders.

5. Where parts or products are produced in regular cycles, the individual lot sizes are constructed to fit in with the cycling, rather than from the balance of setup and inventory holding costs for each individual item.

6. The assumption of constant demand is not met, either as a result of seasonal usage or sales or because demand is *dependent* on the production schedules of other parts, subassemblies, or products. This point will be dealt with in Chapter 12.

Most of the previous reasons for deviating from the concepts of Equations 4 and 9 lead to smaller lot sizes and to reductions of effective capacity. Under these conditions, relatively larger fractions of available machine and worker time are devoted to machine setup. Note that items 1 through 5 in the preceding list all indicate some kind of dependence of the individual lot size on the other orders in the system.

An Example. Table 11-2 gives data on requirements, costs, and production for 10 products that are processed on the same equipment. The capacity of the equipment is limited to 250 days' usage per year. When the daily production rates for each product listed in column 4 are converted to required production days in column 5, we see that the total annual production requirement of 241 days is within the 250 day maximum (setup times are included). Our particular interest is in columns 8 through 11 of Table 11-2. The lot sizes are computed using Equation 9* from

---

* The choice between Equations 4 and 9 depends on whether or not items go into inventory while production progresses. If items do go into inventory during production, inventory builds up at the rate of $(p - r)$, requiring the use of Equation 9, as is assumed in this example. If the situation were such that the entire batch went into inventory at the completion of production, Equation 4 from Chapter 10 would be appropriate.

TABLE 11-3 **Calculation of Production Days Required, Peak Inventory, and Number of Days of Sales Requirements Met by an _EOQ_ for Ten Products**

(1) Product Number	(2) Production Days Required, EOQ/ p_i	(3) Peak Inventory, Production Days $\times (p_i - r_i)$	(4) Days to Deplete EOQ, EOQ/r_i
1	13.0	2457	81.3
2	4.9	2058	30.6[a]
3	10.7	1883	88.8
4	5.4	2980	67.3[a]
5	19.2	8371	149.7
6	3.3	1452	27.5[a]
7	1.2	1162	37.2[a]
8	5.3	4579	131.8
9	3.5	410	55.1[a]
10	4.0	752	66.6[a]
	70.5		

[a] Items that stock out, inventory lasts less than 70.5 days.

Chapter 10, and the number of runs per year, production-days per lot, and costs are computed for independent _EOQ_ scheduling of the 10 products.

Because only one product can be produced at a time, there are problems that result from an attempt to schedule the 10 products independently (see Table 11-3). Each _EOQ_ lot provides inventories to be used at the daily usage rate r_i of that product and will be depleted in EOQ/r_i days, as shown in column 4. Therefore, the cycle inventory must last long enough for that product to be recycled. The total number of production days for all 10 products is shown in column 2 as 70.5 days. Scanning column 4, we see that the inventory for products 2, 4, 6, 7, 9, and 10 will be depleted before the cycle can be repeated. The situation is shown graphically for product 2 in Figure 11-4 and is called _scheduling interference_.

Clearly, independent scheduling will not provide a feasible solution. This infeasibility is not surprising, because the schedule of each product is not independent of the other products since they are all processed on the same equipment, which has limited capacity. We must treat the 10 products as a system. Before considering alternatives, note that our system is operating near capacity, with 241 production days scheduled, or $241 \times 100/250 = 96.4$ percent of the days available. Scheduling interference would probably not occur if we were operating at relatively low loads. The slack capacity under conditions of low load would be available to make the system work.

Common Cycle Scheduling

Perhaps the simplest way to ensure a feasible solution to scheduling interference problems is to adopt some common cycle for all products and produce lot quantities for each that cover usage rates for the cycle. Scanning column 9 of Table 11-2, the number of runs per year ranges from 1.7 to 9.1 (the average is 4.55 runs). A cycle of 4 or 5 runs per year might be reasonable. Table 11-4 gives key results for a cycle of

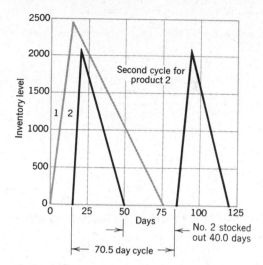

FIGURE 11-4
Inventory levels versus days for products 1 and 2. Product 2 is produced in the quantity $Q_p = 2440$ units, which lasts only 30.5 days at the usage rate of $r_2 = 80$ units per day.

4 runs per year. Each product is scheduled for production of a quantity to provide $250/4 = 62.5$ days' supply.

At the stated usage rates, the inventory of each product will not be depleted before it is recycled. These production lot quantities are computed in column 3 of Table 11-4 as simply $62.5 \times r_i$. The graphs of inventory build up and depletion follow the same general form of Figure 11-4. The inventory costs are computed in column 7 of Table 11-4, and column 8 gives the costs for four setups per year for each product. The

TABLE 11-4
Calculation of Inventory and Setup Costs When Ten Products Are Produced Four Times per Year in a Common Cycle of Length, 250/4 = 62.5 days. Each Product Is Produced in a Lot Size Q_i Sufficient to Cover 62.5 Days' Supply

(1) Product Number	(2) Daily usage Rate, r_i	(3) Production Lot Quantity, $62.5 \times r_i =$ $62.5 \times$ Col. 2	(4) Production Days Required, $Q_i/p_i =$ Col. 3/p_i	(5) Peak Inventory, Col. 4 × $(p_i - r_i)$	(6) Inventory Holding Cost per unit per year, c_{H_i}	(7) Annual Inventory Holding Cost $\frac{(\text{Col. 5} \times \text{Col. 6})}{2}$	(8) Annual Setup Costs, $4 \times c_{p_i}$
1	36	2250	10.00	1890	$0.10	$94.50	$160.00
2	80	5000	10.00	4200	0.20	420.00	100.00
3	24	1500	7.50	1320	0.15	99.00	200.00
4	48	3000	5.00	2760	0.10	138.00	160.00
5	64	4000	8.00	3488	0.02	34.88	200.00
6	60	3750	7.50	3300	0.50	825.00	160.00
7	32	2000	2.00	1936	0.35	338.80	120.00
8	36	2250	2.50	2160	0.05	54.00	240.00
9	8	500	4.00	468	0.55	128.70	100.00
10	12	750	3.75	705	0.20	70.50	80.00
			60.25			$2203.38	$1520.00

TIC = inventory + setup costs = 2203.38 + 1520.00 = $3723.38

TABLE 11-5   Inventory and Setup Costs for Common Cycles of $N = 4, 5, 8,$ and 10 Runs per Year for Ten Products

N, Cycles per Year	Number of Days Supply Produced	Average Annual Inventory Cost	Annual Setup Costs	Total Incremental Costs
4	62.50	$2203.38	$1520.00	$3723.39
5	50.00	1762.70	1900.00	3662.70
8	31.25	1101.69	3040.00	4141.69
10	25.00	881.35	3800.00	4681.35

total incremental costs for the common cycle scheduling system are shown at the bottom of the table as $3723.38, $587.24 greater than for independent scheduling. But independent scheduling did not provide a feasible solution. The total number of production days required is 60.25 days in column 4 of Table 11-4, leaving slack capacity of $62.50 - 60.25 = 2.25$ days, or $2.25 \times 100/62.5 = 3.6$ percent.

Economic Common Cycle Scheduling

Because a common cycle can provide a feasible solution, as long as the total load is within system capacity, the next question is, which cycle should be used, $N = 4, 5,$ 6, and so on? Calculations similar to those in Table 11-4 can be made for various cycles. Intuitively we know that as we increase the number of cycles per year, decreasing lot sizes, annual inventory costs will decrease, but annual setup costs will increase in proportion to the number of cycles per year. Table 11-5 summarizes costs for common cycles of $N = 4, 5, 8,$ and 10 runs per year for the same 10 products. For the alternatives computed, the lowest total incremental cost is associated with $N = 5$ runs to cover $250/5 = 50$ days' supply. If one were to select any of the larger number of runs per year as a plan, involving more rapid cycling, it would be important to consider the extent to which effective capacity would be reduced. If setup times were relatively large, the system capacity limit would be reached at these high loads. Remember that setup *times* are not isolated in our example.

Formal models for economic common cycles for a number of products (m) can be derived by methods similar to those used to develop *EOQ* formulas.* They are slightly more complex, but they are quite parallel in concept. The total incremental cost equation is developed for the entire set of products and similar mathematical operations produce the number of production runs that jointly minimize annual inventory plus setup costs for all products,

$$N_0 = \sqrt{\frac{\sum_{i=1}^{m} c_{H_i} R_i (1 - r_i/p_i)}{2 \sum_{i=1}^{m} c_{P_i}}} \tag{1}$$

* Equations 1 and 2 assume that production takes place over a period of time, and that items go into inventory in smaller quantities as production continues. This was the assumption for Equations 9 and 10 in Chapter 10. If this assumption does not apply, and the entire batch goes into inventory all at once, then the $(1 - r_i/p_i)$ terms in Equations 1 and 2 become 1, and these terms drop out.

TABLE 11-6 **Calculation of the Economic Number of Production Runs per Year, Using Equation 1**

(1) Product Number	(2) $(1 - r_i/p_i)$ from Table 11-2, $(1 - $ Col. 3/Col. 4)	(3) $c_{H_i}R_i(1 - r_i/p_i)$, Col. 6(Table 11-2)x Col. 2(Table 11-2)x Col. 2(this table)	(4) c_{P_i} from Col. 7 of Table 11-2
1	0.840	756.00	$40
2	0.840	3,360.00	25
3	0.880	792.00	50
4	0.920	1,104.00	40
5	0.872	279.04	50
6	0.880	6,600.00	40
7	0.968	2,710.40	30
8	0.960	432.00	60
9	0.936	1,029.60	25
10	0.940	564.00	20
		17,627.00	$380

$$N_0 = \sqrt{\frac{17,627}{2 \times 380}} = 4.82 \text{ runs per year}$$

$$TIC_0 = \sqrt{2 \times 380 \times 17,627} = \$3660.13$$

Equation 1 requires the multiplication of c_{H_i}, R_i, and $(1 - r_i/p_i)$ for each individual product in the numerator, which are then summed for all products. The denominator is simply two times the sum of the setup costs for all products. The total incremental cost of an optimal solution is

$$TIC_0 = \sqrt{2 \sum_{i=1}^{m} c_{p_i} \sum_{i=1}^{m} c_{H_i} R_i \left(1 - \frac{r_i}{p_i}\right)} \qquad (2)$$

Table 11-6 shows the calculations applying Equations 1 and 2 to the 10 product example. The optimal number of production runs is $N_0 = 4.82$ at a cost of $TIC_0 = \$3660.13$. As a practical matter, one would probably select a number of runs close to the optimal number, based on other considerations, because the total incremental cost differences are small near the optimum, as indicated in Table 11-5. In the absence of other overriding considerations, one would probably simply round the number of cycles to $N = 5$ runs per year in our example, because the annual cost difference between $N = 5$ and $N_0 = 4.82$ is only $2.57.

The lot size scheduling problem has been the subject of a great deal of research, and improvements over the costs that result from applying Equation 1 have been developed. For example, rules for running small demand items less often produce cost improvements.

SHOP FLOOR CONTROL

The requirements plan is also a general schedule of production orders to be processed through the shop. Each order is for a lot of a specific part or component and may require a sequence of processing through a number of different functional work centers. Orders go to each work center according to the sequence of operations required and enter a queue of orders to be processed by that work center. The orders are processed according to some priority sequence, the simplest of which is first come–first served.

Looking at the system as a whole, we have a set of service centers with orders that require various sequences of processing and variable process times. We have, in effect, a network of queues, and much of the research work has viewed the scheduling problem for process-focused systems in this context, using large-scale simulation models to test alternate policies. The queue discipline, that is, the sequence of processing orders, has been the focus of many simulation studies. In shop parlance the queue discipline is the "priority system." These are the priority rules used to dispatch an order to be processed within a work center or department.

Priority Dispatching Decision Rules

Rule testing occurred largely during the 1960s, using simulation methods. The main results of these studies indicate that the SOT rule (shortest operation time) provides the lowest mean flow time through the shop, but with a large variance. The SOT rule sequences jobs at each work center according to their estimated operation times, taking the shortest jobs first. The SOT rule is good in that it performs well on the average. But some jobs (those with long operation times) take a long time to get through the system, causing delivery problems.

The other main result of rule testing was the emergence of rules that emphasized getting jobs out on time. The DS/RO rule is effective in this regard, as is COVERT. DS/RO means dynamic slack divided by the remaining number of operations. Dynamic slack is defined as the time remaining until due date in excess of expected remaining processing time.

COVERT sequences jobs according to the largest ratio of downstream waiting time c, to operation process time, t (called c over t, or COVERT). In simulation tests, COVERT was extremely effective in meeting due dates.

Tracking the Progress of Orders

Unfortunately, we cannot predict the flaws in our original plans. Machines may break down, work may pile up behind some critical machine, and dozens of other unexpected production troubles may occur that interfere with original schedules. With hundreds or even thousands of current orders in a shop, the only way to be sure that orders ultimately will meet schedules is to provide information feedback and a system of corrective action that can compensate for delays. Returned job tickets, move orders, and inspection reports can provide formal information that can be compared with schedules.

To be of value, this information flow must be rapid, so that action can be taken on up-to-date reports. Usual company mail systems are much too slow to serve the needs of production control systems. Therefore, special communication systems are in common use, such as special mail services, intercommunication systems, teletype writers interconnected to central offices, pneumatic tube systems, and remote data collection centers tied directly in with automatic computing systems. These systems in combination with rapid data processing can grind out current reports that can be used as a basis for expediting and rescheduling orders.

COMPUTERIZED PLANNING SCHEDULING, AND CONTROL SYSTEMS

Computerized systems are relatively common today. Landmark systems in the past were developed by Bulkin et al. [1966] and LeGrande [1963] at the Hughes Aircraft Company, and a system was developed by Reiter [1966] in a gear manufacturing company. Another system developed by Godin and Jones [1969] at the Western Electric Company is of significant interest because of its interactive nature and application in a small shop. In the Western Electric system the production scheduler or supervisor worked in concert with a scheduling program at a computer terminal. By interacting with the schedule program, one can test the effects of various combinations of possible schedules, simulating effects before selecting a final schedule.

Advanced systems that include the MRP concepts discussed in the next chapter have been installed in many manufacturing plants. Two such systems that have been written up extensively are Markem Corporation and Xerox Corporation. These systems are discussed in Buffa and Miller [1979].

THE TOYOTA PRODUCTION SYSTEM

Because of the Japanese success with products of competitive cost and high quality, there is considerable interest in how they have accomplished their goals. The following is drawn from an account by a Japanese professor visiting the United States, in a paper aptly titled, "What Makes the Toyota Production System Really Tick?" [Monden, 1981]. Rather than an elaborate computer based system that attempts to "optimize" the production system, the "secrets" seem to be in close timing, worker cooperation and control of quality, and a simple information system called *Kanban*.

The overall system is shown in Figure 11-5. In order to achieve continuous flow of production, shown at the top of the inner box leading to "outputs," there are two key concepts on which the system rests: *Just in Time*, and *Autonomation*. *Just in Time* is an objective of producing the necessary units in the quantities needed, at the time they are needed. Certainly the objective is clear and understandable. The methods of achieving the objective are of key interest. *Autonomation* is a Toyota-coined word that means autonomous defects control, that is, "worker controlled" quality control.

Just in Time

Accomplishing the *Just in Time* objective rests on systems for determining production methods, and the information system called *Kanban*. Both of these concepts contribute to the objective of having the right number of parts or components at the right place at the right time.

Production Methods. Processes are designed so that there is less specialization of

371

workers than might be true in U.S. auto plants. The physical layout is arranged so that a worker can operate two or three different machines, thus providing flexibility in processes that might precede the assembly line. The benefits that result from this organization of multifunction workers are:

- reduction of inventory between what would otherwise be separate processes
- decrease in the number of workers required, resulting in a direct increase in productivity

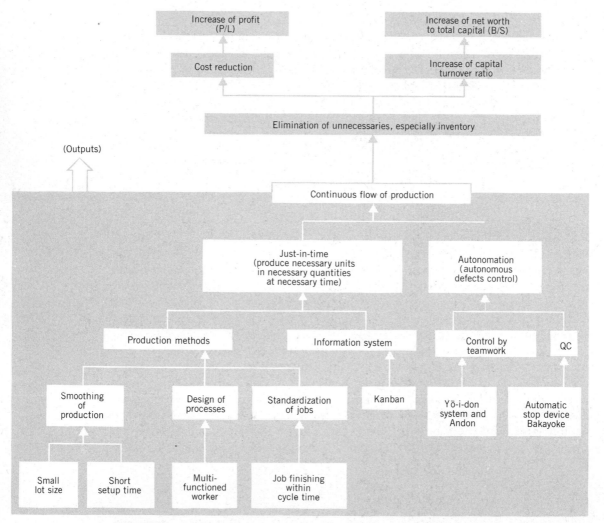

FIGURE 11-5
The Toyota Production System.
SOURCE: Y. Moden. "What Makes the Toyota Production System Really Tick?" *Industrial Engineering,* Vol. 13, No. 1, January 1981, pp. 36–46. Reprinted with permission from *Industrial Engineering* magazine, January 1981. Copyright American Institute of Industrial Engineers, Inc., 25 Technology Park/Atlanta, Norcross, GA 30092.

- increased worker satisfaction because of more broadly defined jobs
- multifunctional workers can engage in teamwork

There are three elements of job standardization that are included on a standard operation sheet tacked up for all workers to see: cycle time, operations routing, and standard quantity of work in process. Based on the computed cycle time that is derived from market demand, the aggregate number of workers required to produce one unit of output in the cycle time is determined. Rebalancing may then be necessary to schedule for minimum labor input for a given output objective. The standard routing indicates the exact activities required of each worker to perform correctly in minimum time. The standard quantity of work in process indicates the in-process inventory required for smooth flow.

The smoothing of production is regarded as the most critical element in the *Just in Time* objective. As will be described in more detail under the heading *Kanban* which follows, workers go to the preceding process to withdraw the required parts and components for their operations. If there are fluctuations in the rates at which these materials are withdrawn, then the preceding process must hold buffer in-process inventories to give off-the-shelf service. Moreover, following the systems dynamics concepts that we discussed in Chapter 8, variability is amplified as we go upstream in such a sequential production process. Therefore, the required in-process inventories would increase also for upstream processes. This results in the objective of minimizing production fluctuations in the final assembly line by scheduling small lots of individual models, and focusing "all out" efforts on minimizing setup times for all processes.

The Kanban System

The other main contribution in addition to the several facets of production methods that we discussed, is the *Kanban* system. The *Kanban* system is a uniquely Japanese information system that "harmoniously" controls the production quantities in each process. It assumes that the three facets of production methods discussed previously are in place.

A *Kanban* is a card of two types: a withdrawal *Kanban,* and a production-ordering *Kanban.* The withdrawal *Kanban* shows the quantity of items that the subsequent process should withdraw from the preceding, and the production-ordering *Kanban* shows the quantity that the preceding process should produce. These cards are used within Toyota, between Toyota and its suppliers, and within the suppliers' plants.

For example, suppose that we are producing products *A, B,* and *C,* and that parts *a* and *b* are produced by the preceding process, as shown in Figure 11-6. The worker on the assembly line producing product *A* goes to the machining line to withdraw the necessary numbers of part *a* from the storage location. The worker withdraws the required number, detaching the production-ordering *Kanban,* leaving it in place of the parts, returning to the assembly line with the withdrawal *Kanban.* The production-ordering *Kanban* is picked up by a worker from the machining line, as a direction to produce that quantity of part *a.* As a result of the *Kanban* system, the various operations in the plant are connected with each other. These connections of processes contribute to better control of production quantities.

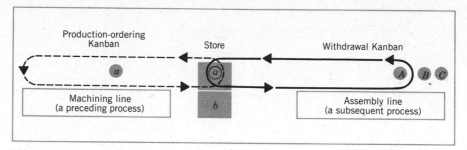

FIGURE 11-6
The flow of two Kanbans.
SOURCE: Y. Moden. "What Makes the Toyota Production System Really Tick?" *Industrial Engineering,* Vol. 13, No. 1, January 1981, pp. 36–46. Reprinted with permission from *Industrial Engineering* magazine, January 1981. Copyright American Institute of Industrial Engineers, Inc., 25 Technology Park/Atlanta, Norcross, GA 30092.

Autonomation

Although the *Just in Time* systems control production quantities, they would be useless if the items delivered were defective. The *Autonomation* system is designed to ensure that theoretically 100 percent good units flow to subsequent operations. It is, therefore, an integral part of a well-operated *Just in Time* system. *Autonomation,* meaning autonomous defects control, depends on both automatic stop devices, and worker teamwork.

"In Toyota factories, almost all machines are autonomous"—meaning that they are equipped with automatic stopping devices to prevent any large output of defects; *Bakayoke* is one such mechanism.

In manual work such as occurs on assembly lines, the concept of *autonomation* is implemented by *Andon;* if a worker observes something abnormal, a stop button can be pushed, thereby stopping the entire line. The problem is then cleared before defective items are produced in any quantity.

In addition, there is a Yō-i-don (which means ready, set, go) system that contributes to *Autonomation,* as well as to smooth work flow. The Yō-i-don system involves teamwork between adjacent operations to make sure that work at stations is balanced, and involves the *Andon* system when necessary. When each worker in each station has completed operations, each will press a button. At the end of the cycle time, a red light automatically goes on at each work station where the work is not complete. The red lights indicate delays, and the entire line stops until all red lights are off. When this happens, the teamwork comes into play, for workers nearby pitch in to help workers who are having difficulty.

It would probably be a mistake to try to transplant the Toyota system. Many of the aspects of it are deeply rooted in the Japanese culture, and in the lifelong employment that supports teamwork and the spirit that results in the entire organization seemingly having common organization goals. Nevertheless, the ideas justify further careful study by operations managers.

IMPLICATIONS FOR THE MANAGER

Although managers prefer to think in terms of comprehensive planning such as the aggregate plans discussed in the last chapter, the managers of productive systems must disaggregate these plans and give careful attention to the product mix. Therefore, the master schedule is of key importance. For them, the issues must also embrace which products must be produced and when; what types of workers must be hired and laid off; what are the projected inventory balances for each product in relation to demand and the production schedule; which raw materials must be available and when to order to key in with the production schedule?

For the managers of product-focused systems, the aggregate plan provides the framework within which the master schedule must function, but the process is relatively simple after that. The detailed plans flow directly from the master schedule, as long as hiring-layoff, overtime, subcontracting, and inventory levels are within the constraints imposed by the aggregate plan. A formalization of the general process has been developed in systems called hierarchical planning.

For managers of process-focused systems, the relationship between capacity and lot size is important to recognize. Capacity can be diluted by responding to the pressures to meet commitments on rush jobs through lot splitting. Scheduling the use of time-shared equipment often results in pressures to reduce lot sizes in order to meet commitments on a variety of orders. The intensity of these kinds of problems is greatest when operating near capacity limits. But the dilution of capacity in such situations has the effect of intensifying the original problem.

Although *EOQ* concepts can help managers to think in terms of balancing the relevant costs, they are seldom applicable in their simple forms. The assumptions of constant demand and lead time are very often not valid, and the assumption of independence between orders fails in most situations unless the system is operating at low load where the interdependent effects are minimal. Managers who understand these effects seek scheduling systems that treat orders as a part of an interdependent system.

Finally, the plans and schedules must be put into effect on the shop floor. Managers need to give careful thought to the nature of the priority system that is used for dispatching. What is the enterprise strategy to be implemented? If on-time delivery to customers is an important part of that strategy, then the priority rule should be selected to give support to that strategy. If in-process inventory cost is a dominant objective, then a different rule should be selected.

IMPORTANT TERMS

Numbers in parentheses indicate page numbers

Andon (374)

Autonomation (374)

Bakayoke (374)

Batch production (363)

Common cycle scheduling (365)

Dependent demand (365)

Economic common cycle scheduling (368)

EOQ schedule (364)

REVIEW QUESTIONS AND PROBLEMS

1. Using Figure 11-1 as a background, discuss the aggregate plan as a constraint to operations scheduling.

2. Under what circumstances is rebalancing of production lines necessary when adjusting to a new aggregate plan?

3. Given the aggregate plan as a constraint to operations scheduling in product-focused systems, what flexibility is left to planners in developing detailed schedules?

4. What flexibility is left to management in product-focused systems for adjusting deviations in actual output from planned levels within a given period?

5. Data for a particular job order are that setup time is 10 hours, and run time is 1 minute per unit once the setup is made; $c_P = \$150$ per setup, $c_H = \$0.12$ per unit per year, $R = 10,000$ units, and $EOQ = 5000$ units.
   What percent dilution of capacity would take place if production were actually in lots of $Q = 1000$ units instead of EOQ?

6. Suppose that the setup time for question 5 were only 1 hour, and setup costs only $c_P = \$15$ per order. EOQ is then $Q_0 = 1581$ units.
   What percent dilution in capacity takes place if production were actually in lots of $Q = 300$ units instead of EOQ?

7. What are the advantages and disadvantages of the practice of lot splitting?

8. Table 11-7 gives data on five products that are produced on the same equipment, assuming 250 productive days available per year. The EOQs and associated costs were computed using Equations 4 and 5 from Chapter 10.
   If the products were produced in EOQ lots, what problems would result?

9. Using the data in Table 11-7, compute lot sizes that would result from using a common cycle for all products of $N = 6$ and 8. How many days supply must be produced for each product? Which common cycle do you prefer? Why?

10. What is a dispatching decision rule? How does it relate to the structure of a waiting line model?

11. If management's objectives place a high value on low in-process inventories, what kind of priority dispatching rule seems best?

12. If management's objectives place a high value on on-time delivery of orders, what kind of priority dispatching decision rule seems best?

TABLE 11-7
Data for Five Products to Be Produced on the Same Equipment

(1) Product Number	(2) Annual Requirements, R_i	(3) Daily Requirements, $R_i/250 = r_i$	(4) Daily Production rate, p_i	(5) Annual Inventory Holding Costs, c_{H_i}	(6) Setup Costs per Run, c_{P_i}	(7) EOQ, Equation 4, Chapter 10	(8) TIC_0, Equation 5, Chapter 10
1	5,000	20	400	$1.00	$40	648.89	$616.44
2	12,500	50	300	0.90	25	912.87	684.65
3	7,000	28	200	0.30	30	1,275.89	329.18
4	16,250	65	300	0.75	27	1,222.14	718.01
5	4,000	16	160	1.05	80	822.95	777.69
					$202		$3,125.97

13. How do you account for the excellent performance of the *COVERT* rule from the point of view of on-time delivery?

14. Job orders are received at a work station with the characteristics indicated by the data in Table 11-8. In what sequence should the orders be processed at the work center if the priority dispatch decision rule is:

  a. FCFS (first come-first served)

  b. SOT (shortest operation time)

  c. SS (static slack, i.e., due date less time of arrival at work center)

  d. FISFS (due date system, first in system-first served)

  e. SS/RO (static slack/remaining number of operations)

  Compute priorities for each rule and list the sequence in which orders would be processed. Which decision rule do you prefer? Why?

SITUATIONS

15. The Mixing and Bagging Company discussed as Situation 26 in Chapter 10 has carried through its plan to install *EOQ* scheduling of its products. The idea expressed by the factory manager is to use an order point trigger for each

TABLE 11-8   Order and Processing Data for Six Jobs

Order Number	Due Date	Date and Time Received at Center	Operation Time, Hours	Remaining Operations
1	May 1	Apr. 18, 9 A.M.	6	3
2	Apr. 20	Apr. 21, 10 A.M.	3	1
3	June 1	Apr. 19, 5 P.M.	7	2
4	June 15	Apr. 21, 3 P.M.	9	4
5	May 15	Apr. 20, 5 P.M.	4	5
6	May 20	Apr. 21, 5 P.M.	8	7

product. He set the order point, P_i, for each product to cover average demand for 2 weeks. When warehouse inventory for an item declines to the order point, an order for the approximate EOQ would be written and released to the foreman.

The delay between actual recognition that the inventory level had triggered an order and the order release to the foreman was 3 days, and the production lead time of 2 days was felt to be normal. The factory manager thought that it should be possible to get an inventory item replenished in mixed and bagged form in the warehouse within the lead time, because of the simple production process. Thus, 5 working days (1 week) of the 2-week supply of inventory was planned to be used in replenishment. This left a 1-week supply as a buffer against the possibility of especially high demand. The factory manager felt that the extra 1-week supply should cover most situations.

The factory manager had classified the 10 product types into *practical* production lot sizes, based on his *EOQ* calculations. There were three high-demand items that were run in lots of 4000 bags (100 pounds per bag), four intermediate-demand items that were run in lots of 2000 bags, and three low-demand items that were run in lots of 1000 bags. These lot sizes were reasonably close to the *EOQ*s and corresponded to units of raw materials and supplies that were easy to deal with. Also, having only three sizes of runs made it a simple system for the foreman and production workers.

Using the factory manager's classification, the product demand, lot sizes, and runs per year are summarized in the following table:

Product	Average Demand, 100-pound sacks/year	Lot Size, 100-pound sacks/run	Average No. of Runs/ Year/Product
3 high demand	160,000	4000	40
4 medium demand	40,000	2000	20
3 low demand	10,000	1000	10

A run of 4000 sacks required about 590 minutes including setup, a run of 2000 sacks about 310 minutes, and a run of 1000 required about 170 minutes (each run includes a 30 minute setup plus 0.14 minutes per bag). Thus the factory manager figured that the average number of runs with the average mix of order sizes required only about 34 hours per week of production time on the equipment, including setup. In other words, the plant was operating at about 85 percent of capacity.

After a short time operating under the new *EOQ* system, the factory manager was puzzled by the results. He was stocking out of some of the high-demand items before the completion of production runs. He examined demand figures and found that the demand for these items had been greater than the average because of some seasonality in demand, but he could not understand why the 1-week supply should not have taken care of the problem.

The foreman said that he had the place "humming," but complained that the factory manager was always and forever telling him to produce a given order first, because of short supply. "Every order can't be run first," he said. The number of orders that he had in his list to produce seemed to be growing, and he processed them strictly in the order in which they were received, unless told to expedite a particular order. When the foreman was asked what he thought the problem was, he said, "The problem is that the runs are too short for the high-demand items. I spend my time constantly changing over to a new product. I suggest that we make all of the lot sizes larger, but particularly the high demand items. Perhaps the lot sizes should be 10,000, 5,000 and 1,000. The small runs of 1000 are OK for the low demand items, since I can sandwich them in easily."

What is the problem? What are your recommendations to the factory manager?

16.   The following material was abstracted from an article by Vincent A. Mabert and Michael J. Showalter, "Priority Rules for Check Processing in Branch Banking," American Production and Inventory Control Society, *Journal of Operations Management,* Vol. 1, No. 1, Summer 1980, pp. 15–22. It is reproduced here with permission. Questions are at the end.

PRIORITY RULES FOR CHECK PROCESSING IN BRANCH BANKING
Vincent A. Mabert
and
Michael J. Showalter

The check-processing activity represents a major function in a commercial bank. If checks are quickly processed through a bank, then funds will be transferred to appropriate accounts and the bank will experience minimum float. This situation discusses the use of priority rules to maximize the dollar value of checks processed each day. A series of experiments are developed to test a set of heuristic priority rules under differing operating conditions of check processing capacity, transit dollar levels, and branch characteristics.

The problem of managing daily float represents an area of major concern to commercial bank management. Float is the amount of funds to which a bank has claim but which are not yet available. Float is created whenever a bank accepts a check written on another institution, commonly referred to as a "transit check." Until the cashing bank presents the transit check to the issuing bank, the cashing bank does not have these funds available for investment. For each day that a transit check is outstanding the cashing bank incurs an opportunity cost in the form of foregone investment income. Any checks received but not forwarded to the issuing bank by the end of each business day represents a single day's holdover opportunity cost. For a large U.S. bank a daily holdover float of $20 to $30 million is not uncommon. If the current yield on short term investment is 10 percent, this daily holdover translates into an annualized opportunity cost of $2 to $3 million.

Banks attempt to minimize daily holdover float by eliminating any processing delays in their internal check-processing system. This requires the availability of adequate daily processing capacity between the time when a transit check is received and the dispatch time at which it must be forwarded to the issuing bank. In the past, banks focused on maintaining a maximum daily processing capacity capable of handling any peak daily check volume. However, this approach resulted in considerable equipment and labor idle time since most of the daily check volume fell below this maximum level. This low utilization rate of equipment and labor also created an opportunity cost in terms of excess investment in capital equipment and wages. Bank management has since come to realize that effective management of daily holdover float requires the minimization of both the opportunity costs of holdover float and the opportunity costs of excess processing capacity.

These opportunity costs are lowest when check volume and check-processing capacity are balanced. In order to match workload and capacity, bank management may (1) adjust the rate of check in-flow, (2) adjust the level of check-processing capacity, or (3) a combination of check volume flow and check-processing capacity adjustment. This paper examines an approach to minimizing the level of holdover float and the resultant opportunity cost for the case in which actual daily check volume exceeds check-processing capacity.

As indicated in the text, there has been a great deal of research in the context of job shop manufacturing systems that indicate that the efficiency of a system's processing capacity can be improved by assigning priorities to the jobs that enter the system. In addition, these concepts have been applied in actual scheduling systems. This study hypothesizes that priority rules can be applied to incoming check volume from different branch bank offices to control order of processing by the central check-processing facility.

Structure of Work Flow

The typical structure of work flow for a Multiple Branch Bank organization is shown in Figure 11-7. Work processed through the central facility arrives from two sources. First, checks and drafts are received at the branches through customer activity. Throughout the day, tellers receive this work and bundle it for pick up by the vehicle messenger system at specific times during the day. These bundled checks are then taken to the central facility for processing.

On receipt at the central facility, each bundle is logged into a control ledger (Receiving). At the next stage, magnetic ink characters are printed on the check (Encoding). These figures indicate the dollar value of the check for machine reading. Next, computer controlled machines read and separate the checks by destination point (Sorting). During sorting two activities occur: first, the account numbers and check values are stored on transaction files for updating later against master files; and second, the checks are sorted by specific destination. Transit checks are sorted by destination points and then dispatched (Distribution) to the appropriate Federal Reserve Bank, clearinghouse, or correspondent bank by a specific deadline each day. For most banks the key deadline occurs late in the evening. Checks which have not cleared by the deadline will usually not be honored until the next business day, thereby creating a daily holdover float.

The second source of work arriving at the central facility is incoming checks from other banks. This work is received from three sources: the Federal Reserve Bank, clearinghouse, and correspondent banks. These institutions act as clearing agencies for moving between Bank X, which cashes a check drawn against Bank Y. Since these incoming checks were encoded by Bank X, the checks move directly to sorting at Bank Y and then to in-house departments for appropriate updating.

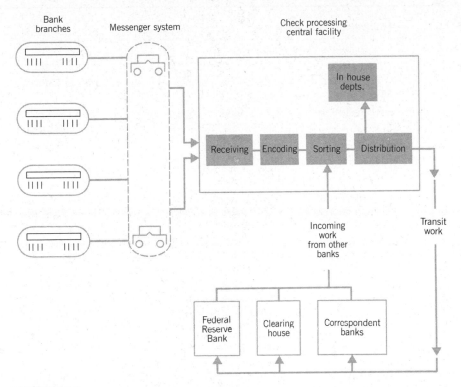

FIGURE 11-7
Bank check handling and processing system.
SOURCE: V. A. Mabert, and M. J. Showalter. "Priority Rules for Check Processing in Multiple Branch Banking: An Experimental Analysis," *Journal of Operations Management,* Vol. 1, No. 1, 1980.

Although such a work flow structure is typical for most multiple branch banks, they tend to differ substantially with respect to the composition of check flow from the branch offices to the central processing facility. Variability of this check flow from branches is characterized by the level of total dollar value, check item volume, proportion of transit checks, and timing of check flow. Since a multiple branch bank may have a different number of branch offices, each of which attracts and serves a unique mix of customers, it is reasonable to expect the workload demands placed on the central processing facility to differ between multiple branch banks. For example, a bank with a large proportion of residential branches may expect a check flow characterized by low dollar value, high unit volume, and a low proportion of transit checks; a bank with a high proportion of metropolitan branches (business district location) will normally generate a check flow characterized by high dollar value, low check unit volume, and a high proportion of transit checks.

Priority Rules

The priority rules shown in Table 11-9 capitalize on the unique characteristics of branch office check flows. Nine priority rules were identified for evaluation. Five are singular in nature, while the other four are combinations of two rules for sequencing work through a central facility.

TABLE 11-9   **Description of Priority Rules**

Rule	Description
First Come–First Served (FCFS)	Bundled work is sequenced in the order that work arrives to the queue. The oldest bundle is processed first.
Largest Bundle First (LBF)	Bundled work is sequenced in the order of the number of checks in the bundle (or weight). The largest bundle is processed first.
Smallest Bundle First (SBF)	Bundled work is sequenced in order of the number of checks in the bundle (or weight). The smallest bundle is processed first.
Largest Total Value First (LTVF)	Bundled work is sequenced in order of the total dollar value of the bundle. The bundle with the largest total dollar value is processed first.
Largest Value per Unit First (LVPUF)	Bundled work is sequenced in order of average dollar value per check (or weight) in the bundle. The bundle with the largest value per unit is processed first.
Branch Priority + FCFS (BP + FCFS)	Bundled work is separated first into two groups, metropolitan and residential branches. Within each group they are sequenced using FCFS. Bundled metropolitan work is processed first as FCFS. Only when all metropolitan bundles are out of the queue will residential bundles be processed in FCFS order.
Branch Priority + Largest Bundle First (BP + LBF)	Bundled work is separated first into two groups, metropolitan and residential branches. Within each group bundles are sequenced by number of checks in a bundle (weight). Bundled metropolitan work is processed first with the largest bundle having top priority. Residential branch bundles will be processed when no metropolitan bundles are present.
Branch Priority + Largest Value per Unit First (BP + LVPUF)	Bundled work is separated first into two groups, metropolitan and residential branches. Within each group they are sequenced by average value per check (weight). Metropolitan bundles are processed first with the largest value per unit priority. Residential bundles are processed when no metropolitan bundles remain in the queue.
Branch Priority + Largest Total Value First (BP + LTVF)	Bundled work is separated first into two groups, metropolitan and residential branches. Within each group they are sequenced by total dollar value. Metropolitan bundles are processed first with the largest total value having first priority. Residential bundles are processed when no metropolitan bundles remain in the queue.

SOURCE. V. A. Mabert, and M. J. Showalter. "Priority Rules for Check Processing in Branch Banking: An Experimental Analysis," *Journal of Operations Management,* Vol. 1, No. 1, Summer 1980, pp. 15–22.

The priority rules are heuristics which attempt to capitalize on particular characteristics of transit checks received at the different branch banks. For example, the composite rules bias selection of work towards metropolitan branches first.

*The **LTVF** and **LVPUF** rules attempt to measure the value of the bundled checks. Generally, control totals are developed by tellers for the bundles to balance their cash drawers. These control totals provide an indication of each bundle's value.*

*The **LBF** and **SBF** rules were developed because of their similarity to the shortest operation time (**SOT**) and longest operation time (**LOT**) rules of the job shop scheduling literature. The **FCFS** rule represents the sequence of check processing at most bank processing centers today.*

Experimental Design

A computer simulation model was programmed to test the nine priority rules. The model replicated the serial operations of the central facility: receiving, encoding, sorting, and distribution. The arrival of work was randomly generated, where all work arrived between 2 PM and 8 PM. All transit checks making it to the dispatch operation by 10 PM cleared the system. Those transit checks remaining in the system are considered to be float and are cleared the next day. All nontransit checks are considered local, have deadlines in the early morning, and can easily be cleared in time.

Other key elements of the model are:

1. *Two queues are present, one before encoding and one before sorting. Bundled work is sequenced in these queues by the priority rule in use and released when capacity is available.*

2. *The capacity of the encoding and sorting are equally balanced.*

3. *When bundled work enters an operation, there is a five-minute delay for set-up prior to processing. This reflects the preparation time to get bundles, unpackage, organize, and then bundle for movement to the next operation.*

4. *There is a delay of 15 minutes between operations for material handling requirements (i.e., receiving, encoding, and sorting).*

5. *The model simulates five working days, with each day's performance independent of the prior day's events.*

To test the priority rules, a series of experiments was designed with four factors controlling the degree of heterogeneity introduced into the general multiple branch banking system.

1. ***Factor one:*** *the ratio of the number of metropolitan to residential branches present. Two ratios were used, 1:1 and 1:4.*

2. ***Factor two:*** *the ratio of transit items in a bundle for metropolitcan to residential branches was set at 3:1.*

3. ***Factor three:*** *The ratio of transit dollar value per check of metropolitan to residential branches. Two ratios were used, 1:1 and 1.2:1.*

4. ***Factor four:*** *The ratio of available capacity to total work load. This was mea-*

383

sured over the time span from the arrival of work to the transit deadline time. Three levels were used, 70 percent, 80 percent, and 90 percent.

Therefore, there were nine priority rules, two levels for factor one, one level for factor two, two levels for factor three, three levels for factor four, and a five-day simulation for each cell. This results in a total of 9 × 2 × 1 × 2 × 3 × 5 = 540 observations.

A second test was also conducted where all factor settings were specified to represent homogeneous branches. In this case there were no differences in numbers of transit items or transit dollars distributed for bundled work of metropolitan and residential branches.

Experimental Results

The results of the simulation tests are summarized in Tables 11-10, 11-11, and 11-12. They provide the proportion mean and standard deviation of transit dollars not cleared to total transit dollars received. Table 11-10 illustrates the performance of the nine rules for the three levels of percent of capacity available when branches are

TABLE 11-10   Proportion Mean and Standard Deviation of Transit Dollars Not Cleared Homogeneous Branches

Priority Rule		Percent Available Capacity		
		70	80	90
First Come-First Served (FCFS)	M[a]	0.307	0.209	0.104
	STD[b]	0.018	0.015	0.019
Largest Bundle First (LBF)	M	0.277	0.176	0.078
	STD	0.017	0.015	0.013
Smallest Bundle First (SBF)	M	0.335	0.230	0.133
	STD	0.026	0.022	0.018
Largest Total Value First (LTVF)	M	0.167	0.087	0.034
	STD	0.018	0.013	0.005
Largest Value/Unit First (LVPUF)	M	0.167	0.086	0.036
	STD	0.011	0.011	0.007
Branch Priority + Largest Bundle First (BP + LBF)	M	0.297	0.190	0.080
	STD	0.012	0.013	0.012
Branch Priority + Largest Value/ Unit First (BP + LVPUF)	M	0.252	0.133	0.043
	STD	0.020	0.020	0.008
Branch Priority + Largest Total Value First (BP + LTVF)	M	0.253	0.128	0.041
	STD	0.017	0.018	0.008

[a]M = proportion mean.
[b]STD = proportion standard deviation.

SOURCE. V. A. Mabert, and M. J. Showalter. "Priority Rules for Check Processing in Branch Banking: An Experimental Analysis," *Journal of Operations Management,* Vol. 1, No. 1, Summer 1980, pp. 15–22.

TABLE 11-11   **Proportion Mean and Standard Deviation of Transit Dollars Not Cleared (Ratio of Metropolitan to Residential Branches = 1:1)**

Priority Rule		Transit Dollar Value/ Check of Metropolitan to Residential Branches Set at 1:1			Transit Dollar Value/ Check of Metropolitan to Residential Branches Set at 1.2:1		
		Percent Available Capacity			Percent Available Capacity		
		70	80	90	70	80	90
First Come–First	M[a]	0.305	0.208	0.104	0.304	0.207	0.104
Served (FCFS)	STD[b]	0.027	0.024	0.019	0.028	0.025	0.019
Largest Bundle First	M	0.276	0.174	0.078	0.275	0.173	0.078
(LBF)	STD	0.026	0.017	0.014	0.027	0.018	0.014
Smallest Bundle First	M	0.344	0.237	0.136	0.343	0.237	0.136
(SBF)	STD	0.039	0.034	0.029	0.041	0.035	0.029
Largest Total Value	M	0.166	0.086	0.033	0.146	0.078	0.030
First (LTVF)	STD	0.018	0.013	0.005	0.019	0.011	0.005
Largest Value/Unit	M	0.171	0.086	0.035	0.138	0.079	0.030
First (LVPUF)	STD	0.014	0.013	0.008	0.017	0.012	0.008
Branch Priority +	M	0.151	0.101	0.032	0.131	0.087	0.045
FCFS (BP + FCFS)	STD	0.006	0.007	0.007	0.005	0.006	0.006
Branch Priority +	M	0.147	0.094	0.040	0.127	0.081	0.034
Largest Bundle First	STD	0.006	0.006	0.006	0.005	0.006	0.005
(BP + LBF)							
Branch Priority +	M	0.124	0.065	0.021	0.108	0.057	0.018
Largest Value/Unit	STD	0.010	0.010	0.004	0.009	0.009	0.003
First (BP + LVPUF)							
Branch Priority +	M	0.125	0.063	0.020	0.108	0.056	0.017
Largest Total Value	STD	0.009	0.009	0.004	0.009	0.009	0.003
First (BP + LTVF)							

[a]M = proportion mean.
[b]STD = proportion standard deviation.

SOURCE. V. A. Mabert, and M. J. Showalter. "Priority Rules for Check Processing in Branch Banking: An Experimental Analysis," *Journal of Operations Management*, Vol. 1, No. 1, Summer 1980, pp. 15–22.

homogeneous. *Tables 11-11 and 11-12 summarize the performance of the nine rules for different heterogeneous environments when the ratio of the number of metropolitan to residential branches was set at 1:1 and when it was set at 1:4.*

QUESTIONS

1.   Which rule would you select if branches were homogeneous? Why? Would you use the same rule under all conditions?

2.   Which rule would you select for heterogeneous branch environments? Why? Would you use the same rule under all conditions?

TABLE 11-12   **Proportion Mean and Standard Deviation of Transit Dollars Not Cleared (Ratio of Metropolitan to Residential Branches = 1 : 4)**

Priority Rule		Transit Dollar Value/ Check of Metropolitan to Residential Branches Set at 1:1			Transit Dollar Value/ Check of Metropolitan to Residential Branches Set at 1.2:1		
		Percent Available Capacity			Percent Available Capacity		
		70	80	90	70	80	90
First Come-First	M[a]	0.308	0.210	0.105	0.308	0.210	0.109
Served (FCFS)	STD[b]	0.030	0.026	0.024	0.032	0.028	0.019
Largest Bundle First	M	0.277	0.177	0.076	0.276	0.177	0.076
(LBF)	STD	0.022	0.012	0.011	0.024	0.013	0.011
Smallest Bundle First	M	0.343	0.242	0.134	0.345	0.245	0.134
(SBF)	STD	0.050	0.040	0.023	0.040	0.044	0.024
Largest Total Value	M	0.166	0.086	0.033	0.154	0.077	0.030
First (LTVF)	STD	0.013	0.012	0.004	0.009	0.007	0.006
Largest Value/Unit	M	0.170	0.087	0.033	0.147	0.080	0.027
First (LVPUF)	STD	0.011	0.006	0.008	0.012	0.007	0.003
Branch Priority +	M	0.216	0.143	0.073	0.199	0.132	0.067
FCFS (BP + FCFS)	STD	0.013	0.013	0.011	0.012	0.007	0.003
Branch Priority +	M	0.199	0.128	0.053	0.183	0.118	0.049
Largest Bundle First (BP + LBF)	STD	0.012	0.009	0.012	0.011	0.008	0.011
Branch Priority +	M	0.137	0.070	0.027	0.126	0.065	0.025
Largest Value/Unit First (BP + LVPUF)	STD	0.007	0.004	0.005	0.007	0.004	0.005
Branch Priority +	M	0.132	0.066	0.025	0.124	0.064	0.025
Largest Total Value First (BP + LTVF)	STD	0.009	0.007	0.004	0.008	0.007	0.004

[a]M = proportion mean.
[b]STD = proportion standard deviation.

SOURCE. V. A. Mabert, and M. J. Showalter. "Priority Rules for Check Processing in Branch Banking: An Experimental Analysis," *Journal of Operations Management,* Vol. 1, No. 1, Summer 1980, pp. 15–22.

3. What do the results of the study suggest for the management of the check processing activity of multiple branch banks?

4. If you were operations manager for a bank, would you install a priority rule as the basis for sequencing work? Would you use it under all conditions of the four factors? How would you implement the use of priority rules; that is, describe the operating procedure?

REFERENCES

Buffa, E. S., and J. G. Miller, *Production-Inventory Systems: Planning and Control* (3rd ed.). Irwin, Homewood, Ill., 1979.

Bulkin, M. H., J. L. Colley, and W. H. Steinhoff, "Load Forecasting, Priority Sequencing, and Simulation in a Job-Shop Control System," *Management Science, 13,* October 1966, pp. 29–51.

Godin, V., and C. H. Jones, "The Interactive Job Shop Supervisor," *Industrial Engineering,* November 1969, pp. 16–22.

Hax, A. C., and H. C. Meal, "Hierarchical Integration of Production Planning and Scheduling," in *Studies in the Management Sciences, Vol. I, Logistics,* edited by M. A. Geisler, North Holland-American Elsevier, Amsterdam, 1975.

LeGrande, E., "The Development of a Factory Simulation System Using Actual Operating Data," *Management Technology, 3,* May 1963.

Magee, J. F., and D. M. Boodman, *Production Planning and Inventory Control* (2nd ed.). McGraw-Hill, New York, 1967.

Monden, Y., "Adaptable Kanban System Helps Toyota Maintain Production," *Industrial Engineering, 13*(5), May 1981, pp. 29–46.

Monden, Y., "What Makes the Toyota Production System Really Tick?" *Industrial Engineering, 13*(1), January 1981, pp. 36–46.

Peterson, R., and E. A. Silver, *Decision Systems for Inventory Management and Production Planning,* Wiley, New York, 1979.

Reiter, S., "A System for Managing Job Shop Production," *Journal of Business, 39* July 1966, pp. 371–393.

CHAPTER 12

Material Requirements Planning

THE DIFFERENCES IN PLANNING, SCHEDULING, AND CONTROL BE-
tween product- and process-focused systems are very substantial. Although
both *may* be producing finished products for inventory, the periodic nature
of production of the latter produces an immensely more complex, detailed
scheduling problem. The nature of forecasting and planning production lot sizes is
unique, because of the dependent nature of the demand for parts and components.
Their demand is dependent on the production schedules of primary products, which
in turn are dependent on market demand. In the case of complex assembled products, which have important subassemblies that are produced for inventory, this dependence may be second or third order.

REQUIREMENTS PLANNING CONCEPTS

Figure 12-1*a* is an illustration of a simple dinette table showing the parts or components required. It consists of a plywood top covered with Formica, four metal legs,
and some miscellaneous hardware.

Figure 12-1*b* is a simplified operation process chart showing the sequence of
major operations required to fabricate and assemble the table. The glue, screws (two
different sizes), plastic feet, and paint are noted as being purchased outside; unlike
the other raw materials of plywood, metal tubing, and so on, they are not processed
before use.

Now, if the table is to be a "one-of-a-kind" custom table, the operation process
chart of Figure 12-1*b* specifies what must be done and the sequences required.
However, if a substantial number of tables are to be made, we have alternatives that
make the problem more complex, but offer planning and scheduling opportunities
for efficient manufacture.

Bills of Materials

We can abstract from Figure 12-1*a* a "bill of materials." This document is not simply
a materials list, but is constructed in a way that reflects the manufacturing process. Of
course, the operation process chart of Figure 12-1 does this also, but we want information useful to a material requirements system in a form that can be maintained in
a computerized file.

The information that will be particularly significant, in addition to the simple list of
parts, will be the dependency structure. For example, if we examine operation 11 in
Figure 12-1, there is a subassembly; the plywood top, skirts, Formica top, and Formica skirts come together in operation 11 to form a unit. Also, the metal tubing,
brackets, paint, and feet form a second subassembly. These two subassemblies can
be produced separately in batches and then can be assembled in operation 12 into
finished tables in batches as needed. Indeed, an important reason for dealing with
these subassemblies as separate units is that the same leg is used in another product,
as we shall see. Therefore, the lot size and timing of the production of legs take on
broader significance.

As a result, one important input to a material requirements planning (*MRP*) system is a bill of materials constructed in a way that recognizes the dependence of

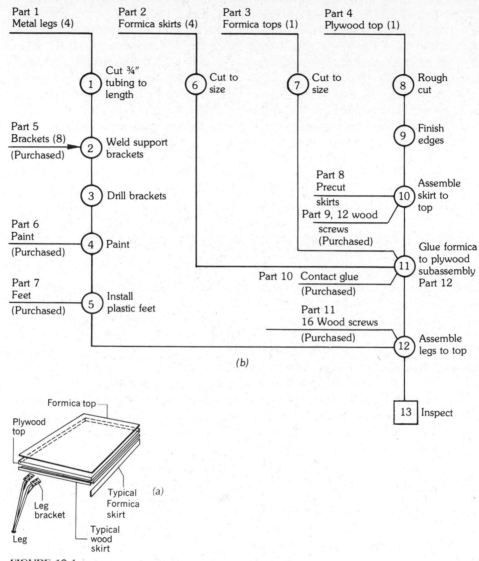

FIGURE 12-1
(a) Part components for dinette table; (b) Operation process chart.

certain components on subassemblies, which in turn are dependent on the final product. In more complex products, there could be several levels of dependency, because subassemblies could contain sub-subassemblies, and so on.

Figure 12-2 is a bill of materials for the square dinette table. It is called an *indented bill* because the dependence of parts and components is indicated by indenting items in the list. The final product is listed first, preceded by the number "1." All the numbers preceding the materials indicate the quantity of that item required for one unit of the item on which it is dependent. For example, each metal leg (part #1) requires two metal brackets (part #5). Then, if we wish to have a bill of materials for

	Part #
1 Square dinette table	#1-80
1 Tabletop subassembly	#12
1 Plywood top	#4
4 Wood skirts	#8
12 Wood screws	#9
1 Formica top	#3
4 Formica skirts	#2
6 oz Contact cement	#10
4 Leg subassemblies	#1
2 3′ Lengths of tubing	#13
2 Metal brackets	#5
2 oz Paint	#6
1 Plastic foot	#7
16 Wood screws	#11

FIGURE 12-2
Bill of materials for square dinette table No. 1-80.

any larger quantity of the final product, a multiplier may be used and the list printed indicating the quantity of each item for the larger lot.

Demand Dependence

Assume that we have translated the current demand for dinette tables into a master schedule and that they are to be produced in lots of 100 every 2 weeks. The production rates for each of the operations in Figure 12-1*b* are relatively fast, therefore the tables are not produced continuously, because low utilization of workers and machines would result. Presumably, the enterprise uses the workers and machines for other products, including other table sizes and designs, chairs, and related products. Therefore, the dinette table will be produced periodically in lots to satisfy demand.

There are several alternatives. We can consider the table as a unit and produce enough legs, tops, and the like to assemble 100 tables every 2 weeks. However, because setup costs and variable production costs for the various operations are different, we may be able to produce more efficiently by considering the manufacture of each component individually. For example, we might produce legs every 4 weeks in lots of 800 to key in with the master schedule.

Let us consider the schedule of producing tables every 2 weeks in lots of 100 and legs every 4 weeks in lots of 800. Because the demand for the legs is entirely dependent on the *production schedule* for tables, the time phasing of the leg lots with respect to table lots has a very important impact on the in-process inventory of legs. Tables are produced in lots of 100 in weeks 3, 5, 7, and so on, as shown in Figure 12-3*c*. In Figure 12-3*a* legs are produced in lots of 800 every 4 weeks in weeks 1, 5, 9, and so on. Legs go into inventory when the lot is completed and are available for use the following week. They are used in table assembly in weeks 3, 5, 7, and so forth, but they are in inventory one full week before 400 are used to produce 100 tables in week 3. The remaining 400 are in inventory during week 4, finally being

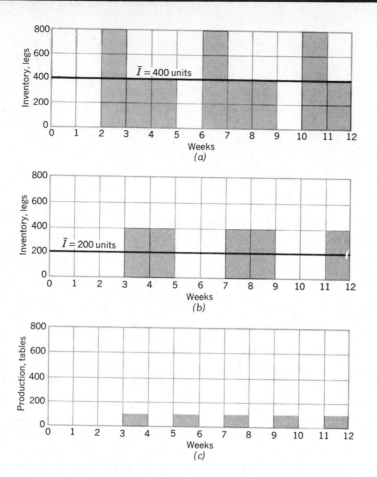

FIGURE 12-3

In-process inventory of table legs when, (a) produced in weeks 1, 5, 9, etc., and (b) produced in weeks 2, 6, 10, etc. (c) Tables are produced in weeks 3, 5, 7, etc.

used to produce 100 tables in week 5. The average in-process inventory of legs is $\bar{I}$ = 400 units.

If we produce legs in weeks 2, 6, 10, and so forth, as in Figure 12-3b, the in-process inventory is reduced to $\bar{I}$ = 200 units. This is true because the revised timing uses 400 legs immediately in week 3 to produce 100 tables. The remaining 400 legs are in inventory during week 4, as with the previous situation, being used to produce 100 tables in week 5. Therefore, the problem is not simply to produce legs in lots of 800 every 4 weeks, but to time phase the production of legs with respect to the production of the table, the primary item. The demand for tables is presumably dependent on market factors. However, the production of legs must become a *requirement* as soon as the table production schedule is set. If the proper time phasing is ignored, the price will be paid in higher in-process inventory of components.

Let us follow through the structure of requirements determination (called the "bill of materials explosion" process) in Figure 12-4. Figure 12-4 culminates in total requirements for metal tubing needed to produce two different models of dinette tables with accompanying sets of four chairs, and a stool. Each product involves the use of

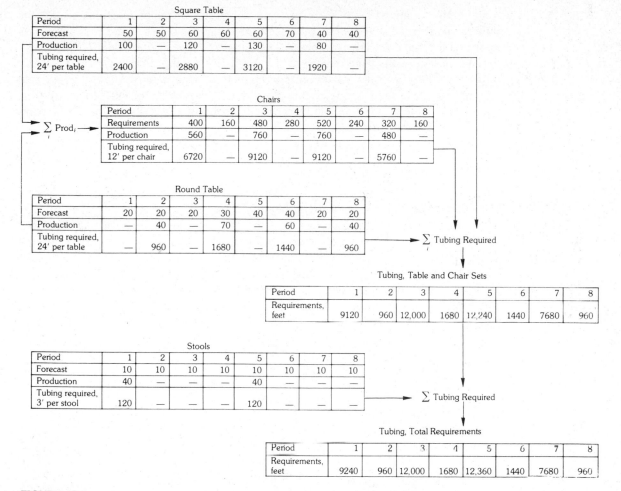

FIGURE 12-4
Requirements determination for square and round tables, chairs, stools, and finally tubing. Requirements for chairs are dependent on the production schedules for tables. Tubing requirements are dependent on the production schedules for all four products.

metal tubing from which the legs are fabricated. First, the primary demand for the two tables and the stools is indicated by the forecasts in each period. Production schedules to meet demand for each of the three primary products are set to anticipate demand for two periods ahead for the tables and for four periods ahead for stools (we will return to the question of lot size at a later point). The chairs are used for both the square and round tables in dinette sets, four chairs per table. Therefore, requirements for chairs are dependent on the production schedules for the two table styles. The chair requirements are derived through a period-by-period summing from the production schedules for the two tables. For example, the requirement for chairs in period 1 is dependent on the sum of the production schedules for the two tables $(100 + 0) \times 4 = 400$. Chairs are produced in batches to cover the next 2 weeks' requirements.

Tubing requirements are, in turn, the period-by-period summation of the tubing requirements derived from the production schedules of tables and chairs, plus the tubing requirements from the production schedule for stools. Note that tubing requirements, even though representing aggregated usage in four different products, have a very uneven usage pattern; that is, 9240 in period 1, 960 in period 2, 12,000 in period 3, and so on. Professionals term such a usage pattern *"lumpy"* demand. Figure 12-4, then, is a requirements plan for the two tables, chairs, stools, and the tubing raw material. A complete plan would provide similar information for all components and raw materials.

Product Structures

Dependency relationships between end-products and components and parts vary widely as indicated in Figure 12-5. Figure 12-5*a* is representative of the structure found in process industries such as paper or steel. For example, in the steel industry, ingots are produced from iron ore, coke, and limestone. Ingots are processed into billets, and then rolled into final shapes such as sheet, I-beams, and so on. In such instances, the dependency structure is linear, involving no assembly.

There are many producers that buy components and parts and assemble them, with little or no fabrication operations, as illustrated in Figure 12-5*b*. Examples are

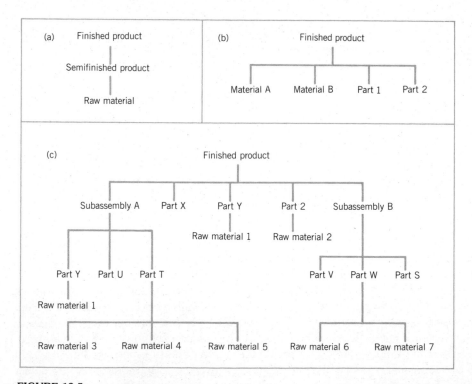

FIGURE 12-5
Typical product structures for dependent demand, (*a*) process industries, (*b*) assemblers who purchase components, and (*c*) integrated fabrication-assembly.
SOURCE: E. S. Buffa, and J. G. Miller. *Production-Inventory Systems: Planning and Control* (3rd ed.). Richard D. Irwin, Inc., Homewood, Ill., 1979.

many producers of electronic products, and some small appliances. In such situations, the product structure is horizontal rather than vertical as with process industries. The master schedule of the finished product requires the supply of all the parts and components at the right time, and in the quantities needed. To accomplish these ends, supply lead times from vendors are of great importance in planning and executing the schedule.

Finally, Figure 12-5c is illustrative of the very complex structures found in an integrated fabrication-assembly operation. These producers fabricate parts, and assemble finished products that may have intervening subassemblies as indicated. The master schedule of end-products again requires the supply of all parts, components, and subassemblies, but must now take account of supply lead times that involve not only vendors, but in-plant fabrication operations. Examples of these hierarchical product structures abound in industry, including automobiles, appliances, machine tools, and so on.

Forecasting Versus Requirements

The required use of metal tubing for the example dinette table is indicated in Figure 12-4. Suppose that we wish to set up an inventory control system for tubing so it can be reordered as needed to maintain stock. If the requirements for tubing in Figure 12-4 represent demand, can we apply standard forecasting techniques?

Figure 12-6 shows the application of an exponential forecasting system with $\alpha = 0.1$ to the requirements as demand data. Average actual demand for the eight periods is 5790 feet, and this is taken as the initial value for S_{t-1}. The forecast has the usual smoothing effect.

Now suppose that tubing is ordered on the basis of the smoothed forecast. If $D_{\max}$ were defined as the maximum demand observed in our small sample, then the buffer stock required would be $B = D_{\max} - \bar{D} = 12{,}360 - 5790 = 6570$ feet, and the average inventory would be $\bar{I} = Q/2 + B = 5790/2 + 6570 = 9465$ feet.

But, in fact, we do not want to smooth demand, because the requirements schedule for tubing is the *best* forecast that we can obtain. Using exponential smoothing (or any other forecasting technique) is a misapplication of forecasting here, because the demand for tubing is dependent. Compare the forecast line with actual demand in Figure 12-6. The forecast errors are very large, MAD = 5049. Note that if we provide inventory according to the requirements schedule, the average inventory would be only 5790 feet, or $9465 - 5790 = 3675$ feet less than if we attempted to cover requirements based on the exponential forecasting methodology. Using the forecasting methodology, we must provide a very large buffer stock, and although this buffer stock cannot be completely eliminated in requirements systems, the time phasing of inventory receipts can drastically reduce it (we will discuss buffer stocks for requirements systems at a later point).

Where then is forecasting applicable in requirements systems? Forecasting is applicable to the primary demand for the tables and stools, not to the dependent components and raw materials. Their requirements are derived directly from the production schedules that have taken into account primary demand and other factors. Therefore, inventory control systems for dependent items will use the requirements schedules directly instead of interposing a forecasting system.

Period	1	2	3	4	5	6	7	8
Actual requirements	9,240	960	12,000	1,680	12,360	1,440	7,680	960
Forecast, $\alpha = 0.1$	5,790	6,135	5,618	6,256	5,798	6,454	5,953	6,126

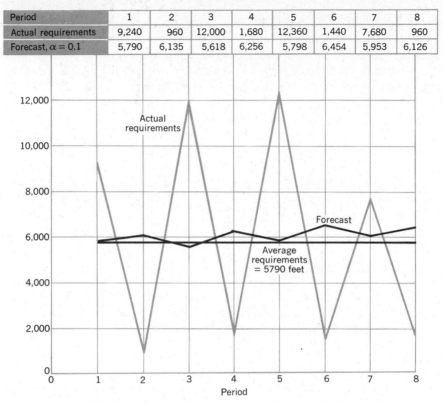

FIGURE 12-6
Effect of using an exponential forecast ($\alpha = 0.1$) for dependent demand of tubing.

The basic ideas of requirements generation developed in connection with the simple example of the tables, chairs, and stools carry forward into larger scale for more complex systems. Figure 12-7 shows that the form of the plan normally includes the master schedule for the *independent item* (the finished product) at the head, followed by requirements plans for dependent components that are keyed in with the master schedule. In addition, requirements plans normally indicate the production lead time, a planned stock record, and the timing of production order releases phased to take account of production lead times.

INVENTORY PLANNING SYSTEMS

The three inventory control systems that we discussed in Chapter 10 are all *reactive* in nature. Action is triggered by inventory status falling to a reorder point or by the inventory status that exists on review. They are backward looking, depending on events that happened.

If we have forecasts, however, why not look forward, making inventory replenishment plans that anticipate events? Forward looking inventory plans would be particularly valuable when we expect increases or decreases in demand, as is common where demand is seasonal.

MASTER ASSEMBLY SCHEDULE—Table 1-80

Week	1	2	3	4	5	6
Planned requirements	100	—	120	—	130	60

Requirements, Part 1 (legs, 4 per assembly)
Production lead time, 2 weeks

	1	2	3	4	5	6
Expected usage	400	—	480	—	520	240
Planned deliveries	400	—	480	—	520	—
Planned stock on hand, end of week	60	60	60	60	60	60
Planned production order release	480	—	520	—	320	—

Requirements, Part 4 (plywood top, 1 per assembly)
Production lead time, 1 week

	1	2	3	4	5	6
Expected usage	100	—	120	—	130	—
Planned deliveries	100	—	120	—	130	—
Planned stock on hand, end of week	20	20	20	20	20	20
Planned production order release	—	120	—	130	—	80

FIGURE 12-7
Requirements plan for master schedule and two dependent components.

Suppose we had an item that was used at the constant rate of $r = 100$ units per week, as shown by the forecast in Table 12-1. The inventory on hand is also shown week by week, beginning initially with 400 units. From the projected schedule of units on hand, we can see that we would run out of stock in the fourth week. Now suppose that lead time is 2 weeks, that we wish to maintain a buffer inventory of $B = 100$ units, and that we have computed $EOQ = 500$ units. It is easy to see from Table 12-1 that we must plan to place an order for $EOQ = 500$ units in week 2 in order to anticipate the projected inventory status of $I = 0$ units in week 4.

The inventory record is revised in Table 12-2 to reflect the planned order. Following the same rationale, a second order must be placed in period 7 to be received in period 9. The second order anticipates the fact that inventory would fall to the buffer level in week 9. Therefore, observing the 2-week lead time, an order must be placed in week 7.

This example illustrates the basic format and functioning of inventory planning systems. One might observe, however, that a fixed reorder quantity system would have produced the same results. We have conveniently observed the constant demand assumption in the example. Suppose that the item were seasonal, with demand increasing by 10 units per week during the 10-week horizon. We can still function with the EOQ system, but orders will need to be placed more often and ordering costs will increase. In this situation, periodic review, coupled with an inventory planning system, has advantages.

Table 12-3 shows a revised schedule of forecasts, with demand increasing by 10 units per week. Beginning inventory is 400 units as before, and we note that inventory would fall to 50 units in period 5 and would go negative after that. Now suppose that each 5 weeks we plan to order projected demand for the next 5 weeks. In placing the order, however, we wish to take account of inventory status and desired buffer inventory of $B = 100$ units. The ordering rule would then be, order an amount to cover 5 weeks projected demand minus $(I - B)$ or

$$D (5 \text{ weeks}) - (I - B)$$

As an example, suppose that the next ordering period for the increasing demand schedule is week 3. The projected number on hand at the end of week 3 is 220 units. Projected demand for the 5 weeks beginning with week 3 is $D = 70 + 80 + 90 + 100 + 110 = 450$ units. This 5-week quantity must then be adjusted for the projected inventory position of 220 units and the desired buffer of 100 units, 220 −

TABLE 12-1
Forecast Versus Projected Inventory on Hand for an Item

Period (weeks)		1	2	3	4	5	6	7	8	9	10
Forecast		100	100	100	100	100	100	100	100	100	100
Scheduled receipts											
On hand	400	300	200	100	0	(100)	(200)	(300)	(400)	(500)	(600)
Planned orders											

TABLE 12-2
Orders Placed in Periods 2 and 7 to Counteract Projected Fall in Inventory Level Below the Desired Buffer of $B = 100$ Units ($Q_o = 500$ units; supply lead time is 2 weeks)

Period (weeks)		1	2	3	4	5	6	7	8	9	10
Forecast		100	100	100	100	100	100	100	100	100	100
Scheduled receipts					500					500	
On hand	400	300	200	100	500	400	300	200	100	500	400
Planned orders			500					500			

TABLE 12-3
Projected Forecasts Versus Inventory on Hand, Forecasts Increasing by 10 Units per Week

Period (weeks)		1	2	3	4	5	6	7	8	9	10
Forecast		50	60	70	80	90	100	110	120	130	140
Scheduled receipts											
On hand	400	350	290	220	140	50	(50)	(160)	(280)	(410)	(550)
Planned orders											

TABLE 12-4
Inventory Planning Systems with Periodic Ordering by the Rule, $Q = D(5 \text{ weeks}) - (I - B)$ (Replenishment Scheduled for Weeks 3 and 8, with Supply Lead time of 2 Weeks)

Period (weeks)		1	2	3	4	5	6	7	8	9	10
Forecast		50	60	70	80	90	100	110	120	130	140
Scheduled receipts				330					750		
On hand	400	350	290	550	470	380	280	170	800	670	530
Planned orders		330						750			

100 = 120 units of excess inventory. The order would then be $Q = 450 - (220 - 100) = 330$ units, set back by the 2-week lead time. The planned order release is said to be *time-phased*. The necessary inventory adjustments are shown in Table 12-4.

Given the planned receipt of the order for 330 units in period 3, we reexamine the projected inventory level 5 weeks later, in period 8. Again, an order would be placed to cover forecast demand for the periods 8 through 12, less the inventory-buffer adjustment. Assuming that forecast demand continues to increase at the same rate, the 5-week forecast demand is $D = 120 + 130 + 140 + 150 + 160 = 700$ units. Projected eighth-week inventory would be 50 units, and therefore, the time-phased order to be placed in the sixth week (again allowing for the 2-week lead time) is $Q = 700 - (50 - 100) = 750$ units. Note that in this instance, the adjustment for current inventory position and desired buffer stock shows a shortage of 50 units compared with the desired buffer stock, so that the adjustment results in an order that rebuilds the buffer to the desired level of 100 units. Table 12-4 also shows the adjustments to the inventory record to reflect the second order.

The periodic ordering rule coupled with an inventory planning system automatically adjusts for the changing forecast. If demand had been decreasing during the review period, the ordering rule would automatically reduce the size of orders to take account of decreased forecasts. When demand is dependent on the production schedule of a product, it may be quite easy to forecast, but extremely variable. These kinds of inventory planning systems are often used in *MRP* systems.

LOT SIZE DECISION POLICIES

In the examples discussed to this point the size of the production run or lot size has been assumed. We now consider some of the alternate lot size decision policies that might be used and how they fit in with requirements planning.

Before considering the alternate policies, however, let us review some key elements concerning requirements systems that may be helpful in deciding the nature of appropriate lot size policies. First, we know that demand for components is dependent and must be thought of as requirements generated to key in with the master schedule of the final product. The nature of the demand distributions that result is not uniform and continuous, as may be true for primary items, such as those discussed in Chapter 10, where demand resulted from the aggregation of independent orders from multiple sources. Demand is lumpy because it is dependent, and demand variations are not the result of random fluctuation. Therefore, some of the assumptions important in traditional inventory control theory are questionable for dependent items. We must keep these assumptions in mind as we discuss alternate lot size policies. The following comparison of three lot size policies is meant to show how the policies react to lumpy demand and is not meant as a valid test of the three policies in *MRP* systems.

Economic Order Quantity (*EOQ*)

In the past the *EOQ* policy or the nonoptimal fixed order quantity alternatives have been used most. In such systems, the order point is set to cover expected usage

TABLE 12-5

Performance of an *EOQ* Model for a Given Requirements Schedule ($\bar{R}$ = 92.1 units per week, c_P = $300 per order, c_H = $2 per unit per week, and *EOQ* = 166 units)

Week number	1	2	3	4	5	6	7	8	9	10	11	12
Requirements	10	10	15	20	70	180	250	270	230	40	0	10
							166		166			
Quantity ordered	166	—	—	—	—	166	166	166	166		—	—
Beginning inventory	166	156	146	131	111	207	359	275	337	107	67	67
Ending inventory	156	146	131	111	41	27	109	5	107	67	67	57

Ordering cost:	$2100
Inventory carrying cost:	3153
Total incremental cost:	$5253

during lead time, an order for a fixed quantity being placed at that time. If the *EOQ* is used, it is computed by the equation, $EOQ = \sqrt{2\bar{R}c_P/c_H}$.

Table 12-5 shows the performance of an *EOQ* model for the requirements schedule given. Instantaneous replenishment is assumed. Seven orders were placed to meet requirements. The order quantity was increased to 2 × *EOQ* in those periods where demand exceeds *EOQ* plus the inventory carried forward. The ordering cost is then 7 × 300 = $2100. Inventory costs are based on the average for beginning and ending inventory in each period. For example, average inventory for period 1 is (166 + 156)/2 = 161 units. The average inventory for the 12 weeks is 89.88 units. The inventory cost for the 12 periods is the sum of the period average inventories multiplied by the unit inventory cost, or 2 × 12 × 131.38 = $3153. The total incremental cost for the *EOQ* model for 12 weeks is $5253. As Berry points out, this example illustrates several problems with the *EOQ* procedure:

> When the demand is not equal from period to period, as is often the case in requirements forecasts, one of the assumptions underlying the EOQ formula is violated. Since demand does not occur at a constant rate, as is assumed by the EOQ formula, the restriction of fixed lot sizes results in larger inventory carrying costs. This occurs because of the mismatch between the order quantities and the demand values, causing excess inventory to be carried forward from week to week [Berry, 1972].

Periodic Reorder System

Recall that we can approximate the economic time interval between replenishment orders by dividing the *EOQ* by the mean demand rate. For our example, $EOQ/\bar{R}$ = 166/92.1 = 1.8, or approximately 2 weeks. When this procedure is applied to the same requirements schedule used to illustrate the *EOQ* policy, the reorder and inventory pattern of Table 12-6 results, where the order quantity is the sum of requirements for the next 2 weeks. The system requires only six orders, but with lot sizes ranging from 20 to 520 units. Therefore, average inventory is 89.4 units, resulting in lower inventory carrying costs of $2145, and total incremental costs of $3945. The periodic system results in a $1303 reduction in total incremental cost, or 25 percent. By being able to vary order size in response to lumpy demand, the periodic system saves one order.

TABLE 12-6
Performance of a Periodic Reorder Model for a Given Requirements Schedule ($\bar{R}$ = 92.1 units per week, c_P = \$300 per order, c_H = \$2 per unit per week, T_O = 2 weeks)

Week number	1	2	3	4	5	6	7	8	9	10	11	12
Requirements	10	10	15	20	70	180	250	270	230	40	0	10
Quantity ordered	20		35		250		520		270			10
Beginning inventory	20	10	35	20	250	180	520	270	270	40	0	10
Ending Inventory	10	0	20	0	180	0	270	0	40	0	0	0

Ordering cost:	\$1800
Inventory carrying cost:	2145
Total incremental cost:	\$3945

SOURCE. W. L. Berry, "Lot Sizing Procedures for Requirements Planning Systems: A Framework for Analysis," *Production and Inventory Management*, 2nd Quarter, 1972.

As Berry points out:

Like the EOQ procedure it, too, ignores much of the information contained in the requirements schedule. That is, the replenishment orders are constrained to occur at fixed time intervals, thereby ruling out the possibility of combining orders during periods of light product demand, e.g., during weeks 1 through 4 in the example. If, for example, the orders placed in weeks 1 and 3 were combined and a single order was placed in week 1 for 55 units, the combined costs can be further reduced by \$160.

Part-Period Total Cost Balancing

Another procedure is to attempt to balance the total incremental costs in each ordering decision. This procedure is called the "part-period algorithm" (part-period means one part carried in inventory for one period). It uses all the information provided by the requirements schedule and attempts to minimize total costs by equating the costs of placing orders and carrying inventories. The procedure considers the alternate lot size choices available at the beginning of week 1, that is, placing an order to cover the requirements for

Week 1 only

Weeks 1 and 2

Weeks 1, 2, and 3

etc.

For example, if we order enough to cover requirements for week 1, the average inventory would be $\bar{I}_1 = 0.5 \times 10 = 5$ units, assuming the same requirements schedule, and that inventory is centered within each week. If we order enough to cover requirements for weeks 1 and 2, the average inventory would be 5 units for week 1 as before, but $\bar{I}_2 = 1.5 \times 10 = 15$ units for the second week, because the 10 units ordered to cover requirements for week 2 would have to be carried in inventory one week longer, or 1.5 weeks, and so on. The inventory cost is then determined by multiplying the average inventory by the inventory cost per unit, $c_H = \$2$, for our example. The inventory carrying cost for these alternatives is as follows:

Week 1: $c_H(\bar{I}_1) = 2 \times 0.5 \times 10 = \$10$

Weeks 1 and 2: $c_H(\bar{I}_1 + \bar{I}_2) = 2(0.5 \times 10 + 1.5 \times 10) = \$40$

Weeks 1, 2, and 3: $c_H(\bar{I}_1 + \bar{I}_2 + \bar{I}_3)$
  $= 2(0.5 \times 10 + 1.5 \times 10 + 2.5 \times 15) = \$115$

Weeks 1, 2, 3, and 4: $c_H(\bar{I}_1 + \bar{I}_2 + \bar{I}_3 + \bar{I}_4)$
  $= 2(0.5 \times 10 + 1.5 \times 10 + 2.5 \times 15 + 3.5 \times 20) = \$225$

Weeks 1, 2, 3, 4, and 5: $c_H(\bar{I}_1 + \bar{I}_2 + \bar{I}_3 + \bar{I}_4 + \bar{I}_5)$
  $= 2(0.5 \times 10 + 1.5 \times 10 + 2.5 \times 15 + 3.5 \times 20 + 4.5 \times 70) = \$885$

By scanning the preceding set of calculations, we see that the fourth alternative, ordering 55 units to cover the demand for the first 4 weeks, approximates the ordering cost of $300. The result is that an order should be placed at the beginning of the first week to cover the first 4 weeks' requirements.

Applying this procedure to the same requirements schedule results in Table 12-7. The total incremental cost is reduced by an additional $460 or 12 percent, compared with the results for the periodic reorder system in Table 12-6. The part-period total cost-balancing procedure allows both the lot size and the time between orders to vary, so that in periods of light demand smaller lot sizes and longer time intervals between orders result, compared with periods of high demand.

Obviously, the part-period balancing procedure has performed best of the three reordering policies reported. The policy performs extremely well because of its flexibility in considering replenishments involving both variable reorder quantity and variable reorder frequency. It considers several different possible horizons and selects the one in which order and inventory costs are approximately equated. Thus, in periods of low requirements for several periods, it will group requirements, saving possible high ordering costs. If demand increases, the policy reacts by closing down its horizon, saving incremental inventory costs. In short, the policy uses the information provided in the requirements plan fully to its advantage.

The part-period balancing procedure, however, does not evaluate all the possible alternatives for lot sizes, and therefore it does not always produce the optimal solu-

TABLE 12-7
Performance of a Total Cost-balancing Model (Part-period Balancing) for a Given Requirements Schedule ($\bar{R}$ = 92.1 units per week, c_P = \$300 per order, c_H = \$2 per unit per week)

Week number	1	2	3	4	5	6	7	8	9	10	11	12
Requirements	10	10	15	20	70	180	250	270	230	40	0	10
Quantity ordered	55				70	180	250	270	270			10
Beginning inventory	55	45	35	20	70	180	250	270	270	40	0	10
Ending inventory	45	35	20	0	0	0	0	0	40	0	0	0

Ordering cost:	$2100
Inventory carrying cost:	1385
Total incremental cost:	$3485

SOURCE. W. L. Berry, "Lot Sizing Procedures for Requirements Planning Systems: A Framework for Analysis," *Production and Inventory Management,* 2nd Quarter, 1972.

tion. The Wagner-Whitin [1958] dynamic programming algorithm produces an optimal solution; however, it is much more complex and requires greater computer time. The result is that it is not used a great deal in practice. Berry included the Wagner-Whitin Algorithm in his study, and it produced a solution that was $240, or 7 percent, lower in cost than the part-period balancing policy. The part-period procedure did not consider the possibility of combining orders placed in weeks 9 and 12. By carrying an extra 10 units in inventory for 3 weeks at a cost of $60, the Wagner-Whitin policy saves placing an order in week 12, and the net cost reduction is $300 − $60 = $240.

Lot Size Policies in Multistage Systems

The discussion of lot size policies to this point has examined each of the three policies in isolated systems. The brief experiments reported are not an adequate test of alternate policies. However, the results of the experiments do give insight into the differing performance characteristics of the policies.

Biggs, Goodman, and Hardy [1977] developed a multistage production-inventory system model that involved a hierarchical system of part and component manufacture, subassembly, and final assembly. The hierarchical system makes it possible to test alternate lot size policies in an operating system where part and component manufacturing schedules are dependent on subassembly and assembly schedules and where subassembly is dependent on final assembly schedules. The final assembly schedule is set in relation to product demand. Thus the structure permits the testing of lot size policies as they would function in the multistage system. Five lot size policies were tested:

Economic order quantity (*EOQ*)

Periodic reorder system, using the *EOQ* to determine the reorder time cycle

Part-period total cost balancing

Lot-for-lot, in which an order is placed for exactly what is needed in the next period.

Wagner-Whitin dynamic programming model

System performance of the lot size models was evaluated using the following four criteria:

1. Total number of stockouts for final products
2. Total units of stockouts for final products
3. Total number of setups, total system
4. Average dollar value of inventory, total system

The results indicate that the part-period total cost balancing and *EOQ* were consistently the best performers in simulation experiments. The dominance of one policy over others depends on the weighting given the four criteria. The reemergence of the *EOQ* policy as a good performer in a multistage system is explained in part by its excellent performance with respect to final product stockouts. The *EOQ* policy places larger orders fewer times per year and is therefore exposed to the risk of stockout less often. Based on the simulation experiments, managers may select policies based on their preference for a given weighting of the criteria.

These results must be regarded as preliminary. As with most early simulation experiments, actual shop conditions are only approximated. In this instance, the simulated shop was loaded well under capacity. There was no lot splitting permitted, and when the "desired" production exceeded capacity, a priority index was used to determine which lots would not be processed. It is difficult to tell how the four lot size policies would have performed if these decision rules had not been imposed and if the load had been varied over a range, including heavy loads. Nevertheless, testing alternate lot size rules within a multistage environment is an important condition and represents a step toward resolving the issue of how different lot size policies actually perform.

BUFFER STOCKS IN REQUIREMENTS SYSTEMS

We have already noted that dependent items are not subject to the kinds of random variations in demand that characterize primary product demand. The demand variability is largely planned and is lumpy in nature. We do not need buffer stocks to absorb these kinds of fluctuations. The nature of the requirements plan is designed to counter the variations with production orders, as shown in Figure 12-7. These kinds of variation are under managerial control.

There are sources of variation, however, for which buffer stocks are a logical countermeasure. Buffer stocks in requirements systems are designed to absorb random variations in the *supply* schedule. The time required for processing orders through process-focused system is variable because of such factors as delays, breakdowns, and plan changes. In addition, the actual quantity delivered from production is variable because of scrap. The result is that we need a cushion to absorb variations in the supply time and the quantity actually delivered.

Buffer Stock Levels

The nature of requirements systems changes the concept of reorder levels in both the *EOQ* and part-period methods of control. In Chapter 10 we noted that the reorder level was set to cover normal usage during the supply lead time *plus* the buffer stock (see Chapter 10, Figure 10-5). In requirements systems, however, the buffer stock level becomes the trigger or reorder level. This is true because we work with future inventory levels in a coordinated plan. A projected fall in inventory level to or below the buffer level can be anticipated by a production order release time-phased by the lead time to be delivered in time to eliminate the impending shortage. Table 12-8 shows an example of how a production order release is scheduled in the third period, triggered by a projected decrease in inventories below the buffer level of 1000 units.

The determination of buffer stock levels can be based on the general experience with supply lead times and an estimate of the maximum usage likely to occur per

TABLE 12-8
Projected Inventory Falls Below the Buffer Stock Level of 1000 Units in Period 5, Triggering a Production Order Release in the Third Period

Period	1	2	3	4	5	6	7	8
Expected usage	—	2400	—	—	2000	1500	—	2000
Planned deliveries	—	—	—	—	2000			
					2600			
Planned stock on hand, end of week	5000	2600	2600	2600	~~600~~			
Planned production order release	—	—	2000					

Buffer stock = 1000 units; lead time = 2 periods; EOQ = 2000 units

period. There are other variables, however, that have the equivalent effect of buffer stocks. First, "safety factors" may be involved in the lead time estimates. If the lead time estimate is, in fact, the time that included 90 percent of the cases and most production orders are received prior to that time, then we have a buffer in effect. Inflated requirements schedules also have an equivalent buffering effect. All of these techniques are used and when used in combination, the equivalent buffer can be large and, unfortunately, partially hidden.

CAPACITY REQUIREMENTS PLANNING

The requirements plans we have discussed have shown ways of exploiting the knowledge of demand dependence and product structure in order to develop production order schedules. These schedules take account of the necessary timing of production orders, but they assume that the capacity is available when needed. However, capacity constraints are a reality that must be taken into account. Because the *MRP* system contains in its files information concerning the processing of each production order, we should be able to use that information to determine whether or not capacity problems will exist.

As an example, consider just the processing of metal legs beginning with the information contained in Figure 12-4. There are two dinette tables that use the same legs, and Table 12-9 summarizes the leg requirements from Figure 12-4. The bottom line of Table 12-9 gives production requirements for legs, if we accumulate 4 weeks' future requirements as production orders. Therefore, it is necessary to receive a lot of 1320 legs in period 1 and 1240 legs in period 5. Because there is a 3-week production lead time, these production orders must be released 3 weeks ahead of the schedule shown in Table 12-9.

TABLE 12-9 **Requirements for Table Legs from Production Schedules for Square and Round Tables shown in Figure 12-4 (Production lead time = 3 weeks)**

Period, weeks	1	2	3	4	5	6	7	8
Leg requirements, square	400	—	480	—	520	—	320	—
Leg requirements, round	—	160	—	280	—	240	—	160
Total leg requirements	400	160	480	280	520	240	320	160
Production requirements	1320	—	—	—	1240	—	—	—

405

TABLE 12-10   **Process Time Requirements for Legs in Lots of 1320 and 1240**

Process	Setup Time, Minutes	Run Time, Minutes/unit	Total Time, Hours, in Lots of	
			1320	1240
1. Cut to length	5	0.25	5.58	5.25
2. Weld brackets	10	1.00	22.16	20.83
3. Drill brackets	20	0.75	16.83	15.50
4. Paint	10	0.25	5.66	5.33
5. Install feet	5	0.10	2.28	2.15

From the operation process chart of Figure 12-1b, let us consider only the load requirements on the fabrication operations of (1) cut to length, (2) weld support brackets, and (3) drill brackets. The time requirements for the three operations are shown in Table 12-10 for each of the two lot sizes we must consider.

If the production orders are released 3 weeks before being needed for assembly, assume that the cutoff operation is planned for the first week, the welding operation for the second week, and the drilling and other minor operations for the third week. Then, the machine hour load on each of the three processes may be projected, as shown in Figure 12-8, completing all operations so that the two orders are available in the first and fifth weeks.

Following the same rationale that produced the load effects on the three processes shown in Figure 12-8, the computer system can pick up load from all orders for all parts and products in the files of the requirements program and print out a projected load for each work center. For example, the projected weekly load on the drill press work center is shown in Figure 12-9. The accumulated load by weeks is shown as "released load," in hours. The capacity for the 8-week horizon is shown as 80 hours, the equivalent of two available machines. The available hours in Figure 12-9 then indicate whether or not capacity problems are projected to occur. In periods 4, 5, and 6, there are projected overloads. Given this information, we may wish to anticipate the problem by changing the timing of some orders, meet the overload through the use of overtime, or possibly subcontract some items. In the example shown in Figure 12-9 there is substantial slack projected in periods 1 and 3, and it may be possible to smooth the load by releasing some orders earlier.

COMPUTERIZED *MRP*

The concepts of *MRP* are relatively straightforward, but clearly require computers for implementation for large numbers of products. When there are many assembled products, perhaps with subassemblies, the number of parts can easily be in the thousands. Requirements generation, inventory control, time phasing of orders, and capacity requirements all need to be carefully coordinated. This is a job for computers. Indeed, *MRP* developed in the computer age for good reasons.

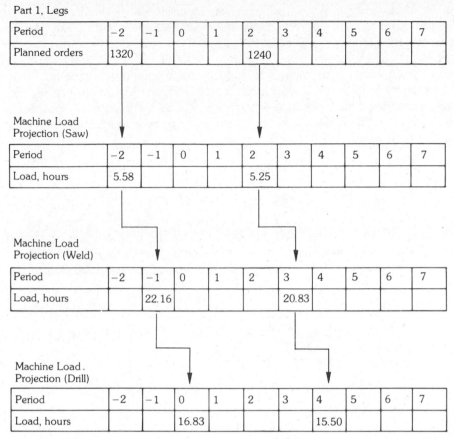

Part 1, Legs

Period	-2	-1	0	1	2	3	4	5	6	7
Planned orders	1320				1240					

Machine Load
Projection (Saw)

Period	-2	-1	0	1	2	3	4	5	6	7
Load, hours	5.58				5.25					

Machine Load
Projection (Weld)

Period	-2	-1	0	1	2	3	4	5	6	7
Load, hours		22.16				20.83				

Machine Load.
Projection (Drill)

Period	-2	-1	0	1	2	3	4	5	6	7
Load, hours			16.83				15.50			

FIGURE 12-8
Load generation for three processes, based on production schedule for legs. Time requirements from Table 12-10.

Projected Weekly Machine Load Report
Work Center 21, Drill Presses   Date: 02/01/80

Period	1	2	3	4	5	6	7	8
Released load, hours	65	71	49	90	81	95	48	62
Capacity, hours	80	80	80	80	80	80	80	80
Available hours	15	9	31	-10	-1	-15	32	18

FIGURE 12-9
Sample projected load report for one work center.

Benefits

It is estimated that somewhat more than 1000 manufacturers are using computerized *MRP* systems with excellent results. Some of the benefits are obvious. Think of changing schedules as a result of market shifts, changed promises to customers, order cancellations, or whatever. A computerized *MRP* system can reflect imme-

diately the effects of changed order quantities, cancellations, delayed material deliveries, and so on. A manager can change the master schedule and quickly see the
effects on capacity, inventory status, or the ability of the system to meet promises to
customers.

One of the important advantages is in capacity requirements adjustments. When
planners examine work center load reports, such as Figure 12-9, they can see immediately possibilities for work load smoothing. It may be possible to pull some
demand forward to fill in slack load. Such actions may reduce idle time and may
eliminate or reduce overtime.

MRP Programs

The structure of *MRP* computer programs is shown in Figure 12-10. The master
schedule drives the *MRP* program. The other inputs are product structures, bills of
materials, and inventory status. The outputs of the *MRP* program are open and
planned orders, net requirements of parts and materials, load reports, and updated
and projected inventory status. A variety of other reports can be generated to suit

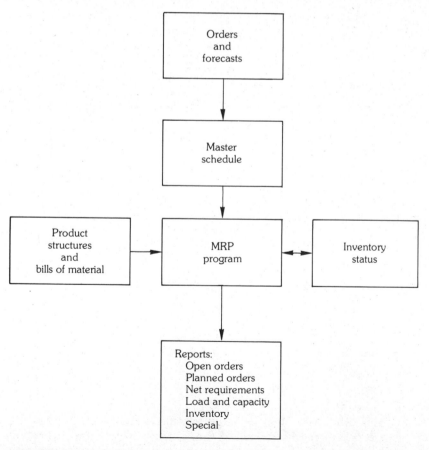

FIGURE 12-10
Structure of *MRP* computer programs.

individual needs, because the files are maintained so that they can be formulated in a variety of formats.

Subprograms include a means of reflecting the effects of engineering design changes on product structures and bills of materials. Also, inventory status requires the reflection of receipts and withdrawals to maintain an up-to-date file of inventory status.

Figure 12-11 shows a flow diagram for the IBM Requirements Generation System. Options are contained for lot size policies that can be called, including the three lot size policies that we discussed.

IMPLICATIONS FOR THE MANAGER

Managers of process-focused systems face extreme complexities of planning, scheduling, and control. These complexities are maximum when the productive system must cope with different levels of dependency of items in assembly, subassembly, and component manufacture. Managers who understand the dependency relationships are better able to create effective systems of planning and control.

The conceptual framework of requirements planning recognizes that the nature of demand for primary products is substantially different than for parts and components of the primary products. Demand for parts and components is dependent on the production schedules of primary items. As is often true, parts and components may be used in more than one primary product, so that the requirements schedule for such an item is derived by summing the needs implied by the master schedule of all primary products. The demand dependence of parts and components has profound effects on the policies used to determine the timing of production orders and the size of production lots.

The demand for parts and components is dependent not only in terms of quantities needed, but also on the timing of supply. Because we are dealing with an interlocking structure, the components must be ready for use at a precise time. If they are too late, production of primary items will be disrupted and delayed. If they are too early, in-process inventory costs will increase.

Because demand for components is dependent and usually lumpy, some of the assumptions in traditional inventory models are not valid. For example, demand is not at a constant rate, nor is it the result of the aggregation of independent demands from multiple sources. In short, demand variations for components are not due to random fluctuations. The result is that the economic order quantity policy sometimes belies its name.

IMPORTANT TERMS

Numbers in parentheses indicate page numbers

Bill of materials (389)   Dependent demand (391)

Bill of materials explosion (392)   Dependent structure (394)

Capacity requirements planning (405)   Independent demand (396)

Basic Input/Output Flowchart

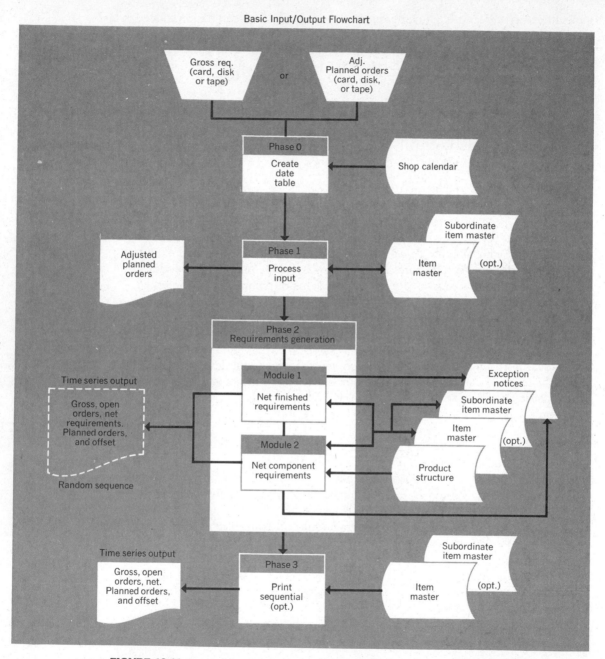

FIGURE 12-11
Computerized requirements generation system. (Courtesy International Business Machines Corporation.)

Inventory planning system (396)

Lumpy demand (394)

Material requirements planning,

Product structure (394)

Reactive inventory systems (396)

Time-phased order release (399)

REVIEW QUESTIONS AND PROBLEMS

1. Figure 12-12 is a cross-classification chart showing the subassemblies, parts, and raw materials that are used in each of nine primary products. For example, reading horizontally, product 1 requires subassembly 11 and part 28; subassembly 11 requires parts 20 and 28; and parts 20 and 28 require purchased parts or raw materials 20(35) and 28(31, 33, 35).

    a. Prepare an indented bill of materials for one unit of product 7.

    b. If one of each of the nine products were produced, how many of part 20 would be required?

2. Using the dinette table shown in Figure 12-1 as an example for requirements planning, why not produce enough components every 2 weeks to key in with a schedule of 100 completed tables per 2 weeks? What are the disadvantages?

3. Still using the dinette table as an example, suppose that they are produced in lots of 400 in weeks 3, 6, 9, and so on. Legs are produced in lots of 3200 every 6 weeks. How should the leg production be phased with respect to the table assemblies? Why?

4. What are the definitions of "dependent" and "independent" demand items? What kinds of forecasting methods are appropriate for each as a basis for production and inventory control?

5. How do inventory planning systems make it possible to adjust to variations in demand? If forecasts are inaccurate, how valid are inventory planning systems?

6. Assuming an inventory planning system with seasonal demand, compare the performance of ordering in preset fixed quantities with ordering variable quantities periodically.

7. The requirements for a motor drive unit to be assembled into a dictating machine follow the assembly schedule for the completed unit. The assembly schedule requires motor drive units with the timing shown in Table 12-11. Other data for the motor drive unit are: average requirements are $\overline{R} = 115.8$ units per week, $c_P = \$400$ per lot, and $c_H = \$4$ per unit per week. What is the

---

TABLE 12-11
Requirements Schedule for a Motor Drive Unit

Week number	1	2	3	4	5	6	7	8	9	10	11	12
Requirements, units	25	30	75	125	200	325	400	100	0	100	0	10

Total requirements for 12 weeks, 1390 units.

inventory record and total incremental cost under each of the following lot size policies?

a.   Economic lot size

b.   Economic periodic reorder model

c.   Part-period total cost balancing

8. Account for the differences in performance of the three lot size policies in problem 7.

9. The requirements for the motor drive unit described in problem 7 have been

Item		Subassembly										Part											Purchased part or raw material							
		10	11	12	13	14	15	16	17	18	19	20	21	22	23	24	25	26	27	28	29	30	31	32	33	34	35	36	
1			1																	1									1
2				1																		1		1					2
3					2							1																	3
4						1							1																4
5							2						2	1															5
6		1						1													1								6
7									1	1			2																7
8			1																1										8
9									1				1																9
10															1	2													10
11											1								1										11
12												1								2									12
13													2		1		2												13
14															3		3	4					1			2			14
15														3		2			2					1					15
16																	2			1							1		16
17																					1						1		17
18												1					2					1		1					18
19												1								1		1		1					19
20																										1			20
21																											1		21
22																						1		1					22
23																							1						23
24																						1				1			24
25																							1					1	25
26																								1					26
27																									1				27
28																						1		2		1			28
29																						1			2		1		29
30																							1		2		1		30

FIGURE 12-12
Cross-classification chart showing the complete explosion of a product line.

TABLE 12-12
Stabilized Requirements Schedule for a Motor Drive Unit

Week number	1	2	3	4	5	6	7	8	9	10	11	12
Requirements, units	300	300	300	300	350	350	400	400	350	350	350	325

Total requirements for 12 weeks, 4075 units

stabilized considerably by compensatory promotion of the dictating machine and by designing a line of portable tape recorders that have general use and a counterseasonal cycle. The tape recorder uses the same motor drive unit. Table 12-12 shows the new requirements schedule. What is the inventory record and total incremental cost of the same three lot size policies? Account for the differences in performance of the three policies.

10. What kinds of variation in demand for dependent items are not taken into account by the straightforward computation of requirements? How can the effects of these kinds of variation be absorbed?

SITUATIONS

11. The Wheel-Pump Company was originally the Pump Company, but many years ago the owner had the opportunity to bid on a contract to produce steel wheels for one of the smaller automobile companies. The Pump Company was successful in this initial venture into a new field, and became a supplier of wheels to the auto industry.

The Wheel Business

The basic process for wheel production involved stamping hub parts from coil strip steel, rolling rim shapes from steel stock, welding the rolled stock into a circular shape, welding hub parts to the rim, and painting. The fabrication processes were connected by conveyor systems, and once set up for a given type and size the system ran smoothly. The main production control problems seemed to be in maintaining material supply and quality control and in scheduling types and sizes to meet customer requirement schedules on two parallel line setups.

The Pump Business

The original pump business was still flourishing. The company manufactured a line of water pumps used in a variety of applications. There were 10 different models that had some common parts. There was a machine shop that fabricated parts which were stocked as semifinished items. Production orders were released for these parts based on a reorder with manufacturing lead times of from 2 to 6 weeks, depending on the item. The intention was to maintain a buffer stock of 6 weeks' supply. A forecast of demand for each item was up-

413

dated monthly, using an exponential smoothing system with $\alpha = 0.3$. The relatively large value of α was used to provide fast reaction to demand changes for inclusion in *EOQ* computations. Purchase parts were handled on an *EOQ*-reorder point basis, again with a buffer stock of 6 weeks' supply.

The basic schedule for the assembly of pumps was set monthly in a master schedule. The master schedule was projected for 3 months, with the first month representing a firm schedule. The most important input to the master scheduling process was a forecast for each model based on an exponential smoothing system merged with knowledge of contracts, orders, and sales estimates from the salespeople. The basic production rule was to produce 1 month's estimated requirements for the four models with heavy demand and 2 months' estimated requirements for the six models with smaller demand. These estimates were then adjusted for back-orders or excess inventory. The intention was to maintain a buffer inventory of finished goods of 2 weeks' supply.

Part shortages at assembly were common, and it was the job of expeditors to get rush orders through the shop to keep the assembly of pumps on schedule. Nevertheless, it was often true that pumps could not be assembled completely because of part shortages and had to be set back in the assembly schedule, resulting in stockouts of finished products.

Material Requirements Planning

The two product lines have always been operated as two separate businesses, both in sales and manufacturing, although the manufacturing facilities were located on the same site. The systems common to both product lines were in the accounting and finance functions. On retirement of the original owner, the firm was sold to a conglomerate, and a new professional manager was installed as president. The new president was satisfied that the manufacturing facilities for the two product lines had to be separate, but felt that the functions of production planning and control could and should be merged. He attended seminars on *MRP* at a local university and was impressed with the integrating nature of the computer based systems available. He felt that the requirements generation system available as software for the company computer could generate material requirements for both the wheel and pump product lines. He believed that production order releases keyed to sales requirements would be beneficial to both product lines and that the use of the capacity requirements concepts would enable forward planning on the use of overtime and the prevention of finished goods stockouts.

The president called in the vice-president of production and suggested the use of the *MRP* concept. The vice-president of production had served under the previous owner for 10 years and objected. "They are two different businesses, it won't work," he said.

What do you recommend?

12. COOKWARE, Inc. (CI) produces a line of pots and pans in various types and sizes. For example, saucepans are produced in three sizes, 1, 2, and 3 quarts. The saucepans and covers are made of stainless steel with plastic handles. The stainless steel parts are fabricated in-plant, and all other parts are purchased

according to specifications. Following the fabrication of stainless steel parts, they are routed to the Sauce Pan (SP) assembly facility for the assembly of handles and covers, packaging, and final movement to the factory warehouse. There are separate assembly facilities for the other products.

Planning and Scheduling

Forecasts for each product are made for 4-week planning periods and a 24-week horizon. Master schedules are constructed based on forecasts, capacities, and inventories on hand, and updated each 4 weeks. The production runs for each product are set in each 4-week period to match the forecast, but the scheduler "eyeballs" the future and tries to average out differences, attempting to stabilize output. Also, inventories of purchased parts are maintained on a monthly basis, with the intention of ordering a month's supply for items that have a 2-week lead time and 2 months' supply for items with a 4-week lead time. The preparation cost of purchase orders is $c_P = \$20$ and the preparation and setup costs for fabrication and assembly orders is $c_P = \$75$. The inventory holding cost is 25 percent of inventory value.

When the master schedule was updated for each 4-week planning period, it was forwarded to the Assembly Department supervisors, the Fabrication Department supervisor, and the Purchasing Department, who were responsible for the coordination necessary to have the required parts available according to the master assembly schedule. However, it was the Assembly Department supervisors who were responsible for the coordination process, and the development of weekly schedules by product for the upcoming 8 weeks (two planning periods), because the maintenance of the assembly master schedule was theirs, and it depended on the availability of all required parts. For example, Joe White, the SP Assembly Department supervisor, coordinated with the Fabrication Department supervisor for the supply of pans, brackets, and covers, and with the Purchasing Department for the supply of the required purchased parts.

When asked, Joe White said that the system worked reasonably well except for part shortages which often occurred. He said that he dealt with problems resulting from the poor matchup between the master schedule and his resources by scheduling short hours or overtime, and by working with the master schedulers to modify the schedule by shifting orders forward or backward in time to smooth the load. He could also lay off, or hire new workers and train them within 2 weeks, because the assembly work involved only simple skills. He preferred not to hire workers for temporary load increases, however, because he would have to lay them off soon, and the CI's policy was to maintain a stable work force size.

The latest forecasts and master schedules for saucepans has just been issued as shown in Table 12-13. Bills of material and other pertinent data are shown in Tables 12-14 to 12-16. Joe is studying the schedule to see if there will be problems with the normal assembly capacity of 4200 pans per week. Joe can increase capacity by scheduling up to 15 percent overtime, or 630 additional pans per week. What actions should he take? What recommendations would

TABLE 12-13
Six Period Forecast and Master Schedule for Saucepans (Planning Period Is 4 Weeks)

Model number	July	July–Aug.	Aug.–Sept.	Sept.–Oct.	Oct.–Nov.	Nov.–Dec.
S1, Forecast	8,000	10,000	11,000	12,000	10,000	9,000
Schedule	9,000	9,000	11,000	11,000	10,000	10,000
S2, Forecast	3,800	3,900	4,000	4,200	4,100	4,000
Schedule	3,800	3,800	3,800	4,200	4,200	4,200
S3, Forecast	1,500	1,800	2,200	2,500	2,000	2,000
Schedule	1,800	1,900	2,000	2,100	2,100	2,100

TABLE 12-14
Bill of Materials and Associated Data for Saucepan S1

Part Number	Description	Number Required per Pan	Cost per Pan	Lead Time, Weeks	Current Inventory
S1	One-Quart Saucepan	1	$2.75	4	400
100	Pan	1	1.50	4	3,400
101	Handle bracket	1	0.15	2	11,200
102	Right handle	1	0.15	4	3,500
103	Left handle	1	0.15	4	3,800
104	Mounting screw	2	0.05	2	4,000
105	Hook ring	1	0.05	2	2,500
106	Pan cover	1	0.45	4	2,600

TABLE 12-15
Bill of Materials and Associated Data for Saucepan S2

Part Number	Description	Number Required per Pan	Cost per Pan	Lead Time, Weeks	Current Inventory
S2	Two-Quart Saucepan	1	$3.25	4	2,300
200	Pan	1	1.90	4	3,400
101	Handle bracket	1	0.15	2	11,200
102	Right handle	1	0.15	4	3,500
103	Left handle	1	0.15	4	3,800
104	Mounting screw	2	0.05	2	4,000
105	Hook ring	1	0.05	2	2,500
206	Pan cover	1	0.55	4	1,000

you make to Joe White in developing a weekly schedule? Do you have recommendations for developing a better planning, scheduling, and control system? What should the schedule be for Part 101, given your weekly schedule?

TABLE 12-16
Bill of Materials and Associated Data for Saucepan S3

Part Number	Description	Number Required per Pan	Cost per Pan	Lead Time, Weeks	Current Inventory
S3	Three-Quart Saucepan	1	$3.50	4	900
300	Pan	1	2.05	4	3,400
101	Handle bracket	1	0.15	2	11,200
102	Right handle	1	0.15	4	3,500
103	Left handle	1	0.15	4	3,800
104	Mounting screw	2	0.05	2	4,000
105	Hook ring	1	0.05	2	2,500
306	Pan cover	1	0.65	4	3,600

REFERENCES

Berry, W. L., "Lot Sizing Procedures for Requirements Planning Systems: A Framework for Analysis," *Production and Inventory Management,* 2nd Quarter, 1972, pp. 13–34.

J. R. Biggs, S. H. Goodman, and S. T. Hardy, "Lot Sizing Rules in a Hierarchical Multi-Stage Inventory System," *Production and Inventory Control Management,* 1st Quarter, 1977.

Buffa, E. S., and J. G. Miller, *Production-Inventory Systems: Planning and Control* (3rd ed.). Irwin, Homewood, Ill., 1979.

Holstein, W. K., "Production Planning and Control Integrated," *Harvard Business Review*, May–June 1968.

Magee, J. F., and D. M. Boodman, *Production Planning and Inventory Control* (2nd ed.). McGraw-Hill, New York, 1967.

"Material Requirements Planning by Computer," *American Production and Inventory Control Society,* 1971, 86 pp.

New, C., *Requirements Planning.* Gower Press Ltd., Epping, Essex, Great Britain, Halsted Press, New York, 1973.

Orlicky, J., *Material Requirements Planning.* McGraw-Hill, New York, 1975.

Peterson, R., and E. A. Silver, *Decisions Systems for Inventory Management and Production Planning.* Wiley, New York, 1979.

Plossl, G., and O. Wight, *Production and Inventory Control: Principles and Techniques.* Prentice-Hall, Englewood Cliffs, N.J., 1967.

Rice, J. W., and T. Yoshikawa, "MRP and Motivation: What Can We Learn from Japan?" *Production and Inventory Management,* 2nd Quarter, 1980, pp. 45–52.

Wagner, H. M., and T. M. Whitin, "Dynamic Version of the Economic Lot Size Model," *Management Science,* 5(1), October 1958.

CHAPTER 13

Large-Scale Projects

O UR SOCIETY PRODUCES BUILDINGS, ROADS, DAMS, MISSILES, ships, and other products of large-scale projects. The problems of managing such projects stem from their great complexity and the nonrepetitive nature of the required activities; when the lot size is only one, there is little chance to take advantage of learning effects. Projects are produced by process-focused systems.

PROJECTS AND PROCESS-FOCUSED SYSTEMS

In the previous two chapters we have dealt with problems of industrial planning and scheduling. Recall from Chapter 2, Table 2-1, that intermittent demand, process-focused systems were divided into those with both inventoriable and noninventoriable outputs.

Systems with inventoriable outputs commonly produce a line of products in various types and sizes. The emphasis in planning and scheduling is on cycling the products through common facilities, lot size determination, the coordination of material requirements with production schedules, capacity requirements planning and control, and so forth. *MRP* represents a system for dealing with the planning and control problems. The focus in these kinds of enterprises is on the system and process for handling a large number of material and production orders. The nature of the complexity requires that we rely on a system, rather than focusing attention on each individual production order. A well-designed system is likely to produce good results.

When the output is not inventoriable, many of the problems shift to the custom order. Each order or job is likely to be unique or at least have some unique characteristics. In the case of a jobbing machine shop, we have a general purpose productive system that processes a large volume of custom orders for metal parts and components. Like the process-focused system for inventoriable products, the focus must still be on the system and process for handling a large number of orders. Here, either centralized or local shop floor control relies on priority decision rule systems. Good performance is measured in part in terms of order tardiness, cost, and the like. A good system will provide good performance, given other enabling factors such as requisite capacity and skills. But an additional factor may be present in some of these custom systems—an explicit penalty for missing deadlines. Most systems, in fact, involve costs that result from poor scheduling and control (idle labor, assembly out of sequence, loss of customers and goodwill). However, when explicit penalties for poor scheduling and control are present, emphasis shifts to more detailed planning, scheduling, and control of each activity to ensure timely completion.

The large-scale project also employs a process-focused system. By its nature, the product is either custom designed or has many features that are custom designed. The activities or operations required flow from the unique design. Because of the large scale, complexity results in terms of the number of activities, their sequence, and timing. The risks that result from failure to meet project completion deadlines are high, and large penalties for missing completion dates are common. These penalties may be explicit or may be in the form of higher costs. Thus the focus for managerial effort in project systems is on detailed planning, scheduling, and control of each major activity in relation to the project as a whole. As we will see, the interdependent nature of the sequence and timing of activities can be exploited to provide project managers with the crucial information they need.

ORGANIZATIONAL STRUCTURES

Given a single project, the manager organizes around the needs of that project, with all functional organizational units focused on achieving the project objectives. The organizational structure is then comparable with the functional organization used commonly in industry. Organizational problems begin when we add a second project. Multiple projects suggest resource sharing with obvious advantages of better utilization. But how will resources be shared? By what schedule? Who will decide these issues, if there are two project managers? The problems can be solved by simply duplicating resources and making the two projects independent, but the potential advantages of economies of the larger scale of operations are lost.

The common organizational form for multiple projects is the matrix organization. Figure 13-1 shows the concept of matrix organization with the functional managers holding the resources and each project manager coordinating the use of designated resources for each project. The advantages of matrix organization are in the efficient use of resources, the coordination across functional departments, and the visibility of project objectives. The disadvantages are in the need for coordination between func-

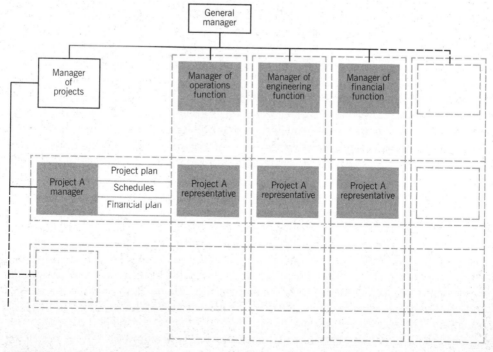

FIGURE 13-1
Structure of matrix organization for project management.

tional and project managers and the often unbearable situation of the person in the middle (the project representative) who is working for two bosses. Vertically, this person reports to the functional manager, but horizontally the project manager is the boss. If conflicts occur, the person in the middle may be caught there.

THE PROJECT MANAGER

The nature of organizational structures for project management and the one-time nature of projects create a difficult situation for project managers. The project manager has less than full authority over the project, being in the position of bargaining for resources and their timing from functional managers. At the same time, the uniqueness of each project creates problems that often cannot be foreseen. These problems commonly result in schedule slippage, replanning, and possibly reallocation of resources in order to maintain the project completion schedule.

If the project manager focuses attention in one critical area to the neglect of other important areas, the secondary areas may become critical problems. In short, the project manager must cope with short deadlines, changing situations, rapid-fire decision making, incomplete information, and skimpy authority. The position has all the potential for being one of simply "putting out fires." The issues are then to devise means for remaining in control.

Thanhain and Wilemon [1975] report on interviews with 100 project managers concerning the primary sources of conflict during a project. The results indicate the following sources of conflict in three broad phases of a project:

1. *Planning Stage.* Priorities, the required activities, and their sequencing.
2. *Buildup Stage.* Priorities, with the scheduling of activities becoming very important.
3. *Execution.* Scheduling of activities the primary source of conflict, with issues concerning the trade-off of the use of resources versus time performance also being very important.

The foregoing typical issues focus on problems of planning, scheduling, and control of activities. For project managers to remain in control, they need mechanisms that provide a clear logic for planning, a detailed schedule that can be easily updated for all activities, and mechanisms for resource trade-off. Network planning and scheduling methods have been developed to meet these special needs.

ORIGIN OF NETWORK PLANNING

Network planning methods were developed independently by two different groups. As an internal project of the DuPont Company, Critical Path Methods (CPM) were developed to plan and control the maintenance of chemical plants. They were subsequently widely used by DuPont for many engineering functions.

Parallel efforts were undertaken by the U.S. Navy at about the same time to develop methods for planning and controlling the Polaris Missile Project. The project involved 3000 separate contracting organizations and was regarded as the most complex of projects experienced to that date. The result was the development of the Performance Evaluation and Review Technique (PERT) methodology.

The immediate success of both the CPM and PERT methodologies may be gauged by the following facts. DuPont's application of their technique to a maintenance project in their Louisville works resulted in reducing downtime for maintenance from 125 to 78 hours. The PERT technique was widely credited with helping to shorten by 2 years the time originally estimated for the completion of the engineering and development program for the Polaris missile.

PERT and CPM are based substantially on the same concepts. As originally developed, PERT was based on probabilistic estimates of activity times that resulted in a probabilistic path through a network of activities and a probabilistic project completion time. CPM, however, assumed constant or deterministic activity times. Actually either the probabilistic or the deterministic model is equally applicable to and usable by either technique.

PERT/CPM PLANNING METHODS

We will use a relatively simple example, the introduction of a new product, to develop the methods used in generating a network representation of a project. The development of a project network may be divided into (1) activity analysis, (2) arrow diagramming, and (3) node numbering.

Activity Analysis

The smallest unit of productive effort to be planned, scheduled, and controlled is called an "activity." For large projects, it is possible to overlook the need for some activities because of the great complexity. Therefore, although professional planning personnel are commonly used, the generation of the activity list is often partially done in meetings and round-table discussions that include managerial and operating personnel. Table 13-1 is an activity list for the introduction of a new product.

Network Diagramming*

A network is developed that takes account of the precedence relationships among activities and must be based on a complete, verified, and approved activity list. The important information required for these network diagrams is generated by the following three questions:

1. Which activities must be completed *before* each given activity can be started?
2. Which activities can be carried out in *parallel*?
3. Which activities immediately *succeed* other activities?

---

* Activities will be diagrammed as occurring on the arcs, or arrows. An alternate network diagramming procedure, where activities occur at the nodes, will be discussed later in the chapter. We can refer to the first as an "arcs" network, and the second as a "nodes" network.

Table 13-1

Precedence Chart Showing Activities, Their Required Sequence, and Time Requirements for the New Product Introduction Project

Activity Code	Description	Immediate Predecessor Activity	Time, Weeks
A	Organize sales office	—	6
B	Hire salespeople	A	4
C	Train salespeople	B	7
D	Select advertising agency	A	2
E	Plan advertising campaign	D	4
F	Conduct advertising campaign	E	10
G	Design package	—	2
H	Set up packaging facilities	G	10
I	Package initial stocks	H, J	6
J	Order stock from manufacturer	—	13
K	Select distributors	A	9
L	Sell to distributors	C, K	3
M	Ship stock to distributors	I, L	5

The common practice is simply to work backwards through the activity list, generating the immediate predecessors for each activity listed, as shown in Table 13-1. The estimated normal time for each activity is also shown in the table, although it is not necessary at this point. The network diagram may then be constructed to represent the logical precedence requirements shown in Table 13-1. It is not particularly important whether or not arcs cross in developing the correct relationships. If the network diagram is to be presented to others, however, there is a value to developing an uncluttered final diagram.

Dummy Activities

Care must be taken in correctly representing the actual precedence requirements in the network diagram. For example, in house construction, consider the immediate predecessor activities for activity s, sand and varnish flooring, and activity u, finish electrical work. Activity s has immediate predecessors o and t, finish carpentry and painting, respectively, whereas u has a predecessor of only activity t, paint. The relationship shown in Figure 13-2a does not correctly represent this situation because it specifies that the beginning of u is dependent on both o and t, and this is not true.

To represent the situation correctly, we must resort to the use of a dummy activity that requires zero performance time. Figure 13-2b represents the stated requirement. The finish electrical work, u, now depends only on the completion of painting, t. Through the dummy activity, however, both finish carpentry and painting must be completed before activity s, sand and varnish flooring, can be started. The dummy activity provides the logical sequencing relationship. But because the dummy activity is assigned zero performance time, it does not alter any scheduling relationships that may be developed.

423

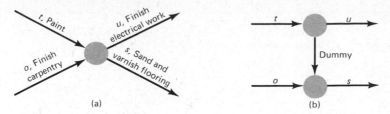

FIGURE 13-2

(a) Diagram does not properly reflect precedence requirements because u seems to be dependent on the completion of both o and t, but actually depends only on t. (b) Creating two nodes with dummy activity between provides the proper predecessors for both activities s and u.

Another use of the dummy activity is to provide an unambiguous beginning and ending event or node for each activity. For example, a functionally correct relationship may be represented by Figure 13-3a, with two activities having the same beginning and ending nodes. If Figure 13-3a were used, however, it would not be possible to identify each activity by its predecessor and successor events because both activities m and n would begin and end with the same node numbers. This is particularly important in larger networks employing computer programs for network diagram generation. The computer is programmed to identify each activity by a pair of node numbers. The problem is solved through the insertion of a dummy activity, as shown in Figure 13-3b. The functional relationship is identical, because the dummy activity requires zero time, but now both m and n are identified by different pairs of node numbers.

Figure 13-4 shows the completed network diagram for the new product introduction project. Activities are identified with their required times in weeks, and all the nodes are numbered. The activity times were not used to this point and were not necessary for the construction of the diagram. However, the activity times will have great significance in the generation of schedule data, critical path determination, and the generation of alternatives for the deployment of resources.

Node Numbering

The node numbering shown in Figure 13-4 has been done in a particular way. Each arc, or arrow, represents an activity. If we identify each activity by its tail (i) and head (j) numbers, the nodes have been numbered so that for each activity, i is always less

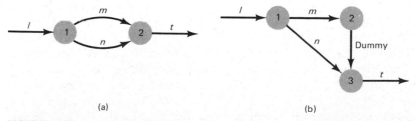

FIGURE 13-3

(a) Activities m and n may be carried out in parallel, but result in identical beginning and end events. (b) Use of dummy activity makes possible separate ending event numbers.

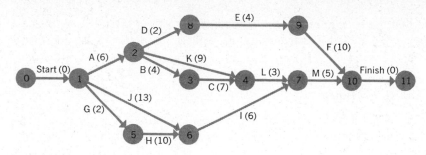

FIGURE 13-4
Arcs network diagram for the new product introduction project.

than j, $i < j$. The numbers for every arrow are progressive, and no backtracking through the network is allowed. This convention in node numbering is effective in computing programs to develop the logical network relationships and to prevent the occurrence of cycling or closed loops.

A closed loop would occur if an activity were represented as going back in time. This is shown in Figure 13-5, which is simply the structure of Figure 13-3b with the activity n reversed in direction. Cycling in a network can result through a simple error, or, when developing the activity plans, if one tries to show the repetition of an activity before beginning the next activity. A repetition of an activity must be represented with additional separate activities defined by their own unique node numbers. A closed loop would produce an endless cycle in computer programs, without a built-in routine for detection and identification of the cycle. Thus, one property of a correctly constructed network diagram is that it is *noncyclical*.

CRITICAL PATH SCHEDULING

With a properly constructed network diagram, it is a simple matter to develop the important schedule data for each activity and for the project as a whole. The data of interest are the earliest and latest start and finish times, the available slack for all activities, and the critical path through the network.

Earliest Start and Finish Times

If we take zero as the starting time for the project, then for each activity there is an earliest starting time (*ES*) relative to the project starting time. This is the earliest

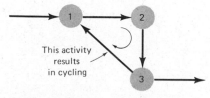

FIGURE 13-5
Example of a closed loop or cycling in a network diagram.

425

possible time that the activity can begin, assuming that all the predecessors also are started at their ES. Then, for that activity, its earliest finish (EF) is simply ES + activity time.

Latest Start and Finish Times

Assume that our target time for completing the project is "as soon as possible." This target is called the "latest finish time" (LF) of the project and of the finish activity. The latest start time (LS) is the latest time at which an activity can start, if the target or schedule is to be maintained. Thus, LS for the finish activity is LF − activity time. Because the finish activity requires zero time units, $LS = LF$.

   Existing computer programs may be used to compute these schedule data automatically, requiring as inputs the activities, their performance time requirements, and the precedence relationships established. The computer output might be similar to Figure 13-6, which shows the schedule statistics for all activities when no slack has been allowed in the overall project completion time. Note, then, that all critical activities have zero total slack in their schedules. All other activities have greater slack.

Slack

The total slack for an activity is simply the difference between computed late and early start times (LS − ES) or between late and early finish times (LF − EF). The significance of total slack (TS) is that it specifies the maximum time that an activity can be delayed without delaying the project completion time. If TS for an activity is used up, then the critical path changes.

THE CRITICAL PATH IS

START → A → B → C → L → M → FINISH

THE LENGTH OF THE CRITICAL PATH IS 25

NODE	DURATION	EARLY START	EARLY FINISH	LATE START	LATE FINISH	TOTAL SLACK	FREE SLACK
START	0.00	0.00	0.00	0.00	0.00	0.00	0.00
A	6.00	0.00	6.00	0.00	6.00	0.00	0.00
B	4.00	6.00	10.00	6.00	10.00	0.00	0.00
C	7.00	10.00	17.00	10.00	17.00	0.00	0.00
D	2.00	6.00	8.00	9.00	11.00	3.00	0.00
E	4.00	8.00	12.00	11.00	15.00	3.00	0.00
F	10.00	12.00	22.00	15.00	25.00	3.00	3.00
G	2.00	0.00	2.00	2.00	4.00	2.00	0.00
H	10.00	2.00	12.00	4.00	14.00	2.00	1.00
I	6.00	13.00	19.00	14.00	20.00	1.00	1.00
J	13.00	0.00	13.00	1.00	14.00	1.00	0.00
K	9.00	6.00	15.00	8.00	17.00	2.00	2.00
L	3.00	17.00	20.00	17.00	20.00	0.00	0.00
M	5.00	20.00	25.00	20.00	25.00	0.00	0.00
FINISH	0.00	25.00	25.00	25.00	25.00	0.00	0.00

FIGURE 13-6
Sample computer output of schedule statistics and critical path for the new product introduction project.

Free slack (*FS*) shown in Figure 13-6 indicates the time that an activity can be delayed without delaying the *ES* of any other activity. *FS* is computed as the difference between *EF* for an activity and the earliest of the *ES* times of all immediate successors. For example, activity F has *FS* = 3 weeks. Its *LF* = 25 weeks, but its *EF* = 22 weeks. If its earliest finish time is delayed up to 3 weeks, no other activity *ES* time is affected, nor is the project completion time affected. Note also that activity K can be delayed 2 weeks without affecting activity L, its successor. To compute *FS* manually, one should examine the network diagram in order to take account of the precedence relationships.

On the other hand, total slack is shared with other activities. For example, activities D, E, and F all have *TS* = 3. If activity D is delayed and thus uses the slack, then E and F no longer have slack available. These relationships are most easily seen by examining the network diagram, where the precedence relationships are shown graphically.

Actually, there are five different paths from start to finish through the network. The *longest*, most limiting path requires 25 weeks by the activity sequence START-A-B-C-L-M-FINISH, which is called a *critical path*. In a small problem such as this one, we could enumerate all the alternate paths to find the longest path, but there is no advantage in doing so, because the critical path is easily determined from the schedule statistics, which are themselves useful.

Manual Computation of Schedule Statistics

Manual computation is appropriate for smaller networks and helps to convey the significance of the schedule statistics. To compute *ES* and *EF* manually from the network, we proceed *forward* through the network as follows, referring to Figure 13-7:

1. Place the value of the project start time in both the *ES* and *EF* positions near the start activity arrow. See the legend for Figure 13-7. We will assume relative

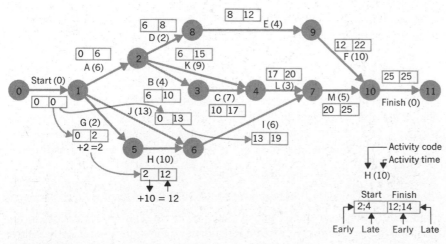

FIGURE 13-7
Flow of calculations for early start (*ES*) and early finish (*EF*) times.

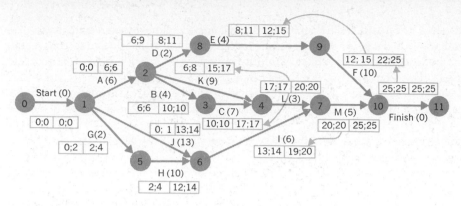

FIGURE 13-8
Flow of calculations for late start (*LS*) and late finish (*LF*) times.

values, as we did in the computer output of Figure 13-6, so the number 0 is placed in the *ES* and *EF* positions for the start activity. (Note that it is not necessary in PERT to include the start activity with zero activity duration. It has been included to make this example parallel in its activity list with the comparable "activities on nodes" example of Figure 13-9. The start and finish activities are often necessary in nodes networks.)

2. Consider any new unmarked activity, *all of whose predecessors have been marked* in their *ES* and *EF* positions, and mark in the *ES* position of the new activity the *largest* number marked in the *EF* position of any of its immediate predecessors. This number is the *ES* time of the new activity. For activity A in Figure 13-7, the *ES* time is 0, because that is the *EF* time of the preceding activity.

3. Add to this *ES* number the activity time, and mark the resulting *EF* time in its proper position. For activity A, $ES + 6 = 6$.

4. Continue through the entire network until the "finish" activity has been marked. As we showed in Figure 13-6, the critical path time is 25 weeks, so $ES = EF = 25$ for the finish activity.

To compute the *LS* and *LF*, we work *backwards* through the network, beginning with the finish activity. We have already stated that the target time for completing the project is as soon as possible, or 25 weeks. Therefore, $LF = 25$ for the finish activity without delaying the total project beyond its target date. Similarly, the *LS* time for the finish activity is *LF* minus activity time. Since the finish activity requires 0 time units, its $LS = LF$. To compute *LS* and *LF* for each activity, we proceed as follows, referring to Figure 13-8.

1. Mark the value of *LS* and *LF* in their respective positions near the finish activity.

2. Consider any new unmarked activity, all of whose successors have been marked, and mark in the *LF* position for the new activity the smallest *LS* time marked for any of its immediate successors. In other words, *LF* for an activity equals the earliest *LS* of the immediate successors for that activity.

3. Subtract from this *LF* number the activity time. This becomes the *LS* for the activity.

4. Continue backwards through the chart until all *LS* and *LF* times have been entered in their proper positions on the network diagram. Figure 13-8 shows the flow of calculations, beginning with the finish activity backwards through several activities.

As discussed previously, the schedule slack for an activity represents the maximum amount of time that it can be delayed beyond its *ES* without delaying the project completion time. Because critical activities are those in the sequence of the longest time path, it follows that these activities will have the minimum possible slack. If the project target date coincides with the *LF* for the finish activity, all *critical activities* will have zero slack. If, however, the target project completion date is later than the *EF* of the finish activity, all critical activities will have slack equal to this time-phasing difference. The manual computation of slack is simply *LS* − *ES* or, alternately, *LF* − *EF*. As noted previously, free slack is computed as the difference between *EF* for an activity and the earliest of the *ES* times of all immediate successors. Thus, free slack is not affected by any time-phasing difference between project earliest finish and target completion times.

ACTIVITIES ON NODES—
NETWORK DIAGRAM DIFFERENCES

Thus far, we have been using the "activities on arcs" network diagramming procedures. The "activities on nodes" procedure results in a slightly simpler network system by representing activities as occurring at the nodes, with the arrows showing only the sequences of activities required. The advantage in this methodology is that it is not necessary to use dummy activities in order to represent the proper sequencing. Figure 13-9 shows the network for the new product introduction project which may be compared with the comparable "activities on arcs" network shown in Figure 13-4.

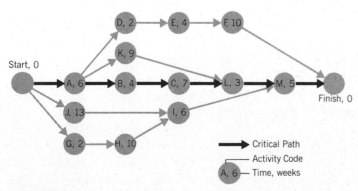

FIGURE 13-9
Project graph of activities on nodes for the new product introduction project.

The analysis developing the early and late start and finish times and slack times is identical with the forward and backward pass procedure previously outlined. The net results of both systems are the schedule statistics that are computed. Because these are the data of interest and because the entire procedure is normally computerized for both methodologies, the choice between the two may fall to other criteria, such as the availability and adaptability of existing computer routines, or the choice may be simply a matter of personal preference.

PROBABILISTIC NETWORK METHODS

The network methods that we have discussed so far may be termed "deterministic," because estimated activity times are assumed to be the expected values. No recognition is given to the fact that the mean or expected activity time is the mean of a distribution of possible values that could occur. Deterministic methods assume that the expected time is actually the time taken.

Probabilistic network methods assume the more realistic situation in which uncertain activity times are represented by a probability distribution. With such a basic model of the network of activities, it is possible to develop additional data important to managerial decisions. Such data help in assessing planning decisions that might revolve around such questions as: What is the probability that the completion of activity A will be later than January 10? What is the probability that the activity will become critical and affect the project completion date? What is the probability of meeting a given target completion date for the project? What is the risk of incurring cost penalties for not meeting the contract completion date? The nature of the planning decisions based on such questions might involve the allocation or reallocation of personnel or other resources to the various activities in order to derive a more satisfactory plan. Thus, a "crash" schedule with extra resources might be justified to ensure the on-time completion of certain activities. The extra resources needed are drawn from noncritical activities or activities where the probability of criticality is small.

The discussion that follows is equally applicable to either the arc or node method of network diagramming. The probability distribution of activity times is based on three time estimates made for each activity.

Optimistic Time

Optimistic time, a, is the shortest possible time to complete the activity if all goes well. It is based on the assumption that there is no more than one chance in a hundred of completing the activity in less than the optimistic time.

Pessimistic Time

Pessimistic time, b, is the longest time for an activity under adverse conditions, but barring acts of nature. It is based on the assumption that there would be no more than one chance in a hundred of completing the activity in a time greater than b.

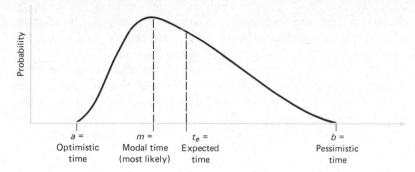

FIGURE 13-10
Time values in relation to a distribution of activity time.

Most Likely Time

Most likely time, m, is the single most likely modal value of the activity time distribution. The three time estimates are shown in relation to an activity completion time distribution in Figure 13-10. The computational algorithm reduces these three time estimates to a single average or expected value, t_e, which is actually used in the computing procedure.* The expected value is also the one used in computing schedule statistics for the deterministic model. The example distribution in Figure 13-10 represents only one possibility. Actually, the time distributions could be symmmetrical or skewed to either the right or the left.

With a probabilistic model we can see that there is a probability that seemingly noncritical activities could become critical, or vice versa. This could happen by the occurrence either of a long performance time for an activity or of a short performance time for an activity already on the critical path. This is a signal that the schedule plans developed are likely to change. As actual data on the progress of activities come in, it may be necessary to make changes in the allocation of resources in order to cope with new critical activities.

Probability theory provides the basis for applying probabilistic network concepts. First, the sum of a reasonable large number ($n > 30$) of random variables is itself a random variable, but is normally distributed, even if the individual random variables are not. Second, the variance of the sum of statistically independent random variables is the sum of the variances of the original random variables.

Translated for network scheduling concepts, we have the following useful statements for larger projects with independent activity times: (1) the mean project com-

---

* The usual model assumes that t_e is the mean of a beta distribution. The estimates of the mean and variance of the distribution may be computed as follows:

$\bar{x} = 1/6\ (A + 4M + B)$

$s^2 = (1/6\ (B - A))^2$

where A, B, and M are estimates of the values of a, b, and m, respectively, and $\bar{x}$ and s^2 are estimates of the mean and variance, t_e and σ_t^2.

pletion time is the mean of a normal distribution, and is the simple sum of the t_e values along a critical path, and (2) the variance of the mean project completion time is the simple sum of the variances of the individual activities along a critical path.

Therefore, we may use the normal tables to determine probabilities for the occurrence of given project completion time estimates. For example, the probability that a project would be completed in less than the mean time is only 0.50. The probability that a project would be completed in less time than the mean plus one standard deviation of the mean is about 0.84; the mean plus two standard deviations, 0.98, and so on.

Simulation of PERT Networks

The probabilistic model we have discussed assumes that each activity time follows a Beta distribution. In some instances this assumption may not be appropriate, and simulation can be used to analyze the network using empirical probability distributions and any significant correlations between activity times.

As an example, assume a simple network involving only seven activities required to install an air conditioning (A/C) plant. The seven activities, their sequence requirements, and expected times are:

Activity	Description	Immediate Predecessors	Expected Time (Weeks)
A	Order A/C plant and materials	Start	4.4
B	Prepare installation site	Start	5.2
C	Prepare application for city permits	Start	4.2
D	Preassemble A/C plant in shop and deliver to site	A	4.4
E	Obtain city permits	C	3.0
F	Install ducting and electrical connections	A	7.6
G	Install A/C system	B, D, E	4.2

The network diagram for the project is shown in Figure 13-11. The critical path can be determined by inspection, because it is the longest time path through the network and there are only four paths. The four paths and their times are as follows:

A—F	12 weeks
B—G	7 weeks
A—D—G	11 weeks
C—E—G	8 weeks

The longest time path is $A—D—G$, requiring 13 weeks. The most important activities to monitor would then be "Order A/C plant and materials," "Preassemble A/C plant in shop and deliver to site," and "Install A/C system."

We now substitute independent empirical probability distributions for the deterministic activity times, assuming that the Beta distribution is not a good approximation to reality. These empirical distributions are superimposed on the network diagram in Figure 13-12. Note that the expected times were calculated directly from

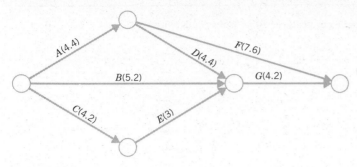

FIGURE 13-11
Network diagram for the air conditioner project, with deterministic activity times.

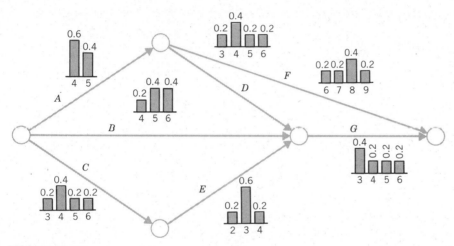

FIGURE 13-12
Network diagram with activity times represented as probability distributions.

these distributions. For example, the expected time for activity B is $0.2 \times 4 + 0.4 \times 5 + 0.4 \times 6 = 5.2$ weeks.

We can simulate the execution of the network using Monte Carlo sampling of the activity times from each of the distributions. (See Appendix E for a review of methods.) After having drawn a set of simulated activity times at random we can determine the critical path for that set of activity times, noting the path and the total project time. By repeating the simulation for a large number of cycles, we can estimate the expected completion time and the probability of shorter or longer project times.

Selection of Random Numbers. For activity A in Figure 13-12, the assumed probability of a time of 4 weeks is 0.6, so only random numbers 1 through 6 will result in a time of 4 weeks. The probability that activity A will require 5 weeks is 0.4, so the random numbers 7 through 0 are assigned. Table 13-2 shows the random number equivalents for the empirical distributions of all seven activities.

Network Simulation. To simulate the network we select at random sets of seven

Table 13-2   **Random Number Equivalents for Seven Network Activities**

Activity	Assumed Probability	These Random Numbers	Select These Activity Times, Weeks
A	0.6	1-6	4
	0.4	7-0	5
B	0.2	1-2	4
	0.4	3-6	5
	0.4	7-0	6
C	0.2	1-2	3
	0.4	3-6	4
	0.2	7-8	5
	0.2	9-0	6
D	0.2	1-2	3
	0.4	3-6	4
	0.2	7-8	5
	0.2	9-0	6
E	0.2	1-2	2
	0.6	3-8	3
	0.2	9-0	4
F	0.2	1-2	6
	0.2	3-4	7
	0.4	5-8	8
	0.2	9-0	9
G	0.4	1-4	3
	0.2	5-6	4
	0.2	7-8	5
	0.2	9-0	6

random numbers from Table G-5 (Appendix G). For example, a set random numbers drawn and equivalent activity times are as follows:

Activity	A	B	C	D	E	F	G
Random number drawn	7	8	7	1	2	3	8
Activity time	5	6	5	3	2	7	5

If these simulated activity times were inserted in the network in Figure 13-12, the four paths and their times would be:

A—F   12 weeks
A—D—G   13 weeks
B—G   11 weeks
C—E—G   12 weeks

and the critical path would be A—D—G, with a project time of 13 weeks. Each simulation run requires this process of selecting random numbers in sets of seven, determining the resulting activity times, critical path determination, and determination of project time. Table 13-3 shows the results of 20 simulation cycles with the critical activities, project times, and other computed data.

Table 13-3   **Simulation of 20 Trials for the Air Conditioner Plant Installation Project Completion Time**

Simulation Cycle Number	Sampled Activity Times (* Indicates "On Critical Path")							Project Completion Time
	A	B	C	D	E	F	G	
1	5*	6	4	4	3	8*	3	13
2	5*	6	5	3*	2	7	5*	13
3	5*	5	4	6*	2	8	5*	16
4	5*	5	5	4*	3	6	3*	12
5	5*	6	3	3	3	9*	4	14
6	5	4	6*	3	3*	7	6*	15
7	5*	6	5	5*	4	8	5*	15
8	4*	4	3	6*	3	6	5*	15
9#	5*	5	6*	4*	3*	6	3*	12
10	5*	5	6	5*	3	6	3*	13
11	4	6	6*	4	3*	8	4*	13
12	5*	5	4	5*	4	8	5*	15
13	4	5	5*	3	3*	7	6*	14
14#	5*	6	4	4*	3	7*	3*	12
15	5*	5	3	4*	2	6	6*	15
16	5*	5	4	4*	4	6	3*	12
17	4	5	6*	3	3*	8	4*	13
18	4*	6	6	6*	3	6	6*	16
19	5*	5	4	3	3	7*	3	11
20#	4*	4	4	6*	3	9*	3*	13
Number of Times Critical	16	0	5	13	5	5	17	273
Critical Ratio	0.80	0.0	0.25	0.65	0.25	0.25	0.85	

Average project completion time = 273/20 = 13.65 weeks

Note that on simulation cycles 9, 14, and 20, there were *two* critical paths. For cycle 9, A—D—G, and C—E—G were both critical with the same project completion time of 12 weeks. For cycles 14 and 20, the critical paths A—D—G, and A—F have the same project completion times.

Interpretation of Results. The average simulated project time is 13.65 weeks, ranging from 12 to 16 weeks. This information is in itself useful to a manager, but the bottom of Table 13-3 has additional information in the form of the number of times that each activity was critical, and the critical ratio.

The critical ratio is the proportion of cycles during which each activity was critical, or an estimate of the probability that the activity will be critical. Note, for example, that activity F has a critical ratio of only 0.25, whereas activity G has a critical ratio of 0.85. Activity B was never on the critical path, and has a ratio of 0.0.

The critical ratios provide new and valuable information to the manager. Activities A, D, and G should receive the most attention because they are likely to be critical in a high proportion of instances. A larger number of cycles would refine these initial estimates of project completion time and critical ratios. For example, the simulated average project time (13.65 weeks for this run), would likely be even closer to the 13-week project time from Figure 13-11. With larger more complex networks and the need for a large sample, network simulation requires the use of a computer.

DEPLOYMENT OF RESOURCES

Given the activity network, the critical path, and the computed schedule statistics, we have a plan for the project. But is it a good plan? We can abstract from the plan some additional data on the demand for resources for the early start schedule. By using the schedule flexibility available through slack in certain activities, we can generate alternate schedules, comparing the use of important resources with the objective of *load leveling.*

Another way to look at the initial or raw plan is in terms of activity costs. The initial activity duration estimates are based on an assumed level of resource allocation. Is it possible to alter activity times by pouring in more or less resources? Activity times for some activities can be directly affected in this way. For example, adding carpenters will usually shorten the time to frame a house. Would it be worthwhile to add more personnel on the critical framing and allocate less to the noncritical brickwork? Would the alternate plan be more or less expensive? Would shortening the critical path be advantageous? *Least-costing* considerations are worth examining.

Finally, in some situations we may be faced with a demand for some important resource that is limited in supply. The raw plan may, in fact, not be feasible if it schedules the use of the only available power shovel in two places at the same time. The raw plan must be examined with the objective of the feasible scheduling of *limited resources,* again using available slack time where possible or even lengthening the project in order to generate a feasible plan.

Load Leveling

What are the costs of not attempting to level loads in an already feasible schedule? Some factors that enter the problem occur in the following example of a major oil refinery repair and overhaul project. After a raw plan was developed, a series of computer runs was made to examine personnel requirements for the refinery project. In the first run it was found that the schedule required 50 boilermakers for the first 4 hours, 20 for the next 6 hours, and 35 for the period immediately following. Similar fluctuations in requirements were found for other crafts. In terms of costs associated with this fluctuation, there is the possible cost of idle or overtime labor.

For example, in the first 10 hours of the refinery project the peak requirement of 50 boilermakers will probably mean productive work of 50×4 hours $+ 20 \times 6$ hours $= 320$ worker-hours. But the likelihood is that it will be difficult to assign the extra 30 workers for the balance of the 8-hour day, so in the first 10 hours of the project the payroll may reflect $50 \times 8 + 20 \times 2 = 440$ worker-hours, 120 of which are idle labor. Figure 13-13 shows the deployment of personnel *after* leveling. Other costs that may be implicit in personnel fluctuation are hiring and separation costs in projects that extend over long periods. Load leveling has the objective of reducing idle labor costs, hiring and separation costs, or the cost of any resource that may be affected by fluctuations in the demand for its use, such as an equipment rental.

For very large and complex projects, a computer-based leveling model may be required. Simulation methodology commonly is used to generate alternate solutions. The starting solution might be the early start schedule, and a first attempt at leveling could then set a maximum of the resource in question just below the highest peak level recorded in the raw plan. The simulation program would then proceed as indicated by the network diagram, beginning all activities leaving node 1, keeping track of the amount of resources used and available. As the calendar is advanced and as activities are completed, resources are returned to the "available" pool. As new activities are started, resources are drawn from the pool. Simulation then proceeds until an activity requires resources from a temporarily exhausted pool. Depending on the decision criteria used by the simulator, the activity may be delayed, even past its latest starting time, until resources are available. Other decision criteria "bump" noncritical jobs and reassign resources to the delayed job when the latest starting time has been reached. By a progressive lowering of the resource limits in such a simulation program, the leveling effect takes place until a satisfactory deployment of resources is achieved.

Least Costing

Least costing concepts are based on cost versus activity time curves, such as in Figure 13-14. Different activities respond differently to changes in the application of resources, and some of the activities may not be responsive to changes in resources. Figure 13-14*a* may be typical of an activity, such as house framing, as we discussed previously, where crash, normal, and slow schedules are progressively less costly. A curve similar to Figure 13-14*b*, where the slow schedule is more costly than the

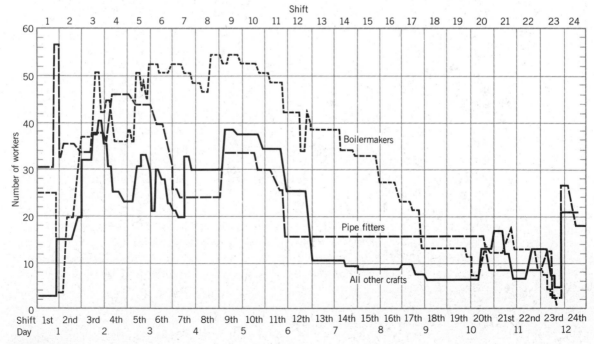

FIGURE 13-13
Personnel usage chart after leveling.
SOURCE: R. D. Archibald, and R. L. Villoria. *Network-Based Management Systems*, John Wiley, New York, 1967, p. 274.

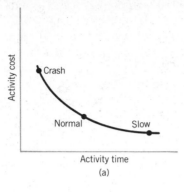
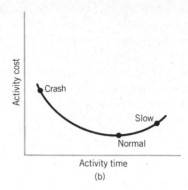

FIGURE 13-14
Typical activity time-cost curves.

normal schedule, could be typical where the meager resources associated with a slow schedule might force the use of inefficient methods. The cost trade-offs are possible partially because of the differential cost-time characteristics of different activities.

Limited Resources

A limited resource model called "SPAR" (Scheduling Program for Allocation of Resources) has been developed by Wiest [1967]. SPAR is a heuristic scheduling model for limited resources designed to handle a project with 1200 single resource activities, 500 nodes, and 12 shops over a span of 300 days. The model focuses on available resources that it allocates, period-by-period, to activities listed in order of their early start times. The most critical jobs have the highest probability of being scheduled first, and as many jobs are initially scheduled as available resources permit. If an available activity fails to be scheduled in one period, an attempt is made to schedule it in the next period. Finally, jobs that have been postponed and become critical then move to the top of the priority list of available activities.

Wiest applied the SPAR program to a space vehicle project that required large block engineering activities with up to five different types of engineers and involving 300 activities. Figure 13-15 shows an overall personnel loading chart for the program. The unlimited resources line resulted from a conventional PERT schedule with all activities at their early start times. The limited resources line results from the SPAR schedule where peak personnel requirements were considerably reduced. The total length of the project was shortened by 5 months, and the number of gross hirings of personnel was reduced by 30 percent as a result of the SPAR schedule.

IMPLICATIONS FOR THE MANAGER

Large-scale projects present managers with unique problems. Although they are process-focused systems, the managerial issues are rather different from the typical manufacturing process-focused system. The project manager's problems center on

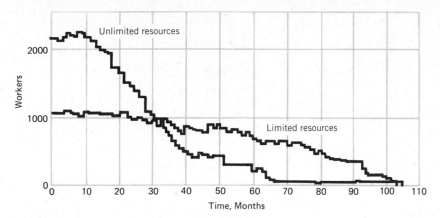

FIGURE 13-15
Personnel loading schedule for the space vehicle project.
SOURCE: J. D. Wiest. "A Heuristic Model for Scheduling Large Projects with Limited Resources," *Management Science*, *13*(6), February 1967, p. B-373.

the detailed schedule of activities and a preoccupation with completion dates of activities, resource budgets, and the project completion date.

The position of project manager requires a particular "breed of cat." A project manager must be someone who can deal with changing deadlines, immediate decisions, and skimpy information all in a general environment of divided authority. The managerial situation requires special concepts and techniques, and network planning and control systems are the best available today.

Davis (1974a) surveyed the top 400 construction firms and found over 80 percent of the 235 respondents were using network planning methods. Thus, it seems clear that many managers have recognized the practical value of network methods; they are not simply theoretical concepts.

Managers need to be involved in formulating the initial network. Perhaps a majority of the benefits of network methods comes at the planning stage. Given the network and time estimates, managers can have a number of computer runs made to assess alternate plans that involve cost-time trade-offs and resource smoothing. This interaction between the manager and the network model can have enormous benefits.

The control phases of network methods are the most costly. Smaller projects may not justify the cost of obtaining updated information and the periodic rescheduling needed for control. Davis also reported that the primary use of network methods in the construction industry was for project planning rather than for control.

IMPORTANT TERMS

Numbers in parentheses indicate page numbers

Activity analysis (422)   Activities on nodes diagram (429)

Activities on arcs diagram (425)   Backward pass (428)

Critical activity (429)

Critical path (427)

Crash schedule (437)

Dummy activity (423)

Early finish (426)

Early start (425)

Forward pass (427)

Free slack (427)

Late finish (426)

Late start (426)

Least costing (437)

Limited resources model (438)

Load leveling (436)

Matrix organization (420)

Most likely time (431)

Network diagram (425)

Node (424)

Optimistic time (430)

Parallel activities (424)

Pessimistic time (430)

PERT/CPM (422)

Probabilistic network (430)

Total slack (426)

REVIEW QUESTIONS AND PROBLEMS

1. What are the characteristics of large-scale projects that focus managerial effort on the detailed scheduling of activities and on project completion dates?

2. Contrast the large project system with the manufacturing process-focused systems discussed in previous chapters. Why does the manufacturing system focus managerial effort on process and system instead of on detailed activity scheduling?

3. Why is the matrix type of organization structure used in project management?

4. In the context of the "activities on arcs" planning methods, define the following terms: activity, event, node, and critical path.

5. For "arcs" planning methods, discuss and interrelate the three phases: (a) activity analysis, (b) network diagramming, and (c) node numbering.

6. What are the functions of dummy activities in an "arcs" network diagram?

7. What is the convention for numbering nodes in an "arcs" network? Why is this convention used?

8. Why must activity networks be noncyclical?

9. Define the following terms: early start (ES), early finish (EF), latest start (LS), latest finish (LF), and slack.

10. Outline the procedure for manual computation of schedule statistics.

11. What are the differences in the construction of the network diagram between the "arcs" and "nodes" methodologies? How can the probabilistic network model provide additional data helpful for managerial decisions?

Table 13-4   **Activities, Sequence, and Time Requirements for the Installation of a Gas-Forced Air Furnace**

Activity Code	Activity Description	Immediate Predecessor Activity	Time, Days
A	Start	—	0
B	Obtain delivery of furnace unit	A	10
C	Delivery of piping	A	5
D	Delivery of dampers and grilles	F	14
E	Delivery of duct work	F	10
F	Design duct layout	A	2
G	Install ducts and dampers	D, E	12
H	Install grilles	G	1
I	Install furnace unit	B	1
J	Install gas piping	C	5
K	Connect gas pipes to furnace	I, J	0.5
L	Install electric wiring	B	2
M	Install controls and connect to electrical system	I, L	1
N	Test installation	H, K, M	0.5
O	Clean up	N	0.5

12. Table 13-4 provides data for the project of installing a gas forced air furnace.

     a. Develop an arcs network diagram for the project.

     b. Identify any dummy activities necessary. Why are they necessary?

     c. Number the nodes of the network so that no cycling would result.

13. For the data of Table 13-4, develop a nodes network diagram. Do you feel that the nodes network is simpler to interpret than the arcs network? If computer programs were available to compute schedule statistics for both models, how would you choose between them?

14. Using the manual computation algorithms, compute the following schedule statistics for the furnace installation project.

     a. *ES, EF, LS, LF* for each activity.

     b. Total slack

     c. Free slack

     d. Critical path

15. Define the following terms: optimistic time, pessimistic time, most likely time, and expected time in probabilistic PERT networks.

16. What is meant by load leveling? How may it be accomplished?

17. Discuss the concepts of least costing in relation to crash, normal, and slow schedules.

18. What is the nature of the SPAR limited resource model?

19. Listed in Table 13-5 is a set of activities, sequence requirements, and estimated

Table 13-5   **Activities, Sequence Requirements, and Times for the Renewal of a Pipeline**

Activity	Activity Code	Code of Immediate Predecessor	Activity Time Requirement (days)	Crew Requirements per Day
Assemble crew for job	A	—	10	—
Use old line to build inventory	B	—	28	—
Measure and sketch old line	C	A	2	—
Develop materials list	D	C	1	—
Erect scaffold	E	D	2	10
Procure pipe	F	D	30	—
Procure valves	G	D	45	—
Deactivate old line	H	B, D	1	6
Remove old line	I	E, H	6	3
Prefabricate new pipe	J	F	5	20
Place valves	K	E, G, H	1	6
Place new pipe	L	I, J	6	25
Weld pipe	M	L	2	1
Connect valves	N	K, M	1	6
Insulate	O	K, M	4	5
Pressure test	P	N	1	3
Remove scaffold	Q	N, O	1	6
Clean up and turn over to operating crew	R	P, Q	1	6

activity times for a pipeline renewal project. Figure 13-16 provides computer output for the project. Which activities can be delayed beyond ES times without delaying the project completion time of 65 days? Which activities can be delayed without delaying the ES of any other activity?

20. For the data of the pipeline renewal project, suppose that activity H is delayed 12 days. What is the total slack remaining for activity I? What is the remaining free slack for activity I?

21. Suppose that activity H is not delayed, but I is delayed 14 days. Which activity or activities will be affected? How, and by how many days?

22. Activity K in the pipeline renewal project is delayed by 2 days. Which activities are affected? How, and by how many days?

23. In Table 13-6 there is additional information in the form of optimistic, most likely, and pessimistic time estimates for the pipeline renewal project. Compute variances for the activities. Which activities have the greatest uncertainty in their completion schedules?

SITUATIONS

24. The manager of the Pipeline Renewal Company had always operated on the basis of having detailed knowledge of the required activities. The manager had

THE CRITICAL PATH IS

START → A → C → D → G → K → O → Q → R → FINISH

THE LENGTH OF THE CRITICAL PATH IS 65

NODE	DURATION	EARLY START	EARLY FINISH	LATE START	LATE FINISH	TOTAL SLACK	FREE SLACK
START	0.00	0.00	0.00	0.00	0.00	0.00	0.00
A	10.00	0.00	10.00	0.00	10.00	0.00	0.00
B	28.00	0.00	28.00	16.00	44.00	16.00	0.00
C	2.00	10.00	12.00	10.00	12.00	0.00	0.00
D	1.00	12.00	13.00	12.00	13.00	0.00	0.00
E	2.00	13.00	15.00	43.00	45.00	30.00	14.00
F	30.00	13.00	43.00	16.00	46.00	3.00	0.00
G	45.00	13.00	58.00	13.00	58.00	0.00	0.00
H	1.00	28.00	29.00	44.00	45.00	16.00	0.00
I	6.00	29.00	35.00	45.00	51.00	16.00	13.00
J	5.00	43.00	48.00	46.00	51.00	3.00	0.00
K	1.00	58.00	59.00	58.00	59.00	0.00	0.00
L	6.00	48.00	54.00	51.00	57.00	3.00	0.00
M	2.00	54.00	56.00	57.00	59.00	3.00	3.00
N	1.00	59.00	60.00	62.00	63.00	3.00	0.00
O	4.00	59.00	63.00	59.00	63.00	0.00	0.00
P	1.00	60.00	61.00	63.00	64.00	3.00	3.00
Q	1.00	63.00	64.00	63.00	64.00	0.00	0.00
R	1.00	64.00	65.00	64.00	65.00	0.00	0.00
FINISH	0.00	65.00	65.00	65.00	65.00	0.00	0.00

FIGURE 13-16
Computer output showing critical path and schedule statistics for the pipeline renewal project.

Table 13-6 **Time Estimates for the Pipeline Renewal Project**

Activity Code	Optimistic Time Estimate of, a	Most Likely Time Estimate of, m	Pessimistic Time Estimate of, b	Expected Time Estimate of, t_e
A	8	10	12	10
B	26	26.5	36	28
C	1	2	3	2
D	0.5	1	1.5	1
E	1.5	1.63	4	2
F	28	28	40	30
G	40	42.5	60	45
H	1	1	1	1
I	4	6	8	6
J	4	4.5	8	5
K	0.5	0.9	2	1
L	5	5.25	10	6
M	1	2	3	2
N	0.5	1	1.5	1
O	3	3.75	6	4
P	1	1	1	1
Q	1	1	1	1
R	1	1	1	1

learned the business from the ground up, seemingly having faced virtually all possible crisis types. The network diagram made good sense, but the manager was really intrigued with the schedule statistics that could be derived from the network and associated activity times.

The manager was bidding on the project for which Table 13-5 represented the basic data. The schedule statistics shown in Figure 13-16 were developed. The estimated times were felt to be realistic and achievable, based on past experience. The bidding was competitive, and time performance was an important factor, because the pipeline operator would lose some revenue, in spite of the fact that an inventory was developed in activity B, since storage was limited. As a result of these facts, it was common to negotiate penalties for late performance in pipeline renewal contracts.

Because of the uncertainties and risks, the manager estimated values for a, m, b, and computed values for t_e in Table 13-6. The manager decided that an attractive completion date would be likely to win the contract. Therefore, the bid promised completion in 70 days, with penalties of $100 per day if actual completion time was greater than 65 days and $200 per day if greater than 70 days. The contract was awarded. Has the manager got a good deal? How likely are the penalties?

After the contract was awarded, the manager became depressed because 5 days were immediately lost because he could not start the job on time due to the interference of other contracts on which he was working. The manager generated the following possible actions to recover schedule time:

a.   Shorten t_e of activity B by 4 days at a cost of $100.

b.   Shorten b of activity G 5 days at a cost of $50.

c.   Shorten t_e of activity A by 2 days at a cost of $150.

d.   Shorten t_e of activity O by 2 days by drawing resources from activity N, thereby lengthening its t_e by 2 days.
    What should the manager do?

25.   The manager of the Pipeline Renewal Company is now concerned with resource utilization. Along with other data, Table 13-5 gave the normal crew requirements per day for each of the activities. When related to the ES schedule given by Figure 13-16, the manager developed the labor deployment chart shown in Figure 13-17.

Based on past experience, the manager had always been aware of the "lumpy" nature of the demand for worker-days on renewal projects. Figure 13-17 verified and dramatized the situation.

The nature of most of the tasks and skill levels was such that a generalized crew was used which could do all the tasks, with few exceptions. For example, activity L has a crew requirement of 25 workers for 6 days, or 150 worker-days. These 150 worker-days may be allocated over many chosen activity times, such as 10 workers for 15 days, or vice versa. The generalized crew provided great flexibility, allowing reallocation of labor between projects being carried on simultaneously. Also, adjustments for absence or vacations were relatively simple.

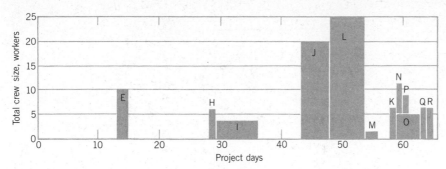

FIGURE 13-17
Worker deployment for the *ES* schedule using normal crew requirements for the pipeline renewal project. Only activities requiring the crew are shown.

The manager was now thinking of alternates to Figure 13-17 as ways of allocating labor to projects. There were a number of reasons for being dissatisfied with the current mode of operation. First, the lumpy nature of the typical situation shown in Figure 13-17 often resulted in idle crew time because of the mismatch of crew sizes and activity times. The company absorbed this idle time. Second, because of similar mismatches and schedule slippage, it was often necessary to work the crews overtime to meet deadlines. Third, the lumpy nature of demand often resulted in layoffs or in short-term hiring, with the usual costs of work force size fluctuation. In addition, the layoffs were a source of discontent among the crews.

In working with alternatives, the manager became aware that alternatives resulted in changes in activity times which sometimes affected the critical path. The manager was impressed, however, that schedule slack could be used to good effect in generating alternatives to Figure 13-17.

What alternate labor deployment do you recommend? Is the critical path affected by your recommendations?

26. Figure 13-18*a* is a nodes network diagram for a construction contract that shows the time in weeks to complete each activity and the normal schedule estimated cost for each activity. Figure 13-18*b* shows the computer output and indicates an overall project time of 11 weeks, the critical path, and the schedule statistics. The total contractor's cost is $31,500, but the contract price is $45,000.

The contractor's problem is that the costs are based on a normal completion of 11 weeks, but the customer insists on a 10-week time and a penalty for late performance of $2000 per week. The price is attractive because it provides the contractor with a $13,500 profit. Therefore, the contractor is interested in alternatives that might achieve the 10-week delivery schedule.

The contractor develops cost-time data for several of the activities; the following list indicates the reduction in weeks and the incremental cost:

A-One week, $1500

B-One week, $6000

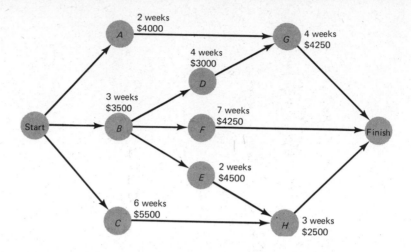

THE CRITICAL PATH IS

START → B → D → G → FINISH

THE LENGTH OF THE CRITICAL PATH IS 11

NODE	DURATION	EARLY START	EARLY FINISH	LATE START	LATE FINISH	TOTAL SLACK	FREE SLACK
START	0.00	0.00	0.00	0.00	0.00	0.00	0.00
A	2.00	0.00	2.00	5.00	7.00	5.00	5.00
B	3.00	0.00	3.00	0.00	3.00	0.00	0.00
C	6.00	0.00	6.00	2.00	8.00	2.00	0.00
D	4.00	3.00	7.00	3.00	7.00	0.00	0.00
E	2.00	3.00	5.00	6.00	8.00	3.00	1.00
F	7.00	3.00	10.00	4.00	11.00	1.00	1.00
G	4.00	7.00	11.00	7.00	11.00	0.00	0.00
H	3.00	6.00	9.00	8.00	11.00	2.00	2.00
FINISH	0.00	11.00	11.00	11.00	11.00	0.00	0.00

(b)

FIGURE 13-18
Construction contract project: (a) CPM network diagram showing time in weeks for the completion of each activity, and normal schedule activity costs, and (b) the computer output indicating the critical path, the overall project-time of 11 weeks, and the schedule statistics.

D-One week, $2000

G-One week, 1500; second week, $2000

The contractor is aware that changes in the activity times are sometimes "tricky," changing the critical path. What action should the contractor take?

*27. An architect has been awarded a contract to prepare plans and specifications

* This situation requires the application of concepts in Appendix E, Monte Carlo Simulation.

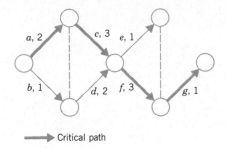

——► Critical path

FIGURE 13-19
Network diagram for the urban renewal project. Critical path is a-c-f-g.

for an urban renewal project. The activities required, their sequencing requirements, and estimated time requirements are as follows:

Activity	Description	Immediate Predecessors	Estimated Time, Days
a	Preliminary sketches	—	2
b	Outline of specifications	—	1
c	Prepare drawings	a	3
d	Write specifications	a, b	2
e	Run off prints	c, d	1
f	Have specifications printed	c, d	3
g	Assemble bid packages	e, f	1

Figure 13-19 is a network diagram for the performance of the project using the deterministic activity times given, showing the critical path as a-c-f-g. The critical path may be identified by inspecting the paths through the network and establishing the critical path as the longest time path or paths.

The architect reexamines the estimated activity times, because he is concerned about the effect of unanticipated events, a common occurrence in his office. He comes up with three time estimates for each activity together with the estimated probabilities of their occurrences as follows:

Activity	Optimistic Time	Optimistic Problem	Estimated Time	Estimated Problem	Pessimistic Time	Pessimistic Problem
a	1	0.1	2	0.6	4	0.3
b	0.5	0.1	1	0.5	2	0.4
c	2	0.2	3	0.6	5	0.2
d	1.5	0.1	2	0.6	3	0.3
e	0.5	0.1	1	0.8	1.5	0.1
f	2	0.3	3	0.4	4	0.3
g	0.5	0.1	1	0.7	1.5	0.2

The architect has agreed to finish the project in 10 days, with a $500 per day penalty for each additional day. What advice would you give the architect?

REFERENCES

Archibald, R. D., and R. L. Villoria, *Network-Based Management Systems.* Wiley, New York, 1967.

Buffa, E. S., and J. G. Miller, *Production-Inventory Systems: Planning and Control* (3rd ed.). Irwin, Homewood, Ill., 1979.

Burgess, A. R., and J. B. Killebrew, "Variation in Activity Level on a Cyclical Arrow Diagram," *Journal of Industrial Engineering, 13*(2), March–April, 1962, pp. 76–83.

Davis, E. W., "CPM Use in Top 400 Construction Firms," *Journal of the Construction Division,* ASCE, *100*(01), Proc. Paper 10295, March 1974, pp. 39–49.(a)

Davis, E. W., "Networks: Resource Allocation," *Industrial Engineering,* April 1974, pp. 22–32.(b)

Davis, E. W., "Project Scheduling Under Resource Constraints—Historical Review and Categorization of Procedures," *AIIE Transactions, 5*(4), December 1973, pp. 297–313.

Dewitte, L., "Manpower Leveling in PERT Networks," *Data Processing Science/Engineering,* March–April 1964.

Glasser, L., and R. Young, "Critical Path Planning and Scheduling: Application to Engineering and Construction," *Chemical Engineering Progress,* Vol. 57, November 1961.

Hanson, R. S., "Moving the Hospital to a New Location," *Industrial Engineering,* November 1972, pp. 32–38.

Levy, F. K., G. L. Thompson, and J. D. Wiest, "Multi-Shop Work Load Smoothing Program," *Naval Research Logistics Quarterly,* March 1963.(a)

Levy, F. K., G. L. Thompson, and J. D. Wiest, "The ABCs of the Critical Path Method," *Harvard Business Review,* September–October 1963, pp. 98–108.(b)

Malcolm, D. G., J. H, Rosebloom, C. E. Clark, and W. Fazar, "Application of a Technique for Research and Development Program Evaluation," *Operations Research, 7*(5), September–October 1959.

Meyers, H. B., "The Great Nuclear Fizzle at Old B. & W.," *Fortune,* November 1969, p. 123.

Moder, J. J., and C. R. Phillips, *Project Management with CPM and PERT* (2nd ed.). Reinhold, New York, 1970.

O'Brian, J., *CPM in Construction Management.* McGraw-Hill, New York, 1965.

Odom, R., and E. Blystone, "A Case Study of CPM in a Manufacturing Situation," *Industrial Engineering,* Vol. 15, No. 6, November–December 1964.

Reeves, E., "Critical Path Speeds Refinery Revamp," *Canadian Chemical Processing,* Vol. 44, October 1960.

Shaffer, L. R., J. B. Ritter, and W. L. Meyer, *The Critical Path Method.* McGraw-Hill, New York, 1965.

Smith, L. A., and P. Mahler, "Comparing Commercially Available CPM/PERT Computer Programs," *Industrial Engineering, 10*(4), April 1978, pp. 37–39.

Thamhain, H., and D. Wileman, "Conflict Management in Project Life Cycles," *Sloan Management Review, 16*(3), 1975, pp. 31–50.

Wiest, J. D., "A Heuristic Model for Scheduling Large Projects with Limited Resources," *Management Science, 13*(6), February 1967, pp. 359–377.

Wiest, J. D., and F. K. Levy, *A Management Guide to PERT/CPM* (2nd ed.). Prentice-Hall, Englewood Cliffs, N.J., 1977.

Wong, Y., "Critical Path Analysis for New Product Planning," *Journal of Marketing,* Vol. 28, No. 4, October 1964.

Woodwoth, B. M., and C. J. Willie, "A Heuristic Algorithm for Resource Leveling in Multi-Project, Multi-Resource Scheduling," *Decision Sciences,* 6(3), 1975, pp. 525–540.

CHAPTER 14

Service Systems and Scheduling Personnel

S ERVICE AND NONMANUFACTURING OPERATIONS HAVE AT LAST
been recognized as interesting and challenging arenas in which to work. The
great diversity of service and nonmanufacturing operations immediately
raises the question of whether or not they have enough in common for us to
generalize. Do they have enough in common with manufacturing systems so that
some of what we have learned in the manufacturing arena can be transferred? Although service and nonmanufacturing operations have some special characteristics,
they are sensitive to similar costs and pressures found in manufacturing. The problems of aggregate, personnel, and detailed planning and scheduling are as important
as they are in manufacturing.

EXAMPLE OF A SERVICE SYSTEM

We will use as an example a report of an outpatient clinic at the University of Massachusetts by Rising, Baron, and Averill [1973]. During the period of the study (1970–
1971) the Outpatient Clinic treated an average 400 to 500 patients per day with a staff
of 12 full-time physicians. Because of a variety of other duties, only 260 physician-hours per week were available during regular clinic hours, or nearly 22 hours per
physician per week. Only about half of the patients were seen by a physician on an
appointment or walk-in basis. The others were treated by nurses under a physician's
supervision or in specialized subclinics, involving tests or immunizations.

In aggregate terms, for the fall 1969 period, approximately 178 patients per day
needed access to an average of 52 available physician-hours. Thus the average time
with a physician was about 17.5 minutes.

Demand for Service

Part of the difficulty in rendering service is seen in Figure 14-1. Demand is not
uniform through the week, being approximately 20 percent above the average on
Mondays, 84 to 88 percent of the average on Thursdays, and increasing slightly on
Friday.

Furthermore, the daily variation is significant. Figure 14-2 shows arrival data for
Monday and Thursday (the days with the heaviest and lightest loads, respectively),
highlighting great demand variation during the day, with peaks at 8 A.M., 10 A.M., and
2 P.M. When the arrival data are placed on an interarrival time basis (time between
arrivals), they exhibit a negative exponential distribution, as shown in Figure 14-3.

Time for Service

The amount of time physicians spent with patients was measured in three separate
categories: walk-in, appointment, and second-service times. Figure 14-4 shows histograms of service times recorded for the three categories. The second-service category represents a return of the patient to the physician following diagnostic tests or
other intervening procedures. Although the three distributions are different, they
share the common general property of being skewed to the right and having relatively large standard deviations. Thus the average appointment service time is only

451

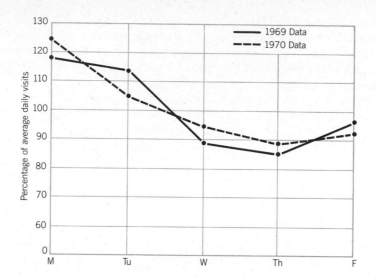

FIGURE 14-1
The percentage of patients arriving at a university health service to see either a physician or a nurse.
SOURCE: E. J. Rising, R. Baron, and B. Averill. "A Systems Analysis of a University-Health-Service Outpatient Clinic," *Operations Research, 21* (5), September–October 1973, p. 1034.

12.74 minutes, but the standard deviation is nearly 10 minutes, and the maximum recorded time is 40 minutes. These typical service time distributions reflect the variety of tasks involved in a consultation, depending on the nature of the complaint.

System Design Problems

With variable arrival patterns on both a day-of-the-week and an hour-of-the-day basis, and with highly variable service times depending on the type of patient, important problems result. First, what can be done to schedule appointments in order to smooth the patient load on physicians? How should appointment schedules be arranged through the week and the day in the light of demand variation? What overall capacity for service is actually needed? How long can patients reasonably be expected to wait for service? Is physician idle time justified? Would a system of priorities help level loading?

SCHEDULES FOR SERVICE SYSTEMS

Service-oriented organizations face unique scheduling problems. In all of these kinds of systems, demands for service and the time to perform the service may be highly variable. It often appears that no sensible schedule can be constructed if arrivals for service and service time are random. The result would be to maintain the capability for service at capacity levels sufficient to keep the waiting line to certain acceptable average levels—the service facility being idle for some fraction of time in order to provide service when needed. In a sense, scheduling of the personnel and physical facilities is simple in such situations, being controlled by policies for the hours during

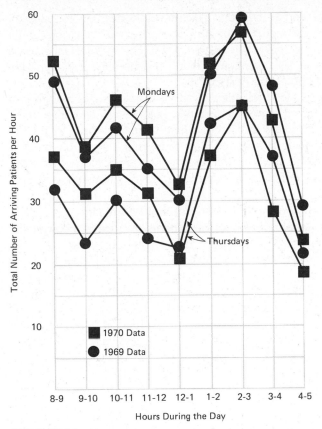

FIGURE 14-2
The hourly arrivals at the Student Health Service (Monday and Thursday averages for the fall semesters in 1969 and 1970).
SOURCE: E. J. Rising, R. Baron, and B. Averill. "A Systems Analysis of a University Health Service Outpatient Clinic," *Operations Research, 21*(5), September–October 1973, pp. 1030–1047.

which the service is to be available and for the service level to be offered. Schedules are then simple statements of "capacity for service," and personnel and other resources are keyed to these levels. The design for the size of maintenance crews has often been on this basis, for example.

Usually, however, we can improve on the system response of simply "keeping hours." Sometimes overall performance can be improved by a priority system, taking arrivals on other than a first-come-first-served basis. Also, improvements often result from examining the demand to see if there is a weekly and/or daily pattern. When a pattern exists, it may be possible to schedule more effectively to improve service facility utilization, shorten average waiting time, or both. Thus, we have three broad groups of situations: the one described by random arrivals at a service center that performs a service requiring variable time, one where priority systems are the basis for improved scheduling, and one in which arrivals follow some dominant pattern.

The random arrival, variable service time case is the classic waiting line or queuing problem. When the distribution of arrivals and service times follow certain known

453

mathematical functions, fairly simple equations describe flow through the system. These computations can be performed for simple situations such as a single-chair barbershop, a multiple server system as in supermarket check-out stands, or a serial set of operations such as an assembly line. Waiting line models are discussed in Appendix D, and Monte Carlo simulation in Appendix E.

One of the variables that may be controllable in waiting line systems is the order of processing of arrivals. For example, in medical facilities, patients will tolerate a priority system that allows emergency cases to be taken first. In machine shops, priority systems are often used to determine the sequence of processing jobs through a service center, as discussed in Chapter 11. Recall that computer simulation of alternate priority rules has shown that certain rules are more effective in getting work through the system on schedule.

When arrivals follow a dominant pattern, we can use that information to schedule personnel and facilities. For example, if arrivals of patients at a clinic followed the weekly pattern shown in Figure 14-1, we could use an appointment system to counterbalance the pattern and smooth the load over the week. Similarly, if the typical daily pattern for physicians' services in a clinic followed that shown in Figure 14-2, it could be counterbalanced both by an appointment system and by having a larger number of physicians on duty during the afternoon hours. If physicians could work different periods or shifts, we may be able to find quite good capacity-service solutions. Thus the entire subject of work shift scheduling becomes an important issue.

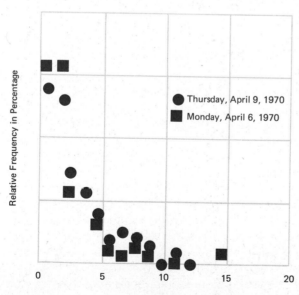

FIGURE 14-3
The frequency distribution of patient interarrival times. Monday, April 6, 1970: $\bar{x} = 2.167$, $s = 2.402$, $n = 237$. Thursday, April 9, 1970: $\bar{x} = 2.626$, $s = 2.838$, $n = 202$.
SOURCE: E. J. Rising, R. Baron, and B. Averill. "A Systems Analysis of a University-Health-Service Outpatient Clinic," *Operations Research, 21* (5), September–October 1973, pp. 1030–1047.

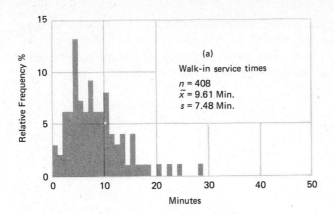

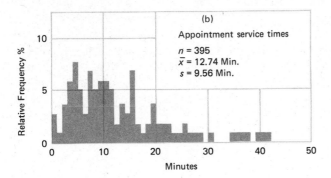

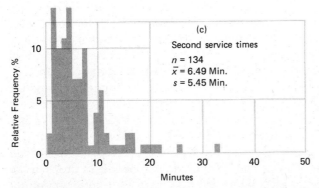

FIGURE 14-4

Histograms of service time for (a) walk-in, (b) appointment, and (c) second-service patients.

SOURCE: E. J. Rising, R. Baron, and B. Averill. "A Systems Analysis of a University-Health-Service Outpatient Clinic," *Operations Research, 21* (5), September–October 1973, pp. 1030–1047.

SCHEDULING PERSONNEL AND WORK SHIFTS

The objective in scheduling personnel and work shifts is to minimize labor costs, given service standards, or to establish some happy compromise between labor cost and service performance. Although our emphasis will be on personnel and shift scheduling itself, it is important to recognize that shift scheduling is a part of a larger process. The demand for the service must be forecast and converted to equivalent labor requirements by the hour of the day, day of the week, and so forth. Scheduling is then done in relation to these requirements, and finally individual workers must be assigned to the work days and shifts.

Noncyclic Personnel Schedules

Suppose that we are faced with hourly requirements that vary from hour to hour, day to day, week to week, and so on. Staffing the operation would require a continuous adjustment to the changing requirements. The demand variations may be caused by trend and seasonal factors, holidays, or weather conditions, depending on the nature of the particular operation. These kinds of personnel scheduling situations can be approached through the application of a simple concept, the "first-hour" principle [Browne and Tibrewala, 1975]. The first-hour principle is: Assign to start to work in the first period a number of workers equal to the number required in that period. For each subsequent period, assign the exact number of additional workers needed to meet requirements. When workers come to the end of their shifts, do not replace them if they are not needed. The procedure is best explained with the aid of an example. Assume the following sequence of worker requirements for the first 12 hours of a continuous operation (once assigned, workers continue working for an 8-hour shift):

Period	1	2	3	4	5	6	7	8	9	10	11	12
Requirement, R_i	5	5	7	8	9	10	15	14	12	10	10	10

In the following schedule, workers are added when they are needed, and we keep a running total of workers on duty in each period. For example, $X_i = 5$ workers are assigned in period 1 to work 8 hours. No additional workers are needed in period 2, because the requirement of 5 workers does not change. However, 2 additional workers must be assigned in period 3 to meet the total requirement of 7. In period 8, a total of $W_i = 15$ workers is on duty, but the 5 who were assigned in period 1 complete their shifts at the end of period 8, leaving a residual of 10 who continue into the ninth period. But 12 workers are required in period 9, so 2 additional workers must be assigned to start their shifts. In period 10, the requirement drops to 10, so no new workers are assigned. But in period 11, the 2 workers who were assigned in period 3 have completed their shifts, so the total on duty in period 11 drops to 10. In period 12, an additional worker must be assigned to maintain a total on duty of 10, because the worker assigned in period 4 goes off duty.

Period	1	2	3	4	5	6	7	8	9	10	11	12
Requirement, R_i	5	5	7	8	9	10	15	14	12	10	10	10
Assigned, X_i	5	—	2	1	1	1	5	—	2	—	—	1
On duty, W_i	5	5	7	8	9	10	15	15	12	12	10	10

The assignment procedure would continue in the same way as new requirements became known, in an endless chain.

Cyclic Personnel Schedules

Now, suppose that we have a stable situation, where the requirements pattern repeats. What is the stable staffing pattern that should be used to meet the cyclic requirements? Propp [1978] has shown that optimal solutions to these cyclic staffing problems can be developed by applying the first hour principle successively to the requirements schedule until the assignment pattern repeats. The repeating schedule is then the optimal cyclic staffing pattern. We choose as an example a 24-hour operation with a 12-hour cyclic requirements schedule where employees work only 4-hour shifts, as might be true if an operation were staffed by students who could work only part-time. This situation keeps the computations simpler for illustrative purposes.

Period	1	2	3	4	5	6	7	8	9	10	11	12
Requirements, R_i	4	6	8	8	9	7	9	7	7	7	6	5

Following the first day principle, the assignments would be:

Period	1	2	3	4	5	6	7	8	9	10	11	12
Requirements, R_i	4	6	8	8	9	7	9	7	7	7	6	5
Assigned, X_i	4	2	2	—	5	—	4	—	3	—	3	—
On duty, W_i	4	6	8	8	9	7	9	9	7	7	6	6

Continuing with the second cycle, 3 workers who started in period 9 complete their shifts at the end of period 12. Therefore, 3 workers continue, and 1 must be assigned to meet the requirement of 4 in the first period of the second cycle. No workers complete their shifts at the end of period 1, so 2 new workers must be assigned in period 2 to meet the requirement of 6, and so on.

Second Cycle

Period	1	2	3	4	5	6	7	8	9	10	11	12
Requirements, R_i	4	6	8	8	9	7	9	7	7	7	6	5
Assigned, X_i	1	2	5	—	2	—	7	—	—	—	6	—
On duty, W_i	4	6	8	8	9	7	9	9	7	7	6	6

Third Cycle

Period	1	2	3	4	5	6	7	8	9	10	11	12
Requirements, R_i	4	6	8	8	9	7	9	7	7	7	6	5
Assigned, X_i	—	—	8	—	1	—	8	—	—	—	6	—
On duty, W_i	6	6	8	8	9	9	9	9	8	8	6	6

Fourth Cycle

Period	1	2	3	4	5	6	7	8	9	10	11	12
Requirements, R_i	4	6	8	8	9	7	9	7	7	7	6	5
Assigned, X_i	—	—	8	—	1	—	8	—	—	—	6	—
On duty, W_i	6	6	8	8	9	9	9	9	8	8	6	6
Slack, $W_i - R_i$	2	0	0	0	0	2	0	2	1	1	0	1

The assignments, and workers on duty, for the third and fourth cycles are identical, would continue to repeat with additional cycles, and are optimal. The staffing pattern shown in the third and fourth cycles should be applied repetitively as long as the requirements pattern remains stable. The resulting slack of 9 worker-hours in the resources applied is shown in the bottom row of the fourth cycle. The sum of the requirements over the 12-hour period is 83 worker-hours, and $83 + 9 = 92$ worker-hours were used.

Weekly Schedules for Seven-Day Operations

Many service and some manufacturing operations must operate on a 7-day per week basis, employing labor that normally works approximately 40 hours. Legal requirements and company-union work rules result in constraints concerning the permissible work periods. One of the simplest constraints is that each worker must be provided with two consecutive days off each week. There are often additional constraints concerning the number of weekend days off, lunch periods, rest breaks, and so on.

Figure 14-5a shows a typical situation in which the number of workers required involves a peak requirement of three workers on Wednesday, Thursday, and Friday, with only two workers being required the other 4 days. The weekly labor requirement is the sum of the daily requirements, or 17 worker-days. If each worker is guaranteed 5 days of work per week, then the minimum number of workers to staff the operation is 4, or 20 worker-days, resulting in three worker-days of slack capacity.

Figure 14-5b shows a configuration of the schedules for four workers that meets

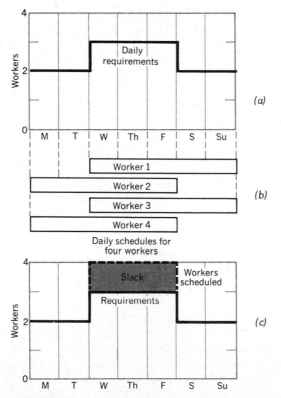

FIGURE 14-5

(a) Requirements for a 7-day per week operation, (b) daily schedule for four workers to meet requirements, and (c) comparison of requirements and workers scheduled with slack shown.

requirements, with each worker having two consecutive days off. Figure 14-5c shows the comparison of workers scheduled versus requirements, indicating the location of the slack associated with the peak days of Wednesday, Thursday, and Friday. Obviously, if part-time workers were available and fit in with other possible work rule constraints, a better solution would be to employ three full-time workers plus one part-time worker for 2 days per week. Such a solution would minimize labor costs, but provide no slack in the system during the peak load days.

Figure 14-5 provides a framework for the general situation that we wish to analyze. Solutions to that simple situation are fairly obvious, but we need a formal model to analyze such situations efficiently when the problems are larger and more complex.

Days Off Personnel Schedules

Suppose that we must staff an operation 7 days per week with personnel requirements each day by the following schedule:

	M	T	W	Th	F	S	Su
Required workers, R_i	2	2	2	2	2	2	3

If each worker is assigned a 5-day week with two consecutive days off, we have a seemingly difficult problem. However, if we sum the requirements, they total 15 worker-days. Theoretically, $15/5 = 3$ workers can be assigned to meet requirements, and in this case the objective can be met by the schedule:

	M	T	W	Th	F	S	Su
Worker 1	O	O	W	W	W	W	W
Worker 2	W	W	O	O	W	W	W
Worker 3	W	W	W	W	O	O	W

Days off are indicated by Os, and Ws are days worked. This schedule of three workers meets requirements and is optimal. The schedule is unique, there being no other way of scheduling the three workers to meet requirements, other than a simple reversal of the days off for workers 1 and 3.

The optimum schedule was generated by the use of simple rules that can be applied to larger problems with somewhat more variable requirements schedules. The computerized algorithm was developed by Browne [1979, 1980]. The algorithm starts with the requirements schedule and assigns days off for worker 1, subtracts the requirements satisfied by worker 1 from the original schedule, and repeats the process until all workers have been assigned days off. Days worked for each worker are simply the 5 days that remain after days off are assigned.

We will use another example to explain the process. The requirements schedule at the time we assign days off to worker 1 is:

	M	T	W	Th	F	S	Su
R_1	3	3	4	3	3	1	2

Note that the total requirements for the week are 19 worker-days. The best possible solution will then require only four workers.

Step 1

Identify the maximum staffing requirement for the 7-day week, the next highest, third highest, and so on, until a unique pair of days off can be identified that includes the lowest level requirements. In case of ties, choose the days off pair with the lowest requirements on an adjacent day. If a tie still remains, arbitrarily choose the first of the available tied pairs, assuming that Monday is the beginning of a cycle. The days off assignment should always involve the lowest requirements in the schedule.

The unique pair for our example is S-Su. That pair is circled as the assigned days off for worker 1. The unique pair could have been in the middle of the week; for example, if the requirements for the Monday through Sunday schedule were 5-5-2-1-4-4-5, the unique days off would be W-Th.

Step 2

The requirements for the work days are reduced by 1, reflecting the days worked by worker 1, to produce a requirements schedule used to assign days off for worker 2. Because none of the S-Su requirements have been satisfied, they are carried forward to R_2. For our example, the original and reduced schedules are:

	M	T	W	Th	F	S	Su
R_1	3	3	4	3	3	(1	2)
R_2	2	2	3	2	2	1	2

Repeat Step 1. In R_2, the maximum requirement is three workers, followed by tied requirements of 2 on Su-M-T, and Th-F. The lowest requirement of 1 is on S, being adjacent to the next lowest requirements of 2 on F and Su. We could choose either F-S or S-Su as the days off assignment for worker 2, and we arbitrarily choose the first of these, F-S. The assignment of F-S as the days off for worker 2 is made by circling these days in R_2, and Step 2 is repeated. One day is subtracted from worker 2's workdays to produce R_3:

	M	T	W	Th	F	S	Su
R_1	3	3	4	3	3	(1	2)
R_2	2	2	3	2	(2	1)	2
R_3	1	1	2	1	2	1	1

In R_3, the maximum requirement is two workers on W and F, followed by ties of one worker required on all other days. We choose the first tied pair on M-T as the days off assignment for worker 3, and one day is subtracted for each work day in R_3 to produce R_4.

	M	T	W	Th	F	S	Su
R_1	3	3	4	3	3	(1	2)
R_2	2	2	3	2	(2	1)	2
R_3	(1	1)	2	1	2	1	1
R_4	1	1	1	0	1	0	0

The unique pair of days off at minimum requirements is S-Su. Reduction of R_4 results in 0 requirements for all days, completing the schedule. The work days and days off are summarized as follows:

Worker	M	T	W	Th	F	S	Su
1	W	W	W	W	W	O	O
2	W	W	W	W	O	O	W
3	O	O	W	W	W	W	W
4	W	W	W	W	W	O	O
Workers, W_i	3	3	4	4	3	1	2
Slack, $S_i = W_i - R_i$	0	0	0	1	0	0	0

The solution is optimal, because requirements have been met with four workers. The total slack is 1 day on Thursday. The slack can be used to generate alternate solutions.

Weekend Peak Example. Now suppose that the personnel requirements emphasize a week-end load. The following schedule has a total weekly requirement of 20 worker-days and can theoretically be satisfied by four workers, each working 5 days, with two consecutive days off:

	M	T	W	Th	F	S	Su
R_1	3	2	2	2	3	4	4

Applying the choice rules, we obtain the following schedule:

	M	T	W	Th	F	S	Su
R_1	3	(2	2)	2	3	4	4
R_2	2	2	(2	1)	2	3	3
R_3	(1	1)	2	1	1	2	2
R_4	1	1	1	(0	0)	1	1
W_i	3	2	2	2	3	4	4
S_i	0	0	0	0	0	0	0

The solution is optimal with no slack. There are variations on the schedule because of the overlapping days off, but these are actually variations of the same basic schedule, with pairs of workers exchanging days off. The following days-off patterns are also optimal.

Worker	Days Off Schedule			
	1	2	3	4
1	TW	TW	MT	WTh
2	MT	MT	TW	MT
3	WTh	ThF	WTh	TW
4	ThF	WTh	ThF	ThF

Rotating Schedules. The schedules illustrated in our examples are assumed fixed. Each employee works a specific cyclic pattern with specified days off. Because of the desire for free weekends, there is the possibility of workers rotating through the several schedules. This creates a different problem, because the number of work days between individual schedules will vary. For example, the schedule that we used to explain the days-off algorithm resulted in,

461

	Work Days	Days Off
Worker 1	M-F	S, Su
Worker 2	Su-Th	F, S
Worker 3	M-F	S, Su
Worker 4	W-Su	M, T

If one rotates through these schedules, the number of work days between days off is variable. Shifting from the first schedule to the second, there are only 4 work days between days off; from the second to the third, 6 work days; from the third to the fourth, zero work days, there being two consecutive sets of days off. If the sequence of the schedules is changed, patterns of work days between days off will also change, but the new pattern will probably also have problems. These variations in numbers of work days between rotating schedules are often unacceptable, even though they average out over a period of time.

Additional Work Rule Constraints. Baker and Magazine [1977] provide algorithms for days-off constraints in addition to the two consecutive days-off situation that we have discussed. These more constraining situations include the following:

1. Employees are entitled to every other weekend off and to 4 days off every 2 weeks.
2. Employees are entitled to every other weekend off and to two pairs of consecutive days off every 2 weeks.

When part-time workers can be used, the problem of scheduling personnel is eased somewhat. The scheduling of the part-time workers themselves then becomes an interesting problem.

Using Part-Time Workers

When demand for service varies significantly, but follows a fairly stable weekly pattern, the use of part-time employees can give managers added flexibility. Mabert and Raedels [1976] reported such an application involving eight branch offices of the Purdue National Bank. Typical demand for service in the branches is shown in Figure 14-6; Mondays and Fridays usually exhibit peak demand. The problem also involved the anticipation of increased demand for service on paydays.

Traditionally, the bank employed only full-time tellers to meet requirements. This policy required staffing to meet peak demand and resulted in relatively poor average staff utilization during the week. Bank management later changed the staffing policy by employing full-time tellers equal to minimum expected demand and by using part-time tellers to staff the peak needs.

Problem Formulation. The basic problem involved determining the minimum cost teller assignments for the eight-branch system and, secondarily, minimizing (1) the number of part-time tellers, and (2) the teller transfers between branches. Although Mabert and Raedels used an integer programming formulation of the problem, the size of the problem limits the use of this technique. The scale of such a mathematical programming problem increases rapidly with the number of branches because of the

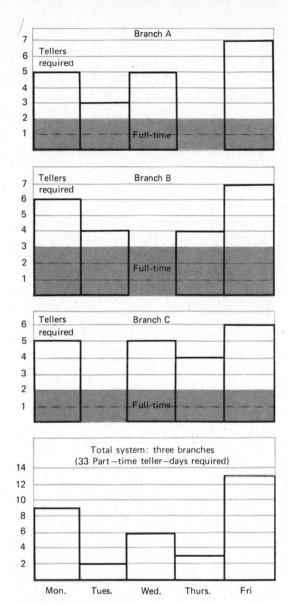

FIGURE 14-6
Teller requirements for three branches and aggregate system part-time teller requirements.
SOURCE: V. A. Mabert, and A. R. Raedels. "The Detail Scheduling of a Part-Time Work Force: A Case Study of Teller Staffing," *Decision Sciences, 8,* January 1977, pp. 109–120.

increasing number of possible alternate work assignments. Therefore, other techniques were needed for a practical solution.

Heuristic Assignment Procedure. The Heuristic Assignment Procedure (HAP) starts with a requirements schedule (such as in Figure 14-6*d*). Because the Friday schedule requires 13 part-time tellers, this is the feasible minimum number of tellers. A decreasing demand histogram, shown in Figure 14-7, is then developed from Figure 14-6*d*. For example:

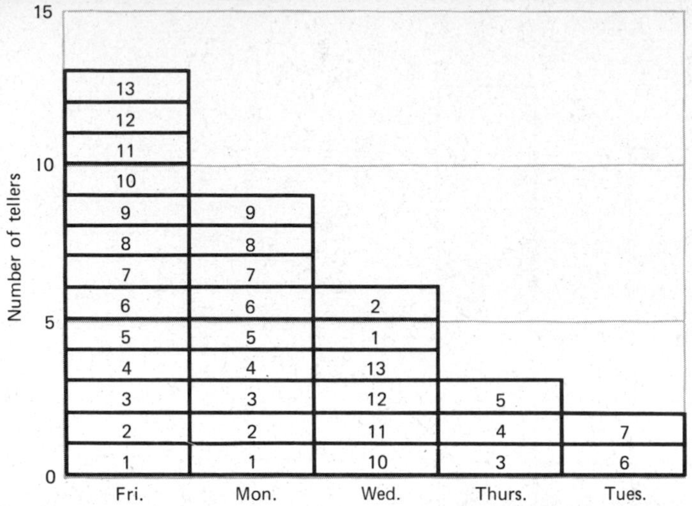

FIGURE 14-7
Assignment of part-time tellers to decreasing-demand histogram. Beginning with the highest-demand day, tellers are assigned in sequence from 1 to 13 in cycles until all 33 teller blocks have been assigned.
SOURCE: V. A. Mabert, and A. R. Raedels, "The Detail Scheduling of a Part-Time Work Force: A Case Study of Teller Staffing," *Decision Sciences, 8,* January 1977, pp. 109–120.

Friday—13 tellers required

Monday—9 tellers required

Wednesday—6 tellers required

Thursday—3 tellers required

Tuesday—2 tellers required

The 13 tellers are then assigned in sequence, beginning with Friday and progressing through the daily requirements, according to the preceding sequence of days. The teller numbers simply are repeated until all 33 requirement blocks have been assigned a part-time teller number. A feasible set of 2- and 3-day teller schedules can be abstracted from Figure 14-7, as follows:

Teller	Daily Work Schedule
1, 2	M, W, F
3, 4, 5	M, Th, F
6, 7	M, Tu, F
8, 9	M, F
10, 11, 12, 13	W, F

The aggregate schedule is disaggregated by assigning schedules to branches by means of a heuristic procedure. First assignments are made within branches until branch requirements are met, as far as possible, without transfers. Then, unassigned tellers are assigned between branches to cover the remaining requirements. For the

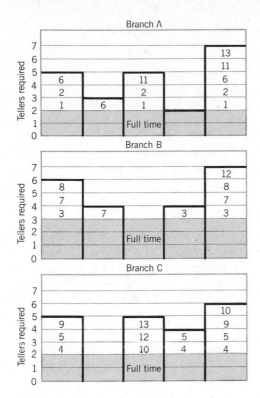

FIGURE 14-8
Assignments of part-time tellers to branches using the *HAP* procedure.
SOURCE: V. A. Mabert, and A. R. Raedels. "The Detail Scheduling of a Part-Time Work Force: A Case Study of Teller Staffing," *Decision Sciences, 8,* January 1977, pp. 109–120.

sample three-branch problem, Figure 14-8 shows that tellers 12 and 13 need to be transferred between branches. Teller 12 transfers between branches B and C, and teller 13 between A and C.

According to Mabert and Raedels, the Purdue National Bank has been using the HAP technique on a manual basis so successfully that the scheduling of part-time tellers save the 8-branch system about $30,000 per year.

WORK SHIFT SCHEDULING

Thus far, we have considered methods for scheduling requirements that vary on a weekly basis. There are many situations where operations are required on a 24-hour basis and where the variations in labor requirements are severe during the work period. Much of the development of methods for dealing with the problem have occurred in the telephone industry, but the applications occur in a wide variety of other service and manufacturing operations also. The following description of a system describes the problem and a practical way of dealing with it.

465

GENERAL TELEPHONE—AN INTEGRATED
WORK SHIFT SCHEDULING SYSTEM

The general concepts of work shift scheduling have been applied at the General Telephone Company of California in an integrated, computerized system. The company has used the system since 1973 to schedule approximately 2600 telephone operators in 43 locations in California. The size of installations ranges approximately from 20 to 220 operators.

The system combines a computerized forecasting system and conversion to operator requirements, the scheduling of tours or shifts, and the assignment of operators to shifts.*

Demand for Service

The service offered is the telephone exchange: operators are assigned to provide directory assistance, coin telephone customer dialing, and toll call assistance. The standard for service is supplied by the Public Utilities Commission in unusually specific terms: Service must be provided at a resource level such that an incoming call can be answered within 10 seconds 89 percent of the time. The difficulty in implementing the response standard lies in the severe demand variability of incoming calls.

Figures 14-9 to 14-12 show typical call variations during the year, the week, the day, and within a peak hour. Figure 14-9 shows the annual variation, highlighting

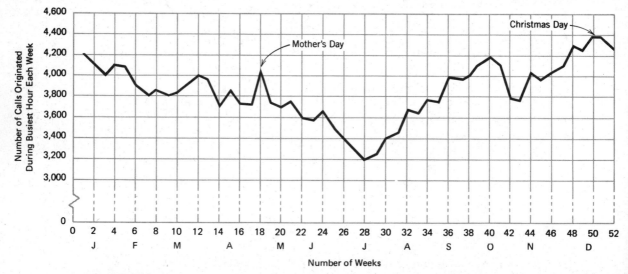

FIGURE 14-9
Typical distribution of calls during the busiest hour for each week during a year.
SOURCE: Figures 14-9 to 14-17 are from E. S. Buffa, M. J. Cosgrove, and B. J. Luce. "An Integrated Work Shift Scheduling System," *Decision Sciences*, 7, October 1976. (Courtesy, General Telephone Company of California.)

* The materials in this section are from E. S. Buffa, M. J. Cosgrove, and B. J. Luce, "An Integrated Work Shift Scheduling System," *Decision Sciences*, 7(October 1976).

the two sharp peaks that were made during the busiest hour in each of the 52 weeks. The minimum occurred in the twenty-eighth week (3200 calls), and the maximum occurred during Christmas (4400 calls). The peak-to-valley ratio is 1.38 to 1. Translating the seasonal scheduling problem, the company must provide about 38 percent more capacity at Christmas time than in the twenty-eighth week, and in general the summer months involve a somewhat lighter load.

Figure 14-10 shows the daily call load for January 1972 at one location. The weekly pattern is very pronounced, and the Saturday and Sunday call load constitutes only about 55 percent of the typical load through the week. Although the telephone company offers somewhat lower weekend toll call rates to help smooth the load, the resultant weekly variation still is very large.

Figure 14-11 shows the half-hourly variation for a typical 24-hour period. Peak call volume is in the 10:30–11:00 A.M. period (2560 calls), and the minimum occurs at 4:30 A.M. (about 20 calls). The peak-to-valley variation for the typical half-hourly load is 128 to 1. Again, the telephone company offers somewhat lower nighttime toll call rates. Figure 14-11 suggests the daily problem of scheduling operator shifts to meet the load.

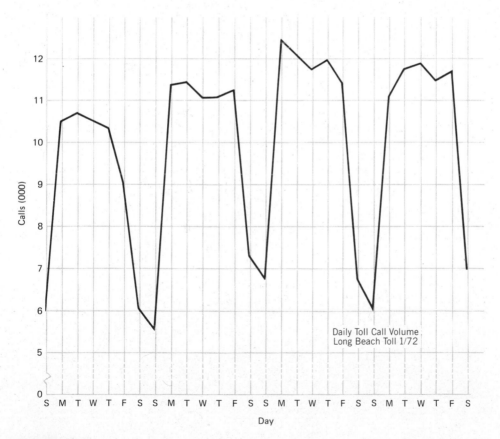

FIGURE 14-10
Daily call load for January.

Finally, Figure 14-12 shows the typical intrahour variation in call load, indicating the number of simultaneous calls by one minute intervals. This variation is random. In fact, continuous tracking of the mean and standard deviation of calls per minute indicates that the standard deviation is equal to the square root of the mean (a reasonably practical test for randomness) or that the arrival rates are described by the Poisson distribution. For the sample of Figure 14-12, $\bar{x} = 15.75$ calls per minute, $s = 4.85$ calls per minute, and $\sqrt{15.75} = 3.99$. Therefore, the variation within the hour is taken as random. We cannot cope with this variation by planning and scheduling. We must simply accept it and provide enough capacity to absorb the random variations.

The overall situation that results from the typical distributions of Figures 14-9 to 14-12 is that a forecastable pattern exists for seasonal, weekly, and daily variation. In addition, the call rate at any selected minute is described adequately by a Poisson distribution.

The Integrated System

Given the description of the demand for service, Figure 14-13 indicates the system developed at General Telephone. There are basically three cycles of planning and

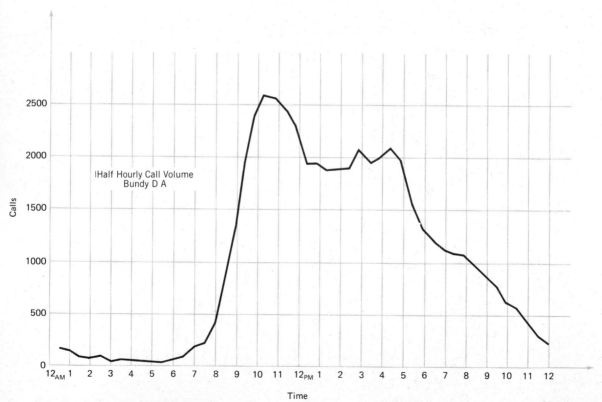

FIGURE 14-11
Typical half-hourly call distribution.

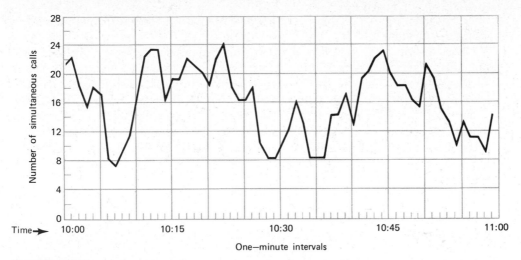

FIGURE 14-12
Typical intrahour distribution of calls, 10:00–11:00 A.M.

scheduling, which involve information feedback concerning actual experience. The forecast of daily calls is the heart of the system. As we will see, the forecast considers seasonal and weekly variation as well as trends. The forecast is converted to a distribution of operator requirements by half-hour increments. Based on the distribution of operator requirements, a schedule of tours or shifts is developed, and finally, specific

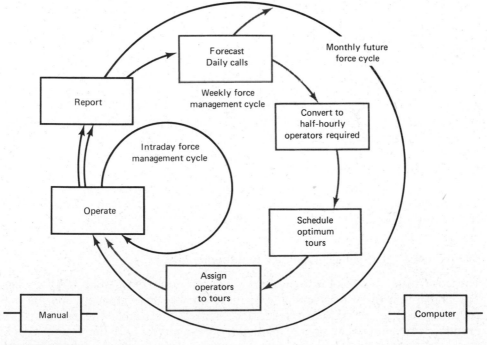

FIGURE 14-13
"Force Management System."

operators are assigned to tours. This sequence of modules is entirely computerized, as indicated in Figure 14-13.

Given the operator schedule, there are two additional cycles that operate on a manual basis. First, a schedule for "today" may be affected by unintended events, such as operator illness or an emergency increase in call load. Supervisors in local installations cope with such events, and this is the "Intraday Management Cycle" shown in Figure 14-13. In addition, there is the "Monthly Future Force Cycle," in which management can make higher level adjustments based on reports of actual operations and on forecasts involving particular trend and seasonal factors. The hiring and training of operators are planned in the future cycle, up to 12 months in advance.

Forecasting Demand

The demand forecasting system involves the following major terms if we are attempting to forecast the number of calls at a specific location for next Monday:

Calls next Monday = calls last Monday
$$+ \text{Weekly growth at this time last year}$$
$$(\text{Monday}_{-52} + \text{Monday}_{-53})$$
$$- \text{error last week} \times \theta$$
$$- \text{error 52 weeks ago} \times \phi$$
$$+ \text{error 53 weeks ago} \times \phi \times \theta$$

where θ is a nonseasonal moving average parameter, and ϕ is a seasonal moving average parameter. In other words, the forecasting model takes account of daily, weekly, and seasonal variations.

In terms of actual operation, the computer inputs are: last week's calls by day and type of service (toll, assistance, directory service); coefficients (work units per call) for the forecasted week by day and type of service; and board load (productivity) by day for the forecasted week. The computer outputs are forecasts of daily calls for up to five weeks in advance and a translation of the forecast into required board hours by day (also for up to five weeks in advance).

Forecast Errors. Figure 14-14 shows a typical record of comparison between forecasted and observed numbers of calls for Santa Monica. The uncanny forecast for day 151 is for Thanksgiving, and people predictably are more interested in dinner and family affairs than in communication. The average error for the forecasting system as a whole is 3.5 percent.

Conversion to Half-Hourly Operator Requirements

The objective at this point is to produce a daily schedule of operator requirements. The profile formed by the requirements curve is called the "topline," and the program required to generate it is called the "topline program." The program itself produces a printout of half-hourly operator requirements for each day in a week, and Figure 14-15 shows the formula for the conversion. The parameter that defines the model is average call duration, based on studies of actual times, efficiency, and the

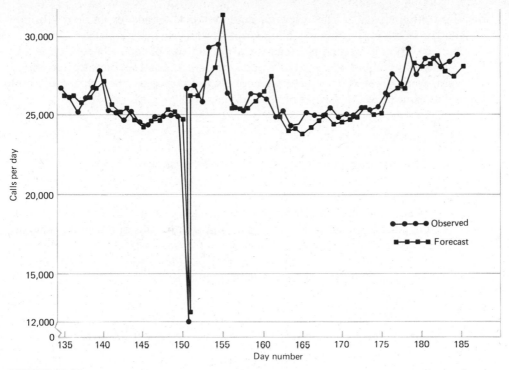

FIGURE 14-14
Sample of forecast versus observed numbers of calls at Santa Monica.

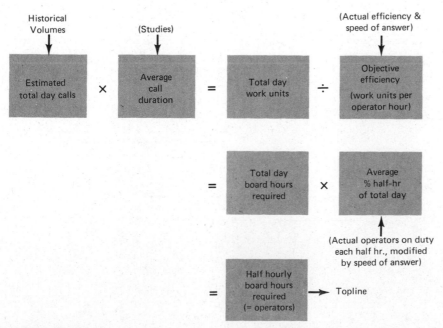

FIGURE 14-15
Model for conversion of calls to half-hourly operator requirements (topline).

response time standard. The response time standard (speed of answer) is a constraint. The result for each day is the information for the topline profile.

Actual half-hourly staffing is based on a percentage of total daily requirements. Exponential smoothing of each half-hourly percent is used to develop the topline program. A table based on a queuing model is used to adjust the actual half-hourly staffing to account for the speed of answering.

Scheduling of Shifts

The graphical representation of a topline profile is shown in Figure 14-16. The problem in assigning tours or shifts involves fitting in shifts so that they aggregate to the topline profile (also shown in Figure 14-16).

The Shift Set. To build up shifts so that they aggregate to the topline profile, we need flexibility in shift types, and we get it in the shift lengths and in the positioning of lunch hours and rest periods. A large shift set provides flexibility. On the other hand, the set of shifts is constrained by state and federal laws, union agreements, company policy, and practical considerations. Shifts in the set are actually selected

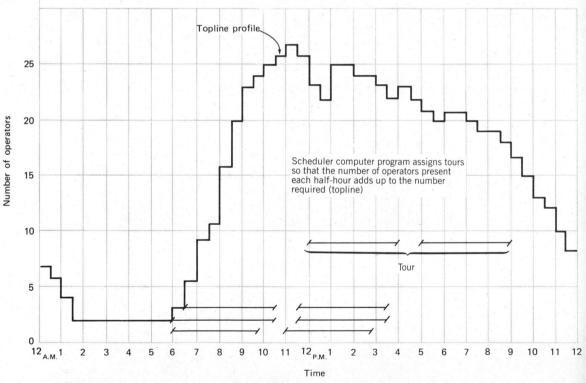

FIGURE 14-16
Topline profile and concept for assigning tours that aggregate to the topline.

based on California state restrictions, company policy, and local management input concerning the desirability of working hours by their employees.

Each shift consists of two working sessions separated by a rest period, which may be the lunch period. Each working session requires a 15-minute rest period near the middle of the session. The following rules enumerate the admissible shift set:

1.   Shifts are 6.5, 7, or 8 hours.
2.   Work sessions are in the range of 3 to 5 hours.
3.   Lunch periods either are a half-hour or an hour.
4.   Split work periods are in the range of 3.5 to 5 hours (split work periods are separated by more substantial nonwork periods).
5.   Eight-hour shifts end before 9 P.M.
6.   Seven-hour shifts end from 9:30 to 10:30 P.M.
7.   Six-and-a-half-hour shifts end at 11:00 P.M. or later.
8.   Earliest lunch period is at 10:00 A.M.

The Scheduling Algorithm. Luce [1973] developed a heuristic algorithm for assigning shifts from the approved set so as to minimize the absolute differences between operators demanded by the topline profile in period i, D_i, and the operators provided, W_i, when summed over all n periods of the day; that is,

$$\text{Minimize} \sum_{i=1}^{n} |D_i - W_i| \tag{1}$$

The strategy is to build up the operator resources in the schedule, one shift at a time, drawing on the universal set of approved shifts. The criterion stated in Equation 1 is used to choose shifts at each step. As the schedule of W_i values is built up, conceptually, we attempt to minimize the distance between the schedules of demand and the number of operators supplied, as illustrated by Figure 14-17.

At each stage in building up the schedule, some remaining distance between D_i and W_i exists. The criterion for the choice of the next shift is the following test on each alternate shift: Add the contributions of the shift to W_i (1 for all working periods and 0 for idle periods, such as lunch and rest periods), and recalculate Equation 1. Choose the shift that minimizes (1). To counteract the shorter length shifts that the preceding rule would favor, weight the different shorter shifts by the ratio of the working times. Thus, if the longest shift is 8 hours, then a 7-hour shift would be weighted $8/7 = 1.14$.

As the number of time intervals and shift types increases, the computing cost increases. Luce states that computing costs are moderate when the number of time intervals is less than 100 and the number of shifts is less than 500.

As indicated in Figure 14-17, the final profiles for D_i and W_i do not coincide perfectly in any real case. Operators provided by the algorithm will be slightly greater or less than the demand, and the aggregate figures are a measure of the effectiveness of a given schedule.

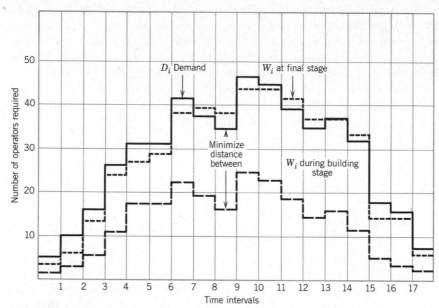

FIGURE 14-17

Concept of the scheduling building process, using the criterion, minimize $\sum_{i=1}^{n} |D_i - W_i|$.

Assigning Operators to Shifts

Given a set of shifts that meets the demand profile, the next step is to assign operators to shifts. The 24-hour day, 7-day week operation complicates this process: Important questions of equity arise regarding the timing of days off and the assignment of overtime work (which carries extra pay). Employee shift and other preferences, as well as seniority status, also must be considered.

Luce [1974b] developed a computing algorithm that makes "days-off" assignments within the following general rules:

1. Give at least 1 day off in a week.
2. Days off are 1 or 2.
3. Maximize consecutive days off.
4. If days off cannot be consecutive, maximize the number of work days between days off.
5. Treat weekends separately on a rotational basis to preserve equity, because:
   a. Overtime pay is given for weekend work.
   b. Weekends are the most desirable days off.
6. Honor requests for additional days off on a first come-first assigned basis.

The days off procedure must be carried out to assure that a final feasible schedule will result. Trading off for work days is allowed. The actual assignment of operators to shifts considers employee shift preferences. Each operator makes up a list of shifts in rank order. The list can have different preferences for each day of the week. The order of satisfying preferences is determined on a seniority basis, and in the matching process, assignments are made to the highest ranked shift available for each operator.

The final employee schedule for each day is a computer output. The schedule specifies for each operator the beginning and end of two work periods (separated by lunch) and the time for each of two rest periods.

During the first year, the company realized a net annual savings of over $170,000 in clerical and supervisory costs, as well as achieving a 6 percent increase in work force productivity. The company continues to use the system.

IMPLICATIONS FOR THE MANAGER

Level staffing of many activities, such as nursing and fire protection, has been the pattern in the past. Certainly, level staffing is the easiest strategy for managers to employ, the peak requirement determining the staffing level. But level staffing will be expensive in most cases, so managers need to consider alternatives. Scheduling to meet variable requirements is a way that managers can counter the system and remain in control.

Our society seems to demand more and more services to be available throughout the week and often on a 24-hour basis. Supermarkets, health services, food service, and even banks are faced with demand for extended hours. At the same time, we are beginning to consider seriously a variety of alternate work patterns, such as the 4-day week, reducing hours to 30 hours per week, 10 hours per day patterns now being discussed. Some of these proposals complicate personnel scheduling, whereas others may provide flexibility. Formal scheduling models will become even more valuable as the variety of work patterns increases. Fortunately, in most instances, rather simple algorithms can be used to schedule personnel within the constraints of work rules.

Work shift scheduling has been formulated as an integer programming problem, but the current state of the integer programming art does not permit the solution of large size real-world problems. Heuristic solutions have been used to obtain very good, although not optimal solutions. Integrated systems for scheduling work shifts have been developed in the telephone industry, in the postal service, and in nurse scheduling. These integrated systems make it possible to schedule shifts and personnel for fairly large operations, based on forecasts. Managers of such systems can meet service performance requirements at minimum cost on a routine basis.

IMPORTANT TERMS

Numbers in parentheses indicate page numbers

Cyclic personnel schedule (457)   First-hour principle (456)

Days-off schedule (459)   Heuristic Assignment Procedure, HAP (463)

Noncyclic personnel schedules (456)

Rotating personnel schedules (461)

Shift set (472)

Topline (470, 472)

Work shift scheduling (456)

REVIEW QUESTIONS AND PROBLEMS

1. What are the reasons why the personnel scheduling problem presents unique problems in service-oriented systems?

2. Table 14-1 provides a requirements schedule for the topline profile in Figure 14-16. Using the first hour principle, what is the staffing pattern for the first 24 hours of operation, assuming a noncyclic situation and 8-hour shifts?

3. Using the requirements data in Table 14-1, what is the staffing pattern assuming a cyclic situation? Employees work an 8-hour shift? Would you expect the first-hour principle to produce a schedule with more or less slack than the work shift scheduling algorithm for The General Telephone Company described in the text?

4. The following Monday through Sunday schedule of requirements is similar to the days off example used in the text, with the exception that the requirement for Thursday is four workers. The result is that no slack would be available if four workers could be scheduled with consecutive days off:

$$R_1: 3\ 3\ 4\ 4\ 3\ 1\ 2$$

Is it still possible to use only four workers to meet requirements? If so, are there alternate solutions?

5. A service operation is offered 7 days per week. Demand for the service converts to four workers required throughout the week. Work rules require that each worker be given two consecutive days off each week. How many workers will be required to staff the operation? Develop the schedule of days worked and days off for each worker.

6. Assume that the schedule of requirements in the previous problem is altered only in that the requirement for Sunday is six workers. Is it still possible to schedule the operation with the same number of workers? Does it make any difference whether or not the requirement of six workers occurs on Sunday or any other day of the week?

7. A service operation requires 5 workers per day, 7 days per week. Total weekly requirements are $5 \times 7 = 35$ worker-days per week. Theoretically, the 35

TABLE 14-1   **Requirements Schedule for the Topline Profile of Figure 14-16**

Period	1	2	3	4	5	6	7	8	9	10	11	12
Requirements, R_i	7	4	2	2	2	2	6	11	20	24	26	27
Period	13	14	15	16	17	18	19	20	21	22	23	24
Requirements, R_i	23	25	24	23	23	21	21	20	19	17	13	10

worker-days can be met with 35/5 = 7 workers, assuming that each worker must have two consecutive days off. Such a solution would have no slack. Is it possible?

8. State the nature of the formulation of the personnel scheduling problem in the bank teller study.

9. For the Mabert-Raedels bank teller study, define the Heuristic Assignment Procedure (HAP).

10. Summarize the results achieved by shift scheduling using part-time workers in the Purdue National Bank.

11. Define the important characteristics of the work shift scheduling problem.

12. What are the various work shift types that may be used? Do they represent constraints to scheduling solutions, or do they make the problem easier?

13. Describe the formal statement or formulation of the work-shift scheduling problem. What solution techniques have been proposed?

SITUATIONS

14. The following situation is based on a paper by Berry, Mabert, and Marcus [1975] dealing with forecasting of teller window demand at the Purdue National Bank and the conversion of demand to teller requirements. An exact count of customer traffic at the teller windows was not normally recorded. However, the system maintained information on the number of transactions processed, such as checks, cash tickets, deposit slips, and the like. It was decided to see if these transaction data could be related to the number of customers served per day. Then, through a knowledge of the average time spent with customers and the time that the tellers' windows were open for service, the number of tellers needed could be computed. The number of cash tickets processed was selected as the transaction, and a 9-week traffic survey was conducted to determine the actual number of customers requiring teller window service. Figure 14-18 shows the results of the survey with a linear regression line fitted to the points. The resulting regression equation is

Number of customers = 64.725 + 1.465 (cash tickets)

with a standard deviation of error of 129.72. The correlation coefficient was $r = 0.84$, and $r^2 = 0.71$.

In addition, the time to service the average customer was measured, based on a sample of 3000 customer transactions, indicating that a teller spent an average of $T = 1.5$ minutes per customer. The number of tellers required was then computed as

$$N = CT/L$$

where: C = number of customers forecast by the regression equation
T = average service time per customer in minutes
L = length of time the teller windows are open for service during the day, in minutes.

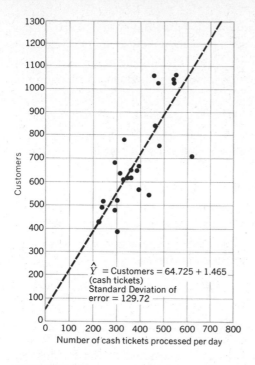

FIGURE 14-18
Customer versus cash ticket regression for the Purdue National Bank, Reserve Square Branch.
SOURCE: W. L. Berry, V. A. Mabert, and M. Marcus. "Forecasting Teller Window Demand with Exponential Smoothing." *Academy of Management Journal,* March 1979.

How do you evaluate this system for converting teller window demand to the number of tellers required? The actual time per transaction varied from as little as 30 seconds to 5 minutes, depending on the nature of the transaction. How can this variability be taken into account? How good would the service be if the average time were used?

15. Figure 14-19 shows the hourly variation in demand for fire service for three typical days in New York City. On the average day the 8 to 9 P.M. peak is 7.7 times the low point that occurs at 6 A.M. The peak of July 4 to 5 is 3.7 times the peak in the low day distribution. Traditional deployment policies in fire departments has been to keep the same number of fire fighters and units on duty around the clock. Also, traditional policies have tried to maintain a "standard response" of personnel and equipment to alarms in most areas at all times.

What staffing strategy should the fire department adopt in attempting to meet the demand for fire protection service? What risks should the department take with respect to the extreme demand days?

16. New York City installed an emergency telephone number (911) that citizens can use. The system has large "trunk" capacity, so that the probability of a busy signal is very small. A call to the system is automatically assigned either to an idle operator or to a first come-first served queue, and the first available operator is given the call automatically. The existence of the automatic system provides data concerning the frequency and timing of calls. Figure 14-20 shows

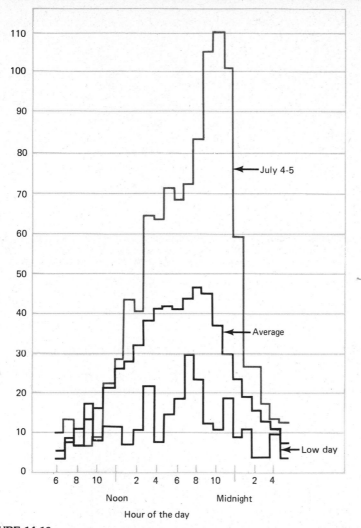

FIGURE 14-19
Total fire alarms received in New York City by hour—1968 data.
SOURCE: E. H. Blum. *Development Research of the New York City Fire Project,* The New York City Rand Institute, R-968, May 1962.

the daily variation in the number of calls in July and August. The high for the 2 months is approximately 22,000 calls per day and the low is 13,000, or a peak-to-valley variation of 1.69 to 1 (41 percent). Such variations have an enormous effect on the personnel planning and scheduling problem and on the resultant costs.

Figure 14-21 shows the hourly variations for Saturday, August 10 (note that most of the peaks in Figure 14-20 occur on Saturdays). Calls are most numerous from approximately 8 P.M. until midnight, occurring at about 1400 per hour, and lowest at 5 A.M., at about 100 calls per hour. This results in a peak-to-valley variation of 14 to 1. Note that the staffing levels for receiving the emergency calls vary only approximately 60 percent. The authors give similar distributions for other days of the week that have lower peaks, and each day

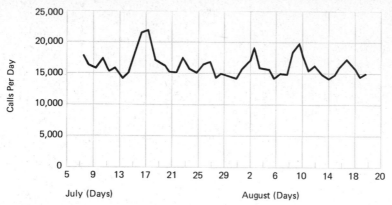

FIGURE 14-20
Number of calls received per day.
SOURCE: Adapted from R. C. Larson. "Improving the Effectiveness of New York City's 911," in *Analysis of Public Systems,* edited by A. W. Drake, R. L. Keeney, and P. M. Moorse. MIT Press, Cambridge, Mass., 1972.

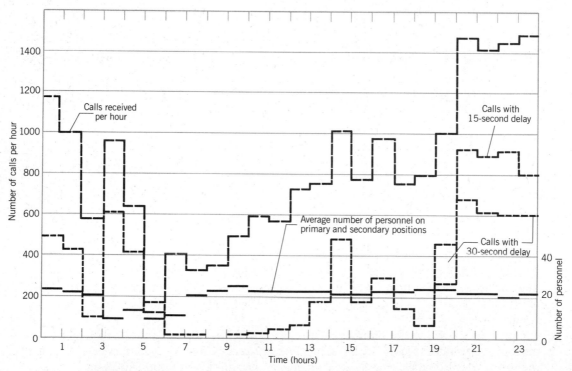

FIGURE 14-21
Distribution of calls, delays, and manning levels (Saturday, August 10).
SOURCE: R. C. Larson. "Improving the Effectiveness of New York City's 911," in *Analysis of Public Systems,* edited by A. W. Drake, R. L. Keeney, and P. M. Morse. MIT Press, Cambridge, Mass., 1972.

the load was met by a somewhat different staffing schedule. Figure 14-21 also contains two additional records of the number of calls per hour that involved a 15-second delay and a 30-second delay.

How do you appraise the staffing strategy indicated by the number of personnel on duty in Figure 14-21? How long a delay in answering is appropriate, or tolerable? What staffing strategy should the police department use for this situation?

17. For this situation, refer to the discussion of the university outpatient clinic near the beginning of the chapter. Figures 14-1 and 14-2 provide data on weekly, daily, and hourly variations of arrivals at the Student Health Service. In addition, Figure 14-4 provides histograms for the service time for three kinds of patients. Reread the materials describing the situation of the outpatient clinic.

What staffing strategy should the outpatient clinic maintain for its physicians? How can one take account of the kinds of weekly, daily, and hourly variations shown? How is this situation different from those described for fire and police protection in situations 15 and 16?

18. After reading the description of the General Telephone Company integrated shift scheduling system in the text, consider the following questions:

a. If in labor negotiations, union and management agreed on a standard 8-hour shift for all personnel, what would the impact be on the work scheduling system?

b. Do you think that the methods of assigning operators to shifts and to days off are fairly typically acceptable throughout industry? If not, why are they acceptable in the telephone industry?

c. How do you appraise the integrated work shift scheduling system installed at the General Telephone Company of California?

*19. The Ushop Department Store is reevaluating its staffing policy in the ready-to-wear department because of customer complaints about service time. The store operates from 9 A.M. to 9 P.M. Sales personnel work in 6-hour shifts either from 9:00 A.M. to 3:00 P.M., or from 3:00 P.M. to 9:00 P.M. Lunch breaks are staggered.

There are currently four salespeople in the department each shift, who are paid $9600 per year, at the hourly rate of $4.80. The manager knows that service could be improved by simply adding another salesperson each shift. However, she hesitates to add to the labor cost because overall sales volume has not changed perceptibly. Instead of taking a seat-of-the-pants approach, she decides to call on the staff of the corporate systems group to study the situation and provide data.

The systems analyst first decides to find out how the existing sales staff spends its time. They perform a work sampling study which results in the data shown in Figures 14-22 and 14-23. Work sampling is a sampling technique that requires a large number of observations of the "state" of employees when being observed. The five states used in the study are indicated in Figures 14-22

---

* This situation requires the application on concepts in Appendix D, waiting lines.

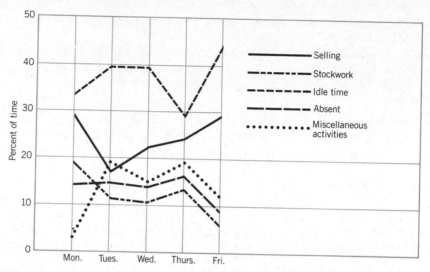

FIGURE 14-22
Store activity by day of week.
SOURCE: R. J. Paul, and R. E. Stevens. "Staffing Service Activities with Waiting Line Models," *Decision Sciences,* Vol. 2, April 1971, pp. 206–218.

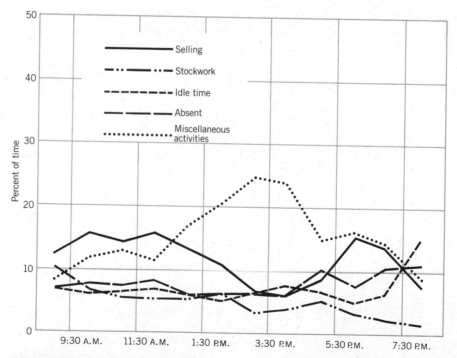

FIGURE 14-23
Store activity by hour of day.
SOURCE: R. J. Paul, and R. E. Stevens. "Staffing Service Activities with Waiting Line Models," *Decision Sciences,* Vol 2, April 1971, pp. 206–218.

TABLE 14-2   **Waiting Line Statistics for Three Allocations of Salespeople**

M, Number of Sales-people	L_q, Average Length of Waiting Line	W_q, Average Customer Waiting Time, Min.	W, Average Customer Time in System, Including Service, Min.	Average percent Utilization of Sales Staff = $\lambda/M\mu \times 100$
4	1.5282	5.1	15.1	75
5	0.3541	1.2	11.2	60
6	0.0991	0.3	10.3	50

and 14-23. By taking a large number of observations, the percent of time spent in each activity can be estimated. The precision of the estimates depends on the sample size. The details of the work sampling technique are covered in Appendix F of the text.

The work sampling study also produced estimates of the average number of customer arrivals as $\lambda = 18$ per hour, and the average service time of $T = 10$ minutes, or an average service rate of $\mu = 60/10 = 6$ per hour. From these data, the analyst produced Table 14-2, based on calculations from a waiting line model, assuming a Poisson distribution of arrivals and a negative exponential distribution of service times. (The data are calculated from the multiple server model discussed in Appendix E, using Table G-3.):

When the data were presented, they seemed generally helpful to the manager. She sees a problem, however, in how to judge the value of customer waiting time versus the cost of sales personnel. She examines the usefulness of contribution and cost data: the contribution of a $100 sale is $30; the major elements of variable costs are $55 for material, $10 for sales labor, and $5 for miscellaneous costs. The manager also wonders what additional useful information might be available from Figures 14-22 and 14-23, and the possibility of variable staffing.

What action should the manager take?

20. Edwards Discount Department Stores, Inc., is a chain that operates throughout the Midwest. They carry an excellent line of merchandise and also try to offer good service at the checkout stands by providing store managers with a relatively good labor budget, 50 percent of which is allocated for checker labor. In the past, the store manager has had the responsibility for allocating the checker labor budget with little or no interference by nor help from corporate headquarters. The result has been good but often variable service in terms of the waiting time that customers have experienced at the checkout stands. Some store managers have been quite successful in scheduling checker operators to match customer arrival patterns, but some have not despite the liberal budget. The result of a poor match is idle checkers at some times and longer than desired customer waiting times at other times, and customer complaints.

Competition has been increasing and Jonathan Edwards, president and chief executive officer of Edwards feels that they can tighten up checker labor budgets and still maintain or even improve their excellent service by providing store managers with better information and training that should enable them to obtain improved utilization of what they intend will be smaller checker labor budgets. Mr. Edwards has therefore hired a consultant to recommend a scheduling system that can be used by store managers. Mr. Edwards wants to provide help to store managers by improved information and systems, but recognizes that short-term local conditions require the scheduling decisions to be made locally.

Elements of the Consultant's Recommendations

The basic structure of the consultant's recommended system is shown in Figure 14-24. The output of the system is the required number of checker hours for each hour of each day for the upcoming week. Given this requirements schedule, the store manager could develop work assignments for each checker using a form provided by the system. The requirements reflected the weekly sales forecast, the mix of purchases through the AT (average transaction amount,

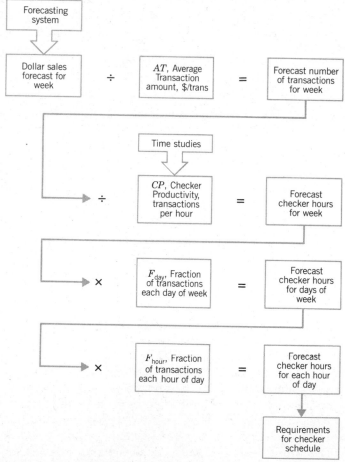

FIGURE 14-24
Calculation of checker operator requirements.

which changed with the season and price adjustments), the *CP* (checker productivity), the pattern of transactions each day of the week through F_{day} (the fraction of weekly transactions that occur each day of the week), and the pattern of transactions each hour of the day through F_{hour} (the fraction of daily transactions that occur each hour of the day). Seasonality was reflected through the sales forecast and through the figure used for *AT*. Inflation and changing consumer purchase mix was reflected through periodic updating of the values for *AT*. The values of *CP*, F_{day}, and F_{hour} were all fairly stable. If the checkout system itself should change, then new time studies would be required to determine new average values for *CP*.

Implementation of the Recommendations

The system had to be one that the store managers could use manually, because no computers were available for each store. Therefore, the consultant had developed straightforward forms to be used in the necessary calculations. As a trial the consultant was asked to train Jeff Higgins, manager of store No. 43. Jeff's record as a scheduler was relatively poor, and Mr. Edwards felt that if the consultant could make the system work well with Jeff, then it had promise for the system as a whole. Higgins was no fuddyduddy, for his store had a good general performance record, but he controlled costs very tightly and, Mr. Edwards thought, too tightly on checker labor.

On being approached by the consultant, Jeff saw the opportunity to get the scheduling done for the upcoming week while gaining an understanding of the proposals, so he suggested that they use that data as an example.

The Upcoming Week as an Example

The consultant pointed out that they would have to generate some important data based on Jeff's particular operations, such as the load patterns on days of the week and hours of the day, and so on. There were six forms involved and the consultant suggested that they simply march through what would be required in each. When the consultant displayed the forms, Jeff shuddered and moaned, "more forms!"

Form 1 (Figure 14-25). The purpose of this form was to determine the daily pattern of customer arrivals by hour of the day, and the amount of transactions so that other important data could be computed. Fortunately, all the raw data needed was available from the cash register tapes, but to make it useful, the tapes had to be read at the end of each hour, and the total dollar transactions recorded at the end of the day for each register.

The consultant explained that at the end of the day the manager need only enter the dollar sale for the register, and successively subtract the register readings to obtain the differences for each register. These differences represented the number of transactions in each hour for the register. Then by totaling the columns for each hour he could obtain the total number of transactions in each hour for all registers. Then, F_{hour} was easily computed by dividing each hourly total by the grand total of transactions for each day (shown at the bot-

Form 1							Day of Week Wednesday							
Register No.	10 AM	11 AM	12 N	1 PM	2 PM	3 PM	4 PM	5 PM	6 PM	7 PM	8 PM	9 PM	Final Read	Final Sales
1	4592	4592	4592	4592	4607	4639	4663	4672	4672	4672	4674	4680	4680	$1248
Diff.		0	0	0	15	32	24	9	0	0	2	6	0	
2	8296	8296	8296	8298	8298	8319	8349	8349	8354	8354	8354	8354	8354	$ 464
Diff.		0	0	12	0	21	30	0	5	0	0	0	0	
.														
.														
.														
.														
.												Total sales in day		$6249
Tot. Col. Diff.	33	65	28	85	83	54	42	63	51	89	16		0 (Sum of diff = 609)	
F_{hour}, Diff/ Sum	0.054	0.107	0.046	0.140	0.136	0.088	0.069	0.103	0.084	0.146	0.026	0		

FIGURE 14-25

Form 1 for calculating F_{hour}, and amount of transactions.

tom of Form 1). For example, $F_{10-11} = 33/609 = 0.054$ is the fraction of transactions that occurred between 10 A.M. and 11 A.M. for the Wednesday used as an example.

"It looks like a lot of fussy work," said Jeff. The consultant admitted that it was, but stated that once you have the data on F_{hour} you need not repeat the data gathering phase day after day and week after week because the fractions seem to remain stable. "How do you know that?" replied Jeff. The consultant said that he had performed an analysis of variance to determine if there were differences in the fractions of transactions from hour to hour on different days of the week. He said that the F test showed that the F value from the test was considerably less than the F value required for the 90 percent confidence level. Jeff just stared at the consultant, but what he was thinking could not be aired on TV. Jeff said, "I guess you are taking the long way around to tell me that you have scientific evidence that the F_{hour} values don't change from day to day." Then the consultant hedged a bit, saying that the pattern was very stable from Monday through Friday, but the F test rejected the Monday through Sunday sequence. Somehow, Saturdays and Sundays were different. "We may have to continue to gather Saturday–Sunday data and perform some more statistical tests." Jeff decided to accept the consultant's appraisal for the moment. "OK, what do we do next?"

Form 2 (Figure 14-26). The purpose of Form 2 was to calculate F_{day} (fraction of transactions that occur on each day of the week) and AT (average transaction amount). As the consultant explained, the data required for this form come

Form 2   Sales and Transaction Summary, Week Ending _____

Trans-actions	Mon.	Tues.	Wed.	Thurs.	Fri.	Sat.	Sun.	Weekly Total
No., N	484	518	609	578	714	1,473	884	5,260
Sales, $	4871	5648	6249	6663	9012	14,613	10,593	$57,649
$F_{DAY} =$ N_i/N_{week}	0.092	0.098	0.116	0.110	0.136	0.280	0.168	

$$AT = \frac{\text{Total weekly sales}}{\text{Total weekly transactions}} = \frac{\$57,649}{5,260} = \$10.96$$

FIGURE 14-26
Form 2 for calculating F_{day}, and average transaction amount (AT).

directly from Form 1. Form 1 was completed for a Wednesday, but similar data is accumulated for each day, and the total number of transactions and daily dollar sales is entered as indicated.

Anticipating a question, the consultant said, "I also made an analysis of variance—," but before he could finish, Jeff said, "Look, I don't care about your $\alpha\rho^*\beta\gamma$ tests. You say that the F_{day} values don't change. OK, you better be right or Mr. Edwards will hang you. How about the value of AT? Are you going to tell me that it doesn't change either? If you do I'll throw you out!" The consultant agreed that AT changes with the seasons, depending on the purchase mix, and with changes in the price level and perhaps changing consumer habits and preferences. He explained that AT needs to be recomputed to track what is going on, and that you would have to use a "Thanksgiving" value of AT if you were scheduling for that period. He said that the value of $AT = \$10.96$ just calculated was a low season value, and that his best estimates for current values were $16 (high season), $13 (medium season), and $11 (low season).

Form 3 (Figure 14-27). The consultant pulled a clipboard and a stopwatch from his briefcase and asked which of the checkers did Jeff feel was representative of an ordinary well-trained checker. Jeff suggested two who had been on the job for 6 months, and then asked, "Hey wait a minute, what do you think you're going to do? We need to make a time study of one or two checkers to determine the value of CP (checker productivity). We'll need it to compute the checker hours needed. I'll show you how to do it. It's simple, but takes about an hour to get a reasonable sample of what a checker puts out in the way of transactions per hour."

Jeff got red-faced. "You can't do that; you'll upset my checkers and the customers too. Besides, I can tell you that they get out about 30 customers per hour. What kind of a manager would I be if I didn't know that?" The consultant soothed Jeff, "We really need to get good information. We'll explain it to the checkers, and you won't have to do this continually. The productivity figures should remain stable once we have them—they shouldn't change unless

Form 3   Computation of Checker Productivity, Checker Stephanie

(1) Customer Number	(2) Time: Start of Transaction Hrs:Min:Sec	(3) Time: End of Transaction Hrs:Min:Sec	(4) Payment Form: 1 = cash 2 = check	(5) Amount of Payment, $	(6) Transaction Time. Col. 3–Col. 2 (Convert to seconds)
1	5:26:00	5:29:20	1	4.23	200
2	5:29:25	5:30:25	2	18.29	60
3	5:30:30	5:31:10	1	0.52	40
.	.	.	.	.	.
.	.	.	.	.	.
.	.	.	.	.	.
12	5:43:00	5:45:20	1	3.17	40
					1160

Compute:

Cashier productivity (transactions per hour) = $\dfrac{\text{Number customers in sample}}{\text{Total elapsed time, seconds}}$

$$CP = \frac{12}{1160} \times 3600 = 37.2$$

Forms of payment: Cash   7
                         Check   5

FIGURE 14-27
Form 3 for calculating checker productivity (CP), average transactions per hour.

you change the system for checkout." Jeff finally agreed, and they talked to the two checkers who agreed also to being observed.

The consultant explained the form, which was largely self-explanatory. The consultant obtained the time readings and notations for columns 1 to 5, and computed the values in column 6 and the values called for at the bottom of the form.

The consultant commented that Jeff wasn't too far off in his estimate, but because of the importance of the CP figure, more precision was justified. But Jeff said, "You measured productivity only when my checker was checking someone out. There were times when she was idle. When I said 30 per hour, I was taking overall productivity. I don't like your figure." The consultant didn't answer, but was mulling over what he should say if Jeff insisted on an answer. He thought that going on to Form 4 would divert Jeff's attention for the moment.

Form 4 (Figure 14-28). At last a checker requirements schedule! Form 4 puts the previous data together with a weekly sales forecast provided by corporate headquarters. The consultant said, "I'll go through one day's computation with you and then you can go ahead and prepare a complete schedule for the upcoming week. The week's forecast from corporate is $89,587. The form really just follows the flow chart I gave you (Figure 14-24). We use all of the basic numbers that we have generated, except that we will use a seasonal AT

Form 4 Weekly and Daily Checker Requirements, Week of _____

Sales forecast: $89,587
AT, Average Transaction (seasonal) $11.00
CP, Checker Productivity (average value):   36.3

Compute required checker hours for week = $\dfrac{\text{Sales Forecast}}{AT \times CP} = \dfrac{89{,}587}{11.00 \times 36.3} = 224$

Hours/week   224 $\times F_{day}$ (Form 2)   = Hours for day

224	$\times F_{Mon}$	0.092 = Mon.	21
224	$\times F_{Tue}$	0.098 = Tue.	22
224	$\times F_{Wed}$	0.116 = Wed.	26
224	$\times F_{Thur}$	0.110 = Thur.	25
224	$\times F_{Fri}$	0.136 = Fri.	31
224	$\times F_{Sat}$	0.280 = Sat.	63
224	$\times F_{Sun}$	0.168 = Sun.	38
			226

FIGURE 14-28
Form 4 for calculating weekly and daily checker requirements.

rather than the number we computed. Also, we will use an average figure for CP that involves a longer term study that I made."

Jeff objects to the fact that the process yields 226 hours for the week, though the initial figure was 224 (see Form 4). The consultant says that he always rounded up, but if Jeff wanted to round down on days where he thought he could squeak by, that was all right.

Then Jeff reflects on the 226-hour total. "That is really awfully tight. I'm regarded as being tight-fisted in my use of checker labor, but I would use more than that at this time of year. If I cut it that close, I would have some pretty long lines behind those checkers. You know, people don't organize themselves to come in according to schedule, even if your F_{days} and F_{hours} do come right from this store."

The consultant replied, "You're right, and that's why I recommend that you take those daily totals and bump them up 25 percent to allow for the variations that are sure to occur. Sure checkers will be idle for short periods, but you will end up giving good service. But by following the patterns through the system, you will have the proportionate amount of labor here when you need it.

Form 5 (Figure 14-29). Seven copies of Form 5 are used, one for each day that the checkstands must be staffed. Jeff groaned again. The purpose of Form 5 is to convert the daily allocations of checker hours to hourly requirements, using the F_{hour} values computed in Form 1. The consultant said he would go through the Wednesday calculations and let Jeff carry on from there.

"How do I schedule 0.42 or 0.86 hours? We don't work like that here." The consultant suggested going to the nearest quarter-hour for scheduling purposes. "But, what does this schedule of hours mean? Doesn't it mean that I should have 1.76 checkers on duty between 10 and 11 A.M.?"

"Well, yes and no," the consultant responded. "It could mean that the second checker opens up 15 minutes later than the first. Then at 11 A.M. a third opens up; at 11:30 a fourth opens. Then at noon you send two to lunch for an

Form 5   Projected Checker Hours by Hour of Day: Week ——————, Day ——Wed.——

Hours allocated from Form 4 __26__ × 1.25 = __32.5__ hours

32.5	× F_{10-11}	0.054	=	1.76
32.5	× F_{11-12}	0.107	=	3.48
32.5	× F_{12-1}	0.046	=	1.50
32.5	× F_{1-2}	0.140	=	4.55
32.5	× F_{2-3}	0.136	=	4.42
32.5	× F_{3-4}	0.088	=	2.86
32.5	× F_{4-5}	0.069	=	2.24
32.5	× F_{5-6}	0.103	=	3.35
32.5	× F_{6-7}	0.084	=	2.73
32.5	× F_{7-8}	0.146	=	4.75
32.5	× F_{8-9}	0.026	=	0.85

Total   32.49

FIGURE 14-29
Form 5 for calculating hourly checker requirements.

hour; at 12:30 you send a third to lunch for only a half-hour, and so on. Isn't that the kind of thing you do now?"

"Look, I still don't have a schedule. We use people here you know, not numbers." The consultant agreed, pointing out that the people schedule was the purpose of Form 6. "You just list the people and your assignment of hours to them. Of course, you have to take account of union rules, seniority, and whatever number of hours per week that you have agreed to provide. Form 6 simply provides the hours across the top and the names of people down the side. The hours are in 15 minute blocks, and you just check the hours to be worked, lunch breaks, and two 15 minute rest breaks as per the union agreement."

Form 6 (Figure 14-30). This form looked reasonable to Jeff, but he had one more question before attempting to schedule for the week. "This system seems as though it is going to take a lot of my time. You know we store managers don't have a staff of lackeys to do our work, we do it ourselves. How much of my time do you think that it will take?"

The consultant knew that this question was coming and was ready. "It will take some time to get it set up, that is, to get good values for the Fs, AT, and CP. Once set up, however, I think that you will find that it saves time and will help you develop better schedules. I figure that it should take a day overall to get good values for F_{hour}, a couple of hours for AT and for F_{day}, and a day to perform good time studies for all of your checkers. That's really not bad to get it set up. Then, it's going to take perhaps five or six hours per week to keep it going, with some extra time during high seasons to update AT, and to keep sampling now and then to be sure that the Fs have remained stable. Also, if you change the checker system some way, you will have to do those time studies over again.

a.   How would you answer Jeff's concerns?

Form 6   Work Schedule for _____ ; _____

Name:	Day of Week		Date								
	10-	11-	12-	1-2	2-3	3-4	4-5	5-6	6-7	7-8	8-9
	:----:	----:	----:	----:	----:	----:	----:	----:	----:	----:	----:
	:----:	----:	----:	----:	----:	----:	----:	----:	----:	----:	----:
	:----:	----:	----:	----:	----:	----:	----:	----:	----:	----:	----:
	:----:	----:	----:	----:	----:	----:	----:	----:	----:	----:	----:
	:----:	----:	----:	----:	----:	----:	----:	----:	----:	----:	----:
	:----:	----:	----:	----:	----:	----:	----:	----:	----:	----:	----:
	:----:	----:	----:	----:	----:	----:	----:	----:	----:	----:	----:
	:----:	----:	----:	----:	----:	----:	----:	----:	----:	----:	----:
	:----:	----:	----:	----:	----:	----:	----:	----:	----:	----:	----:
	:----:	----:	----:	----:	----:	----:	----:	----:	----:	----:	----:
	:----:	----:	----:	----:	----:	----:	----:	----:	----:	----:	----:
Number scheduled:	:----:	----:	----:	----:	----:	----:	----:	----:	----:	----:	----:
Number allocated:	:----:	----:	----:	----:	----:	----:	----:	----:	----:	----:	----:
Difference:	:----:	----:	----:	----:	----:	----:	----:	----:	----:	----:	----:

FIGURE 14-30
Form 6 for developing checker daily work schedules.

b. How do you evaluate the scheduling system developed by the consultant? Should Mr. Edwards install the system? Why, or why not?

c. What schedule should Jeff develop for the example week, assuming that each checker has two consecutive days off? If each checker works 6 hours with at least 1 hour as a break for lunch, how many checkers would be required for monday? What is a feasible schedule for them?

*d. What service level is provided by the schedule developed in c?

†21. The manager of a large bank has the problem of providing teller service for customer demand, which varies somewhat during the business day from 10 A.M. to 4 P.M. She has a total capacity of 6 windows and can assign unneeded tellers to other useful work about 60 percent of the time. She also wishes to give excellent service, which she defines in terms of customer waiting time as $W_q \le 2$ minutes. There is controversy about this service standard, however,

* This question requires the application of concepts in Appendix D, Waiting Lines.
† This situation requires the application of concepts in Appendix D, Waiting Lines.

some feeling that the average waiting time should be no longer than 1 minute, whereas others feel a 4-minute standard would be adequate.

To give the best service for any situation, the manager has arranged the layout so that customers form a single waiting line from which the customer at the head of the line goes to the first available teller. The arrival pattern is as follows:

10:00 A.M.–11:30 A.M., λ = 1.8 customers per minute
11:30 A.M.–1:30 P.M., λ = 4.8 customers per minute
1:30 P.M.–3:00 P.M. λ = 3.8 customers per minute
3:00 P.M.–4:00 P.M., λ = 4.6 customers per minute

The arrival distributions follow the Poisson distribution; that is, the mean value of arrivals varies, but always forms a Poisson distribution. The average service time is 1 minute and the distribution of service times is approximated by the negative exponential distribution. Tellers are paid $4 per hour.

The manager wishes to compare the cost of the several service standard policies. Because of the difficulty with reassigning tellers to useful work in all instances, she is also considering the use of part-time tellers.

What action should be taken by the bank manager?

*22. A university must maintain a large and complex physical plant, so that plant maintenance is an important support function. The plant maintenance department maintains a crew of 6 maintenance mechanics who respond to calls for service from department heads and other authorized personnel on the campus. They respond to a wide variety of calls that range from simple adjustments of room thermostats to actual repair of plant and equipment. In some instances, extensive work involving specialized personnel may be required, and this is scheduled separately.

During the work day, there are 5 calls per hour, and the distribution of the call rate is approximated by a Poisson distribution. The average time for service is 60 minutes, including travel time both ways and the time to actually perform the required work and is approximated by the negative exponential distribution. The wage rate of the mechanics is $8 per hour.

One of the mechanics has just resigned for personal reasons, and the university business manager has refused to replace him because of the budget squeeze. The head of the plant maintenance department is furious and produces a file of complaints from department heads about the slow response to calls for service. The business manager implies that the slow service reflects inefficiency and that it is time for the plant maintenance department to "shape up."

How many maintenance mechanics are economically justified? What action do you feel should be taken?

* This situation requires the application of concepts in Appendix D, Waiting Lines.

REFERENCES

Baker, K. R., and M. Magazine, "Workforce Scheduling with Cyclic Demands and Days-Off Constraints," *Management Science, 24*(2), October 1977, pp. 161–167.

Berry, W. L., V. A. Mabert, and M. Marcus, "Forecasting Teller Window Demand with Exponential Smoothing," *Academy of Management Journal*, March 1979.

Browne, J. J., "Simplified Scheduling of Routine Work Hours and Days Off," *Industrial Engineering,* December 1979, pp. 27–29.

Browne, J. J., and J. Propp, "Supplement to Scheduling Routine Work Hours," *Industrial Engineering,* July 1980, p. 12.

Browne, J. J., and R. K. Tibrewala, "Manpower Scheduling," *Industrial Engineering,* August 1975, pp. 22, 23.

Browne, J. J., and R. K. Tibrewala, "A Simple Method for Obtaining Employee Schedules," *Proceedings, Conference on Disaggregation,* Columbus, Ohio, 1977.

Buffa, E. S., M. J. Cosgrove, and B. J. Luce, "An Integrated Work Shift Scheduling System," *Decision Sciences,* 7(4), October 1976, pp. 620–630.

Chase, R. B., "Where Does the Customer Fit in a Service Operation," *Harvard Business Review,* Vol. 56, 1978, pp. 137–142.

Connel, B. C., E. E. Adam, Jr., and A. N. Moore, "Aggregate Planning and Scheduling in Foodservice Systems With Varying Technologies," forthcoming.

Fitzsimmons, J. A., and R. S. Sullivan, *Service Operations Management,* McGraw-Hill, New York, 1982.

Luce, B. J., "A Shift Scheduling Algorithm." ORSA 44th National Meeting, November 1973.

Luce, B. J., "Employee Assignment System," ORSA/TIMS Joint National Meeting, April 1974b.

Mabert, V. A., and A. R. Raedels, "The Detail Scheduling of a Part-Time Work Force: A Case Study of Teller Staffing," *Decision Sciences,* 7(4), October 1976.

Mabert, V. A., and M. J. Showalter, "Priority Rules for Check Processing in Branch Banking," *Journal of Operations Management,* Vol. 1, No. 1, Summer 1980.

Propp, J. A., *Greedy Solution for Linear Programs With Circular Ones,* IBM Corporation Internal Report, 1978.

Rising, E. J., R. Baron, and B. Averill, "A Systems Analysis of a University-Health-Service Outpatient Clinic," *Operations Research, 21*(5), September–October 1973, pp. 1030–1047.

Sasser, W. E., R. P. Olsen, and D. D. Wyckoff, *Management of Service Operations: Text, Cases, and Readings,* Allyn & Bacon, Boston, 1978.

Tibrewala, R. K., D. Philippe, and J. J. Browne, "Optimal Scheduling of Two Consecutive Idle Periods," *Management Science, 19*(1), September 1972, pp. 71–75.

CHAPTER 15

Maintaining System Reliability

F THE OUTPUT OF A PRODUCTIVE SYSTEM MAINTAINS STANDARD
quality, quantity, and cost, we think of it as being reliable; that is, it continues to
do what it was designed to do. In our discussion of operations planning and
control systems (see Chapter 8, Figure 8-6), we established basic control loops
for performance. Control was accomplished by monitoring the output, comparing it
with standards, interpreting differences, and taking action to readjust processes so
that they conformed to standards. We also discussed broader level control systems
with which to seek a system optimum.

It is not sufficient to think only in terms of average standards of performance; if the
system is erratic in its performance, it is unreliable. It is somewhat harder to maintain
system reliability with complex systems than it is with simple ones, and an analogy to
machines will explain why.

RELIABILITY OF MACHINES

Complex machines may break down often, even though they are designed and
manufactured according to the highest standards. We can view machines as being
made up of a sequence of components, each of which performs a function. For
example, when we strike a key on an electric typewriter, an electric switch is closed.
This actuates a solenoid, which causes the mechanical action of the type to strike the
ribbon, which in turn transfers carbon to the paper. The type linkage returns to its
normal position, and the carriage indexes one space to make ready for the next
cycle. The number of individual and mechanical-electrical components required to
perform correctly in sequence (series) is surprisingly large. If any single component
fails to function correctly—owing either to breakdown or faulty adjustment—the
system as a whole fails to function correctly. We are interested in how this affects
system reliability.

If we are dealing with a machine that is made up of $n = 50$ independent components in series, each with an average reliability of 99.5 percent, the reliability of the
machine as a whole is only about 77 percent (see Figure 15-1). In other words, if the
average probability of breakdown of each of the 50 components were $1.00 - 0.995
= 0.005$, then the probability that the machine might break down because any one
of the components broke down is 0.23. As complexity increases, in terms of the
number of components in series, the reliability of the system as a whole declines very
rapidly.

The reliability of a system in which the components are in parallel differs. With
parallel components, there are two or more components that perform the same
function. Therefore, if the system is to fail, both parallel components must fail, thus
increasing the system's reliability. Increasing reliability through parallel components
and systems is expensive, but when the possible losses are great, it may be justified.
In space vehicle systems, for example, parallel systems are often used because of the
potential costs of system failure. In productive systems, a way to provide parallel
paths is by having more than one machine that can perform the same operation.

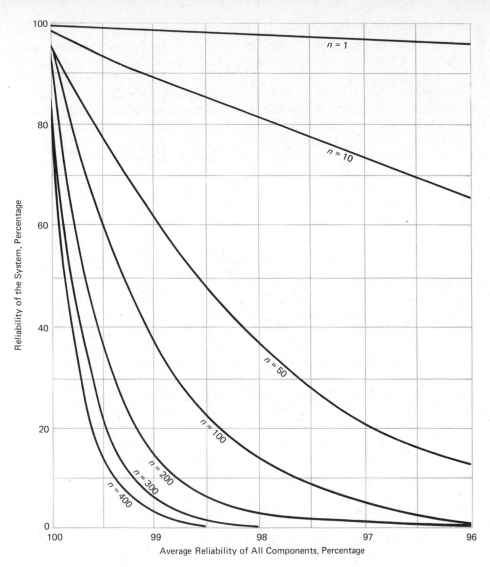

FIGURE 15-1
Overall system reliability as a function of complexity (number of components) and component reliability with components in series.
SOURCE: *R. Lusser. "The Notorious Unreliability of Complex Equipment," Astronautics, 2, February 1958.*

RELIABILITY IN PRODUCTIVE SYSTEMS

There are close parallels between the reliability of machines and of organizations producing services and products. When the *number* of sequential operations required is small and the reliability of each operation is high, the reliability of the system as a whole can be quite good. When the number of sequential operations is large and an error or defect in quality can come from any one operation, then there is a potential for unreliable performance, just as with machine components. We can extend the analogy to include the functioning of entire organizations. Complexity creates the possibility of unreliable performance. This is one of the most important reasons why larger, more complex organizations must use formal procedures in dealing with many kinds of standardized problems. Such organizations become bureaucratic to become more reliable, although the bureaucracy may create problems of its own.

One characteristic of machines is that they can perform repetitive operations fairly consistently, reproducing the same activities. Variations in quality and output quantity tend to be minimized. On the other hand, operations dominated by humans exhibit relatively wide variation in measures of performance. When we combine all the wide variations found in manual operations into a complex sequence (as is common in some service operations), the maintenance of system reliability becomes difficult. In such service operations, consistent output quality may depend on individuals following exacting procedures, and variation can have important consequences. For example, if a nurse fails to identify the patient before administering medication and a mixup occurs, the results can be disastrous.

We try to control the reliability of output through general schemes, as diagrammed in Figure 15-2. The output quality and quantity are monitored in some way, and the results are compared with standards. Although we generally are interested in quality measures, changes in output quantity also may be symptomatic of reliability problems. Associated costs of quality and quantity control are derivatives of reliability. When the results are interpreted, we may conclude that the processes are out of adjustment or that something more fundamental is wrong, therefore requiring machine repair or possibly retraining in manual operations. If equipment actually breaks down, then the maintenance control loop is called directly. Information on output quality and quantity also may be used to form preventive maintenance pro-

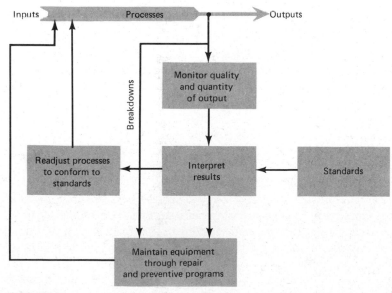

FIGURE 15-2
Control loops for maintaining system reliability by monitoring quality and quantity of output.

grams designed to anticipate breakdown. Thus, although other important interactions have their effects, the control of system reliability centers on quality control and equipment maintenance.

THE RELIABILITY SYSTEM

Figure 15-2 suggests the nature of control loops for quality and maintenance control. However, it is local in nature and leaves a great deal unsaid. We must ask: Where did the standards come from? What is the nature of the productive system, and is it appropriate?

Figure 15-3 places the reliability system in context. The organization must set policies regarding the desired quality in relation to markets and needs, investment requirements, return on investment, potential competition, and so forth. For profit-making organizations, this involves the judgment of where in the market they have a relative advantage.

For nonprofit organizations, policy setting may involve meeting standards set by legislation and/or by the organization to maximize its position. For example, one reason that universities acquire superior academic staffs is to raise funds, improve the physical plant, obtain outstanding students, and enhance research output. Hospitals may set high standards of care partially to attract the best-known physicians, support fund-raising programs, and attract interns with the best qualifications. The post office may set standards for delivery delay that accommodate current budgetary levels.

The policies set by management in box 1 of Figure 15-3 provide the guidelines for the design of the organization's products and services. This design process is an interactive one, in which the productive system design is both considered in and influenced by the design of products and services, as shown in boxes 2 and 3. For manufacturing systems, the design of products in this interactive fashion is termed *production design*. The interaction affects quality considerations, because equipment capability must be good enough to produce at least the intended quality.

Out of the process of the design of products/services and productive system design comes specifications of quality standards, as shown in box 4 of Figure 15-3. Here, we are dealing with a system of quality standards for materials that are consumed in processes, as well as raw materials; for the standards for the output of processes, such as the specification of dimensions, tolerances, weights, and chemical compositions; and for the performance standards for the outputs. The nature of performance standards for products is well known. For example, manufacturers state the capabilities of their product: the fidelity range of an amplifier, the acceleration of an auto, the waterproof finish of a table surface, and the like.

The performance standards of services seem (so far) to be somewhat less formalized. What performance do we expect from postal systems, educational systems, police and fire protection, and medical care systems? This relative lack of formal standards, and the difficulty of defining them, may be the reason for the paucity of our knowledge about the control of the quality of services.

Given standards, however, we can set up controls for incoming materials in box 5, and for the processes and performance of products and services in box 7. An inter-

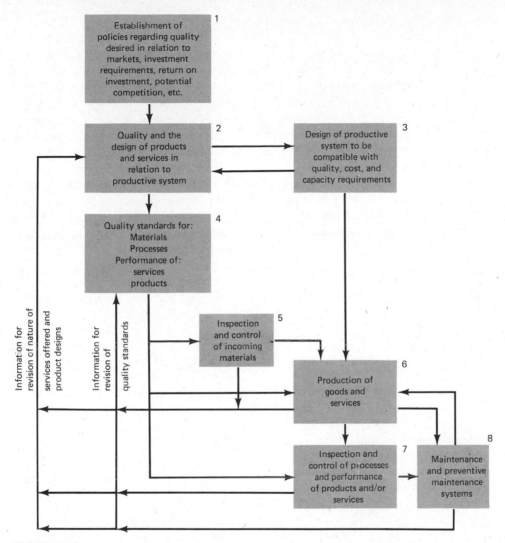

FIGURE 15-3
Schematic representation of the relationships between policies, design of products and services, design of productive system, and the maintenance of the system reliability for quality and quantities.

related control loop concerns the maintenance of the capabilities of the physical system in box 8, through repair and preventive maintenance programs.

Secondary control loops that seek a system optimum are shown in Figure 15-3. These appear as information flow from boxes 5, 6, 7, and 8 to boxes 2 and 4. Their function is to influence the nature of services and products offered and to help revise quality standards, respectively.

CHOICE OF PROCESSES AND RELIABILITY

Management has basic choices to make in balancing processing costs and the costs to maintain reliability. The process choices may involve more or less expensive equipment. The less expensive equipment may not be capable of holding high quality standards. Or it may hold adequate quality standards, but only at a higher maintenance cost or by more labor input. So the balance of costs may involve low process cost, but higher maintenance and quality control costs, and perhaps lower quality (more rejected product and poorer market acceptance of low quality).

The opposite balance of costs may occur with more expensive processes and equipment. The better processes and equipment may be able to hold improved quality standards, resulting in fewer rejected products and perhaps less equipment maintenance and labor input. Some of the best examples of these process choices are in the mechanical industries. A lower-quality lathe may be capable of holding tolerances within ± 0.001 inch. But a precision lathe may be capable of holding tolerances within ± 0.0001 inch or better. However, the choice is certainly not always for the precision lathe; it depends on the product requirements and the balance of costs. These kinds of choices exist generally, although they are not always as clearcut as the lathe example. Sometimes a more expensive process involves greater labor input with more steps in the productive process.

Figure 15-4 shows the balance between the costs of process choice and the costs of maintaining reliability. The manager's choice among alternatives should be in the middle range shown, near the minimum cost of the total incremental cost curve. The reason for not stating that the choice should be simply to minimize cost is that the manager's choice should be influenced by nonquantifiable factors such as market image and acceptance, flexibility of operations, availability of labor with skills to match equipment requirements, and so on.

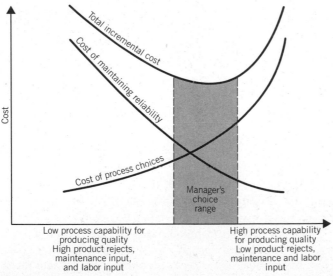

FIGURE 15-4
Cost basis for manager's choice of processes and system reliability.

CONTROL OF QUALITY

Our general block diagram for control calls for a measurement system to generate information on which to base control actions. In industry, this is the inspection function. Inspectors make measurements that are called for by the quality standards, thereby separating acceptable from nonacceptable units. However, no control or corrective action is implied. When we link measurement, investigation to determine why an unacceptable product has been produced, and corrective action, we have completed the control loop.

The measures of quality in productive systems are diverse. These measures are perhaps most obvious in manufacturing systems where quality characteristics can be related to objective standards of dimensions, chemical composition, and actual performance tests. Standards for these measures can then be established and regular procedures used to measure the critical characteristics to determine if standards are maintained. In service-oriented systems, measures of quality are often not as objective. The personal contact required may emphasize the *way* service is given, even though the service was technically adequate. Waiting time is often a criterion for service quality. Following are typical quality measures of the outputs of productive systems:

Type of System	Measure of Output
Manufacturing	Dimensions
	Tolerances on dimensions
	Chemical composition
	Surface finish
	Performance tests
Medical service	False positive diagnosis
	False negative diagnosis
Postal service	Waiting time at post office
	Errors in delivery
	Overall delivery time
Banks	Waiting time at windows
	Clerical errors

Liability and Quality

Liability for poor product quality has been well established. Although negligence on the part of the manufacturer is central to liability, the concept in legal practice extends to include foreseeable use and misuse of the product. Product warranty includes both that expressed by the manufacturer (written and oral) and the implied warranty that the product design will be safe for the user. The uses are not legally restricted to those specified in warranties, but include those that may be foreseen. The latter concept of "foreseeable usage" has often been interpreted to mean that if the product *was* misused, then such use was foreseeable. These legal doctrines place

501

a particularly heavy responsibility on the quality control function, for liability suits can have an important bearing on enterprise survival. See Bennigson and Bennigson [1974] and Eginton [1973] for further discussion of product liability.

Medical malpractice liability has become an important factor in health care costs. Insurance premiums have skyrocketed, and physicians' fees have reflected the increases. Controversy over the control of health care quality has resulted, with emphasis on establishing standards.

Variation and Control

All processes exhibit variation, and the manager's task is to distinguish between tolerable variation that is representative of the stable system and major changes that result in an unacceptable product. The manager must be aware of the system's inherent capability in order to know when system behavior is abnormal. Thus, because we are dealing with systems that exhibit variation, the manager's control model must be a probabilistic one.

Sampling Information

Because of the ongoing nature of processes and their inherent variability, we must base quality control decisions on samples. First, we cannot usually examine all the data, because the process is continuous and, at best, we have access to a sample at a particular point in time. Second, even if the entire universe of data were available, it might be uneconomical to analyze it. Third, measurement and inspection sometimes require destruction of the unit; and fourth, with some products, any additional handling is likely to induce defects and therefore should be avoided. Thus, the sampling of information about the state of incoming raw materials and of control of processes is the common approach on which to base decisions and control actions.

The amount of sampling justified represents another managerial choice. As the amount of sampling increases, approaching 100 percent inspection, the probability of passing defective items decreases, and vice versa. The combined incremental cost curve is again dish-shaped. The manager's range of choices is near the minimum cost, but is a range because nonquantifiable factors must influence the decision.

Risks and Errors

Because we normally must use samples of data drawn from a system that naturally exhibits variation, we can make mistakes, even in controlled experiments. Figure 15-5 summarizes the nature of errors and risks taken; here, we classify the actual state of the system and the decision taken. The process either is in control or it is not; or, similarly, we have a batch of parts or materials that has been generated by a system that either was or was not in control.

As Figure 15-5 shows, we can decide either to accept or reject the output. If the process is in control—and if, based on our information, we would reject the output—then we have made an error called a *Type I error*. We, the producer, risk making such an erroneous decision on the basis of the probabilities that are associated with the inherent variability of the system and the sample size. Logically, this

True state of system	Decision	
	Reject output as bad	Accept output as good
Process is in control	Type-I error (Producer's risk)	Correct decision
Process is out of control	Correct decision	Type-II error (Consumer's risk)

FIGURE 15-5
Errors and risks in quality control decisions.

risk is called the *producer's risk*, because—if the decision is made—it is the producer who absorbs the loss.

Similarly, there is a risk that we may accept output as a good product when, in fact, the process is out of control. This decision is called a *Type II error* and is termed the *consumer's risk*. In statistical control models, we can preset the probabilities of Type I and Type II errors.

Kinds of Control

Figure 15-3 shows that, fundamentally, we control quality by controlling (1) incoming materials, (2) processes at the point of production, and (3) the final performance of products and services, with the maintenance system acting in a supporting role. For some products, quality control of product performance includes the distribution, installation, and use phases.

From the point of view of control methods, we can apply statistical control concepts by sampling a *lot* of incoming materials to see whether it is acceptable (acceptance sampling) or by sampling the output of a process to keep that process in a state of statistical control (process control).

Acceptance sampling lets us control the level of outgoing quality from an inspection point to ensure that, on the average, no more than some specified percentage of defective items will pass. This procedure assumes that the parts or products already have been produced. We wish to set up procedures and decision rules to ensure that outgoing quality will be as specified or better. In the simplest case of acceptance sampling, we draw a random sample of size n from the total lot N and decide, on the basis of the sample, whether or not to accept the entire lot. If the sample signals a decision to reject the lot, the lot either may be subjected to 100 percent inspection, in which all bad parts are sorted out, or the lot may be returned to the original supplier. Parallel acceptance sampling procedures can be used to classify parts as simply good or bad (sampling by attributes) or to make some kind of actual measurement that indicates how good or bad a part is (sampling by variables).

In process control, we monitor the actual ongoing process that makes the units. This allows us to make adjustments and corrections as soon as they are needed, so

503

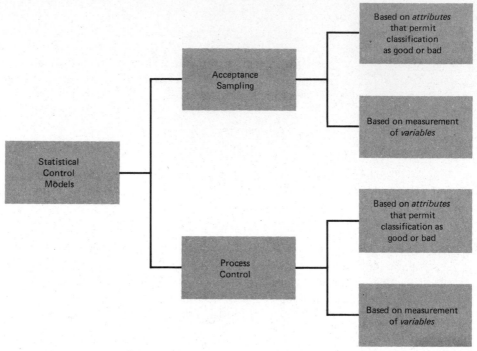

FIGURE 15-6
Classification of statistical control models.

that bad units in any quantity are never produced. This procedure is a direct application of the statistical control chart, and, as with acceptance sampling, parallel procedures are available for those situations in which sampling is done by attributes and for those in which measurements are made of variables that measure quality characteristics. Figure 15-6 summarizes the classification of statistical control models.

The Supplement to this chapter covers the statistical quality control models shown in Figure 15-6.

Controlling the Quality of Services

The previous material dealing with industrial quality control has clear objectives on what to measure and control and sophisticated methodology for accomplishing these ends. In nonprofit organizations, however, the objectives and outputs seem less well defined and the control methodology relatively crude.

The profit motive provides a focus for all kinds of managerial controls including quality. By contrast, nonprofit organizations exist to render service, and their success is judged in those terms. Measuring the quality of services is difficult in part because the attributes of quality are somewhat more diffuse. Is quality health care measured by the death rate, length of hospital stay, or the treatment process used for specific disease? Is the quality of police protection measured by the crime rate, feeling of security by citizens, or indexes of complaints of police excesses? (Note the following anomaly: If the size of the police force is increased, crime rates have been observed to increase, because more of the crimes committed are acted on and reported.) Is the quality of fire service measured by reaction time, the annual extent of fire damage, or some other factor? In partial answer to these questions, we must note that the quality characteristics of most of these kinds of services are multidimensional and often controversial, and reducing quality measurement to something comparable to specific dimensions or chemical composition may be impossible.

A Framework for Controlling Quality of Services. Adam, Hershauer, and Ruch [1978] have proposed a process for developing standards and measures of quality in services and have applied it in banking. Their approach provides a framework and process for creating a unique set of measures for each service within each organization. It assumes that the knowledge needed to create a measurement system exists within the minds of current systems managers. The group processes involved are designed to coalesce from the managers the definition of the system from a quality point of view, the specific kinds of deviations from accepted norms that affect quality, and ways of measuring each specific deviation.

A shirt-laundering service is used as an example to explain their processes to system managers. Shirt laundering involves operations that are simple and well understood. The major steps in this process are as follows:

1. *Define unit operations.* A unit operation is associated with an identifiable change in state in processing that occurs. For example, in the shirt-laundering service, the unit operations are (1) receive and tag, (2) wash and clean, (3) dry and press, and (4) package and deliver. The unit operation that results from the process is defined by the managers through a carefully designed group process.

2. *Generate key quality deviations.* Deviations represent technical system requirements that are subject to variability and that need to be controlled. Through carefully designed group processes, the managers generate *what* and *where* in the process deviations may occur. A second step in the process is then to distill from the deviations list the key quality deviations. Compared with the industrial quality control systems discussed previously, key quality deviations are equivalent to the dimensions and attributes that need to be controlled because they affect product performance and quality. The key quality deviations are caused by the nature of the items being processed (at entry, in process, or at output) or the nature of the processes used. In the shirt-laundering example, the key quality deviations and the unit operation location where they occur (in parentheses) are as follows:

   a. Number, type, and size of stains in shirts (input, wash and clean)
   b. Number of buttons missing (input, wash and clean, dry and press)
   c. Item identification missing (receive and tag, wash and clean, dry and press)
   d. Wrong availability (package and deliver)
   e. Days until delivery (wash and clean, dry and press, package and deliver)

3. *Generate measures.* Using the key quality deviations as a basis, the managers develop related measures through group processes. For example, for the deviation "number, type, and size of stains," the measures were:

  a. Customer stain complaints per customer
  b. Worker-hours expended removing stains
  c. Cost of shirt replacements divided by standard for replacements
  d. Number of shirts with a stain divided by total number of shirts received

4. *Evaluation of measures.* As a basis for finalizing the measures developed in step 3, participants are asked to rate each measure in terms of its value in the outcome of the deviation and to rate the strengths of their convictions of that rating. Only measures whose average rating is above a certain threshold are retained in the measurement system.

Applications in Banking. The system for developing quality measures was applied to check processing and to the personnel function in three banks.

For check processing, seven unit operations were defined in two banks as:

1. Receipt of transfer documents
2. Preparation for processing
3. Processing
4. Reconciling and settlement
5. Preparation for dispatch
6. Dispatch
7. Post processing

In bank C, 93 deviations were defined which were reduced to seven key quality deviations. Sixty measures were then defined related to the key deviations. These measures were evaluated by executives in the organization through the rating processes, and a final list of 25 measures was retained. In addition to the more detailed measures, five systemwide measures for check processing were accepted at bank A:

1. Percentage of error-free outgoing cash letters divided by total worker-hours in check processing
2. Dollar amount of "as of" adjustments divided by total dollars processed
3. Percentage of error-free outgoing cash letters divided by cost of 1000 letters
4. Total dollar expense of adjusting key deviations divided by total dollar expense in check processing
5. Total worker-hours in adjusting key deviations divided by total worker-hours in check processing

For the personnel function, five unit operations were defined in two banks as:

1. Recruit and employ staff
2. Evaluate employee job assignments
3. Compensate employees: review and adjustment for wages, salaries, and benefits

4. Train

5. Administer personnel services to employees and the public

In bank A, 42 deviations were defined which were reduced to 11 key quality deviations. Forty-eight measures were defined related to the key quality deviations. These measures were evaluated by executives through the rating process, and 48 were retained.

Given the measures of *what* to control for service operations, it is necessary to close the control loop. Standards must be set concerning levels of each of the measures that represent acceptable and unacceptable quality, and corrective action must be taken when measurements signal that the system is out of control. Statistical control procedures similar to those used in industrial quality control may then be used.

Although the process for establishing quality measures is complex, it reflects the technical-behavioral emphasis of service systems. It is the first comprehensive effort to establish quality measures in service-type operations. The emphasis of the framework on quality measures of service productivity is unique. Most quality control measures in the past have been taken in isolation and do not attempt to relate the measure and quality control effort to input-output values. The validity of the quality control effort in relation to productivity has been the result of a separate judgment that is usually not explicit.

Quality Control in Health Care. Mounting costs, complaints, and the enormous increase in public funds allocated to health care have focused attention on the development of formal mechanisms for assessing quality. In 1972, Congress created the Professional Standards Review Organizations (PSROs) as a means of self-regulation in health care. The general thrust of these organizations is to set standards for health care and mechanisms for review to ensure that these standards are maintained in practice. The organizations are intended to be relatively local, and physicians who practice medicine in local medical service areas are to be held responsible for the quality of their practices.

Development of Health Care Standards. Current efforts to establish health care standards and control mechanisms focus on an evaluation of outcomes (did the patient die, recover, or recover at what level?). An inquiry into the treatment process used is conducted if the outcomes are outside of standardized limits.

A general model for evaluating the quality of patient care has been developed by Williamson [1971] in this outcomes-process assessment format. In Williamson's format, four factors are evaluated in the following order:

1. The data required to determine the need for care, specific therapy, and prognosis (diagnostic outcomes)

2. The health status of the patients at a given time period following treatment (therapeutic outcomes)

3. The procedures carried out in order to furnish the physician with facts on which to base diagnoses (diagnostic process)

4. The planning, implementation, and evaluation of therapy (therapeutic process)

The heart of the quality control process is in the establishment of standards for outcome criteria. For example, a criterion for death as an outcome might be established by determining the maximum acceptable case fatality rate for patients with a given health problem. "Peer judgment offers a practical method for setting standards." The measurement problems for the four elements in the program are significant; however, the data base is available and can be analyzed.

Definition of Risks and Errors. Although the definitions are not couched in decision theory terms, the medical profession has developed equivalents for Type I and II errors, acceptable quality level, unacceptable quality, and risks. The key definitions are as follows.

False positive, individuals receiving care who did not need it, Type I error.

False negative, individuals needing care who did not receive it, Type II error.

One can then state a maximum false positive for a given health problem as something equivalent to acceptable quality level and the probability of rejecting samples at this level as an equivalent to the producer's risk.

Similarly, one can state a maximum false negative for a given health problem as the limit of bad quality and the probability of accepting this poor quality as the equivalent of the consumer's risk. In fact, both risks are absorbed by the patient (consumer) in the medical system, because a false positive results in a patient's receiving unneeded care that is billed and could be injurious, and a false negative results in a patient's not receiving needed care.

Process Study and Action. In the Williamson control format, measured findings with established criteria reveal whether detailed study of the medical care process is indicated. He suggests that a 95-percent confidence interval covering the measured findings be used. For example, if the maximum acceptable case fatality rate were set at 5 percent, a measured rate of 10 percent with confidence limits of 4 to 15 percent would not differ sufficiently from the criterion to warrant process study. The result of process study, when it is invoked, might bring the standards into question or might result in the alteration of health care procedures.

Example 1

A study was made of urinary tract infections diagnosed in a community hospital in the Midwest involving over 6000 consecutive admissions. Criteria were independently established by group judgment, taking into account the sensitivity and specificity of methods for detecting urinary tract infections and the seriousness of implications to the patient of a "missed diagnosis" or a "misdiagnosis."

The maximum acceptable percentage of false negatives was set at 15 percent and of false positives at 20 percent.

Measurement of actual outcomes revealed that 265 of the 6145 consecutive admissions probably required urinary tract care; however, 187 of these patients did not receive this care from the regular hospital staff, resulting in a false negative rate of over 70 percent. Of 110 patients thought by the hospital staff to have urinary tract infections, 32 had negative urine tests results, producing a false positive rate of 29 percent. Process study in this example was indicated because maximum acceptable criteria for both false negative and false positive diagnoses were exceeded by measured findings [Gonella et al., 1970].

Example 2

Another study of urinary tract infections used the same criteria of maximum acceptable outcomes established for Example 1. Measurement of outcomes was accomplished by an independent study team who examined 133 consecutive new patients admitted to the medical clinic. Over 3 months later the patients' charts were examined, and recorded results were compared with the findings of the study team. Of 18 patients requiring urinary tract care, 10 (56 percent) were missed by the clinic staff. There were no false positives [Williamson, 1971].

Example 3

A study of heart failure was conducted in a city hospital in the East that was interested in applying the quality control strategy to the study of patients in the emergency room. The first sample consisted of 113 consecutive admissions suspected of having acute coronary artery disease. Criteria were based on staff judgment and set at 5 percent as the maximum acceptable levels for both false negatives and false positives in diagnostic results. Measurement of diagnostic outcomes indicated a false negative rate of 3 percent and a false positive rate of 0 percent. Process study was not indicated, because the criteria were not exceeded.

Example 4

A study assessing the health status of patients at the end of a 1-year follow-up was made of 75 patients among the 113 consecutive emergency room patients who were suspected of having an acute coronary occlusion. The criterion of maximum acceptable fatility rate set by the medical staff by peer judgment techniques was 30 percent. Measurement of outcomes on 1-year follow-up revealed that 31 percent had died. Process study was not indicated, because the 95 percent confidence limits were not exceeded [Williamson, 1971].

The examples indicate that setting standards for desired outcomes, monitoring performance with comparisons to standard, and taking corrective action in the traditional control loop conception may have valid use in health care systems. Although the idea of setting standards for recovery or death rates may be shocking to some, it is realistic in decision theory terms and may result in improvements of care quality and some basis for the control of institutions providing substandard care. In fact, the health care quality control example is most encouraging, because it shows that rigorous concepts of quality control in services may be possible.

Japanese Quality Circles

Many years ago a product marked, "Made in Japan," conveyed an image of cheapness and shoddy workmanship. In fact the mark was often amplified with the slogan, "Cheaply Made in Japan." As we know, this image has been completely reversed, and Japanese products are now well regarded as being of the highest quality. How did the reversal take place? Do they have more effective statistical control models? No, as a matter of fact, they use concepts and models of statistical quality control that were imported from the United States in the 1950s.*

* S. Konz, "Quality Circles: Japanese Success Story," *Industrial Engineering, 11*(10), October 1979, pp. 24–27.

There are slogans about quality generated by quality control specialists in the United States that the Japanese learned very well, such as "quality is built in, not inspected in," and "quality is everyone's job." The Japanese success with quality control appears to be not only that they learned the techniques of quality control, but that they applied the spirit of the slogans in their own unique way.

While in the United States, the quality control function developed as a technical staff that functioned by obtaining the cooperation of management and the workers, the Japanese trained the workers themselves in the techniques, as well as management and the technical staff. By training the workers, who are the ones most familiar with the day-to-day problems, the Japanese concept reduced resistance to the introduction of these quantitative models.

Workers are organized into teams (3 to 25 members per team), and select, analyze, and present proposed solutions to quality problems. These quality circles as they are called, involve thousands of people working on problems, rather than the technical specialist attempting to solve quality problems and install them through a sales approach. By the beginning of 1979, there were 95,000 registered quality circles, involving over 900,000 members. It is estimated that only about 15 percent are actually registered, therefore, it appears that over 600,000 workers are involved. In Japan, quality really is everyone's job!

In addition to improvements in quality, a large proportion of the solutions to quality problems developed by quality circles also result in improved productivity.

THE MAINTENANCE FUNCTION

Quality control procedures are designed to track characteristics of quality and to take action to maintain quality within limits. In some instances the action called for may be equipment maintenance. The maintenance function then acts in a supporting role to keep equipment operating effectively to maintain quality standards, as well as to maintain the quantitative and cost standards of output.

There are alternate policies that may be appropriate, depending on the situation and the relative costs. First, is routine preventive maintenance economical, or will it be less costly to wait for breakdowns to occur and repair the equipment? Are there guidelines that may indicate when preventive maintenance is likely to be economical? What service level for repair is appropriate when breakdowns do occur? How large should maintenance crews be to balance the costs of downtime versus the crew costs? In addition, there are longer range decisions regarding the possible overhaul or replacement of a machine.

The decision concerning the appropriate level of preventive maintenance rests on the balance of costs, as indicated in Figure 15-7. Managers will want to select that policy which minimizes the sum of preventive maintenance plus repair costs.

Curve *a* in Figure 15-7 represents the increase in costs that result from higher levels of preventive maintenance. These costs increase because increased level means that more often we replace parts before they fail, and/or we replace more components when preventive maintenance is performed. In addition, there may be more frequent lubrication and adjustment schedules for higher levels of preventive maintenance. Curve *b* of Figure 15-7 represents the declining cost of breakdown and

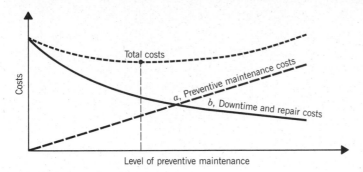

FIGURE 15-7
Balance of costs defining an optimal preventive maintenance policy.

repair as the level of preventive maintenance increases. These costs represent the cost of repair plus downtime costs that result from a breakdown. With higher levels of preventive maintenance, we should experience fewer actual breakdowns.

The total incremental cost curve is the sum of curves a and b. The optimal policy regarding the level of preventive maintenance is defined by the minimum of that curve.

There is a combination of costs that leads to the decision not to use preventive maintenance. Suppose that the breakdown and repair costs did not decline as the level of preventive maintenance increased or declined more slowly than preventive costs increased. Then preventive maintenance would not be justified, because the minimum total cost occurs with no preventive maintenance. The optimal policy would then be simply to repair the machine when breakdowns occurred.

In order to develop a framework for preventive maintenance policy, we need basic data concerning breakdowns.

Breakdown Time Distributions

Breakdown time distribution data are basic to the formulation of any general policies concerning maintenance. Breakdown time distributions show the frequency with which machines have maintenance-free performance for a given number of operating hours. Ordinarily, they are shown as distributions of the fraction of breakdowns that exceed a given run time. Breakdown time distributions are developed from distributions of run time free of breakdowns, as shown in Figure 15-8.

Figure 15-9 shows three breakdown time distributions. These distributions take different shapes, depending on the nature of the equipment with which we are dealing. For example, a simple machine with a few moving parts would tend to break down at nearly constant intervals following the last repair. That is, it would exhibit minimum variability in breakdown time distributions. Curve a of Figure 15-8 would be fairly typical of such a situation. A large percentage of the breakdowns occur near the average breakdown time, T_a, and only a few occur at the extremes.

In a more complex machine with many parts, each part would have a failure distribution. When all these parts were grouped together in a single distribution of the breakdown time of the machine for any reason, we would expect to find greater variability. The machine could break down for any one of a number of reasons.

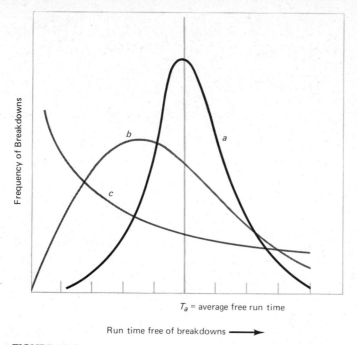

FIGURE 15-8
Frequency distribution of run time free of breakdowns representing three degrees of variability in free run time.

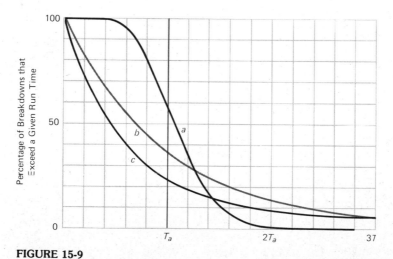

FIGURE 15-9
Breakdown time distributions. Curve *a* exhibits low variability from the average breakdown time T_a. Curve *b* is the negative exponential distribution and exhibits medium variability. Curve *c* exhibits high variability; vertical line shows constant breakdown times.
SOURCE: *Adapted from P. M. Morse. Queues, Inventories, and Maintenance. John Wiley, New York, 1958.*

Some breakdowns could occur shortly after the last repair, or at any time. Therefore, for the same average breakdown time T_a, we would find much wider variability of breakdown time, as in curve b of Figure 15-8.

To complete the picture of representative breakdown time distributions, curve c is representative of distributions with the same average breakdown time T_a, but with wider variability. A large proportion of the breakdowns with a distribution such as curve c occur just after repair; on the other hand, machines may have a long running life after repair. Curve c may be typical of machines that require "ticklish" adjustments. If the adjustments are made just right, the machinery may run for a long time; if not, readjustment and repair may be necessary almost immediately.

In models for maintenance, we normally deal with distributions of the percentage of breakdowns that exceed a given run time, as shown in Figure 15-9. They are merely transformations of the distributions of free run time typified by those in Figure 15-8. By examining curve a in Figure 15-9 we see that almost 60 percent of the breakdowns exceeded the average breakdown time T_a, and that very few of the breakdowns occurred after $2T_a$.

In practice, actual breakdown time distributions often can be approximated by standard distributions, three of which are shown in Figure 15-9. Curve c is the negative exponential distribution.

Preventive Maintenance

Assume a preventive maintenance policy for a single machine that provides for an inspection and perhaps replacement of parts after the machine has been running for a fixed time, called the *preventive maintenance period*. The maintenance crew takes an average time, T_m, to accomplish the preventive maintenance. This is the *preventive maintenance cycle*. A certain proportion of the breakdowns will occur before the fixed cycle has been completed. For these cases, the maintenance crew will repair the machine, taking an average time, T_s, for the repair. This is the *repair cycle*. These two patterns of maintenance are diagrammed in Figure 15-10. The probability of occurrence of the two different cycles depends on the specific breakdown time distribution of the machine and the length of the standard preventive maintenance period. If the distribution has low variability and the standard period is perhaps only 80 percent of the average run time without breakdowns, T_a, actual breakdown would occur rather infrequently, and most cycles would be preventive maintenance

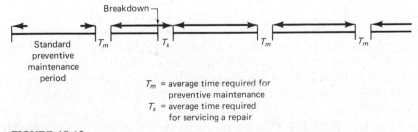

FIGURE 15-10
Illustrative record of machine run time, preventive maintenance time T_m, and service time for actual repairs T_s.

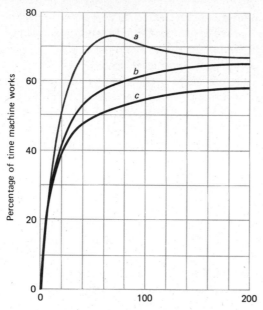

FIGURE 15-11
Percentage of time a machine is working for the three distributions of breakdown time shown in Figure 15-9. Preventive maintenance time, T_m, is 20 percent of T_a; repair time is 50 percent of T_a.
SOURCE: *Adapted from P. M. Morse. Queues, Inventories, and Maintenance. John Wiley, New York, 1958.*

cycles. If the distribution were more variable for the same standard preventive maintenance period, more actual breakdowns would occur before the end of the standard period. Shortening the standard period would result in fewer actual breakdowns, and lengthening it would have the opposite effect for any distribution.

Assuming that either a preventive maintenance or a repair puts the machine in shape for a running time of equal probable length, the percentage of machine running time depends on the ratio of the standard maintenance period and the average run time, T_a, for the breakdown time distribution. Figure 15-11 shows the relationship between the percentage of time that the machine is working and the ratio of the standard maintenance period to average run time, T_a, for the three distributions of breakdown times shown in Figure 15-9. In general, when the standard period is short (say less than 50 percent of T_a), the machine is working only a small fraction of the time. This is because the machine is down so often owing to preventive maintenance. As the standard period is lengthened, more actual breakdowns occur that require repair. For curves b and c, this lengthening of the standard period improves the fraction of time during which the machine is running because the combination of preventive maintenance time and repair time produces a smaller total downtime.

Curve a, however, contains an optimum preventive maintenance period, which maximizes the percentage of machine working time. What is different about curve a? It is based on the low variability breakdown time distribution from Figure 15-9. For curve a, lengthening the maintenance period beyond about 70 percent of T_a reduces the fraction of machine working time because actual machine breakdowns are more likely. For the more variable distributions of curves b and c, this is not true, because breakdowns are more likely throughout the distributions of these curves than they are are in curve a. Comparable curves can be constructed showing the percentage of time that the machine is in a state of preventive maintenance and the percentage of time that the machine is being repaired because of breakdown.

Guides to a Preventive Maintenance Policy

First, preventive maintenance generally is applicable to machines with breakdown time distributions that have low variability, exemplified by curve a of Figure 15-9. In general, distributions with less variability than the negative exponential, curve b, are in this category because low variability means that we can predict with fair precision when the majority of breakdowns will occur. A standard preventive maintenance period can then be set that anticipates breakdowns fairly well.

Equally important, however, is the relation of preventive maintenance time to repair time. If it takes just as long to perform a preventive maintenance as it does to repair the machine, there is no advantage in preventive maintenance, because the amount of time that the machine can work is reduced by the amount of time it is shut down for repairs. In this situation, the machine will spend a minimum amount of time being down for maintenance if we simply wait until it breaks down.

The effect of downtime costs can modify these conclusions. Suppose that we are dealing with a machine in a production line. If the machine breaks down, the entire line may be shut down, and very high idle labor costs will result. In this situation, preventive maintenance is more desirable than repair *if* the preventive maintenance can take place during second or third shifts, vacations, or lunch hours, when the line normally is down anyway. This is true even when $T_m \geq T_s$. The determination of the standard preventive maintenance period would require a different, but similar, analysis in which the percentage of machine working time is expressed as a function of repair time only, because preventive maintenance takes place outside of normal work time.

An optimal solution would minimize the total of downtime costs, preventive maintenance costs, and repair costs. The effect of the downtime costs would be to justify shorter standard preventive maintenance periods and to justify making repairs more quickly (at higher cost) when they do occur. There are many situations, however, in which extra personnel on a repair job would not speed it up. In such cases, total downtime might be shortened by overtime on multiple shifts and weekends, with higher costs. Optimal solutions would specify the standard preventive maintenance period, the machine idle time, and the repair crew idle time, striking a balance between downtime costs and maintenance costs.

Overhaul and Replacement

In maintaining system reliability, sometimes more drastic maintenance actions are economical. These decisions renew machines through overhauls or replace them when obsolete. Overhaul and replacement decisions can be related to the capital and

515

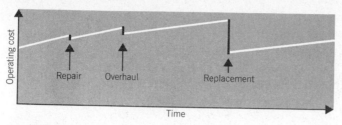

FIGURE 15-12
Operating cost increase with time with temporary improvements resulting from repair, overhaul, and replacement.

operating costs (including maintenance) of the equipment. Figure 15-12 shows that although the operating costs are temporarily improved through preventive maintenance, repair, and overhaul, there is a gradual cost increase until replacement is finally justified.

Repair Versus Overhaul. The decisions concerning the choice between repair and major overhaul normally occur at the time of a breakdown. Many organizations also have regular schedules for overhaul. For example, trucking companies may schedule major engine overhauls after a given number of miles of operation. These major preventive maintenance actions are meant to anticipate breakdowns and the occurrence of downtime at inconvenient times and perhaps to minimize downtime costs.

Because renewals through overhaul involve future costs, these values must be discounted. For example, suppose that a machine breakdown has just occurred. It will cost $500 to repair the equipment, after which the annual operating costs are expected to be $2000, $2500, and $3000 per year for the next 3 years, at which time replacement is planned. If a major overhaul is performed now, the cost will be $1500, with operating costs of only $1800, $2000, and $2300 in the following 3 years, with the replacement decision probably postponed. Let us first examine just the next 3 years of cost to see if the overhaul is justified in that time frame. The two alternatives are compared in Table 15-1 by discounting all future costs to present values, using a 10 percent interest rate.* In this instance, the present value of overhaul is lower and tentatively would be the more economical strategy.

Replacement Decisions. If the choice is only between overhaul and repair, the foregoing analysis may be adequate. However, the replacement alternatives lurk in the background and need to be considered as a part of a sequential decision strategy. The possible sequences could include repair, overhaul, perhaps a second overhaul, replacement, repair, overhaul, and so on.

An Example. Suppose that a machine is used in a productive system and that it is usually overhauled after 2 years of operation, or replaced. The present machine was purchased 2 years ago, and a decision must now be made concerning overhaul or possible replacement. The machine costs $9000 installed, and annual operating costs (including maintenance) are $2000 the first year and $3000 during the second year. The machine can be overhauled for $5000, but operating costs for the next 2 years will be $2800 and $4000 for the first overhaul and $3500 and $5000 for the second overhaul.

* Present value methods are reviewed in Appendix A, Capital Costs and Investment Criteria.

TABLE 15-1 **Present Values of Repair and Overhaul Alternatives for a Machine (Assume that salvage value is zero. Interest rate = 10 percent)**

(1) Year	(2) Present Value Factor for Future Single Payments[a]	(3) Repair Costs	(4) Present Value of Repair Costs, Col. 2 × Col. 3	(5) Overhaul Costs	(6) Present Value of Overhaul Costs, Col. 2 × Col. 5
Initial	1.000	$500	$500	$1500	$1500
1	0.909	2000	1818	1800	1636
2	0.826	2500	2065	2000	1652
3	0.751	3000	2253	2300	1727
			$6636		$6515

[a] Present value factors from Table G-1 in Appendix G.

In deciding whether to overhaul or replace at this time, we should consider the available alternate sequences of decisions. For example, we can overhaul at this time or replace. For each of these possible decisions, we have the same options 2 years hence, and so on. Figure 15-13 shows the simple decision tree structure.

In order to compare the alternatives, the future costs are discounted to present value, using the present value methods reviewed in Appendix A. The calculations are summarized in Table 15-2 for the four sequences indicated in the decision tree of Figure 15-13. The four alternate strategies are:

1.   Replace now and in 2 years (R-R).
2.   Replace now and overhaul in 2 years (R-OH).

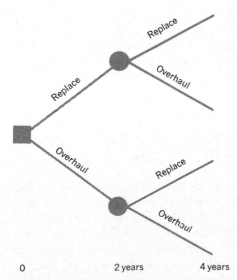

FIGURE 15-13
Decision tree for the overhaul-replacement example.

TABLE 15-2
Present Values for Four Alternate Strategies Involving Overhaul and Replacement (Assume that salvage values are zero. Interest rate = 10 percent)

(1) Year	(2) Present Value Factor for Future Single Payments[a]	(3) Costs for R-R Sequence	(4) Present Value of R-R, Col. 2 × Col. 3	(5) Costs for R-OH Sequence	(6) Present Value of R-OH, Col. 2 × Col. 5	(7) Costs for OH-R Sequence	(8) Present Value of OH-R, Col. 2 × Col. 7	(9) Costs for OH-OH Sequence	(10) Present Value of OH-OH, Col. 2 × Col. 9
Initial	1.000	$9,000.00	$9,000.00	$9,000.00	$9,000.00	$5,000.00	$5,000.00	$5,000.00	$5,000.00
1	0.909	2,000.00	1,818.00	2,000.00	1,818.00	2,800.00	2,545.20	2,800.00	2,545.20
2	0.826	3,000.00	2,478.00	3,000.00	2,478.00	4,000.00	3,304.00	4,000.00	3,304.00
Replace or overhaul at end of									
2nd year	0.826	9,000.00	7,434.00	5,000.00	4,130.00	9,000.00	7,434.00	5,000.00	4,130.00
3	0.751	2,000.00	1,502.00	2,800.00	2,102.80	2,000.00	1,502.00	3,500.00	2,628.50
4	0.683	3,000.00	2,049.00	4,000.00	2,732.00	3,000.00	2,049.00	5,000.00	3,415.00
			$24,281.00		$22,260.80		$21,834.20		$21,022.70

[a] Present value factors from Table G-1 in Appendix G.

3. Overhaul now and replace in 2 years (OH-R).
4. Overhaul now and again in 2 years (OH-OH).

The 4-year present value totals in Table 15-2 indicate that the best strategy for this example is to overhaul each 2 years (OH-OH) and that the next best strategy is to overhaul now and replace in 2 years (OH-R). This is true in spite of the rapidly mounting operating costs.

Because operating costs do increase so rapidly, perhaps it will be worthwhile to see what happens if we adopt a 6-year planning horizon. If a third overhaul is scheduled, the next 2 years' operating costs will be $4500 and $5500. On the other hand, if we add an overhaul cycle to the third alternative, it will enjoy the relatively low operating cost of a first overhaul. Adding a third cycle to each of the four alternatives results in the following strategies (we are ignoring the additional sequences created by a third branching to reduce computations for this example):

1. R-R-R
2. R-OH-R
3. OH-R-OH
4. OH-OH-OH

Table 15-3 summarizes the calculations for the third cycle, the present values for the first 4 years, and the 6-year present value totals. Alternative 3 (OH-R-OH) is now the lowest-cost strategy. This change in result demonstrates the importance of choosing a horizon that fairly represents all the alternatives. If a fourth 2-year cycle were added to the evaluation, it might seem that strategies 3 and 4 are the same, but reversed in sequence. But they are not the same because we start from an existing situation with a 2-year old machine. Strategy 2 places two replacements in sequence, whereas strategy 3 alternates overhauls and replacements.

TABLE 15-3
Present Values for Third Cycle, and Six-Year Totals for Four Alternate Strategies Involving Overhaul and Replacement (Assume that salvage values are zero. Interest rate = 10 percent)

(1) Year	(2) Present Value Factor for Single Payments[a]	(3) Costs for R-R Sequence	(4) Present Value of R-R, Col. 2 × Col. 3	(5) Costs for R-OH Sequence	(6) Present Value of R-OH, Col. 2 × Col. 5	(7) Costs for OH-R Sequence	(8) Present Value of OH-R, Col. 2 × Col. 7	(9) Costs for OH-OH Sequence	(10) Present Value of OH-OH, Col. 2 × Col. 9
Replace or overhaul at end of 4th year	0.683	$9,000.00	$6,147.00	$9,000.00	$6,147.00	$5,000.00	$3,415.00	$5,000.00	$3,415.00
5	0.621	2,000.00	1,242.00	2,000.00	1,242.00	2,800.00	1,738.80	4,500.00	2,794.50
6	0.564	3,000.00	1,692.00	3,000.00	1,692.00	4,000.00	2,256.00	5,500.00	3,102.00
			$9,081.00		$9,081.00		$7,409.80		$9,311.50
First 4 years from Table 15-2			24,281.00		22,260.80		21,834.20		21,022.70
6-year totals			$33,362.00		$31,341.80		$29,244.00		$30,334.20

[a] Present value factors from Table G-1 in Appendix G.

This example assumes replacement with an identical machine, but it is often true that alternate machines will have rather different capital and operating costs characteristics. New machine designs often have improvements (owing to mechanization or automation) that reduce labor and maintenance costs, and these cost advantages would affect replacement decisions.

IMPLICATIONS FOR THE MANAGER

The general concepts of system reliability are important for managers to understand. When productive systems involve a network of activities with many required sequences, it will be difficult to maintain the reliability of the system as a whole. This system unreliability would be true even though each individual operation might be 99 percent reliable. Managers can improve the reliability by providing parallel capabilities and slack capacity, although these remedies may be expensive.

The most important techniques available to managers to sustain reliability are through quality control and equipment maintenance systems. The quality control system functions as a primary control loop, with the maintenance system providing reliability in the longer term through a secondary control loop.

Quality control begins in the preproduction planning phases of an enterprise, where policies regarding market strategies are developed. Quality standards are then developed out of the iterative process of product/service design and productive system design. The productive system must be designed so that it is capable of producing the required quality level at reasonable cost.

Monitoring quality levels of output is necessarily a sampling process, because the entire population of output is seldom available for screening. The techniques of statistical quality control are often valid and cost-effective mechanisms for managers to employ.

Quality control of services is difficult for a variety of reasons related to the unique character of services. Attempts are being made to establish a framework for control. Legislation has placed great emphasis on quality control in health care systems, and self-regulation experiments are now developing. Nevertheless, quality control techniques in service operations are underdeveloped, partly because rigorous standards for quality of services are not available.

Managers often regard the maintenance function as ancillary to operations, ignoring its crucial role in supporting the reliability system. It is important to understand when preventive maintenance is likely to be appropriate. Analysis of breakdown time distributions provides guidelines to the development of preventive maintenance policies. In general, these policies are appropriate when breakdown time distributions exhibit low variability and when the average time for preventive maintenance is less than the average repair time following breakdown. Also, when downtime costs are large, preventive maintenance is preferable to repair if it can be performed when the facilities are normally down anyway.

The maintenance function extends into decisions involving major overhaul and replacement. These kinds of decisions involve a longer time horizon and the proper handling of capital costs. Present value techniques for the evaluation of alternate strategies may be used, and the strategies need to consider sequences of decisions involving repair, overhaul, and replacement.

IMPORTANT TERMS

Numbers in parentheses indicate page numbers

Acceptance sampling (503)	Producer's risk (503)
Breakdown time distribution (511)	Production design (498)
Consumer's risk (503)	Quality circles (509)
False negative (508)	Repair cycle (513)
False positive (508)	Replacement (515)
Key quality deviations (505)	Sampling by attributes (503)
Overhaul (515)	Sampling by variables (503)
Preventive maintenance (513)	Type I error (502)
Preventive maintenance cycle (513)	Type II error (503)
Preventive maintenance period (513)	Unit operations (505)
Process control (503)	

REVIEW QUESTIONS AND PROBLEMS

1. If the *reliability* of a productive system means its capability to maintain quality, schedule, and cost standards, which of the following kinds of systems are likely

to encounter the greatest quality-reliability problems? Schedule-reliability problems? Why?

   a. Skyscraper construction project

   b. Automobile engine plant

   c. Restaurant

   d. Hospital

2. Compare the reliability of systems with components in series versus components in parallel.

3. How does variability of performance affect system reliability?

4. What are the primary and secondary feedback control loops in the overall reliability system?

5. What measures of quality of output do you think might be important in the following kinds of systems? Be as specific as possible.

   a. Fast-food operation such as McDonalds

   b. Motel

   c. Luxury hotel

   d. Space vehicle manufacture

6. How can you control the aspects of quality that you suggest be measured in your answer to question 5?

7. Define the following terms:

   a. Type I error

   b. Type II error

   c. Producer's risk

   d. Consumer's risk

8. What kinds of control can be exercised in maintaining quality standards?

9. What conditions make acceptance sampling appropriate?

10. What are the criteria of quality in the following?

   a. Banking service

   b. The Postal Service

   c. An institution of higher learning

   d. A hospital

   e. The Internal Revenue Service

11. In controlling the quality of health care, what is the meaning of a *false positive? A false negative?*

12. In the Williamson control model for health services, under what conditions do we examine the treatment processes that are used?

13. What kinds of costs are associated with machine breakdown?

14. Discuss the general methods by which the reliability of productive systems can be maintained.

TABLE 15-4   **Operating Costs for Problem 21.**

Year	New Machine	First Overhaul	Second Overhaul	Third Overhaul	Fourth Overhaul
1	$1000	$1100	$1300	$1700	$2300
2	1100	1300	1700	2300	3200

15. What is a breakdown time distribution?

16. Discuss the types of situations of machine breakdown that are typified by curves *a, b,* and *c,* respectively, in Figure 15-8.

17. What are the general conditions for which preventive maintenance is appropriate?

18. If it takes just as long to perform a preventive maintenance operation as it does a repair, is there an advantage to preventive maintenance? How can high downtime costs modify this?

19. Rationalize why the operating costs for equipment should increase with time, as indicated in Figure 15-12.

20. If the decision tree of Figure 15-13 were developed through decisions made at the end of 4 years, how many alternate sequences result? Enumerate them.

*21. A company is considering whether to overhaul or replace a machine. The machine was purchased 4 years ago and was overhauled 2 years ago.

A new machine costs $2000, and an overhaul costs $500 and lasts 2 years. Experience indicates that annual operating costs increase with time owing to increased maintenance charges. Table 15-4 shows operating costs for new and overhauled machines.

Analyze the situation and indicate what decision should be made. Assume that machines have no salvage value at any time, and that the cost of capital is 15 percent per year.

REFERENCES

Adam, E. E., J. C. Hershauer, and W. A. Ruch, *Measuring the Quality Dimension of Service Productivity,* National Science Foundation No. APR 76-07140, University of Missouri—Arizona State University, 1978.

Bennigson, L. A., and A. I. Bennigson, "Product Liability: Manufacturers Beware!", *Harvard Business Review,* May–June 1974.

Boere, N. J., "Air Canada Saves with Aircraft Maintenance Scheduling," *Interfaces,* 7(3), May 1977, pp. 1–13.

Dodge, H. F., and H. G. Romig, *Sampling Inspection Tables* (2nd ed.), Wiley, New York, 1959.

---

* This problem requires the application of present value concepts in Appendix A, Capital Costs and Investment Criteria.

Duncan, A. J., *Quality Control and Industrial Statistics* (4th ed.), Irwin: Homewood, Ill., 1974.

Eginton, W. W., "Minimizing Product Liability Exposure," *Quality Control,* January 1973.

Fitzsimmons, J. A., and R. S. Sullivan, *Service Operations Management*, McGraw-Hill, New York, 1982.

General Electric Company, *User's Guide to Preventive Maintenance Planning and Scheduling*, FAME—Facilities Maintenance Engineering, New York, General Electric Company, 1973.

Gilbert, J. O. W., *A Manager's Guide to Quality and Reliability*, Wiley, New York, 1968.

Gonella, J. A., M. J. Goran, and J. W. Williamson et al., "The Evaluation of Patient Care," *Journal of the American Medical Association, 214* (8), 1970, pp. 2040–2043.

Grant, E. L., and R. S. Leavenworth, *Statistical Quality Control* (5th ed.), McGraw-Hill, New York, 1980.

Jardine, A. K. S., *Maintenance, Replacement and Reliability*, Wiley, New York, 1973.

Juran, J. M., and F. M. Gryna, *Quality Planning and Analysis: From Product Development Through Usage*, McGraw-Hill, New York, 1970.

Kirkpatrick, E. G., *Quality Control for Managers and Engineers*, Wiley, New York, 1970.

Smith, C. S., *Quality and Reliability: An Integrated Approach*, Pitman, New York, 1969.

Williamson, J. W., "Evaluating Quality of Patient Care," *Journal of the American Medical Association, 218* (4), October 25, 1971, pp. 564–569.

SUPPLEMENT
Statistical Quality Control

This supplement assumes that one has read the relevant materials in Chapter 15. The classification of the kinds of control is shown in Figure 15-6, and we resume at that point with a discussion of acceptance sampling by attributes.

ACCEPTANCE SAMPLING BY ATTRIBUTES

The inspection procedure for attributes sampling results in the simple classification of parts or items as "good" or "not good." For part dimensions, this can often be accomplished by the use of snap or plug gauges that incorporate a go- not-go feature. If the inspection is for surface paint defects or some other attribute of appearance, again the two-part classification of good or not good is made. The statistical methods are based on distributions such as the binomial, or Poisson distributions. (The appropriateness of these and other distributions in specific situations is beyond our scope.)

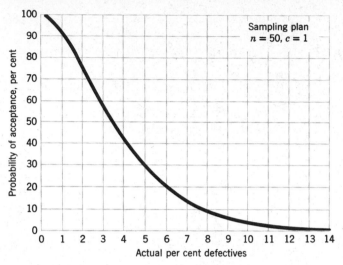

FIGURE 15-14

Operating characteristic (*OC*) curve for a sampling plan with *n* = 50, *c* = 1.

Operating Characteristic (OC) Curves

To specify a particular sampling plan, we indicate the random sample size *n* and the number of defectives in the sample *c* (acceptance number) permitted before the entire lot from which the sample was drawn is to be rejected. The *OC* curve for a particular combination of *n* and *c* shows how well the plan discriminates between good and bad lots. Figure 15-14 is an *OC* curve for a sampling plan with sample size *n* = 50 and acceptance number *c* = 1. Figure 15-14 shows the probability of acceptance of a lot for various values of percent defectives in the lot. For example, if the actual lot quality were 2 percent, samples of *n* = 50 would accept the lot as satisfactory about 73 percent of the time, and reject it about 27 percent of the time. In other words, the probability of finding zero or one defective in random samples from such a lot is 73 percent, whereas the probability of finding more than one defective is only 27 percent. Note, however, that if the actual quality of the lot were somewhat worse than 2 percent defective, say 5 percent, the probability of accepting these lots falls drastically to about 27 percent. Therefore, if the actual quality is good, we want a high probability of acceptance, but if the actual quality is poor, we want the probability of acceptance to be low. Thus, the *OC* curve shows how well a given plan discriminates.

The discriminating power of a sampling plan depends heavily on the size of the sample, as we might expect. Figure 15-15 shows the *OC* curves for sample sizes of 100, 200, and 300, with the acceptance number remaining in proportion to the sample size. Note that the *OC* curve becomes somewhat steeper as the sample size goes up. If we compare the discrimination power of the three plans represented in Figure 15-15, we see that all three would accept lots of about 0.7 percent defectives about 83 percent of the time (approximately the crossover point of the three curves). However, if actual quality falls to 3.0 percent defectives, the plan with *n* = 100 accepts lots about 20 percent of the time, *n* = 200, about 6 percent of the time, and

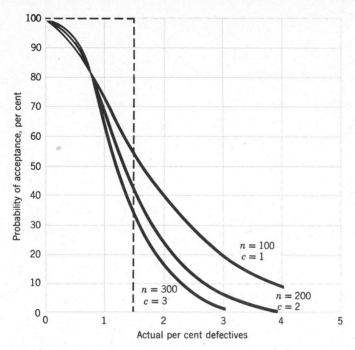

FIGURE 15-15
OC curves for different sample sizes with acceptance numbers in proportion to sample sizes.

$n = 300$, less than 1 percent of the time. Plans with larger sample sizes are definitely more effective.

What happens to the *OC* curve if only the acceptance number changes? Figure 15-16 shows *OC* curves for a sample of $n = 50$ and acceptance numbers of $c = 0$, 1, 2, and 3. Note that the effect is mainly to change the level of the *OC* curve, so that lower acceptance numbers make the plan "tighter"; that is, hold outgoing quality to lower percents.

A sampling plan that discriminates perfectly between good and bad lots would have a vertical *OC* curve; that is, it would follow the dashed line of Figure 15-15. For all lots having percent defectives to the right of the line, the probability of acceptance is zero. Unfortunately, the only plan that could achieve this discrimination is one requiring 100 percent inspection. Therefore, the justification of acceptance sampling turns on a balance between inspection costs and the probable cost of passing bad parts.

By making sampling plans more discriminating (increasing sample sizes) or tighter (decreasing acceptance numbers), we can approach any desired level of outgoing quality that we please, but at increasing inspection costs. This increased inspection effort would result in lower probable costs of passing defective parts. At some point the combination of these incremental costs is a minimum. This minimum point defines the most economical sampling plan for a given situation.

To justify a 100 percent sample, the probable losses due to the passing of bad products would have to be large in relation to inspection costs, perhaps resulting in the loss of contracts and customers. It is on this basis that the Japanese objective of

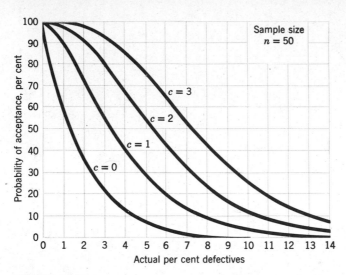

FIGURE 15-16
OC curves with different acceptance numbers for a sample size of $n = 50$.

"zero defects" can be justified. On the other hand, to justify no inspection at all, inspection costs would have to be very large in relation to probable losses due to passing bad parts. The most usual situation is between these extremes, where there is a risk of not accepting lots that are actually good and a risk of accepting lots that are bad. As we discussed in this chapter, the first risk is called the producer's risk and the second, the consumer's risk.

Producer's and Consumer's Risks. The definition of these risks can be made specific by referring to a typical *OC* curve. Figure 15-17 shows graphically the following four definitions:

AQL = acceptable quality level—Lots of this level of quality are regarded as good, and we wish to have a high probability of their acceptance.

α = producer's risk—the probability that lots of the quality level AQL will *not* be accepted. Usually $\alpha = 5$ percent in practice.

risk of rejecting a good

$LTPD$ = lot tolerance percent defective—the dividing line selected between good and bad lots. Lots of this level of quality are regarded as poor and we wish to have a low probability for their acceptance.

β = consumer's risk—the probability that lots of the quality level $LTPD$ will be accepted. Usually $\beta = 10$ percent in practice.

risk of accepting a bad

When we set levels for each of these four values, we are determining two critical points on the *OC* curve that we desire, points a and b in Figure 15-17.

Specification of a Specific Sampling Plan. To specify a plan that meets the requirements for AQL, α, $LTPD$, and β, we must find a combination of n and c with an *OC* curve that passes through points a and b in Figure 15-17. The mechanics of actually finding specific plans that fit can be accomplished by using standard tables, charts, or formulas, which result in the specification of a combination of sample size

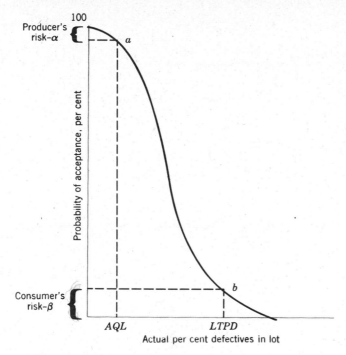

FIGURE 15-17
Complete specification of a sampling plan. An *OC* curve that goes through points *a* and *b* meets the requirements stated by *AQL* and *α*, and *LTPD* and *β*, thus specifying a sampling plan defined by a sample size *n* and acceptance number *c*.

and acceptance number that closely approximates the requirements set for *AQL*, *α*, *LTPD*, and *β*.*

Averages Outgoing Quality (AOQ) Curves

If we assume that when a sampling plan rejects a lot, the lot is then subjected to 100 percent inspection and defectives are replaced by good items, the sampling plan gives definite assurance that the average outgoing quality will not exceed certain limits. We now develop a curve for any given sampling plan that shows the *AOQ* for any level of incoming quality. Such a curve can be plotted by assuming different values of actual incoming quality, determining from the *OC* curve the probability of acceptance for that incoming quality, P_a. These figures can then be substituted in a formula to compute *AOQ*. Each calculation for different incoming quality levels determines a point on the *AOQ* curve, as indicated in Figure 15-18. The *AOQ* curve of Figure 15-18 is based on a sampling plan with $n = 50$, $c = 1$, and a total lot size of $N = 1000$, the *OC* curve of which is shown in Figure 15-14.

Note the interesting characteristics of the *AOQ* curve. First, there is a maximum or limiting quality that can be passed on the average. This peak of the curve is called the average outgoing quality limit (*AOQL*). There is an *AOQL* for every sampling plan that depends on the characteristics of the plan. The reason that the *AOQ* curve

---

* For example, see Dodge and Romig [1959] or Duncan [1974].

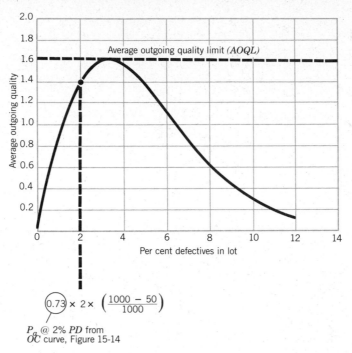

$$0.73 \times 2 \times \left(\frac{1000 - 50}{1000} \right)$$

P_a @ 2% PD from
OC curve, Figure 15-14

FIGURE 15-18
Average outgoing quality (AOQ) curve for a sampling plan with $n = 50$, $c = 1$, and lot size $N = 1000$; OC curve shown in Figure 15-14.

takes the shape illustrated is as follows: When good quality is presented to the sampling plan, for example, 0 to 3 percent, the probability of acceptance is relatively high, so most defectives will be passed. As we go beyond 3 percent incoming quality, however, the probability of acceptance is declining. Therefore, the probability of 100 percent inspection is increasing, so a larger share of defectives is screened out. This accounts for the fact that the outgoing quality improves as incoming quality becomes worse.

The essence of the characteristics of the sampling plan represented by the AOQ curve of Figure 15-18 is simply that average outgoing quality will never exceed approximately 1.6 percent, regardless of the incoming quality level. The amount of inspection required to maintain quality standards automatically adjusts to the situation.

The level of $AOQL$ that should be selected for a given situation depends on the consequences of bad quality. If subsequent operations can catch further defectives without disrupting production, $AOQL$ can be fairly loose. These probability controls are ideal. We can first specify the level of quality demanded by technical and economic considerations, and then set up controls that guarantee the average performance needed. A great deal of inspection labor is used when bad lots occur and only slightly used when good lots occur.

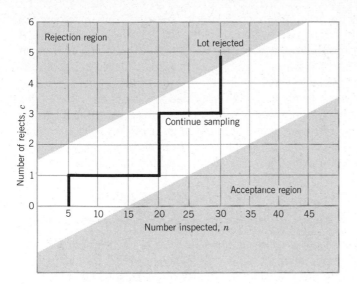

FIGURE 15-19
Sequential sampling plan.

Sequential Sampling Plans

In sequential sampling, samples are drawn at random, as before. But after each sample is inspected, the cumulated results are analyzed and a decision made to (a) accept the lot, (b) reject the lot, or (c) take another sample. The sequential sample sizes can be as small as $n = 1$.

Figure 15-19 shows the graphical structure of a sequential sampling plan. The main advantage of sequential sampling is a reduction in the total amount of inspection required to maintain a given level of protection. In the plan shown in Figure 15-19, a minimum of 15 items must be inspected in order to accept a lot. If the number of rejects on the graph rises such that the point falls on or above the upper line, the lot is rejected. If the point should fall on or below the lower line, the lot is accepted. Until one of these events occurs, sampling is continued. The disadvantage of sequential sampling is that inspection loads vary considerably. As before, a sequential sampling plan is specified by the four requirements: AQL, α, $LTPD$, and β. In turn, these requirements determine OC curves of sequential plans that meet requirements.

ACCEPTANCE SAMPLING BY VARIABLES

In acceptance sampling by variables, we make and record actual measurements instead of simply classifying items as good or bad as in attributes sampling. This difference in procedure changes the details of determining a plan that meets our specifications of AQL, α, $LTPD$, and β, because the appropriate statistical distribution is now the *normal* distribution instead of distributions for proportions. Conceptually, however, the basic ideas on which the control of outgoing quality is maintained remain the same. The discriminating power of a plan still is represented by an *OC* curve, which shows the probability of acceptance for different levels of actual quality presented to the plan. To specify a plan that gives the desired protection requires basically the same procedure.

Upper and lower tolerance levels are often specified on measurements of part dimensions, chemical content, and so on, as part of variables sampling plan specifications. In these instances, the variables sampling must provide two-sided protection from defectives occurring because the measured characteristic may be too small or too large to be useful. A sampling plan then would specify a sample size, an upper acceptance average, and a lower acceptance average.

Obviously, inspection, recording, and computing costs per unit will normally be higher with variables sampling inspection plans than with attributes plans. Then, why use variables plans? The most important reason is that, for a given level of protection, variables plans require smaller samples and less total inspection than do attributes plans. From an economic point of view, variables inspection should be used where the smaller sample size tips the balance of costs of inspection, recording, and computing. In addition to the possible cost advantages, the data generated by variables inspection (mean and standard deviation) provide valuable diagnostic information for controlling processes.

PROCESS CONTROL CHARTS

In general, variations that occur in a production process fall into two broad categories: *chance* variations and those due to *assignable causes*. The chance variations may be due to a complex of minor actual causes, none of which can account for any significant part of the total variation. The result is that these variations occur in a random manner, and there is very little that we can do about them, given the process. On the other hand, variations due to assignable causes are relatively large and can be traced. In general, assignable causes are:

1. Differences among workers
2. Differences among machines
3. Differences among materials
4. Differences due to the interaction between any two or all three of the above factors

When a process is in a state of statistical control, variations that occur in the number of defects, the size of a dimension, chemical composition, weight, and so on, are due to chance variation only. With the control chart, we set up standards of expected normal variation due to chance causes. Thus, when variations due to one or more of the assignable causes are superimposed, they "stick out like a sore thumb" and tell us that something basic has changed. The *natural tolerance* of a process is commonly taken as $\bar{x} \pm 3s$.

Control Charts for Attributes

p-Charts. Control charts for the proportion or fraction of defectives (*p-charts*) occurring are based on the binomial distribution. Recall that:

$$\bar{p} = \frac{x}{n} = \frac{\text{number of defectives}}{\text{total number observed}}$$

$$s_p = \sqrt{\frac{\bar{p}(1-\bar{p})}{n}}$$

where $n =$ the size of the subsample.

Following general practice for quality control charts, the control limits are set at the process average of defectives plus and minus three standard deviations; that is, they are set at $\bar{p} \pm 3s_p$.

Table 15-5 shows a set of data covering 24 consecutive production days on the number of defectives found in daily samples of 200. We wish to determine first if the data exhibit statistical control and to set up a control chart. The daily fraction defective is calculated by dividing each daily figure by the sample size, $n = 200$. Preliminary figures for $\bar{p}$, s_p, and the upper and lower control limits, UCL and LCL, are also calculated in Table 15-5. These preliminary figures are used to determine if the process generating the data is in control. Figure 15-20 shows the resulting plot of the daily fraction defective in relation to the preliminary control limits. Two points are outside of limits and the point for day 7 is nearly outside the upper limit. Investiga-

---

TABLE 15-5   **Record of Number of Defectives and Calculated Fraction Defective in Daily Samples of $n - 200$**

Production Day	Number of Defectives	Fraction Defective	Production Day	Number of Defectives	Fraction Defective
1	10	0.05	14	14	0.07
2	5	0.025	15	4	0.02
3	10	0.05	16	10	0.05
4	12	0.06	17	11	0.055
5	11	0.055	18	11	0.055
6	9	0.045	19	26	0.13
7	22	0.11	20	13	0.065
8	4	0.02	21	10	0.05
9	12	0.06	22	9	0.045
10	24	0.12	23	11	0.055
11	21	0.105	24	12	0.06
12	15	0.075	Total	294	
13	8	0.04			

$$\bar{p} = \frac{294}{24 \times 200} = 0.061$$

$$s_p = \sqrt{\frac{0.061 \times 0.939}{200}} = 0.017$$

$3s_p = 3 \times 0.017 = 0.051$
$UCL = \bar{p} + 3s_p = 0.061 + 0.051 = 0.112$
$LCL = \bar{p} - 3s_p = 0.061 - 0.051 = 0.010$

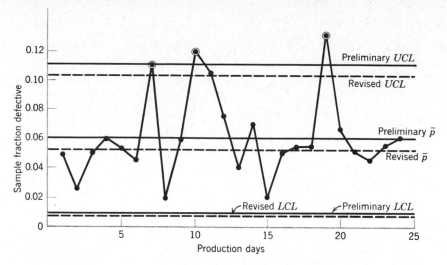

FIGURE 15-20
A p-chart for examining past data and establishing preliminary and revised control limits.

tion shows nothing unusual for the first point, day 7. For the second point, day 10, it appears that a logical explanation is that three new workers were taken on that day. The supervisor contends that the following day's defectives were also affected by the breaking in of these workers. The last point, day 19, was explained by the fact that the die had worn and finally fractured that day.

To set up standards for normal variation, we eliminate the data for days on which we have established assignable causes (days 10 and 19), and recompute $\bar{p}$, UCL, and LCL as follows:

$$\bar{p} = \frac{244}{200 \times 21} = 0.058$$

$$UCL = 0.058 + 3 \sqrt{\frac{0.058 \times 0.942}{200}} = 0.108$$

$$LCL = 0.058 - 3 \sqrt{\frac{0.058 \times 0.942}{200}} = 0.008$$

These revised values reflect the variation due to chance causes. We now use them as standards by which we judge future samples of fraction defective. If any future samples fall outside these limits, our immediate reaction is that it is highly probable that there is an assignable cause for the unusual observation of fraction defective. We then attempt to determine the cause and correct it before more scrap has been produced.

Another control chart for attributes is based on the number of defects per unit of product. On a painted surface these might be dimples, paint runs, and so on. A measure of the quality might be the number of these blemishes per unit or per unit area sampled. Control charts set up on this basis are called *c-charts*.

Control Charts for Variables

Control charts for variables could be constructed for individual measurements. Usually, however, these charts are constructed for sample means rather than for individual measurements. One important reason for this is that *although a universe distribution may depart radically from normality, the sampling distribution of means of random samples will be approximately normal if the sample size is large enough.* This statement, known as the central limit theorem, is very important for it gives us some assurance that the probabilities associated with the 3s limits will apply. Figure 15-21 demonstrates that the deviation from normality can be fairly great and yet the sampling distribution of the means of samples as small as $n = 5$ follow the normal distribution quite closely.

If we take samples of four from the distribution of individual measurements of shaft diameters in Figure 15-22, and determine an average for each sample, we have a new distribution. We regard each sample mean as an observation; if we plot a frequency distribution of the sample means, it will have a mean and a standard deviation of its own. The distribution is called a *sampling distribution of means of $n = 4$.* To distinguish the *statistics* from those of the distribution of individual observations, we use the notation $\bar{x}$ for the grand mean of the sampling distribution and $s_{\bar{x}}$ for the standard deviation. We expect that $\bar{x}$ and $\bar{\bar{x}}$ will be very nearly the same and that they will be equal in the limit as the number of subsamples increases. The standard deviation will be much smaller for the sampling distribution of means, however, because the variation is reduced by the averaging process within each sample. The resulting relationship between the two distributions for the shaft data is shown in Figure 15-22. The functional relationship between s and $s_{\bar{x}}$ is given by

$$s_{\bar{x}} = \sqrt{s^2/n}$$

where n is the size of the subsample.

Now to construct a control chart for the means ($\bar{X}$-charts), we first need to establish standard values for $\bar{x}$ and $s_{\bar{x}}$, which are based on the normal conditions of whatever it is that we wish to control. The upper and lower control limits are established as $\bar{x} \pm 3s_{\bar{x}}$. Means of subsequent samples are plotted; again, action would be called for if a sample mean should fall outside the control limits.

The reasons why sample means may fall outside the control limits are related to the technology of the processes being controlled. For example, if parts were being produced on a lathe, they would tend to become oversized as the cutting tool became worn. Changes of this general nature tend to reflect themselves in the *mean* of the sampling distribution. If, however, the bearings of the lathe spindle had worn, this situation would be reflected by an increase in *variability* of the sampling distribution, and we would expect points to go outside of both control limits. The control chart can reveal changes in the mean of the distribution actually being generated, changes in the standard deviation (or range), and combinations of changes in the mean and changes in variability. Where changes in variability are particularly important, a special control chart on a measure of variability can be constructed.

533

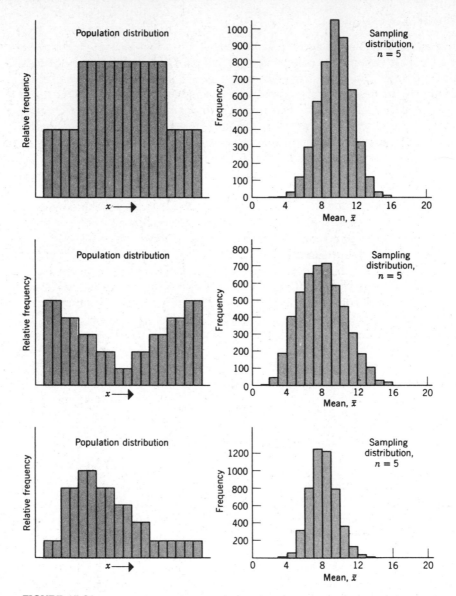

FIGURE 15-21
Normality of sampling distributions. The three distributions on the left are populations from which 5000 samples of $n = 5$ were drawn at random. The resulting sampling distributions are shown at the right.

IMPORTANT TERMS

Numbers in parentheses indicate page numbers

Acceptable quality level, AQL (526)

Assignable cause (530)

Attributes sampling (523)

Average outgoing quality, AOQ (527)

Average outgoing quality limit, AOQL (527)

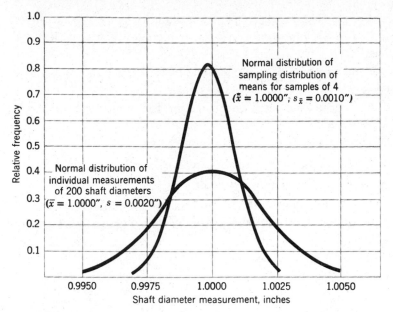

FIGURE 15-22
Relation between the distribution for individual observations and the sampling distribution of samples of $n = 4$ for shaft diameter data.

Consumer's risk, β (526)

Control chart (530)

c-charts (532)

Lot tolerance percent defective,
   LTPD (526)

Natural tolerance (530)

Operating characteristic (OC)
   curve (524)

p-chart (531)

Percent defectives (524)

Producer's risk, α (526)

Sequential sampling (529)

Variables sampling (529)

$\bar{x}$-charts (533)

REVIEW QUESTIONS AND PROBLEMS

1. What kind of control can be exercised in maintaining quality standards?

2. What conditions make acceptance sampling appropriate?

3. What is an OC curve and what information does it convey?

4. What is the effect of increasing sample size on the OC curve? What practical
    result does it achieve in terms of the discriminating power of a sampling plan?

5. What is the effect of decreasing acceptance numbers on the OC curve? What
    practical result does it achieve in terms of outgoing quality levels?

6. Define AQL, α, $LTPD$, and β. Relate these definitions to a typical OC curve.

7. Discuss the significance of the shape of the average outgoing quality (AOQ) curve. Relate this to the amount of inspection required at various levels of incoming quality.

8. What is the general structure for sequential sampling? What are its advantages and disadvantages?

9. Contrast the differences in concept and statistical technique for sampling by attributes and by variables.

10. What conditions favor the use of sampling by variables?

11. What are the sources of assignable causes of variation in quality control?

12. Discuss the procedure for setting up a p-chart.

13. What is the significance of the fact that the sampling distribution of means can be normal even though the distribution of individual measurements departs radically from normality?

14. What is the relationship between s and $s_{\bar{x}}$?

PROBLEMS

15. A large medical insurance company maintains an office staff that processes claims, computing the payment amounts under the terms of the insurance contracts. Because errors in payment are important to both the company and subscribers, a sampling plan is to be installed. At the end of the day a random sample of $n = 50$ claims is taken and the benefits recomputed. Any variance in the computed benefits is regarded as an error or "defective." The claims manager feels that acceptable quality is 1 percent defectives, and wants the probability of acceptance of such quality to be 90 percent. What sampling plan would yield this performance: If the consumer's risk is 10 percent, what percent defectives represent poor quality for the plan? (See OC curves.)

16. A large hardware distributor has a staff that prepares invoices to be sent to customers. Problems with clerical accuracy have led to the installation of probability controls. Any variance in the invoice is regarded as an error. In order to establish a control chart, initial samples of 200 invoices are taken over a period of several days as shown in Table 15-6.

    a. What are the control limits for a p-chart for the invoice operation?

    b. Plot the samples on a p-chart.

    c. Is the invoice operation in control?

17. The manager of the invoice department in Problem 16 notes the relatively high error rates in the samples taken on May 11. On investigation he finds that the air conditioning system was broken down that day and is satisfied that it is an assignable cause for the high error rates. Should the control limits be altered? If so, what are the revised control limits?

18. The Stamped Metal Products Company (StaMPCo), which makes the V-belt pulley shown in Figure 15-23 has decided to employ certain statistical control

TABLE 15-6   **Errors in Invoice Samples**

		Time	Sample Size	Number of Errors	Error Rate in Sample (Percent)
May	7	A.M.	200	3	1.5
		P.M.	200	12	6.0
	8	A.M.	200	0	0.0
		P.M.	200	11	5.5
	9	A.M.	200	5	2.5
		P.M.	200	7	3.5
	10	A.M.	200	9	4.5
		P.M.	200	6	3.0
	11	A.M.	200	16	8.0
		P.M.	200	18	9.0
	14	A.M.	200	9	4.5
		P.M.	200	5	2.5
	15	A.M.	200	7	3.5
		P.M.	200	0	0.0
	16	A.M.	200	13	6.5
		P.M.	200	2	1.0
	17	A.M.	200	11	5.5
		P.M.	200	7	3.5
	18	A.M.	200	4	2.0
		P.M.	200	1	0.5
	21	A.M.	200	6	3.0
		P.M.	200	12	6.0
	22	A.M.	200	6	3.0
		P.M.	200	1	2.0
	23	A.M.	200	4	2.0
Total			5000	178	

techniques to reduce the cost of inspection and to improve quality control. StaMPCo buys 0.875-inch diameter rolled bar stock on a contract basis from a large, dependable supplier. Shipments are made in lots of 400 as required. At the present production rate of pulleys having 0.875-inch diameter hubs, 400 bars roughly correspond to 6 to 7 days' usage.

To match the pulley flanges produced on punch presses properly, the bar stock cannot vary more than 0.002 inch from the nominal diameter. Therefore, the specification for bar stock diameter is 0.875 inch ±0.002 inch. If the bar diameter exceeds the upper specification limit, the flanges tend to split excessively when forced onto the hub by the arbor press. If the diameter is smaller than specified, the flange-hub fit is loose and the spot welding operation tends to pull the flanges off the axis of rotation. As a result, a large number of pulleys must be rejected because of excessive "wobble." The company's contract with the steel supplier specifies that 95 percent of the bars are to meet the diameter specification of 0.875 inch ±0.002 inch.

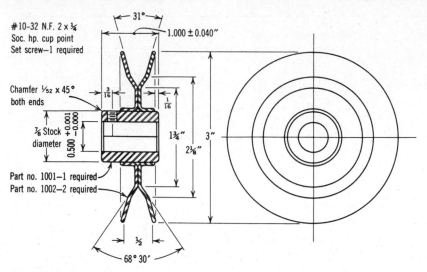

FIGURE 15-23
Drawing of a V-belt pulley.

The production manager and purchasing agent have decided that the company should not accept an individual shipment in which more than 17.5 percent of the bars are oversized or undersized. What are the values of the parameters that would define an acceptance sampling plan?

19. After several months the production manager of StaMPCo feels that the receiving inspection department has been accepting too many lots in which the actual number of defective bars exceeds 17.5 percent. Therefore, the manager recommends reducing the probability of accepting lots that have more than 17.5 percent defectives by one-half. How must the plan discussed in Problem 17 be modified to carry out this recommendation?

REFERENCES

Dodge, H. F., and H. G. Romig, *Sampling Inspection Tables* (2nd ed.), Wiley, New York, 1959.

Duncan, A. J., *Quality Control and Industrial Statistics* (4th ed.), Irwin, Homewood, Ill. 1974.

Grant, E. L., and R. S. Leavenworth, *Statistical Quality Control* (4th ed.), McGraw-Hill, New York, 1980.

Kirkpatrick, E. G., *Quality Control for Managers and Engineers,* Wiley, New York, 1970.

CHAPTER 16

The Operating Manager

T HROUGHOUT THE BOOK, WE HAVE TALKED A GREAT DEAL about operating systems, their problems, and the nature of analysis and decisions in production/operations management. But operating systems are managed by people who make the judgments.

The managers who run the shops, services, or projects have important and exciting positions. They are "in the line" in organizational terms. From a social point of view, they contribute *directly* to the creation of goods and services—they are not leeches on society, and it is a good feeling!

The operating management positions themselves involve the development of strategies as well as the day-to-day management of resources and people. The decisions made are crucial to the success of the organization. They determine whether or not the products and services are of appropriate quality and cost and whether they are delivered to the consumers in timely fashion. Image makers can build on product attributes that exist, but only the operating managers can build the base on which the image can be erected.

THE "FIRING LINE"

The operating manager is in the vortex of action. Customers and clients want products and services; they complain about quality and availability. Sales personnel make promises that are kept by the operating manager, if they are kept. Suppliers create problems with faulty materials, delays, and shortages. Equipment breaks down. Workers go on strike. Within this madhouse of "action," the operating manager is somehow supposed to produce the products and services in the quantities needed, available when needed, and at a controlled cost and quality.

Surely the operating manager's position must be one of putting out fires. Each of the problems must be dealt with, and sometimes emergencies must be faced. But the firefighting approach to managing operations is seldom a winning philosophy. If for no other reason, operating managers cannot physically survive for long. How then can operating managers cope?

Managers cope by creating rational systems for handling the great bulk of problems. They do not attempt to reinvent the wheel for each problem that comes along. We have examined many of these systems in this book. They deal with forecasting and scheduling systems and a variety of controls to ensure that the systems are continuing to function properly.

The operating manager's decisions invariably seem to seek balance. There is a price for everything, and you cannot usually get something for nothing. "Free cheese is in mousetraps!" The decision problems reflect a recognition of these realities, and managers are constantly balancing one cost against another. Sometimes the costs are obvious, and we try to construct models that formalize them. Then managers can use the models to help price the nonquantitative aspects of decisions, as well as using them in the decision-making process.

While staff specialists are busy dissecting problems and trying to analyze them, operating managers must try to see relationships and integrate the results. Managers are probably the true systems philosophers. They must continually think in holistic terms. They must anticipate interacting effects and the unintended effects of decisions. Managers must take to heart Lord Acton's admonition, "You can't change just one thing." There will be unintended effects, and a system-oriented manager will anticipate them with counterbalancing actions.

THE FUTURE OF PRODUCTION/OPERATIONS MANAGEMENT

The impact of pollution and natural resource limits, the overbearing increase in population, and our changing values seem destined to change industrialized society. Predicting the form of the changes may require a crystal ball, and we will not attempt it. However, the impact of these events on Production/Operations Management is somewhat more clear.

First, the importance of well-managed productive systems will increase rather than decrease as even greater importance is placed on the efficient use of resources. In line with the external pressures, more emphasis will be placed on analytical approaches to problems within the framework of systems analysis.

At the same time, we will become masters of technology in productive systems, and jobs will be designed in ways that use the unique capability of both humans and machines appropriately. This latter process will face a severe test if the predictions of doom are correct. Because, if the collapse of modern technology and a breakdown of industrial society should actually occur, we will once again find ourselves doing work more appropriate for machines in order to survive.

More likely in my view, is that robotics and progressive automation will drastically change the nature of work in society. These effects will be more evident in manufacturing where we are already experiencing an actual decline in the percent of the work force employed in that sector. Predictions are that by the year 2000, manufacturing employment will decline to the range of 2 to 10 percent. We are following the pattern of agriculture, where the work force percentage declined from 90 percent in the 18th century to only 4 percent today. Just as mechanization and science in agriculture made possible the conversion from an agrarian to an industrial society, managerial competence and automation will make possible the conversion from an industrial to a service-oriented society. More, not less emphasis will be placed on operations management, partly because of the burgeoning service industries. But, even for the manufacturing sector, the reduction of the work force requirements does not mean that the operating problems disappear, for the demand for goods will be even greater than it is today. The emphasis of operations management simply shifts.

The interesting question is: What changes will be effected in the management of service operations? Will we find ways to increase productivity in service operations just as we did in the earlier cycles of agriculture and manufacturing? It is not clear at this point that we will; however, it was not clear in the 1800s that agricultural productivity could increase so dramatically. If many aspects of service are automated, we may have to rename it.

PART
FOUR

APPENDIXES

APPENDIX A

Capital Costs and
Investment Criteria

C APITAL COSTS AFFECT DECISION PROBLEMS IN PRODUCTION/ Operations Management whenever a physical asset or expenditure is involved that provides a continuing benefit or return. From an accounting point of view, the original capital expenditure must be recovered through the mechanism of depreciation and must be deducted from income as an expense of doing business. The number of years over which the asset is depreciated and the allocation of the total amount to each of these years (i.e., whether depreciation is straight-line or some accelerated rate) represent alternative strategies that are directed toward tax policy. We must remember that all of these depreciation terms and allocations are arbitrary and have not been designed from the point of view of cost data for decision making.

A SIMPLE EXAMPLE

We have just installed a piece of equipment that performs a highly specialized operation. The installation was a custom job that fit our particular situation. Because of the specialized nature of the equipment and the custom installation, the equipment has no salvage value.

The useful physical life of the equipment can be prolonged almost indefinitely by maintenance and repair, so it is difficult to say yet what the life of the equipment will be. Because the equipment has no salvage value, the entire $10,000 seems to go down some sort of economic sink the minute the equipment becomes ours. We say that the $10,000 is a *sunk cost*, meaning simply that it is gone forever, regardless of what we may list as the "book value" of the equipment. Because the $10,000 is sunk, it is completely irrelevant to any future decisions because no future decision can affect it.

The cost of owning the equipment is simply $10,000. We hope to spread this total over a period of time so that the *average* annual cost of ownership will not be too great. In 5 years, the average cost of owning the equipment is only $10,000/5 = $2000 per year. In 10 years, the average annual cost is down to $1000 per year. Regardless of how long we keep the equipment, this cost of owning is irrelevant because it is a past cost. The only future costs that we shall incur for this equipment are the costs of operating and maintaining it. Once the machine is installed, these are the only costs that are subject to managerial control by future decisions.

Assume that two workers are required to operate the equipment at $4000 per year per worker. Maintenance costs are expected to be $2000 the first year, thereafter increasing by $200 per year. Figure A-1 shows the total of these costs in relation to time. We assume that there are no other pertinent costs. The original cost of the equipment is sunk, and the only future costs are the operating and maintenance costs. Therefore, we are in a position to determine under what conditions we would consider this machine to be obsolete and would replace it. We would replace it any time that we could find a functionally equivalent machine which could offer a total average annual cost of owning plus operation and maintenance that fell below the cost curve of Figure A-1.

Assume that during the *fourth* year of operation of the present machine a new equipment design is developed. This *new equipment design* has an important ad-

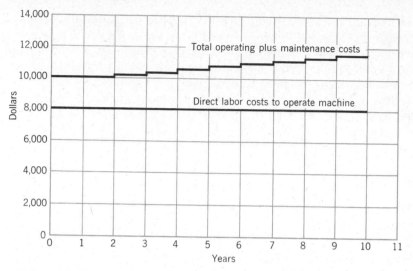

FIGURE A-1
Operating and maintenance costs, showing rising costs of maintenance.

vantage over the old one. Because it is more automatic, it can be operated by one person. The more automatic features require an additional $1000 maintenance input, however. Therefore, the first-year operating and maintenance cost is expected to be $4000 operating labor plus $3000 maintenance. This total of $7000 is expected to increase by $200 per year as before, because of mounting maintenance charges. The improved design costs $12,000, installed. Now we want to see whether the average annual total of the costs of owning plus operating and maintaining the improved equipment design are less than the $10,600 current annual expense (fourth year) for the present machine. Although we ignore the original sunk cost of the present machine, we cannot ignore the installed cost of the improved design. It is still a future cost.

The average annual cost of owning (capital cost) and the annual operating and maintenance costs for the improved equipment design are plotted in Figure A-2. The total cost curve is developed simply by adding the cost of owning to the operating and maintenance costs for each year. The total cost is very high during the first 2 years, it reaches a minimum during the eighth year, and then it begins to rise again. It is high in the early years because the annual average costs of owning the equipment are very high during those years. It begins to rise again after the eighth year because of the influence of rising maintenance costs.

For the present machine, the total incremental cost for the fourth year is $10,600, a sum that we expect will become larger in future years. However, the total average annual cost for the proposed machine will be less than $10,600 after its fourth year. It seems clear that a decision to replace the present machine is needed.

What criteria for comparison are we using here? We are looking at the best possible future cost performance for both the present and proposed machines. The best cost performance possible for the present design is $10,600, which is this year's operating and maintenance cost. The best cost performance possible for the proposed design is achieved if it is held in service for 8 years; its total cost would average only $9900 per year for the entire 8-year span. As long as the best performance of the proposed design (represented by the minimum of the total cost curve) is less than the best performance of the present design, it would be economical to make the switch. We must temper this statement by recognizing important intangible values and the accuracy of the cost estimates.

OPPORTUNITY COSTS

Suppose that we are discussing an asset that is used for more general purposes, such as an over-the-road semitrailer truck. Assume that we own such a truck and that the question is: How much will it cost us to *own* this truck for one more year? These costs of owning, or capital costs, cannot be derived from the organization's ordinary accounting records. The cost of owning it for one more year depends on its current value. If the truck can be sold on the secondhand market for $5000, this is a measure of its economic value. Because it has value, we have two basic alternatives: We can sell it for $5000 or we can retain it. If we sell, the $5000 can earn interest or a return on an alternate investment. If we keep the truck, we forgo the return, which then becomes an *opportunity cost* of holding the truck one more year. Similarly, if we keep the truck, it will be worth less a year from now, so there is a second opportunity cost, measured by the fall in salvage value during the year.

The loss of opportunity to earn a return and the loss of salvage value during the year are the costs of continued ownership. They are opportunity costs rather than costs paid out. Nevertheless, they can be quite significant in comparing alternatives

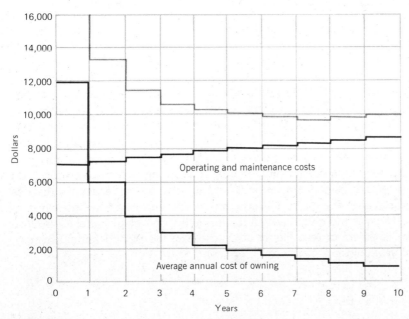

FIGURE A-2
Year-by-year average costs for a proposed replacement machine costing $12,000 initially and having no salvage.

TABLE A-1   Year-by-Year Capital Costs for a Semitrailer Truck, Given a Salvage Schedule (Interest at 10%)

Year	Year-End Salvage Value	Fall in Salvage Value during Year	Interest on Opening Salvage Value	Capital Cost, Sum of Fall in Value, and Interest
New	$10,000	—	—	—
1	8,300	$1,700	$1,000	$2,700
2	6,900	1,400	830	2,230
3	5,700	1,200	690	1,890
4	4,700	1,000	570	1,570
5	3,900	800	470	1,270
6	3,200	700	390	1,090
7	2,700	500	320	820
8	2,300	400	270	670
9	1,950	350	230	580
10	1,650	300	195	495

that require different amounts of investment. There is one more possible component of capital cost for the next year if the truck is retained—the cost of possible renewals or "capital additions." We are not thinking of ordinary maintenance, but of major overhauls such as a new engine or an engine overhaul that extends the physical life for some time. In summary, the capital costs, or costs of owning the truck for one more year, are as follows:

1. Opportunity costs:
    a. Interest on opening salvage value
    b. Loss in salvage value during the year
2. Capital additions or renewals required to keep the truck running for at least an additional year

By assuming a schedule of salvage values, we can compute the year-by-year capital costs for an asset. This is done in Table A-1 for a truck that cost $10,000 initially and for which the salvage schedule is indicated. The final result is the projected capital cost that is incurred for each year. If we determine the way in which operating and maintenance costs increase as the truck ages, we can plot a set of curves of yearly costs. The combined capital plus operating and maintenance cost curve will have a minimum point. This minimum of the combined cost curve defines the best cost performance year in the life of the equipment. Beyond that year, the effect of rising maintenance costs more than counterbalances the declining capital costs. Note that such a plot is different from Figure A-2, in which we plotted annual average costs instead of yearly costs.

OBSOLESCENCE AND ECONOMIC LIFE

By definition, when a machine is obsolete, an alternate machine or system exists that is more economical to own and operate. The existence of the new machine does not cause any increase in the cost of operating and maintaining the present machine. Those costs already are determined by the design, installation, and condition of the present machine. However, the existence of the new machine causes the salvage value of the present machine to fall, inducing an increased capital cost. For assets in technologically dynamic classifications, the salvage value schedule falls rapidly in anticipation of typical obsolescence rates. Economic lives are very short. On the other hand, when the rate of innovation is relatively slow, salvage values hold up fairly well.

Table A-2 compares year-by-year capital costs for two machines that initially cost $10,000, but that have different salvage schedules. The value of machine 1 holds the best; machine 2 has more severe obsolescence reflected in its salvage schedule. The result is that capital costs in the initial years are greater for machine 2 than for machine 1. The average capital costs for the first five years are:

Machine 1 $1913
Machine 2 $2198

Therefore, if the schedules of operating expenses for the two machines were identical, machine 1 would seem more desirable. However, because the timing of the capital costs is different for the two machines, we adjust all figures to their equivalent present values.

PRESENT VALUES

Because money has a time value, future expenditures and opportunity costs will have different present values. Because money can earn interest, $1000 in hand now is equivalent to $1100 a year from now if the present sum can earn interest at 10

TABLE A-2   **Comparison of Capital Costs for Two Machines Costing $10,000 Initially but with Different Salvage Schedules (Interest at 10%)**

	Machine 1				Machine 2		
Year-End Salvage Value	Fall in Value During Year	Interest at 10% on Opening Value	Capital Cost	Year-End Salvage Value	Fall in Value During Year	Interest at 10% on Opening Value	Capital Cost
$10,000	—	—	—	$10,000	—	—	—
8,330	$1,670	$1,000	$2,670	7,150	$2,850	$1,000	$3,850
6,940	1,390	833	2,223	5,100	2,050	715	2,765
5,780	1,160	694	1,854	3,640	1,460	510	1,970
4,820	960	578	1,538	2,600	1,040	364	1,404
4,020	800	482	1,282	1,860	740	260	1,000
3,350	670	402	1,072	1,330	530	186	716
2,790	560	335	895	950	380	133	513
2,320	470	279	749	680	270	95	365
1,930	390	232	622	485	195	68	263
1,610	320	193	513	345	140	49	189

percent. Similarly, if we must wait a year to receive $1000 that is due now, we should expect not $1000 a year from now, but $1100. When the time spans involved are extended, the appropriate interest is compounded, and its effect becomes much larger. The timing of payments and receipts can make an important difference in the value of various alternatives.

Future Single Payments

We know that if a principal amount P is invested at interest rate i, it will yield a future total single payment S in n years hence, if all the earnings are retained and compounded. Therefore, P in the present is entirely equivalent to S in the future by virtue of the compound amount factor. That is,

$$S = P(1 + i)^n \tag{1}$$

where $(1 + i)^n$ = the compound amount factor for interest rate i and n years.

Similarly, we can solve for P to determine the present worth of a single payment to be paid n years hence:

$$P = \frac{S}{(1 + i)^n} = S \times PV_{sp} \tag{2}$$

where $PV_{sp} = 1/(1 + i)^n$, the present value of a single payment of $1 to be made n years hence with interest rate i. Therefore, if we were to receive a payment of $10,000 in 10 years, we should be willing to accept a smaller but equivalent amount now. If interest at 10 percent were considered fair and adequate, that smaller but equivalent amount would be

$$P = 10{,}000 \times 0.3855 = \$3855$$

because

$$\frac{1}{(1 + 0.10)^{10}} = PV_{sp} = 0.3855$$

Table G-1 in Appendix G gives the present values for single future payments or credits; Table G-2 gives present values for annuities for various years and interest rates.

Annuities, Annual Amounts

An *annuity* is a sum that is received or paid annually, and is defined by the relationship in Equation 3.

$$P = A \times PV_a \tag{3}$$

where

$$PV_a = \frac{1 - (1 + i)^{-n}}{i} \tag{4}$$

where
A = amount of periodic (annual) payment
PV_a = the present value of an annuity
i = interest rate in decimals
n = years

TABLE A-3
Present Value of Capital and Operating Costs for the Two Machines from Table A-2 [Schedule of operating costs is the same for both machines (interest at 10%)]

Year (1)	Operating Cost (2)	Capital Costs (from Table A-2)		Combined Operating and Capital Costs		Present Worth Factor for Year Indicated[b]	Present Worth of Combined Costs for Year Indicated	
		Machine 1 (3)	Machine 2 (4)	Machine 1 (5)	Machine 2 (6)	(7)	Machine 1 (8)	Machine 2 (9)
1	$3,000	$2,670	$3,850	$5,670	$6,850	0.909	$5,154	$6,227
2	3,200	2,223	2,765	5,423	5,965	0.826	4,490	4,939
3	3,400	1,854	1,970	5,254	5,370	0.751	3,946	4,033
4	3,600	1,538	1,404	5,138	5,004	0.683	3,509	3,418
5	3,800	1,282	1,000	5,082	4,800	0.621	3,156	2,981
6	4,000	1,072	716	5,072	4,716	0.565	2,866	2,665
7	4,200	895	513	5,095	4,713	0.513	2,614	2,418
8	4,400	749	365	5,149	4,765	0.467	2,405	2,225
9	4,600	622	273	5,222	4,873	0.424	2,214	2,066
10	4,800	513	189	5,313	4,989	0.386	2,051	1,926
Totals							$32,405	$32,898

Machine 1, present worth of all future values is total of column (8) less present worth of tenth-year salvage value, i.e., $32,405   1610[a] × 0.386 = 32,405 − 621 − $31,784.
Machine 2, $32,898 − 345[a] × 0.386 = 32,898 − 133 = 32,765.
[a] Tenth-year salvage values from Table A-2.
[b] From Table G-1 (Appendix G).

The factors in Table G-2 convert the entire series of annual sums to present values for various interest rates and years.

Consider the present value of receiving $10,000 per year for 10 years with an interest rate of 10 percent.

$$P = \$10,000 \times 6.145 = \$61,450$$

$$PV_a = \frac{1 - (1 + 0.10)^{-10}}{0.10} = 6.145 \text{ (check in Table G-2)}$$

As a check of logic, note that the present value of an annuity is simply the sum of the individual single payment present values of the $10,000 amounts received in year one plus year two, and so on. Therefore, the PV_a factor for 10 years at 10 percent (6.145) should be equal to the sum of the individual single payment factors, PV_{sp}, for the years one to ten in the 10 percent column in Table G-1. If you add those factors, they total 6.144. The difference is due to rounding in the table.

Now let us return to the example of the two machines. The capital costs for each machine occur by different schedules because of different salvage values. If all future values were adjusted to the present as a common base time, we could compare the totals to see which investment alternative was advantageous. We have done this in Table A-3, where we have assumed an operating cost schedule in column 2, determined combined operating and capital costs in columns 5 and 6, and listed present values in columns 8 and 9. The present value of the entire stream of expenditures and opportunity costs is $32,405 for machine 1. The net difference in present values for the two machines is shown at the bottom of Table A-3. Because the operating cost schedule was identical for both machines, the contrast reflects differences in the present worth of capital costs. Obviously, the method allows for different operating cost schedules as well.

There are some difficulties with the methods just described. First, we have assumed that the schedule of salvage values is known, which is not usually true. Second, at some point in the life of the machines it becomes economical to replace them with identical models. Therefore, a chain of identical machines should be considered for comparative purposes; the machine is replaced in the year in which operating and capital costs are exactly equal to the interest on the present worth of all future costs. The essence of this statement is that we are seeking a balance between this year's costs (operating and capital costs) and opportunity income from disposal (interest on the present worth of all future costs). When the opportunity income from disposal is the greater of the two, replacement with the identical machine is called for. Most common criteria for comparing alternate capital investments circumvent these problems by (1) assuming an economic life, and (2) assuming some standard schedule for the decline in value of the asset. We will now consider some of these criteria.

COMMON CRITERIA FOR COMPARING ECONOMIC ALTERNATIVES

Some of the common criteria used to evaluate proposals for capital expenditures and compare alternatives involving capital assets are (1) present values, (2) rate of return, and (3) payoff period.

Present Value Criterion

Present value methods for comparing alternatives take the sum of present values of all future out-of-pocket expenditures and credits over the economic life of the asset. This figure is compared for each alternative. If differences in revenue also are involved, their present values also must be accounted for.

An Example. Suppose we are considering a machine that costs $15,000, installed. We estimate that the economic life of the machine is 8 years, at which time its salvage value is expected to be about $3000. For simplicity's sake, we take the average operating and maintenance costs to be $5000 per year. At 10 percent interest, the present value of the expenditures and credits is

Initial investment	$15,000 \times PV_{sp} =$	$15,000 \times 1.000 = 15,000$
Annual operating and maintenance costs	$5,000 \times PV_a =$	$5,000 \times 5.335 = \dfrac{26,675}{41,675}$
Less credit of present value of salvage to be received in 8 years	$3,000 \times PV_{sp} =$	$3,000 \times 0.467 = \dfrac{1,401}{\$40,274}$

The net total of $40,274 is the present value of the expenditures and credits over the 8-year expected life of the machine. The initial investment is already at present value; that is, $PV_{sp} = 1$. The annual costs of operation and maintenance are an 8-year annuity, so the entire stream of annual costs can be adjusted to present value by the multiplication of PV_a from Table G-2. Finally, the present value of the salvage is deducted. This total could be compared with similar figures for other alternatives over the same 8-year period.

Suppose that another alternate machine is estimated to have a different economic life (perhaps 4 years). Then, to make the present value totals comparable, we compare two cycles of the 4-year machine with one cycle of the 8-year machine. If the operating and maintenance costs increased as the machine aged, the present value of the expenditure in each year would be determined separately by PV_{sp}.

Rate of Return Criterion

One common method of evaluating new projects or comparing alternate courses of action is to calculate a rate of return, which is then judged for adequacy. Usually, no attempts are made to consider interest costs, so the resulting figure is referred to as the "unadjusted" rate of return (i.e., unadjusted for interest values). It is computed as follows:

$$\text{Unadjusted rate of return} = \frac{100 \text{ (net monetary operating advantage-amortization)}}{\text{average investment}}$$

The net monetary advantage reflects the algebraic sum of incremental costs of operation and maintenance and possible differences in revenue. If the rate computed is a "before-tax" rate, then the amortization

$$\text{incremental investment/economic life}$$

is subtracted, and the result is divided by average investment and multiplied by 100 to obtain a percentage return. If an "after-tax" rate is sought, the net increase in income taxes due to the project is subtracted from the net monetary advantage, and the balance of the calculation is as before. Obviously, the adequacy of a given rate of return changes drastically if it is being judged as an after-tax return.

An Example. Assume that new methods have been proposed for the line assembly of a product, each assembly being completed by one individual. The new methods require the purchase and installation of conveyors and fixtures that cost $50,000 installed, including the costs of relayout. The new line assembly methods require five fewer assemblers. After the increased maintenance and power costs are added, the net monetary operating advantage is estimated as $20,000 per year. Economic life is estimated at 5 years. The unadjusted before-tax return is

$$\frac{20,000 - \dfrac{50,000}{5}}{\dfrac{50,000}{2}} \times 100 = 40 \text{ percent}$$

The after-tax return requires that incremental taxes be deducted. Incremental taxable income will be the operating advantage less increased allowable tax depreciation. Assuming straight-line depreciation and an allowed depreciation term of 8 years, incremental taxable income is $20,000 less $50,000/8, or $20,000 − $6,250 = $13,750. Assuming an income tax rate of 50 percent, the incremental tax due to the project is $6875. The after-tax return is therefore

$$\frac{20,000 - 6,875 - 10,000}{25,000} \times 100 = \frac{3,125 \times 100}{25,000} = 12.5 \text{ percent}$$

Whether or not either the before- or after-tax rates calculated in this example are adequate must be judged in relation to the risk involved in the particular venture and the returns possible through alternate uses of the capital.

Payoff Periods

The payoff period is the time required for an investment to "pay for itself" through the net operating advantage that would result from its installation. It is calculated as follows:

$$\text{Payoff period in years} = \frac{\text{net investment}}{\text{net annual operating advantage after taxes}}$$

The payoff period for the conveyor installation that we discussed previously is

$$\frac{\$50,000}{\$20,000 - \$6875} = 3.8 \text{ years}$$

It is the period of time for the net after-tax advantage to equal exactly the net total amount invested. Presumably, after that period, "it is all gravy"; the $13,125 per year is profit, because the invested amount has been recovered. If the economic life of the equipment is 5 years and 10 percent is regarded as an appropriate rate of after-tax return for the project, what *should* the payoff period be?

Obviously, the period for both capital recovery and return is the 5-year economic life. The period that recovers capital only, but also allows enough time in the economic life to provide the return, will be somewhat shorter and will depend on the required rate of return. The payoff period is another interpretation that can be given to the present value factors for annuities, PV_a, given in Table G-2 (Appendix G).

As an example, for an economic life of 5 years and a return rate of 10 percent, $PV_a = 3.791$ from Table G-2. This indicates that capital recovery takes place in 3.791 years. The equivalent of 10 percent compound interest takes place in 5.000 − 3.791 = 1.209 years. Therefore, any of the PV_a values in Table G-2 for a given economic life in years and a given return rate indicate the shorter period in years required to return the investment; they give the payoff period directly.

The proper procedure would be to estimate economic life and to determine the applicable return rate. Determine from the present value tables the payoff period associated with these conditions. Then compute the actual payoff period of the project in question and compare it with the standard period from the tables. If the computed period is less than, or equal to, the standard period, the project meets the payoff and risk requirements that are imposed. If the computed value is greater than the table value, the project would earn less than the required rate.

IMPORTANT TERMS

Numbers in parentheses indicate page numbers

Annuity (550)	Present value of an annuity (550)
Cost of operating (546)	Present value criterion (552)
Cost of owning (546)	Present value of a single payment (550)
Economic life (549)	Rate of return criterion (553)
Obsolescence (548)	Salvage loss (548)
Payoff period (554)	Salvage value (547)

REVIEW QUESTIONS AND PROBLEMS

1. A trucking firm owns a 5-year old truck that it is considering replacing. The truck can be sold for $5000, and Blue Book values indicate that this salvage value would be $4000 1 year from now. It also appears that the trucker would need to spend $500 on a transmission overhaul if the truck were to be retained. What are the trucker's projected capital costs for next year? Interest is at 10 percent.

2. What is the present value of the salvage of a machine that can be sold 10 years hence for $2500? Interest is at 10 percent.

3. What is the future value in 25 years of a bond that earns interest at 10 percent and has a present value of $10,000?

4. What interest rate would a $10,000 bond have to earn to be worth $50,000 in 10 years?

5. At 8 percent interest, how many years will it take money to double itself?

6. What is the present value of an income stream of $1500 for 15 years at 10 percent interest?

7. What is the value of an annuity of $2000 per year for 10 years at the end of its life? Interest is at 10 percent.

8. The proud owner of a new automobile states that she intends to keep her car for only 2 years in order to minimize repair costs, which she feels should be near zero during the initial period. She paid $4000 for the car new, and Blue Book value schedules suggest that it will be worth only $2000 2 years hence. She normally drives 10,000 miles per year, and she estimates that her cost of operation is $0.10 per mile. What are her projected capital costs for the first 2 years, if interest of 6 percent represents a reasonable alternate investment for her?

9. Suppose that we are considering the installation of a small computer to accomplish internal tasks of payroll computation, invoicing, and other routine accounting. The purchase price is quoted as $300,000 and the salvage value 5

years later is expected to be $100,000. The operating costs are expected to be $100,000 per year, mainly for personnel to program, operate, and maintain the computer. What is the present value of the costs to own and operate the computer over its 5-year economic life? The value of money in the organization is 15 percent.

10. An aggressive marketer of a new office copier has made its machine available for sale as well as lease. The idea of buying a copying machine seems revolutionary, but less so when we examine our present costs, which come to $6500 per year for lease plus per copy charges of 2 cents per page. If we own a machine, the cost of paper and maintenance is projected to be $1500 per year. The new copier costs $10,000, installed, and is assumed to have an economic life of 5 years and a salvage value of $2000 (assume 50,000 pages per year).

   a. What is the projected unadjusted rate of return if we install the copier?

   b. If incremental taxes for the project are $1000, what is the adjusted rate of return?

11. What is the actual payoff period for the office copier project discussed in problem 10? If interest is 10 percent, what should the minimum payoff period be to make the investment economically sound? Does the office copier project meet the payoff standard?

REFERENCES

Anthony, R. N., and G. A. Welsch, *Fundamentals of Management Accounting* (3rd ed.), Irwin, Homewood, Ill., 1981.

Grant, E. L., and W. G. Ireson, *Principles of Engineering Economy* (5th ed.), Ronald Press, New York, 1970.

Reisman, A., *Managerial and Engineering Economics*, Allyn & Bacon, Boston, 1971.

Thuesen, H. G., W. J. Fabrycky, and G. J. Thuesen, *Engineering Economy* (5th ed.), Prentice-Hall, Englewood Cliffs, N.J., 1977.

APPENDIX B*

Linear Programming

NATURE OF LINEAR OPTIMIZATION MODELS

Linear optimization models are characterized by linear mathematical expressions. In addition, they are usually deterministic in nature; that is, they do not take account of risk and uncertainty. The parameters of the model are assumed to be known with certainty. Finally, linear programming is used most often when we are attempting to allocate some limited or scarce resource in order to make decisions that use the resource in question in such a way that a single stated criterion is optimized (either minimized or maximized). The solution technique for linear optimization models is linear programming.

The Meaning of Linearity

In linear models, we *must* use only linear mathematical expressions. In Figure B-1 we show equations of both linear and nonlinear mathematical expressions, together with their graphs. In Figure B-1, (a) and (b) are graphs of linear expressions and appear as straight lines. Figures B-1 (c) and (d) are graphs of nonlinear expressions, because (c) contains an x^2 term and (d) the cross product of $x_1 x_2$.

Figure B-1 also illustrates the mathematical form of constraints. In Figure B-1(b) in the shaded portion, we see the expression $x_1 - 2x_2 \geq 4$, which states that $(x_1 - 2x_2)$ must be greater than or equal to ($\geq$) 4. When it is equal to 4, we have the straight line. Otherwise, the inequality expression constrains all combinations of x_1 and x_2 to be in the shaded portion of the graph. Conversely, all combinations of x_1 and x_2 that fall above the straight line are not admissible, because they do not satisfy the constraint $x_1 - 2x_2 \geq 4$.

Figure B-1(d) shows a nonlinear constraint expression in the shaded portion of the graph. That expression contrains combinations of x_1 and x_2 to be above the curve (in the shaded portion), because the expression states that $(x_1 - 2x_1 x_2)$ must be less than or equal to ($\leq$) 4. Again, when the statement on the left-hand side of the expression is equal to 4, all points fall on the curve.

Mathematical statements of constraints may be less than or equal to ($\leq$), equal to ($=$), and greater than or equal to ($\geq$). *Linear* constraints, illustrated by the expression in the shaded portion of Figure B-1b, will be very important in linear optimization models.

Elements of the Model-Building Process

To develop a linear optimization model, we use the following process:

1. Define the decision variables.
2. Define the objective function, Z, a linear equation involving the decision variables that identifies our objective in the problem-solving effort. This equation predicts the effects on the objective function of choosing different values for the decision variables.

* The materials in this appendix were drawn from Chapters 3 and 5 of E. S. Buffa, and J. S. Dyer, *Management Science/Operations Research: Model Formulation and Solution Methods* (2d ed.), John Wiley & Sons, Inc. New York, 1981. For a more complete coverage see Chapters 3 to 6 of that text.

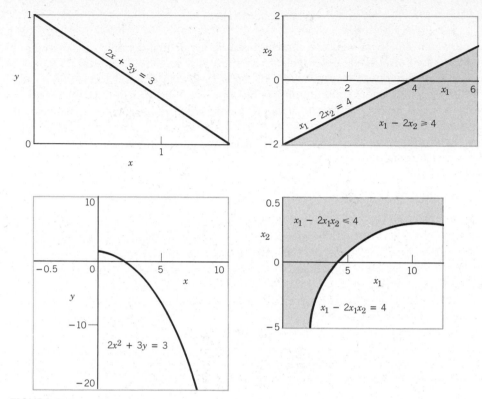

FIGURE B-1
Examples of linear and nonlinear expressions; (a) and (b) are linear, and (c) and (d) are nonlinear, because (c) has an x^2 term, and (d) contains the cross product term x_1x_2. The shaded portions of both (b) and (d) contain inequality expressions describing constraints; that is, values of x_1 and x_2 falling within the shaded areas are admissible, but points beyond the curve are not

3. Define the constraints—linear expressions involving the decision variables that specify the restrictions on the decisions that can be made. *Feasible alternatives can be generated* by selecting values for the decision variables that satisfy these constraints.

FORMULATION OF A TWO-PRODUCT MODEL

A chemical manufacturer produces two products, which we shall call chemical x and chemical y. Each product is manufactured by a two-step process that involves blending and mixing in machine A and packaging on machine B. The two products complement each other because the same production facilities can be used for both products, thus achieving better utilization of these facilities.

Definition of Decision Variables

Because these facilities are shared, and costs and profits from each product are different, there is the question of how to utilize the available machine time in the most profitable way. Chemical x is seemingly more profitable, but the manager once tried producing the maximum amount of chemical x within market limitations, using the balance of his capacity to produce chemical y. The result, however, was that such an allocation of machine time resulted in poor profit performance. The manager now feels that some appropriate balance between the two products is best and wishes to determine the production rates for each product per 2-week period.

Thus, the decision variables are

x, the number of units of chemical x to be produced

y, the number of units of chemical y to be produced

Definition of the Objective Function

The physical plant and basic organization exists and represents the fixed costs of the organization. These costs are irrelevant to the production scheduling decision, and they are ignored. The manager, however, has obtained price and variable cost information and has computed the contribution to profit and overhead per unit of each product sold as shown in Table B-1. The objective is to maximize profit, and the contribution rates have a linear relationship to this objective. Therefore, the objective function is to maximize the sum of the total contribution from chemical x ($60x$) plus the total contribution from chemical y ($50y$), or

$$\text{maximize } Z = 60x + 50y$$

Definition of Constraints

The processing times for each unit of the two products on the mixing machine (A) and the packaging machine (B) are as follows:

Product	Machine A (hours/unit)	Machine B (hours/unit)
x	2	3
y	4	2

For the upcoming 2-week period, machine A has available 80 hours and machine B has available 60 hours of processing time.

TABLE B-1

Sales Prices, Variable Costs, and Contributions per Unit for Chemicals x and y

	Sales Price (p)	Variable Costs (c)	Contribution to Profit and Overhead ($r = p - c$)
Chemical x	$350	$290	$60
Chemical y	450	400	50

Machine A Constraint. Because we are limited by the 80 hours available on the mixing machine A, the total time spent in the manufacture of chemical x and chemical y cannot exceed the total time available. For machine A, because chemical x requires 2 hours per unit and y requires 4 hours per unit, the total time spent on the two products must be less than or equal to 80 hours, that is,

$$2x + 4y \leq 80$$

Machine B Contraint. Similarly, the available hours on the packaging machine B are limited to 60, and because chemical x requires 3 hours per unit and y requires 2 hours per unit, the total hours for the two products must be less than or equal to 60 hours, or

$$3x + 2y \leq 60$$

Marketing Constraints. Forecasts of the markets indicate that we can expect to sell a maximum of 16 units of chemical x and 18 units of chemical y. Therefore,

$$x \leq 16$$
$$y \leq 18$$

Minimum Production Constraints. The minimum production for each product is zero, therefore,

$$x \geq 0$$
$$y \geq 0$$

The Linear Optimization Model

We can now summarize a statement of the linear optimization model for the two-product chemical company in the standard linear programming format, as follows:

maximize $Z = 60x + 50y$
subject to

$2x + 4y \leq 80$	(machine A)
$3x + 2y \leq 60$	(machine B)
$x \leq 16$	(demand for chemical x)
$y \leq 18$	(demand for chemical y)
$x \geq 0$	(minimum production for chemical x)
$y \geq 0$	(minimum production for chemical y)

A Graphical Solution

We can gain some insight into the solution of a linear optimization model by analyzing it graphically. Although this is not a practical approach to the solution of large linear optimization models of real-world problems, the basic concepts do carry over into these problems.

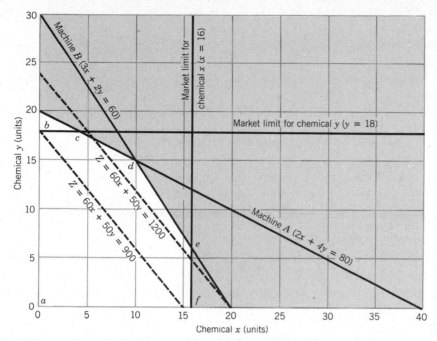

FIGURE B-2
Graphic representation of the limitations imposed by machine capacity, marketing, and minimum production constraints. The area enclosed by *abcdef* includes all feasible solutions to the model

The constraints of the linear optimization model are shown in Figure B-2. To see how they were plotted, suppose we consider the machine A constraint

$$2x + 4y \leq 80 \tag{1}$$

The simplest way to show the values of x and y that satisfy an inequality is to plot the straight line corresponding to the equation obtained by replacing the inequality sign with an equality sign; that is, we plot the line corresponding to the equality

$$2x + 4y = 80 \tag{2}$$

for our example. Generally, the easiest way to plot an equality is to find the x-intercept—the point on the x axis representing the value of x that satisfies this equality constraint when $y = 0$—and the y-intercept, the value of y satisfying the equality when $x = 0$.

If $y = 0$ in Equation 2, then $2x + 4(0) = 80$, or $2x = 80$. Therefore, $x = 80/2 = 40$ is the x-intercept value for Equation 2 as shown in Figure B-2. If $x = 0$, then $2(0) + 4y = 80$, so $y = 20$ is the y-intercept value. Because we know that Equation 2 passes through the two points $(40, 0)$ and $(0, 20)$, the line can be plotted easily.

This straight line represents all the values of x and y that satisfy Equation 2, but what about the (x, y) pairs that satisfy Inequality 1? All the points that satisfy an inequality lie the line on one side of the corresponding equation, and all the points that violate that inequality lie on the other side. On which side of the line representing Equation 2 are the points satisfying Inequality 1? The simplest way to decide is often to consider the origin (0, 0) and check to see if the values $x = 0$ and $y = 0$ satisfy the inequality. If they do, then the origin and all other points on the same side of the equality line 2 satisfy Inequality 1. Otherwise, all points on the side of (2) away from the origin satisfy (1). In our example, $2(0) + 4(0) = 0$ and $0 \leq 80$, so the origin satisfies Inequality 1.

The solution to a linear optimization model must simultaneously satisfy *all* the constraints of the model. Points that violate one or more of the constraints of the two product model are in the shaded areas of Figure B-2. For example, the values $x = 0$ and $y = 20$ satisfy the constraints $2x + 4y \leq 80$ and $3x + 2y \leq 60$, but violate the constraint $y \leq 18$. Therefore, the point (0, 20) is in the shaded region of Figure B-2. The solution to our problem lies somewhere within the set of feasible decisions, the solution space *abcdef*. Any production schedule with a combination of amounts x and y that falls outside this solution space is not feasible because it does not simultaneously satisfy all the constraints.

We have also plotted in Figure B-2 the linear objective function for two values of total contribution, $Z = \$900$ and $Z = \$1200$. When we set $Z = \$900$, for example,

$$60x + 50y = 900$$

Then, when $x = 0$, we must have $y = 18$ as the y-intercept because $60(0) + 50(18) = 900$, and when $y = 0$, we have $60x + 50(0) = 900$ and $x = 900/60 = 15$. The resulting straight line is very simple to plot in Figure B-2. The "900" line within the solution space of points simultaneously satisfying all the constraints defines all the feasible solutions that would produce a contribution of $Z = \$900$. Because our objective is to maximize contribution, what happens if we increase Z to $\$1200$? Because the slope of the objective function has not changed, the line for $Z = \$1200$ is parallel to the $\$900$ line, and closer to point d, as we note in Figure B-2. It is now rather obvious for this simple problem that if we substituted larger and larger values of Z in the objective function, lines parallel to the $\$900$ and $\$1200$ lines would result, and a line through point d would define a combination of x and y with the maximum possible contribution within the feasible solution space. Now we will see how this same solution point might be found using a computer program for solving linear optimization models.

Solution and Interpretation of the Two-Product Model

We will assume that we have a mechanism for solving linear optimization models when they are formulated in the preceding standard format. Indeed, linear programming computing codes are commonly available both in interactive mode (available from a time-share terminal) and in batch mode for large-scale linear programming problem solutions. In order to use either of these computing programs for the solution of linear optimization models, the problem must be presented to the "black box" in the precise form required. This input format is usually more user oriented in interactive time-share systems, and we shall use one of these programs to illustrate solutions to problems in this appendix (see Buckley et al., 1974).

Now, let us return to the chemical production problem for which we just formulated the linear optimization model in standard form. Figure B-3 shows a portion of the computer printout for the problem.

Computer Input. In Figure B-3a we see the input steps following the "sign on" and "call up" of the linear programming subroutine. The objective function and constraints are entered as shown. We need not enter the last two constraints of $x \geq 0$ and $y \geq 0$, because the computer program assumes that none of the decision variables can take on negative values.

Computer Output. Figure B-3b shows the solution output. First, the terminal prints the optimum value of the objective function, $1350. In other words, it states that $Z = 1350$ in the objective function for an optimal solution.

Next, the terminal prints the values of the variables in the optimum solution. Note that scientific notation is used; that is, the value of each variable is followed by "E" and some number. This notation means that the number preceding the E is to be multipled by that number of 10s. For example, E1 means multiply by 10, E2 by 100, and so on. E0 indicates that the multiplier is "1," or simply that the value of the variable needs no modification.

Now let us consider only the first two variables listed in the solution we have named $CHEMX$ and $CHEMY$. The solution states that their optimal values are 10 and 15 units, respectively. Note that this is point d in Figure B-2, the point where the capacity constraint lines for machines A and B intersect, as we expected, based on our graphical analysis of this problem. This is an important observation that we shall use in understanding how the linear programming algorithm actually works.

Using the solution values of $CHEMX$ and $CHEMY$, we insert them in the objective function and compute Z,

$$Z = 60 \times 10 + 50 \times 15 = 1350$$

```
     LPENTER
ENTER THE NAME OF THIS PROJECT CHEMICAL PRODUCTION
MAXIMIZE OR MINIMIZE:  MAXIMIZE
OBJECTIVE FUNCTION: Z=60CHEMX+50CHEMY
ENTER CONSTRAINT EQUATIONS (STRIKE JUST A CARRIAGE RETURN TO STOP INPUT)
[1] 2CHEMX+4CHEMY≤80
[2] 3CHEMX+2CHEMY≤60
[3] CHEMX≤16
[4] CHEMY≤18
```

(A)

```
     LPRUN

                CHEMICAL PRODUCTION

THE OPTIMAL VALUE OF THE OBJECTIVE FUNCTION IS:    1350.000

            THE VARIABLES IN THE SOLUTION ARE

VARIABLE   CHEMX   AT LEVEL     1.0000E1
           CHEMY                1.5000E1
           SLK3                 6.0000E0
           SLK4                 3.0000E0
```

(B)

FIGURE B-3
The chemical production problem: (a) computer input and (b) computer solution

This result checks with the optimal value of Z given by the computer solution.

Checking one further bit of logic, if the solution to our problem is at the intersection of the two capacity constraint equations, then we should be able to solve the equations for the two lines simultaneously to determine the values of CHEMX and CHEMY that are common to the equations. First, let us use the equation for machine A and solve for x,

$$2x + 4y = 80$$

Therefore,

$$x = 80/2 - 4y/2 = 40 - 2y$$

We then substitute this value of x in the constraint equation for machine B,

$$3(40 - 2y) + 2y = 60$$
$$(120 - 6y) + 2y = 60$$
$$4y = 60$$
$$y = 15$$

This value of y checks with our computer solution. Now, substitute $y = 15$ in the machine A constraint equation to determine the value of x,

$$2x + 4(15) = 80$$
$$x = (80 - 60)/2 = 10$$

Thus, we have verified that the solution to our problem is at point d of Figure B-2 where the two constraint equations intersect. Another interpretation of this fact is that machines A and B, our two productive resources, are completely utilized in this solution—there is no residual slack machine capacity. This fact is important because any of the other feasible solutions in the polygon $abcdef$ of Figure B-2 would have involved some slack capacity in one or both of the two machines. If there had been slack capacity for either of the machines in the optimum solution, that fact would have been indicated in the computer output for the optimum solution. In some more complex problems, there might be slack capacity of a productive resource in an optimum solution.

Now, note that the computer output gave us the value of variables that we did not ask for explicitly, $SLK3$ and $SLK4$. These are the slack values related to constraints (3) and (4), the market constraints. Constraint (3), $CHEMX \le 16$ was the market limit for that product. The solution simply points out to us that if we produce according to the optimum solution where $CHEMX = 10$, there will be unsatisfied demand (slack) of 6, and this fits in with the market constraint because $CHEMX + SLK3 = 10 + 6 = 16$. Similarly, the value of $SLK4 = 3$ agrees with the market constraint, $CHEMY \le 18$, because $CHEMY + SLK4 = 15 + 3 = 18$.

These interpretations of the optimum solution to the chemical production problem are rather simple. The important point is that equivalent interpretations of more complex problems are a straightforward extension of these ideas. The solution will state the combination of variables that optimizes the objective function. Some but not necessarily all of the constraints will be the controlling ones, and there will be slack in some of the resources; that is, they will not all be fully utilized. In our example, the slack was in the demands for the two products. Note, however, that if the demand for *CHEMY* dropped to only 14, that is ($y = 14$), it would have become one of the controlling ("tight") constraints as may be seen from Figure B-2, and there would have been some slack capacity in machine *A*.

SENSITIVITY ANALYSIS AND INTERPRETATION OF RESULTS

If we wanted only the solution to the problem—the optimal combination of variables, the value of slack variables, and the optimum value of the objective function—we could stop at this point. However, additional valuable information can be obtained from the sensitivity analysis.

Although the optimum solution states what to do now, given the objective function and the constraints, the sensitivity analysis raises questions about opportunities and perhaps about what could or should be done to improve the solution to the managerial problem.

Figure B-4 presents the sensitivity analysis in tabular form, first for each constraint and then for the prices (contributions) for each product. For each constraint there is listed a "*SHADOW*" (shadow price), the "*LB*" (lower bound of the right-hand side of the constraint), "*CURRENT*" (current value of the right-hand side), and "*UB*" (upper bound of the right-hand side).

Shadow Prices

The shadow prices indicate the value of a marginal unit in the right-hand side of the constraint. For example, recall the meaning of the first constraint for machine *A* (2 *CHEMX* + 4 *CHEMY* ≤ 80. It states that the total available capacity for machine *A* is 80 hours. What would be the marginal value (in the objective function) of one additional unit of capacity? The answer is given in Figure B-4 as $3.75. If the capacity of machine *A* were 81 hours, the extra hour would add $3.75 to the total contribution (Z). Conversely, if only 79 hours were available, this amount would be subtracted from total contribution.

Now observe that the shadow price for machine *B* capacity is $17.50. The marginal value of capacity for machine *B* is 17.50/3.75 = 4.7 times that for machine *A*. The shadow prices tell the manager that the opportunity provided by increasing

```
DO YOU WISH SENSITIVITY ANALYSIS? YES
                        SHADOW          LB         CURRENT         UB
CONSTRAINT       1     3.7500E0     5.6000E1     8.0000E1     8.8000E1
                 2     1.7500E1     4.8000E1     6.0000E1     7.2000E1
                 3     0.0000E0     1.0000E1     1.6000E1     7.2370E75
                 4     0.0000E0     1.5000E1     1.8000E1     7.2370E75


PRICE        CHEMX                  2.5000E1     6.0000E1     7.5000E1
             CHEMY                  4.0000E1     5.0000E1     1.2000E2

-<END>-
```

FIGURE B-4
Sensitivity analysis for the chemical production problem

machine B capacity is relatively large and allow for appraisal of expansion proposals for both machines.

The shadow prices for constraints 3 and 4 (demands) are zero because these constraints do not limit us in the current solution. If demand for *CHEMY* dropped to 14, then it would become one of the controlling constraints, as we noted previously. The optimum solution would change, but in addition, the shadow price for constraint 4 would become some positive value, indicating a marginal value to increasing demand for *CHEMY*, perhaps providing the manager with information to appraise programs to stimulate demand.

Lower, Current, and Upper Bounds

We just stated the meaning of the shadow prices, that is, the value of marginal units of resources. But, for what ranges are these marginal rates valid? Can we increase capacity for machine B to two or three times its present capacity and expect to obtain an additional $17.50 per unit in the objective function? No, there are limits, and the bounds tell us exactly what they are. Taking the capacity of machine B as an example, it is currently 60 hours as shown in Figure B-4 under the *"CURRENT"* column, but we see that the shadow price is valid in the range of 48 to 72 hours.

If we could increase the capacity of machine B to 72 hours, we would obtain an additional $17.50 \times 12 = $210 in total contribution. We would be able to increase contribution by $210 \times 100/1350 = 15.6$ percent. On the down side, if we had a breakdown of machine B, for example, and available hours fell to the lower bound of 48, we would lose $210 in total contribution. The interpretation for the bounds on the capacity of machine A is similar.

Now let us examine the significance of the bounds on the demand for the two products. Take constraint (4), the demand for *CHEMY*, for example. Its lower bound is 15. A shadow price of zero applies if demand falls to 15, that is, the constraint is ineffective in that range. But, as we have already noted, if demand falls below 15, the constraint becomes one of those controlling the solution.

Now, the upper bound for constraint (4) is listed as 7.2370E75. This is the code for infinity in this particular linear programming computer program. In effect there is no upper bound.

Price Sensitivity

The contribution rates in the objective function are termed generally "prices." Recall that the contribution of a unit of *CHEMX* was $60 and of *CHEMY* $50, and these are shown as the *"CURRENT"* values in Figure B-4. But, what if "prices" change? Would the changes affect the solution? The lower and upper bounds for prices shown in Figure B-4 indicate the range of prices (contribution rates) for which the optimum solution ($x = 10, y = 15$) is still optimum. For example, the contribution rate for *CHEMX* could be anywhere in the range of $25 to $75 and the optimum amount of *CHEMX* and *CHEMY* would still be as indicated in the present solution: Produce 10 units of *CHEMX* and 15 units of *CHEMY*. Of course, the total contribution would change because of the change in the contribution rate, but the optimal *decision* would remain the same.

There is a practical significance to the price sensitivity. For example, the manager might estimate contribution for *CHEMX* at $60, but these kinds of figures are seldom absolutely precise. Suppose that the contribution is somewhere in the $55 to $65 range. In this case, the same solution applies. The result is that the use of *rough* estimates for the contribution rate is adequate, and we should not spend additional time and money to refine the estimate. Thus, the calculated bounds in relation to managerial judgments help indicate how we should allocate time and money to refine cost information—if the bounds are tight, it may be worthwhile to be precise, but if they are loose we would gain nothing by attempting to improve the estimates.

Summary

Given a linear optimization model stated in the format we have specified, we can use a computer program to provide the optimum combination of the decision variables, the optimum value of the objective function, and the values of slack capacity or other resources in the system. In interpreting the solution, however, we can also obtain the value of a marginal unit of each resource (shadow prices) and the range over which the shadow price is valid. In addition, we can obtain the range of prices (contribution rates in our example) in the objective function for which the printed solution is valid.

Understanding the significance of the optimum solution and the sensitivity analysis in the context of the real problem has great value. Decision makers are in a position to appraise various proposals for changing the optimum solution. They should not look on the optimum solution as necessarily the final decision, but as a basis for asking "what if" questions. The sensitivity analysis provides information regarding many possible "what if" questions, and may also suggest variations of the model that may require additional computer runs.

THE SIMPLEX METHOD

We will use a modification of the chemical production problem as a vehicle for discussion. Because we can represent that problem in graphic form, and we already know the optimal solution, we can see readily what is happening at each stage of the algorithm. We will simplify the problem slightly by eliminating the demand constraints. Recall that for the stated problem, these constraints were not effective in dictating the optimal solution anyway. Eliminating them provides a simpler, more direct explanation of the procedure.

Formulation

The statement of the problem was one of allocating time on machines *A* and *B* to the two products, *x* and *y*, in such a way that contribution to profit and overhead would be maximized. The time requirements on the two machines for each product were

569

given and the total available time on the two machines was limited. Therefore, the resulting modified linear optimization model is

$$\text{maximize } Z = 60x + 50y$$
subject to

$2x + 4y \leqslant 80$	(machine A)
$3x + 2y \leqslant 60$	(machine B)
$x \geqslant 0$	(minimum production for chemical x)
$y \geqslant 0$	(minimum production for chemical y)

Graphic Solution

Figure B-5 shows the constraints plotted on a graph and identifies the feasible solution space, *abcd,* and the previously determined optimal allocation of machine time at point *c*; that is, produce $x = 10$ units and $y = 15$ units. Recall also that the contribution for the optimal solution was $1350.

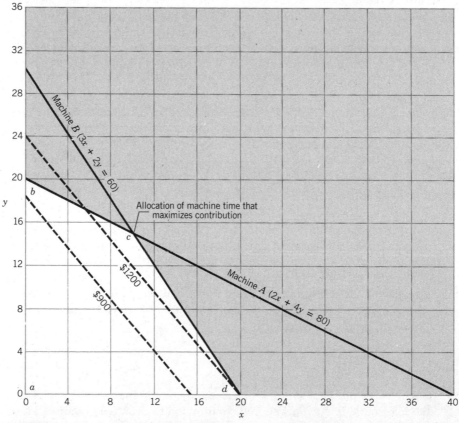

FIGURE B-5
Graphic solution of example used for interpretation of the simplex method

We have plotted in Figure B-5 the linear objective function for two values of total contribution, $Z = \$900$ and $Z = \$1200$. It is now rather obvious for this simple problem that if we substituted larger and larger values of Z in the objective function, lines parallel to the $\$900$ and $\$1200$ lines would result, and a line through point c would define a combination of x and y with the maximum possible contribution within the feasible solution space. Figure B-5 then provides us with a clear picture of the problem and the relationships for various solutions evaluated by the objective function.

Slack Variables

First, we note the physical meaning of the constraints on available time for machines A and B. For machine A, because x requires 2 hours per unit and y requires 4 hours per unit, and we are limited to a total of 80 hours, we write the inequality constraint

$$2x + 4y \leq 80 \tag{1}$$

and for machine B,

$$3x + 2y \leq 60 \tag{2}$$

The inequalities state that the use of machines A and B is *less* than or equal to 80 and 60 hours, respectively; that is, there *could* be idle machine time. If we account for any slack available, we could convert Inequalities 1 and 2 into equations by defining *slack variables* to represent the possible idle time. Therefore,

$$2x + 4y + W_A = 80 \tag{3}$$

$$3x + 2y + W_B = 60 \tag{4}$$

where W_A is the idle time for machine A, and W_B is the idle time for machine B. We also require W_A and W_B to be nonnegative ($W_A, W_B \geq 0$). The constraints plotted in Figure B-5 are then lines that indicate the full use of machine A when $W_A = 0$ and of machine B when $W_B = 0$. Solutions that involve some idle time are permissible and would fall below one or both of the constraint lines, and would be within the solution space *abcd*.

The effect of solutions involving slack (idle machine time) is easy to see through examples. Assume that the production schedule is 9 units of chemical x, and 14 units of chemical y. Because 2 hours per unit of x and 4 hours per unit of y are required of machine A time, and machine A has a total of 80 hours available, we have from Equation 3

$$W_A = 80 - (2)(9) - (4)(14) = 80 - 74 = 6 \text{ hours}$$

There are 74 productive hours, and the slack in machine A time is taken up as idle time of 6 hours.

Similarly, the idle time on machine B from Equation 4 would be

$$W_B = 60 - (3)(9) - (2)(14) = 60 - 55 = 5 \text{ hours}$$

Now examine Figure B-5 and note that the point ($x = 9$, $y = 14$) falls inside the feasible solution space, but not on any of the constraint lines. This type of solution is called *nonbasic*.

With the slack variables now in the formulation, the objective function is actually

$$\text{maximize } Z = 60x + 50y + (0)W_A + (0)W_B$$

The zero coefficients for the slack variables are appropriate, because they make no contribution to profit. The total contribution of the nonbasic solution is

$$Z = (60)(9) + (50)(14) + (0)(6) + (0)(5) = 540 + 700 + 0 + 0 = 1240$$

Let us return to our two Equations, 3 and 4, with four unknown variables, plus the objective function. Now, recall from simple algebra that we can solve equations simultaneously if there are the same number of unknowns as equations. If we set any two of the four variables to zero, we can solve the two equations simultaneously to find the values of the other two. This is exactly what we will be doing in the following step-by-step procedure.

THE SIMPLEX ALGORITHM

We used simple problems to explain linear optimization models and the simplex solution technique. The power of linear programming, however, is in the solution of large-scale problems, and the key to their solution has been the simplex algorithm. When the algorithm has been developed in a rigorous way, the computing effort can be further reduced by programming the algorithm for computers. Large-scale problems of resource allocation can then be formulated and solved at reasonable cost. Without the simplex algorithm and without computers, the solution of large-scale problems would be impossible.

We will now present a more rigorous description of the simplex method. This description is based on an approach for solving several simultaneous linear equations.

In reducing the simplex algorithm to a set of rigorous rules, there is a risk that we may begin to think of it as a mechanical procedure, losing contact with what is being accomplished at each stage of solution. We will try to maintain contact with the meaning of each step by using the chemical production problem as an example again, and relating our manipulations to the graphic solution shown in Figure B-5.

After the addition of the slack variables to account for idle time, our two restricting equations for machines A and B were

$$2x + 4y + W_A = 80 \tag{5}$$
$$3x + 2y + W_B = 60 \tag{6}$$

An initial solution to this set of equations is found by setting $x = y = 0$, which gives $W_A = 80$ and $W_B = 60$. This solution is easy to see, because W_A has a coefficient of $+1$ in (5) but does not appear in (6), and W_B has a coefficient of $+1$ in (6) but does not appear in (5).

The objective function for this problem can be written as

$$Z = 60x + 50y + (0)W_A + (0)W_B \tag{7}$$

because idle time contributes nothing to profits or overhead. Substituting the initial solution of $W_A = 80$ and $W_B = 60$ into Equation 7 gives

$$Z - 60x - 50y = (0)80 + (0)60 = 0 \qquad\qquad (8)$$

as the corresponding value of the objective function.

Because (8) is also an equation, we can combine it with (5) and (6) and write

$$
\begin{array}{llll}
Z - 60x - 50y & & = 0 & \text{(row 0)} \\
2x + 4y + W_A & & = 80 & \text{(row 1)} \\
3x + 2y & + W_B & = 60 & \text{(row 2)}
\end{array}
$$

where all the variables must also be nonnegative. This is our set of *initial equations* associated with the initial solution $x = y = 0$, $W_A = 80$, and $W_B = 60$.

Improving the Initial Solution

To improve the initial solution, we use the test for optimality: "Are there coefficients in the objective function which indicate that Z can be increased?" If there are, we know we can substitute a variable in the solution that has a higher contribution rate to the objective function than one of the variables now in the solution. Variables with *negative* coefficients in row 0 will improve the objective function if they are brought into the solution.

Identifying the Entering Variable and Key Column. Any variable with a negative coefficient in row 0 will improve (increase) the objective function if its value is increased from 0. The following rule is useful in selecting the entering variable:

Rule I

If there are variables with negative coefficients in row 0, choose the one with the most negative coefficient as the *entering variable.* If there are no variables with negative coefficients in row 0, the current solution is optimal.

In this example, we choose x as the entering variable according to Rule I. This choice determines the "direction of change" in the solution.

The coefficients of the entering variable x, -60 in row 0, 2 in row 1, and 3 in row 2, will play a key role in the computations of the simplex algorithm. Because these coefficients are arranged vertically as a column of numbers in rows 0, 1, and 2, we designate them as the *key column.*

Identifying the Key Row. If x increases by 1 unit, W_A must decrease by 2 units (the coefficient of x in row 1) in order to maintain the equality in row 1, and W_B must decrease by 3 units (the coefficient of x in row 2) to maintain the equality in row 2. If W_A decreases from its initial value of 80 units to 0, x could increase to $80/2 = 40$; if W_B decreases from its initial value of 60, x could increase to $60/3 = 20$. The latter, 20, would be reached first as x increases. Therefore, the relationship between W_B and x in row 2 *limits* the size of x, so we designate row 2 as the *key row* in our calculations.

Notice that this result was determined by dividing the right-hand side of each row (ignoring row 0) by the corresponding number in the key column. If the coefficient in the key column in a row were negative or zero, the row would be ignored, because increasing the entering variable would not force another variable to zero. This idea can be implemented in the simplex algorithm with a second rule.

Rule II

Taking the ratios of the right-hand sides of the rows to the corresponding coefficients of the key column (ignoring zero or negative coefficients), choose the row with the smallest ratio as the *key row.*

Rule II determines the "amount of change" in the solution.

Pivoting. We now know the entering variable x, the key column of the coefficients of x, and the key row, row 2. The coefficient of the entering variable x that is in the key column and in the key row, 3, also plays a special role in the simplex algorithm, so we call it the *key number.* We are prepared to carry out the *pivoting operation* that determines a revised solution to our linear optimization problem.

The key row was determined by identifying the first nonzero variable to be *decreased to zero* as the entering variable is *increased from zero.* From our Rule II calculations, we know that the variable x will be increased to 20 and the variable W_B will be decreased to 0 in the new solution.

Pivoting requires the following steps:

1. Divide each coefficient in the key row and its right-hand side by the key number.
2. For each row *except* the key row:

    a. Multiply each coefficient of the newly transformed key row (found in step 1 above) by the negative of the coefficient in the key column in the nonlimiting row.

    b. Add the result to the nonlimiting row.

In our example problem, we carry out these steps by dividing row 2 (the key row) by the key number, 3. The result is

$$x + \frac{2y}{3} + \frac{W_B}{3} = 20 \qquad (9)$$

Next, we modify rows 0 and 1 as indicated.

Row 0: multiply (9) by 60 and add to row 0

Row 1: multiply (9) by -2 and add to row 1

For row 0, the calculations would be

$$
\begin{array}{lll}
Z - 60x - 50y & = 0 & \text{(row 0)} \\
\underline{\quad 60x + 40y \quad + 20W_B = 1200} & & \text{[Eq. (9) multiplied by 60]} \\
Z \qquad\quad - 10y \quad + 20W_B = 1200 &
\end{array}
$$

After carrying out similar calculations for row 1 (check them for yourself), the revised set of equations is

$$
\begin{array}{lll}
Z \qquad -10y \qquad + 20W_B = 1200 & \text{(row 0)} \\[2mm]
\qquad\quad \frac{8y}{3} + W_A \; - \frac{2W_B}{3} \quad = 40 & \text{(row 1)} \\[2mm]
\qquad\quad x + \frac{2y}{3} \qquad + \frac{W_B}{3} \quad = 20 & \text{(row 2)}
\end{array}
$$

Notice that in each row there is one variable with a coefficient of 1 and with coefficients of 0 in the other rows (including row 0). This variable is "in the solution" with a value equal to the number on the right-hand side of the equal sign. In row 0, this variable is Z, which equals 1200; in row 1, $W_A = 40$; and in row 2, $x = 20$. The variables that are "in the solution" are called *basic variables*. The other variables, y and W_A in this case, are required to equal 0, and are called *nonbasic variables*.

When examined closely, pivoting is simply an approach for solving a system of simultaneous equations. Although the arithmetic is a bit tedious, there is nothing about this basic solution strategy that is particularly sophisticated or mathematically "advanced."

In fact, step 2 of the pivoting procedure can be made even more mechanical by using a simple formula. For each row *except* the key row, all the numbers in the revised row can be obtained from the following relationship:

$$\text{new number} = \text{old number} - \frac{\left(\begin{array}{c}\text{corresponding} \\ \text{number of} \\ \text{key row}\end{array}\right) \times \left(\begin{array}{c}\text{corresponding} \\ \text{number of} \\ \text{key column}\end{array}\right)}{\text{key number}} \tag{10}$$

For example,

1. row 1, constant column
    new number = $80 - (60 \times 2)/3 = 40$
2. row 1, x column
    new number = $2 - (3 \times 2)/3 = 0$
3. row 0, x column
    new number = $-60 - (3 \times -60)/3 = 0$

The remaining coefficients in row 0 and row 1 can be calculated in the same way (check this yourself).

Accomplishing the pivoting operation completes one *iteration* of the simplex algorithm. One iteration corresponds to a movement from one corner point of the solution space to another adjacent corner point, or from one basic solution to another.

Improving the Solution

The variable y has the only negative coefficient in row 0, and so we know that it should enter the solution by Rule I. The coefficients of y, -10 in row 0, 8/3 in row 1, and 2/3 in row 2, become the key column. We can determine the key row from the ratios shown in Table B-2. The minimum ratio of 15 corresponds to row 1, which is designated as the key row according to Rule II. The key number is the coefficient in both the key row and the key column, 8/3.

Performing the pivoting operation, we first divide each coefficient in the key row, row 1, by the key number, 8/3, and obtain

$$y + \frac{3W_A}{8} - \frac{W_B}{4} = 15 \tag{11}$$

TABLE B-2	**Applying Rule II**		
Row	Current Right-Hand Side	Coefficient of y	Ratio
1	40	8/3	15
2	20	2/3	30

We modify rows 0 and 2 as indicated.

Row 0: multiply (11) by 10 and add to row 0.

Row 2: multiply (11) by $-2/3$ and add to row 2.

Alternately, rows 1 and 2 could be determined by applying formula (10). The resulting system of equations is

$$Z \qquad + \frac{15W_A}{4} + \frac{35W_B}{2} = 1350 \qquad \text{(row 0)}$$

$$y \;\; + \;\; \frac{3W_A}{8} - \frac{W_B}{4} = 15 \qquad \text{(row 1)}$$

$$x \;\; - \;\; \frac{W_A}{4} + \frac{W_B}{2} = 10 \qquad \text{(row 2)}$$

By identifying the variable in each row with a coefficient of 1 and with coefficients of 0 in the other rows, we see that the solution is $Z = 1350$, $x = 10$, and $y = 15$, with $W_A = W_B = 0$. Now both x and y are basic variables, whereas W_A and W_B are nonbasic.

Because there are no variables in row 0 with negative coefficients, this solution is optimal. Note that the coefficients in row 0 yield shadow prices obtained previously for W_A and W_B.

Summary of the Procedure

The steps of the simplex algorithm may be summarized as follows:

1. Formulate the constraints and the objective function.
2. Develop the set of *initial equations,* using the slack variables in the initial solution.
3. Identify the *entering variable,* the variable with the most negative coefficient in row 0, and the *key column* of coefficients of the entering variable.
4. Identify the *key row,* the row with the minimum ratio, determined by dividing the right-hand side of each row by the positive coefficient in the key column in that row (if the coefficient is zero or negative, the row is ignored). This is the limiting row, and all other rows are nonlimiting.
5. Perform the *pivoting operation.*

```
          LPRUN
                        CHEMICAL PRODUCTION


THE OPTIMAL VALUE OF THE OBJECTIVE FUNCTION IS:    1350.000


                THE VARIABLES IN THE SOLUTION ARE


VARIABLE   X        AT LEVEL        1.0000E1
           Y                        1.5000E1


DO YOU WISH SENSITIVITY ANALYSIS? Y

                        SHADOW        LB         CURRENT        UB
CONSTRAINT      1     3.7500E0    4.0000E1      8.0000E1     1.2000E2
                2     1.7500E1    4.0000E1      6.0000E1     1.2000E2


PRICE          X                  2.5000E1      6.0000E1     7.5000E1
               Y                  4.0000E1      5.0000E1     1.2000E2
```

FIGURE B-6
Computer solution and sensitivity analysis for the simplified chemical production problem.

a. Divide the key row by the *key number,* the coefficient at the intersection of the key row and the key column.

b. For each nonlimiting row:

   (1) Multiply the newly transformed key row [found in (a) above] by the negative of the coefficient in the key column of the nonlimiting row.

   (2) Add the result to the nonlimiting row.

Alternately, the coefficients for the nonlimiting rows can be calculated from the formula:

$$\text{new number} = \text{old number} - \frac{\left(\begin{array}{c}\text{corresponding}\\\text{number of}\\\text{key row}\end{array}\right) \times \left(\begin{array}{c}\text{corresponding}\\\text{number of}\\\text{key column}\end{array}\right)}{\text{key number}}$$

6. Repeat steps 3 through 5 until all the coefficients in row 0 are nonnegative. An optimal solution then results.

7. The resulting optimal solution is interpreted in the following manner: In each row there is exactly one basic variable with a coefficient of 1 and with coefficients of 0 in the other rows. This variable is equal to the right-hand side of the row. The value of the objective function is given by the value of Z. All other nonbasic variables are zero. The shadow prices, which indicate the value of a marginal unit of each variable not in the solution, are the coefficients of the slack variables in row 0.

The output for the computer solution, including sensitivity analysis for the simplified chemical production problem, is shown in Figure B-6.

THE SIMPLEX TABLEAU

The logic and calculations of the simplex algorithm can be simplified even further by the use of the simplex tableau format for organizing the data. To minimize recopying of x, y, W_A, W_B, and Z, let us rearrange the two restricting equations (5) and (6) and the objective function equation (8) with the variables at the heads of columns and the coefficients of these variables in rows to represent the equations. The equal signs have also been dropped.

Z	x	y	W_A	W_B		
1	-60	-50	0	0	0	(row 0)
0	2	4	1	0	80	(row 1)
0	3	2	0	1	60	(row 2)

Next, to the right beside constants 80 and 60, we place two columns that identify the variables in the solution and their contribution rates in the objective function, as shown in Table B-3. This format for a linear optimization model is called the *simplex tableau*. The column of constants plus these two new columns is called the *stub* of the tableau.

Before proceeding, let us name the various parts of the tableau shown in Table B-3. The variable row simply identifies the variable associated with each of the coefficients in the various columns. Row 0 is the objective function row and contains the negative of the coefficients that show the contribution rates for each of the variables in the objective function. For example, the contribution of each unit of x is $60 per unit, y is $50 per unit, W_A is zero, and so on.

The solution stub always contains three columns. The variable column shows the variables that have positive values (basic variables) at a given stage of solution, *and the variables not shown in the variable column have a value of zero*. The constant column shows the value of each of the variables in the solution. The objective column shows the contribution rates of the variables in the solution, and these coeffi-

TABLE B-3   **Initial Simplex Tableau**

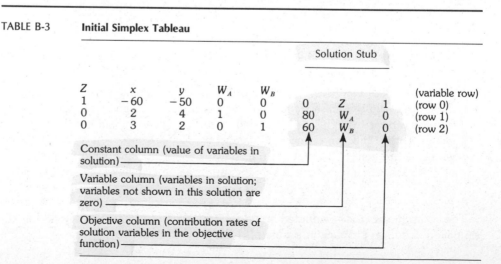

						Solution Stub		
Z	x	y	W_A	W_B				(variable row)
1	-60	-50	0	0	0	Z	1	(row 0)
0	2	4	1	0	80	W_A	0	(row 1)
0	3	2	0	1	60	W_B	0	(row 2)

Constant column (value of variables in solution)——

Variable column (variables in solution; variables not shown in this solution are zero)——

Objective column (contribution rates of solution variables in the objective function)——

cients come from the objective row. For example, in the initial solution, the coefficients below W_A and W_B are zeros.

We must not lose sight of the fact that the numbers in the tableau are the coefficients of the variables in the variable row, and that the numbers in the constant column are the numerical values of the right-hand side of the objective function row 0 and of the constraint equations, rows 1 and 2.

Improving the Initial Solution

The simplex algorithm can be applied just as before, except that the tableau format allows some additional streamlining of the calculations.

Selecting the Key Column, Key Row, and Key Number. We can apply Rule I of the simplex algorithm to the tableau, which says that we should select the variable with the most negative contribution in row 0 as the *entering variable*. From Table B-3, we can see that the most negative coefficient is $-\$60$, which is associated with the variable x. Therefore, we designate the column of coefficients of x as the *key column*.

We select the *key row* by applying Rule II of the simplex algorithm. That is, *we divide each number in the constant column by the corresponding number in the key column* (ignoring zero or negative entries in the key column). The key row is the row yielding the smallest quotient. For our problem, the ratios are:

$$\text{first row, } 80/2 = 40$$

$$\text{second row, } 60/3 = 20 \text{ (key row)}$$

The number at the intersection of the key row and the key column is designated the *key number*. Table B-4 shows the initial tableau with the key column, key row, and key number identified.

The pivoting operation can now be accomplished in a mechanistic fashion by creating a new tableau. The first step in developing the new tableau is to calculate the coefficients for the *main row*. The main row appears in the same relative position in the new tableau as the key row in the preceding tableau. It is computed by dividing the coefficients of the key row by the key number; Table B-5 shows this development. The variable and its objective number from the head of the key column, that is, x and 60, are placed in the stub of the main row, replacing W_B and 0 from the previous tableau. The balance of the objective and variable columns in the stub is

---

TABLE B-4   **Initial Simplex Tableau with Key Column, Key Row, and Key Number Identified**

Tableau I

	Z	x	y	W_A	W_B				
	1	-60	-50	0	0	0	Z	1	(row 0)
	0	2	4	1	0	80	W_A	0	(row 1)
Key row →	0	3	2	0	1	60	W_B	0	(row 2)

Key column _____   Key number

TABLE B-5   **Simplex Tableau with Main Row of New Tableau**

Tableau I

Z	x	y	W_A	W_B				
1	−60	−50	0	0	0	Z	1	(row 0)
0	2	4	1	0	80	W_A	0	(row 1)
0	3	2	0	1	60	W_B	0	(row 2)

Tableau II

0	1	2/3	0	1/3	20			Main row

copied from the previous tableau and the new tableau developed to this point now appears in Table B-6.

Now all the remaining coefficients in the new tableau can be calculated by applying Equation 10. The completed improved solution is shown in Tableau II in Table B-7. Note that the solution at this stage is $x = 20$, $W_A = 40$, $y = 0$, and $W_B = 0$, and that the value of the objective function is 1200, as shown in the solution stub.

Third and Optimal Solution

Next, we examine row 0 of Tableau II in Table B-7, and we see that potential improvement still exists, because the coefficient −10 appears under the variable y. Thus, y is selected as the key column of Tableau II. Proceeding as before, we obtain the new solution in Tableau III of Table B-8, which is optimal.

To summarize, the use of the tableau helps to organize the data and calculations of the simplex algorithm, but the results obtained are identical.

The optimum solution is interpreted in the following manner: The solution appears in the stub. The variables shown in the variable column have the values shown in the corresponding rows of the constant column. The value of the objective function is shown in the constant column, row 0. All variables not shown in the stub are zero. The shadow prices that indicate the value of a marginal unit of each variable in the solution are shown in row 0 of the final solution.

TABLE B-6   **Simplex Tableau with Variable and Objective Columns Completed**

Tableau I

Z	x	y	W_A	W_B				
1	−60	−50	0	0	1200	Z	1	(row 0)
0	2	4	1	0	80	W_A	0	(row 1)
0	3	2	0	1	60	W_B	0	(row 2)

Tableau II

						Z	1	
						W_A	0	
0	1	2/3	0	1/3	20	x	60	

TABLE B-7   **Simplex Tableau with First Iteration Completed**

Tableau I

	Z	x	y	W_A	W_B				
	1	-60	-50	0	0	0	Z	1	(row 0)
	0	2	4	1	0	80	W_A	0	(row 1)
	0	3	2	0	1	60	W_B	0	(row 2)

Tableau II

	1	0	-10	0	20	1200	Z	1	(row 0)
	0	0	8/3	1	-2/3	40	W_A	0	(row 1)
	0	1	2/3	0	1/3	20	x	60	(row 2)

TABLE B-8   **Simplex Tableau, Second and Third Iterations Completed**

Tableau I

	Z	x	y	W_A	W_B				
	1	-60	-50	0	0	0	Z	1	(row 0)
	0	2	4	1	0	80	W_A	0	(row 1)
	0	3	2	0	1	60	W_B	0	(row 2)

Tableau II

	1	0	-10	0	20	1200	Z	1	(row 0)
	0	0	8/3	1	-2/3	40	W_A	0	(row 1)
	0	1	2/3	0	1/3	20	x	60	(row 2)

Tableau III

	1	0	0	15/4	35/2	1350	Z	1	(row 0)
	0	0	1	3/8	-1/4	15	y	50	(row 1)
	0	1	0	-1/4	1/2	10	x	60	(row 2)

IMPORTANT TERMS

Numbers in parentheses indicate page numbers

Basic solution (575)	Key row (563, 579)
Basic variable (575)	Linearity (559)
Bounds, lower, current, upper (568)	Linear optimization model (562)
Constraint (579, 561)	Linear programming (559)
Decision variable (561)	Model building process (559)
Entering variable (573)	Nonbasic solution (571)
Iteration (575)	Nonbasic variable (575)
Key column (573, 579)	Objective function (561)
Key number (574, 579)	Pivot (574)

REVIEW QUESTIONS AND PROBLEMS

1. Which of the following mathematical expressions are linear? Why?
   a. $x + y = 1$
   b. $x^2 + y^2 = 10$
   c. $1/x + 2x = 10$
   d. $x + xy + y = 1$
   e. $x_1 + x_2 + x_3 + x_4 = 1$

2. Outline the model-building process used for developing linear optimization models.

3. Suppose that in the chemical production problems, the availability of time on machine A is drastically reduced to only 40 hours because of a breakdown. How does this change the solution space shown in Figure B-2? Is it likely to change the optimum number of units of each chemical to produce?

4. Explain the concept of shadow prices. How can a manager use a knowledge of shadow prices in decision making?

5. What is the interpretation of the upper and lower bounds on the shadow prices indicated in Figure B-4? Of what value is this information to a manager?

6. What is the interpretation of the upper and lower bounds on the "prices" given in Figure B-4? Of what value is this information to the manager?

7. What may be the practical value of knowing that the bounds on one or more prices may be "tight"?

8. What is the function of slack variables in the simplex method of solution?

9. What is the physical meaning of slack variables in the following types of constraints?
   a. Constraint on the capacity of a machine
   b. Constraint on the size of the market
   c. Constraint on the total expenditure on advertising in various media

10. What is a feasible solution? A basic solution? Identify both kinds of solutions in Figure B-5. Can a feasible solution be basic? Must a feasible solution be basic?

PROBLEMS

11. Once upon a time Lucretia Borgia invited 50 enemies to dinner. The piece de resistance was to be poison. In those crude days only two poisons were on the

market, poison X and poison Y. Before preparing the menu, however, the remarkably talented young lady considered some of the restrictions placed on her scheme:

a. If she used more than one-half pound of poison, the guests would detect it and refuse to eat.

b. Lucretia's own private witch, a medieval version of the modern planning staff, once propounded some magic numbers for her in the following doggerel:
One Y and X two,
If less than half,
Then woe to you.

c. Poison X will kill 75 and poison Y will kill 200 people per pound.

d. Poison X costs 100 solid gold pieces per pound, and poison Y 400 solid gold pieces per pound.

After devising a menu to cover up the taste of the poison, Lucretia found she was very short of solid gold pieces. In fact, unless she were very careful she would not be able to have another scheduled poisoning orgy that month. So she called in her alchemist, a very learned man, and told him about her problem. The alchemist had little experience in solving problems of this type, but he was able to translate the four restrictions into mathematical statements.

1. $X + Y \leq 1/2$
2. $2X + Y \geq 1/2$
3. $75X + 200Y \geq 50$
4. $100X + 400Y = \text{cost}$

Assist the alchemist in solving this problem, using graphic methods. The penalty for failure will be an invitation to next month's dinner.

12. A manufacturer has two products, both of which are made in two steps by machines A and B. The process times for the two products on the two machines are as follows:

Product	Machine A (hr)	Machine B (hr)
1	4	5
2	5	2

For the coming period, machine A has 100 hours available and B has 80 hours available. The contribution for product 1 is $10 per unit and for product 2, $5 per unit. Using the methods of the simplex algorithm, formulate and solve the problem for maximum contribution.

13. Consider the following linear optimization model:

maximize $Z = 3x_1 + x_2 + 4x_3$

subject to $6x_1 + 3x_2 + 5x_3 \leqslant 25$
$3x_1 + 4x_2 + 5x_3 \leqslant 20$
$x_1, x_2, x_3 \geqslant 0$

After adding slack variables and performing one simplex iteration, we have the following tableau:

1	−3/5	11/5	0	0	4/5	16	Z	1
0	3	−1	0	1	−1	5	x_4	0
0	3/5	4/5	1	0	1/5	4	x_3	4

If the above result is not optimal, perform the next iteration. Indicate the resulting values of the variables and the objective function.

14. Consider the following linear optimization model:

maximize $Z = 3x_1 + 6x_2 + 2x_3$

subject to $3x_1 + 4x_2 + x_3 \leqslant 2$ (resource A)

$x_1 + 3x_2 + 2x_3 \leqslant 1$ (resource B)

$x_1, x_2, x_3 \geqslant 0$

Solve this problem for the optimal solution using the simplex method.

REFERENCES

Bierman, H., C. P. Bonini, and W. H. Hausman, *Quantitative Analysis for Business Decisions* (6th ed.), Irwin, Inc., Homewood, Ill., 1981.

Buckley, J. W., M. R. Nagarai, D. L. Sharp, and J. W. Schenck, *Management Problem-Solving with APL,* Wiley, New York, 1974.

Buffa, E. S., and J. S. Dyer, *Management Science/Operations Research: Model Formulation and Solution Methods* (2nd ed.), Wiley, New York, 1981.

Daellenbach, H. G., and E. J. Bell, *User's Guide to Linear Programming,* Prentice-Hall, Englewood Cliffs, N.J., 1970.

Eppen, G. D., and F. J. Gould, *Quantitative Concepts for Management: Decision Making Without Algorithms,* Prentice-Hall, Englewood Cliffs, N.J., 1979.

Krajewski, L. J., and H. E. Thompson, *Management Science: Quantitative Methods in Concepts,* Wiley, New York, 1981.

Thierauf, R. J., and R. Klekamp, *Decision Making Through Operations Research,* (2nd ed.), Wiley, New York, 1975.

APPENDIX C

Linear Programming— Distribution Methods

EXAMPLE PROBLEM

Assume the distribution situation of the Pet Food Company. There are three factories located in Chicago, Houston, and New York, that produce some identical products. There are five major distribution points that serve various market areas in Atlanta, Buffalo, Cleveland, Denver, and Los Angeles. The three factories have capacities that determine the availability of product, and the market demand in the five major areas determines the requirements to be met. The problem is to allocate available product at the three factory locations to the five distribution points so that demand is met and distribution cost is minimized for the system.

Data for our illustrative problem are shown in Table C-1. There are 46,000 cases per week available at the Chicago plant, 20,000 at Houston, and 34,000 at New York, or a total of 100,000 cases per week of pet food. Similarly, demands in the five market areas are indicated in the bottom row of the table and also total 100,000 cases per week. Equality of availability and demand is not a necessary requirement for solution, and this issue is discussed later in this appendix.

These figures of units available and required are commonly termed the "rim conditions." Table C-1 also shows the distribution costs per 1000 cases for all combinations of factories and distribution points. These figures are shown in the small boxes; for example, the distribution cost between the Chicago plant and the Atlanta distribution point is $18 per 1000 cases. For convenience in notation the plants are labeled A, B, and C, and the distribution points V, W, X, Y, and Z. Table C-1 is called the "transportation or distribution table."

An Initial Solution

We will establish an initial solution in an arbitrary way, ignoring the distribution costs. Beginning in the upper left-hand corner of the transportation table (called the northwest corner) note that A has 46 (1000) cases available and V needs 27 (1000). We

TABLE C-1 Transportation Table for the Pet Food Company. Quantities of Product Available at Factories and Required at Distribution Points, and Distribution Costs per Thousand Cases

To Distr. Points / From Factories	Atlanta (V)	Buffalo (W)	Cleveland (X)	Denver (Y)	Los Angeles (Z)	Available from Factories, 1000's
Chicago (A)	18	16	12	28	54	46
Houston (B)	24	40	36	30	42	20
New York (C)	22	12	16	48	44	34
Required at distribution points, 1000's	27	16	18	10	29	100

assign the 27 from A to V. (See Table C-2, where circled numbers represent assigned product; e.g., 27 in box AV means 27,000 cases are to go from A to V.) We have not used up A's supply, so we move to the right under column W and assign the maximum possible to the route AW, 16. We still have not used up A's supply, so we move to the right under column X and assign the balance of A's supply, 3, to X.

Examining the requirements for X, we note that it has a total requirement of 18, so we drop down to row B and assign the balance of X's requirements, 15, from B's supply of 20. We then move to the right again and assign the balance of B's supply to Y, 5. We continue in this way, stair-stepping down the table, until all the arbitrary assignments have been made as in Table C-2. The distribution costs, $2984, are calculated below Table C-2. Note that we have seven squares with assignments (n rows + m columns − 1) and eight open squares without assignments. This requirement for $m + n - 1$ assignments avoids degeneracy, to be discussed later. Table C-2 is the northwest corner initial solution.

Methods for obtaining better starting solutions, and simplifications will be discussed later in this appendix.

Test for Optimality

Because the northwest corner solution in Table C-2 was established arbitrarily, it is not likely to be the best possible solution. Therefore, we need to develop a method for examining each of the open squares in the transportation table to determine if improvements can be made in total distribution costs by shifting some of the units to be shipped to these routes. In making the shifts, we must be sure that any new

TABLE C-2   **Northwest Corner Initial Solution**

To Distr. Points / From Factories	Atlanta (V)	Buffalo (W)	Cleveland (X)	Denver (Y)	Los Angeles (Z)	Available from Factories, 1000's
Chicago (A)	18 ㉗	16 ⑯	12 ③	28	54	46
Houston (B)	24	40	36 ⑮	30 ⑤	42	20
New York (C)	22	12	16	48 ⑤	44 ㉙	34
Required at distribution points, 1000's	27	16	18	10	29	100

Total distribution cost:
AV, 27×18 =   486
AW, 16×16 =   256
AX, 3×12 =   36
BX, 15×36 =   540
BY, 5×30 =   150
CY, 5×48 =   240
CZ, 29×44 =   1276
                 $2984

solution satisfies the supply and demand restrictions shown in the rim conditions of the transportation table.

In evaluating each open square, the following steps are used:

Step 1

Determine a closed path, starting at the open square being evaluated and "stepping" from squares with assignments back to the original open square. Right angle turns in this path are permitted only at squares with assignments, and at the original open square. Because only the squares at the turning points are considered to be on the closed path, both open and assigned squares may be skipped over.

Step 2

Beginning at the square being evaluated, assign a plus sign and then alternate minus and plus signs at the assigned squares on the corners of the path.

Step 3

Add the unit costs in the squares with plus signs, and subtract the unit costs in the squares with minus signs. If we are minimizing costs, the result is the net change in cost per unit from the changes made in the assignments. If we are maximizing profits, the result is the net change in profit.

Step 4

Repeat steps 1, 2, and 3 for each open square in the transportation table.

Steps 1 and 2 involve the assignment of a single unit to the open square and then adjusting the shipments in the squares with assignments until all the rim conditions are satisfied.

Step 3 simply calculates the cost (or contribution to profit) that would result from such a modification in the assignments. If we are minimizing costs, and if the net changes are all greater than or equal to zero, for all open squares, we have found an optimal solution. If we are maximizing profits, and all net changes are less than or equal to zero for all open squares, we have found an optimal solution.

The application of these steps to open square BV is shown in Table C-3. In this case, the closed path forms a simple rectangle. The net change in total distribution cost resulting from shifting one unit to route BV is

$$24 - 18 + 12 - 36 = -18$$

This value is entered in the bottom left-hand corner of the square BV in Table C-3. The evaluation of open squares does not always follow the simple rectangular path. For example, the closed path of evaluating square CV is shown in Table C-4, and the net change in total distribution cost resulting from shifting one unit to route CV is

$$22 - 18 + 12 - 36 + 30 - 48 = -38$$

The net changes in total distribution cost for all the open squares are shown in Table C-3, in the lower left-hand corner of each open square.

TABLE C-3   Evaluation of Square BV for Possible Improvement. The Change in Total Distribution Cost Resulting from Shifting One Unit to Route BV is: 24 − 18 + 12 − 36 = − 18

To Distr. Points / From Factories	Atlanta (V)	Buffalo (W)	Cleveland (X)	Denver (Y)	Los Angeles (Z)	Available from Factories, 1000's
Chicago (A)	(−) [18] ⟨27⟩	[16] ⟨16⟩	(+) [12] ⟨3⟩	[28] +22	[54] +52	46
Houston (B)	[24] (+) −18	[40] 0	[36] ⟨15⟩ (−)	[30] ⟨5⟩	[42] +16	20
New York (C)	[22] −38	[12] −46	[16] −38	[48] ⟨5⟩	[44] ⟨29⟩	34
Required at distribution points, 1000's	27	16	18	10	29	100

TABLE C-4   Evaluation of Square CV for Possible Improvement. The Change in Total Distribution Cost Resulting from Shifting One Unit to Route CV is: 22 − 18 + 12 − 36 + 30 − 48 = −38

To Distr. Points / From Factories	Atlanta (V)	Buffalo (W)	Cleveland (X)	Denver (Y)	Los Angeles (Z)	Available from Factories, 1000's
Chicago (A)	(−) [18] ⟨27⟩	[16] ⟨16⟩	(+) [12] ⟨3⟩	[28]	[54]	46
Houston (B)	[24]	[40]	[36] (−)⟨15⟩	[30] ⟨5⟩ (+)	[42]	20
New York (C)	[22] (+) −38	[12]	[16]	[48] ⟨5⟩ (−)	[44] ⟨29⟩	34
Required at distribution points, 1000's	27	16	18	10	29	100

Improving the Solution

Because each negative net change indicates the amount by which the total distribution cost will decrease if one unit were shifted to the route of that cell, we will be guided by these evaluations as indexes of potential improvement. Notice in Table C-3 that four of the open squares indicate potential improvement, three indicate that costs would increase if units were shifted to those routes, and one indicates that costs would not change if units were shifted to its route, Which change should be made first in determining a new improved solution? One reasonable rule for small problems and hand solutions is to select the square with the most negative index number when we are minimizing costs. Therefore, we choose square CW.

To improve the solution, we carry out the following steps for square CW:

Step 1

Identify again the closed path for the chosen open square, and assign the plus and minus signs around the path as before. Determine the minimum number of units assigned to a square on this path that is marked with a minus sign.

Step 2

Add this number to the open square and to all other squares on the path marked with a plus sign. Subtract this number from the squares on the path marked with a minus sign. This step is a simple accounting procedure for observing the restrictions of the rim conditions.

The closed path for open square CW is +CW −AW + AX − BX + BY − CY. The minimum number of units in a square with a minus sign is five in CY. Thus, we add five units to squares CW, AX, and BY, and subtract five units from squares AW, BX, and CY. This reassignment of units generates a new solution, as shown in Table C-5.

Taking Table C-5 as the current solution, we repeat the process, reevaluating all open squares, as shown in Table C-5. Note that there are now only two open squares with negative index numbers, indicating potential improvement. Following our previous procedure, open square BZ indicates that the largest improvement could be made by shifting assignments to that route.

An Optimal Solution

The process is continued until all open squares show no further improvement. At this point, an optimal solution has been obtained and is shown in Table C-6, where all the index numbers for open squares are either positive or zero. The total distribution cost required by the optimal solution is $2446, which is $538 less than the original

TABLE C-5   **New Solution Resulting After Shifting Five Units to Square CW. The Number of Units That Could Be Shifted to CW Was Limited to Five by Square CY in the Previous Solution**

To Distr. Points / From Factories	Atlanta (V)	Buffalo (W)	Cleveland (X)	Denver (Y)	Los Angeles (Z)	Available from Factories, 1000's
Chicago (A)	18 / (27)	16 / (11)	12 / (8)	28 / +22	54 / +6	46
Houston (B)	24 / −18	40 / 0	36 / (10)	30 / (10)	42 / −30	20
New York (C)	22 / +8	12 / (5)	16 / +8	48 / +46	44 / (29)	34
Required at distribution points, 1000's	27	16	18	10	29	100

TABLE C-6   **An Optimal Solution. Evaluation of All Open Squares in This Table Results in No Further Improvement. Total Distribution Cost = $2446**

From Factories \ To Distr. Points	Atlanta (V)	Buffalo (W)	Cleveland (X)	Denver (Y)	Los Angeles (Z)	Available from Factories, 1000's
Chicago (A)	18 ㉗	16 +6	12 ⑱	28 ①	54 +14	46
Houston (B)	24 +2	40 +30	36 +22	30 ⑨	42 ⑪	20
New York (C)	22 0	12 ⑯	16 0	48 +16	44 ⑱	34
Required at distribution points, 1000's	27	16	18	10	29	100

northwest corner solution. Although this 18 percent improvement is impressive, we should note that we started with a rather poor initial solution. Better starting solutions can be obtained for simple problems by making initial assignments to the most promising routes while observing the restrictions of the rim conditions and being sure that there are exactly $n + m - 1$ assignments. Solutions with $n + m - 1$ assignments are called basic solutions; solutions with fewer assignments are called degenerate, and solutions with more than $n + m - 1$ assignments are called nonbasic solutions.

Alternate Optimal Solutions

The fact that open squares CV and CX in Table C-6 have zero evaluations is important and gives us flexibility in determining the final plan of action. These zero evaluations allow us to generate other solutions that have the same total distribution costs as the initial optimal solution generated in Table C-6.

As an example, because open square CV has a zero evaluation, we may make the shifts in allocations indicated by its closed path and generate the alternate basic optimal solution shown in Table C-7. Still another alternate optimum solution could be generated by shifting assignments to square CX.

We are not yet finished, because we can generate literally dozens of other optimal solutions from each of the basic solutions. In generating the alternate basic optimum solution in Table C-7, we shifted 9000 units to open square CV, which had a zero evaluation. It was not necessary for us to shift the entire 9000 units, however. We could have shifted only 5000 units, or 4000, or 3000, or any fractional amount of the 9000 units. All the basic alternate optimum solutions could also be varied in this way, producing nonbasic alternate optimum solutions.

Where we have optimum solutions containing open squares with zero evaluations, we have great flexibility in distribution at minimum cost. Where fractional units are permitted, we have in fact a tremendous number of alternate optimal solutions. This

TABLE C-7   **Alternate Basic Optimum Solution**

To Distr. Points From Factories	Atlanta (V)	Buffalo (W)	Cleveland (X)	Denver (Y)	Los Angeles (Z)	Available from Factories, 1000's
Chicago (A)	18 (18)	16 +8	12 (18)	28 (10)	54 +14	46
Houston (B)	24 +4	40 +30	36 +16	30 0	42 (20)	20
New York (C)	22 (9)	12 (16)	16 0	48 +16	44 (9)	34
Required at distribution points, 1000's	27	16	18	10	29	100

may often make it possible to satisfy subjective factors in the problem and still retain minimum distribution costs.

UNEQUAL SUPPLY AND DEMAND

Now suppose that supply exceeds demand as shown in Table C-8. The total available supply is still 100,000 cases; however, the aggregate demand at the five distribution points totals only 95,000 cases. This situation can be handled in the problem by creating a dummy distribution point to receive the extra 5000 cases. The nonexistent distribution point is assigned zero distribution costs as shown, because the product will never be shipped. The optimal solution then assigns 95,000 of the

TABLE C-8   **Distribution Table with Supply Exceeding Demand: Optimum Solution**

To Distr. Points From Factories	Atlanta (V)	Buffalo (W)	Cleveland (X)	Denver (Y)	Los Angeles (Z)	Dummy	Available from Factories, 1000's
Chicago (A)	18 (25)	16 8	12 (11)	28 (10)	54 14	0 4	46
Houston (B)	24 4	40 30	36 22	30 0	42 (20)	0 2	20
New York (C)	22 0	12 (15)	16 (7)	48 16	44 (7)	0 (5)	34
Required at distribution points, 1000's	25	15	18	10	27	5	100

100,000 available units in the most economical way to the five real distribution points and assigns the balance to the dummy distribution point. Table C-8 shows an optimal distribution plan for this situation.

When demand exceeds supply, we can resort to a modification of the same technique. Create a dummy factory to take up the slack. Again zero distribution costs are assigned to the dummy factory, because the product will never be shipped. The solution then assigns the available product to the distribution points in the most economical way, indicating which distribution points should receive "short" shipments, so that the total distribution costs are minimized.

TRANSSHIPMENT

It often happens that direct routes between all origins and destinations are not used. Major routes may exist through distribution centers on the way to smaller receipt points. The transshipment model is a modification of the distribution model that allows transshipment points. See Buffa and Dyer [1977] for methods.

DEGENERACY IN DISTRIBUTION PROBLEMS

Another aspect of the mechanics of developing a solution is the condition known as *degeneracy*. Degeneracy occurs in distribution problems when, in shifting assignments to take advantage of a potential improvement, more than one of the existing assignments goes to zero. Degeneracy also can occur in an initial solution that does not meet the $m + n - 1$ requirement for the number of allocations. Examination of the problem in Table C-9 shows that degeneracy is about to happen. This problem was set up in the usual way, and an initial northwest corner solution was established. The open squares were evaluated column by column, as before, and changes in assignments were made when they indicated potential improvement.

In Table C-9, we are evaluating square AX by the closed path pattern. Potential improvement is indicated, because a unit of allocation reduces transportation costs by \$4 per thousand. We wish to press this advantage to the maximum by shifting as much as possible to AX. We are limited, however, by both squares AV and BX, each of which has an allocation of 6000 units assigned to it. When the shift in assignment is made, both AV and BX go to zero. This is shown in Table C-10. We now have only six allocations instead of the seven we had before, and we do not meet the restriction on the method of solution that we stated earlier: that the number of allocations must be $m + n - 1$. The practical effect of this is that several of the open squares, namely AV, BW, CW, BX, CX, AY, and AZ, cannot be evaluated in the usual way because a closed path cannot be established for them.

We can resolve the degeneracy, however, by regarding one of the two squares in which allocations have disappeared as an allocated square with an extremely small allocation, which we will call an ϵ (*epsilon*) allocation. This is illustrated in Table

TABLE C-9   **Evaluation of Square AX Produces Degeneracy**

From \ To	V	W	X	Y	Z	Available from Factories, 1000's
A	42 (−) ⑥	42 ⑬	44 (+)	40	44	19
B	34 (+) ⑥	42	40 ⑥ (−)	46 ⑯	48	28
C	46	44	42	48 ①	46 ㉔	25
Required 1000s →	12	13	6	17	24	72

TABLE C-10   **Problem Now Degenerate; Squares AV, BW, CW, BX, CX, AY, and AZ Cannot be Evaluated**

From \ To	V	W	X	Y	Z	Available from Factories, 1000's
A	42	42 ⑬	44 ⑥	40	44	19
B	34 ⑫	42	40	46 ⑯	48	28
C	46	44	42	48 ①	46 ㉔	25
Required 1000s →	12	13	6	17	24	72

TABLE C-11   **Degeneracy Resolved by Use of the ε Allocation**

From \ To	V	W	X	Y	Z	Available from Factories, 1000's
A	42 / (ε)	42 / (13)	44 / (6)	40	44	19
B	34 / (12)	42	40	46 / (16)	48	28
C	46	44	42	48 / (1)	46 / (24)	25
Required 1000s →	12	13	6	17	24	72

C-11. Conceptually, we will regard the ε allocation as infinitesimally small, so that it does not affect the totals indicated in the rim. The ε allocation, however, does make it possible to meet the $m + n - 1$ restriction on the number of allocations so that evaluation paths may be established for all open squares. The ε allocation is simply manipulated as though it were no different from the other allocations.

If, in subsequent manipulations, the ε allocation square is the one that limits shifts in assignments, it simply is shifted to the square being evaluated, and the usual procedures are then continued. This is illustrated in Table C-12, where we are attempting to evaluate square AZ by the closed path shown. A potential improvement of $8 per 1000 units is indicated, but the limiting allocation at a negative square is the ε allocation. The net effect of adding and subtracting the ε allocation around the closed path is to move the ε allocation from square AV to square AZ. The procedure then is continued as before, until an optimal solution is obtained.

As the procedure continues, the ε allocation may disappear. This is illustrated in Table C-13, in which we are evaluating the open square CX. Potential improvement of $4 per 1000 units is indicated, and here we are limited not by the ε allocation, but by the allocation of 6000 units at AX. In making the adjustments, we add and subtract 6000 units around the closed path according to the signs indicated, and the result is that the ε allocation at AZ becomes 6000 units. We now have seven squares with positive allocations, and the ε allocation is no longer needed. In carrying through the solution of larger-scale problems, we may find that degeneracy appears and disappears in the routine solution of a problem or that more than one ε allocation exists. Also, optimal solutions may be degenerate.

TABLE C-12   **Shift of ε Allocation When it is Limiting**

From \ To	V	W	X	Y	Z	Available from Factories, 1000's
A	42 (−) (ε)	42 (13)	44 (6)	40	44 (ε) (+)	19
B	34 (+) (12)	42	40	46 (−) (16)	48	28
C	46	44	42	48 (+) (1)	46 (24) (−)	25
Required 1000s →	12	13	6	17	24	72

TABLE C-13   **Disappearance of the ε Allocation When It Falls at a Positive Corner of an Evaluation Path**

From \ To	V	W	X	Y	Z	Available from Factories, 1000's
A	42	42 (13)	44 (−) (6)	40	44 (+) (ε)	19
B	34 (12)	42	40	46 (16)	48	28
C	46	44	42 (+)	48 (1)	46 (24) (−)	25
Required 1000s →	12	13	6	17	24	72

TECHNIQUES FOR SIMPLIFYING PROBLEM SOLUTION

We can simplify the arithmetic complexity considerably by using two methods. A little thought about the example we used will convince us that it is the cost *differences* which are important in determining the optimal allocation, rather than their absolute values. Therefore, we can reduce all costs by a fixed amount, and the resulting allocation will be unchanged. In our illustrative example, we may subtract 12 from all distribution cost values, so that the numbers with which we must work are of such magnitude to allow many evaluations to be accomplished by inspection. Another simplification in the arithmetic may be accomplished by expressing the rim conditions in the simplest terms. For example, in our illustration, we expressed the rim conditions in thousands of units, thus enabling us to work with two-digit numbers only.

Getting an Advantageous Initial Solution

The northwest corner initial solution is not used in practice, because ordinarily it is a rather poor solution, which involves a number of steps to develop an optimal solution. Placing the lowest cost cell in the northwest corner gives an advantageous start. The usual procedure is to start with some solution by inspecting the most promising routes and entering allocations that are consistent with the rim conditions. In establishing such an initial solution, the only rules to be observed are that there must be exactly $m + n - 1$ allocations, so that it is possible to evaluate all open squares by the closed path methods.

If the initial solution turns out to be degenerate, it is simple to increase the allocations to the exact number required by resorting to the ϵ allocation. There are a number of short-cut methods commonly used, such as row minimum, column minimum, matrix minimum, and VAM. Although they all have merits, we will discuss VAM in some detail because it seems particularly valuable for hand computation of fairly large-scale problems. Of course, computer solutions should be used for large-scale problems.

Vogel's Approximation Method (VAM)

VAM facilitates a very good initial solution, which usually is the optimal solution. The technique is a simple one, and it considerably reduces the amount of work required to generate an optimal solution. We will use a new problem to illustrate. Table C-14 shows a distribution table with the distribution costs all reduced by the constant amount, $34. The steps in determining an initial VAM solution are as follows:

1. *Determine the difference between the two lowest distribution costs for each row and each column.* This has been done in Table C-14, and the figures at the heads of columns and to the right of the rows represent these differences. For example, in column V, the three distribution costs are 8, 0, and 12. The two lowest costs are 8 and 0, and their difference is 8. In row A, the two lowest distribution costs are 6 and 8, or a difference of 2. The other figures at the heads

TABLE C-14   **Distribution Table with Initial VAM Row and Column Differences Shown**

From \ To	↓ 8 V	0 W	2 X	6 Y	2 Z	Available from Factories, 1000's	
A	8	8	10	6	10	19	2
B	0	8	6	12	14	28	6
C	12	10	8	14	12	25	2
Required 1000s →	11	13	7	17	24	72	

of the columns and to the right of the rows have been determined in a similar way.

2. *Select the row or column with the greatest difference.* For the example, the row or column with the greatest difference is column V, which has a difference of 8.

3. *Assign the largest possible allocation within the restrictions of the rim conditions to the lowest cost square in the row or column selected.* This has been done in Table C-15. Under column V, the lowest cost square is BV, which has a cost of 0, and we have assigned 11 units to that square. The 11 unit assignment is the largest possible because of the restriction imposed by the number required at distribution point V.

4. *Cross out any row or column that has been completely satisfied by the assignment just made.* For the assignment just made at BV, the requirements for V are entirely satisfied. Therefore, we may cross out the other squares in that column, because we can make no future assignments to them. This is shown in Table C-15.

5. *Recalculate the differences as in step 1, except for rows or columns that have been crossed out.* This has been done in Table C-15, where row B is the only one affected by the assignment just made.

6. *Repeat steps 2 to 5 until all assignments have been made.*

   a. Column Y now exhibits the greatest difference; therefore, we allocate 17

TABLE C-15   **First VAM Assignment Satisfies V's Requirement (Row and Column VAM Differences Are Recalculated)**

From \ To	V	W	X	Y	Z	Available from Factories, 1000's	
↓ 8	**0**	**2**	**6**	**2**			
A	X [8]	[8]	[10]	[6]	[10]	19	2
B	⑪ [0]	[8]	[6]	[12]	[14]	28	62
C	X [12]	[10]	[8]	[14]	[12]	25	2
Required 1000s →	11	13	7	17	24	72	

units to AY, because it has the smallest distribution cost in column Y. Because Y's requirements are completely satisfied, the other squares in that column are crossed out. Differences are recalculated. This entire step is shown in Table C-16.

b.   The recalculated differences now show five of the columns and rows with a difference of 2. The lowest cost square in any column or row is BX, which has a cost of 6. We assign 7 units to BX, which completely satisfies the requirements at X. Table C-17 shows the allocation of 7 units at BX, the crossing out of the other squares in column X, and the recalculation of cost differences for the remaining rows and columns.

c.   Row B now shows a cost difference of 6, and we allocate 10 units to the low cost square BW, as shown in Table C-18. This completes row B. Recalculated cost differences now show that all remaining cost differences in rows and columns are 2. The lowest cost square available is AW, so we allocate 2 units there to complete row A. This step is also shown as part of Table C-18.

d.   The last two allocations at CW and CZ are made by inspection of the rim conditions (shown in Table C-19). An evaluation of the open squares in Table C-19 shows that this solution is optimal.

TABLE C-16   **Second VAM Assignment Satisfies Y's Requirement (Row and Column VAM Differences Are Recalculated)**

From \ To	V (8̶)	W (0)	X (2)	Y (6̶) ↓	Z (2)	Available from Factories, 1000's	
A	[8] X	[8]	[10]	[6] (17)	[10]	19	2
B	[0] (11)	[8]	[6]	[12] X	[14]	28	6̶2
C	[12] X	[10]	[8]	[14] X	[12]	25	2
Required 1000s →	11	13	7	17	24	72	

TABLE C-17   **Third VAM Assignment**

From \ To	V (8̶)	W (0)	X (2̶) ↓	Y (6̶)	Z (2)	Available from Factories, 1000's	
A	[8] X	[8]	[10] X	[6] (17)	[10]	19	2
B	[0] (11)	[8]	[6] (7)	[12] X	[14]	28	6̶2̶6
C	[12] X	[10]	[8] X	[14] X	[12]	25	2
Required 1000s →	11	13	7	17	24	72	

TABLE C-18   **Fourth and Fifth VAM Assignments**

From \ To	V	W	X	Y	Z	Available from Factories, 1000's	
	8̸	0	2	¢	2		
A	[8] X	[8] (2)	[10] X	[6] (17)	[10] X	19	2←
B	[0] (11)	[8] (10)	[6] (7)	[12] X	[14] X	28	626←
C	[12] X	[10]	[8] X	[14] X	[12]	25	2
Required 1000s →	11	13	7	17	24	72	

TABLE C-19   **Final Assignments at CW and CZ Balance with Rim Restrictions and Yield VAM Initial Solution Which is Optimal**

From \ To	V	W	X	Y	Z	Available from Factories, 1000's
A	[8] X	[8] (2)	[10] X	[6] (17)	[10] X	19
B	[0] (11)	[8] (10)	[6] (7)	[12] X	[14] X	28
C	[12] X	[10] (1)	[8] X	[14] X	[12] (24)	25
Required 1000s →	11	13	7	17	24	72

IMPORTANT TERMS

Numbers in parentheses indicate page numbers

Degeneracy (594)   Transshipment (594)

Distribution table (593)   Transportation table (587)

Epsilon (ϵ) allocation (594)   Vogel's Approximation Method, VAM (598)

PROBLEMS

1. A company has factories at A, B, and C, which supply warehouses at D, E, F, and G. Monthly factory capacities are 70, 90, and 115, respectively. Monthly warehouse requirements are 50, 60, 70, and 95, respectively. Unit shipping costs are as follows:

	To			
From	D	E	F	G
A	$17	$20	$13	$12
B	$15	$21	$26	$25
C	$15	$14	$15	$17

Determine the optimum distribution for this company to minimize shipping costs.

2. A company with factories at A, B, and C supplies warehouses at D, E, F, and G. Monthly factory capacities are 20, 30, and 45, respectively. Monthly warehouse requirements are 10, 15, 40, and 30, respectively. Unit shipping costs are as follows:

	To			
From	D	E	F	G
A	6	$10	$ 6	$ 8
B	$7	$ 9	$ 6	$11
C	$8	$10	$14	$ 6

Determine the optimum distribution for this company to minimize shipping costs.

3. A company has factories at A, B, and C, which supply warehouses D, E, F, and G. Monthly factory capacities are 300, 400, and 500, respectively. Monthly warehouse requirements are 200, 240, 280, and 340, respectively. Unit shipping costs are as follows:

	To			
From	D	E	F	G
A	$7	$ 9	$ 9	$ 6
B	$6	$10	$12	$ 8
C	$9	$ 8	$10	$14

Determine the optimum distribution for this company to minimize shipping costs.

4. A company has factories at A, B, and C, which supply warehouses at D, E, F, and G. Monthly factory capacities are 160, 150, and 190, respectively. Monthly warehouse requirements are 80, 90, 110, and 160, respectively. Unit shipping costs are as follows:

	To			
From	D	E	F	G
A	$42	$48	$38	$37
B	$40	$49	$52	$51
C	$39	$38	$40	$43

Determine the optimum distribution for this company to minimize shipping costs.

5. A company has factories at A, B, C, and D, which supply warehouses at E, F, G, H, and I. Monthly factory capacities are 200, 225, 175, and 350, respectively. Monthly warehouse requirements are 130, 110, 140, 260, and 180, respectively. Unit shipping costs are as follows:

	To				
From	E	F	G	H	I
A	$14	$19	$32	$ 9	$21
B	$15	$10	$18	$ 7	$11
C	$26	$12	$13	$18	$16
D	$11	$22	$14	$14	$18

Determine the optimum distribution for this company to minimize shipping costs. (*Hint:* Use VAM for initial solution.)

6. A company has factories at A, B, and C, which supply warehouses at D, E, F, and G. Monthly factory capacities are 250, 300, and 200, respectively for regular production. If overtime production is utilized, the capacities can be increased to 320, 380, and 210, respectively. Incremental unit overtime costs are $5, $6, and $8 per unit, respectively. The current warehouse requirements are 170, 190, 230, and 180, respectively. Unit shipping costs between the factories and warehouses are:

	To			
From	D	E	F	G
A	$8	$ 9	$10	$11
B	$6	$12	$ 9	$ 7
C	$4	$13	$ 3	$12

Determine the optimum production-distribution for this company to minimize costs.

7. A company with factories at A, B, C, and D supplies warehouses at E, F, G, and H. Monthly factory capacities are 100, 80, 120, and 90, respectively, for regular

production. If overtime production is utilized, the capacities can be increased to 120, 110, 160, and 140, respectively. Incremental unit overtime costs are $5, $2, $3, and $4, respectively. Present incremental profits per unit, excluding shipping costs, are $14, $9, $16, and $27, respectively, for regular production. The current monthly warehouse requirements are 110, 70, 160, and 130, respectively. Unit shipping costs are as follows:

From	To E	F	G	H
A	$3	$4	$5	$7
B	$2	$9	$6	$8
C	$4	$3	$8	$5
D	$6	$5	$4	$6

Determine the optimum production-distribution for this company. (*Hint:* This problem requires that you maximize profits.) What simple change in the procedures makes it possible to maximize rather than minimize?

REFERENCES

Bierman, H., C. P. Bonini, and W. H. Hausman, *Quantitative Analysis for Business Decisions* (6th ed.), Irwin, Homewood, Ill., 1981.

Buffa, E. S., and J. S. Dyer, *Management Science/Operations Research: Model Formula and Solution Methods* (2nd ed.), Wiley, New York, 1981.

Eppen, G. D., and F. J. Gould, *Quantitative Concepts for Management: Decision Making Without Algorithms,* Prentice-Hall, Englewood Cliffs, N.J., 1979.

Krajewski, L. J., and H. E. Thompson, *Management Science: Quantitative Methods in Concepts,* Wiley, New York, 1981.

Reinfeld, N. V., and W. R. Vogel, *Mathematical Programming,* Prentice-Hall, Englewood Cliffs, N.J., 1958.

Thierauf, R. J., and R. C. Klekamp, *Decision Making through Operations Research* (2nd ed.), Wiley, New York, 1975.

APPENDIX D

Waiting Line Models

WAITING LINE OR QUEUING CONCEPTS PROVIDE INSIGHT INTO many problems in productive systems. The original work in waiting line theory was done by A. K. Erlang, a Danish telephone engineer. Erlang started his work in 1905 in an attempt to determine the effect of fluctuating demand (arrivals) on the utilization of automatic dial telephone equipment. Since the end of World War II, Erlang's work has been extended and applied to a variety of situations that are now recognized as being described by the general waiting line model.

Structure of Waiting Line Models

There are four basic waiting line structures that describe the general conditions at the service facility. The simplest structure, shown in Figure D-1a, is our basic module. It is called the *single server case.* There are many examples of the simple module: the cashier at a restaurant, any single-window operation in a post office or bank, a one-chair barber shop.

If the number of processing stations is increased but still draws on a single waiting line, we have the *multiple servers case* shown in Figure D-1b. A post office with several open windows but drawing on a single waiting line is a common example of a multiple server waiting line structure.

A simple assembly line or a cafeteria line has, in effect, a number of service facilities in series and is an example of the *single servers in series case* shown in Figure D-1c.

Finally, the *multiple servers in series case* can be illustrated by two or more parallel assembly lines as shown in Figure D-1d. Combinations of any or all of the basic four structures could also exist in networks in very complex systems.

The analytical methods for waiting lines divide into two main categories for any of the basic structures in Figure D-1, depending on the size of the source population of the inputs. When the source population is very large, and in theory at least the length of the waiting line could grow without fixed limits, the applicable models are termed *infinite waiting line models.* On the other hand, when the arriving unit comes from a small fixed-size population, the applicable models are termed *finite waiting line models.* For example, if we are dealing with the maintenance of a bank of 20 machines and a machine breakdown represents an arrival, the maximum waiting line is 20 machines waiting for service, and a finite waiting line model is needed. On the other hand, if we operated an auto repair shop, the source population of breakdowns is very large and an infinite waiting line model would provide a good approximation. We will discuss both infinite and finite models.

There are other variations in waiting line structures that are important in certain applications. The "queue discipline" describes the order in which the units in the waiting line are selected for service. In Figure D-1, we imply that the queue discipline is first come–first served. Obviously there are many other possibilities involving priority systems. For example, in a medical clinic, emergencies and patients with appointments are taken ahead of walk-in patients. In production scheduling systems there has been a great deal of experimentation with alternate priority systems. Because of the mathematical complexity involved, Monte Carlo simulation has been the

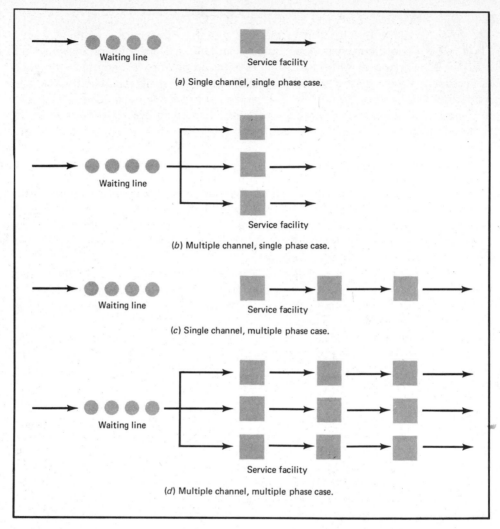

(a) Single channel, single phase case.

(b) Multiple channel, single phase case.

(c) Single channel, multiple phase case.

(d) Multiple channel, multiple phase case.

FIGURE D-1
Four basic structures of waiting line situations.

common mode of analysis for systems involving queue disciplines other than first come–first served. Table D-1 shows the waiting line elements for a number of common situations.

Finally, the nature of the distributions of arrivals and service is an important structural characteristic of waiting line models. Some mathematical analysis is available for distributions that follow the Poisson or the Erlang process (with some variations), or that have constant arrival rates or constant service times. If distributions are different from those mentioned or are taken from actual records, simulation is likely to be the necessary mode of analysis, as we will describe in Appendix E.

INFINITE WAITING LINE MODELS

We will not cover all possibilities of infinite waiting line models, but will restrict our discussion to situations involving the first come–first served queue discipline and the Poisson distribution of arrivals. We will deal initially with the single server case (our basic service facility module), but later we will also discuss the multiple server case. Our objective will be to develop predictions for some important measures of performance for waiting lines, such as the mean length of the waiting line, and the mean waiting time for an arriving unit.

Poisson Arrivals

The Poisson distribution function has been shown to represent arrival rates in a large number of real-world situations. It is a discrete function dealing with whole units of arrivals, so that fractions of people, products, or machines do not have meaning, nor do negative values. The Poisson distribution function is given by

$$f(x) = \frac{\lambda^x e^{-\lambda}}{x!} \tag{1}$$

TABLE D-1	**Waiting Line Model Elements for Some Commonly Known Situations**		
	Unit Arriving	Service or Processing Facility	Service or Process Being Performed
Ships entering a port	Ships	Docks	Unloading and loading
Maintenance and repair of machines	Machine breaks down	Repair crew	Repair machine
Assembly line, not mechanically paced	Parts to be assembled	Individual assembly operations or entire line	Assembly
Doctor's office	Patients	Doctor, staff and facilities	Medical care
Purchase of groceries at a supermarket	Customers with loaded grocery carts	Checkout counter	Tabulation of bill, receipt of payment and bagging of groceries
Auto traffic at an intersection or bridge	Automobiles	Intersection or bridge with control points such as traffic lights or toll booths	Passage through intersection or bridge
Inventory of items in a warehouse	Order for withdrawal	Warehouse	Replenishment of inventory
Machine shop	Job order	Work center	Processing

609

where

$$f(x) = \text{Poisson distribution function}$$
$$\lambda = \text{the mean arrival rate}$$
$$x = \text{the number arriving in one unit of time}$$
$$x! = x \text{ factorial}$$

[*Note:* $x!$ is simply (x) $(x - 1)$ . . . (3) (2) (1). For example, $4! = 4 \times 3 \times 2 \times 1 = 24$. $0! = 1$.]

For example, if $\lambda = 4$ per hour, then the probability of $x = 6$ in 1 hour is

$$f(6) = \frac{4^6 e^{-4}}{6!} = \frac{4096 \times 0.0183}{720} = 0.104$$

The Poisson distribution for an average arrival rate of $\lambda = 4$ per hour (as well as for other values of λ) is shown in Figure D-2. The Poisson distribution is typically skewed to the right. The distribution is simple in that its standard deviation is expressed solely in terms of the mean, $\sigma_\lambda = \sqrt{\lambda}$.

Evidence that the Poisson distribution in fact represents arrival patterns in many applications is indeed great. Many empirical studies have validated the Poisson arrival distribution in general industrial operations, traffic flow, and various service operations.

Arrival distributions are sometimes given in terms of the time between arrivals, or interarrival times. The distributions of the time between arrivals often follow the negative exponential distribution. However, if the *number* of arrivals in a given interval is Poisson distributed, then necessarily the times *between* arrivals have a negative exponential distribution, and vice versa.

Although we cannot say that all distributions of arrivals per unit of time are adequately described by the Poisson distribution, we can say that it is usually worth checking to see if it is true, for then a fairly simple analysis may be possible. It is logical that arrivals may follow the Poisson distribution when many factors affect arrival time, because the Poisson distribution corresponds to completely random arrivals. This means that each arrival is independent of other arrivals as well as of any condition of the waiting line. The practical question is whether or not the Poisson distribution is a reasonable approximation to reality.

Poisson Arrivals—Service Time Distribution Not Specified

Because Poisson arrivals are common, a useful waiting line model is one that depends on Poisson arrivals, but accepts any service time distribution. We assume that the mean service rate is greater than the mean arrival rate, otherwise the system would be unstable and the waiting line would become infinitely large. We also assume the single server case, first come–first served queue discipline, and arrivals wait for service; that is, they neither fail to join the line nor leave it because it is too long. Under these conditions the expected length of the waiting line is

$$L_q = \frac{(\lambda \sigma)^2 + (\lambda / \mu)^2}{2(1 - \lambda / \mu)} \qquad (2)$$

where

$$L_q = \text{the expected length of the waiting line}$$

λ = the mean arrival rate from a Poisson distribution

μ = the mean service rate

σ = the standard deviation of the distribution of service times

We define the average service facility utilization as $\rho = \lambda/M\mu$, where M is the number of servers in the waiting line system. In the single server case, $M = 1$ and ρ is simplified to λ/μ. Because λ is the mean arrival rate and μ is the mean service rate, then ρ may be interpreted as the proportion of time that at least one server is

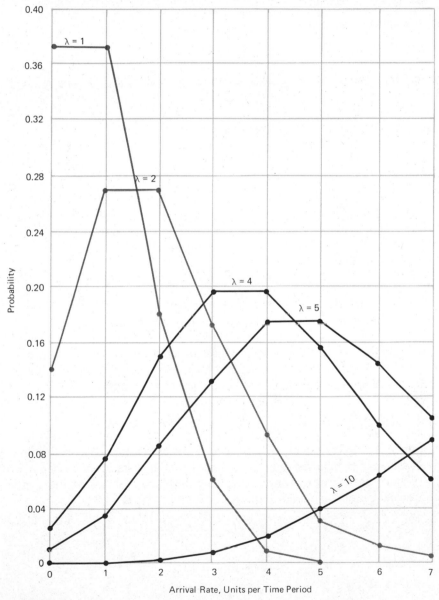

FIGURE D-2
Poisson distributions for several mean arrival rates.

busy. For example, if $\lambda = 2$, $\mu = 4$, and $M = 1$, then on the average two units arrive per time unit and the single server has the capacity to process four units during the same time interval. Therefore, the server will be busy $\rho = \lambda/M\mu = 2/(1 \times 4) = 0.5$, or half the time.

In the single server case, $\rho = \lambda/\mu$ represents the proportion of time that the service facility is in use. Therefore, the probability that a unit will have to wait for service is $P_w = \lambda/\mu$. Also, $(1 - \rho)$ is the fraction of service facility idle time, or the fraction of time when no one is being served. Because ρ is the expected number being served, the total number in the waiting line plus the expected number being served is the total number in the system, L,

$$L = L_q + \lambda/\mu \tag{3}$$

Similar simple logic leads to the formula for expected waiting time in line W_q, and time in the system including service W. The reciprocal of the mean arrival rate is the mean time between arrivals $(1/\lambda)$. For example, if $\lambda = 2$ units per hour on the average, then the expected time between arrivals of any two units is $1/2 = 0.5$ hours. The multiplication of the mean time between arrivals and the line length gives the waiting time

$$W_q = L_q/\lambda \tag{4}$$

Therefore, if $\lambda = 2$ units per hour and $L_q = 3$, then one unit arrives in the system every 0.5 hours on the average, but the line is three units long. Then, units waiting in line must wait three times as long as the time between arrivals, or $3 \times 0.5 = 1.5$ hours, that is, $L_q/\lambda = 3/2 = 1.5$ hours.

Also, the multiplication of the mean time between arrivals and the mean total number in the system, L, gives the mean time in the system including service, that is,

$$W = L/\lambda = W_q + 1/\mu \tag{5}$$

The latter equality in Equation 5 is true because the total time in the system must equal the waiting time plus the time for service. Equations 2, 3, 4, and 5 are useful relationships. The general procedure would be to compute L_q from (2), and compute the values of L, W_q, and W as needed, given the value of L_q. Note that Equations 2 through 5 deal only with average or long-run equilibrium conditions.

An Example. Trucks arrive at the truck dock of a wholesale grocer at the rate of eight per hour and the distribution of arrivals is Poisson. The loading and/or unloading time averages 5 minutes, but the estimate s of the standard deviation of service time is 6 minutes. Truckers are complaining that they must spend more time waiting than unloading and the following calculations verify their claim:

$$\lambda = 8/\text{hour}; \mu = 60/5 = 12/\text{hour}; s = 6/60 = 1/10 \text{ hours}$$

$$L_q = \frac{(8/10)^2 + (8/12)^2}{2(1 - 8/12)} = 1.63 \text{ trucks in line}$$

$L = 1.63 + 8/12 = 2.30$ trucks in the system
$W_q = 1.63/8 = 0.204$ hours, or 12.24 minutes in line waiting for service
$W = 2.30/8 = 0.288$ hours, or 17.28 minutes in the system

The calculations yield another verification of logic in that the average truck waits 12.24 minutes in line plus 5 minutes for service, or 17.28 minutes in the system. Thus, $W = W_q + 1/\mu$ as indicated in Equation 5.

Let us pause for a moment to reflect on this model. Which are the decision variables and which are the uncontrollable parameters? The service-related variables can be altered by the manager if there is a willingness to invest capital in new capacity or if new procedures can be devised that can reduce the variability of service time. On the other hand, the arrival rate of trucks is presumably not under managerial control, and thus is a parameter.

The grocer knows, of course, that the problem could probably be solved by expanding the truck dock so that two trucks could be handled simultaneously. This solution, however, would require a large capital expenditure and disruption of operations during construction. Instead, the grocer notes the very large standard deviation of service time, and on investigation finds that some orders involve uncommon items which are not stored in a systematic manner. Locating these items takes a great deal of search time.

The grocer revamps the storage system so that all items can be easily located. As a result, the standard deviation is reduced to 3 minutes. Assuming that mean service time is not affected, we have an indication of the sensitivity of the system to changes in the variability of service time. The new values are $L_q = 0.91, L = 1.57, W_q = 6.8$ minutes, and $W = 11.8$ minutes. Waiting time has been cut almost in half. The truckers are happier, and the grocer has improved the system without a large capital expenditure.

SERVICE TIME DISTRIBUTIONS

Although there is considerable evidence that arrival processes tend to follow the Poisson distributions as has been indicated, service time distributions seem to be much more varied in their nature. This is why the previous model involving Poisson arrivals and an unspecified service time distribution is so valuable. With Equation 2, one can compute the waiting line statistics, knowing only the mean service rate and the standard deviation of service time.

The negative exponential distribution has been one of the prominent models for service time, and there is evidence that in some instances the assumption is valid. However, Nelson's study [1959] of distributions of arrivals and service times in a Los Angeles machine shop did *not* indicate that the exponential model fit the actual service time distributions adequately for all of the machine centers.

Model for Poisson Input and Negative Exponential Service Times

The negative exponential distribution is completely described by its mean value, because its standard deviation is equal to its mean. We can describe this model as a special case of Equation 2. If the service times are adequately described by a negative exponential distribution, then the mean of the distribution is the reciprocal of the mean service rate, that is, $1/\mu$. Therefore, $1/\mu$ is also the standard deviation of the distribution of service times when the distribution is the negative exponential.

Equation 6 can easily be derived from Equation 2 when $1/\mu$ is substituted for σ (verify this derivation yourself):

$$L_q = \frac{\lambda^2}{\mu(\mu - \lambda)} \tag{6}$$

Also, the probability of n units in the system at any point in time is

$$P_n = \left(\frac{\lambda}{\mu}\right)^n \left(1 - \frac{\lambda}{\mu}\right) \tag{7}$$

The other relationships between L_q, L, W_q, and W, expressed by Equations 3, 4, and 5, hold for the negative exponential service time distributions as well as for the case where no service time distribution is specified. For the sake of simplicity, many individuals prefer to use Equation 2, using the appropriate value of σ to reflect the special case.

We can now check to see the effect of exponential service times on waiting line statistics for the truck dock problem. If we assume that the service time in that situation was represented by a negative exponential distribution, then $\sigma = 1/\mu = 1/12$, and the value of L_q from Equation 2 is 1.33. The other waiting line model statistics are $L = 2$, $W_q = 10$ minutes, and $W = 15$ minutes. The values are intermediate between the previous two calculations for the grocer's problem, because the value of σ is between the two previous values.

Model for Poisson Input and Constant Service Times

Although constant service times are not usual in actual practice, they may be reasonable assumptions in cases where a machine processes arriving items by a fixed-time cycle. Also, constant service times represent a boundary or lower limit on the value of σ in Equation 2. As such, a constant service time is also a special case of Equation 2. The resulting equation for constant service times is

$$L_q = \frac{\lambda^2}{2\mu(\mu - \lambda)} \tag{8}$$

You should derive Equation 8 from Equation 2 by substituting $\sigma = 0$ in Equation 2.

Again, for comparison, and to gain insight into what happens in waiting lines, let us see what the result would have been if the grocer could have made service time constant at 5 minutes, that is, reduced the standard deviation to zero. Substituting in Equation 8, we have $L_q = 0.67$, $L = 1.33$, $W_q = 5$ minutes, and $W = 10$ minutes. Again, the other relationships between L_q, L, W_q, and W expressed by Equations 3, 4, and 5 hold for the constant service time distribution as well as for the case where no service time distribution is specified.

We can consider Equation 2 as a fairly general model with service time distributions described by the negative exponential, or constant service times as special cases. Figure D-3 shows a graph of L_q for various values of the standard deviation, including the values for the negative exponential distribution and for constant service times. Values of the standard deviation greater than that for the negative exponential distribution occur in distributions termed *hyperexponential*. The extreme values of standard deviation are not representative of values found in practice; however, the tail of the curve in Figure D-3 is shown to indicate how rapidly L_q increases with variability in the service time distribution.

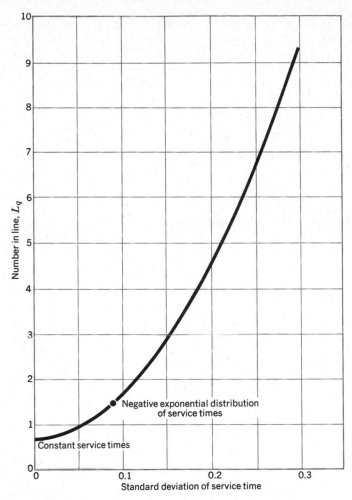

FIGURE D-3
Relationship between waiting line length L_q and standard deviation of service time for the grocer's truck dock problem (Poisson input).

Relationship of Queue Length to Utilization

Recall that $\rho = \lambda/M\mu$ represents the service facility utilization. If $\lambda = \mu$, then $\rho = 1$ for the single server case where $M = 1$, and theoretically the service facility is used 100 percent of the time. But let us see what happens to the length of the queue as ρ varies from zero to one. Figure D-4 summarizes the result for Poisson input and exponential service times for a single server. As ρ approaches unity, the number waiting in line increases rapidly and approaches infinity. We can see that this must be true by examining Equations 2, 6, and 8 for L_q. In all cases, the denominator goes to zero as ρ approaches unity and the value of L_q becomes infinitely large.

We see now that one of the requirements of any practical system is that $\mu > \lambda$; otherwise we cannot have a stable system. If units are arriving faster on the average than they can be processed, the waiting line and waiting time will increase continuously and no steady state can be achieved. This simple fact also indicates that there is a value to be placed on idle time in the service facility. *We must trade off the value of rapid service against service facility costs that may include substantial service facility idle time.*

Multiple Servers

In the multiple servers case we assume the conditions of Poisson arrivals, exponential service times, first come–first served queue discipline, and all servers drawing on a single waiting line. The effective service rate $M\mu$ must be greater than the arrival rate λ, where M is the number of servers. The facility utilization factor is $\rho = \lambda/M\mu$, and we define $r = \lambda/\mu$. First, it is necessary to calculate L_q, the mean number in the waiting line. The formula for L_q becomes relatively complex in the multiple server case, so we have computed L_q for various values of M (the number of servers) and $r = \lambda/\mu$ in Table G-3 of Appendix G.

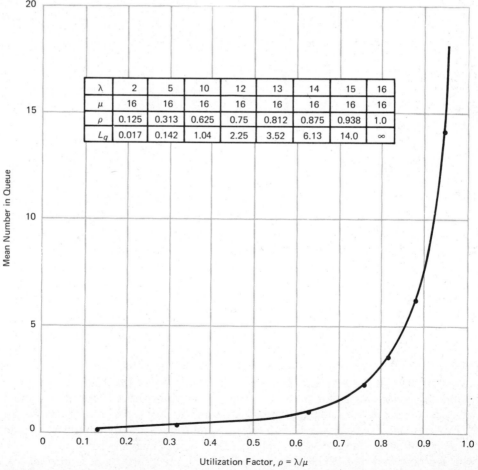

λ	2	5	10	12	13	14	15	16
μ	16	16	16	16	16	16	16	16
ρ	0.125	0.313	0.625	0.75	0.812	0.875	0.938	1.0
L_q	0.017	0.142	1.04	2.25	3.52	6.13	14.0	∞

Mean Number in Queue (y-axis)

Utilization Factor, $\rho = \lambda/\mu$ (x-axis)

FIGURE D-4
Relationship of queue length to the utilizaition factor ρ for a single server system where $M = 1$.

TABLE D-2   **Summary of Waiting Line Model Statistics for the Wholesale Grocer Example. λ = 8/hour, μ = 12/hour**

	Single Dock, M = 1				Two Docks, M = 2, Negative Exponential Service Time
	s = 6 min.	s = 3 min.	Negative Exponential Service Time, s = $1/\mu$ = 5 min.	Constant Service Time, s = 0	
L_q, trucks in line	1.63	0.91	1.33	0.67	0.085
L, trucks in system	2.30	1.57	2.00	1.33	0.752
W_q, minutes	12.24	6.80	10.00	5.00	0.64
W, minutes	17.28	11.80	15.00	10.00	5.64

Given the value of L_q, then L, W_q, and W are easily computed from Equations 3, 4, and 5. The probability that all servers are busy (the probability that there will be a wait), P_w, can be computed using the values of L_q in Table G-3 as

$$P_w = \frac{L_q (M - r)}{r} \qquad (9)$$

As an example, assume that the wholesale grocer decides to expand facilities and add a second truck dock. What is the effect on average truck waiting time? Recall the basic data: λ = 8 per hour, μ = 12 per hour, but now M = 2. From Table G-3, for M = 2 and r = λ/μ = 8/12 = 0.67, we find, by interpolating, that L_q = 0.085 trucks in line. Then W_q = L_q/λ = 0.085/8 = 0.0106 hours or 0.64 minutes. Compare these results with the single server solution for exponential service time of W_q = 10 minutes. Obviously, adding the second dock eliminates the truck waiting problem. Note that overall utilization of the facilities declines from ρ = $\lambda/M\mu$ = 0.67 to ρ = 0.34. Table D-2 provides a summary of the waiting line model statistics for all the models constructed for the wholesale grocer example.

The effect of increasing the number of servers can be seen from Figure D-5. For M = 1, ρ = $\lambda/M\mu$ = 8/12 = 0.67. Reading from Figure D-5, we can approximate the line length as L_q = 1.3. However, for M = 2, ρ = 8/(2 × 12) = 0.33. The approximate value of line length from Figure D-5 is L_q = 0.8, or 0.9. The effects in reducing L_q by increasing the number of servers are dramatized by the graphical representation. Figure D-5 can be used conveniently to make gross estimates of L_q. When more precise estimates are needed, Table G-3 should be used.

The Effect of Pooling Facilities

Sometimes managers have the option of organizing the needed capacity into two or more independent facilities or pooling the resources into one large facility. If for example, we were faced with a situation where r = 0.9 for the single server case, then L_q is approximately 8 from Table G-3. Adding a second server reduces the average line length to L_q = 0.23. Adding a third server reduces it to L_q = 0.03. The

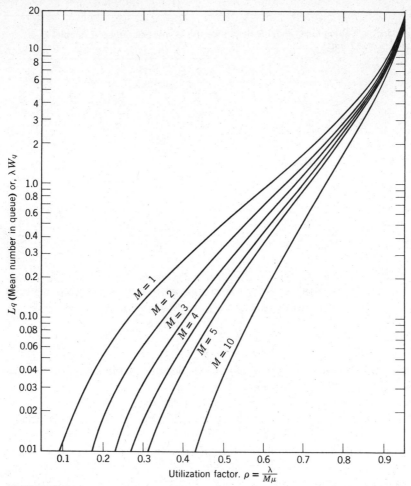

FIGURE D-5
L_q for different values of M, in relation to the utilization factor ρ (Poisson arrivals, negative exponential service time distributions).

effects on L_q are surprisingly large; that is, we can obtain disproportionate gains in reducing waiting time by increasing the number of servers. We can see intuitively that this might be true from Figure D-4, because queue length (and waiting time) begins to increase very rapidly at about $\rho = 0.8$, for the single server case represented. A rather small increase in the capacity of the system (decrease in ρ) at these high loads can produce a large decrease in waiting line length and waiting time.

When we design a system with waiting lines, we can increase its service level by increasing the speed of a server, adding another server at the same physical location that draws on the same waiting line, or adding another server at a different physical location. Intuitively, we might expect these alternatives to produce essentially identical results. To investigate this issue, let us compare the doubling of capacity within the same service facility by doubling the service rate, doubling capacity by adding a second server within the same facility, and doubling capacity through parallel service facilities. Assume that $\lambda = 8$, $\mu = 10$, and $r = \lambda/\mu = 0.8$ for the base case with a single server. From Table G-3 and the equations, the mean number waiting is $L_q = 3.2$, the mean number in the system is $L = 4$, the mean waiting time is $W_q = 0.4$ hours or 24 minutes, and the mean time in the system is $W = 0.5$ hours, or 30 minutes. These data are summarized in Table D-3.

If we double capacity by doubling the service rate within the same facility, all the waiting line model statistics improve dramatically as shown in Table D-3. If we double capacity by adding a second server, service improves, but not as dramatically.

Now, however, suppose that we double capacity by establishing a second service facility in another location so that there must be two independent waiting lines. The arrivals are divided equally between the two facilities, and $\lambda = 4$, $\mu = 10$, and $r = 0.4$. The information for comparison is given by the right-hand column in Table D-3. Each service facility will provide the service indicated.

Now look at just the two alternatives of providing the same capacity with one large facility, either by doubling service rate or by adding a second server (the third and fourth columns of Table D-3). Comparing them with two equivalent small facilities in the right-hand column, it is clear that either of the alternatives involving an enlarged single facility gives better service. One large facility definitely provides better service than two equivalent smaller facilities. Looking just at the two alternate ways of doubling capacity within the existing facility, doubling service rate is superior. Although doubling service rate results in a larger waiting line ($L_q = 0.27$ versus 0.15, because sometimes two are being served simultaneously in the $M = 2$ case) and waiting time is proportionately greater, this condition is compensated for by faster service, and the mean number in the system as well as the *total* time in the system are smaller for the system with the higher service rate.

When capacity is doubled by adding a second parallel facility, service is improved, but not as dramatically as for either of the other two alternatives; the reason is that service is being provided by two independent systems with two independent waiting lines. Idle capacity in one system cannot be used by the other as would be true if they were both drawing from a single waiting line.

TABLE D-3   **Effects of Doubling Capacity Within the Same Service Facility by Doubling Service Rate Versus Adding a Second Server**

		Capacity Doubled		
	Base Case $(M = 1,$ $r = 0.8)$	Within Same Facility $(M = 1,$ $r = 0.4)$	By Adding Second Server $(M = 2,$ $r = 0.8)$	Second Facility each $(M = 1,$ $r = 0.4)$
L_q*	3.2000	0.2666	0.1533	0.2666
$L = L_q + \lambda/\mu$	4.0000	0.6666	0.9533	0.6666
$W_q = L_q/\lambda$	0.4000 hr	0.0333 hr	0.0192 hr	0.0667 hr
$W = L/\lambda$	0.5000 hr	0.0833 hr	0.1192 hr	0.1667 hr
	or	or	or	or
	30.0 min	5.0 min	7.15 min	10.0 min

*Values from Table G-3 of Appendix G.

An Example. A large manufacturing concern with a 100-acre plant had a well-established medical facility, which was located at the plant offices at the eastern edge of the property. Over the years the plant had grown from east to west and currently travel time to the medical facility was so great that management was considering dividing the facility. The second unit was to be established near the center of the west end of the plant. A study had been made of weighted travel times for the present single facility and for the proposed two-facility system. The result indicated that average travel time for the present large medical facility was 15 minutes. The volume averaged 1000 visits per week, or 250 worker hours for travel time. The two-facility plan would reduce the average travel time to 8 minutes, or 133 worker hours per week.

The question now was, what would happen to waiting time in the waiting rooms? For the one large facility, $\lambda = 25$ per hour, and average service time was 20 minutes, or a service rate of $\mu = 3$ per hour, and $r = 25/3 = 8.33$. There were 10 physicians who handled the load. Interpolating in Table G-3, $L_q = 2.45$, and $W_q = 2.45 \times 60/25 = 5.88$ minutes per person or 98 worker-hours per week. Therefore, the travel time plus the waiting time was $250 + 98 = 348$ worker-hours per week.

The plan was to divide the medical staff for the two facilities, and it was assumed that the load would divide equally, so comparable data for the divided facilities are $\lambda = 12.5$ per hour per facility, $\mu = 3$ per hour, $M = 5$, and $r = 4.2$. From Table G-3 of Appendix G, $L_q = 3.3269$ and $W_q = 16$ minutes per person or 267 worker hours per week. The travel plus waiting time for the dual facility plan was therefore $133 + 267 = 400$ worker hours per week, compared with 348 for the single large facility. Other alternatives could be computed, probably involving an increased medical staff.

The waiting time for the single large facility was 5.88 minutes per person compared with 16.0 minutes per person for the two-facility plan. The large facility gives better service than the two smaller facilities. If we visualize the two decentralized facilities functioning side-by-side, we can see intuitively why waiting time increases. If facility *1* were busy and had patients waiting while at the same time facility *2* happened to be idle, someone from the facility *1* waiting room could be serviced immediately by facility *2*, thereby reducing average waiting time. In this situation the two facilities are drawing from one waiting line. When they are physically decentralized, the facilities must draw on two independent waiting lines and *the idle capacity of one cannot be used by the waiting patients of the other.*

Costs and Capacity in Waiting Line Models

Although many decisions concerning service systems may turn on physical factors of line length, waiting time, and the service facility utilization, very often system designs will depend on comparative costs for alternatives. The costs involved are commonly the costs of providing the service *versus* the waiting time costs. In some instances the waiting time costs are objective, as when the enterprise is employing both the servers and those waiting. The company medical facility just discussed is such a case. The company absorbed all the travel time and waiting time costs, as well as the cost of providing the service. In such an instance, a direct cost-minimizing approach can be taken balancing the waiting costs, or the time-in-system costs, against the costs of providing the service.

TABLE D-4

Utilization, Waiting Time, and Costs for Different Levels of Medical Service

	Number of Physicians		
	9	10	11
Utilization ($\rho = \lambda/M\mu$)	0.93	0.83	0.76
Mean waiting time (min)	23.4	5.88	2.26
Weekly waiting time (hr)	390	98	38
Cost of waiting time/week	$1950	$ 490	$ 190
Physicians' cost/week	6235	6928	7620
Total affected cost	$8185	$7418	$7810

When the arriving units are customers, clients, or patients, the cost of making them wait is less obvious. If they are customers, excessive waiting may cause irritation and loss of goodwill and eventually sales. Placing a value on goodwill, however, is not a straightforward exercise. In public service operations and other monopoly situations, the valuation of waiting cost may be even more tenuous because the individual cannot make alternate choices. In these situations where objective costs cannot be balanced, it may be necessary to set a standard for waiting time; for example, to adjust capacity to keep average waiting time at or below a given number of minutes at supermarket checkout counters.

Example. Let us refer to the data for the company internal medical facility. Recall that there were 10 physicians, whom we will assume are paid $3000 per month, or about $6928 per week for the 10 physicians. We also assume that the average hourly wage of employees coming to the medical facility is $5. Computations for the single central facility yield a travel time cost of $250 \times 5 = \$1250$ per week, and a waiting time cost of $98 \times 5 = \$490$ per week. The total weekly cost is then $8668, including physicians' salaries. First, with the central facility only, how many physicians will minimize affected costs? Using Table G-3, we can determine average waiting time for 9, 10, and 11 physicians, and the resulting weekly costs. The results are shown in Table D-4. Consequently, the present policy of having 10 physicians is a little less costly than having either 9 or 11.

Now, let us consider the dual facility concept, where travel cost is also affected. The travel, waiting, and physicians' cost for the central facility was $5(250 + 98) + $6928 = $8668 per week. The comparable figures for the dual facilities were $5 (133 + 267) + $6928 = $8928. Would increased capacity in either or both of the dual facilities improve affected costs? The answer is no. The weekly travel and waiting costs and service costs for 5 physicians in each facility, 5 in one and 6 in the other, and 6 in each are $8928, $9109, and $9292.

An important observation concerning the company medical facility is that the unit cost of providing the service is very large and tends to dominate, compared with unit waiting time costs. The physician is paid $3000 per month, whereas the average employee waiting is paid only about $866 per month. If the unit costs change relative to each other, the best solution may be different.

621

FINITE WAITING LINE MODELS

Many practical waiting line problems that occur have the characteristics of finite waiting line models. This is true whenever the population of machines, people, or items that may arrive for service is limited to a relatively small finite number. The result is that we must express arrivals in terms of a unit of the population rather than as an average rate. In the infinite waiting line case the average length of the waiting line is effectively independent of the number in the arriving population, but in the finite case the number in the waiting line may represent a significant proportion of the arriving population, and therefore the probabilities associated with arrivals are affected. For example, suppose there are 10 machines being serviced by a mechanic and one breaks down (arrives for service). Then, there are only 9 that could possibly break down, because one has been eliminated from the arriving population.

The resulting mathematical formulations are somewhat more difficult computationally than those for the infinite waiting line case. Fortunately, however, finite queuing tables [Peck and Hazelwood, 1958] are available that make problem solution very simple. Although there is no definite number that we can point to as a dividing line between finite and infinite applications, the finite queuing tables have data for populations from 4 up to 250, and these data may be taken as a general guide. We have reproduced these tables for populations of 5, 10, 20, and 30 in Table G-4 of Appendix G, to illustrate their use in the solution of finite waiting line problems. The tables are based on a finite model for negative exponential times between arrivals and negative exponential service times, and a first come–first served queue discipline.

Use of the Finite Queuing Tables

The tables are indexed first by N, the size of the population. For each population size, data are classified by X, the service factor (comparable with the utilization factor in infinite waiting line models), and by M, the number of parallel servers. The service factor X is computed from the following formula:

$$X = \text{service factor} = \frac{\lambda}{\lambda + \mu}$$

where μ is the service rate as before, but λ is the mean arrival rate *per population unit*. For example, if our time unit is hours and *each population unit* arrives for service every 4 hours on the average, then $\lambda = 1/4 = 0.25$ per hour.

For a given N, X, and M, three factors are listed in the tables: D (the probability of a delay; that is, if a unit calls for service, the probability that it will have to wait), F (an efficienty factor, used to calculate other important data), and L_q (the mean number in the waiting line). To summarize, we define the following factors:

$$W_q = \text{mean waiting time} = \frac{1}{\mu X}\frac{(1-F)}{(F)}$$

$$L = \text{mean number waiting plus being served} = L_q + FNX$$
$$W = \text{mean time in system} = W_q + 1/\mu$$
$$H = \text{mean number of units being serviced} = FNX = L - L_q$$

J = mean number of units not being served = $FN(1 - X)$

$M - H$ = mean number of servers idle

The procedure for a given case is as follows:

1. Determine the mean service rate μ and the mean arrival rate λ per population unit, based on data or measurements of the system being analyzed.
2. Compute the service factor $X = \lambda/(\lambda + \mu)$.
3. Locate the section of the tables listing data for the population size N.
4. Locate the service factor calculated in (2) above, for the given population.
5. Read the values of D, F, and L_q for the number of servers M, interpolating between values of X when necessary.
6. Compute values for W_q, H, and J as required by the nature of the problem.

Example. A hospital ward has 30 beds in one section, and the problem centers on the appropriate level of nursing care. The hospital management believes that patients should have immediate response to a call at least 80 percent of the time because of possible emergencies. The mean time between calls is 95 minutes *per patient,* for the 30 patients. The service time is approximated by a negative exponential distribution and mean service time is 5 minutes.

The hospital manager wishes to staff the ward to give service so that 80 percent of the time there will be no delay. Nurses are paid $5 per hour, and the cost of idle time at this level of service must be considered. Also, the manager wishes to know how much more patients will have to pay for the 80 percent criterion compared with a 50 percent service level for immediate response, which is the current policy.

The *solutions* to the problems posed by the hospital manager are developed through a finite waiting line model. The situation requires a finite model because the maximum possible queue is 30 patients waiting for nursing care, and if a patient calls for service, there are only 29 patients who could now possibly call for service. Thus, because of the relatively small population, the potential for more arrivals has been changed by the occurrence of an arrival.

In terms of the finite waiting line model for this situation, the mean service time is 5 minutes (μ = 0.2/min., or 12/hr), the mean time between calls is 95 minutes *per patient* (λ = 0.0105/min., or 0.632/hr), and therefore the service factor is $X = \lambda/(\lambda + \mu)$ = 0.632/12.632 = 0.05.

Scanning the finite queuing tables (Table G-4) under Population N = 30, and X = 0.05, we seek data for the probability of a delay of D = 0.20, because we wish to establish service such that there will be no delay 80 percent of the time. The closest we can come to providing this level of service is with M = 3 nurses and corresponding data (see Table G-4) of D = 0.208, F = 0.994, and L_q = 0.18. Note that we must select an integer number of servers (nurses).

The cost of this level of service is the cost of employing 3 nurses or $5 \times 3 = \$15$ per hour, or $360 per day, assuming day and night care. The average number of calls waiting to be serviced will be L_q = 0.18 and the mean waiting time will be

$$W_q = \frac{1}{\mu X}\left(\frac{1 - F}{F}\right) = \frac{1}{0.2 \times 0.05}\left(\frac{1 - 0.994}{0.994}\right) = 0.6 \text{ minutes}$$

The waiting time due to waiting line effects is, of course, negligible, which is intended.

The average number of patients being served will be $H = FNX = 0.994 \times 30 \times 0.05 = 1.49$, and the average number of nurses idle will be $3 - 1.49 = 1.51$. The equivalent value of this idleness is $1.51 \times 5 \times 24 = \$181.20$ per day.

Finally, the number of nurses needed to provide immediate service 50 percent of the time is $M = 2$ from Table G-4 ($D = 0.571$, $F = 0.963$, and $L_q = 1.11$). The average waiting time under this policy is $W_q = 3.84$ minutes. The average cost to patients of having the one additional nurse to provide the higher level of service is $5 per hour or $120 per day. Divided among 30 patients, the cost is $4 per patient per day.

IMPORTANT TERMS

Numbers in parentheses indicate page numbers

Arrival rate, λ (611)

Constant service time model (614)

Facility utilization, ρ (611,615)

Finite waiting line model (607,622)

Infinite waiting line model (607)

Mean line length, L_q (610)

Mean number in system, L (612)

Mean time in system, W (612)

Mean waiting time, W_q (612)

Multiple server model (616)

Negative exponential service times (613)

Poisson arrivals (609)

Probability of a wait, P_w (617)

Probability of n units in system, P_n (614)

Service factor, X (622)

Service rate, μ (611)

Single server model (610)

Time between arrivals (610)

REVIEW QUESTIONS AND PROBLEMS

(Table D-5 provides a summary of waiting line models.)
1.   Classify the following in terms of the four basic waiting line structures.
    a.   Assembly line
    b.   Large bank—six tellers (one waiting line for each)
    c.   Cashier at a restaurant
    d.   One-chair barbershop
    e.   Cafeteria line
    f.   Jobbing machine shop
    g.   General hospital
    h.   Post office—four windows drawing from one waiting line

2.   Define the following terms

TABLE D-5
Summary of Waiting Line Models; Poisson Arrivals and First-Come First-Served Queue Discipline

	Infinite Models			Finite Model, Negative Exponential Service Time, $N = 4 - 250$, Multiple Servers
	Single Server Models		Multiple Server Model, Negative Exponential Service Time	
Service Time Distribution Not Specified	Negative Exponential Service Time	Constant Service Time		
$L_q = \dfrac{(\lambda\sigma)^2 + (\lambda/\mu)^2}{2(1 - \lambda/\mu)}$	$L_q = \dfrac{\lambda^2}{\mu(\mu - \lambda)},$ or use Table G-3 for $M = 1$	$L_q = \dfrac{\lambda^2}{2\mu(\mu - \lambda)}$	Compute $r = \lambda/\mu$. Use Table G-3 to find L_q for a given value of M	Compute $X = \dfrac{\lambda}{\lambda + \mu}$. Use Table G-4 to find values of L_q, D, and F for value of M wanted.
$W_q = L_q/\lambda$	$W_q = L_q/\lambda$	$W_q = L_q/\lambda$	$W_q = L_q/\lambda$	$W_q = \dfrac{1}{\mu X}\dfrac{(1 - F)}{(F)}$
$L = L_q + \lambda/\mu$	$L = L_q + \lambda/\mu$	$L = L_q + \lambda/\mu$	$L = L_q + \lambda/\mu$	$L = L_q + FNX$
$W = W_q + 1/\mu = L/\lambda$	$W = W_q + 1/\mu = L/\lambda$	$W = W_q + 1/\mu = L/\lambda$	$W = W_q + 1/\mu = L/\lambda$	$W = W_q + 1/\mu$
$\rho = \lambda/M\mu$	$\rho = \lambda/M\mu$	$\rho = \lambda/M\mu$	$\rho = \lambda/M\mu$	$H = FNX = L - L_q$ = mean number being served
	$P_w = \lambda/\mu$ = probability an arrival must wait		$P_w = L_q(M - r)/r$ = probability an arrival must wait	$J = FN(1 - X)$ = mean number not being served
	$P_n = (\lambda/\mu)^n(1 - \lambda/\mu)$			
	$P_0 = 1 - \lambda/\mu$		$P_0 = \dfrac{L_q(M - 1)!(M - r)^2}{(r)^{M+1}}$	$M - H$ = servers idle

    a.   Arrival process

    b.   Queue discipline

    c.   Infinite waiting line model

    d.   Finite waiting line model

    e.   Single-server model

    f.   Multiple-server model

3.   Given a Poisson distribution of arrivals with a mean of $\lambda = 5$ per hour, what is the probability of an arrival of $x = 4$ in 1 hour? What is the probability of the occurrence of 15 minutes between arrivals?

4.   The barber of a one-chair shop finds that sometimes customers are waiting, but sometimes he has nothing to do and can therefore read sports magazines. He prefers to keep a rather steady pace when he is working, hoping to get blocks of time for reading and keeping up on sports. In the hope of improving his situation, he kept records for several weeks and found that an average of one customer per hour comes in for haircuts (Poisson distribution). It takes him an average of 20 minutes per haircut and the standard deviation of his sample of service times is 5 minutes.

    a.   What is the average number of customers waiting for service?

    b.   What is the average customer waiting time?

    c.   How much of the time does the barber have to read sports magazines?

d. The other barber in town has fallen ill, and our barber's business increases to an average number of two customers per hour. What happens to the average number of customers waiting, the average waiting time, and the time available for reading sports magazines?

e. After practicing at home on his children, the barber finds that he can reduce both the haircutting time to 10 minutes and the variance to virtually zero by using a bowl and only electric clippers (no scissors). Will this solve the waiting time problem in the interim while the other barber is ill? How would it affect the barber's available reading time?

f. With the other barber ill, our barber finds that his customers are screaming for better service and that his reading time is available only in small increments. He feels under great pressure, but is afraid to try the technological improvements he has developed. How can he solve his problem?

5. A taxicab company has four cabs that operate out of a given taxi stand. Customer arrival rates and service rates are described by the Poisson distribution. The average arrival rate is 10 per hour, and the average service time is 20 minutes. The service time follows a negative exponential distribution.

a. Calculate the utilization factor.

b. From Table G-3, determine the mean number of customers waiting.

c. Determine the mean number of customers in the system.

d. Calculate the mean waiting time.

e. Calculate the mean time in the system.

f. What would be the utilization factor if the number of taxicabs were increased from four to five?

g. What would be the effect of the change in part (f) on the mean number in the waiting line?

h. What would be the effect of reducing the number of taxicabs from four to three?

6. Why is queuing felt to be an unacceptable method for dealing with overload conditions in medical systems?

7. A stenographer has five persons for whom he performs stenographic services. Arrival rates are adequately represented by the Poisson distribution, and service times follow the negative exponential distribution. The arrival rate is five jobs per hour. The average service time is 10 minutes. Assume that once an individual assigns a job, she will not bring another job until the first is completed.

a. Calculate the mean number in the waiting line.

b. Calculate the mean waiting time.

c. Calculate the mean number of units being served.

d. What is the probability that an individual bringing work to the stenographer will have to wait?

8. In the manufacture of photographic film, there is a specialized process of perforating the edges of the 35-mm film used in movie and still cameras. A bank of

TABLE D-6

Expected Changes in Breakdown Rates, Service Time, and Cost of Repair Parts for Three Levels of Preventive Maintenance

Level of Preventive Maintenance	Breakdown Rate (%)	Service Time (%)	Cost of Repair Parts (%)
L_1	−30	+20	+ 50
L_2	−40	+35	+ 80
L_3	−50	+75	+120

20 such machines is required to meet production requirements. The severe service requirements cause breakdowns that must be repaired quickly because of high downtime costs. Because of breakdown rates and downtime costs, management is considering the installation of a preventive maintenance program that they hope will improve the situation.

The present breakdown rate is three per hour per machine, or a time between breakdowns of 20 minutes. The average time for service is only 3 minutes. The breakdown rate follows a Poisson distribution, and the service times follow a negative exponential distribution. The crew simply repairs the machines in the sequence of breakdown. Machine downtime is estimated to cost $9 per hour, and present repair parts cost an average of $1 per breakdown. Maintenance repairmen are paid $6 per hour. The breakdown rates, service times, and repair parts costs are expected to change with different levels of preventive maintenance, as indicated in Table D-6.

What repair crew size and level of preventive maintenance should be adopted to minimize costs?

REFERENCES

Bierman, H., C. P. Bonini, and W. H. Hausman, *Quantitative Methods for Business Decisions* (6th ed.), D. Irwin, Homewood, Ill., 1981.

Bleuel, W. H., "Management Science's Impact on Service Strategy," *Interfaces,* *6*(1), Part 2, November 1975, pp. 4–12.

Buffa, E. S., and J. S. Dyer, *Management Science/Operations Research: Model Formulation and Solution Methods* (2nd ed.), Wiley, New York, 1981.

Cosmetatos, G. P., "The Value of Queueing Theory—A Case Study," *Interfaces,* *9*(3), May 1979, pp. 47–51.

Erikson, W. J., "Management Science and the Gas Shortage," *Interfaces, 4*(4), August 1974, pp. 47–51.

Foote, B. L., "A Queuing Case Study of Drive-In Banking," *Interfaces, 6*(4), August 1976, pp. 31–37.

Gilliam, R. R., "An Application of Queueing Theory to Airport Passenger Security Screening," *Interfaces, 9*(4), August 1979, pp. 117–123.

Krajewski, L. J., and H. E. Thompson, *Management Science: Quantitative Methods in Concepts,* Wiley, New York, 1981.

McKeown, P. G., "An Application of Queueing Analysis to the New York State Child Abuse and Maltreatment Register Telephone Reporting System," *Interfaces, 9*(3), May 1979, pp. 20–25.

Nelson, R. T., "An Empirical Study of Arrival, Service Time, and Waiting Time Distributions of a Job Shop Production Process," Research Report No. 60, *Management Sciences Research Project,* UCLA, 1959.

Paul, R. J., and R. E. Stevens, "Staffing Service Activities with Waiting Line Models," *Decision Sciences, 2,* April 1971, pp. 206–227.

Peck, L. G., and R. N. Hazelwood, *Finite Queuing Tables*, Wiley, New York, 1958.

Vogel, M. A., "Queueing Theory Applied to Machine Manning," *Interfaces, 9*(4), August 1979, pp. 1–8.

APPENDIX E

Monte Carlo Simulation

S IMULATED SAMPLING, KNOWN GENERALLY AS MONTE CARLO, makes it possible to introduce into a system data that have the statistical properties of an empirical distribution. If the model involves the flow of orders according to the actual demand distribution experienced, we can simulate the "arrival" of an order by Monte Carlo sampling from the distribution; the timing and flow of orders in the simulated system will then parallel experience. If we are studying the breakdown of a certain machine as a result of bearing failure, we can simulate typical breakdown times through simulated sampling from the distribution of bearing lives.

A COMPUTED EXAMPLE

Suppose we are dealing with the maintenance of a bank of 30 machines, and, initially, we wish to estimate what level of service can be maintained by one mechanic. We have the elements of a waiting line situation, with machine breakdowns representing arrivals, the mechanic being the service facility, and repair time representing service time. If the distributions of the time between breakdowns and service times followed the negative exponential distribution, the simplest procedure would be to use the formulas and calculate the average time that a machine waits, the mechanic's idle time, and so forth. We can see by inspection of Figures E-1 and E-2 that the distributions are not similar to the negative exponential, so simulation is an alternative. The procedure is as follows:

1. *Determine the distributions of time between breakdowns and service time.* If these data were not available directly from records, we would have to make a study to determine the distributions. Figures E-1 and E-2 show the distributions of breakdowns and repair times for 73 breakdowns.
2. *Convert the frequency distribution to cumulative probability distributions (see Figures E-3 and E-4).* This conversion is accomplished by summing the frequencies that are less than or equal to each breakdown or repair time and plotting them. The cumulative frequencies are then converted to probabilities by assigning the number 1.0 to the maximum value.

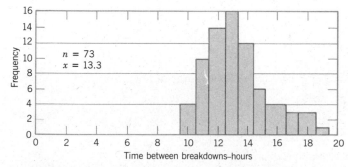

FIGURE E-1
Frequency distribution of the time between breakdowns for 30 machines.

631

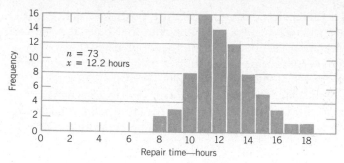

FIGURE E-2
Frequency distribution of the repair time for 73 breakdowns.

As an example, let us take Figure E-1 and convert it to the cumulative distribution of Figure E-3. Beginning at the lowest value for breakdown time, 10 hours, there are four occurrences. Four is plotted on the cumulative chart for the breakdown time of 10 hours. For the breakdown time, 11 hours, there were 10 occurrences, but there were 14 occurrences of 11 hours or less, so the value 14 is plotted for 11 hours. For the breakdown time, 12 hours, there were 14 occurrences recorded, but there were 28 occurrences of breakdowns for 12 hours or less.

Figure E-3 was constructed from Figure E-1 by proceeding in this way. When the cumulative frequency distribution was completed, a cumulative probability scale was constructed on the right of Figure E-3 by assigning the number 1.0 to the maximum value, 73, and dividing the resulting scale into 10 equal parts. This results in a cumulative empirical probability distribution. From Figure E-3, we can say that 100 percent of the breakdown time values were 19 hours or less; 99 percent were 18 hours or less, and so on. Figure E-4 was constructed from Figure E-2 in a comparable way.

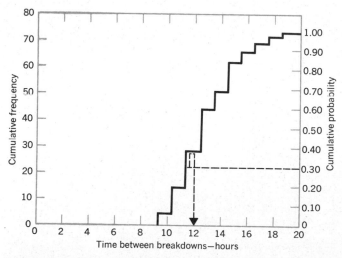

FIGURE E-3
Cumulative distribution of breakdown times.

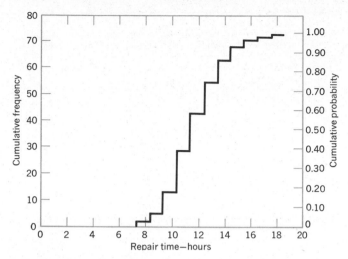

FIGURE E-4
Cumulative distribution of repair times.

3. Sample at random from the cumulative distributions to determine specific breakdown times and repair times to use in simulating the repair operation. We do this by selecting numbers between 001 and 100 at random (representing probabilities in percentage). The random numbers could be selected by any random process, such as drawing numbered chips from a box. The easiest way is to use a table of random numbers, such as those included in Table G-5 of the Appendix G. (Pick a starting point in the table at random and take two-digit numbers in sequence in that column, for example.)

The random numbers were used to enter the cumulative distributions to obtain time values. An example is shown in Figure E-3. The random number 30 is shown to select a breakdown time of 12 hours. We can now see the purpose behind the conversion of the original distribution to a cumulative distribution. Only one breakdown time can be associated with a given random number. In the original distribution, two values would result because of the bell shape of the curve.

By using random numbers to obtain breakdown time values in this fashion from Figure E-3, we will obtain breakdown time values in proportion to the probability of occurrence indicated by the original frequency distribution. We can construct a table of random numbers that selects certain breakdown times. For example, reading from Figure E-3, the random numbers 6 through 19 result in a breakdown time of 11 hours, and so on. This is the same as saying that 5 percent of the time we would obtain a value of 10 hours, 14 percent of the time we would obtain a breakdown time of 11 hours, and so forth. Table E-1 shows the random number equivalents for Figures E-3 and E-4.

Sampling from either the cumulative distributions of Figures E-3 and E-4 or from Table E-1 will produce breakdown times and repair times in proportion to the original distributions, just as if actual breakdowns and repairs were happening. Table E-2 gives a sample of 20 breakdown and repair times determined in this way.

4. Simulate the actual operation of breakdowns and repairs. The structure of the simulation of the repair operation is shown by the flowchart of Figure E-5. This

TABLE E-1

Random Numbers Used to Draw Breakdown Times and Repair Times in Proportion to the Occurrence Probabilities of the Original Distributions

Breakdown Times		Repair Times	
These Random Numbers ⟶	Select These Breakdown Times	These Random Numbers ⟶	Select These Repair Times
1–5	10 hours	1–3	8 hours
6–19	11	4–7	9
20–38	12	8–18	10
39–60	13	19–40	11
61–77	14	41–59	12
78–85	15	60–75	13
86–90	16	76–86	14
91–95	17	87–93	15
96–99	18	94–97	16
0=100	19	98–99	17
		0=100	18

operation involves the selection of a breakdown time and determining whether or not the mechanic is available. If the mechanic is not available, the machine must wait until one is, and the wait time may be computed. If the mechanic is available, the question is: Did the mechanic have to wait? If waiting was required, we compute the mechanic's idle time. If the mechanic did not have to wait, we select a repair time and proceed according to the flowchart, repeating the overall process as many times as desired, stopping the procedure when the desired number of cycles has been completed.

TABLE E-2

Simulated Sample of Twenty Breakdown and Repair Times

Breakdown Times		Repair Times	
Random Number	Breakdown Time from Figure E-3	Random Number	Repair Time from Figure E-4
83	15	91	15
97	18	4	9
88	16	72	13
12	11	12	10
22	12	30	11
16	11	32	11
24	12	91	15
64	14	29	11
37	12	33	11
62	14	8	10
52	13	25	11
9	11	74	13
64	14	97	16
74	14	70	13
15	11	15	10
47	13	43	12
86	16	42	12
79	15	25	11
43	13	71	13
35	12	14	10

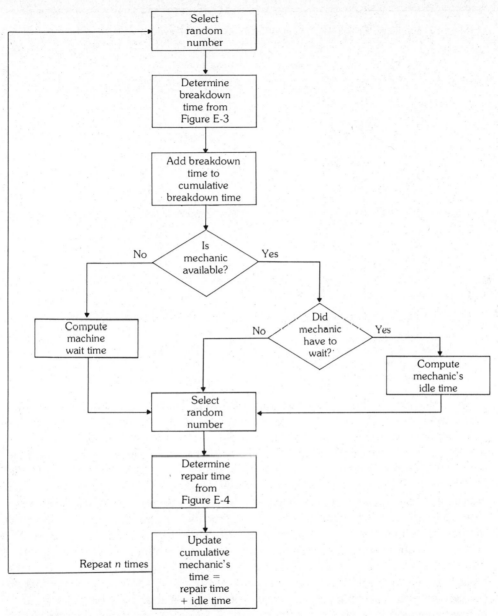

FIGURE E-5
Flowchart showing structure of repair simulation.

TABLE E-3   **Simulated Breakdown and Repair for Twenty Breakdowns**

Time of Breakdown	Time Repair Begins	Time Repair Ends	Machine Wait Time	Repair Mechanics Idle Time
0	0	15	0	0
18	18	27	0	3
34	34	47	0	7
45	47	57	2	0
57	57	68	0	0
68	68	79	0	0
80	80	95	0	1
94	95	106	1	0
106	106	117	0	0
120	120	130	0	3
133	133	144	0	3
144	144	157	0	0
158	158	174	0	1
172	174	187	2	0
183	187	197	4	0
196	197	209	1	0
212	212	224	0	3
227	227	238	0	3
240	240	253	0	2
252	253	263	1	0

Total machine wait time = 11 hours
Total mechanic's idle time = 26 hours

The simulation of the repair operation is shown in Table E-3, using the breakdown times and repair times selected by random numbers in Table E-2. We assume that time begins when the first machine breaks down and calculate breakdown time from that point. The repair time required for the first breakdown was 15 hours, and because this is the first occurrence in our record, neither the machine nor the mechanic had to wait. The second breakdown occurred at 18 hours, but the mechanic was available at the end of 15 hours, waiting 3 hours for the next breakdown to occur.

We proceed in this fashion, adding and subtracting, according to the requirements of the simulation model to obtain the record of Table E-3. The summary at the bottom of Table E-3 shows that for the sample of 20 breakdowns, total machine waiting time was 11 hours, and total mechanic's idle time was 26 hours. To obtain a realistic picture we would have to use a much larger sample. Using the same data on breakdown and repair time distributions, 1000 runs using a computer yielded 15.9 percent machine wait time and 7.6 percent mechanic's idle time. Of course, the mechanic is presumably paid for an 8-hour day regardless of the division between idle and service time; however, knowing idle time available may be a guide to the assignment of "fill-in" work.

PROBLEMS

1. A sample of 100 arrivals of customers at a check-out station of a small store occurs according to the following distribution:

Time Between Arrivals, Minutes	Frequency
0.5	2
1.0	6
1.5	10
2.0	25
2.5	20
3.0	14
3.5	10
4.0	7
4.5	4
5.0	2
	100

A study of the time required to service the customers by adding up the bill, receiving payment, making change, placing packages in bags, and so on, yields the following distribution:

Service Time, Minutes	Frequency
0.5	12
1.0	21
1.5	36
2.0	19
2.5	7
3.0	5
	100

a. Convert the distributions to cumulative probability distributions.
b. Using a simulated sample of 20, estimate the average percentage customer waiting time and the average percentage idle time of the server.

2. The manager of a drive-in restaurant is attempting to determine how many carhops he needs during his peak load period. As a policy, he wishes to offer service such that average customer waiting time does not exceed 2 minutes.

a. How many carhops does he need if the arrival and service distributions are as follows and if any carhop can service any customer?
b. Simulate for various alternate numbers of carhops with a sample of 20 arrivals in each case.

Time Between Successive Arrivals, Minutes	Frequency	Carhop Service Time, Minutes	Frequency
0.0	10	0.0	0
1.0	35	1.0	5
2.0	25	2.0	20
3.0	15	3.0	40
4.0	10	4.0	35
5.0	5		100
	100		

3. A company maintains a bank of machines exposed to severe service, causing bearing failure to be a common maintenance problem. There were three bearings in the machine that caused trouble. The general practice had been to replace bearings when they failed. However, excessive downtime costs raised the question of whether or not a preventive policy was worthwhile. The company wished to evaluate three alternate policies:

a. The current practice of replacing bearings that fail.

b. When a bearing fails, replace all three.

c. When a bearing fails, replace that bearing plus other bearings that have been in use 1700 hours or more.

Time and cost data are as follows:

Maintenance mechanics time:
   Replace 1 bearing   5 hours
   Replace 2 bearings   6 hours
   Replace 3 bearings   7 hours
Maintenance mechanic's wage rate $3 per hour
Bearing cost $5 each
Downtime costs $2 per hour

A record of the actual working lives of 200 bearings results in the following distribution:

Bearing Life, Hours	Frequency
1100	3
1200	10
1300	12
1400	20
1500	27
1600	35
1700	30
1800	25
1900	18
2000	15
2100	4
2200	1
	200

Simulate approximately 20,000 hours of service for each of the three alternate policies.

REFERENCES

Buffa, E. S., and J. S. Dyer, *Management Science/Operations Research: Model Formulation and Solution Methods* (2nd ed.), Wiley, New York, 1981.

Fetter, R. B., and J. D. Thompson, "The Simulation of Hospital Systems," *Operations Research*, 13(5), 1965, pp. 689–711.

Kwak, N. K. P., P. J. Kuzdrall, and H. H. Schmitz, "The GPSS Simulation of Scheduling Policies for Surgical Patients," *Management Science, 22*(9), May 1976, pp. 982–989.

Law, A. M., and W. D. Kelton, *Simulation Modeling and Analysis,* McGraw-Hill, New York, 1982.

Maisel, H., and G. Gnugnuoli, *Simulation of Discrete Stochastic Systems,* SRA, Chicago, 1972.

Moore, L. J., and B. W. Taylor, III, Experimental Investigation of Priority Scheduling in a Bank Check Processing Operation," *Decision Sciences, 8*(4), October 1977.

Reitman, J., *Computer Simulation Applications*, Wiley, New York, 1971.

Schriber, T. J., *Simulation Using GPSS*, Wiley, New York, 1974.

APPENDIX F

Work Measurement

PERFORMANCE STANDARDS

Performance standards provide data that are basic to many decision-making problems in production/operations management. The performance standard is of critical importance because labor cost is a predominant factor, influencing many decisions that must be made. For example, decisions to make or buy, to replace equipment, or to select certain manufacturing processes require estimates of labor costs. These decisions necessarily require an estimate of how much output can be expected per unit of time.

Performance standards also provide basic data used in the day-to-day operation of a plant. For example, scheduling or loading machines demands a knowledge of the projected time requirements. For custom manufacture, we must be able to give potential customers a bid price and delivery date. The bid price is ordinarily based on expected costs for labor, materials, and overhead, plus profit. Labor cost is commonly the largest single component in such situations. To estimate labor cost requires an estimate of how long it will take to perform the various operations.

Finally, performance standards provide the basis for labor cost control. By measuring worker performance in comparison with standard performance, indexes can be computed for individual workers, whole departments, divisions, or even plants. These indexes make it possible to compare performance on completely different kinds of jobs. Standard labor costing systems and incentive wage payment systems are based on performance standards.

INFORMAL STANDARDS

Every organization has performance standards of sorts. Even when they do not seem to exist formally, supervisors have standards in mind for the various jobs based on their knowledge of the work and past performances. These types of standards are informal. Standards based on supervisor's estimates and past performance data have weaknesses, however. First, in almost all such situations, methods of work performance have not been standardized. Therefore, it is difficult to state what output rate, based on past records, is appropriate, because past performance may have been based on various methods. Because it has been demonstrated that output rates depend heavily on job methods, standards based on past performance records might not be dependable. A second major defect in standards based on estimates and past performance records is that they are likely to be too strongly influenced by the working speeds of the individuals who held the jobs. Were those workers high or low performers?

THE CORE OF THE WORK MEASUREMENT PROBLEM

We wish to set up standards that are applicable to the working population, not just to a few selected people within that population. The standards problem is comparable in some ways with that of designing a lever with the proper mechanical advantage to match the capabilities of workers. But not just any worker: The force required to pull the lever should accommodate perhaps 95 to 99 percent of the population, so that anyone who comes to the job will have the necessary arm strength.

We require a knowledge of the distribution of performance times for the entire working population doing the job. For example, suppose that we have 500 people all doing an identical task; we make sample studies on all of them and plot the data. Figure F-1 shows the results of such a study. The distribution shows that average performance time varies from 0.28 to 0.63 minute per piece. If past records reflected data from one or more individuals taken at random from the population of 500, a standard based on their performance might not fit the whole population very well. On the other hand, if we have good data concerning the entire distribution, as in Figure F-1, we can set up standards that probably would be appropriate for everyone. One way to do this is to set the standard so that it accommodates about 95 percent of the population. For Figure F-1, a standard performance time of about 0.48 minute is one that about 95 percent of the individuals exceeded. If we pegged the standard at this level, we would expect that practically all employees on the job should be able to meet or exceed the standard.

Some managers feel that it is not wise to quote minimum performance standards such as these for fear that they will encourage relatively poor performance as acceptable. These people prefer to say that the standard performance is about the average of the distribution (0.395 minute for Figure F-1) and expect that most workers will produce about standard, that some will fall below, and that some will exceed standard. Both systems of quoting standards are used, although the practice of quoting *minimum acceptable values* is more common than that of quoting average values.

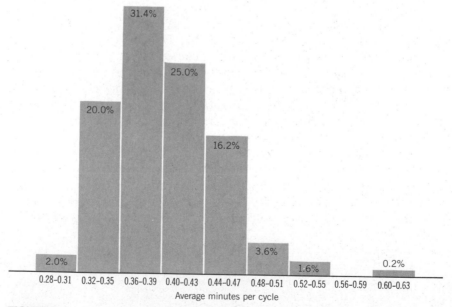

FIGURE F-1
Percentage distribution of the performance of 500 people performing a wood block positioning task. About 5.4 percent of the people averaged 0.48 minute per cycle or longer.
SOURCE: Adapted from R. M. Barnes. Motion and Time Study: Design and Measurement of Work *(7th ed.). John Wiley, New York, 1980.*

The distribution of Figure F-1 shows how long it took on the average to perform the task. Using the minimum acceptable level as a standard of performance, we will call the actual work time at that level the *normal time.* The normal time for the data of Figure F-1 is 0.48 minute; the total standard time is then

Standard time = Normal time + standard allowance for personal time
$$+ \text{ allowance for measured delays normal to the job}$$
$$+ \text{ fatigue allowance}$$

We will discuss the several allowances later, but the central question now is: How do we determine normal time in the usual situation when only one or a few workers are on the job? The approach to this problem used in industry is called performance rating.

PERFORMANCE RATING

Performance rating is a critically important part of any formal means of work measurement. To be able to rate accurately requires considerable experience. A pace or performance level is selected as standard. An analyst observes this pace, compares it with various other paces, and learns to judge pace level in percentage of the standard pace. For Figure F-1, we called the cycle time of 0.48 minute "normal," and the pace or rate of output associated with this time is normal pace. A pace of work that is 25 percent faster would require proportionately less time per cycle, or $0.48/1.25 = 0.381$ minute. If a skilled analyst observed a worker performing the task on which Figure F-1 is based and rated performance at 125 percent of normal while simultaneously measuring the actual average performance time as 0.381 minute, 25 percent would be added to observed time to adjust it to the normal level. In this instance, performance rating is perfect, because $0.381 \times 1.25 = 0.48$. Other perfect combinations of rating and actual observed time are 150 percent and 0.32 minute, 175 percent and 0.274 minute, 90 percent and 0.533 minute, and so forth.

In an actual work measurement situation, the analyst does not have the answer beforehand, so actual time taken to do the task and performance rating must be done simultaneously. The normal time is then computed as

$$\text{Normal time} = \text{actual observed time} \times \frac{\text{performance rating}}{100}$$

All formal work measurement systems involve this rating or judgment of working pace, or some equivalent procedure. Alternate methods will be considered later in this appendix.

How Accurate Is Performance Rating?

In the actual work measurement situation, it is necessary to compare a mental image of "normal performance" with what is observed. This rating enters the computation of performance standards as a factor, and the final standard can be no more accurate than the rating. How accurately can experienced people rate? Controlled studies in which films have been rated indicate a standard deviation of 7 to 10 percent. In other words, experienced people probably hold these limits about 68 percent of the time. Therefore, the effect of the element of judgment in current work measurement practice is considerable.

WORK MEASUREMENT SYSTEMS

All practical work measurement systems involve (1) the measurement of actual observed time and (2) the adjustment of observed time to obtain "normal time" by means of performance rating. The alternate systems that we will discuss combine these factors in somewhat different ways.

Stopwatch Methods

The most prevalent approach to work measurement currently used involves a stopwatch time study and simultaneous performance rating of the operation to determine normal time. Electronic timing devices are now often used instead of the conventional stopwatch. The general procedure is as follows:

1. Standardize methods for the operation; that is, determine the standard method, specifying work place layout, tools, sequence of elements, and so on. Record the resulting standard practice.
2. Select for study an operator who is experienced and trained in the standard methods.
3. Determine the elemental structure of the operation for timing purposes. This may involve a breakdown of the operation into elements and the separation of the elements that occur during each cycle from those that occur only periodically or randomly. For example, tool sharpening might be required each 100 cycles to maintain quality limits. Machine adjustments might occur at random intervals.
4. Observe and record the actual time required for the elements, making simultaneous performance ratings.
5. Determine the number of observations required to yield the desired precision of the result based on the sample data obtained in step 4. Obtain more data as required.
6. Compute normal time = average observed actual time × average rating factor/ 100.
7. Determine allowances for personal time, delays, and fatigue.
8. Determine standard time = normal times for elements + time for allowances.

Breakdown of Elements. Common practice is to divide the total operation into elements rather than to observe the entire cycle as a whole. There are several reasons why this practice is followed:

1. The element breakdown helps to describe the operation in some detail, indicating the step-by-step procedure followed during the study.

2. More information is obtained that may be valuable in comparing times for like elements on different jobs and for building up a handbook of standard data times for common elements in job families. With standard data for elements, cycle times for new sizes can be forecast without additional study.

3. A worker's performance level may vary in different parts of the cycle. With an element breakdown, different performance ratings can be assigned to different elements where the overall cycle is long enough to permit separate evaluation of performance.

In breaking down an operation into elements, it is common practice to make elements a logical component of the overall cycle, as illustrated in Figure F-2. For example, element 1, "pick up piece and place in jig," is a fairly homogeneous task. Note that element 4, "drill ¼-inch hole," is the machining element, following the general practice to separate machining time from handling time. Finally, constant elements are usually separated from elements that might vary with size, weight, or some other parameter.

Taking and Recording Data. Figure F-2 is a sample study in which 20 cycles were timed by the continuous method, that is, the stopwatch is allowed to run continuously, being read at the breakpoints between elements. Elapsed times for elements are then obtained by successive subtraction. *Repetitive* or "snap-back" methods of reading the watch are also common. In repetitive timing, the observer reads the watch at the end of each element and snaps the hand back to zero, so that each reading gives the actual time without the necessity of subtraction. Comparative studies indicate that the two methods are equally accurate.

Other data recorded in Figure F-2 identify the part, operation, operator, material, and so on, as well as check data of elapsed time of the study and the number of completed units. The "selected times" represent averages of the element times; the cycle "selected time" is merely the sum of the element averages. A single performance rating of 100 percent was made for the study, and a 5 percent allowance was added to obtain the standard time of 1.17 minutes per piece.

Adequacy of Sample Size. We are attempting to estimate, from the sample times and performance ratings observed, a normal time of performance. The precision desired will determine how many observations will be required. For example, if we wanted to be 95 percent sure that the resulting answer, based on the sample, was within ±5 percent, we would calculate the sample size n required from a knowledge of the mean and standard deviation of our sample data. If we wanted greater confidence or closer precision, the sample size would have to be larger.

Figure F-3 is a convenient chart for estimating required sample sizes to maintain a ±5 percent precision in the answer for 95 and 99 percent confidence levels. To use the chart, we merely calculate the mean value, $\bar{x}$, and the standard deviation based on the sample data. The "coefficient of variation" is simply the percentage variation, $100(s_x/\bar{x})$. The chart is entered with the calculated coefficient of variation, and the sample size is read off for the confidence level desired. The most common confidence level is 95 percent in work measurement.

Let us test the adequacy of the sample taken in the study of Figure F-2. First, was $n = 20$ adequate for estimating the overall cycle within a precision of ±5 percent

OBSERVATION SHEET

SHEET 1 OF 1 SHEETS **DATE**

OPERATION Drill ¼" Hole **OP. NO.** D-20

PART NAME Motor Shaft **PART NO.** MS-267

MACHINE NAME Avey **MACH. NO.** 2174

OPERATOR'S NAME & NO. S.K. Adams 1347 **MALE** [✓] **FEMALE** [ ]

EXPERIENCE ON JOB 18 Mo. on Sens. Drill **MATERIAL** S.A.E. 2315

FOREMAN H. Miller **DEPT. NO.** DL 21

BEGIN 10:15 **FINISH** 10:38 **ELAPSED** 23 **UNITS FINISHED** 20 **ACTUAL TIME PER 100** 115 **NO. MACHINES OPERATED** 1

ELEMENTS	SPEED	FEED	T/R	1	2	3	4	5	6	7	8	9	10	SELECTED TIME
1. Pick Up Piece and Place in Jig			T	.12	.11	.12	.13	.12	.10	.12	.12	.14	.12	
			R	.12	.29	.39	.54	.66	.77	.92	8.01	14	.32	
2. Tighten Set Screw			T	.13	.12	.12	.14	.11	.12	.12	.13	.12	.11	
			R	.25	.41	.51	.68	.77	.89	7.04	.14	.26	.43	
3. Advance Drill to Work			T	.05	.04	.04	.04	.05	.04	.04	.04	.03	.04	
			R	.30	.45	.55	.72	.82	.93	.08	.18	.29	.47	
4. DRILL ¼" HOLE	980	H	T	.57	.54	.56	.51	.54	.68	.52	.53	.59	.56	
			R	.87	.99	3.11	4.23	5.36	6.51	.60	.71	.88	11.03	
5. Raise Drill from Hole			T	.04	.03	.03	.03	.03	.03	.03	.03	.04	.03	
			R	.91	2.02	.14	.26	.39	.54	.63	.74	.92	.06	
6. Loosen Set Screw			T	.06	.06	.07	.06	.06	.06	.06	.06	.07	.08	
			R	.97	.08	.21	.32	.45	.60	.69	.80	.99	.14	
7. Remove Piece from Jig			T	.08	.09	.08	.08	.09	.08	.07	.08	.09	.07	
			R	1.05	.17	.29	.40	.54	.68	.76	.88	10 08	.21	
8. Blow Out Chips			T	.13	.10	.12	.14	.13	.12	.13	.12	.12	.11	
			R	.18	.27	.41	.54	.67	.80	.89	9.00	.20	.32	
9.			T											
			R											
10. (1)			T	.12	.11	.13	.14	.12	.12	.11	.13	.12	.12	.12
			R	11.44	.56	.69	.82	.87	17011	8.09	.21	.31	.42	
11. (2)			T	.12	.14	.12	.11	.12	.10	.13	.15	.12	.11	.12
			R	.56	.70	.81	.93	.99	.11	.22	.36	.43	.53	
12. (3)			T	.04	.04	.04	.03	.04	.04	.04	.04	.04	.04	.04
			R	.60	.74	.85	.96	16.03	.15	.26	.40	.47	.57	
13. (4)			T	.64	.53	.55	.52	.57	.54	.50	.53	.65	.54	.54
			R	12.14	13.27	14.40	15.48	.60	.69	.76	.93	21 02	22.11	
14. (5)			T	.03	.03	.03	.03	.03	.03	.03	.03	.03	.03	.03
			R	.17	.30	.43	.51	.63	.72	.79	.96		.14	
15. (6)			T	.06	.06	.06	.07	.06	.05	.06	.06	.05	.06	.06
			R	.23	.36	.49	.58	.69	.77	.85	20.02	.10	.20	
16. (7)			T	.08	.08	.09	.08	.08	.07	.08	.06	.08	.08	.08
			R	.31	.44	.58	.66	.77	.84	.93	.08	.18	.28	
17. (8)			T	.14	.12	.10	.09	.12	.14	.15	.11	.12	12	.12
			R	.45	.56	.68	.75	.89	.98	19.08	.19	.30	22.40	
18.			T											1.11
			R											

SELECTED TIME 1.11 **RATING** 100% **NORMAL TIME** 1.11 **TOTAL ALLOWANCES** 5% **STANDARD TIME** 1.17

Overall Length 12" Drill ¼" Hole 1" ¾" 1½"

TOOLS, JIGS, GAUGES: Jig No. D-12-33
Use H.S. Drill ¼" Diam.
Hand Feed
Use Oil - S4

TIMED BY J.B.M.

FIGURE F-2
Stopwatch time study of a drilling operation made by the continuous method.
SOURCE: *R. M. Barnes. Motion and Time Study: Design and Measurement of Work (7th ed.). John Wiley, New York, 1980.*

and a confidence level of 95 percent? Table F-1 shows the calculation of the coefficient of variation for the cycle times as about 5 percent; that is, the standard deviation of 0.057 minute is about 5 percent of the mean cycle time of 1.12 minutes. From Figure F-3, we see that a sample of $n = 4$ would be adequate to maintain a precision within ±5 percent of the correct mean cycle time, 95 percent of the time. For a confidence level of 99 percent, $n = 10$. Our actual sample of 20 was more than adequate.

The reason that the small sample size was adequate is easy to understand. The variability of the readings is small in relation to the mean cycle time, so a good estimate of cycle time is obtained by only a few observations. This is commonly true of operations dominated by a machine cycle. In this case, the actual drill time is almost half of the total cycle, and the machining time itself does not vary much.

If all we wanted was an estimate of cycle time, we could stop at this point. Suppose, however, that we want estimates of each of the average element times to be adequate for future use as elemental standard data. Was the sample size of $n = 20$ adequate for each of these elements? Take element 1 as an example. The mean element time is $\bar{x} = 0.121$ minute, the standard deviation is $s = 0.0097$ minute, and

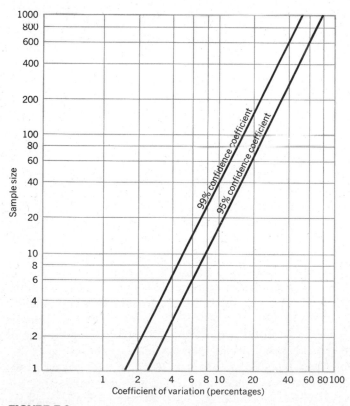

FIGURE F-3
Chart for estimating the sample size required to obtain maximum confidence intervals of ±5 percent for given coefficient of variation values.
SOURCE: A. Abruzzi. Work Measurement. Columbia University Press, New York, 1952.

TABLE F-1 **Cycle Times from Figure F-2, and Calculated Mean Value, Standard Deviation, Coefficient of Variation and Required Sample Sizes from Figure F-3**

Cycle Number	Cycle Time (minutes)	Cycle Time (squared)	Cycle Number	Cycle Time (minutes)	Cycle Time (squared)
1	1.18	1.395	11	1.13	1.280
2	1.09	1.190	12	1.11	1.235
3	1.14	1.300	13	1.12	1.255
4	1.13	1.280	14	1.07	1.145
5	1.13	1.280	15	1.14	1.300
6	1.13	1.280	16	1.09	1.190
7	1.09	1.190	17	1.10	1.215
8	1.11	1.235	18	1.11	1.235
9	1.20	1.440	19	1.11	1.235
10	1.12	1.255	20	1.10	1.215
			Sum	22.40	25.150

$$\bar{x} = \frac{22.40}{20} = 1.12$$

$$s = \sqrt{\frac{\sum x_i^2 - \frac{(\sum x_i)^2}{n}}{n - 1}}$$

$$= \sqrt{\frac{25.150 - \frac{(22.40)^2}{20}}{19}} = 0.057$$

$$\text{Coefficient of variation} = \frac{0.057 \times 100}{1.12} = 5.09\%$$

From Figure F-3:

$$n \approx = \quad 4 \text{ @ 95\% confidence level.}$$

$$n \approx = 10 \text{ @ 99\% confidence level.}$$

the coefficient of variation is 8 percent. From Figure F-3, we see that we should have taken a sample of $n = 10$ for a 95 percent confidence level and $n = 20$ for a 99 percent confidence level. The reason why a larger sample is needed for element 1 than for the entire cycle is that element 1 is somewhat more variable than is the total cycle (coefficient of variation of 8 percent compared with only 5 percent for the cycle). Therefore, if data on each of the elements are needed, the element for which the largest sample size is indicated, from Figure F-3, dictates the minimum sample size for the study. This procedure ensures the precision and confidence requirements for the limiting element and yields better results than this on all other elements.

Procedures for Ensuring Consistency of Sample Data. A single study always leaves open the question: Were the data representative of usual operating conditions? If a similar study were made on some other day of the week or some other hour of the day, would the results be different? This question suggests the possibility of dividing the total sample into smaller subsamples taken at random times. Then, by setting up control limits based on an initial sample, we can determine if the subsequent data taken are consistent. That is, did all the data come from a common universe?

This situation is comparable with that found in quality control. If a point falls outside of the $\pm 3s$ control limits, we know that the probability is high that some assignable cause of variation is present which has resulted in an abnormally high or low set of sample readings. These assignable causes could be anything that could have an effect on the time of production, such as material variations from standard or changes in tools, work place, methods of work, or the working environment. As with quality control, we would attempt to determine the nature of these assignable causes and eliminate data where abnormal readings have an explanation.

The general procedure is as follows:*

1. Standardize methods, select operator, and determine elemental breakdown as before.
2. Take an initial sample study.
   a. Compute preliminary estimates of $\bar{x}$ and s.
   b. Determine estimate of total sample needed from Figure F-3.
   c. Set up control limits for the balance of the study based on preliminary estimates of $\bar{x}$ and s.
3. Program and execute the balance of the study:
   a. Divide the total sample by the subsample size to find the number of separate subsamples to obtain. Subsample sizes are commonly 4 to 5.
   b. Randomize the time when these subsamples will be taken. A random number table is useful.
   c. At the random times indicated, obtain subsample readings and plot points on a control chart. If points fall outside limits, investigate immediately to determine the cause. Eliminate data from computations for standards where causes can be assigned.
   d. When the study is complete, make a final check to be sure that the precision and confidence level of the result are at least as good as desired.
4. Compute normal time, determine allowances, and compute standard time as before.

Work Sampling

The unique thing about work sampling is that it accomplishes the results of stopwatch study without the need for an accurate timing devise. Work sampling was first introduced to industry by L. H. C. Tippett in 1934. However, it has been in common use only since about 1950.

We can illustrate the basic idea of work sampling by a simple example. Suppose we wish to estimate the proportion of time that a worker, or a group of workers, spends working and the proportion of time spent not working. We can do this by long-term studies in which we measure the work time, the idle time, or both. This

---

* For detailed procedures with appropriate charts for estimating sample sizes, precision limits, and control limits, see Barnes [1980].

	Tally	Number	Per cent
Working	~~THL~~ ~~THL~~ ~~THL~~ ~~THL~~ ~~THL~~ ~~THL~~ ~~THL~~ ~~THL~~ ~~THL~~ ~~THL~~ ~~THL~~ ~~THL~~ ~~THL~~ ~~THL~~ ~~THL~~ ~~THL~~ ~~THL~~ ~~THL~~ /	96	88.9
Idle	~~THL~~ ~~THL~~ //	12	11.1
Total		108	100.0

FIGURE F-4
Work sampling tally of working and idle time.

would probably take a day or longer, and after measuring we would not be sure that the term of the study covered representative periods of work and idleness.

Instead, suppose that we make a large number of *random* observations in which we simply determine whether the operator is working or idle and tally the result (see Figure F-4). The percentages of the tallies recorded in the "working" and "idle" classifications are estimates of the actual percentage of time that the worker was working and idle. Herein lies the fundamental principle behind work sampling: *The number of observations is proportional to the amount of time spent in the working or idle state.* The accuracy of the estimate depends on the number of observations, and we can preset precision limits and confidence levels.

Number of Observations Required. The statistical methods of work sampling depend on the distributions for proportions. Recall that

$$\bar{p} = \frac{x}{n} = \frac{\text{number observed in classification}}{\text{total number of observations}}$$

and

$$s_p = \sqrt{\frac{\bar{p}(1 - \bar{p})}{n}}$$

From these simple formulas for mean proportion and the standard deviation of a proportion, charts and tables have been developed that give directly the number of observations required for a given value of $\bar{p}$, precision limits, and the 95 percent confidence level. Estimates of sample sizes can be obtained from Figure F-5.*

Note that the number of observations required is fairly large. For example, to maintain a precision in the estimate of $\bar{p}$ of ± 1.0 percentage point at 95 percent confidence, 10,000 observations are required if $\bar{p}$ is in the neighborhood of 50 percent; that is, to be 95 percent sure that an estimate of $\bar{p} = 50$ percent is between 49 and 51 percent. About 3600 observations are required to hold an estimated $\bar{p} = 10$ percent between 9 and 11 percent. Smaller samples are required for looser limits. Although these numbers of observations seem huge, we must remember that the nature of the observation required is merely a recognition of whether or not the employee is working, or possibly a classification of worker activity into various reasons for idleness.

Measuring Delays and Allowances. One common use of work sampling is to determine the percentage of time that workers are actually spending for personal time, and delays which are a part of the job. The resulting information could then be

* More complete information on sample sizes is available in Barnes [1957].

used as the basis for the percentage allowances that enter into the calculation of standard time.

Consider as an example the determination of delay and personal allowances in a lathe department of a machine shop. There are 10 workers involved. The delays of which we are speaking are a part of the job, such as waiting for tools, materials, and instructions; machine cleanup; securing an inspector's approval; change of jobs; and minor mechanical difficulties. We wish to determine the extent of the delays and how much time workers are using for personal time. The procedure is as follows:

1. *Design work sampling study.*

   a. Estimate preliminary values for the percentage of time spent in the three

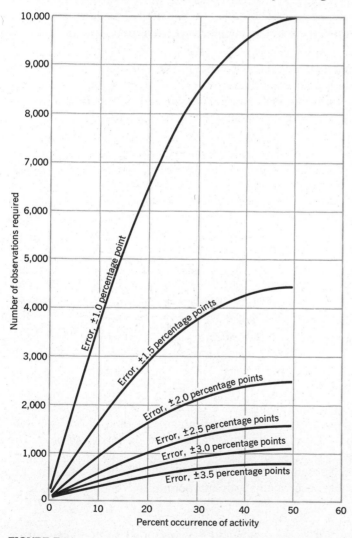

FIGURE F-5

Curves for determining the number of observations required to maintain precision within the percentage points indicated at the 95 percent confidence level.

categories of work, delay, and personal time from past knowledge, studies, supervisor's estimates, or a preliminary study of the jobs. These preliminary estimates are necessary to gauge the magnitude of the data-taking phase. Based on a composite of past information and foremen's estimates, our best guesses are:

Work	85 percent
Delay	10 percent
Personal time	5 percent

b. Set desired precision limits of estimates to be obtained. We decide that ±1.0 percentage point at 95 percent confidence on the delay estimate will be controlling. Thus, if the estimate for delays is actually 10 percent, we want to be 95 percent sure that it is not less than 9 percent or more than 11 percent, with 10 percent being the most probable value.

c. Estimate the total number of readings from Figure F-5. For $\bar{p} = 10$ percent, $N = 3600$ for ±1.0 percentage point error. Note from Figure F-5 that our precision for personal time of 5 percent would then be slightly better than ±1.0 percentage point and for working time, slightly worse.

d. Program the total number of readings over the desired time span of the study. We decide that 3600 readings over a 2-week period (10 working days) will cover a representative period. Therefore, we propose to obtain $3600/10 = 360$ observations per day. Because there are 10 workers involved, we will obtain 10 observations each time we sample. So we need to program $360/10 = 36$ random sampling times each day for 10 days to obtain the total of 3600 readings. The easiest way to select 36 random sampling times is to use a random number table.

e. Plan the physical aspects of the study. This includes an appropriate data sheet, as well as a determination of the physical path, observation points, and the like, so that the results are not biased because workers see the observer coming and change activities accordingly.

2. *Take the data as planned.* Table F-2 shows a summary of the actual data taken in this instance with a breakdown between morning and afternoon observations. The percentages for "work," and "delay," and "personal time" have been computed for each half-day and for the total sample.

3. *Recheck precision of results and consistency of data.* A final check of the delay percentage of 9.97 percent shows that the number of readings taken was adequate to maintain the ±1.0 percentage point precision on the delay time. The consistency of the data could be checked by setting up a control chart for proportions to see if any subsample points fell outside the limits. Other statistical tests comparing morning observations with afternoon observations could also be carried through.

Based on the work sampling study, we could then conclude that the delay part of the work in the lathe department was about 10 percent. We are 95 percent sure that the sampling error has been held to no more than ±1.0 percentage point, and it is

TABLE F-2   **Summary of Work Sampling Data for Lathe Department Study**

Date		Total Observations	Work		Delay		Personal	
			Obs.	Percent	Obs.	Percent	Obs.	Percent
10-2	A.M.	190	152	80.0	24	12.6	14	7.4
	P.M.	170	145	85.3	14	8.2	11	6.5
10-3	A.M.	160	144	90.0	10	6.3	6	3.7
	P.M.	200	158	79.0	19	9.5	23	11.5
10-4	A.M.	150	127	84.7	15	10.0	8	5.3
	P.M.	210	182	86.6	23	11.0	5	2.4
10-5	A.M.	180	142	78.9	24	13.3	14	7.8
	P.M.	180	148	82.2	20	11.1	12	6.7
10-6	A.M.	220	189	85.9	24	10.9	7	3.2
	P.M.	140	114	81.4	17	12.1	9	6.5
10-9	A.M.	210	185	88.2	14	6.6	11	5.2
	P.M.	150	135	90.0	9	6.0	6	4.0
10-10	A.M.	190	155	81.6	25	13.2	10	5.2
	P.M.	170	146	85.9	14	8.2	10	5.9
10-11	A.M.	200	166	83.0	22	11.0	12	6.0
	P.M.	160	136	85.0	14	8.8	10	6.2
10-12	A.M.	140	118	84.3	15	10.7	7	5.0
	P.M.	220	185	84.1	25	11.4	10	4.5
10-13	A.M.	210	181	86.2	19	9.1	10	4.7
	P.M.	150	130	86.7	12	8.0	8	5.3
		3600	3038	84.4	359	9.97	203	5.63

probable that it is less. We have based these conditions on a study that covered 2 weeks of time, with any time of the day being equally likely as a sampling time. The personal time of 5.6 percent is slightly greater than the company standard practice of allowing 5 percent; however, 5 percent is within the probable range of error of estimate.

Determining Production Standards. The previous example showed the use of work sampling to determine percentage allowances for noncyclical elements such as delays and for personal time. Why not carry the idea forward one more step and utilize the observations on percenage work time to establish production standards? What additional data do we need? If we knew (1) how many pieces were produced during the total time of the study and (2) the performance rating for each observation of work time, we could compute normal time as follows:

$$\text{Normal time} = \frac{\left(\begin{array}{c}\text{total}\\\text{time of}\\\text{study in}\\\text{minutes}\end{array}\right) \times \left(\begin{array}{c}\text{work time}\\\text{in decimals}\\\text{from work}\\\text{sampling study}\end{array}\right) \times \left(\begin{array}{c}\text{average}\\\text{performance}\\\text{rating in}\\\text{decimals}\end{array}\right)}{\text{total number of pieces produced}}$$

Standard time is then computed as before:

Standard time = normal time + allowances for delays, fatigue, and personal time

We have already seen how the allowances for delays and personal time can be determined from work sampling. Here we see the complete determination of a production standard without the use of a precise timing device. All that was needed was a calendar from which we might calculate the total available time.

Although work sampling can be used in most situations, its most outstanding field of application is in the measurement of noncyclical types of work where many different tasks are performed, but where there is no set pattern of cycle or regularity. In many jobs, the frequency of tasks within the job is based on a random demand function. For example, a storeroom clerk may fill requisitions, unpack and put away stock, deliver material to production departments, clean up the storeroom, and so on. The frequency and time requirements of some of these tasks depend on factors outside the control of the clerk. To determine such production standards by stopwatch methods would be difficult or impossible. Work sampling fits this situation ideally because, through its random sampling approach, reliable estimates of time and performance for these randomly occurring tasks can be obtained.

Standard Data Work Measurement Systems

Two kinds of standard data are used: universal data based on minute elements of motion (often called universal or microdata) and standard data for families of jobs (often called macrodata or element standard data).

Universal Standard Data. Universal standard data give time values for fundamental types of motions, so complete cycle times can be synthesized by analyzing the motions required to perform the task. Fundamental time values of this nature can be used as building blocks to forecast the standard time, provided that the time values are properly gathered and that the various minute motion elements required by the tasks are analyzed perfectly.

The result provided by these synthetic standards is an estimate of normal time for the task. Standard time is then determined as before by adding allowances for delay, fatigue, and personal time.

Does performance rating enter into standards developed from universal data? Not for each standard developed, because the analyst simply uses the time value from the table for a given motion. However, performance rating was used to develop the time values that are in the tables. So the rating factor enters the system, but not for each occasion that the data are used.

Many people feel that universal standard data lead to greater consistency of standards, because analysts are not called on to judge working pace in order to develop a standard. This does not mean that judgment is eliminated from the use of universal standard data systems, however. A great deal of judgment is required in selecting the appropriate classifications of motion to use in analyzing an operation. An inexperienced person ordinarily will not be able to perform these selections accurately enough for the purpose of determining production standards.

Using universal standard data as the sole basis for determining production standards is not common. In most cases where data of this kind are used, they are employed in conjunction with some other technique, such as stopwatch study or work sampling. The reason for this methodology seems to be that most organizations feel more comfortable when some actual direct measurement of the work involved has been made.

Standard Data for Job Families. Standard data for job families give normal time values for major elements of jobs (macrostandard data). Also, time values for machine setup and for different manual elements are given, so a normal time for an entirely new job can be constructed by an analysis of blueprints to see what materials are specified, what cuts must be made, how the work piece can be held in the machine, and so forth. Unlike the universal standard data discussed previously, however, the time values for these elements have been based on actual previous stopwatch or other measurement of work within the job family.

In these previous studies, the operations were consistently broken down into common elements until finally a system of data emerged that showed how "normal element time" varied with size, depth of cut, material used, the way the work piece was held in the machine, and the like. At that point the data themselves could be used to estimate production standards without a separate study actually being performed on every different part. Again, although individual performance rating does not enter each application of the standard data, it was used in constructing the data originally. As before, final production standards are determined by adding allowances for delays, fatigue, and personal time to the normal cycle time derived from the standard data. Macrostandard data are in common use, especially in machine shops where distinct job families have a long-standing tradition. The occurrence of this kind of standard data is likely to exist wherever job families exist or when parts or products occur in many sizes and types. Macrostandard data have a large field of application where short runs of custom parts and products occur. In these instances, if we attempt to determine production standards by actual measurement, the order may be completed by the time the production standard has been determined. The result will be of no value unless the identical part is reordered.

ALLOWANCES IN PERFORMANCE STANDARDS

Allowances are commonly added to the computed normal time for delay, fatigue, and personal time. Allowances for delay and fatigue depend on the nature of the operation. They may not exist for some activities. The usual approach is to express allowances in percentage of the total available time. Thus, a 10 percent allowance over an 8-hour (480-minute) day is the equivalent of 48 minutes.

Delay Allowances

Delay allowances must be based on actual measurement of the magnitude of the delays. Although stopwatch study can be used, work sampling provides a much more efficient means of obtaining accurate data because delays often occur randomly. Work sampling expresses its measurement of delays directly in terms of percent of the total available time.

Fatigue and Personal Allowances

For some very heavy industrial jobs, an employee might work 20 minutes and rest 20 minutes. This type of very heavy work is not common today, but it occurs often

655

enough for a continuing interest to be maintained on the subject of physical fatigue and rest allowances.

Unfortunately, we still lack an accepted framework for the establishment of rest allowances based on any rational or scientific measurements. In most instances, schedules of *fatigue allowances* for various types of work are used based on general acceptability and are often the subject of agreements between labor and management.

Allowances for *personal time* provide at least a minimum of time that the worker can be away from the job. This personal time allows a break from both the physical and psychological stresses that a job may contain and is, in a sense, a minimum fatigue allowance. The minimum allowance is normally 5 percent of the total available time.

Application of Allowances in Performance Standards

The usual interpretation of the meaning of percentage allowances is that they allow a percentage of the total available time. A personal time allowance of 5 percent translates into $0.05 \times 480 = 24$ minutes of personal time in a normal 8-hour day. If the normal time has been measured as 1.20 minutes per piece, then the personal time must be prorated properly to the normal time in computing standard time per piece:

$$\text{Standard time} = \text{normal time} \times \frac{100}{100 - \text{percentage allowance}}$$

$$= 1.20 \times \frac{100}{95} = 1.263 \text{ minutes per piece}$$

If all the allowances for delay, fatigue, and personal time are expressed as percentages of total available time, they can be added together to obtain a single total percentage allowance figure. Then, standard time can be computed from normal time by a single calculation using the preceding formula.

IMPORTANT TERMS

Numbers in parentheses indicate page numbers

REFERENCES

Barnes, R. M., *Motion and Time Study: Design and Measurement of Work* (7th ed.), Wiley, New York, 1980.

Barnes, R. M., *Work Sampling* (2nd ed.), Wiley, New York, 1957.

Mundel, M. E., *Motion and Time Study* (5th ed.), Prentice-Hall, Englewood Cliffs, N.J., 1978.

Niebel, B. W., *Motion and Time Study* (7th ed.), Irwin, Homewood, Ill., 1982.

Rice, R. S., "Survey of Work Measurement and Wage Incentives," *Industrial Engineering, 9*(7), July 1977, pp. 18–31.

APPENDIX G

Tables

TABLE G-1 PV_{sp}, Present-Value Factors for Future Single Payments

Years Hence	1%	2%	4%	6%	8%	10%	12%	14%	15%	16%	18%	20%
1	0.990	0.980	0.962	0.943	0.926	0.909	0.893	0.877	0.870	0.862	0.847	0.833
2	0.980	0.961	0.925	0.890	0.857	0.826	0.797	0.769	0.756	0.743	0.718	0.694
3	0.971	0.942	0.889	0.840	0.794	0.751	0.712	0.675	0.658	0.641	0.609	0.579
4	0.961	0.924	0.855	0.792	0.735	0.683	0.636	0.592	0.572	0.552	0.516	0.482
5	0.951	0.906	0.822	0.747	0.681	0.621	0.567	0.519	0.497	0.476	0.437	0.402
6	0.942	0.888	0.790	0.705	0.630	0.564	0.507	0.456	0.432	0.410	0.370	0.335
7	0.933	0.871	0.760	0.665	0.583	0.513	0.452	0.400	0.376	0.354	0.314	0.279
8	0.923	0.853	0.731	0.627	0.540	0.467	0.404	0.351	0.327	0.305	0.266	0.233
9	0.914	0.837	0.703	0.592	0.500	0.424	0.361	0.308	0.284	0.263	0.225	0.194
10	0.905	0.820	0.676	0.558	0.463	0.386	0.322	0.270	0.247	0.227	0.191	0.162
11	0.896	0.804	0.650	0.527	0.429	0.350	0.287	0.237	0.215	0.195	0.162	0.135
12	0.887	0.788	0.625	0.497	0.397	0.319	0.257	0.208	0.187	0.168	0.137	0.112
13	0.879	0.773	0.601	0.469	0.368	0.290	0.229	0.182	0.163	0.145	0.116	0.093
14	0.870	0.758	0.577	0.442	0.340	0.263	0.205	0.160	0.141	0.125	0.099	0.078
15	0.861	0.743	0.555	0.417	0.315	0.239	0.183	0.140	0.123	0.108	0.084	0.065
16	0.853	0.728	0.534	0.394	0.292	0.218	0.163	0.123	0.107	0.093	0.071	0.054
17	0.844	0.714	0.513	0.371	0.270	0.198	0.146	0.108	0.093	0.080	0.060	0.045
18	0.836	0.700	0.494	0.350	0.250	0.180	0.130	0.095	0.081	0.069	0.051	0.038
19	0.828	0.686	0.475	0.331	0.232	0.164	0.116	0.083	0.070	0.060	0.043	0.031
20	0.820	0.673	0.456	0.312	0.215	0.149	0.104	0.073	0.061	0.051	0.037	0.026

TABLE G-2 PV_a, Present-Value Factors for Annuities

Years (n)	1%	2%	4%	6%	8%	10%	12%	14%	15%	16%	18%	20%
1	0.990	0.980	0.962	0.943	0.926	0.909	0.893	0.877	0.870	0.862	0.847	0.833
2	1.970	1.942	1.886	1.883	1.783	1.736	1.690	1.647	1.626	1.605	1.566	1.528
3	2.941	2.884	2.775	2.673	2.577	2.487	2.402	2.322	2.283	2.246	2.174	2.106
4	3.902	3.808	3.630	3.465	3.312	3.170	3.037	2.914	2.855	2.798	2.690	2.589
5	4.853	4.713	4.452	4.212	3.993	3.791	3.605	3.433	3.352	3.274	3.127	2.991
6	5.795	5.601	5.242	4.917	4.623	4.355	4.111	3.889	3.784	3.685	3.498	3.326
7	6.728	6.472	6.002	5.582	5.206	4.868	4.564	4.288	4.160	4.039	3.812	3.605
8	7.652	7.325	6.733	6.210	5.747	5.335	4.968	4.639	4.487	4.344	4.078	3.837
9	8.566	8.162	7.435	6.802	6.247	5.759	5.328	4.946	4.772	4.607	4.303	4.031
10	9.471	8.983	8.111	7.360	6.710	6.145	5.650	5.126	5.019	4.833	4.494	4.192
11	10.368	9.787	8.760	7.887	7.139	6.495	5.988	5.453	5.234	5.029	4.656	4.327
12	11.255	10.575	9.385	8.384	7.536	6.814	6.194	5.660	5.421	5.197	4.793	4.439
13	12.134	11.343	9.986	8.853	7.904	7.103	6.424	5.842	5.583	5.342	4.910	4.533
14	13.004	12.106	10.563	9.295	8.244	7.367	6.628	6.002	5.724	5.468	5.008	4.611
15	13.865	12.849	11.118	9.712	8.559	7.606	6.811	6.142	5.847	5.575	5.092	4.675
16	14.718	13.578	11.652	10.106	8.851	7.824	6.974	6.265	5.954	5.669	5.162	4.730
17	15.562	14.292	12.166	10.477	9.122	8.022	7.120	6.373	6.047	5.749	5.222	4.775
18	16.398	14.992	12.659	10.828	9.372	8.201	7.250	6.467	6.128	5.818	5.273	4.812
19	17.226	15.678	13.134	11.158	9.604	8.365	7.366	6.550	6.198	5.877	5.316	4.844
20	18.046	16.351	13.590	11.470	9.818	8.514	7.469	6.623	6.259	5.929	5.353	4.870

TABLE G-3   Values of L_q for $M = 1 - 15$, and Various Values of $r = \lambda/\mu$. Poisson Arrivals, Negative Exponential Service Times

	Number of Service Channels M														
r	1	2	3	4	5	6	7	8	9	10	11	12	13	14	15
0.10	0.0111														
0.15	0.0264	0.0008													
0.20	0.0500	0.0020													
0.25	0.0833	0.0039													
0.30	0.1285	0.0069													
0.35	0.1884	0.0110													
0.40	0.2666	0.0166													
0.45	0.3681	0.0239	0.0019												
0.50	0.5000	0.0333	0.0030												
0.55	0.6722	0.0449	0.0043												
0.60	0.9000	0.0593	0.0061												
0.65	1.2071	0.0767	0.0084												
0.70	1.6333	0.0976	0.0112												
0.75	2.2500	0.1227	0.0147												
0.80	3.2000	0.1523	0.0189												
0.85	4.8166	0.1873	0.0239	0.0031											
0.90	8.1000	0.2285	0.0300	0.0041											
0.95	18.0500	0.2767	0.0371	0.0053											
1.0		0.3333	0.0454	0.0067											
1.2		0.6748	0.0904	0.0158											
1.4		1.3449	0.1778	0.0324	0.0059										
1.6		2.8444	0.3128	0.0604	0.0121										
1.8		7.6734	0.5320	0.1051	0.0227	0.0047									
2.0			0.8888	0.1739	0.0398	0.0090									
2.2			1.4907	0.2770	0.0659	0.0158									
2.4			2.1261	0.4305	0.1047	0.0266	0.0065								
2.6			4.9322	0.6581	0.1609	0.0426	0.0110								
2.8			12.2724	1.0000	0.2411	0.0659	0.0180								
3.0				1.5282	0.3541	0.0991	0.0282	0.0077							
3.2				2.3856	0.5128	0.1452	0.0427	0.0122							
3.4				3.9060	0.7365	0.2085	0.0631	0.0189							
3.6				7.0893	1.0550	0.2947	0.0912	0.0283	0.0084						
3.8				16.9366	1.5184	0.4114	0.1292	0.0412	0.0127						

TABLE G-3   Values of L_q for $M = 1 - 15$, and Various Values of $r = \lambda/\mu$, Poisson Arrivals, Negative Exponential Service Times (Continued)

r	Number of Service Channels M														
	1	2	3	4	5	6	7	8	9	10	11	12	13	14	15
4.0					2.2164	0.5694	0.1801	0.0590	0.0189						
4.2					3.3269	0.7837	0.2475	0.0827	0.0273						
4.4					5.2675	1.0777	0.3364	0.1142	0.0389	0.0087					
4.6					9.2885	1.4867	0.4532	0.1555	0.0541	0.0128					
4.8					21.6384	2.0708	0.6071	0.2092	0.0742	0.0184					
5.0						2.9375	0.8102	0.2786	0.1006	0.0260	0.0125				
5.2						4.3004	1.0804	0.3680	0.1345	0.0361	0.0175				
5.4						6.6609	1.4441	0.4881	0.1779	0.0492	0.0243	0.0085			
5.6						11.5178	1.9436	0.6313	0.2330	0.0663	0.0330	0.0119			
5.8						26.3726	2.6481	0.8225	0.3032	0.0883	0.0443	0.0164			
6.0							3.6828	1.0707	0.3918	0.1164	0.0590	0.0224			
6.2							5.2979	1.3967	0.5037	0.1518	0.0775	0.0300	0.0113		
6.4							8.0768	1.8040	0.6454	0.1964	0.1008	0.0398	0.0153		
6.6							13.7692	2.4198	0.8247	0.2524	0.1302	0.0523	0.0205		
6.8							31.1270	3.2441	1.0533	0.3222	0.1666	0.0679	0.0271	0.0105	
7.0								4.4471	1.3471	0.4090	0.2119	0.0876	0.0357	0.0141	
7.2								6.3135	1.7288	0.5172	0.2677	0.1119	0.0463	0.0187	
7.4								9.5102	2.2324	0.6521	0.3364	0.1420	0.0595	0.0245	0.0097
7.6								16.0379	2.9113	0.8202	0.4211	0.1789	0.0761	0.0318	0.0129
7.8								35.8956	3.8558	1.0310	0.5250	0.2243	0.0966	0.0410	0.0168
8.0									5.2264	1.2972	0.6530	0.2796	0.1214	0.0522	0.0220
8.2									7.3441	1.6364	0.8109	0.3469	0.1520	0.0663	0.0283
8.4									10.9592	2.0736	1.0060	0.4288	0.1891	0.0834	0.0361
8.6									18.3223	2.6470	1.2484	0.5286	0.2341	0.1043	0.0459
8.8									40.6824	3.4160	1.5524	0.6501	0.2885	0.1298	0.0577
9.0										4.4806	1.9368	0.7980	0.3543	0.1603	0.0723
9.2										6.0183	2.4298	0.9788	0.4333	0.1974	0.0899
9.4										8.3869	3.0732	1.2010	0.5287	0.2419	0.1111
9.6										12.4189	3.9318	1.4752	0.6437	0.2952	0.1367
9.8										20.6160	5.1156	1.8165	0.7827	0.3588	0.1673
10.0										45.4769	6.8210	2.2465	0.9506	0.4352	0.2040

TABLE G-4   Finite Queuing Tables

POPULATION 5

X	M	D	F	L_q
0.012	1	0.048	0.999	0.005
0.019	1	0.076	0.998	0.010
0.025	1	0.100	0.997	0.015
0.030	1	0.120	0.996	0.020
0.034	1	0.135	0.995	0.025
0.036	1	0.143	0.994	0.030
0.040	1	0.159	0.993	0.035
0.042	1	0.167	0.992	0.045
0.044	1	0.175	0.991	0.045
0.046	1	0.183	0.990	0.050
0.050	1	0.198	0.989	0.055
0.052	1	0.206	0.988	0.060
0.054	1	0.214	0.987	0.065
0.056	2	0.018	0.999	0.005
	1	0.222	0.985	0.075
0.058	2	0.019	0.999	0.005
	1	0.229	0.984	0.080
0.060	2	0.020	0.999	0.005
	1	0.237	0.983	0.085
0.062	2	0.022	0.999	0.005
	1	0.245	0.982	0.090
0.064	2	0.023	0.999	0.005
	1	0.253	0.981	0.095
0.066	2	0.024	0.999	0.005
	1	0.260	0.979	0.105
0.068	2	0.026	0.999	0.005
	1	0.268	0.978	0.110
0.070	2	0.027	0.999	0.005
	1	0.275	0.977	0.115
0.075	2	0.031	0.999	0.005
	1	0.294	0.973	0.135
0.080	2	0.035	0.998	0.010
	1	0.313	0.969	0.155
0.085	2	0.040	0.998	0.010
	1	0.332	0.965	0.175
0.090	2	0.044	0.998	0.010
	1	0.350	0.960	0.200
0.095	2	0.049	0.997	0.015
	1	0.368	0.955	0.255
0.100	2	0.054	0.997	0.015
	1	0.386	0.950	0.250
0.105	2	0.059	0.997	0.015
	1	0.404	0.945	0.275
0.110	2	0.065	0.996	0.020
	1	0.421	0.939	0.305
0.115	2	0.071	0.995	0.025
	1	0.439	0.933	0.335
0.120	2	0.076	0.995	0.025
	1	0.456	0.927	0.365
0.125	2	0.082	0.994	0.030
	1	0.473	0.920	0.400
0.130	2	0.089	0.993	0.035
	1	0.489	0.914	0.430
0.135	2	0.095	0.993	0.035
	1	0.505	0.907	0.465
0.140	2	0.102	0.992	0.040
	1	0.521	0.900	0.500
0.145	3	0.011	0.999	0.005
	2	0.109	0.991	0.045
	1	0.537	0.892	0.540
0.150	3	0.012	0.999	0.005
	2	0.115	0.990	0.050
	1	0.553	0.885	0.575
0.155	3	0.013	0.999	0.005
	2	0.123	0.989	0.055
	1	0.568	0.877	0.615
0.160	3	0.015	0.999	0.005
	2	0.130	0.988	0.060
	1	0.582	0.869	0.655
0.165	3	0.016	0.999	0.005
	2	0.137	0.987	0.065
	1	0.597	0.861	0.695
0.170	3	0.017	0.999	0.005
	2	0.145	0.985	0.075
	1	0.611	0.853	0.735
0.180	3	0.021	0.999	0.005
	2	0.161	0.983	0.085
	1	0.638	0.836	0.820
0.190	3	0.024	0.998	0.010
	2	0.177	0.980	0.100
	1	0.665	0.819	0.905
0.200	3	0.028	0.998	0.010
	2	0.194	0.976	0.120
	1	0.689	0.801	0.995
0.210	3	0.032	0.998	0.010
	2	0.211	0.973	0.135
	1	0.713	0.783	1.085
0.220	3	0.036	0.997	0.015
	2	0.229	0.969	0.155
	1	0.735	0.765	1.175
0.230	3	0.041	0.997	0.015
	2	0.247	0.965	0.175
	1	0.756	0.747	1.265
0.240	3	0.046	0.996	0.020
	2	0.265	0.960	0.200
	1	0.775	0.730	1.350
0.250	3	0.052	0.995	0.025
	2	0.284	0.955	0.225
	1	0.794	0.712	1.440
0.260	3	0.058	0.994	0.030
	2	0.303	0.950	0.250
	1	0.811	0.695	1.525
0.270	3	0.064	0.994	0.030
	2	0.323	0.944	0.280
	1	0.827	0.677	1.615
0.280	3	0.071	0.993	0.035
	2	0.342	0.938	0.310
	1	0.842	0.661	1.695
0.290	4	0.007	0.999	0.005
	3	0.079	0.992	0.040
	2	0.362	0.932	0.340
	1	0.856	0.644	1.780
0.300	4	0.008	0.999	0.005
	3	0.086	0.990	0.050
	2	0.382	0.926	0.370
	1	0.869	0.628	1.860
0.310	4	0.009	0.999	0.005
	3	0.094	0.989	0.055
	2	0.402	0.919	0.405
	1	0.881	0.613	1.935
0.320	4	0.010	0.999	0.005
	3	0.103	0.988	0.060
	2	0.422	0.912	0.440
	1	0.892	0.597	2.015
0.330	4	0.012	0.999	0.005
	3	0.112	0.986	0.070
	2	0.442	0.904	0.480
	1	0.902	0.583	2.085
0.340	4	0.013	0.999	0.005
	3	0.121	0.985	0.075
	2	0.462	0.896	0.520
	1	0.911	0.569	2.155
0.360	4	0.017	0.998	0.010
	3	0.141	0.981	0.060
	2	0.501	0.880	0.600
	1	0.927	0.542	2.290
0.380	4	0.021	0.998	0.010
	3	0.163	0.976	0.120
	2	0.540	0.863	0.685
	1	0.941	0.516	2.420
0.400	4	0.026	0.997	0.015
	3	0.186	0.972	0.140
	2	0.579	0.845	0.775
	1	0.952	0.493	2.535
0.420	4	0.031	0.997	0.015
	3	0.211	0.966	0.170
	2	0.616	0.826	0.870
	1	0.961	0.471	2.645
0.440	4	0.037	0.996	0.020
	3	0.238	0.960	0.200
	2	0.652	0.807	0.965
	1	0.969	0.451	2.745
0.460	4	0.045	0.995	0.025
	3	0.266	0.953	0.235
	2	0.686	0.787	1.065
	1	0.975	0.432	2.840
0.480	4	0.053	0.994	0.030
	3	0.296	0.945	0.275
	2	0.719	0.767	1.165
	1	0.980	0.415	2.925
0.500	4	0.063	0.992	0.040
	3	0.327	0.936	0.320
	2	0.750	0.748	1.260
	1	0.985	0.399	3.005
0.520	4	0.073	0.991	0.045
	3	0.359	0.927	0.365
	2	0.779	0.728	1.360
	1	0.988	0.384	3.080

TABLE G-4 *(Continued)*

POPULATION 5, Cont.

X	M	D	F	L_q
0.540	4	0.085	0.989	0.055
	3	0.392	0.917	0.415
	2	0.806	0.708	1.460
	1	0.991	0.370	3.150
0.560	4	0.098	0.986	0.070
	3	0.426	0.906	0.470
	2	0.831	0.689	1.555
	1	0.993	0.357	3.215
0.580	4	0.113	0.984	0.080
	3	0.461	0.895	0.525
	2	0.854	0.670	1.650
	1	0.994	0.345	3.275
0.600	4	0.130	0.981	0.095
	3	0.497	0.883	0.585
	2	0.875	0.652	1.740
	1	0.996	0.333	3.335
0.650	4	0.179	0.972	0.140
	3	0.588	0.850	0.750
	2	0.918	0.608	1.960
	1	0.998	0.308	3.460
0.700	4	0.240	0.960	0.200
	3	0.678	0.815	0.925
	2	0.950	0.568	2.160
	1	0.999	0.286	3.570
0.750	4	0.316	0.944	0.280
	3	0.763	0.777	1.115
	2	0.972	0.532	2.340
0.800	4	0.410	0.924	0.380
	3	0.841	0.739	1.305
	2	0.987	0.500	2.500
0.850	4	0.522	0.900	0.500
	3	0.907	0.702	1.490
	2	0.995	0.470	2.650
0.900	4	0.656	0.871	0.645
	3	0.957	0.666	1.670
	2	0.998	0.444	2.780
0.950	4	0.815	0.838	0.810
	3	0.989	0.631	1.845

POPULATION 10

X	M	D	F	L_q
0.016	1	0.144	0.997	0.03
0.019	1	0.170	0.996	0.04
0.021	1	0.188	0.995	0.05
0.023	1	0.206	0.994	0.06
0.025	1	0.224	0.993	0.07
0.026	1	0.232	0.992	0.08
0.028	1	0.250	0.991	0.09
0.030	1	0.268	0.990	0.10
0.032	2	0.033	0.999	0.01
	1	0.285	0.988	0.12
0.034	2	0.037	0.999	0.01
	1	0.302	0.986	0.14
0.036	2	0.041	0.999	0.01
	1	0.320	0.984	0.16
0.038	2	0.046	0.999	0.01
	1	0.337	0.982	0.18
0.040	2	0.050	0.999	0.01
	1	0.354	0.980	0.20
0.042	2	0.055	0.999	0.01
	1	0.371	0.978	0.22
0.044	2	0.060	0.998	0.02
	1	0.388	0.975	0.25
0.046	2	0.065	0.998	0.02
	1	0.404	0.973	0.27
0.048	2	0.071	0.998	0.02
	1	0.421	0.970	0.30
0.050	2	0.076	0.998	0.02
	1	0.437	0.967	0.33
0.052	2	0.082	0.997	0.03
	1	0.454	0.963	0.37
0.054	2	0.088	0.997	0.03
	1	0.470	0.960	0.40
0.056	2	0.094	0.997	0.03
	1	0.486	0.956	0.44
0.058	2	0.100	0.996	0.04
	1	0.501	0.953	0.47
0.060	2	0.106	0.996	0.04
	1	0.517	0.949	0.51
0.062	2	0.113	0.996	0.04
	1	0.532	0.945	0.55
0.064	2	0.119	0.995	0.05
	1	0.547	0.940	0.60
0.066	2	0.126	0.995	0.05
	1	0.562	0.936	0.64
0.068	3	0.020	0.999	0.01
	2	0.133	0.994	0.06
	1	0.577	0.931	0.69
0.070	3	0.022	0.999	0.01
	2	0.140	0.994	0.06
	1	0.591	0.926	0.74
0.075	3	0.026	0.999	0.01
	2	0.158	0.992	0.08
	1	0.627	0.913	0.87
0.080	3	0.031	0.999	0.01
	2	0.177	0.990	0.10
	1	0.660	0.899	1.01
0.085	3	0.037	0.999	0.01
	2	0.196	0.988	0.12
	1	0.692	0.883	1.17
0.090	3	0.043	0.998	0.02
	2	0.216	0.986	0.14
	1	0.722	0.867	1.33
0.095	3	0.049	0.998	0.02
	2	0.237	0.984	0.16
	1	0.750	0.850	1.50
0.100	3	0.056	0.998	0.02
	2	0.258	0.981	0.19
	1	0.776	0.832	1.68
0.105	3	0.064	0.997	0.03
	2	0.279	0.978	0.22
	1	0.800	0.814	1.86
0.110	3	0.072	0.997	0.03
	2	0.301	0.974	0.26
	1	0.822	0.795	2.05
0.115	3	0.081	0.996	0.04
	2	0.324	0.971	0.29
	1	0.843	0.776	2.24
0.120	4	0.016	0.999	0.01
	3	0.090	0.995	0.05
	2	0.346	0.967	0.33
	1	0.861	0.756	2.44
0.125	4	0.019	0.999	0.01
	3	0.100	0.994	0.06
	2	0.369	0.962	0.38
	1	0.878	0.737	2.63
0.130	4	0.022	0.999	0.01
	3	0.110	0.994	0.06
	2	0.392	0.958	0.42
	1	0.893	0.718	2.82
0.135	4	0.025	0.999	0.01
	3	0.121	0.993	0.07
	2	0.415	0.952	0.48
	1	0.907	0.699	3.01
0.140	4	0.028	0.999	0.01
	3	0.132	0.991	0.09
	2	0.437	0.947	0.53
	1	0.919	0.680	3.20
0.145	4	0.032	0.999	0.01
	3	0.144	0.990	0.10
	2	0.460	0.941	0.59
	1	0.929	0.662	3.38
0.150	4	0.036	0.998	0.02
	3	0.156	0.989	0.11
	2	0.483	0.935	0.65
	1	0.939	0.644	3.56
0.155	4	0.040	0.998	0.02
	3	0.169	0.987	0.13
	2	0.505	0.928	0.72
	1	0.947	0.627	3.73
0.160	4	0.044	0.998	0.02
	3	0.182	0.986	0.14
	2	0.528	0.921	0.79
	1	0.954	0.610	3.90
0.165	4	0.049	0.997	0.03
	3	0.195	0.984	0.16
	2	0.550	0.914	0.86
	1	0.961	0.594	4.06
0.170	4	0.054	0.997	0.03
	3	0.209	0.982	0.18
	2	0.571	0.906	0.94
	1	0.966	0.579	4.21
0.180	5	0.013	0.999	0.01
	4	0.066	0.996	0.04
	3	0.238	0.978	0.22
	2	0.614	0.890	1.10
	1	0.975	0.549	4.51
0.190	5	0.016	0.999	0.01
	4	0.078	0.995	0.05
	3	0.269	0.973	0.27

TABLE G-4 (Continued)

POPULATION 10, Cont.

X	M	D	F	L_q	X	M	D	F	L_q	X	M	D	F	L_q
						2	0.918	0.672	3.28		2	0.996	0.454	5.46
						1	0.999	0.345	6.55	0.460	8	0.011	0.999	0.01
					0.300	6	0.026	0.998	0.02		7	0.058	0.995	0.05
	2	0.654	0.873	1.27		5	0.106	0.991	0.09		6	0.193	0.979	0.21
	1	0.982	0.522	4.78		4	0.304	0.963	0.37		5	0.445	0.930	0.70
0.200	5	0.020	0.999	0.01		3	0.635	0.872	1.28		4	0.747	0.822	1.78
	4	0.092	0.994	0.06		2	0.932	0.653	3.47		3	0.947	0.646	3.54
	3	0.300	0.968	0.32		1	0.999	0.333	6.67		2	0.998	0.435	5.65
	2	0.692	0.854	1.46	0.310	6	0.031	0.998	0.02	0.480	8	0.015	0.999	0.01
	1	0.987	0.497	5.03		5	0.120	0.990	0.10		7	0.074	0.994	0.06
0.210	5	0.025	0.999	0.01		4	0.331	0.957	0.43		6	0.230	0.973	0.27
	4	0.108	0.992	0.08		3	0.666	0.858	1.42		5	0.499	0.916	0.84
	3	0.333	0.961	0.39		2	0.943	0.635	3.65		4	0.791	0.799	2.01
	2	0.728	0.835	1.65	0.320	6	0.036	0.998	0.02		3	0.961	0.621	3.79
	1	0.990	0.474	5.26		5	0.135	0.988	0.12		2	0.998	0.417	5.83
0.220	5	0.030	0.998	0.02		4	0.359	0.952	0.48	0.500	8	0.020	0.999	0.01
	4	0.124	0.990	0.10		3	0.695	0.845	1.55		7	0.093	0.992	0.08
	3	0.366	0.954	0.46		2	0.952	0.617	3.83		6	0.271	0.966	0.34
	2	0.761	0.815	1.85	0.330	6	0.042	0.997	0.03		5	0.553	0.901	0.99
	1	0.993	0.453	5.47		5	0.151	0.986	0.14		4	0.830	0.775	2.25
0.230	5	0.037	0.998	0.02		4	0.387	0.945	0.55		3	0.972	0.598	4.02
	4	0.142	0.988	0.12		3	0.723	0.831	1.69		2	0.999	0.400	6.00
	3	0.400	0.947	0.53		2	0.961	0.600	4.00	0.520	8	0.026	0.998	0.02
	2	0.791	0.794	2.06	0.340	7	0.010	0.999	0.01		7	0.115	0.989	0.11
	1	0.995	0.434	5.66		6	0.049	0.997	0.03		6	0.316	0.958	0.42
0.240	5	0.044	0.997	0.03		5	0.168	0.983	0.17		5	0.606	0.884	1.16
	4	0.162	0.986	0.14		4	0.416	0.938	0.62		4	0.864	0.752	2.48
	3	0.434	0.938	0.62		3	0.750	0.816	1.84		3	0.980	0.575	4.25
	2	0.819	0.774	2.26		2	0.968	0.584	4.16		2	0.999	0.385	6.15
	1	0.996	0.416	5.84	0.360	7	0.014	0.999	0.01	0.540	8	0.034	0.997	0.03
0.250	6	0.010	0.999	0.01		6	0.064	0.995	0.05		7	0.141	0.986	0.14
	5	0.052	0.997	0.03		5	0.205	0.978	0.22		6	0.363	0.949	0.51
	4	0.183	0.983	0.17		4	0.474	0.923	0.77		5	0.658	0.867	1.33
	3	0.469	0.929	0.71		3	0.798	0.787	2.13		4	0.893	0.729	2.71
	2	0.844	0.753	2.47		2	0.978	0.553	4.47		3	0.986	0.555	4.45
	1	0.997	0.400	6.00	0.380	7	0.019	0.999	0.01	0.560	8	0.044	0.996	0.04
0.260	6	0.013	0.999	0.01		6	0.083	0.993	0.07		7	0.171	0.982	0.18
	5	0.060	0.996	0.04		5	0.247	0.971	0.29		6	0.413	0.939	0.61
	4	0.205	0.980	0.20		4	0.533	0.906	0.94		5	0.707	0.848	1.52
	3	0.503	0.919	0.81		3	0.840	0.758	2.42		4	0.917	0.706	2.94
	2	0.866	0.732	2.68		2	0.986	0.525	4.75		3	0.991	0.535	4.65
	1	0.998	0.384	6.16	0.400	7	0.026	0.998	0.02	0.580	8	0.057	0.995	0.05
0.270	6	0.015	0.999	0.01		6	0.105	0.991	0.09		7	0.204	0.977	0.23
	5	0.070	0.995	0.05		5	0.292	0.963	0.37		6	0.465	0.927	0.73
	4	0.228	0.976	0.24		4	0.591	0.887	1.13		5	0.753	0.829	1.71
	3	0.537	0.908	0.92		3	0.875	0.728	2.72		4	0.937	0.684	3.16
	2	0.886	0.712	2.88		2	0.991	0.499	5.01		3	0.994	0.517	4.83
	1	0.999	0.370	6.30	0.420	7	0.034	0.993	0.07	0.600	9	0.010	0.999	0.01
0.280	6	0.018	0.999	0.01		6	0.130	0.987	0.13		8	0.072	0.994	0.06
	5	0.081	0.994	0.06		5	0.341	0.954	0.46		7	0.242	0.972	0.28
	4	0.252	0.972	0.28		4	0.646	0.866	1.34		6	0.518	0.915	0.85
	3	0.571	0.896	1.04		3	0.905	0.700	3.00		5	0.795	0.809	1.91
	2	0.903	0.692	3.08		2	0.994	0.476	5.24		4	0.953	0.663	3.37
	1	0.999	0.357	6.43	0.440	7	0.045	0.997	0.03		3	0.996	0.500	5.00
0.290	6	0.022	0.999	0.01		6	0.160	0.984	0.16	0.650	9	0.021	0.999	0.01
	5	0.093	0.993	0.07		5	0.392	0.943	0.57		8	0.123	0.988	0.12
	4	0.278	0.968	0.32		4	0.698	0.845	1.55		7	0.353	0.954	0.46
	3	0.603	0.884	1.16		3	0.928	0.672	3.28		6	0.651	0.878	1.22

TABLE G-4 *(Continued)*

POPULATION 10, Cont.

X	M	D	F	L_q
	5	0.882	0.759	2.41
	4	0.980	0.614	3.86
	3	0.999	0.461	5.39
0.700	9	0.040	0.997	0.03
	8	0.200	0.979	0.21
	7	0.484	0.929	0.71
	6	0.772	0.836	1.64
	5	0.940	0.711	2.89
	4	0.992	0.571	4.29
0.750	9	0.075	0.994	0.06
	8	0.307	0.965	0.35
	7	0.626	0.897	1.03
	6	0.870	0.792	2.08
	5	0.975	0.666	3.34
	4	0.998	0.533	4.67
0.800	9	0.134	0.988	0.12
	8	0.446	0.944	0.56
	7	0.763	0.859	1.41
	6	0.939	0.747	2.53
	5	0.991	0.625	3.75
	4	0.999	0.500	5.00
0.850	9	0.232	0.979	0.21
	8	0.611	0.916	0.84
	7	0.879	0.818	1.82
	6	0.978	0.705	2.95
	5	0.998	0.588	4.12
0.900	9	0.387	0.963	0.37
	8	0.785	0.881	1.19
	7	0.957	0.777	2.23
	6	0.995	0.667	3.33
0.950	9	0.630	0.938	0.62
	8	0.934	0.841	1.59
	7	0.994	0.737	2.63

POPULATION 20

X	M	D	F	L_q
0.005	1	0.095	0.999	0.02
0.009	1	0.171	0.998	0.04
0.011	1	0.208	0.997	0.06
0.013	1	0.246	0.996	0.08
0.014	1	0.265	0.995	0.10
0.015	1	0.283	0.994	0.12
0.016	1	0.302	0.993	0.14
0.017	1	0.321	0.992	0.16
0.018	2	0.048	0.999	0.02
	1	0.339	0.991	0.18
0.019	2	0.053	0.999	0.02
	1	0.358	0.990	0.20
0.020	2	0.058	0.999	0.02
	1	0.376	0.989	0.22
0.021	2	0.064	0.999	0.02
	1	0.394	0.987	0.26
0.022	2	0.070	0.999	0.02
	1	0.412	0.986	0.28
0.023	2	0.075	0.999	0.02
	1	0.431	0.984	0.32
0.024	2	0.082	0.999	0.02
	1	0.449	0.982	0.36
0.025	2	0.088	0.999	0.02
	1	0.466	0.980	0.40
0.026	2	0.094	0.998	0.04
	1	0.484	0.978	0.44
0.028	2	0.108	0.998	0.04
	1	0.519	0.973	0.54
0.030	2	0.122	0.998	0.04
	1	0.553	0.968	0.64
0.032	2	0.137	0.997	0.06
	1	0.587	0.962	0.76
0.034	2	0.152	0.996	0.08
	1	0.620	0.955	0.90
0.036	2	0.168	0.996	0.08
	1	0.651	0.947	1.06
0.038	3	0.036	0.999	0.02
	2	0.185	0.995	0.10
	1	0.682	0.938	1.24
0.040	3	0.041	0.999	0.02
	2	0.202	0.994	0.12
	1	0.712	0.929	1.42
0.042	3	0.047	0.999	0.02
	2	0.219	0.993	0.14
	1	0.740	0.918	1.64
0.044	3	0.053	0.999	0.02
	2	0.237	0.992	0.16
	1	0.767	0.906	1.88
0.046	3	0.059	0.999	0.02
	2	0.255	0.991	0.18
	1	0.792	0.894	2.12
0.048	3	0.066	0.999	0.02
	2	0.274	0.989	0.22
	1	0.815	0.881	2.38
0.050	3	0.073	0.998	0.04
	2	0.293	0.988	0.24
	1	0.837	0.866	2.68
0.052	3	0.080	0.998	0.04
	2	0.312	0.986	0.28
	1	0.858	0.851	2.98
0.054	3	0.088	0.998	0.04
	2	0.332	0.984	0.32
	1	0.876	0.835	3.30
0.056	3	0.097	0.997	0.06
	2	0.352	0.982	0.36
	1	0.893	0.819	3.62
0.058	3	0.105	0.997	0.06
	2	0.372	0.980	0.40
	1	0.908	0.802	3.96
0.060	4	0.026	0.999	0.02
	3	0.115	0.997	0.06
	2	0.392	0.978	0.44
	1	0.922	0.785	4.30
0.062	4	0.029	0.999	0.02
	3	0.124	0.996	0.08
	2	0.413	0.975	0.50
	1	0.934	0.768	4.64
0.064	4	0.032	0.999	0.02
	3	0.134	0.996	0.08
	2	0.433	0.972	0.56
	1	0.944	0.751	4.98
0.066	4	0.036	0.999	0.02
	3	0.144	0.995	0.10
	2	0.454	0.969	0.62
	1	0.953	0.733	5.34
0.068	4	0.039	0.999	0.02
	3	0.155	0.995	0.10
	2	0.474	0.966	0.68
	1	0.961	0.716	5.68
0.070	4	0.043	0.999	0.02
	3	0.165	0.994	0.12
	2	0.495	0.962	0.76
	1	0.967	0.699	6.02
0.075	4	0.054	0.999	0.02
	3	0.194	0.992	0.16
	2	0.545	0.953	0.94
	1	0.980	0.659	6.82
0.080	4	0.066	0.998	0.04
	3	0.225	0.990	0.20
	2	0.595	0.941	1.18
	1	0.988	0.621	7.58
0.085	4	0.080	0.997	0.06
	3	0.257	0.987	0.26
	2	0.643	0.928	1.44
	1	0.993	0.586	8.28
0.090	5	0.025	0.999	0.02
	4	0.095	0.997	0.06
	3	0.291	0.984	0.32
	2	0.689	0.913	1.74
	1	0.996	0.554	8.92
0.095	5	0.031	0.999	0.02
	4	0.112	0.996	0.08
	3	0.326	0.980	0.40
	2	0.733	0.896	2.08
	1	0.998	0.526	9.48
0.100	5	0.038	0.999	0.02
	4	0.131	0.995	0.10
	3	0.363	0.975	0.50
	2	0.773	0.878	2.44
	1	0.999	0.500	10.00
0.105	5	0.046	0.999	0.02
	4	0.151	0.993	0.14
	3	0.400	0.970	0.60
	2	0.809	0.858	2.84
	1	0.999	0.476	10.48
0.110	5	0.055	0.998	0.04
	4	0.172	0.992	0.16
	3	0.438	0.964	0.72
	2	0.842	0.837	3.26
0.115	5	0.065	0.998	0.04
	4	0.195	0.990	0.20
	3	0.476	0.958	0.84
	2	0.870	0.816	3.68
0.120	6	0.022	0.999	0.02

TABLE G-4 *(Continued)*

X	M	D	F	L_q	X	M	D	F	L_q	X	M	D	F	L_q
POPULATION 20, Cont.					5	0.248	0.983	0.34	0.260	9	0.039	0.998	0.04
						4	0.513	0.945	1.10		8	0.104	0.994	0.12
						3	0.838	0.830	3.40		7	0.233	0.983	0.34
	5	0.076	0.997	0.06		2	0.993	0.587	8.26		6	0.446	0.953	0.94
	4	0.219	0.988	0.24	0.180	7	0.044	0.998	0.04		5	0.712	0.884	2.32
	3	0.514	0.950	1.00		6	0.125	0.994	0.12		4	0.924	0.755	4.90
	2	0.895	0.793	4.14		5	0.295	0.978	0.44		3	0.995	0.576	8.48
0.125	6	0.026	0.999	0.02		4	0.575	0.930	1.40	0.270	10	0.016	0.999	0.02
	5	0.088	0.997	0.06		3	0.879	0.799	4.02		9	0.049	0.998	0.04
	4	0.245	0.986	0.28		2	0.996	0.555	8.90		8	0.125	0.992	0.16
	3	0.552	0.942	1.16	0.190	8	0.018	0.999	0.02		7	0.270	0.978	0.44
	2	0.916	0.770	4.60		7	0.058	0.998	0.04		6	0.495	0.943	1.14
0.130	6	0.031	0.999	0.02		6	0.154	0.991	0.18		5	0.757	0.867	2.66
	5	0.101	0.996	0.08		5	0.345	0.971	0.58		4	0.943	0.731	5.38
	4	0.271	0.983	0.34		4	0.636	0.914	1.72		3	0.997	0.555	8.90
	3	0.589	0.933	1.34		3	0.913	0.768	4.64	0.280	10	0.021	0.999	0.02
	2	0.934	0.748	5.04		2	0.998	0.526	9.48		9	0.061	0.997	0.06
0.135	6	0.037	0.999	0.02	0.200	8	0.025	0.999	0.02		8	0.149	0.990	0.20
	5	0.116	0.995	0.10		7	0.074	0.997	0.06		7	0.309	0.973	0.54
	4	0.299	0.980	0.40		6	0.187	0.988	0.24		6	0.544	0.932	1.36
	3	0.626	0.923	1.54		5	0.397	0.963	0.74		5	0.797	0.848	3.04
	2	0.948	0.725	5.50		4	0.693	0.895	2.10		4	0.958	0.708	5.84
0.140	6	0.043	0.998	0.04		3	0.938	0.736	5.28		3	0.998	0.536	9.28
	5	0.131	0.994	0.12		2	0.999	0.500	10.00	0.290	10	0.027	0.999	0.02
	4	0.328	0.976	0.48	0.210	8	0.033	0.999	0.02		9	0.075	0.996	0.08
	3	0.661	0.912	1.76		7	0.093	0.995	0.10		8	0.176	0.988	0.24
	2	0.960	0.703	5.94		6	0.223	0.985	0.30		7	0.351	0.967	0.66
0.145	6	0.051	0.998	0.04		5	0.451	0.954	0.92		6	0.592	0.920	1.60
	5	0.148	0.993	0.14		4	0.745	0.874	2.52		5	0.833	0.828	3.44
	4	0.358	0.972	0.56		3	0.958	0.706	5.88		4	0.970	0.685	6.30
	3	0.695	0.900	2.00		2	0.999	0.476	10.48		3	0.999	0.517	9.66
	2	0.969	0.682	6.36	0.220	8	0.043	0.998	0.04	0.300	10	0.034	0.998	0.04
0.150	7	0.017	0.999	0.02		7	0.115	0.994	0.12		9	0.091	0.995	0.10
	6	0.059	0.998	0.04		6	0.263	0.980	0.40		8	0.205	0.985	0.30
	5	0.166	0.991	0.18		5	0.505	0.943	1.14		7	0.394	0.961	0.78
	4	0.388	0.968	0.64		4	0.793	0.852	2.96		6	0.639	0.907	1.86
	3	0.728	0.887	2.26		3	0.971	0.677	6.46		5	0.865	0.808	3.84
	2	0.976	0.661	6.78	0.230	9	0.018	0.999	0.02		4	0.978	0.664	6.72
0.155	7	0.021	0.999	0.02		8	0.054	0.998	0.04		3	0.999	0.500	10.00
	6	0.068	0.997	0.06		7	0.140	0.992	0.16	0.310	11	0.014	0.999	0.02
	5	0.185	0.990	0.20		6	0.306	0.975	0.50		10	0.043	0.998	0.04
	4	0.419	0.963	0.74		5	0.560	0.931	1.38		9	0.110	0.993	0.14
	3	0.758	0.874	2.52		4	0.834	0.828	3.44		8	0.237	0.981	0.38
	2	0.982	0.641	7.18		3	0.981	0.649	7.02		7	0.438	0.953	0.94
0.160	7	0.024	0.999	0.02	0.240	9	0.024	0.999	0.02		6	0.684	0.893	2.14
	6	0.077	0.997	0.06		8	0.068	0.997	0.06		5	0.892	0.788	4.24
	5	0.205	0.988	0.24		7	0.168	0.989	0.22		4	0.985	0.643	7.14
	4	0.450	0.957	0.86		6	0.351	0.969	0.62	0.320	11	0.018	0.999	0.02
	3	0.787	0.860	2.80		5	0.613	0.917	1.66		10	0.053	0.997	0.06
	2	0.987	0.622	7.56		4	0.870	0.804	3.92		9	0.130	0.992	0.16
0.165	7	0.029	0.999	0.02		3	0.988	0.623	7.54		8	0.272	0.977	0.46
	6	0.088	0.996	0.08	0.250	9	0.031	0.999	0.02		7	0.483	0.944	1.12
	5	0.226	0.986	0.28		8	0.085	0.996	0.08		6	0.727	0.878	2.44
	4	0.482	0.951	0.98		7	0.199	0.986	0.28		5	0.915	0.768	4.64
	3	0.813	0.845	3.10		6	0.398	0.961	0.78		4	0.989	0.624	7.52
	2	0.990	0.604	7.92		5	0.664	0.901	1.98	0.330	11	0.023	0.999	0.02
0.170	7	0.033	0.999	0.02		4	0.900	0.780	4.40		10	0.065	0.997	0.06
	6	0.099	0.995	0.10		3	0.992	0.599	8.02		9	0.154	0.990	0.20

TABLE G-4 *(Continued)*

X	M	D	F	L_q	X	M	D	F	L_q	X	M	D	F	L_q
POPULATION 20, Cont.						7	0.907	0.785	4.30		8	0.976	0.713	5.74
						6	0.980	0.680	6.40		7	0.996	0.625	7.50
						5	0.998	0.568	8.64	0.580	16	0.015	0.999	0.02
	8	0.309	0.973	0.54	0.460	14	0.014	0.999	0.02		15	0.051	0.997	0.06
	7	0.529	0.935	1.30		13	0.043	0.998	0.04		14	0.129	0.991	0.18
	6	0.766	0.862	2.76		12	0.109	0.993	0.14		13	0.266	0.978	0.44
	5	0.933	0.748	5.04		11	0.228	0.982	0.36		12	0.455	0.952	0.96
	4	0.993	0.605	7.90		10	0.407	0.958	0.84		11	0.662	0.908	1.84
0.340	11	0.029	0.999	0.02		9	0.620	0.914	1.72		10	0.835	0.847	3.06
	10	0.079	0.996	0.08		8	0.815	0.846	3.08		9	0.941	0.772	4.56
	9	0.179	0.987	0.26		7	0.939	0.755	4.90		8	0.986	0.689	6.22
	8	0.347	0.967	0.66		6	0.989	0.651	6.98		7	0.998	0.603	7.94
	7	0.573	0.924	1.52		5	0.999	0.543	9.14	0.600	16	0.023	0.999	0.02
	6	0.802	0.846	3.08	0.480	14	0.022	0.999	0.02		15	0.072	0.996	0.08
	5	0.949	0.729	5.42		13	0.063	0.996	0.08		14	0.171	0.988	0.24
	4	0.995	0.588	8.24		12	0.147	0.990	0.20		13	0.331	0.970	0.60
0.360	12	0.015	0.999	0.02		11	0.289	0.974	0.52		12	0.532	0.938	1.24
	11	0.045	0.998	0.04		10	0.484	0.944	1.12		11	0.732	0.889	2.22
	10	0.112	0.993	0.14		9	0.695	0.893	2.14		10	0.882	0.824	3.52
	9	0.237	0.981	0.38		8	0.867	0.819	3.62		9	0.962	0.748	5.04
	8	0.429	0.954	0.92		7	0.962	0.726	5.48		8	0.992	0.666	6.68
	7	0.660	0.901	1.98		6	0.994	0.625	7.50		7	0.999	0.583	8.34
	6	0.863	0.812	3.76	0.500	14	0.033	0.998	0.04	0.650	17	0.017	0.999	0.02
	5	0.971	0.691	6.18		13	0.088	0.995	0.10		16	0.061	0.997	0.06
	4	0.998	0.555	8.90		12	0.194	0.985	0.30		15	0.156	0.989	0.22
0.380	12	0.024	0.999	0.02		11	0.358	0.965	0.70		14	0.314	0.973	0.54
	11	0.067	0.996	0.08		10	0.563	0.929	1.42		13	0.518	0.943	1.14
	10	0.154	0.989	0.22		9	0.764	0.870	2.60		12	0.720	0.898	2.04
	9	0.305	0.973	0.54		8	0.908	0.791	4.18		11	0.872	0.837	3.26
	8	0.513	0.938	1.24		7	0.977	0.698	6.04		10	0.957	0.767	4.66
	7	0.739	0.874	2.52		6	0.997	0.600	8.00		9	0.990	0.692	6.16
	6	0.909	0.777	4.46	0.520	15	0.015	0.999	0.02		8	0.998	0.615	7.70
	5	0.984	0.656	6.88		14	0.048	0.997	0.06	0.700	17	0.047	0.998	0.04
	4	0.999	0.526	9.48		13	0.120	0.992	0.16		16	0.137	0.991	0.18
0.400	13	0.012	0.999	0.02		12	0.248	0.979	0.42		15	0.295	0.976	0.48
	12	0.037	0.998	0.04		11	0.432	0.954	0.92		14	0.503	0.948	1.04
	11	0.095	0.994	0.12		10	0.641	0.911	1.78		13	0.710	0.905	1.90
	10	0.205	0.984	0.32		9	0.824	0.846	3.08		12	0.866	0.849	3.02
	9	0.379	0.962	0.76		8	0.939	0.764	4.72		11	0.953	0.783	4.34
	8	0.598	0.918	1.64		7	0.987	0.672	6.56		10	0.988	0.714	5.72
	7	0.807	0.845	3.10		6	0.998	0.577	8.46		9	0.998	0.643	7.14
	6	0.942	0.744	5.12	0.540	15	0.023	0.999	0.02	0.750	18	0.031	0.999	0.02
	5	0.992	0.624	7.52		14	0.069	0.996	0.08		17	0.113	0.993	0.14
0.420	13	0.019	0.999	0.02		13	0.120	0.992	0.16		16	0.272	0.980	0.40
	12	0.055	0.997	0.06		12	0.311	0.972	0.56		15	0.487	0.954	0.92
	11	0.131	0.991	0.18		11	0.509	0.941	1.18		14	0.703	0.913	1.74
	10	0.265	0.977	0.46		10	0.713	0.891	2.18		13	0.864	0.859	2.82
	9	0.458	0.949	1.02		9	0.873	0.821	3.58		12	0.952	0.798	4.04
	8	0.678	0.896	2.08		8	0.961	0.738	5.24		11	0.988	0.733	5.34
	7	0.863	0.815	3.70		7	0.993	0.648	7.04		10	0.998	0.667	6.66
	6	0.965	0.711	5.78		6	0.999	0.556	8.88	0.800	19	0.014	0.999	0.02
	5	0.996	0.595	8.10	0.560	15	0.035	0.998	0.04		18	0.084	0.996	0.08
0.440	13	0.029	0.999	0.02		14	0.095	0.994	0.12		17	0.242	0.984	0.32
	12	0.078	0.995	0.10		13	0.209	0.984	0.32		16	0.470	0.959	0.82
	11	0.175	0.987	0.26		12	0.381	0.963	0.74		15	0.700	0.920	1.60
	10	0.333	0.969	0.62		11	0.586	0.926	1.48		14	0.867	0.869	2.62
	9	0.540	0.933	1.34		10	0.778	0.869	2.62		13	0.955	0.811	3.78
	8	0.751	0.872	2.56		9	0.912	0.796	4.08		12	0.989	0.750	5.00

TABLE G-4 *(Continued)*

POPULATION 20, Cont.

X	M	D	F	L_q
	11	0.998	0.687	6.26
0.850	19	0.046	0.998	0.04
	18	0.201	0.988	0.24
	17	0.451	0.965	0.70
	16	0.703	0.927	1.46
	15	0.877	0.878	2.44
	14	0.962	0.823	3.54
	13	0.991	0.765	4.70
	12	0.998	0.706	5.88
0.900	19	0.135	0.994	0.12
	18	0.425	0.972	0.56
	17	0.717	0.935	1.30
	16	0.898	0.886	2.28
	15	0.973	0.833	3.34
	14	0.995	0.778	4.44
	13	0.999	0.722	5.56
0.950	19	0.377	0.981	0.38
	18	0.760	0.943	1.14
	17	0.939	0.894	2.12
	16	0.989	0.842	3.16
	15	0.999	0.789	4.22

POPULATION 30

X	M	D	F	L_q
0.004	1	0.116	0.999	0.03
0.007	1	0.203	0.998	0.06
0.009	1	0.260	0.997	0.09
0.010	1	0.289	0.996	0.12
0.011	1	0.317	0.995	0.15
0.012	1	0.346	0.994	0.18
0.013	1	0.374	0.993	0.21
0.014	2	0.067	0.999	0.03
	1	0.403	0.991	0.27
0.015	2	0.076	0.999	0.03
	1	0.431	0.989	0.33
0.016	2	0.085	0.999	0.03
	1	0.458	0.987	0.39
0.017	2	0.095	0.999	0.03
	1	0.486	0.985	0.45
0.018	2	0.105	0.999	0.03
	1	0.513	0.983	0.51
0.019	2	0.116	0.999	0.03
	1	0.541	0.980	0.60
0.020	2	0.127	0.998	0.06
	1	0.567	0.976	0.72
0.021	2	0.139	0.998	0.06
	1	0.594	0.973	0.81
0.022	2	0.151	0.998	0.06
	1	0.620	0.969	0.93
0.023	2	0.163	0.997	0.09
	1	0.645	0.965	1.05
0.024	2	0.175	0.997	0.09
	1	0.670	0.960	1.20
0.025	2	0.188	0.996	0.12

X	M	D	F	L_q
	1	0.694	0.954	1.38
0.026	2	0.201	0.996	0.12
	1	0.718	0.948	1.56
0.028	3	0.051	0.999	0.03
	2	0.229	0.995	0.15
	1	0.763	0.935	1.95
0.030	3	0.060	0.999	0.03
	2	0.257	0.994	0.18
	1	0.805	0.918	2.46
0.032	3	0.071	0.999	0.03
	2	0.286	0.992	0.24
	1	0.843	0.899	3.03
0.034	3	0.083	0.999	0.03
	2	0.316	0.990	0.30
	1	0.876	0.877	3.69
0.036	3	0.095	0.998	0.06
	2	0.347	0.988	0.36
	1	0.905	0.853	4.41
0.038	3	0.109	0.998	0.06
	2	0.378	0.986	0.42
	1	0.929	0.827	5.19
0.040	3	0.123	0.997	0.09
	2	0.410	0.983	0.51
	1	0.948	0.800	6.00
0.042	3	0.138	0.997	0.09
	2	0.442	0.980	0.60
	1	0.963	0.772	6.84
0.044	4	0.040	0.999	0.03
	3	0.154	0.996	0.12
	2	0.474	0.977	0.69
	1	0.974	0.744	7.68
0.046	4	0.046	0.999	0.03
	3	0.171	0.996	0.12
	2	0.506	0.972	0.84
	1	0.982	0.716	8.52
0.048	4	0.053	0.999	0.03
	3	0.189	0.995	0.15
	2	0.539	0.968	0.96
	1	0.988	0.689	9.33
0.050	4	0.060	0.999	0.03
	3	0.208	0.994	0.18
	2	0.571	0.963	1.11
	1	0.992	0.663	10.11
0.052	4	0.068	0.999	0.03
	3	0.227	0.993	0.21
	2	0.603	0.957	1.29
	1	0.995	0.639	10.83
0.054	4	0.077	0.998	0.06
	3	0.247	0.992	0.24
	2	0.634	0.951	1.47
	1	0.997	0.616	11.52
0.056	4	0.086	0.998	0.06
	3	0.267	0.991	0.27
	2	0.665	0.944	1.68
	1	0.998	0.595	12.15
0.058	4	0.096	0.998	0.06
	3	0.288	0.989	0.33
	2	0.695	0.936	1.92

X	M	D	F	L_q
	1	0.999	0.574	12.78
0.060	5	0.030	0.999	0.03
	4	0.106	0.997	0.09
	3	0.310	0.987	0.39
	2	0.723	0.927	2.19
	1	0.999	0.555	13.35
0.062	5	0.034	0.999	0.03
	4	0.117	0.997	0.09
	3	0.332	0.986	0.42
	2	0.751	0.918	2.46
0.064	5	0.038	0.999	0.03
	4	0.128	0.997	0.09
	3	0.355	0.984	0.48
	2	0.777	0.908	2.76
0.066	5	0.043	0.999	0.03
	4	0.140	0.996	0.12
	3	0.378	0.982	0.54
	2	0.802	0.897	3.09
0.068	5	0.048	0.999	0.03
	4	0.153	0.995	0.15
	3	0.402	0.979	0.63
	2	0.825	0.885	3.45
0.070	5	0.054	0.999	0.03
	4	0.166	0.995	0.15
	3	0.426	0.976	0.72
	2	0.847	0.873	3.81
0.075	5	0.069	0.998	0.06
	4	0.201	0.993	0.21
	3	0.486	0.969	0.93
	2	0.893	0.840	4.80
0.080	6	0.027	0.999	0.03
	5	0.088	0.998	0.06
	4	0.240	0.990	0.30
	3	0.547	0.959	1.23
	2	0.929	0.805	5.85
0.085	6	0.036	0.999	0.03
	5	0.108	0.997	0.09
	4	0.282	0.987	0.39
	3	0.607	0.948	1.56
	2	0.955	0.768	6.96
0.090	6	0.046	0.999	0.03
	5	0.132	0.996	0.12
	4	0.326	0.984	0.48
	3	0.665	0.934	1.98
	2	0.972	0.732	8.04
0.095	6	0.057	0.999	0.03
	5	0.158	0.994	0.18
	4	0.372	0.979	0.63
	3	0.720	0.918	2.46
	2	0.984	0.697	9.09
0.100	6	0.071	0.998	0.06
	5	0.187	0.993	0.21
	4	0.421	0.973	0.81
	3	0.771	0.899	3.03
	2	0.991	0.664	10.08
0.105	7	0.030	0.999	0.03
	6	0.087	0.997	0.09
	5	0.219	0.991	0.27

TABLE G-4 (Continued)

POPULATION 30, Cont.

X	M	D	F	L_q	X	M	D	F	L_q	X	M	D	F	L_q
					5	0.580	0.944	1.68		8	0.303	0.980	0.60
					4	0.860	0.849	4.53		7	0.515	0.952	1.44
					3	0.991	0.665	10.05		6	0.758	0.892	3.24
	4	0.470	0.967	0.99	0.155	9	0.029	0.999	0.03		5	0.938	0.782	6.54
	3	0.816	0.879	3.63		8	0.077	0.997	0.09		4	0.995	0.634	10.98
	2	0.995	0.634	10.98		7	0.177	0.992	0.24	0.220	11	0.041	0.999	0.03
0.110	7	0.038	0.999	0.03		6	0.357	0.976	0.72		10	0.095	0.996	0.12
	6	0.105	0.997	0.09		5	0.622	0.935	1.95		9	0.197	0.989	0.33
	5	0.253	0.988	0.36		4	0.887	0.830	5.10		8	0.361	0.974	0.78
	4	0.520	0.959	1.23		3	0.994	0.644	10.68		7	0.585	0.938	1.86
	3	0.856	0.857	4.29	0.160	9	0.036	0.999	0.03		6	0.816	0.868	3.96
	2	0.997	0.605	11.85		8	0.090	0.997	0.09		5	0.961	0.751	7.47
0.115	7	0.047	0.999	0.03		7	0.201	0.990	0.30		4	0.998	0.606	11.82
	6	0.125	0.996	0.12		6	0.394	0.972	0.84	0.230	12	0.023	0.999	0.03
	5	0.289	0.985	0.45		5	0.663	0.924	2.28		11	0.056	0.998	0.06
	4	0.570	0.950	1.50		4	0.910	0.811	5.67		10	0.123	0.994	0.18
	3	0.890	0.833	5.01		3	0.996	0.624	11.28		9	0.242	0.985	0.45
	2	0.998	0.579	12.63	0.165	9	0.043	0.999	0.03		8	0.423	0.965	1.05
0.120	7	0.057	0.998	0.06		8	0.105	0.996	0.12		7	0.652	0.923	2.31
	6	0.147	0.994	0.18		7	0.227	0.988	0.36		6	0.864	0.842	4.74
	5	0.327	0.981	0.57		6	0.431	0.967	0.99		5	0.976	0.721	8.37
	4	0.619	0.939	1.83		5	0.702	0.913	2.61		4	0.999	0.580	12.60
	3	0.918	0.808	5.76		4	0.930	0.792	6.24	0.240	12	0.031	0.999	0.03
	2	0.999	0.555	13.35		3	0.997	0.606	11.82		11	0.074	0.997	0.09
0.125	8	0.024	0.999	0.03	0.170	10	0.019	0.999	0.03		10	0.155	0.992	0.24
	7	0.069	0.998	0.06		9	0.051	0.998	0.06		9	0.291	0.981	0.57
	6	0.171	0.993	0.21		8	0.121	0.995	0.15		8	0.487	0.955	1.35
	5	0.367	0.977	0.69		7	0.254	0.986	0.42		7	0.715	0.905	2.85
	4	0.666	0.927	2.19		6	0.469	0.961	1.17		6	0.902	0.816	5.52
	3	0.940	0.783	6.51		5	0.739	0.901	2.97		5	0.986	0.693	9.21
0.130	8	0.030	0.999	0.03		4	0.946	0.773	6.81		4	0.999	0.556	13.32
	7	0.083	0.997	0.09		3	0.998	0.588	12.36	0.250	13	0.017	0.999	0.03
	6	0.197	0.991	0.27	0.180	10	0.028	0.999	0.03		12	0.042	0.998	0.06
	5	0.409	0.972	0.84		9	0.070	0.997	0.09		11	0.095	0.996	0.12
	4	0.712	0.914	2.58		8	0.158	0.993	0.21		10	0.192	0.989	0.33
	3	0.957	0.758	7.26		7	0.313	0.980	0.60		9	0.345	0.975	0.75
0.135	8	0.037	0.999	0.03		6	0.546	0.948	1.56		8	0.552	0.944	1.68
	7	0.098	0.997	0.09		5	0.806	0.874	3.78		7	0.773	0.885	3.45
	6	0.226	0.989	0.33		4	0.969	0.735	7.95		6	0.932	0.789	6.33
	5	0.451	0.966	1.02		3	0.999	0.555	13.35		5	0.992	0.666	10.02
	4	0.754	0.899	3.03	0.190	10	0.039	0.999	0.03	0.260	13	0.023	0.999	0.03
	3	0.970	0.734	7.98		9	0.094	0.996	0.12		12	0.056	0.998	0.06
0.140	8	0.045	0.999	0.03		8	0.200	0.990	0.30		11	0.121	0.994	0.18
	7	0.115	0.996	0.12		7	0.378	0.973	0.81		10	0.233	0.986	0.42
	6	0.256	0.987	0.39		6	0.621	0.932	2.04		9	0.402	0.967	0.99
	5	0.494	0.960	1.20		5	0.862	0.845	4.65		8	0.616	0.930	2.10
	4	0.793	0.884	3.48		4	0.983	0.699	9.03		7	0.823	0.864	4.08
	3	0.979	0.710	8.70	0.200	11	0.021	0.999	0.03		6	0.954	0.763	7.11
0.145	8	0.055	0.998	0.06		10	0.054	0.998	0.06		5	0.995	0.641	10.77
	7	0.134	0.995	0.15		9	0.123	0.995	0.15	0.270	13	0.032	0.999	0.03
	6	0.288	0.984	0.48		8	0.249	0.985	0.45		12	0.073	0.997	0.09
	5	0.537	0.952	1.44		7	0.446	0.963	1.11		11	0.151	0.992	0.24
	4	0.828	0.867	3.99		6	0.693	0.913	2.61		10	0.279	0.981	0.57
	3	0.986	0.687	9.39		5	0.905	0.814	5.58		9	0.462	0.959	1.23
0.150	9	0.024	0.999	0.03		4	0.991	0.665	10.05		8	0.676	0.915	2.55
	8	0.065	0.998	0.06	0.210	11	0.030	0.999	0.03		7	0.866	0.841	4.77
	7	0.155	0.993	0.21		10	0.073	0.997	0.09		6	0.970	0.737	7.89
	6	0.322	0.980	0.60		9	0.157	0.992	0.24		5	0.997	0.617	11.49

TABLE G-4 *(Continued)*

X	M	D	F	L_q	X	M	D	F	L_q	X	M	D	F	L_q
POPULATION 30, Cont.					9	0.795	0.876	3.72		18	0.041	0.998	0.06
					8	0.927	0.799	6.03		17	0.087	0.996	0.12
					7	0.985	0.706	8.82		16	0.167	0.990	0.30
0.280	14	0.017	0.999	0.03	6	0.999	0.606	11.82		15	0.288	0.979	0.63
	13	0.042	0.998	0.06	0.340 16	0.016	0.999	0.03		14	0.446	0.960	1.20
	12	0.093	0.996	0.12	15	0.040	0.998	0.06		13	0.623	0.929	2.13
	11	0.185	0.989	0.33	14	0.086	0.996	0.12		12	0.787	0.883	3.51
	10	0.329	0.976	0.72	13	0.169	0.990	0.30		11	0.906	0.824	5.28
	9	0.522	0.949	1.53	12	0.296	0.979	0.63		10	0.970	0.755	7.35
	8	0.733	0.898	3.06	11	0.468	0.957	1.29		9	0.994	0.681	9.57
	7	0.901	0.818	5.46	10	0.663	0.918	2.46		8	0.999	0.606	11.82
	6	0.981	0.712	8.64	9	0.836	0.858	4.26	0.460 19	0.028	0.999	0.03
	5	0.999	0.595	12.15	8	0.947	0.778	6.66		18	0.064	0.997	0.09
0.290	14	0.023	0.999	0.03	7	0.990	0.685	9.45		17	0.129	0.993	0.21
	13	0.055	0.998	0.06	6	0.999	0.588	12.36		16	0.232	0.985	0.45
	12	0.117	0.994	0.18	0.360 16	0.029	0.999	0.03		15	0.375	0.970	0.90
	11	0.223	0.986	0.42	15	0.065	0.997	0.09		14	0.545	0.944	1.68
	10	0.382	0.969	0.93	14	0.132	0.993	0.21		13	0.717	0.906	2.82
	9	0.582	0.937	1.89	13	0.240	0.984	0.48		12	0.857	0.855	4.35
	8	0.785	0.880	3.60	12	0.392	0.967	0.99		11	0.945	0.793	6.21
	7	0.929	0.795	6.15	11	0.578	0.937	1.89		10	0.985	0.724	8.28
	6	0.988	0.688	9.36	10	0.762	0.889	3.33		9	0.997	0.652	10.44
	5	0.999	0.575	12.75	9	0.902	0.821	5.37	0.480 20	0.019	0.999	0.03
0.300	14	0.031	0.999	0.03	8	0.974	0.738	7.86		19	0.046	0.998	0.06
	13	0.071	0.997	0.09	7	0.996	0.648	10.56		18	0.098	0.995	0.15
	12	0.145	0.992	0.24	0.380 17	0.020	0.999	0.03		17	0.184	0.989	0.33
	11	0.266	0.982	0.54	16	0.048	0.998	0.06		16	0.310	0.977	0.69
	10	0.437	0.962	1.14	15	0.101	0.995	0.15		15	0.470	0.957	1.29
	9	0.641	0.924	2.28	14	0.191	0.988	0.36		14	0.643	0.926	2.22
	8	0.830	0.861	4.17	13	0.324	0.975	0.75		13	0.799	0.881	3.57
	7	0.950	0.771	6.87	12	0.496	0.952	1.44		12	0.910	0.826	5.22
	6	0.993	0.666	10.02	11	0.682	0.914	2.58		11	0.970	0.762	7.14
0.310	15	0.017	0.999	0.03	10	0.843	0.857	4.29		10	0.993	0.694	9.18
	14	0.041	0.998	0.06	9	0.945	0.784	6.48		9	0.999	0.625	11.25
	13	0.090	0.996	0.12	8	0.988	0.701	8.97	0.500 20	0.032	0.999	0.03
	12	0.177	0.990	0.30	7	0.999	0.614	11.58		19	0.072	0.997	0.09
	11	0.312	0.977	0.69	0.400 17	0.035	0.999	0.03		18	0.143	0.992	0.24
	10	0.494	0.953	1.41	16	0.076	0.996	0.12		17	0.252	0.983	0.51
	9	0.697	0.909	2.73	15	0.150	0.992	0.24		16	0.398	0.967	0.99
	8	0.869	0.840	4.80	14	0.264	0.982	0.54		15	0.568	0.941	1.77
	7	0.966	0.749	7.53	13	0.420	0.964	1.08		14	0.733	0.904	2.88
	6	0.996	0.645	10.65	12	0.601	0.933	2.01		13	0.865	0.854	4.38
0.320	15	0.023	0.999	0.03	11	0.775	0.886	3.42		12	0.947	0.796	6.12
	14	0.054	0.998	0.06	10	0.903	0.823	5.31		11	0.985	0.732	8.04
	13	0.113	0.994	0.18	9	0.972	0.748	7.56		10	0.997	0.667	9.99
	12	0.213	0.987	0.39	8	0.995	0.666	10.02	0.520 21	0.021	0.999	0.03
	11	0.362	0.971	0.87	0.420 18	0.024	0.999	0.03		20	0.051	0.998	0.06
	10	0.552	0.943	1.71	17	0.056	0.997	0.09		19	0.108	0.994	0.18
	9	0.748	0.893	3.21	16	0.116	0.994	0.18		18	0.200	0.988	0.36
	8	0.901	0.820	5.40	15	0.212	0.986	0.42		17	0.331	0.975	0.75
	7	0.977	0.727	8.19	14	0.350	0.972	0.84		16	0.493	0.954	1.38
	6	0.997	0.625	11.25	13	0.521	0.948	1.56		15	0.633	0.923	2.31
0.330	15	0.030	0.999	0.03	12	0.700	0.910	2.70		14	0.811	0.880	3.60
	14	0.068	0.997	0.09	11	0.850	0.856	4.32		13	0.915	0.827	5.19
	13	0.139	0.993	0.21	10	0.945	0.789	6.33		12	0.971	0.767	6.99
	12	0.253	0.983	0.51	9	0.986	0.713	8.61		11	0.993	0.705	8.85
	11	0.414	0.965	1.05	8	0.998	0.635	10.95		10	0.999	0.641	10.77
	10	0.608	0.931	2.07	0.440 19	0.017	0.999	0.03					

TABLE G-4 (Continued)

X	M	D	F	L_q	X	M	D	F	L_q	X	M	D	F	L_q
POPULATION 30, Cont.						22	0.059	0.997	0.09		19	0.946	0.842	4.74
						21	0.125	0.993	0.21		18	0.981	0.799	6.03
						20	0.230	0.986	0.42		17	0.995	0.755	7.35
0.540	21	0.035	0.999	0.03		19	0.372	0.972	0.84		16	0.999	0.711	8.67
	20	0.079	0.996	0.12		18	0.538	0.949	1.53	0.800	27	0.053	0.998	0.06
	19	0.155	0.991	0.27		17	0.702	0.918	2.46		26	0.143	0.993	0.21
	18	0.270	0.981	0.57		16	0.837	0.877	3.69		25	0.292	0.984	0.48
	17	0.421	0.965	1.05		15	0.927	0.829	5.13		24	0.481	0.966	1.02
	16	0.590	0.938	1.86		14	0.974	0.776	6.72		23	0.670	0.941	1.77
	15	0.750	0.901	2.97		13	0.993	0.722	8.34		22	0.822	0.909	2.73
	14	0.874	0.854	4.38		12	0.999	0.667	9.99		21	0.919	0.872	3.84
	13	0.949	0.799	6.03	0.650	24	0.031	0.999	0.03		20	0.970	0.832	5.04
	12	0.985	0.740	7.80		23	0.076	0.996	0.12		19	0.991	0.791	6.27
	11	0.997	0.679	9.63		22	0.158	0.991	0.27		18	0.998	0.750	7.50
	10	0.999	0.617	11.49		21	0.281	0.982	0.54	0.850	28	0.055	0.998	0.06
0.560	22	0.023	0.999	0.03		20	0.439	0.965	1.05		27	0.171	0.993	0.21
	21	0.056	0.997	0.09		19	0.610	0.940	1.80		26	0.356	0.981	0.57
	20	0.117	0.994	0.18		18	0.764	0.906	2.82		25	0.571	0.960	1.20
	19	0.215	0.986	0.42		17	0.879	0.865	4.05		24	0.760	0.932	2.04
	18	0.352	0.973	0.81		16	0.949	0.818	5.46		23	0.888	0.889	3.03
	17	0.516	0.952	1.44		15	0.983	0.769	6.93		22	0.957	0.862	4.14
	16	0.683	0.920	2.40		14	0.996	0.718	8.46		21	0.987	0.823	5.31
	15	0.824	0.878	3.66		13	0.999	0.667	9.99		20	0.997	0.784	6.48
	14	0.920	0.828	5.16	0.700	25	0.039	0.998	0.06		19	0.999	0.745	7.65
	13	0.972	0.772	6.84		24	0.096	0.995	0.15	0.900	29	0.047	0.999	0.03
	12	0.993	0.714	8.58		23	0.196	0.989	0.33		28	0.200	0.992	0.24
	11	0.999	0.655	10.35		22	0.339	0.977	0.69		27	0.441	0.977	0.69
0.580	23	0.014	0.999	0.03		21	0.511	0.958	1.26		26	0.683	0.953	1.41
	22	0.038	0.998	0.06		20	0.681	0.930	2.10		25	0.856	0.923	2.31
	21	0.085	0.996	0.12		19	0.821	0.894	3.18		24	0.947	0.888	3.36
	20	0.167	0.990	0.30		18	0.916	0.853	4.41		23	0.985	0.852	4.44
	19	0.288	0.980	0.60		17	0.967	0.808	5.76		22	0.996	0.815	5.55
	18	0.443	0.963	1.11		16	0.990	0.762	7.14		21	0.999	0.778	6.66
	17	0.612	0.936	1.92		15	0.997	0.714	8.58	0.950	29	0.226	0.993	0.21
	16	0.766	0.899	3.03	0.750	26	0.046	0.998	0.06		28	0.574	0.973	0.81
	15	0.883	0.854	4.38		25	0.118	0.994	0.18		27	0.831	0.945	1.65
	14	0.953	0.802	5.94		24	0.240	0.986	0.42		26	0.951	0.912	2.64
	13	0.985	0.746	7.62		23	0.405	0.972	0.84		25	0.989	0.877	3.69
	12	0.997	0.690	9.30		22	0.587	0.950	1.50		24	0.998	0.842	4.74
	11	0.999	0.632	11.04		21	0.752	0.920	2.40					
0.600	23	0.024	0.999	0.03		20	0.873	0.883	3.51					

TABLE G-5   **Table of Random Digits**

03689	33090	43465	96789	56688	32389	77206	06534	10558	14478
43367	46409	44751	73410	35138	24910	70748	57336	56043	68550
45357	52080	62670	73877	20604	40408	98060	96733	65094	80335
62683	03171	77109	92515	78041	27590	42651	00254	73179	10159
04841	40918	69047	68986	08150	87984	08887	76083	37702	28523
85963	06992	65321	43521	46393	40491	06028	43865	58190	28142
03720	78942	61990	90812	98452	74098	69738	83272	39212	42817
10159	85560	35619	58248	65498	77977	02896	45198	10655	13973
80162	35686	57877	19552	63931	44171	40879	94532	17828	31848
74388	92906	65829	24572	79417	38460	96294	79201	47755	90980
12660	09571	29743	45447	64063	46295	44191	53957	62393	42229
81852	60620	87757	72165	23875	87844	84038	04994	93466	27418
03068	61317	65305	64944	27319	55263	84514	38374	11657	67723
29623	58530	17274	16908	39253	37595	57497	74780	88624	93333
30520	50588	51231	83816	01075	33098	81308	59036	49152	86262
93694	02984	91350	33929	41724	32403	42566	14232	55085	65628
86736	40641	37958	25415	19922	65966	98044	39583	26828	50919
28141	15630	37675	52545	24813	22075	05142	15374	84533	12933
79804	05165	21620	98400	55290	71877	60052	46320	79055	45913
63763	49985	88853	70681	52762	17670	62337	12199	44123	37993
49618	47068	63331	62675	51788	58283	04295	72904	05378	98085
26502	68980	26545	14204	34304	50284	47730	57299	73966	02566
13549	86048	27912	56733	14987	09850	72817	85168	09538	92347
89221	78076	40306	34045	52557	52383	67796	41382	50490	30117
97809	34056	76778	60417	05153	83827	67369	08602	56163	28793
65668	44694	34151	51741	11484	13226	49516	17391	39956	34839
53653	59804	59051	95074	38307	99546	32962	26962	86252	50704
34922	95041	17398	32789	26860	55536	82415	82911	42208	62725
74880	65198	61357	90209	71543	71114	94868	05645	44154	72254
66036	48794	30021	92601	21615	16952	18433	44903	51322	90379
39044	99503	11442	81344	57068	74662	90382	59433	48440	38146
87756	71151	68543	08358	10183	06432	97482	90301	76114	83778
47117	45575	29524	02522	08041	70698	80260	73588	86415	72523
71572	02109	96722	21684	64331	71644	18933	32801	11644	12364
35609	58072	63209	48429	53108	59173	55337	22445	85940	43707
73703	70069	74981	12197	48426	77365	26769	65078	27849	41311
42979	88161	56531	46443	47148	42773	18601	38532	22594	12395
12279	42308	00380	17181	38757	09071	89804	15232	99007	39495

INDEX

673